OUR NAVY

DURING THE GREAT REBELLION,

1861–1865.

FARRAGUT

AND

OUR NAVAL COMMANDERS.

Eng'd by H. B. Hall N.Y.

D. G. Farragut

ADM. DAVID G. FARRAGUT.

Engraved expressly for Headley's Naval Work.

FARRAGUT

AND OUR

NAVAL COMMANDERS.

BY

HON. J. T. HEADLEY,

AUTHOR OF "WASHINGTON AND HIS GENERALS," "NAPOLEON AND HIS MARSHALS," "SACRED MOUNTAINS," &C., &C., &C.

A COMPANION VOLUME TO HEADLEY'S "GRANT AND SHERMAN."

COMPRISING

THE EARLY LIFE AND PUBLIC SERVICES OF THE PROMINENT NAVAL COMMANDERS WHO, WITH GRANT AND SHERMAN AND THEIR GENERALS, BROUGHT TO A TRIUMPHANT CLOSE

THE GREAT REBELLION

OF

1861-1865.

WITH NUMEROUS

Fine Steel Portraits and Battle Scenes.

SOLD ONLY BY SUBSCRIPTION.

NEW YORK:

E. B. TREAT & CO., PUBLISHERS.

CHICAGO, ILL.: C. W. LILLEY. CINCINNATI, O.: G. B. FESSENDEN
ST. LOUIS, MO.: I. S. BRAINARD. DETROIT, MICH.: B. C. BAKER.
CLEVELAND, O.: A. O. BRIGGS. BOSTON, MASS.: M. PITMAN & CO.
SAN FRANCISCO, CAL.: E. E. SHEAR.

1867.

ERRATA.

Page 35—Three lines from bottom, for "Northern," read "Southern."
" 85—Twelve lines from bottom, for "passed," read "paved."
" 144—Four lines from top, for "commander," read "commanders."
" 148—Last paragraph on the page should be omitted.
" 225—Fifteen lines from top, for "at Natchez," read "on the Natchez."
" 338—Fourteenth line from top, for "ship," read "ships."
" 403—For "Mazatlin," read "Mazatlan."
" 446—Fifteenth line from top, for "her," read "the."
" 457—Fifteenth line from top, for "end," read "bend."

JOHN F. TROW & CO,
PRINTERS, STEREOTYPERS, & ELECTROTYPERS,
50 GREENE STREET, N. Y.

PREFACE.

The object of the following work is twofold: first, to bring out into distinct relief the important actions of our navy during the recent war; and, second, to give a personal history of the brave officers who covered themselves and the nation with honor.

Our navy has always been the pride and boast of the people, for its record is without a blot. Disgrace and defeat have often been visited on our arms on the land, but the former never, and the latter rarely on the sea. We have never lost a vessel in a fair combat, so that no commander, however unfortunate in the loss of his vessel, has ever lost his reputation with it—nay, rather, he has added to his renown by the gallant and determined manner in which he fought it.

Isolated, and so far from the great powers of the world, we could protect ourselves at home; but without a navy with a brilliant record, we could not command respect abroad. Our honor on the deep and in foreign ports had therefore to be entrusted to our naval commanders, and nobly did they fulfil their trust. We have never been, till now, scarce a third-rate power in our maritime strength, yet the navy, by its deeds of renown, has made us to be regarded as a first-rate one throughout the world. Our national flag seemed almost lost amid the swarming fleets of England and France; still, wherever it floated, it asserted its supremacy and claimed and received that respect which hitherto had been awarded only to numbers. This high character, won by no other navy of our size in the civilized world, has not only been sustained, but elevated by our commanders in the recent struggle for self-preservation. They therefore deserve a separate place in history. Besides, our naval commanders seem not so much a part of the people as the volunteer generals, who step from their office and ordinary employments to the head of our armies. From boyhood their home is on the ocean, and they are lost to view except by their immediate friends; and we know them only by their deeds of renown. A volunteer navy is impossible, except in its crews. The sailing and manœuvring and fighting of a ship can be done only by those who have had years of practical training—only the results of which we see. We have thought, therefore, that the early history, experience, and struggles of those men who have covered our flag with glory, would be interesting to the American people. Besides, the new instruments of warfare—the heavy ordnance and monster shells and unparalleled range which have been reached—the iron-clad vessels and destructive rams and novel modes of attack and defence which have characterized this naval contest, have made it unique and worthy of a separate and distinct notice.

It is not to be inferred, that, because some admirals and commodores are omitted in the following sketches, and others of lower rank inserted, the distinction is meant as a test of their respective merits. Those have been selected who performed marked service or fought separate engagements. Officers in command of navy-yards, or on peaceful stations, may have rendered equal service to the nation, but the character of it was such as to furnish no material for a biographical sketch; yet their rank indicates the high appreciation of their worth and services by the Government.

We have only to add that, in almost every case, the facts and personal details in the biographical sketches have been furnished either by the commanders themselves, or their friends, with their approval. Hence they can be relied on.

LIST OF ILLUSTRATIONS.

CONTENTS.

CHAPTER I.

CHAPTER II.

ADMIRAL DAVID GLASCOE FARRAGUT.

CHAPTER III.

REAR-ADMIRAL CHARLES WILKES.

CHAPTER IV.

REAR-ADMIRAL SILAS H. STRINGHAM.

CHAPTER V.

REAR-ADMIRAL SAMUEL FRANCIS DUPONT.

CHAPTER VI.

REAR-ADMIRAL ANDREW HULL FOOTE.

CHAPTER VIII.

COMMODORE CHARLES STUART BOGGS.

CHAPTER IX.

REAR-ADMIRAL LOUIS MALESHERBES GOLDSBOROUGH.

CHAPTER X.

COLONEL CHARLES ELLET.

CHAPTER XI.

REAR-ADMIRAL THEODORUS BAILEY.

CHAPTER XII.

REAR-ADMIRAL CHARLES HENRY DAVIS.

PAGE.

CHAPTER XIII.

COMMANDER HOMER C. BLAKE.

CHAPTER XIV.

COMMODORE JOHN A. WINSLOW.

CHAPTER XV.

VICE-ADMIRAL DAVID D. PORTER.

CHAPTER XVI.

COMMANDER WILLIAM B. CUSHING.

CHAPTER XVII.

REAR-ADMIRAL STEPHEN C. ROWAN.

CHAPTER XVIII.

COMMODORE S. P. LEE.

CHAPTER XIX.

COMMODORE THORNTON A. JENKINS.

CHAPTER XX.

REAR-ADMIRAL HENRY KNOX THATCHER.

CHAPTER XXI.

COMMODORE WILLIAM D. PORTER.

CHAPTER XXIII.

REAR-ADMIRAL JOHN A. DAHLGREN.

CHAPTER XXIV.

REAR-ADMIRAL HIRAM PAULDING.

CHAPTER XXV.

REAR-ADMIRAL JAMES S. PALMER.

CHAPTER XXVI.

CAPTAIN JOHN LORIMER WORDEN.

CHAPTER XXVII.

REAR-ADMIRAL HENRY H. BELL.

CHAPTER XXVIII.

COMMODORE MELANCTHON SMITH.

PAGE.

CHAPTER XXIX.

COMMODORE JOHN ROGERS.

CHAPTER XXX.

APPENDIX.

Eng^d by H.B. Hall, N.Y.

Engraved expressly for Headley's Naval Work.

CHAPTER I.

MODERN SCIENCE IN NAVAL WARFARE.—EARLIEST NAVAL ENGAGEMENT ON RECORD.—BATTLE OF SALAMIS.—ROMAN MODE OF FIGHTING.—ANCIENT ENGINES AND IMPLEMENTS OF DESTRUCTION.—CANNON FIRST USED IN NAVAL COMBATS.—THE TERRIBLE BATTLE OF LEPANTO.—RAPIDITY WITH WHICH ANCIENT NAVAL EXPEDITIONS WERE FITTED OUT.—IMPROVEMENT IN SHIP-BUILDING.—THE PAIXHAN GUN.—EXPLOSION OF SHELLS BY CONCUSSION.—OUR SECOND WAR WITH ENGLAND.—ASTOUNDING RESULTS OF THE VARIOUS COMBATS.—CHIEF CAUSE OF OUR VICTORIES.—SIGHTS ON CANNON.—INFERIORITY OF OUR NAVY AT THE COMMENCEMENT OF THE REBELLION.—IMPROVEMENTS IN GUNS.—DAHLGREN GUN.—DESCRIPTION OF THE PARROTT GUN.—CONSTRUCTION OF IRON-CLADS.—THE MONITOR, GALENA, AND IRONSIDES.—FOUNDATION OF THE IRON-CLAD NAVY.—STRENGTH OF THE NAVY AT THE COMMENCEMENT OF THE WAR.—ITS DIVISION.—EXTENT OF COAST TO BE BLOCKADED.—NUMBER OF VESSELS BUILT AND PURCHASED.—EUROPE ON THE BLOCKADE.—ENGLAND.—SOUTHERN EFFORTS TO BREAK THE BLOCKADE. BLOCKADE RUNNERS.—NUMBER CAPTURED THE FIRST YEAR.—TOTAL NUMBER DURING THE WAR.—INCREASE OF OUR NAVAL FORCE DURING THE WAR. —AMOUNT EXPENDED BY OUR NAVY DEPARTMENT.

MODERN science has worked greater changes in naval warfare since the breaking out of the recent rebellion than ever before in the same period of time. These changes have been not only in the size and destructive power of cannons, but in the mode of constructing ships of war.

The earliest naval engagement on record was fought by Eurythus, a prince who controlled the Red Sea.

The most noted one of ancient times was that of Salamis, between the Greeks and Persians. The fleet of the latter consisted of twelve hundred galleys, manned by five hundred thousand men, while the former had but four hundred vessels. Xerxes caused his throne to be placed on a mountain overlooking the scene of combat, in which he sat surrounded with secretaries, pen in hand, to note the heroic deeds of individual commanders, and to mark the laggards in the conflict. The mountain ridges near the Acropolis and the Hill of Mars were crowded with spectators of the fight, which ended in the dispersion and destruction of the whole Persian fleet. This was five hundred years before Christ.

The Romans were accustomed to advance to the attack with their galleys arranged in the form of a triangle—the admiral's vessel at the head. Then, as now, human ingenuity multiplied the engines of destruction. Turrets were erected on the prow or stern, from which arrows could be discharged in showers; huge engines arose from the centre, from which rocks were hurled with a power that sent them, like round-shot, through the bottoms of the vessels; battering-rams swung from the masts, to beat in their sides; while pots of live coals and melted pitch and combustible compounds were added to the battle-axe and spear. It is said that the ancestor of Hannibal threw pots of live and poisonous serpents on board his enemy's ships, which, darting around on deck, spread consternation among the crew.

The invention of cannon introduced a new element into naval warfare. The Venetians and Genoese, the great naval powers of the 16th century, first used them in naval combats. The first great battle fought after their introduction was that of Lepanto, in 1571, between the

Venetians and Spanish on one side, and the Turks on the other, in which the great question was decided whether Christianity or Mohammedanism should control Northern Europe. The Turks had two hundred and thirty galleys and transports, with six vessels carrying heavy artillery. The Christians had two hundred and fifty, manned with fifty thousand men. Nearly five hundred vessels, with two mighty armies on board, met in mortal combat. No time was lost in distant firing, for the vessels rushed on each other in a close death-grapple. Modern naval warfare furnishes no such an imposing array of force. It was a frightful struggle, and when it closed nearly a hundred of the Turkish vessels had sunk to the bottom of the sea, and twenty-five thousand men lay dead on the decks, or had disappeared beneath the waves. Ten thousand Christians also had fallen, making the total number of victims in this terrific sea-fight thirty-five thousand. Such a loss of life in a naval combat at the present day can hardly be conceived of.

In those old barbarous times, as we are accustomed to call them, grand naval expeditions were fitted out with a rapidity that even in these days would be regarded with astonishment. Rome once fitted out an immense fleet in ninety days after the trees were standing in the forest. Piso built and equipped a fleet, to sail against the king of Syracuse, of two hundred and twenty vessels in forty-five days.

War-vessels kept pace with improvements in shipbuilding, till huge fabrics with three gun-decks, and throwing a terrific amount of metal in a single broadside, were launched by the great maritime powers of the world.

Hollow shot or shells were very early introduced into

the navy; but being thrown from mortars, were used chiefly in assailing fortified places on land. The Paixhan gun, though invented by an American, about 1812, received but little attention here until it was introduced into France by Captain Paixhan. This was a great improvement in naval warfare, for with this piece of ordnance shell were fired point-blank like round-shot. Before they were thrown in a curve, and hence of but little use on the water. The explosion of shells by concussion was a great step forward. With this exception, however, the improvement in cannon was very slight. There is, however, a great difference between the howitzer of 1693 and the Dahlgren howitzer, which is used for firing grape and canister at close quarters.

In our second war with England we made a great stride forward in naval warfare. England had been regarded by the world as "mistress of the sea," and the attempt to contend with her on her favorite element was considered the world over to be a piece of madness on our part.

The first conflict took place between the Constitution and Guerrière, and lasted less than an hour, yet so terribly was the English frigate cut up, that she went down in the waves while yet crimson with the blood of her slain.

In the single-handed fight that occurred not long after between the United States and Macedonian, the latter had a third of her entire crew and officers, numbering three hundred men, killed and wounded, while the American frigate lost but twelve, all told. So also the United States suffered but very little in her hull, while the Macedonian received a hundred shot below her bulwarks. In the fight between the Constitution and Java, the former came out of it with every spar standing, and ready for another antagonist, while the latter resembled a slaughter-pen, and sank a helpless wreck to the bottom. In nearly every contest the same result followed. Not only were we the victors, but the disparity between the killed in the two ships, and the frightful manner in which the enemy was cut up, while we suffered but little, caused the most unbounded astonishment. The English accounted for it on the ground of a slight difference in the weight of the respective broadsides, or attributed it to mere accident. We made as great a mistake in boasting that our success arose from superior bravery or seamanship. The simple truth was, we had introduced an improvement in gunnery, of which the English at that time were ignorant. *We had placed sights on our cannon.* The English regulated their firing by a pendulum, swinging in the square of the hatchway, by which the inclination of the ship was indicated, and which enabled them to know when the guns were in a horizontal position, and thus, if in a smooth sea, on a level with the hostile ship. But with a vessel rolling on a swell it was a very uncertain guide. On the contrary, we had sights on the guns, sometimes on the muzzle-ring, answering to the forward sight of the rifle, and sometimes tubes were laid along the gun, and capable of being adjusted to suit the range. Hence our gunners took *aim* when they fired, and the consequence was, that in a broadside engagement, we, in an incredibly short space of time, made a wreck of the enemy. This rifle-practice with cannon on board ships was an entirely new thing in naval warfare.

This new improvement was soon adopted by the naval powers of Europe, and others made,—so that at the commencement of the recent civil war, our navy was hardly equal to one of the third-rate maritime powers. The country was living on the fame of its former achievements, and had we been suddenly thrown into war with either France or England, we would have been amazed and mortified at the sorry exhibition our navy would have made. Our ports would have been blockaded and our ships shut up in harbors, until we could have built vessels and created a navy of respectable proportions. We were, however, making improvements in guns as well as England. The Dahlgren gun differs from ordinary cannon only in that the metal is taken from the forward part of the piece and put around the breech. The great strain always being in the back part of a cannon, the strength is concentrated here, so that a Dahlgren gun and one constructed on the old principle of the same weight, would have very different calibres—the former throwing a much larger shot. Almost endless experiments have been made to make guns of large calibre that would be safe. The casting of so large a mass as a gun that should be capable of throwing one hundred or two hundred pound shot, and yet have it, in the cooling process, retain its strength, was very difficult. Throwing a jet of water in the bore while the atmosphere cooled the outside has overcome some of the difficulty.

The rifled cannon of Parrott attracted but little attention from the public at large, until the breaking out of the war. It seems strange that the superior accuracy of the rifle to the musket did not suggest rifled cannon before, but the great difficulty was to make any large iron ball fit so closely as to get a spiral motion from the grooves. This was at last overcome by having the ball long instead of round, and slightly conical, and a band of copper metal around the base, which would expand into the grooves by the air being forced underneath it when the charge was fired. A tumbling shot from a rifled piece would, of course, be worse than a round shot from a smooth bore.

But a charge of thirty or forty pounds of powder required great strength in the breech of the piece, and to secure this, Parrott resorted to an ingenious contrivance. After the gun was cast, the surface of the breech was made of polished smoothness. Then a wrought-iron bar, several inches square, was rolled by machinery into a spiral coil, and the inside dressed off perfectly smooth, yet a fraction too small in bore to slip over the gun. This was then heated to make it expand, when it was driven over the breech. Contracting in cooling, it hugged the piece almost as close as though it had been welded to it. This wrought-iron reinforcement gives the rifled cannon prodigious strength, for the strain on the former is lengthwise of the metal. The various English rifled guns, such as the Whitworth, Armstrong, and others, differ only in the manner of producing the spiral motion of the shot or in being breech-loading.

But the greatest improvements have been in the construction of iron-clad vessels. France and England had both for a long time been experimenting on a large scale in their construction, and though our attention had been directed to it, but little had been done except to encourage by large appropriations the completion of the famous Stevens Battery at New York. But the breaking out of the civil war stimulated at once the proverbial ingenuity of Americans, and a great variety of models were proposed. The increased size of ordnance rendered a corresponding power of resistance in ships necessary, and Congress made an appropriation for the carrying out of some experiments in building iron-clad steamers. The

Secretary of the Navy was also authorized to appoint a board of three skilful naval officers to investigate the plans and specifications that might be submitted for their construction, and report on the same. The Navy Department immediately issued an advertisement for the construction of "one or more iron-clad steam vessels of war" for sea or river service, "to carry an armament of from eighty to one hundred and twenty tons' weight, with provisions and stores for from one hundred and eighty-five to three hundred persons, according to armament, for sixty days, with coal for eight days." This was in the forepart of August, 1861. The board consisted of Joseph Smith, H. Paulding, and C. H. Davis. By the middle of the next month their report was ready. Some seventeen propositions with specifications were sent in, of which only three were accepted. One was the Monitor of Ericsson, the price of which was to be $275,000; length of vessel 172 feet, breadth of beam 41 feet, depth of hold 10 feet, displacement 1,255 tons; speed per hour, nine statute miles. The second was the famous Ironsides, of Philadelphia, offered by Merrick & Sons. The price of this was to be $780,000; length of vessel 220 feet, breadth of beam 60 feet, depth of hold 23 feet, draught of water 13 feet, displacement 3,296 tons, speed per hour, nine and a half knots. The third proposition accepted, was that of Bushnell & Co., New Haven (the Galena). The price of this was $235,250; length of vessel 180 feet, breadth of beam — feet, depth of hold 12½ feet, draught of water 10 feet, displacement, —— tons; speed per hour, twelve knots. Of these it will be seen that the Ironsides was to be a very large vessel, and the contractors asked for nine months' time in which to complete her. In accordance with the recommendation of the Board the

Navy Department immediately made a contract with the three parties named above, and our iron-clad navy was commenced. Ericsson's model was a novel one—the vessel being made to lie very low in the water, and to carry but two guns of large calibre, which were to be mounted in a shot-proof turret that revolved by machinery placed within it, so that, without manœuvring the vessel, the broadside of two guns could be brought to bear on any desired point.

These were not to be made for exhibition, and to awaken criticism or excite doubts, but for actual immediate combat. No time could be wasted on target practice. The ponderous shot and shell already in use and to which wooden vessels presented no resistance, were to be tested on these, and the question settled at once for the whole world whether anything that would resist them could be made to float.

The Board did not think it desirable to go into the question of large sea-going steamers; for in the first place the appropriation was not sufficient, and in the second place, in this war, upon which we had entered, we should have little need of these, as the contest on the water was to be chiefly in our harbors and shoal rivers.

Various minor improvements, of course, followed these, but the three vessels contracted for settled the question of iron-clads, and revolutionized naval warfare.

But some months would necessarily elapse before these would be ready for service, and in the mean time the rebel ports must be blockaded, and such war-vessels as the enemy had stolen, or could extemporize, met and disposed of.

The coast was to be guarded over three thousand miles in extent, while our little navy was scattered over the world at the time of the breaking out of hostilities, so that the home squadron consisted on the 4th of March, 1861, the time of Mr. Lincoln's inauguration, of but twelve vessels, only a few of which were in Northern ports. These were the Pawnee, screw, at Washington, Crusader and Mohawk steamers, and a supply and store-ship at New York. Before the month closed, however, the Powhatan, Pocahontas, and Cumberland arrived.

The old navy, all told, consisted of but seventy-six vessels, carrying 1,783 guns. Fifteen vessels returned during the year, which, as fast as they could, were ordered on duty.

It can scarcely be wondered at, that European powers at first ridiculed the idea of our blockading so great an extent of coast with such an insignificant fleet.

At the outset our naval force was divided into two squadrons—the Atlantic, extending south of Cape Florida, under Stringham, and the Gulf squadron, its line of blockade reaching from Cape Florida to Grand Gulf, under G. W. Mason, who, in September, was superseded by McKean. Besides these there was the Potomac flotilla, necessary to keep open the water communication with Washington. Added to this, the Mississippi River must be opened, and a flotilla was at once ordered to be built on our western waters. Of course the necessities of the Government in a war of such gigantic proportions, and thrown so suddenly upon it, were too urgent to permit it to wait for the building of a sufficient number of vessels, and those to be used as a part of the navy, or that could be easily transformed into war-vessels, were purchased. One hundred and thirty-six were thus bought the first year, and fifty-two built, which, added to the old navy, made the new one to consist of 264 vessels, in all carrying 2,557 guns, with an aggregate of 218,000 tons and 22,000 seamen.

Although the seaports of Wilmington, Newbern, Charleston, Mobile, and New Orleans were very important ones in a military point of view, and their occupation by our forces necessary in the great plan for the overthrow of the rebel army, it was not expected they would be taken at once. Hence the sudden and great accession of naval strength was for the purpose of blockading them, for the South being a non-manufacturing country, its guns, ammunition, clothing, etc., must be brought from abroad. It was of the utmost importance to cut off these supplies; and the vessels which brought them belonging in the main to neutral powers, and the South having nothing deserving the name of a navy at sea, comparatively weak vessels would answer for blockading purposes. Speed was the first consideration; number and size of guns a secondary one. The South being filled with cotton, the want of which had stopped many mills in England, it furnished a tempting prize to adventurous ship-owners, especially as the articles which they brought in exchange for it would command fabulous prices. It had long ago been established as a law of nations that a *paper blockade*, or a blockade simply declared by proclamation, was not binding. There must be an adequate force to maintain it, or neutral powers were not obliged to regard it. Hence the enormous efforts of our Government to accumulate sufficient force at the various Southern seaports to sustain the President's proclamation. Of course, we could not have maintained the blockade of such an extent of coast had we been at a war with even a third-rate maritime power. The Southern Government, aware of this, began at once to construct a powerful ram, for the purpose of running down our vessels and breaking up the blockade. Rams, or vessels constructed with an iron beak to sink vessels by running into them, had been talked of before the war, and Col. Ellet urged on Congress the advantage to the Government of building such vessels. Their final adoption was another new feature in naval warfare. On our rivers and the smooth waters of our harbors they became powerful engines of destruction.

Great efforts were made by Southern emissaries to get France and England to deny the blockade, and it was fondly believed by the rebel Government that England would do this, on account of the cotton, on which her mills depended. It had been repeated so often by Southern speakers that "Cotton was king," that the South believed it, and that England, to keep her great manufactories going, and her millions from starving, would risk a war rather than do without it. But the British Government dreaded nothing so much as a collision with us, for although at the outset her powerful navy might overwhelm us, her statesmen well knew our vast resources, great inventive capacity, national pride, and indomitable perseverance in anything that we undertook; in short, that if we fell, like Samson, we would carry the pillars of her commercial temple with us in our overthrow.

But though, as a nation, she did not dare to disregard our blockade, she was not at all anxious to interfere with the private enterprise of her citizens in their efforts to render it ineffectual. The amount of shipping engaged in this nefarious business may be gathered from the fact that the very first year, with our inadequate naval force, we captured a hundred and sixty-one blockade-runners, and during the war, of both small and great, more than a thousand were taken or destroyed. When it is remembered that only a small percentage of those actually employed in this business were taken, at least in their first voyage, some estimate may be made of the number of times the blockade was run.

From this brief summary it may be seen how weak our naval force was at the outset of the war—the urgency of the Government in getting those vessels home that were scattered over different seas, and the prodigious efforts it put forth to obtain a naval force sufficient for the vast work it had to do. How great this work was, may be gathered from the fact that during the war, two hundred and eight vessels were commenced, and most of them completed, and four hundred and eighteen purchased, while the number of men in the service was increased from 7,600 to 51,500, and the number of artisans and laborers in the various navy-yards from 3,844 to 16,880, exclusive of an almost equal number engaged in private shipyards and establishments under contracts. The total sum expended by the Navy Department during the war was $314,170,960 68, or an annual average expenditure of $72,500,990 93.

Designing this brief outline of naval affairs as an introduction to the heroic deeds of our naval commanders, we refer the reader to the Appendix for fuller and more complete statistics.

CHAPTER II.

ADMIRAL DAVID GLASCOE FARRAGUT.

HIS PARENTAGE.—HIS FATHER SERVES IN THE REVOLUTIONARY ARMY.—NATIVITY OF DAVID.—APPOINTED MIDSHIPMAN WHEN NINE YEARS OF AGE.—SERVES UNDER CAPTAIN PORTER.—HIS FIRST CRUISE.—DESCRIPTION OF THE FIGHT IN VALPARAISO HARBOR.—DAVID'S HEROIC CONDUCT.—IS WOUNDED.—SENT HOME ON PAROLE.—PUT TO SCHOOL.—SENT TO THE MEDITERRANEAN.—STUDIES UNDER THE CHAPLAIN.—HIS PROMOTION.—STATIONED AT NORFOLK.—HIS MARRIAGE.—COMMANDS THE NAVY-YARD AT SAN FRANCISCO.—SECOND MARRIAGE.—REMAINS LOYAL AT THE BREAKING OUT OF THE REBELLION.—COMPELLED TO LEAVE NORFOLK.—COMMANDS THE EXPEDITION AGAINST NEW ORLEANS.—PASSAGE OF THE FORTS.—CAPTURE OF THE CITY.—HIS CAREER ON THE MISSISSIPPI.—DARING PASSAGE OF THE REBEL BATTERIES.—ANECDOTE.—EXPEDITION AGAINST MOBILE.—PASSES THE FORTS LASHED TO THE MAINMAST.—HIS AFTER-SERVICES AND PROMOTION.

EVER since the second war with England the navy has been the pride of the country. When the sea closed over the Guerrière, a new era dawned on naval history. From that moment the supremacy of England on the seas was broken, and ever since, wherever the national flag has been borne over the waters of the world, it has been looked on with respect. Our navy, in that war, obtained a character which commanders and sailors have been proud to maintain, until the "blue coats" have been synonymous with bravery. The shout that shook the land when Hull returned with the news of that first victory in a fair broadside-to-broadside engagement with one of England's finest frigates, kindled a feeling of pride in the heart of the people that has never since died out. Defeats may be expected on the land, but never on the sea. With such names heading the list of naval heroes as Hull and Bainbridge and Lawrence and Decatur and Porter and Perry and McDonough and Blakely and others, our commanders at the commencement of this war had a difficult task before them to maintain the high reputation which these illustrious captains had given the navy.

But no better name could be found than Farragut's with which to recommence that roll of renown. His father was born on the island of Minorca, in the Mediterranean Sea, but came to this country in 1776, at the opening of the great struggle for our independence. Entering at once into the spirit of that contest, like Kosciusko, Steuben, and Pulaski, he joined the ragged, ill-paid army of the colonies, and by his gallant conduct rose to the rank of Major. At the close of the war he married Miss Shire, of North Carolina, and settled down on our western frontier near Knoxville, Tennessee. Here, at Campbell's station, in 1801, David Glascoe Farragut was born. Although his early childhood was passed among the great forests of the West, his mind turned to the distant ocean, and in 1810, though but nine years of age, he obtained a midshipman's berth under Capt. Porter. This place was probably secured through the influence of his father, who was a warm friend of the captain, they being at that time sailing-masters in the navy together. A mere boy, of an age needing a mother's care, and scarce big enough to climb to the top of the bulwarks of his vessel, he was launched forth on the sea and the world together. Two years after, the war with England broke out, and he put to sea in the Essex, bearing on her defiant flag, "Free Trade and Sailors' Rights." Porter sailed in April, and as he passed down by the battery, he sent five shots into Castle William, to "try its strength;" then floating through the Narrows, swept off into the broad Atlantic. Young Farragut's first experience of a battle on that element which was to be his future home and field of renown, was in August. On the 13th the English sloop-of-war Alert hove in sight, and thinking to make an easy prey of the Essex, ran boldly down on her weather quarter, and giving three cheers, poured in a broadside. The Essex returned it with such fury that in eight minutes the English vessel had seven feet of water in her hold, and struck her colors. Young Farragut had gone to school in a wild sort of fashion, and his first lesson was one he was not likely ever to forget. A fortnight after, Porter came in sight of an English frigate just at dark, and fearing his powerful antagonist might lose him in the night, he hoisted a light, but in the morning the enemy was nowhere to be seen. Four days later he found himself near St. George's bank, close upon two ships of war, which immediately gave chase. As night came on he found the enemy gaining rapidly on him, and so he determined to heave about, and try to pass the largest ship unobserved, and in case he failed to do so, to give him one broadside and board him. He called the crew about him and made known his plans. Three cheers greeted the bold determination, and soon the vessel was bowling along in the darkness in the direction where his powerful adversary was last seen. He, however, passed him without being observed.

Not long after Farragut received another lesson in naval matters which his after-career shows was not lost on him. Sir James Yeo, of the frigate Southampton, sent a challenge to Porter in which, after presenting his compliments, he said he "would be glad to have a *tête-à-tête* anywhere between the Capes of Delaware and the Havana, when he would have the pleasure to break his own sword over his d—d head, and put him down forward in irons." To this Porter replied that he "accepted with pleasure his polite invitation," and "would prefer meeting near the Delaware Capes, where Capt. P. pledges his honor that no other American vessel shall interrupt their *tête-à-tête.* The Essex may be known by a flag bearing the motto: 'Free Trade and Sailors' Rights.' And when that is struck to the Southampton, Capt. Porter will deserve the treatment promised by Sir James." The blustering Englishman, however, did not take advantage of the offer, but one can see that the boy Farragut was to study his profession under a competent teacher.

But young David was soon transferred to a different scene. In October, Commodore Bainbridge having sailed from Boston with the Constitution and Hornet, Porter, then lying in the Delaware with the Essex, was ordered to join him in Port Praya, in St. Jago, or at Fernando, Norenha. But the capture of the Java by the Constitution, and of the Peacock by the Hornet, caused a change in the plans of Bainbridge; and Porter not finding him at either of the places above mentioned, or off Frio, another rendezvous designated by the Commodore, he was left to cruise where he thought best. After revolving various schemes, he at length, in midwinter, took the bold resolution to go alone into the Pacific, where he had not a depot of any kind, or a place in which a vessel could be refitted, while all the neutral ports were under the influence of our enemy, and make a dash at the British fishermen, and obtain his supplies from them. His prow was at once turned southward. Fierce storms off Cape Horn again and again beat him back; but he held on, and at length took the breezes of the Pacific, and stretched northward. Cruising here, he captured several vessels, until he had quite a little fleet. One of them, the Atlantic, he named the Essex Junior, and put it under the command of Lieut. Downes. Finding at length it was necessary to refit, and hearing that English cruisers were after him, he repaired to the Marquesas islands, and there, in a sequestered bay, repaired his vessels. The natives were at first friendly, but at length the Typees, a warlike tribe, succeeded in arousing the others to hostilities, and a plan was laid to murder all the American crews. Porter saw that he must make them feel his power, and so taking nearly his whole crew with him, he boldly entered the mountains, swarming with thousands of the natives, and marched towards the Typee villages. Compelled at first to retreat, he at length, after incredible hardships, reached the summit of the mountains, from which he descended in wrath on the beautiful plain below, and driving the natives into a fortress, set fire to their towns, and returned to the ship. David was now only twelve years old, yet he was eager to join the expedition; but much to his disappointment was left behind with the few that remained to take care of the ships. In the noontide of his fame, his attention being called to this period of his boyhood, he was asked why he did not accompany the captain in his notable campaign against the Typees. He replied, with his usual humor: "*I was ruled out—my legs being considered too short to cross the mountains.*"

It may easily be imagined that they *were* altogether too short for such a rough land-cruise as that of the captain's against the hostile tribes.

But all these new and trying scenes were merely preparatory to the great trial which was to fix his character for all future time. Porter, having finished his repairs, and leaving his two prizes behind, set sail in December, and arrived in Valparaiso the 12th of January. Here he determined to wait for the British ship Phœbe, which, he learned, had been sent out on purpose to capture him. She at length arrived; but not alone—the Cherub, sloop-of-war, bearing her company. These vessels bore flags with the mottoes: "God and our country—British sailors' best rights—Traitors offend them." Porter immediately hoisted at his mizen: "God, our country, and liberty—Tyrants offend them."

The English ships having taken in supplies, cruised outside for six weeks, completely blockading the Essex. Porter tried in vain to bring on an engagement with the Phœbe, but the latter steadily avoided it, though superior both in weight of metal and the number of men. Porter, finding that he had got to fight both vessels at once or not at all, and hearing that other British cruisers were on their way to the port, resolved to put to sea. So on the 28th of March, the wind blowing fresh, he stood out of port. But in doubling the Point of Angels to clear the harbor, a squall struck the vessel, carrying away the maintop-mast, and with it several men, who were drowned. It would not do to go to sea in this crippled condition, and unable to beat back to his former anchorage ground, he ran to the northeast side of the harbor and dropped anchor within three miles of the city, and a mile and a half from the Castello Viego. He was clearly on neutral ground, and where now, in the same circumstances, no nation on the globe would dare to fire into an American man-of-war. Yet Captain Hillyar moved down on him with both his vessels, and choosing his position, opened his broadsides on the Essex. Porter saw at once that to conquer was impossible, yet he resolved to fight his vessel to the last, and ordered the decks cleared for action. With the few guns he could bring to bear, he opened such a terrific fire that in a short time both vessels had to haul off for repairs. The cannonading had aroused the inhabitants, and they came thronging by thousands to see the unequal fight, and soon darkened the surrounding heights. Hillyar, having completed his repairs, came back and took his position where Porter could not bring a gun to bear. Proud and unyielding, he lay there for a while a helpless target on the water. Seeing that he would soon be sent to the bottom, he determined to make a desperate effort to board the largest vessel. But his sheets and halyards had been so shot away, that not a sail could be set except the flying jib. Giving this to the wind and cutting his cable, he drifted slowly down on his foes, and getting them at length within range of his carronades, opened a terrible fire. The cannonade on both sides now became swift and awful. The Essex, being set on fire and swept by the broadsides of both vessels, at length became almost totally unmanageable; but still she worked slowly forward, hoping to close, when Porter knew his inferior but brave crew would carry the vessel like a storm. But the English commanders, seeing their advantage, kept away. It was a painful sight to behold that crippled vessel, bravely limping up to grapple with her powerful adversary, and that adversary as slowly moving off, and pouring in the while a rapid, murderous fire. Hulled at almost every shot, her decks ripped up, and strewed with the dead, her guns torn from their carriages and rendered useless, it was evident the noble frigate could not be fought much longer. Porter saw his hopeless condition and, as a last resort, rather than strike his flag, resolved to run his vessel ashore and blow her up. Her head was with difficulty turned towards the beach and had actually got within musket-shot of it when the unsympathizing wind suddenly veered and blew him straight back on the Phœbe and under her raking broadsides. Still unyielding, Porter hoped by this untoward event to get foul and board the enemy. It was a last vain effort—fate was against him; the Phœbe kept edging away, raking the Essex as she retired.

The scene on board the frigate at this time was horrible. The cock-pit was crowded with the wounded; men by the dozen were mowed down at every discharge; fifteen had fallen successively at one gun, and scarcely a quarter-deck officer was left standing. And where was the boy Farragut all this time? A midshipman, it is true, he was, but nevertheless a lad only twelve years of age, too young to be standing in such a human slaughter-house. Only old and war-hardened hearts should beat unmoved amid such a wild scene. Yet there he stood—his delicate form rigid as iron, and his young heart fearless and proud as that of his commander. The deck ran blood beneath his tender feet, the splintered timbers crashed and shivered around him, and the murderous shot lifted the locks from his fair young head as they shrieked past him. The gore and clotted flesh of the brave men falling around him covered his garments, and the blood was trickling from a wound in his own side; yet there he stood manfully to the guns, his childish voice sounding strangely in that wild uproar, and his innocent blue eyes blazing with unnatural light amid that carnival of death as they turned unblenchingly on his beloved commander. Porter's case was evidently hopeless; but disdaining to yield, he made one more final attempt to bring his vessel around so as to make his broadside bear. He let go his sheet-anchor, and the staggering vessel, swinging slowly around again, presented her guns to the astonished foe. But the hawser parted in the strain, and the vessel lay an unmanageable wreck on the water, while to complete the disaster, the flames burst from the hatchway and rolled away towards the magazine. Porter now saw that his doom was inevitably sealed; and seeing that his boats had all been shot away, he ordered those of his crew who could swim, to jump overboard and attempt to reach the shore, three quarters of a mile distant. He then, with the few who chose to remain on board, among whom was young Farragut, extinguished the flames, and again shotted the few guns that could be brought to bear. It was, however, the last feeble effort of despair, for the water being smooth, and the enemy able to choose his own positions, he soon made a riddle of the American frigate. Her wounded were killed while under the hands of the surgeons, and only one of the carpenter's crew remained to stop the shot-holes, though the water was now pouring through in torrents. Porter would have gone down with his flag flying, but for the number of wounded that he would be compelled to take to the bottom with him; and so, after this unparalleled struggle of two hours and a half, he gave the melancholy orders to lower his flag.

I have given a lengthy description of this naval combat, because of its important bearing on Farragut's character. The future Admiral was christened in this awful baptism of fire. It was his first great lesson in naval combat, and it could not have been otherwise than stamped in indelible lines on his young heart. It was a fearful trial for one so youthful; but as he had chosen the navy for his profession, it was important he should see how a ship ought to be fought. To one of his age it would naturally occur that such was the *only* way a gallant commander would act, and of course he would settle it in his mind at once and forever, that it was the way he must act if ever called to command a vessel. That his future character was fixed in this unparalleled combat, his after-life clearly shows. In his daring passage of the forts below New Orleans, which to common men seemed madness—in his entrance to Mobile harbor, lashed to the maintop to direct the battle, he only acted over again the scenes of his boyhood. As one contemplates him in these daring enterprises, the mind involuntarily goes back to that battle in Valparaiso harbor. They are the lessons of boyhood put into practice in maturer years. We see simply the soul of Porter transferred to the soul of the boy that stood and battled by his side.

That his bearing on this occasion was gallant and heroic beyond his years, is evident from the fact that it attracted the especial attention of Porter. A hero of the grandest mould himself, and surrounded by heroic men—witnessing a devotion and courage seldom seen—he yet was struck by the conduct of this boy of twelve, and made special mention of him in his report to the Secretary of the Navy, adding, evidently with regret, that notwithstanding his meritorious conduct, he was "too young for promotion." Only twelve years old, he yet had behaved with such distinguished gallantry that he deserved a lieutenant's commission. The history of our navy records no other such instance. That such a boy, if he lived and circumstances permitted it, would be heard from again, was evident. He received his first wound in this engagement; but young as he was, it did not keep him from his post of duty. He was sent home in the Essex Junior, among the paroled officers. Porter's interest in the boy was enhanced by his heroic conduct in this battle, and he had him put to school at Chester and taught military tactics. He however was soon afloat again, being attached to the Mediterranean squadron. In 1816, we find him on board a ship of the line, where he became acquainted with the chaplain, the Rev. Charles Folsom, who took a great interest in him, and to whose instructions Farragut attributes much of his after-success in life. Afterwards, the chaplain was appointed our consul at Tunis, and David was sent with him. From this intimacy of three years' duration, sprung up a friendship which neither change of circumstances nor years of separation ever weakened. Mr. Folsom, in a letter respecting Farragut's life during the long peace that followed, says that it differed little from that of other officers. By slow degrees he worked his way up the difficult ladder of promotion, but did not reach the rank of lieutenant till the year 1825. He then married a lady of Norfolk; but it proved a less happy connection than he had anticipated, for she soon became a great sufferer, and continued so till relieved by death. Her trials, however, were relieved as much as they could be by a care and devotion and tenderness, such as a great soul like his alone can exhibit.

In 1841 he was made commander, and in 1851 captain. Promotion comes so slow in "piping times of peace" that it took him forty-one years to reach the rank of captain. He by turns sailed in almost every sea visited by our fleets, and by his studies and intercourse with other nations became proficient in several modern languages. At one time he was stationed at the Norfolk navy-yard, and afterwards was placed in command of the navy-yard at San Francisco. He also held the post of assistant inspector of ordnance for three years. In the mean time he married again, and this time also took his wife from Norfolk, Miss Virginia Loyall, daughter of a prominent citizen of the place. By her he had one son, now a cadet at West Point—choosing the military rather than the naval service.

He thus passed through his youth and manhood, and bade fair to pass through life without exhibiting any of those extraordinary qualities for which his boyhood was distinguished. He was nearly threescore years old when the rebellion broke out, having seen forty-eight years of service.

At this time he was living at Norfolk, and being a Southerner by birth and connected with the South by marriage, it was supposed by his Southern friends that he would cast in his lot with them. The tide seemed all to set that way. Officers went over by the dozen, whole messes resigned; and it was held dishonorable not "to go with their States," as it was termed. Very few Southern officers were proof against this feeling, especially as it was fully believed by them that the North and South would hereafter be separate nations. Even Lee said that if he thought the Union would ever be restored, he would go with the North, but as the two portions must inevitably constitute separate nationalities, he felt it his duty to cast his future in with the South. A few, however, remained true; and among these was Farragut. He had grown up from childhood with the old flag waving morning and night over his head; and from the time when, a mere boy, he had watched its bright folds gleaming amid the storm of battle in Valparaiso harbor—and with a great sorrow, such as his young heart never felt before, had seen it lowered to the foe—his love for it had grown with his growth and strengthened with his strength; and now he could not desert it. It was dearer to him than kindred, and he would stand by it to the last, and if fall he must in the deadly strife, it should be beneath it waving in all its pristine glory. He made no concealment of his views, and his Southern friends were at first astonished at what they considered his treason to the South; and then became indignant, and plainly hinted to him that it might be unsafe to remain longer in the South. "Very well," said he, "I will then go where I can live with such sentiments." At length Fort Sumter fell, and then came the conspiracy to seize the Norfolk navy-yard. Farragut now saw that if he expected to render his country any service in the awful struggle on which she was being so wildly launched, he must leave Norfolk; and so, on the night of the 18th of April, 1861, he bade adieu to his home, and turned his face northward. The very next day the navy-yard was set on fire. The Government was thunderstruck at the abyss opening beneath it, and knew not whom to trust amid the general defection. It had but few ships; and Farragut's services being uncalled for, he took up his abode on the Hudson River, just below Tarrytown, and watched with gloomy forebodings the increasing storm.

Being a stranger in the vicinity, his solitary walks in the fields were watched with suspicion, and it was whispered about that he was one of a band of conspirators to cut the Croton Aqueduct.

The Administration seemed asleep or stupefied; but after the battle of Bull Run, the following summer, it aroused from its lethargy, and began to act as though the country was really in the midst of civil war. In the autumn it resolved to make a bold push for the capture of New Orleans. The West Gulf Blockading Squadron, with twenty bomb-schooners, was to constitute the naval force, with which a land force of eighteen hundred men under Maj. Gen. Butler was to coöperate. Preparations were set on foot before the naval commander was determined on—an unwise step to start with; but the blunder was more than compensated by the fortunate selection of Farragut. The country knew but little about him, and when his name was published as the head of the expedidion, vastly more was expected from Porter, who commanded the bomb vessels, than from him.

He received his orders on the 20th of January, 1862, and on the 3d of next month sailed from Hampton Roads in the flag-ship Hartford—a vessel destined to assume a place in our naval history second only to that of the Old Constitution. The place of rendezvous was Ship Island, at which he arrived in seventeen days, and immediately began to make the arrangements necessary for the herculean task before him. He would have entered into a combat on the deep without any hesitation; but the work to which he was assigned—to beat down or run the batteries lining both sides of a river—was an entirely different undertaking. It was a new, untried experiment, and presented difficulties that to some seemed impossible to surmount;

but indomitable energy, he well knew, could overcome the greatest obstacles, and the fleet set sail and arrived safely at the entrance of the Mississippi. It was desirable to get the powerful steam frigate Colorado, Captain Bailey commanding, over the bars at the mouth of the river; but as she drew, with her armament aboard, twenty-two feet of water, and the deepest soundings gave only fifteen, this was found to be impossible. The Mississippi and Pensacola were got over only by great labor; and at length the fleet was safely anchored at the head of the Pass à l'Outre and the Southwest Pass. Those who saw with what care Farragut attended to the minutest details—the thorough preparation which he made for every contingency—felt that his bravery was equalled by his prudence and forethought.

The expedition, when it sailed on its secret, unknown destination from the North, created the liveliest interest; and when, at last, it was discovered that its object was the capture of New Orleans, the greatest enthusiasm prevailed, for the opening of the Mississippi was the first great object of the administration. But the long delays that followed, cooled down the public expectation, and it was at last almost lost sight of in the stirring victories that were taking place farther north under the gallant Foote. But Farragut, patient as well as daring, was biding his time.

Six war steamers, sixteen gunboats, twenty-one mortar vessels, with five other national vessels, comprised the fleet which had now fairly entered on its work.

It was a grand spectacle when, on the 16th of March, this formidable fleet at last opened its fire. The low banks of the river on both sides seemed inherent with flame, and the deep reverberations of the guns rolled like heavy thunder up the lordly Mississippi. All day long the earth trembled under the heavy explosions, and by night two thousand shells had been hurled against the forts.*

Farragut and Porter had obtained the exact distance of the forts by triangulation, performed by the coast survey under Captain Gerdes—Messrs. Harris and Oltmanns doing the work. Thus, surveyors' instruments prepared the way for the direct cannon shot. The rebels had not been idle during the delays of the previous weeks, but had contrived and constructed every possible instrument of destruction and defence. On the first morning of the bombardment they set adrift a fire-ship made of a huge flatboat piled with lighted pitch-pine cord-wood. It came drifting slowly down the sluggish stream, burning with a fierce crackling roar, and darkening all the sky with its volumes of black eddying smoke. Shot and shell had no effect on it, save to fill the air with flying sparks and blazing brands, and it kept steadily on its flaming path, straight towards our vessels. Two of the advance steamers were in danger of getting foul of it, and, slipping their cables, moved down the stream. On swept the unwieldy, blazing mass, and, keeping the middle of the stream, passed the entire fleet without inflicting any damage. As it disappeared below, the taunts and jeers of the sailors followed it. To be prepared for another, Captain Porter ordered all the row-boats of the flotilla, a hundred and fifty in number, to be supplied with grapnels, ropes, and buckets, ready at a moment's notice to seize it and tow it ashore. At night the rebels set another adrift, and as it towered majestically in the darkness near the forts,

* The account of the bombardment by the mortars will be found in the sketch of Vice-Admiral Porter.

signal-lights were run up on all the vessels, and those hundred and fifty boats leaped forth on the water as though created by magic. Down came the pyramid of flame, lighting the reed-fringed shores with a ruddy glow, and turning the muddy waters into molten flame. Swinging easily on the mighty current, it moved steadily down till its baleful glare was cast over the vessels at anchor along the banks. Suddenly out of the surrounding darkness, right into the blazing light the Westfield dashed with a full head of steam on, and, steering straight for the burning pile, buried its bows in the crackling mass, while her hose poured a torrent of water upon it. The next moment the diminutive row-boats shot into the light, and, sweeping swiftly over the ruddy waters, each sailor and oar painted in dark lines against the fiery background, fastened boldly to the burning structure, not knowing but that it was filled with torpedoes and missiles of death that might explode at any moment. They then gave way with a will, and in a short time the grand and imposing structure that seemed fraught with destruction, was consuming ignobly away against the shore. Loud cheers from the whole fleet greeted the gallant exploit.

The bombardment which had commenced was kept up steadily for a week, and although the fire, when the exact range was got, was very severe, setting the citadel of Fort Jackson on fire and driving the gunners from their pieces, the forts seemed as far from being reduced as ever. In the mean time shells, fuses, cartridge-boxes, coal, and hospital stores were getting short; the gunners on the mortar-boats were worn out, and when relieved from their guns would fall down exhausted on deck. It was evident that something else must be tried, or the expedition be abandoned. In this extremity a council of war was called on board the flag-ship, composed of the different commanders, and the question was put, What next shall be done? After it was over, Farragut issued his order: "The flag-officer, having heard all the opinions expressed by the different commanders, is of the opinion that whatever is to be done will have to be done quickly. When, in the opinion of the flag-officers, the propitious time has arrived, the *signal will be made to weigh, and advance to the conflict.* * * * He will make the signal for close action, No. 8, and abide the result—*conquer or be conquered.*"

A short time before, a French vessel had gone up to the forts, and on its return, one of its officers told Farragut he never could get by them. He replied, "I am ordered to go to New Orleans, and I intend to do so."

This decision having been reached, it only remained to get his wooden fleet in the best possible state of preparation for the terrible ordeal to which it was to be exposed. How this was done cannot be better described than in Farragut's own language. He says: "Every vessel was as well prepared as the ingenuity of her commander and officers could suggest, both for the preservation of life and of the vessel; and perhaps there is not on record such a display of ingenuity as has been evinced in this little squadron. The first was by the engineer of the Richmond, Mr. Moore, by suggesting that the sheet cables be stopped up and down on the sides, in the line of the engines, which was immediately adopted by all the vessels. Then each commander made his own arrangements for stopping the shot from penetrating the boilers or machinery, that might come in forward or abaft, by hammocks, coal, bags of ashes, bags of sand, clothes-bags, and, in fact, every device imaginable. The bulwarks were lined with hammocks by some, by splinter-nettings made with ropes by others. Some rubbed their vessels over with mud, to make their ships less visible, and some white-washed their decks, to make things more visible by night during the fight. In the afternoon, I visited each ship, in order to know positively that each commander understood my orders for the attack, and to see that all was in readiness. I had looked to their efficiency before. Every one appeared to understand his orders well, and looked forward to the conflict with firmness, but with anxiety, as it was to be in the night, or two o'clock in the morning."

The following order had been previously issued to the various commanders:

You will prepare your ship for service in the Mississippi river in the following manner:

Send down the top-gallant masts. Rig in the flying jib-boom, and land all the spars and rigging, except what are necessary for the three topsails, foresail, jib, and spanker. Trice up the topmast stays, or land the whiskers, and bring all the rigging into the bowsprit, so that there shall be nothing in the range of the direct fire ahead.

Make arrangements, if possible, to mount one or two guns on the poop and top-gallant forecastle; in other words, be prepared to use as many guns as possible ahead and astern, to protect yourself against the enemy's gun-boats and batteries, bearing in mind that you will always have to ride head to the current, and can only avail yourself of the sheer of the helm to point a broadside gun more than three points forward of the beam.

Have a kedge in the mizzen chains (or any convenient place) on the quarter, with a hawser bent and leading through in the stern chock, ready for any emergency; also grapnels in the boats, ready to hook on to, and to tow off, fire-ships. Trim your vessel a few inches by the head, so that if she touches the bottom she will not swing head down the river. Put your boat howitzers in the foremaintops, on the boat carriages, and secure them for firing abeam, &c. Should any injury occur to the machinery of the ship making it necessary to drop down the river, you will back and fill down under sail, or you can drop your anchor and drift down, but in no case attempt to turn the ship's head down stream. You will have a spare hawser ready, and when ordered to take in tow your next astern, do so, keeping the hawser slack so long as the ship can maintain her own position, having a care not to foul the propeller.

No vessel must withdraw from battle, under any circumstances, without the consent of the flag-officer. You will see that force and other pumps and engine hose are in good order, and men stationed by them, and your men will be drilled to the extinguishing of fire.

Have light Jacob-ladders made to throw over the side for the use of the carpenters in stopping shot holes, who are to be supplied with pieces of inch board lined with felt and ordinary nails, and see that the ports are marked in accordance with the "ordnance instructions" on the berth deck, to show the locality of the shot hole.

Have many tubs of water about the decks, both for the purpose of extinguishing fire and for drinking. Have a heavy kedge in the port main-chains, and a whip on the main-yard, ready to run it up and let fall on the deck of any vessel you may run alongside of, in order to secure her for boarding.

You will be careful to have lanyards on the lever of the screw, so as to secure the gun at the proper elevation, and prevent it from running down at *each fire*. I wish you to understand that the day is at hand when you will be called upon to meet the enemy in the worst form for our profession. You must be prepared to execute all those duties to which you have been so long trained in the navy without having the opportunity of practising. I expect every vessel's crew to be well exercised at their guns, because it is required by the regulations of the service, and it is usually the first object of our attention; but they must be equally well trained for stopping *shot holes* and extinguishing fire. Hot and cold shot will, no doubt, be freely dealt to us, and there must be stout hearts and quick hands to extinguish the one and stop the holes of the other.

I shall expect the most prompt attention to signals and verbal orders either from myself or the captain of the fleet, who, it will be understood, in all cases acts by my authority.

D. G. FARRAGUT,
Flag-Officer, Western Gulf Blockading Squadron.

Having at last made all the preparations that he could with the means allowed him, and the mortar-boats having accomplished all that was in their power to do for the present, the 26th day of April was fixed for the passage of the forts. The chain across the channel had been cut a few nights before, and a daring reconnoissance by Lieutenant Caldwell, on the night preceding the intended movement, showed that it had not been repaired.

It was determined to start at two o'clock in the morning, and, the evening before, Farragut visited his ships for a last interview with the commanders. These brave men were anxious as he himself was, as he went from ship to ship on that momentous afternoon, to see that his orders were understood; for there were two powerful forts, mounted with heavy guns, with their terrific cross-fire, to be passed, while fire-ships, rams, and iron-clad gunboats lay beyond this gate of death, ready to receive what might remain of the crippled squadron, if any portion should succeed in getting through. Hopes, fears, doubts of success, and anticipations of glory, by turns filled their hearts, but on none did such a heavy load lay as on Farragut.

That quiet spring evening was passed as the few hours that precede a desperate battle always is. Some, gay and reckless, laughed and joked over the coming encounter, with all the thoughtlessness of sailors; others spent it in indicting last letters to loved ones at home, and entrusting keepsakes to friends, should they fall; while some God-fearing men knelt in prayer, and committed their lives calmly into the hands of Him whose purposes are ever right. The mighty river swept placidly by, fanned by the balmy breeze, and the quiet stars came out one by one and looked down, tranquil as ever, on the unconscious stream, giving no token of the coming earthquake. Some, inured to danger, lay down and slept soundly as ever; others paced the deck, taking, as they believed, their last look of the tranquil heavens.

Thus the hours wore away, and midnight came, and still all was quiet on land and water, save the solemn boom, at short intervals, of a gun from the boats on watch far up stream. At length, at two o'clock, two lanterns were seen to rise slowly to the mizzen peak of the Hartford. The hour of action had come, and quickly the boatswain's shrill call rung over the water, "Up all hammocks," and the drums beat to quarters.

In a moment that quiet scene was changed to one of intense activity and bustle. The rattling of chains, the "yo heave ho" at the anchors, and quick, stern commands of the officers, and slow revolving of wheels, and answering signal-lights sparkling through the gloom, sent the blood with a quicker flow through every heart. The surrounding darkness imparted a mystery to these sounds of preparation, and added a deeper interest to the scene. In one hour everything was ready, and the low, black masses were moving steadily up towards the slumbering forts.

The attack was to be made in two columns. The right, led by Captain Bailey in the Cayuga, was composed of the Pensacola, Mississippi, Oneida, Varuna, Katahdin, Kineo, and Wissahickon; the left, led by Farragut in the Hartford, of the Brooklyn, Richmond, Sciota, Iroquois, Kennebec, Spinola, Itasca, and Winona. The latter was to engage Fort Jackson, and the former St. Philip. Porter, with the Harriet Lane, Westfield, Owasco, Miami, Clifton, and Jackson, was to take up a position where he could pour in an enfilading fire while the fleet was passing the forts.

The enemy was on the look-out, and the vessels had scarcely got under way when signal-lights flashed along the batteries, and then a belt of fire gleamed through the darkness, and the next moment the heavy shot came shrieking along the bosom of the stream. All eyes were now turned on the Hartford, as she silently steamed on —the signal "close action" blazing from her rigging. In the mean time the mortar-boats below opened their fire, and the hissing shells rose in graceful curves, and, weaving an arch of fiery network over the advancing fleet, dropped with a thunderous sound into the forts above. In a few minutes the advanced vessels opened, firing at the flash from the forts. The white smoke rolled and heaved in vast volumes along the shuddering waters, and one of the wildest scenes in the history of war now commenced. The fleet, with full steam on, was soon abreast of the forts, and its rapid broadsides mingling in with the deafening explosions on shore, turned night into fiery day. Louder than redoubled thunders the heavy guns sent their deafening roar through the gloom, not in distinct explosions, but in one long, wild, protracted crash, as though the ribs of nature were breaking in final convulsion. Amid this hell of terrors, a fire-raft, pushed steadily forward by the ram Manassas, loomed through the smoke like a phantom from the unseen world. As if steered by adverse fate, it bore straight down on the Hartford. Farragut sheered off to avoid the collision, and in so doing ran aground, when the fire-ship came full against him. In a moment the hungry flames leaped up the rigging and darted along the smoking sides of the Hartford. It seemed all up with the gallant Farragut, and but for that stern discipline he always maintains, his fate would have been sealed. There was no panic on board at this awful catastrophe—every man was in his place, and in a moment the hose was manned and a stream of water turned on the flames. The powerful engines were reversed, and soon forced the vessel off into deep water, though all aflame. The firemen, cool and collected, plied their hose, while the gunners still stood to their guns, and poured in their broadsides, and still the signal, "close action," flamed above the staggering ship. The fire was at length got under, and Farragut again moved at the head of his column. And now came down the rebel fleet of thirteen gunboats and two iron-clad rams to mingle in the combat. Broadside to broadside, hull crashing against hull, it became at once a gladiatorial combat of ships. The Varuna, Captain Boggs, sent five to the bottom one after another; and, finally overcome by her unparalleled exertions, the noble boat went down to join her adversaries beneath the turbid Mississippi.

Farragut at last found himself past all the forts, with thirteen out of the seventeen vessels of the fleet. The Itasca, Winona, and Kennebec were so terribly cut up that they had to turn back, and floated in a crippled condition down the river. The Kineo was accidentally run into by the Brooklyn, and badly stove—receiving besides twelve shots in her hull; yet she gallantly fought her way through. The Hartford, Cayuga, and Varuna encountered the greatest apparent dangers; yet every vessel, especially the Brooklyn, humanly speaking, ought to have been lost, for never before were such frail boats exposed to such a terrible fire and lived. The several commanders were worthy to fight under such a glorious leader, and carried their ships forward with a steadiness and nerve that have covered their names with imperishable renown.

When the sun struggled up through the morning mist, he looked down on a scene never to be forgotten while naval deeds are honored by the nation. There lay the forts with the rebel flags still flying. But their doom was sealed. And there, too, driven ashore or wrecked or captured, were thirteen of the enemy's gunboats out of the seventeen he had brought down to assist the forts in demolishing our fleet.

Our total loss in this unparalleled combat was one hundred and seventy-one.

Farragut now steamed up the river towards New Orleans, having first dispatched Captain Boggs in an open boat, through a bayou inlet, to announce to Porter his success. In his letter to the latter he says, with a *sang froid* and brevity that provoke a smile: "We have had a rough time of it, as Boggs will tell you;" and then adds, that as soon as he has captured New Orleans he will return and finish the forts. As he passed up, he heard cannonading ahead, for Bailey in advance had come upon powerful batteries at English Town, and was getting severely handled. But the Hartford coming to his rescue, they were soon finished.

The way these were disposed of cannot be given better than in Farragut's own language: "They permitted us to approach within a mile and a quarter before they opened on us. Captain Bailey, in the Cayuga, Lieutenant-Commander Harrison, was in advance of me, and received the most of the first fire; but, although the shooting was good, they did not damage his little vessel much. He fell back, and the Hartford took her place. We had only two guns, which I had placed on the top-gallant forecastle, that could bear on them, until we got within half a mile. We then sheered off, and gave them such a fire 'as they never dreamed of in their philosophy.' The Pensacola ran up after a while, and took the starboard battery off our hands; and in a few moments the Brooklyn ranged and took a chance at my friends on the left bank. They were silenced in, I should say, twenty minutes or half an hour. But I cannot keep a note of time on such occasions. I only know that half of the vessels did not get a chance at them. The river was too narrow for more than two or three vessels to act to advantage; but all were so anxious, that my greatest fear was that we should fire into each other; and Captain Wainwright and myself were hallooing ourselves hoarse at the men not to fire into our ships. This last affair," he says, "was what I call one of the little elegances of the profession—a dash and a victory." But in speaking of the passage of the forts, in the same letter, he says: "It was one of the most awful sights and events I ever saw or experienced. The smoke was so dense that it was only now and then you could see anything but the flash of the cannon and the fire-ships and rafts."

New Orleans was now at his mercy, and Lovell, commanding the rebel troops in the city, took himself off and left it once more under the control of the mayor, Monroe From him Farragut, through Captain Bailey, demanded the surrender of the city, and that the national flag be hoisted by noon on the City Hall, Mint, and Custom House, which were the property of the United States. To this summons the Mayor sent a long, windy, ridiculous answer. In regard to the raising of the flags, he said: "As to the hoisting any flag other than the flag of our adoption and allegiance, let me say to you that the man lives not in our midst whose hand and heart would not be paralyzed at the *mere thought of such an act;* nor could I find in my entire constituency so wretched and desperate a renegade as would dare to profane with his hand the sacred emblem of our aspirations." He then goes on to compliment Farragut as much as he could concerning his "noble but deluded nature," and winds up with an appeal to be very careful of the feelings of his gallant constituency, assuming an air of superiority and injured innocence that entitle him to a preëminence among all conquered rulers of cities. To this piece of fustian and rhodomantade Farragut returned the following quiet, brief reply:

UNITED STATES FLAG-SHIP HARTFORD,
OFF THE CITY OF NEW ORLEANS, *April* 26.

To his Honor the Mayor of New Orleans:

Your Honor will please give directions that no flag but that of the United States will be permitted to fly in the presence of this fleet so long as it has the power to prevent it; and as all displays of that kind may be the cause of bloodshed, I have to request that you will give this communication as general a circulation as possible.

I have the honor to be, very respectfully,
Your obedient servant,
D. G. FARRAGUT.

No bluster in this, but a very plain hint, that his honor, pompous and inflated as he is, may easily understand. "No flag but the stars and stripes will kiss the air in my sight while my guns, shotted and ready, bear on your city." Stern and inflexible in the discharge of his duty, yet humble and meek before his Creator, he, on the same day on which this curt message was sent to the mayor, issued the following order:

UNITED STATES FLAG-SHIP HARTFORD,
OFF THE CITY OF NEW ORLEANS, *April* 26, 1862.

GENERAL ORDER:

Eleven o'clock this morning is the hour appointed for all the officers and crews of the fleet to return thanks to Almighty God for His great goodness and mercy in permitting us to pass through the events of the last two days with so little loss of life and blood. At that hour the church pennant will be hoisted on every vessel of the fleet, and their crews assembled will, in humiliation and prayer, make their acknowledgments therefor to the Great Dispenser of all human events.

D. G. FARRAGUT,
Flag-Officer Western Gulf Blockading Squadron.

Although he had refused to confer further with the impudent Mayor, he ordered Captain Morris to hoist the flag on the Mint. The latter sent a party on shore, and soon the old flag swung once more to the breeze in sight of the enraged population. The officer in charge warned the spectators that the guns of the Pensacola would open fire on the building if any one attempted to haul it down. Leaving no guard to protect it, he returned to the ship and directed the howitzers in the maintop to be loaded with grape and trained on it.

At eleven o'clock, in accordance with the order given above, the crews were all assembled on deck for prayers, and only one look-out left in the maintop to watch the flag. The solemn service had been progressing perhaps twenty minutes when the deep silence was broken by the discharge of the howitzers overhead. It at once aroused every man from his devotions, and as all eyes turned towards the Mint they saw four men on the roof of the building tearing down the flag. In an instant the gunners, without waiting for orders, sprang to the guns and pulled the lanyards. The next moment a whole broadside was expected to pour into the city; but not a gun went off. As it looked like rain, the gunners had removed the "wafers" by which they were discharged, before the service commenced, so that only the click of the locks was heard. But for this, fearful destruction would have ensued.

Farragut also had trouble with Clouet, the commander of a French man-of-war, who, choosing to consider the order of the former as threatening the city with immediate bombardment, had protested indignantly against it.

Wearied out with the ridiculous proceedings all round, he gladly turned over the city to Butler, and advanced up the river with his fleet. He sent Captain Palmer ahead to demand the surrender of Baton Rouge, and, while the correspondence with the Mayor was going on, arrived himself and took possession. He then directed the Captain to proceed to Natchez and seize it, while S. P. Lee continued on to Vicksburg and demanded its surrender. To this the military governor, Antry, replied that Mississippians did not know how to surrender, and if Farragut could teach them, to come on and try.

After a somewhat spicy correspondence with Lovell, with regard his to taking vengeance on the inhabitants of a place near which the latter chose to place guns to fire into our passing vessels, Farragut proceeded to test the batteries of Vicksburg. Porter was ordered up with his mortar flotilla to shell out the heights, and at two o'clock on the 28th of June the signal to weigh anchor was given, and with the Iroquois (Roland commanding), the Oneida (S. P. Lee), the Richmond (James Alden), and Sciota, Pinola, and Winona, slowly steamed up into the fire of the batteries.

The rebel guns opened on the fleet, the shot apparently being directed principally on the flag-ship. As the Hartford slowly approached, moving only fast enough to give steerage way, she opened a fearful fire from her starboard battery. She was so near that the gunners on shore could be plainly seen working their guns and waving their hats in defiance. Farragut, with his accustomed audacity, mounted to the mizen rigging to direct the movements; but his life there was not worth a farthing, for the enemy fired too high, and hence their concentrated storm of shot and shell tore through the rigging of the vessel, shrieking in a perfect hurricane around him. He therefore descended to the deck, and not two minutes after, the rigging where he had been standing was torn into shreds. Had he remained a little longer, he undoubtedly would have fallen a dead or wounded man on the deck below.

For two hours he lay broadside to the batteries, pouring in an incessant fire, when, finding that he could not bring his guns to bear any longer, he put on steam and shot past, up the river. He had been struck by a splinter, which, however, only made a bruise. The Richmond, Oneida, Pinola, Sciota, ran the batteries with him. Captain Craven, of the Brooklyn, had received orders not to leave any batteries behind him without silencing them, and after sustaining the same fire for two hours, dropped down the river, remaining with the Kennebeck, Katahdin, and Porter mortar fleet. The loss on those which succeeded in passing the batteries was forty-five.

Farragut now sent dispatches to Captain Davis, commanding the squadron of the Upper Mississippi, and Halleck, asking their coöperation in the movements against Vicksburg. In the mean time, he wrote to the Government, that, though he might be able to silence the batteries of Vicksburg, and could go up and down when he chose, yet the place could not be captured without the aid of ten or twelve thousand men to approach it from the rear. The bombardment, however, was kept up, though with but little effect.

About the middle of July, Farragut again steamed past the batteries, and anchored below with the rest of his fleet. The next month he fulfilled his threat against Donaldsonville, unless the inhabitants ceased the practice of firing on his vessels as they passed up and down the river, and opened his guns on the place and nearly destroyed it.

He also dispatched a part of his force to take Galveston, Corpus Christi, and Sabine City. Commander W. B. Renshaw captured the former, and G. W. Kittredge seized Corpus Christi, and Acting-master F. Crocker Sabine Pass. Lieut.-commander Thos. McKean Buchanan was also dispatched to the Southwest Pass; and up the Teche he had a sharp engagement with rebel batteries, and the rebel gunboat Cotton.

The next month we find Farragut again down the river, in front of Baton Rouge—a part of his fleet assisting in the engagement on land, in which the gallant General Williams fell in the very moment of victory.

His career during the rest of the season was distinguished chiefly for hard work, without any great battles. Among the incidents illustrative of his character that abound on the Mississippi, is one which showed his *sang froid.* In order to show how impervious iron-clads could be made against the heaviest shot, he was asked one time to accompany the Benton, the strongest boat in Davis's fleet, in a reconnoissance of a new battery that had been erected near Vicksburg. He did so; but the vessel had been but a short time under the fire of the battery, when a heavy shot crashed through the mailed sides, and, striking a person beside him, tore him to fragments, throwing the blood and clotted flesh over his own person. Gazing a moment at the frightful spectacle, he coolly turned to the officer beside him and said: "I am not going to stay here; I am going on deck." It seemed a curious place to go for safety; but the anecdote throws a world of light on the character of the man. When the storm raged fiercest, and shot and shell fell thickest on the vessel, he wished to stand on her exposed deck.

But the next year, in the very month (April) in which he passed the batteries of forts Philip and Jackson, he again showed what wooden vessels could do against formidable shore batteries. Grant was working his slow, toilsome way towards Vicksburg, and Farragut was ordered up to coöperate with him. But since he was there the year before, the rebels, owing to the stupidity of the War Department, which, in the face of Porter's earnest representations, refused to occupy Port Hudson, had erected formidable works, which were more difficult to pass than the batteries at Vicksburg.

With the flag-ship Hartford, accompanied by the Richmond, armed with twenty-six eight and nine-inch Columbiads, the Mississippi, with twenty-one, the Monongahela with sixteen heavy guns, and the gunboats Kineo, Albatross, Sachem, and Gennessee, carrying each three Columbiads and two rifled 32-pounders (all screw propellers except the Mississippi), he, on the morning of the 14th of April, anchored below the place. Here the preparations were all completed, and as Farragut determined to run the terrible gauntlet in the night, and hence could have no lights aboard the vessels, the decks, gun-carriages and nettings were whitewashed, so that the gunners could distinguish enough to work their pieces. The next morning he reached Prophet's Island, in full view of the rebel batteries. Four mortar-boats were anchored some three miles distant, to throw shells into the hostile works. At one o'clock these opened fire, and all the afternoon the blazing shells swept in long curves over the stream and dropped amid the hostile guns. They seemed, however, to produce but little effect. A small land force had been sent to the rear of the garrison to distract their attention; for Farragut, notwithstanding his former success, saw clearly enough that his vessels were to be put to a severer test than ever before.

That night, when all was ready, the Hartford ran up a red light—the signal to weigh anchor—and the little fleet moved cautiously up the stream. The Hartford, with the Albatross lashed to her side, led the van, followed by the Richmond with the Gennessee, and the Monongahela with the Kineo. The Mississippi and Sachem came last. The rebel batteries extended for nearly four miles along the banks, tier above tier. The experience of the past year had not been lost on the enemy, and they had fortified the place so that it was thought impossible for boats to get past it. Made perfectly aware by their men on watch of the movements of Farragut, the latter had scarcely started, when signal-lights flashed from battery to battery, and then a blaze leaped up on the shore from a pile of combustibles gathered for the purpose, which soon swelled to a conflagration that made the whole bosom of the stream in front, light as day. Notwithstanding all his precaution, it was plain that Farragut would have light enough on his awful passage. When the silent, dark vessels entered this illuminated space, the fire of the rebel batteries was awful beyond conception. The vessels at once poured in their starboard broadsides, as rapidly as the guns could be loaded and fired. There was but little air stirring. The huge volumes of smoke, rolling out in fierce contortions over the ruddy bosom of the stream, added indescribably to the terror of the combat, while above it the shells rose and fell incessantly, with shrieks that ribbed the continuous thunder-peal below with a strange, unearthly sound. The immense volumes of smoke soon wrapped river and shore in impenetrable darkness, rent only by the solid sheets of fire that burst through. Amid this terrific uproar there arose from the water the despairing cry of "Help! oh, help!" from a drowning man who had fallen overboard. But amid this wild hurricane of death no help could be given, and the cry grew fainter and fainter, as the poor fellow was borne down by the swift current, till it was lost in the distance. The river was narrow at this point, and soon the ships, in the smoke and darkness, could not see each other, and again and again barely escaped firing a broadside into each other. The shouts of the officers rose over the din, and the whole scene became one of complete bewilderment; yet the brave ships struggled on, stemming the mighty current, in the stern endeavor to pass this gateway of hell. An officer stood on the prow of each vessel, striving to pierce the gloom, while a line of men stretched from him to the stern, to transmit orders; for if she should run aground in the darkness, her doom was sealed. For an hour and a half this fearful nightly combat lasted, before the Hartford, with the Albatross lashed to her side, succeeded in passing beyond the batteries. Farragut now turned his eye down stream, to see what had become of the rest of his fleet; but not a vessel greeted his eye, except, through the intervening darkness, now and then a black hull would start out amid the gushes of flame, that, like a blaze of lightning, illuminated the river, showing that they were still struggling below. The Richmond came next to him, but a shell had entered her starboard port, bursting inside with a terrific explosion that almost lifted the strong ship from the water. Soon after a storm of shot burst through her bulwarks, sending everything to wreck in its passage. Lieut.-Commander Cummings, with speaking trumpet in hand, was shouting out over the uproar to his crew at the time, and by his side stood Captain Alden, and both fell at once to the deck—the former with his left leg torn off just below the knee. As they bore him away, he said: "Put a tourniquet on my leg, boys. Send my letters to my wife, and tell her I fell in doing my duty." As the surgeon took off the shattered limb, he said, "I would willingly give my other leg, if we could but pass those batteries." The vessel struggled on amid flame and smoke, and succeeded in passing the most powerful batteries, when a shot entered her steam-chest, which so disabled her that she began to drift helplessly down stream. Just then a torpedo burst under her stern, with a force that made all her timbers quiver. The Gennessee, which was alongside, now took her in tow, and steamed rapidly down stream. The Monongahela, with the Kineo, that came next, fared but little better. Her commander (McKinstry) fell early in the battle, and the command devolved on Lieutenant Thomas. In the smoke and darkness, she lost the channel, and suddenly found herself aground directly under the fire of a heavy battery, where she lay for nearly a half an hour, riddled and torn by shot and shell. At length she succeeded in backing off, and once more boldly turned her prow up stream, and began to stem the rapid current. But the tremendous fire to which she had been so long exposed had disabled her machinery, and it was soon evident that the gallant struggle was in vain, and she too dropped down to the mortar fleet at Prophet's Island. Last of all came the noble Mississippi, with a crew of three hundred aboard, sweeping proudly over the waters whose name she bore, with the Selma lashed to her larboard side, to assist her in case her machinery gave way. She got opposite the town, and, feeling that her greatest danger was over, put on steam and shot swiftly ahead.

The next moment she struck bottom near the western shore, having lost her course in the darkness. There she lay, a moveless target. The enemy saw her, and immediately concentrated an awful fire upon her. Captain Smith ordered the gunners to keep up their fire, and her broadsides exploded so rapidly that one could scarcely count the reports, and in the mean time he put forth every effort to get the vessel afloat. Her decks were soon slippery with blood, and the dead and wounded lay strewn around like autumn leaves. The ship, however, under her great headway, had buried herself so deep in the mud that she could not be forced off, and Smith resolved to destroy her. Amid the raining shot, combustibles were piled fore and aft, to be fired as soon as the crew had taken to the boats. By some mistake the torch was applied forward before the order was given, and while the crew still crowded the deck. A panic followed, and some flung themselves overboard, many of whom were drowned. Captain Smith, however, coolly lighted his segar, and quietly, but rapidly, hurried the men ashore; and then, spiking the guns—many of them with his own hand—he, with Lieutenant Dewey and Engineers Boekelder and Tower, who had stood by him to share his fate, left the vessel, and stepped on board the iron-clad Essex, which had come to his assistance, commanded by Captain Caldwell, and amid the tempest of shot and shell that incessantly swept both vessels, removed all the sick and wounded, and dropped down stream. As the light of the burning vessel arose on the midnight air, the enemy on shore sent up frantic yells of delight. The next moment two shells burst in the abandoned ship, scattering several casks of turpentine amid the blazing combustibles. A torrent of fire immediately rolled over the vessel, which, lightened by the removal of her crew and the action of the flames, now slowly floated off; and her bow, catching the downward current, swung heavily down stream, bringing her other broadside to bear, which had not yet been used. The guns, heated by the fire, soon began to go off, one after another, as though fired by an invisible hand. The flag was still floating above the flaming ruin, and the grand old vessel, as if conscious that the country's honor was committed to her keeping, swept steadily down stream, flaunting her colors in the face of the foe, and in her death-struggles still thundering on the hostile batteries. It was a wild and grand spectacle that she presented, as, erect amid the roaring flames—not wildly swaying with the current, but moving steadily, as though steered by an unseen hand, with her flag still flying and her guns roaring—she passed proudly and all alone, out of the desolating fire. Still drifting with the current, she swept on till Prophet's Island concealed her form. Then there suddenly arose a pyramid of fire and smoke, lighting up the shores like a conflagration, followed by an earthquake sound. The fire had reached her magazine, and in one loud explosion the proud vessel, which had so long braved the seas, went to the bottom, carrying her flag with her. Of about three hundred that composed her crew, sixty-five, or nearly a quarter, were killed, wounded, or taken prisoners. Seventy, who reached the western shore, made their way through the woods and swamps, and finally reached the ships below.

Farragut, with the Albatross, was now above the place, but all alone. His fleet was cut off from him. He had not only been lucky in getting safely through, but his vessel had been handled with consummate skill; for it was necessary to strike the rapid current running almost at right angles to his course, as he passed the point, so as to keep his bows from being swept around, and the vessel borne back down the stream under the batteries. In the darkness, this was a very difficult matter.

Though he had not succeeded in getting the vessels he needed above the place, he at once began to bombard it, while the fleet attacked it from below.

In the subsequent siege of the place by Banks, Farragut did good service, inflicting severe injury on the rebel batteries.

While at Port Hudson he heard, in the latter part of June, that Donaldsonville was about to be attacked by the rebels, and moved down before it, and on the day of attack opened such a flanking fire on the enemy that he was obliged to withdraw, although the storming party had already got inside. He also bombarded Grand Gulf.

Much impatience was exhibited East at the slowness with which operations went on around Vicksburg. Farragut was blamed by a portion of the press. Among other papers which showed dissatisfaction with his course was the *Journal of Commerce.* This one he took notice of in a letter to the Secretary of the Navy, saying that he did so because he heard that the information of the writer was obtained from the War Department.

His duties on the waters of the Mississippi and coast of Texas, the blockading of which was under his charge, were not of the kind most congenial to his tastes, for a great part of the time he was compelled to keep his squadron scattered on every side. Guerrillas had to be attacked in one place, an annoying little battery silenced in another, streams and channels opened to our forces, or shut to blockade runners, and rebel property destroyed where it was of use to the Confederate government—making those duties varied and harrassing. Here and there, too, losses were sustained which he had no means of preventing, as most of the work had to be done by subordinates that, from the peculiar circumstances in which they were placed, had to act without specific orders.

Hence it was with satisfaction that he heard he was to to be removed from this sort of guerrilla warfare on the water, and once more hoist his pennant on the deep. The strongholds on the Mississippi having fallen, the Government next turned its attention to Mobile. It was decided that a land and naval force combined should operate against it—the former under Generals Canby and Granger, and the latter under Farragut. In January, 1864, he sailed for Mobile Bay to make a reconnoissance of the forts and batteries, and vessels commanding its entrance, for the purpose of obtaining an accurate knowledge of their strength. Morgan and Gaines were the chief forts barring it, and he gives the following as the results of his investigations:

On the morning of the 20th instant I made a reconnoissance of Forts Morgan and Gaines. I went in over the bar in the gunboat Octorara, Lieutenant Commander Lowe, taking the Itasca in company as a precaution against accident. We passed up to Land Island, and laid abreast of the light-house on it. The day was uncommonly fine and the air very clear. We were distant from the forts three (3) and three and a half (3½) miles, and could see everything distinctly, so that it was easy to verify the statements of the refugee McIntosh, in respect to the number of guns visible on the bastions of the fort. I could count the guns and the men who stood by them; could see the piles that had been driven across from Fort Gaines to the channel opposite Fort Morgan—the object of which is to force the ships to keep as close as possible to the latter. There were no vessels in the bay except one transport steamer.

I am satisfied that if I had one iron-clad at this time, I could destroy their whole force in the bay, and reduce the forts at my leisure, by coöperation with our land forces—say five thousand men. We must have about two thousand and five hundred men in the rear of each fort, to make regular approaches by land, and to prevent the garrison's receiving supplies and reinforcements; the fleet to run the batteries, and fight the flotilla in the bay. But without iron-clads, we should not be able to fight the enemy's vessels of that class with much prospect of success, as the latter would lie on the flats where our ships could not go to destroy them. Wooden vessels can do nothing with them unless by getting within one or two hundred yards, so as to ram them or pour in a broadside.

I am told by Mr. Shock, the first engineer, that two of the iron-clads now being constructed at St. Louis are finished, and that three or four ought to be by this time. If I could get these, I would attack them at once.

There was a very full and elaborate description of the rebel works in and about Mobile bay and harbor furnished by a mechanic from New Hampshire who was employed in the South when the rebellion broke out, and who took work at his trade at Mobile on half-pay to escape conscription. Taking advantage of a furlough granted him that he might visit his father in Alabama or Florida, he escaped to Pensacola, and at this time was on board the Octorara. According to his statement Fort Morgan mounted some thirty guns in all—a portion of them carrying an enormous weight of metal—and Fort Gaines twenty-one. There were also three steamers and four rams inside, waiting to receive any vessels that might succeed in passing the forts. Batteries also lined the shore, and torpedoes passed the bed of the channel. That Farragut thought "with one iron-clad he could destroy all the force in the bay" shows a daring and consciousness of power that would be alarming in any one but a commander who was not born to be beaten.

The latter part of next month (February), he shelled Fort Powell on Shell Island in Grant's Pass for a week, but made but little impression on it, as he could not, on account of the shallowness of the water, get his vessels nearer than 4000 yards. The powerful rebel ram Tennessee had not at this time got over Dog River Bar into the harbor, and Farragut wished to make his attack before she did.

On the 1st of March he again bombarded Fort Powell, and in an hour and a half silenced it. During the day, however, to his great surprise, he saw the Tennessee steam slowly up opposite Grant's Pass, where his squadron lay. He now wrote to the Department that it would be "much more difficult to take Mobile with wooden vessels than it would have been a week ago."

A month later he says:

I fully understand and appreciate my situation. The experience I had of the fight between the Arkansas and Admiral Davis's vessels on the Mississippi, showed plainly how unequal the contest is between iron-clads and wooden vessels in loss of life, unless you succeed in destroying the iron-clad. I therefore deeply regret that the Department has not been able to give us ONE of the many iron-clads that are off Charleston and on the Mississippi. I have always looked for the latter, but it appears that it takes us twice as long to build an iron-clad as any one else. It looks as if the contractors and the fates were against us. While the rebels are bending their whole energies to the war, our people are expecting the war to close by default: and if they do not awaken to a sense of their danger soon, it will be so.

But be assured, sir, that the navy will do its duty, let the issue come when it may, or I am greatly deceived.

I think you have many ready and willing to make any sacrifice their country can require of them.

All I ask of them is *to do their whole duty*; the result belongs to God.

A few weeks subsequent to this he says:

My mail from New Orleans this morning is very discouraging. Our army is not only falling back to that most demoralizing of places, New Orleans, but I am informed by Lieutenant-Commander Cook, at Matagorda, that General Banks has ordered Matagorda to be abandoned, and the forts and earthworks to be destroyed. The general is in New Orleans; the army said to be at Morganzia, just above Port Hudson, on the western shore.

I ran in shore yesterday, and took a good look at the iron-clad Tennessee. She flies the blue flag of Admiral Buchanan. She has four ports of a side, out of which she fights, I understand from the refugees, four 7-inch Brooks rifles, and two 19-inch columbiads. She has a torpedo fixture on the bow. Their four iron-clads and three wooden gunboats make quite a formidable appearance.

* * * * * * * * *

The Department has not yet responded to my call for the iron-clads in the Mississippi, which I was led to believe were intended for this squadron.

I am placing heavy iron cutters on the bows of my vessels, and shall also have torpedoes to place me on an equality with my enemy, if he comes outside. No doubt he will have the advantage of me inside, as they are planting them every day; we can see them distinctly when at work.

Torpedoes are not so agreeable when used on both sides; therefore I have reluctantly brought myself to it, and have always deemed it unworthy of a chivalrous nation; but it does not do to give your enemy such a decided superiority over you.

Thus the winter and spring wore away, and mid-summer came before the preparations were completed for the contemplated attack. Farragut was at length informed that the iron-clad Tecumseh had arrived at Pensacola. There she was detained for want of coal, and had it not been for Captain Jenkins, of the Richmond, Craven said on his arrival, "God knows when I should have got here." He worked incessantly to carry out Farragut's wishes, and the latter said of him, "He carries out the spirit of one of Lord Collingwood's best sayings, 'Not to be afraid of doing too much; those who are, seldom do as much as they ought.'"

On the 8th of July he had an interview with General Canby, and it was finally agreed that the latter should first invest Fort Gaines with the army; and the troops were landed for that purpose, and began to throw up works. He, in the mean time, had issued the following order:

Strip your vessels and prepare for the conflict. Send down all your superfluous spars and rigging. Trice up or remove the whiskers. Put up the splinter-nets on the starboard side, and barricade the wheel and steersmen with sails and hammocks. Lay chains or sand-bags on the decks over the machinery, to resist a plunging fire. Hang the sheet-chains over the side, or make any other arrangement for security that your ingenuity may suggest. Land your starboard boats, or lower and tow them to the port side, and lower the port boats down to the water's edge. Place a leadsman and the pilot in the port-quarter boat, or the one most convenient to the commander.

The vessels will run past the forts in couples, lashed side by side, as hereinafter designated. The flag-ship will lead, and steer from Sand Island N. by E. by compass, until abreast of Fort Morgan; then N.W. half N., until past the Middle Ground; then N. by W.; and the others, as designated in the drawing, will follow in due order, until ordered to anchor; but the bow and quarter line must be preserved, to give the chase-guns a fair range; and each vessel must be kept astern of the broadside of the next ahead. Each vessel will keep a very little on the starboard quarter of his next ahead, and when abreast of the fort will keep directly astern, and as we pass the fort will take the same distance on the port-quarter of the next ahead, to enable the stern guns to fire clear of the next vessel astern.

It will be the object of the admiral to get as close to the fort as possible before opening fire; the ships, however, will open fire the moment the enemy opens upon us, with their chase and other guns, as fast as they can be brought to bear. Use short fuses for the shell and shrapnell, and as soon as within three or four hundred yards, give the grape. It is understood that heretofore we have fired too high; but with grape-shot it is necessary to elevate a little above the object, as grape will dribble from the muzzle of the gun. If one or more of the vessels be disabled, their partners must carry them through, if possible; but if they cannot, then the next astern must render the required assistance; but as the admiral contemplates moving with the flood-tide, it will only require sufficient power to keep the crippled vessels in the channel.

Vessels that can, must place guns upon the poop and topgallant forecastle, and in the tops on the starboard side. Should the enemy fire grape, they will remove the men from the topgallant forecastle and poop to the guns below, out of grape range.

The howitzers must keep up a constant fire from the time they can reach with shrapnell until out of its range.

D. G. FARRAGUT,
Rear-Admiral, Commanding W. G. B. Squadron.

The preparations having been completed, the signal was hoisted at daylight, August 5th, to weigh anchor and get under way. The wooden vessels were lashed in the following order: The Brooklyn, Captain James Alden, commander, led the fleet with the Octorara, Lieutenant-Commander C. H. Greene, on the port side. Next came the flag-ship Hartford, Captain Percival Drayton, with the Metacomet, Lieutenant-Commander J. E. Jewett; the Richmond, Captain T. A. Jenkins, with the Port Royal,

Lieutenant-Commander B. Gheradi; the Lackawana, Captain G. B. Marchand, with the Seminole, Commander E. Donaldson; the Monongahela, Commander F. H. Strong, with the Kennebec, Lieutenant-Commander W. P. McCann; the Ossipee, Commander W. E. LeRoy, with the Itasca, Lieutenant-Commander George Brown; and the Oneida, Commander R. M. Mullany, with the Galena, Lieutenant-Commander C. H. Wells, completed the line.

It was a novel position for Farragut to find himself in—following instead of leading—and one which he took very reluctantly, and only at the earnest solicitations of the officers, who said that the Brooklyn, having four chase guns to the Hartford's one, and also an ingenious machine for picking up torpedoes, with which they knew the channel to be lined, should be the leading vessel. They stated, moreover, that in their judgment the flag-ship, on the movements and signals of which all the other movements depended, should not be so much exposed as she would be at the head of the line, for she might be crippled before they came up with the forts. Farragut demurred very much to this arrangement, saying that "exposure was one of the penalties of rank in the navy;" besides, it did not matter where the flag-ship was, as "she would always be the main target of the enemy."

The fleet, with the Brooklyn ahead, steamed slowly on, and at a quarter to seven the Tecumseh fired the first gun. Twenty minutes later the forts opened their fire, when the Brooklyn replied with two 100-pounder Parrott rifles, and the battle fairly commenced. The rebel rams and iron-clads, lying under the protection of the fort, added their fire, playing almost exclusively on the wooden vessels.

Farragut had lashed himself near the maintop, so as to

be able to overlook the whole scene, and watched with absorbing anxiety the progress of the fleet through the tremendous fire now concentrated upon it. Suddenly, to his utter amazement, he saw the Brooklyn stop and begin to back, causing the order to reverse engines to pass down through the whole fleet, and bringing it to a sudden halt just as it was entering the fiery vortex. "What could this mean," had hardly leaped to the lips of Farragut, when he heard the cry, "The Tecumseh is going down!" Glancing his eye towards the spot where she lay, he saw only the top of her turrets rapidly disappearing beneath the water. The sight at this moment was enough to try the stoutest heart, and it brought out, like a flash of lightning, all the heroism in the man. What! his whole line halted—the Tecumseh, for which he had waited so long, as the only match in his fleet for the ram Tennessee, gone to the bottom with all her noble crew, and the fiery tempest full upon him! With his usually mild face now blazing with the light of battle, and unalterable resolution written on every lineament, he shouted out, in a voice that rung over the thunder of cannon, to start the engines and steam right on; and, dashing to the head of the line, with his bold signal fluttering aloft "close action," he drove straight for the blazing fort, followed by the squadron,—the commanders believing, as he said, "that they were going to a noble death with their commander-in-chief." The buoys were right ahead which had turned the Brooklyn back, indicating where torpedoes were supposed to be sunk, ready to lift his ship into the air as they had the Tecumseh; but, pointing between them, the order was to move on, and with the foam dashing from the bows of his vessel he swept forward, "determined," he said, "to take the chances." The fleet followed, gun answering gun, in one continuous thunder-peal that shook land and water.

Wheeling to the northwest as he kept the channel, he brought his whole broadside to bear with fearful effect on the fort. As he moved in flame and smoke past it, still standing high up in the rigging, he saw the ram Tennessee steam out to attack him. He, however, did not stop to engage her, but, giving her one broadside, kept on towards the rebel gunboats Selma, Gaines, and Morgan, that were raking him with a scourging fire. The Selma, especially, by keeping on his bows, made sad havoc with her stern-guns, while his own 100-pounder rifle could not be brought to bear, as its carriage had been shattered by a shell. He therefore cast off his consort, the Metacomet, with orders to pursue her. She at once gave chase, and, after a sharp race of an hour, captured her. The Morgan and Gaines ran into shallow water under the guns of the fort, where the latter was set on fire, but the former in the night escaped up the Mobile river.

The other vessels following in the wake of the flag-ship, one after another swept past the batteries, the crews loudly cheering, and were signalled by Farragut to come to anchor. But the officers had scarcely commenced clearing decks when the rebel ram was seen boldly standing out into the bay, and steering straight for the fleet, with the purpose of attacking it. The moment Farragut discovered it, he signalled the vessels to run her down, and, hoisting up his own anchor, ordered the pilot to drive the Hartford full on the monster. The Monongahela, under the command of the intrepid Strong, being near the rear of the line, was still moving up the bay when he saw the ram heading for the line. He instantly sheered out, and, ordering on a full head of steam, drove with tremendous force straight on the iron-clad structure. He struck her fair, then, swinging round, poured a broadside of eleven-inch shot, which, fired at such close range, fell with the weight of descending rocks on her mailed side. Yet they bounded back, and dropped harmlessly into the water. Wheeling, he again struck her, though he had carried away his own iron prow and cutwater.* The Lackawana came next, and striking the ram while under full headway, rolled her over on her side. Such was the force of the shock that her own stern was cut and crushed to the planks for a distance of three feet above the water's edge to five feet below, springing her aleak. If his yards and topmasts had not been down, they would have gone overboard under the shock. As the vessel swung around broadside to, a gunner succeeded in planting a nine-inch shell, fired within twelve feet of the ram, into one of the shutters, breaking it into fragments, which were driven into the casemate. The rebels could be seen through the portholes making defiant gestures, while they cursed and blackguarded our crew in revolting language, which so exasperated them that they fired on them with muskets, and even hurled a spittoon and holy-stone at them, which made them scatter. The next moment, down came Farragut in the Hartford, but just before the vessel struck, the ram sheered so that the blow was a glancing one, and the former rasped along her iron-plated hull and fell alongside. Recoiling for some ten or twelve feet, the Hartford poured in at that short distance a whole broadside of nine-inch solid shot, hurled with charges of thirteen pounds of powder. The heavy metal, though sent with such awful force, and in such close proximity, made no

* Strong, by this bold movement, doubtless saved some of the vessels, and ought to have been promoted.

CAPTURE OF THE RAM TENNESSEE BY FARRAGUT (MOBILE BAY).

impression, but broke into fragments on the mailed sides, or dropped back into the water. The shot and shell from the Tennessee, on the other hand, went crashing through and through the wooden sides of the Hartford, strewing her deck with the dead. One 150-pound shell, exploding inside, prostrated men on the right hand and left, one of the fragments going through the spar and berth decks, and clean through the launch into the hold below among the wounded.

Farragut now stood off, and began to make a circuit in order to come down again, when the Lackawana, which was driving the second time on the monster, struck by accident the Hartford a little forward of the mizzen mast, and cut her down to within two feet of the water. She was at first thought to be sinking, and "the Admiral! the Admiral!—save the Admiral!" rang over the shattered deck. But Farragut, seeing that the vessel would still float, shouted out to put on steam, determined to send her, crushed and broken as she was, full on the ram.

By this time the monitors had crawled up, and were pouring in their heavy shot. The Chickesaw got under the stern and knocked away the smokestack, while the Manhattan sent one shot clean through the vessel, and disabled her stern port shutter with a shell, so that the gun could not be used, while a third carried away the steering gear. Thus, with her steering-chains gone, her smokestack shot away, many of her port shutters jammed, the Tennessee stood amid the crowding gunboats like a bleeding stag at bay among the hounds, while the Ossipee, Le Roy commanding, was now driving towards her under full headway; and a little farther off, bearing down on the same awful errand, were coming the Hartford, Monongahela and Lackawana. The fate of the poor vessel was now sealed, and her commander hoisted the white flag, but not until the Ossipee was so near, that Le Roy could not prevent a collision, and his vessel rasped heavily along the iron sides of the ram. He received her surrender from commander Johnson—the admiral, Buchanan, having been previously wounded in the leg. This ended the morning's work, and, at ten minutes past ten, Farragut brought his fleet to anchor within four miles of Fort Morgan.

The killed and wounded on board the fleet amounted to two hundred and twenty-two—among the latter was Captain Mallory, of the Galena. Fifty-two were killed, of which twenty-five, or about half, were killed on board the Hartford, showing to what a fearful fire the flag-ship had been exposed. The Brooklyn was the next severest sufferer, receiving the heaviest fire of the fort.

The loss of the Tecumseh, with her gallant commander Craven and his crew, nearly all of whom went to the bottom, chastened somewhat the joy over this great victory. Craven was in the turret when the torpedo exploded, which almost lifted the iron-clad from the water, and blowing such a huge opening in her bottom that she sunk before the men from below could get on deck. Farragut, when he saw her go down, and just as he was starting to the head of the line, sent Acting Ensign Henry C. Nields with a boat to rescue any of the survivors that might be swimming in the water, and nobly did he perform the perilous duty assigned him. Sitting in the stern of the boat, he gave his orders coolly as his great commander could have done, and the rowers bent steadily to their oars while shot and shell fell in a perpetual shower around them. He succeeded in picking up ten within six hundred yards of the fort. A smile of pleasure lighted for a moment Farragut's face as he saw from his high perch how faithfully and heroically the daring youth performed his perilous task.

The only other vessel lost was the Philippi, which followed the fleet against orders, and being struck by a shot was run ashore by her commander and deserted, when the rebels burned her.

Some idea of the terrible fire that had rolled over the waters that morning may be obtained by reflecting what an enormous amount of powder must have been exploded, since the Hartford and Brooklyn alone fired nearly five thousand pounds. The fleet and batteries together must have expended enough, if put together, to have lifted the city of Mobile bodily from its firm foundations.

The spirit of the commander in this great combat seemed to have actuated every officer and man. Farragut said of his flag-lieutenant, G. Crittenden Watson, who stood on the poop during the entire action, attending to the signals, "He is a scion worthy of the noble stock he sprang from." Drayton, the flag-captain, said that although many of the crew had never before seen a battle, not one flinched. At different times the greater part of four guns' crews were swept away, yet in every case the killed and wounded were quietly removed, the injury at the guns made good, and in a few moments, except from the crimson deck, nothing could lead one to suspect that anything out of the ordinary routine had happened. Charles Melville, knocked down and wounded with fifteen others, and presenting a ghastly spectacle, no sooner got his wounds dressed than he returned to his gun, and, though scarcely able to stand, worked it bravely to the last. Thomas Fitzpatrick set the same splendid example, moving a hero amid the crew, though his face was streaming with blood. The same could be said of James R. Garrison, Thomas O'Connel, James E. Sterling, and Alexander Mack, all wounded—and all fighting bravely till the last shot was fired. But to mention all who bore themselves worthily and well, one would have to give the entire list of the officers and crews.

Two days after the victory, Farragut issued the following order:

FLAG-SHIP HARTFORD,
Mobile Bay, Aug. 7th, 1864.

The admiral desires the fleet to return thanks to Almighty God for the signal victory over the enemy on the morning of the 5th instant.

D. G. FARRAGUT,
Rear-Admiral Commanding W. G. B. Squadron.

Thus, after every battle, this great yet humble commander exclaimed, "Not unto us, but to Thy name be all the praise and glory!" His dependence on God was full and complete, yet all his plans were laid with care and consummate skill. He showed admirable forethought in lashing his ships together; for the one on the farther side from the fort would necessarily receive but little injury; and therefore, if her consort was disabled by the enemy's fire, could carry her out of range, and, if she sunk, pick up her crew. Hence, though he lost half his fleet, he would have the other half safe in Mobile Bay for further service. By this arrangement he also shortened his line of battle one half, and consequently it was only half as long under fire as if he had advanced in single line. If they had sailed two abreast without being lashed together, there would have been great danger of getting fouled.

The night after the battle, Fort Powell was evacuated, the rebels blowing it up. The next morning the Chickesaw went down and shelled Fort Gaines, and the following morning Colonel Anderson, the commander, sent a note to Farragut, offering to surrender, and asking for terms. The reply was, first, unconditional surrender. When this was done the prisoners should be treated in conformity with the custom of civilized nations, and private property, with the exception of arms, be respected. These terms were accepted, and at a quarter to ten o'clock the same morning the rebel flag came down, and the stars and stripes went up, amid the loud and prolonged cheers of the fleet.

Fort Morgan still refused to surrender, and Granger having perfected his siege operations, Farragut moved down on Sunday night, the 21st, with his fleet, and next morning at daybreak opened a terrific bombardment upon it. The batteries on shore joined in with their overwhelming fire, and all day long it rained a horrible tempest on the devoted fort. Farragut said: "A more magnificent fire has rarely been kept up." The inhabitants of Mobile gathered on the shores and house-tops and towers to gaze on the terrific scene, while the buildings, though miles away, rattled under the awful explosions, and one vast sulphurous cloud heaved and tossed above the quiet waters of the bay. Just at twilight the citadel of the fort took fire, and the garrison, finding themselves unable to extinguish the flames, which now shot heavenward in the increasing darkness, flooded the magazine to prevent its blowing up, and threw large quantities of powder into the wells.

All night long the bombardment was kept up, ribbing the darkness with ghastly seams of light, as shells crossed and recrossed each other in their fiery track.

Thus the fearful night wore on, and at six in the

morning a dull, heavy explosion came over the bay from the smoking fort, and half an hour later a white flag was seen to wave from its ramparts. General Page offered to surrender the fort, and asked the terms. The same as those given to Fort Gaines were offered and accepted. In his impotent rage, however, the commander ordered all the guns to be spiked, the carriages disabled, and arms, ammunition, &c., destroyed. He also, with some other officers, broke their swords, under the silly impression that this would lessen the humiliation of the surrender.

"The whole conduct of the officers of Fort Gaines and Fort Morgan," said Farragut, "presents such a striking contrast in moral principle that I cannot fail to remark upon it. Colonel Anderson, who commanded the former, finding himself in a position perfectly untenable, and encumbered with a superfluous number of conscripts, many of whom were mere boys, determined to surrender a fort which he could not defend, and in this determination was supported by all his officers save one; but, from the moment he hoisted the white flag, he scrupulously kept everything intact, and in that condition delivered it over; whilst General Page and his officers, with a childish spitefulness, destroyed the guns which they had said they would defend to the last, but which they never defended at all, and threw away or broke those weapons which they had not the manliness to use against their enemies; for Fort Morgan never fired a gun after the commencement of the bombardment, and the advanced pickets of our army were actually on its glacis."

As before stated, the ceremony of surrender took place at two P. M., and that same afternoon the garrison was sent to New Orleans in the United States steamers Tennessee and Bienville, where they arrived safely.

Farragut remained for awhile blockading the place, and sending off expeditions to destroy public property; but his health needing some relaxation from his duties, he at length received permission to return home.

He sailed in the Hartford on the 20th of November, and on the 12th of December reached New York harbor. The city, apprised of his coming, made preparations to receive him with fitting ceremonies.

A revenue cutter, with the committee of reception on board, met him down in the Narrows, and a crowd welcomed him at the docks in New York. He was then driven to the Custom House, where a more formal reception took place. Collector Draper welcomed him to the city in a flattering address, to which Admiral Farragut made the following reply, which we give as being, in our estimation, the most characteristic, unstudied, and best one of any that he has made:

"MY FRIENDS: I can only reply to you as I did before, by saying that I receive these compliments with great thankfulness and deep emotions. I am entirely unaccustomed to make such an address as I would desire to do upon this occasion; but, if I do not express what I think of the honor you do me, trust me I feel it most deeply. I don't think, however, that I particularly deserve anything from your hands. I can merely say that I have done my duty to the best of my abilities. I have been devoted to the service of my country since I was eight years of age, and my father was devoted to it before me. I have not specially deserved these demonstrations of your regard. I owe everything, perhaps, to chance, and to the praiseworthy exertions of my brother officers serving with me. That I have been fortunate is most true, and I am thankful, deeply thankful for it, for my country's sake. I return my thanks to the committee for their resolutions, especially for the one in regard to the creation of an additional rank."

On the last day of the year another reception took place at the collector's headquarters, when the sum of $50,000—a gift from the wealthy men of New York—was presented to him.

Wherever he went ovations awaited him—even the little village of Hastings, to which he retired with his wife in the winter, made an imposing display on his arrival.

His reception at this place contrasted strikingly with his first entrance into it, an unknown man, three years before. Suspected of conspiracy, his movements were then watched; now the wintry heavens rang with acclamations and the shout of "See, the conquering hero comes!"

Farragut was no more afloat during the war; and now, raised to the rank of Admiral, modestly wears the honors a grateful nation loves to heap on his head.

In person Farragut is spare, but his form is firmly knit and very supple. He has always prided himself on the latter quality, and it has been his custom almost daily for years, to interlace his fingers in front of him and thrust his legs, one after another, through the letter "O" made by his clasped hands. A few months ago, however, he caught a severe tumble while going through this difficult operation, which has caused him to abandon it. He finds that age and hard work will tell on limbs, however vigorous and elastic.

Although Farragut possesses the originality, in conception and plan, belonging to true genius, he is not like Napoleon the First, who rarely called a council of war. He advises with his commanders, hears their suggestions, grafts the good ones on to his own plan, and thus makes an admirable use of the ability which surrounds him.

Brave as a lion, he has the dash and daring which a sailor loves, and which, if joined with success, makes a commander the idol of the people. To see him drive on through the deadly fire of batteries towards the enemy's vessels beyond, one would think him a reckless, desperate man, to whom success, if it came at all, would be pure luck. But this would be an erroneous conclusion, for no man ever planned more carefully his blow beforehand than Farragut. He endeavors to ascertain from the enemy's defences and preparations where he least expects that blow to fall, then plants it so suddenly that he has no time to interpose a new defence, and so terribly that it grinds everything to powder. His crouch is as careful and stealthy as the panther, and his leap as sudden and deadly. The awful fury with which he presses the attack when once commenced, does not arise from the frenzied excitement of battle, but from the well-settled conviction that he has chosen the best course that could be adopted, and victory must be reached right onward in it, if reached at all.

Genius, prudence, and judgment in preparing for battle; unconquerable energy and desperate vehemence in pushing it; imperturbable coolness in the most unexpected and sudden disaster, and total unconsciousness of danger, though death and havoc reign supreme on his decks; loving to lead his line where the peril is greatest, and asking his subordinates only to follow him—he possesses all those qualities which go to make up a great and successful commander. Modest and unassuming, he dislikes the pompous ceremony of public ovations—retaining still his boyish frankness of nature and geniality of heart, that make him accessible to the humblest and beloved by all. Many anecdotes are told of the kindness of his heart, playfulness of disposition, and boyish freshness of nature, that add greatly to the interest one takes in his character. Among others, a friend of his has related to us the following, that occurred on a trip the Admiral recently made to the White Mountains. At Conway, a man brought his little daughter, at her own urgent request, some fifteen miles to see him, for she would not be content till she had looked on the great Admiral. Farragut took the child in his arms, kissed her, and talked playfully with her. He was dressed in citizen's costume, and looked in her eyes very much like any other man, and totally unlike the hero whose praises had been so long ringing over the land. In her innocent surprise, she said, "Why, you do not look like a great general. I saw one the other day, and he was covered all over with gold." The Admiral laughed, and, to please her, actually took her to his room, and put on his uniform, when she went away satisfied. One such little incident as this throws a flood of light on one phase of his character, showing that he is kind and good as he is brave and great. The nation may well be proud of him, not only for the aid he brought to our cause by his astonishing victories, but for the lustre he has shed on our navy the world over.

CHAPTER III.

REAR-ADMIRAL CHARLES WILKES.

HIS NATIVITY.—A MIDSHIPMAN.—HIS FIRST CRUISE.—HIS EARLY SERVICES.—APPOINTED TO THE DEPOT OF CHARTS AND INSTRUMENTS.—HIS EFFORTS TO CREATE A NATIONAL OBSERVATORY DECLARED UNCONSTITUTIONAL.—SENT TO SURVEY ST. GEORGE'S BANK.—APPOINTED TO COMMAND THE ANTARCTIC EXPEDITION.—ACCOUNT OF HIS EXPLORATIONS.—TAKES VENGEANCE ON THE CANNIBALS FOR THE MURDER OF HIS NEPHEW.—HIS AFTER-VOYAGE ROUND THE WORLD.—COURT-MARTIALLED.—NAMES OF THE VARIOUS WORKS THAT HE PUBLISHED.—AT THE BEGINNING OF THE WAR PLACED IN COMMAND OF THE FRIGATE SAN JACINTO, AND SENT TO THE WEST INDIES TO CAPTURE THE PRIVATEER SUMTER.—SEIZES THE BRITISH MAIL-STEAMER TRENT, AND CARRIES OFF MASON AND SLIDELL.—EXCITEMENT IN BOTH HEMISPHERES OVER THE SEIZURE.—THE ACT FINALLY CONDEMNED BY THE PRESIDENT.—MADE COMMODORE, AND PLACED FIRST ON THE LIST.—ASSIGNED TO THE COMMAND OF THE POTOMAC FLOTILLA.—MADE ACTING REAR-ADMIRAL, AND SENT TO PROTECT OUR COMMERCE IN THE WEST INDIES.—SUSPENDED.—PLACED ON THE RETIRED LIST.

CHARLES WILKES is a native of the city of New York, where he was born in the year 1801. A mere lad, he entered the navy as midshipman, when he was fifteen years old. In 1819 and 1820 he was attached to the squadron of McDonough in the Mediterranean. The two following years he served in the Pacific under Commodore Stewart, and exhibited so much nautical skill that he was selected for a separate command. In 1826.

when twenty-five years old, he, after ten years' service, was promoted to the rank of lieutenant. In 1830 he was appointed over dépôt of charts and instruments, and was the first man in the country to set up fixed astronomical instruments and make observations with them. He placed the observatory in his own garden; but, on attempting to build a firm inclosure around the stone piers erected to sustain his instruments, he received an informal notice from the Navy Department, that it would not be allowed. On inquiring the reason, he was told that a *national observatory was unconstitutional.* It seems hardly credible that this could have happened a little over thirty years ago. The constitution has been made to play a very curious *rôle* in our national history. He was taken from this post and sent to survey St. George's Bank, which was a great bugbear to navigators, and performed the service with entire satisfaction.

He was now transferred to a position of still greater responsibility. For some time the Government had been contemplating an expedition into the Antarctic Ocean, to see what lay beyond the stormy seas of Cape Horn, and at length organized it, and placed him at its head. It consisted of five ships, and set sail August 18th, 1838.

Reaching the Pacific Ocean, he explored various groups of islands lying south of the equator, and discovered many never before known. Having finished his surveys here, he, at the end of the year 1839, turned his prow for the Antarctic. Pushing boldly toward the south pole, he at length reached the icy barrier that surrounds it, and discovered the Antarctic Continent, never before seen by explorers. With the American flag flying in the strange breezes of this unknown, mysterious region, he boldly sailed along the barrier of ice in full sight of the land he could not reach,—running half as many degrees of longitude as it is across the Atlantic Ocean. The next year he explored the Fejee Islands, where a nephew of his was killed by the cannibals, for which act he took summary vengeance. He thus opened these islands to future navigators and missionary establishments, which were subsequently planted by the Christian world. He then set sail north, and visited the Hawaiian Islands, the Northwest Coast of North America, and made explorations by land in California. Crossing thence to Asia, he visited Manilla, Loochoo, Borneo and Singapore; and, returning by way of the Cape of Good Hope and the isle of St. Helena, completed his voyage around the world, and reached home June 10th, 1842, having been gone four years. The next month he was made commander. During the year charges were made against him, by some of his officers, and he was court-marshalled. He was, however, acquitted of all, except of illegally punishing some of his crew, for which he was reprimanded. He published a narrative of his explorations in five octavo volumes, which made his name widely known in both hemispheres. Eleven other volumes and atlases were subsequently published, of which he was the author of the one on meteorology. In 1849 he published another book, giving an account of his observations in California and Oregon. In 1855 he was made Captain. The next year he published his "Theory of Wind." Five years of comparative quiet now passed, but on the breaking out of the rebellion in 1861, he was sent to the West Indies in the frigate San Jacinto, to capture the privateer Sumter.

While cruising in the region he learned that Messrs. Mason and Slidell had reached Havana from Charleston on their way to England, as accredited ministers for the

Confederate States to Great Britain and France. He immediately sailed for that port, and there ascertained that they had taken passage on board the English mail steamer Trent, which was to sail from St. Thomas on the 1st of November. He immediately determined to capture them, and for that purpose cruised in the neighborhood of the course it was supposed the vessel would take on her voyage to England. On the 8th he saw her smoke rising over the water, and immediately beat to quarters, and ordered Lieutenant Fairfax to have two boats manned for the purpose of boarding her. The steamer, as she approached the waiting frigate, hoisted English colors. Wilkes ran up the American flag, and, as she drew near, fired a shot across her bow as a sign to heave to. She however paid no attention to the summons, and kept steadily on ; he then fired a shell across her bow, which was saying, "the next will be a broadside." The English commander understood it, and hove to. Lieutenant Fairfax then proceeded with his boats alongside, and mounted the deck. The captain being pointed out to him, he informed him that he was Lieutenant Fairfax of the American frigate San Jacinto, commanded by Captain Wilkes, and asked to see the passenger list. The request was peremptorily declined.

The Lieutenant then told him that he was informed that Messrs. Mason, Slidell, Eustis, and McFarland, were on board, and he meant to find them. These gentlemen, hearing the discussion, then came forward. Lieut. Fairfax quietly communicated to them the object of his visit. They at once protested against being taken on board of the American vessel. The passengers now began to crowd around, in a state of great excitement. The lieutenant, fearing that violence would be used, ordered the lieutenant in the boat alongside to come on board with a party of marines. The appearance of these armed men on deck of the British vessel was the signal of still greater excitement. "Marines on board!" was shouted on every side. "What an outrage!" "What a piratical act!" "England will open the blockade for this," and various other exclamations which showed the bitter feeling that was aroused. Fairfax was in the cabin, and the lieutenant, hearing the altercation and angry threats, marched his marines in among the startled passengers, who fell back at their presence. Amid the confusion was heard a woman's voice, which proved to be that of Slidell's daughter, who stood before the door of the state-room into which her father had retired, declaring that no one should take him away. Finding that the prisoners would not go without force, the lieutenant took Mr. Mason by the collar and called on Mr. Hall to assist him. Slidell now came through the window of the state-room, when he too was seized, and the party hurried off into the boats. The families of the gentlemen preferring to keep on to England, they were allowed to remain on board the steamer, and she resumed her course.

The news of the arrest of these men in our port caused the wildest excitement. Washington was thrown into fever heat, and the whole nation aroused. Some were delighted at the capture of these arch traitors, others alarmed at the consequences that would result from their capture. "What would England say to it?" was asked on every side. Pages of argument were written to show that the seizure was in accordance with the law of nations, and past history was ransacked for precedents to justify it. The Secretary of the Navy indorsed the act by a letter of thanks to Capt. Wilkes, and Congress passed a vote of thanks. A banquet was given to the Captain in Boston, and the country seemed determined to sustain the act at all hazards. The news caused still greater excitement in England. "The British flag had been insulted," was the angry exclamation on every side. The deck of an English vessel had been invaded by a hostile force, and the cry of "redress or war" rolled over the land. After the first burst of passion had subsided with us, the affair did not wear so gratifying an aspect. We were not in a condition just then to go to war with England, and whatever else might be the result, it was plain that such a catastrophe at this critical juncture would give the South its independence. This was not a pleasant alternative; yet Congress and the Secretary of the Navy had indorsed the act, and if the President did the same, we must abide the decision, whatever the results might be. The British government at once denounced it as an affront to the British flag, a violation of international law, and demanded the restoration of the prisoners. The press throughout the country laughed at this extreme sensitiveness to the obligations of international law on the part of a nation which had violated it more than all other maritime powers put together. Still her crimes in this respect could not sanction us in committing similar ones. The wrong, if one, was the same, whatever her conduct may have been. The feeling, however, was very general, that, because Great Britain was the chief of sinners in the invasion of maritime rights, therefore we had a right to sin also. But fortunately our Government took a more statesmanlike view of it. What England *deserved* was one thing; what precedent we should establish to be used in future complications was quite another. Our record must be kept clean, without any reference to feelings of pride or passion.

The demand of the British government for the return of the prisoners on board an English ship was finally acceded to, and the threatened storm averted. Some, who believed the North could conquer both the South and Canada, and at the same time maintain the blockade, whip the English navy, and chase her commerce from the seas, were disappointed and offended at the humiliation, as they termed it, of the Government. But none, judging from the tone of their press, were more chagrined than the rebels. They professed to be ashamed of the poltroonery of American blood, and scoffed at the base self-degradation. But the truth was, this unfortunate occurrence seemed to be such a stroke of good fortune for them that they did not want to lose the benefits of it. Mason and Slidell were sent abroad to secure the intervention of foreign governments in their behalf, and their mission promised to be successful before it was begun. In their imaginations, the storm of foreign war was already darkening over the North, and they saw their independence secured. To see it dissipated so suddenly, aroused all their anger and derision.

Many at the North accepted the action of our Government on the ground of expediency alone, but it was in fact justified on the strict ground of international law. Much ingenious argument was expended to justify Capt. Wilkes, but men forgot that international law, like the laws of civilized warfare, is not based on the strict rule of justice, but of mutual benefit. They are simply general rules, adopted for the good of all parties, under the present order of things ; nothing more.

The Secretary of State gave several reasons to show the propriety of the decision which the government came to, but only one was needed. Capt. Wilkes' duty under international law was, if he regarded the carrying of

Mason and Slidell as a violation of neutral rights, to seize the vessel and carry her into a neutral port, and have the case decided by a prize court. This was the first step to be taken; and until this was done, all requirements about the status of these men, and what constituted articles contraband of war, were out of place. Neither the press, nor the people, nor Capt. Wilkes, were to be judges of that. The first step which he did take being a wrong one, there was no use of discussing the intrinsic merits of the case.

To justify Capt. Wilkes would be to lay down the extraordinary doctrine, that any sloop-of-war may turn her deck into a *prize court and adjudicate on its own* seizures. This would be a monstrous principle for our government to establish, and yet this is exactly what it would have done, had it sustained Capt. Wilkes. It evidently dawned on his own mind, after his first report was sent to the Government, that his action was unjustifiable on this very ground, for he made a second, in which he apologizes for not bringing the vessel in, on the ground of inability to do so. But this was plainly an afterthought, and had no foundation in fact.

On the reorganization of the navy in 1862, he was promoted to the rank of Commodore, and placed first on the list. He was then assigned the command of the flotilla in the James River. The rebel troops at City Point having attacked our transports, he moved up and shelled it, leaving it a heap of ruins. Afterwards he was made acting rear-admiral, and was sent in command of a squadron to the West Indies, to protect our commerce there. His presence in those waters annoyed the English much, who imagined that it was done to insult them, because of their denunciations of his conduct in the

Trent affair. The scene of his discomfiture was made to witness his promotion and a still larger exercise of power granted him.

Afterward, having allowed some Governmental documents to be made public, he was court-martialled, and the trial told so heavily against him, that he was suspended for awhile, and eventually placed on the retired list, where he now is. He is an able man, and stands among the first of American explorers, and as such is more widely known than any other regular naval commander.

CHAPTER IV.

REAR-ADMIRAL SILAS H. STRINGHAM.

HIS NATIVITY.—ENTERS THE NAVY.—SAILS UNDER RODGERS.—AFFAIR OF THE PRESIDENT AND LITTLE BELT.—WAR DECLARED.—CHASE OF THE BELVIDERE.—SERVES UNDER DECATUR ON THE COAST OF ALGIERS.—RESCUES THE CREW OF A FRENCH BRIG AT GIBRALTAR.—A GALLANT FEAT.—CAPTURES SLAVERS ON THE AFRICAN COAST AND SENT HOME WITH HIS PRIZES.—MADE LIEUTENANT, AND SENT TO THE WEST INDIA STATION.—CAPTURES A NOTORIOUS SLAVER.—TRANSFERRED TO THE BROOKLYN NAVY YARD.—COMMANDS THE OHIO IN THE BOMBARDMENT OF VERA CRUZ.—COMMANDS THE BRAZILIAN SQUADRON.—SENT TO THE MEDITERRANEAN.—PLACED OVER GOSPORT NAVY YARD.—AT COMMENCEMENT OF THE REBELLION MADE FLAG-OFFICER OF THE ATLANTIC BLOCKADING SQUADRON.—COMMANDS THE EXPEDITION SENT TO CAPTURE HATTERAS.—THE BOMBARDMENT.—JOY OVER HIS VICTORY.—BLAMED FOR NOT PROSECUTING IT, AND IS RELIEVED OF HIS COMMAND.—PLACED ON THE RETIRED LIST.

ADMIRAL STRINGHAM was born in New York State, and entered the service in 1809, in 1810 as midshipman, and served under the gallant Rodgers in the frigate President till 1815. In 1811, the year before the second war with England was declared, though then but thirteen years of age, he got a taste of the life he might expect in his profession. In May of that year, Commodore Rodgers, whose vessel was then lying at Annapolis, heard that an American had been impressed on board an English frigate, near Sandy Hook. Impressment of Americans on board of British men-of-war was at that time one of the outrages against which we remonstrated, and for which we finally declared war. Its repetition, right on our coast, was too gross an insult to be overlooked, and he immediately weighed anchor and hastened northward to get the man released, or fight the English vessel. On the 16th of May, at noon, a sail was made, and the President immediately stood towards it. The latter bore away, and the President gave chase. Rodgers did not come up with the stranger till after dark, and so did not know his strength. But when he got within hail, he demanded the name of the ship. No answer being returned, except to send back, word for word, his own hail, the question, after a short interval, was again put, when a shot came for a reply from the stranger, striking the mainmast of the frigate. Three more guns followed, in quick succession, when the President opened her broadsides. After a few shots, Rodgers, finding that his insolent enemy made but feeble resistance, ordered the fire to cease, and again hailed the vessel. This time he got an answer. Seeing that his antagonist was disabled, and having finally compelled him to answer his hail, he though he had given him a sufficient lesson in good manners, and so gave the name of his own ship. He then wore round, and, running a short distance to leeward, hove to for the night. The next morning he sent an officer aboard, who reported the vessel to be the English ship of war Little Belt. She was sadly cut up, having lost thirty-one of her crew by the President's broadsides. The captain, Bingham, angrily refusing any assistance, both vessels bore away to their respective ports, to report this momentous event to the two nations, already on the verge of war, and needing only a spark to kindle the smouldering embers into a blaze. No one at this day can imagine the tremendous excitement this affair created on both sides of the water. Rodgers was assailed on all sides; but his officers stood by him.

The next year war was declared. Our little navy at this critical period was so insignificant, compared to that of the English, that it was at first determined not to send it to sea at all, but to keep it for harbor defences; but this fatal decision was changed by the resolute determination of two naval officers—Bainbridge and Stewart.

A large fleet of Jamaica men was reported to have sailed, and should be at this time off our coast, and Rodgers, who was then in New York harbor, was ordered to intercept it. The amount of abuse he had received for his attack on the Little Belt had not lessened his antipathy to the English; and, in an hour after he received the orders—as if fearing they might be revoked—his squadron, with all sail set, was standing proudly down the bay. Stringham was now fourteen years old, and the scene he witnessed left an indelible impression on his memory. The gallant officers and sailors of that squadron had none of the misgivings of the Government. They wanted no shelter in port, and asked no favors but an unfettered command and the broad ocean, and the privilege, with their flag flying in the breeze, to lay alongside of the proudest frigate in the proud English navy. When the order to weigh was given, never was anchor to the cathead sooner, or with a heartier "yo-heave-ho," nor topsail sheeted home sooner, for every pulse on board that little squadron was bounding with joy. As the vessels bore majestically down the bay, the men were beat to quarters, and all told, if any among them disliked the coming contest, or a single one who had not rather sink alongside, giving gun for gun, than surrender, he might leave at once and go ashore in the pilot boat. Fore-and-aft, like a rising storm, went "*not one, not* ONE!" and then three thundering cheers rolled over the placid waters of the bay. Stringham's voice joined in the shout, and, though a mere lad, he panted for the fight. That little squadron was to make the first claim for equal rights on the sea. Two days after, just at sunrise, an English frigate was seen in the northeast, and all sail crowded in pursuit. The chase led down the wind, and the President being a fast sailer, when going free, soon left the squadron far astern, and all day long bore steadily down on the Englishman, gaining slowly but steadily. At four o'clock he got within gunshot, and in a very short time the excited crew expected to be alongside. But at this critical moment the wind lulled, and the Englishman began to creep away from the President. Rodgers then determined to cripple his antagonist, so that he could come up, and, training the first gun himself, pulled the lanyard. The well-aimed shot struck the stern of the British frigate, and, crashing through her timbers, plunged into the gun-room. Shot after shot was now fired in quick succession; but at the fourth discharge the gun burst, killing and wounding sixteen of our own men, and flinging the Commodore into the air, who fell back on the deck with such violence that his leg was broken. The enemy, seeing the accident, now opened fire; but the President, recovering from her disaster, soon began to heave her shot with such precision, that the Belvidere (the name of the English vessel) was compelled to cut away her anchors, throw overboard her boats, and spring fourteen tons of water, in order to lighten herself. By this sacrifice she gained in the desperate chase, and the President was compelled to give up the pursuit. This was the first real engagement with a foe of equal size that young Stringham was in, and his disappointment at the result was intense. He was in no after engagement during the war, though the navy covered itself with imperishable glory. In 1815, he was transferred to the brig Spark, Capt. Gamble, which constituted a part of Decatur's squadron in the Algerine war, and helped to take an Algerine frigate. The next year, while his vessel was lying at Gibraltar, he performed one of those acts of gallant daring that have always distinguished our navy. A French brig, attempting to come into the bay in a heavy gale, was capsized, and lay wallowing in the sea, totally helpless. The crew of the Spark saw her distress, and Stringham, though a stripling of only eighteen years of age, volunteered to go to her assistance. Gamble gave his consent, and the former, with six seamen, leaped into a small boat and pulled through the turbulent sea towards the Frenchman. He reached the brig, and, with great difficulty and danger to his boat, succeeded in taking off five of the crew, and then bore away to transfer his burden to his vessel and return. But the wind and waves beat him back, and he could make no headway in that direction. He then turned and pulled for the Algerian shore; but as he approached it he saw the surf, lashed by the gale, breaking furiously upon it. There was now no alternative, however, but to pass through it; and the rowers bent to their oars with all their strength. The breakers caught the frail, heavily-laden boat, and, lifting it high into the air, hurled it, bottom side up, on the beach. Each one now had to struggle for his life. Stringham got ashore; but one of his crew and two of the Frenchmen were borne away by the surf and drowned.

In 1819 we find Stringham on board the Cyane, conveying the first settlers to Liberia. While on the African coast he was put with an armed crew in command of a boat, and sent out in search of slavers. He succeeded in capturing four, and was made prize-master, and sent home with his prizes. In 1821 he was promoted to a first-lieutenancy, and ordered to the Hornet, then on the West India station. There he captured a notorious pirate-ship and slaver. From 1825 to 1829 he was at the Brooklyn navy yard, and afterward went as first-lieutenant of the Peacock in search of the Hornet, supposed to be lost. During the search he was transferred to the Falmouth, and sent to Carthagena, and in 1830 returned to New York. For the next five years he was engaged on shore duty. He then was sent to the Mediterranean, but in 1837 was again in command of the Brooklyn navy yard. In 1842 he was ordered to the razee Independence, but the next year returned to the navy yard. He was here when Marshal Bertrand visited the country, and helped to honor the illustrious Frenchman. In 1846 he was placed in command of the ship-of-the-line Ohio, and took part in the bombardment of Vera Cruz during its investment by Scott. Afterward, for a short time, he commanded the Brazilian squadron, but in 1851 took charge of the Gosport navy yard. The three subsequent years he commanded the Mediterranean squadron—his flag-ship being the ill-fated Cumberland. He was then ordered again to the Gosport navy yard, where he remained till 1859. In March, 1861, he was called to Washington as a member of a naval court-martial. The rebellion breaking out, he was appointed flag-officer of the Atlantic blockading squadron. In August he was sent with General Butler, commanding a land force, to capture Fort Hatteras. This fort commanded the inlet to Pamlico and Albermarle Sounds—a great rendezvous for rebel privateers, and the waters of which commanded nearly the whole coast of North Carolina. No secret was made of the expedition, and the Confederate authorities had ample time and notice to prepare for defence. The expedition consisted of the flag-ship Minnesota, the United States steamers Wabash, Monticello, Pawnee, Harriet Lane, and the chartered steamers Adelaide, Peabody, and the tug Fanny. The Adelaide and Peabody were transports carrying the troops, and towing schooners loaded with surf-boats, in which to land them. These were a part of two regiments—five hundred of the Twentieth New York Volunteers, Colonel Weber commanding, and two hundred and twenty of the Ninth, Colonel Hawkins commanding, with one hundred of the coast-guard, under Captain Nixon, and sixty of the Second United States Artillery, under Lieutenant Larned—making nine hundred in all. The expedition sailed on the 26th of August, 1861, at one o'clock, and the news of its departure was soon telegraphed all over the country, causing the greatest excitement,—for all were eager to have something done to offset the mortification caused by the defeat of Bull Run.

Light summer airs prevailed, and the next morning, at half past nine o'clock, Cape Hatteras was sighted. At five the squadron came to anchor south of the Cape, and the boats were hoisted out ready to commence landing the troops in the morning. At four next morning the drum roused the men, and, a hasty breakfast being taken, between six and seven the signal was made to disembark the troops—the Pawnee, Monticello, and Harriet Lane, in the mean time to cover the landing, which was to take place about two miles east of Fort Clark. Fort Hatteras, a regularly constructed earthwork, with bomb-proofs, and guns mounted en barbette, was some one hundred and thirty rods inland, while fort Clark was a redoubt lying between it and the ships, and near the shore.

At ten o'clock the Wabash, Cumberland, and Minnesota opened their broadsides, and, running backwards and forwards past the battery, rained shot and shell without intermission upon it. An hour later, the Susquehannah came up, and the four vessels poured in a continuous fire on the doomed earthwork. The smoke from fifty-seven guns rolled away over the water, and, settling in the still air, shut out, except at intervals, the fort, whose guns replied, but could not reach the ships. While this tremendous cannonading was going on, three miles away the surf-boats were pulling for the shore. Although the weather was calm, a heavy southerly gale had prevailed just before the fleet arrived, and was evidently still blowing farther down the coast, from the effect of which the surf was breaking with tremendous power on the exposed beach and momentarily increasing in force. The boats, as soon as they entered the breakers, were hurled violently forwards, then left aground, so that the soldiers had to wade ashore, wetting their guns and ammunition. It was impossible in the heavy seas, to launch the boats again, and return after the remaining troops, lying off in smooth water. All this time Stringham kept up the bombardment, though expecting every moment the signal of the land attack, which was to be the signal to cease firing. But, despite all their exertions, but three hundred men could be got on shore, with only two howitzers, one of which was disabled in the landing. This little force however, immediately formed and marched along the beach toward the fort. The vessels ceased firing, and watched its steady progress. The garrison at the battery also saw it advancing, and fled inland to the protection of Fort Hatteras. At two o'clock the American flag was flying above it. The Monticello, Capt. Gillis, was now ordered to feel her way into the inlet. In doing so, however, she came within range of the guns of Fort Hatteras, and was struck several times; while inside, a rebel steamer was seen towing a schooner filled with troops, toward the fort. Stringham immediately hoisted the signal "engage batteries," and the ponderous shot and shell again rained against the fortifications. The cannonade was kept up till a little after six, when the signal "cease firing" was displayed from the flag-ship, and silence once more reigned over the waters. The wind now rising, the squadron hauled off to get an offing in case of a gale, with the exception of the Monticello, Pawnee, and Harriet Lane, which were ordered to lie close in shore and protect the troops. The condition of the latter was any thing but pleasant. Cut off from their comrades, cut off from the ships, and., if a storm arose, which might be expected at any moment on that inhospitable coast, sure to be captured, the prospect before them was gloomy enough. Wet through, with but little ammunition, and no provisions, they, as night came on, fell back toward the shore. As they did so they luckily came upon some sheep and geese, which they at once appropriated and carried back to the beach. Camp fires were then built, and the hastily dressed mutton and fowls spitted on bayonets and cutlasses, and roasted. As darkness closed around them, the rain began to fall, foretelling a stormy night. The few fires burned dimly along the strand, on which all night long the white-crested billows broke with a deep motononous roar. The hours passed slowly away, and the poor fellows looked forward to a southern prison as their doom. But at length it began to lighten in the east, and as the early dawn brightened over the broadly heaving Atlantic, they saw with joy the vessels again standing towards the land. A little after seven the signal was again run up "engage batteries," and now Fort Hatteras took all the storm. After a couple of hours, however, Stringham saw that many of his shot fell short, and ordered the firing to cease, and the gunners use fifteen-second fuses only, with ten-inch guns. He had been using ten-second fuses. The fire was then renewed, and, the Harriet Lane coming up with her rifled guns, the fort took a terrible pounding. Commodore Barron, of the rebel navy,—in whose charge the defences of the North Carolina coast had been placed, —came to the fort the previous evening, and assumed command. A few months before, his flag had waved from the Wabash, that he as a federal officer commanded, and now he saw her guns turned on him, a traitor. He soon noticed that the guns of the fort were too light to reach the ships, which with their heavy metal could, while keeping out of his range, hurl shells and shot, with unerring precision, into his works. He saw at once it was a hopeless fight, yet he could have kept to his bomb-proofs, and waited for a storm to disperse the fleet, which might be expected any hour on that coast; but the wooden ventilator of his magazine taking fire from our shells, a panic, it was supposed, seized the troops, and they demanded that the fort should be surrendered. So just before noon a white flag went up—the firing ceased, and the little band on shore began to move towards the fort. The crews of the squadron, when they saw this, simultaneously sent up three rousing cheers.

Gen. Butler went in to receive the surrender, and soon returned with Barron and the officers on board. Seven hundred and fifteen men, a thousand stand of arms, seventy-five kegs of powder, five stand of colors, thirty-one cannon, besides provisions, stores, and cotton, were the fruits of this victory. The wild delight with which the news was received, showed how deeply the nation had felt the disgrace of Bull Run, and how eager it was to seize on any success that would help to wipe out its remembrance.

The Harriet Lane, in trying to cross the bar, grounded, and it was feared for a while that she would be lost, but she was finally got off. The fleet returned to Fortress Monroe amid the acclamations of the people, and ovations were freely tendered to Stringham. But the plaudits that were rained on him soon gave way to unmeasured and unmerited blame, for not taking his fleet into the sound, and prosecuting his victories along the coast. It was said that he was in a hurry to get back, and be fêted and lionized, and an attempt was made to throw ridicule upon him. It afterwards turned out that his vessels drew too much water to go over the bar, and, moreover, that his orders were to return immediately, after the reduction of the forts, to Fortress Monroe. When this was finally ascertained, the denunciations were turned from him on the navy department, for its shiftless management; but too late to soothe the wounded feelings of the brave commander. Whether it was owing to the unmerited abuse he received, causing him to be dissatisfied with the service, or not, he, for some reason, the next month, at his own request, was relieved from his command. The next year, Aug. 1st, he was made rear-admiral on the retired list.

Engd by H.B. Hall, N.Y.

S. F. Du Pont

Rear Adm. SAMUEL F. Du PONT.

Engraved expressly for Headley's Naval Work.

CHAPTER V.

REAR-ADMIRAL SAMUEL FRANCIS DUPONT.

HIS NATIVITY.—MADE MIDSHIPMAN AT TWELVE YEARS OF AGE.—FIRST CRUISE UNDER COMMODORE STEWART.—COMMANDER IN 1845.—COMMANDS THE CONGRESS DURING THE MEXICAN WAR.—RESCUES A PARTY BELEAGUERED IN THE MISSION OF SAN JOSE.—MADE CAPTAIN AND PLACED IN COMMAND OF THE STEAM FRIGATE MINNESOTA, AND CONVEYS OUR MINISTER TO CHINA.—CRUISE IN THE CHINESE WATERS.—AT THE BREAKING OUT OF THE REBELLION PLACED OVER THE PHILADELPHIA NAVY YARD.—PROPOSES THE CAPTURE OF PORT ROYAL.—PLACED IN COMMAND OF THE EXPEDITION.—EXCITEMENT OF THE COUNTRY ON ITS DEPARTURE.—MYSTERY RESPECTING ITS DESTINATION.—A TERRIFIC STORM.—FOREBODINGS OF THE PEOPLE AND EXULTATION OF THE SOUTH.—THE FLEET SCATTERED.—SHIPWRECK AND DEATH.—SINKING OF THE GOVERNOR.—FRIGHTFUL SCENES.—ARRIVAL AT PORT ROYAL.—THE ATTACK.—A THRILLING SPECTACLE.—SURRENDER OF THE FORTS.—ENTHUSIASM OVER THE VICTORY.—DUPONT'S CONQUESTS ALONG THE COAST OF SOUTH CAROLINA, GEORGIA, AND FLORIDA.—HIS STRINGENT BLOCKADE.—RAID OF THE REBEL RAMS OF CHARLESTON ON HIS FLEET.—THE MERCEDITA AND KEYSTONE STATE.—COMMANDS THE IRON-CLAD FLEET IN THE GREAT ATTACK ON CHARLESTON.—DESCRIPTION OF THE COMBAT.—DISAPPOINTMENT OVER THE FAILURE.—DUPONT BLAMED FOR NOT RENEWING THE ATTACK.—HIS DEFENCE.—COURT-MARTIALS THE CHIEF ENGINEER.—RELIEVED OF HIS COMMAND.—ADMIRAL FOOTE PUT IN HIS PLACE.—HIS SUDDEN DEATH.—ADMIRAL DAHLGREN SUCCEEDS HIM.—RETIREMENT OF DUPONT.—HIS DEATH.—HIS CHARACTER.

DUPONT, as his name indicates, is of French extraction, his father and grandfather both having emigrated to this country in 1799.

He was born at Bergen Point, New Jersey, September 27th, 1803. The remembrance of the vital aid rendered us by the French nation in our struggle for independence being fresh in our memories, it was not difficult to get a son of one of its recent citizens into our navy; and Samuel, in 1817, at twelve years of age, obtained a midshipman's warrant and sailed on his first cruise in the seventy-four gunship Franklin, under the gallant Commodore Stewart. Being an apt scholar, he rapidly acquired the knowledge of his profession, but, promotion coming slowly in times of peace, he, though steadily rising step by step in rank, did not reach the position of commander till 1845. All this time he faithfully fulfilled his duties in whatever waters he sailed. In 1845 he was ordered to the Pacific to the command of the Congress, and saw much service, during the Mexican war, on the coast of California.

In 1848, hearing that Lieutenant Heywood, with a small party, was beleaguered in the Mission House at St. Jose by some five hundred Mexicans, he landed a hundred marines and sailors, and boldly advancing against this force, five times as great as his own, scattered them in confusion, and rescued the lieutenant. His gallant "blue jackets" were received by the rescued party with rousing cheers, which they returned with a sailor's heartiness.

In 1856 he was made captain, and the next year placed in command of the steam-frigate Minnesota, and ordered to convey Mr. Reed, the American minister, to China. He remained cruising in the Chinese waters for two years, when he returned to the United States, and, on the 1st of January, 1861, was appointed over the Philadelphia navy yard. In the summer, while Stringham was preparing the expedition against Hatteras, the

Secretary of the Navy consulted with him respecting the seizure of some Southern harbor occupying a central position, which would answer for a depot and place of rendezvous, etc., for our fleets in the South Atlantic and Gulf of Mexico. He recommended Port Royal, a place but little known at the time in the North. His views being adopted, he was put in command of the Atlantic blockading squadron, and directed to fit out an expedition to capture it.

A fleet of fifty sail—transports and all—was assembled in Hampton Roads, attached to which was a land force, some twenty thousand strong, under Gen. W. T. Sherman. The Government, having learned wisdom by experience, determined that the destination of this expedition should be kept secret; and each commander was furnished with sealed orders, which were not to be opened till out to sea. Bad management in some of the minor details delayed the sailing of the fleet later than was intended, and the beautiful month of October slipped away, leaving it still in the waters of the Chesapeake. Dupont had sent off some twenty coal vessels, with directions to rendezvous off Savannah, in order to deceive the enemy as to the real point of attack; and, at length, on the 24th of October, gave the signal to the fleet to weigh anchor. No such imposing naval force had ever before been seen in our waters, and the appearance it presented as it moved down the bay, was most grand and striking. When the news was received that it was fairly out to sea, the most intense excitement prevailed throughout the country. The secret of its destination had been well kept; and hence a mystery enveloped it which served to increase the excitement. Various conjectures were made respecting the point along the coast on which the descent was to be made. Some suggested Wilmington, others Savannah and Charleston; while but a few guessed its real destination. All were agreed in one thing, however, that it would send consternation through the South. But in a few days, however, the elation of the people was changed into gloomy forebodings, for a storm of unprecedented fury swept along the Atlantic coast, carrying wreck and destruction in its path. One might have well been filled with anxiety had the fleet been composed of thorough-going sea vessels; but it was known that many of those used as transports were never intended for the sea—being mere river steamers, and even ferry-boats. Loaded to their utmost capacity with stores and ammunition, and precious lives, how could they outride such a hurricane? Men in Washington turned pale as they heard, hour after hour, the heavy storm surging by, and it began to look as though God's frown was on the enterprise. The Southern papers overflowed with exultation and thanksgiving, and every one called to mind the Spanish Armada, whose strength and pride were humbled by just such a storm, and left a helpless wreck on the waters.

Rumors of wreck and disaster came at intervals from along the coast; but it was many days before any definite information was received.

The fleet took the storm on the most dangerous part of our coast—off Cape Hatteras—and was scattered by it like autumn leaves in a gale. From four o'clock, Friday morning, till midnight, the tempest was at its height. Signal lights were hoisted after dark in the rigging of the vessels, which rose and fell like fireflies along the heaving deep. Now up and now down, as the laboring ships reeled from the watery summits to the yawning gulfs below; they one moment gleamed dimly through the blinding storm and rain, that fell in torrents, and then disappeared, as if quenched for ever, in the tumultuous billows. Some of the vessels soon became unmanageable, others endeavored to lay-to, and all were fearful, even could they outride the hurricane, that they would be dashed against each other in the darkness. The wind howled and shrieked through the rigging, and the thousands of soldiers, unaccustomed to the sea, stood appalled at the might and terror of the angry elements. The Winfield Scott, loaded with nearly five hundred troops, labored fearfully, and soon sprung a leak. Hoisting signals of distress, she cut away her masts. This failing to relieve her, she tumbled overboard her three rifled cannon. Next, the tents, equipments, and muskets were thrown into the sea, while the pumps were kept vigorously at work. The Bienville saw her signal of distress and hove-to. It did not seem possible that a small boat could live a moment in such a sea, and Captain Steedman, unwilling to order any of his crew to attempt the perilous task of carrying a hawser to her, shouted, "Who will volunteer to save the Winfield Scott?" "I," "I," replied a score of brave sailors, and three boats were at once lowered, and the next moment were riding like cockle-shells on the careering waves. Two were swamped, but the lives of the crew saved. At length the two vessels drifted together, with a crash. Taking advantage of the collision, fifty soldiers leaped aboard the Bienville—some fell between, and, with a shriek, disappeared in the boiling waters. Three were caught between the grinding timbers, and, crushed out of the form of humanity, dropped silently into the deep. The chief-engineer and his assistants, panic-stricken, also escaped over the sides of the vessel while in contact with the Bienville. The remaining soldiers were now wild with terror; but the captain of the vessel, seeing the dastardly escape of the engineer, came on board, and, putting him in irons, took him and the crew back. It was midnight, and five feet of water was in the hold, and terror and death were on every side. But the return of the captain, with the engineer and crew, restored order, and the soldiers became calm and steady again. The storm at length began to abate, when they then gained on the leak, and the vessel was saved.

The crew of the transport Peerless were taken from her in a sinking condition; but the steamer Governor, with the Marine battalion on board, was soon left helpless and sinking. Under the blows of the heavy seas the brace-chains of the smoke-stack parted, and it went overboard; but breaking three feet above the hurricane-deck, a little steam could be kept up. Then the steam-pipe burst, while the frail vessel was leaking badly. At dark a vessel was seen in the distance, and a rocket was sent up through the storm, asking for help. An answering signal flashed out, filling every heart with hope. But she was unable to render any assistance, and kept on her way. Rocket after rocket was now sent up in the darkness—mute cries of distress, till all were gone—and then the soldiers were ordered to keep up a fire of musketry; but the vollies scarcely made a sound in the louder tumult of the wind and waves. A hundred men were kept at the pumps, others held on to the braces, that threatened to part every moment, and thus the fearful night wore away.

As daylight broke slowly over the wild and stormy waste, two vessels were descried off the starboard bow. One, the Isaac Smith, commanded by Lieut. Nicholson, saw the signal of distress and stood towards her. At ten o'clock the former hailed, saying he would take off the crew. By great exertion a hawser was got on board; but through some carelessness was soon lost and dragged in the water. The Smith then stood off, and the Young Rover came up, the captain of which said he would stand by them to the last, which was answered by a loud cheer from the deck of the Governor. The Smith soon came back, and another hawser was got aboard, but again parted. All this while the water was rapidly gaining on the vessel, and every moment she threatened to go down with all on board. The Young Rover, seeing a frigate in sight, stood toward her with a signal of distress. It proved to be the Sabine, Capt. Ringgold, who soon was within hail, giving the comforting assurance that he would take all on board. But night was now coming on again, and it was not until eight or nine o'clock that her stern could be brought near enough to the bow of the Sabine to allow a boom to be rigged out, along which thirty were "whipped" aboard, when hawsers and cables parted, under the tremendous plunges of the vessels. Ringgold now determined to get alongside, hazardous as the attempt was. It seemed impossible to do this without coming in collision with the Governor with a force that would crush her like an egg-shell. It was, however, done; though the Sabine had twenty feet of her hurricane-deck carried away by the former. Forty were then got on board, while one, falling between the vessels, was crushed to death. The Sabine now started ahead, determined to tow the disabled vessel till morning. The hearts of those left on board sunk at the prospect. There were three feet of water in the hold, and rapidly gaining; and the sea running mountains high. That she could be kept afloat till morning seemed hardly possible. But every thing movable was thrown overboard, and the water casks started to lighten the ship; so that, though slowly settling, she floated nobly through the rest of the night. At daybreak, the boats of the Sabine put off to her relief, though a fearful sea was running at the time. They dared not approach the guards of the vessels lest they should be swamped, and so lay off and called on the soldiers and crew to jump overboard. It was a fearful alternative; but no other was left. The ranks were kept in military order, and one soldier after another stepped out as he was ordered and leaped into the sea, and was hauled aboard the boats. Thus all were saved, with the exception of one corporal and six privates, who left the ranks in their fright, and were lost. The hawser was then cast loose, and the vessel wallowed for a short time heavily in the sea, and then with a heavy lurch went to the bottom.

At length the gale spent its fury, and the scattered vessels, some far out to sea, resumed their course, and, by Sabbath evening, fourteen of them were in sight of each other, though the flag-ship Wabash was nowhere to be seen.

On Monday these vessels arrived off Port Royal, and at noon the Wabash hove in sight, with the Susquehannah—which Dupont had taken from blockading duty off Charleston harbor—and some thirty-six more of the fleet and the gunboats.

This and the next day, while the gunboats were feeling their way up the channel and marking it out for the passage of the larger vessels, three rebel gunboats came down and attacked them, but were easily driven off. Preparations were now made to land the troops; but on consultation it was deemed best, for several reasons, that the navy should first attack alone. The following day, Wednesday, was spent in completing preparations, and every thing got ready for action in the morning.

The two islands of Hilton Head and Bay Point guard the entrance of Port Royal Sound and are nearly three miles apart. On the extreme point of these two islands two fortifications had been erected—Fort Walker, on Hilton Head, mounting twenty-three guns; and Fort Beauregard, on Bay Point, mounting fifteen guns. There was, besides, a mortar battery, mounting four guns.

Thursday morning dawned calm and beautiful, and the waters of the bay flashed like a mirror in the early moonlight. At nine o'clock the signal from the Wabash to get under way was run up, and thirteen vessels, the Wabash leading, moved majestically off toward the batteries. Dupont could get none of his large frigates up, and the battle was to be fought by the Wabash, Susquehanna, Mohican, Seminole, Pawnee, Unadilla, Pembina, Bienville, Seneca, Curlew, Penguin, Ottawa, and Vandalia. In single file, with ports open and bristling with heavy guns, these vessels swept rapidly up toward Fort Walker, presenting a majestic spectacle. Beyond the entrance of the harbor lay the little rebel fleet, under command of Tatnall, formerly of our navy, and, still farther in, a fleet of steamers loaded with spectators, that had come down from Charleston to witness the destruction of the Yankee fleet. Dupont, in the Wabash, led the imposing column, and every eye watched with the intensest interest his movements, as he steadily approached the low silent structure on Hilton Head. As he came near, it poured in a tremendous fire, but Dupont kept on in dead silence, till the second steamer came abreast, when the three forward vessels opened at once with their powerful broadsides, and the shot and shell from seventy-five guns fell in one wild crash on the fort. Dupont had determined to fight the forts while in motion, so as not to let his wooden vessels be stationary targets for the enemy's fire; and, having delivered his broadsides, moved on. Each vessel as it came opposite the fort delivered its broadside, so that there was no cessation to the fire till the whole had passed. Having got beyond the fort, Dupont wheeled, still followed by the vessels in single file, and poured his fire into Fort Beauregard. Thus these thirteen vessels moved in the form of a flat letter O, flaming and thundering all the while with a power and terror indescribable. An eighty-pound rifle ball went clean through the mainmast of the Wabash, making an ugly hole. Another pierced her after-magazine, letting the water into it, yet she still kept on her sublime way, proudly leading the long file of flaming ships. Captain Rogers, acting as aid to Dupont, says: "The Wabash was a destroying angel—hugging the shore; calling the soundings with cold indifference; slowing the engine so as only to give steerage way; signalling the vessels their various evolutions; and at the same time raining shell, as with target practice, too fast to count. Shell fell in the fort, not twenty-eight in a minute, but as fast as a horse's feet beat the ground in a gallop. The resistance was heroic, but what could flesh and blood do against such a fire? I watched two men particularly, in red shirts; I saw them seated at the muzzle of a gun, apparently waiting, exhausted, for more ammunition. They were so still that I doubted whether they were men. This terrible fire fell around them—I saw them move, and I knew they were men. They loaded the gun—a shell burst near them, and they dropped, doubtless blown to atoms."

In the mean time the gunboats, having found that in a cove they could get an enfilading fire on Hilton Head, took up their position there, and rendered good service. A little after noon the signal "cease firing" was made from the flag-ship, and the steamers swept beyond the reach of the batteries to rest the men and give them some refreshment before returning to their terribly exhausting work. The gunboats, however, from their enfilading position, kept up a galling fire. About three o'clock, just as the vessels were getting ready for action again, the rebel flag was struck. The firing ceased, and Captain Rogers jumped into a boat lowered from the flag-ship, and rowed swiftly toward the shore. He found the works deserted, the ramparts desolate, and planted the stars and stripes upon them.

When the thousands on board the fleet, who for five long hours had watched the terrible conflict, saw our flag go up, the excitement was unbounded. Many of the officers wept like children, but a wild enthusiasm overrode every other feeling, and from ship to ship, down the whole mighty fleet, there went up a cheer such as never before stirred the placid waters of that bay, while the various bands struck up "The Star-spangled Banner," making the air ring with the stirring strains. Upon seeing this fort abandoned, the garrison of the other left also and fled inland.

A portion of the troops were now landed, and General Sherman assumed command of the place, and issued a proclamation to the people of the State of South Carolina. This was General T. W. Sherman, not W. T. Sherman, the hero of Atlanta. Savannah could probably have been taken at this time, had he marched promptly forward, such was the terror occasioned by this victory of Dupont. His orders, however, were to fortify himself there, build piers, docks, &c., and fit up the port for a naval depot.

Port Royal, from this time through the war, sustained a prominent position in all our naval movements along the Atlantic coast.

The victory created the wildest enthusiasm throughout the North. The national flag had been planted on the traitorous soil of South Carolina, never to be displaced till every stronghold of the State was in our possession. Dupont at once became the hero of the day. Naval men were especially delighted. Our ill-successes on land thus far had been a cause of deep mortification, and this first great essay of the navy recalled to mind the halo of glory it hung round the nation during the first year of the second war with England, when successive defeats on land made the people's cheeks crimson with shame. Whenever one met a naval man the eye of the latter brightened, and with a proud shake of the head he would say, "I told you how it would be when the 'blue jackets' got a chance." "Ah! we are all sure of the navy," was the common remark. It is said that Commodore Barron, then a prisoner in Fort Warren, when he read a description of the fight, and how gallantly his old ship, the Wabash, bore herself, forgot he was a rebel prisoner, and exclaimed, "By heavens! *our* navy can beat the world."

Dupont's career was now one of continued success along the coast. Fort Clinch surrendered—the first national fort reclaimed. Captain Drayton, sending a boat's crew on shore to raise the American flag, pushed on to Old Fernandina, where a white flag was displayed. Shortly after, and when passing New Fernandina, a few rifle-shots were fired from some bushes, and a railroad train was perceived just starting. As it was naturally supposed to contain soldiers escaping, he directed Lieutenant-Commanding Stevens to try and stop it; and the road passing for some distance near the river, "and we going at full speed, there was an opportunity of firing several shots at the two locomotives attached to the train, which, however, did not prevent its escape across the railroad bridge, which is four miles from the town, and it was soon lost in the woods on the other side. We afterwards found on the track the bodies of two men who had been killed by our shots, one of whom was a soldier; and the report was that ex-Senator Yulee was on board one of the cars, and had also been struck, but this, I think, was a mistake." Thus was presented the novel spectacle of a vessel-of-war attacking a railroad train.

Dupont also visited the coast of Florida, and captured St. Augustine, keeping the whole Southern seaboard in a state of alarm. The slaves crowded to the protection of his flag, and were left sole occupants of their late masters' plantations.

The waters of Warsaw and Ossibaw Sounds, Brunswick, Darien, and other places, owned the sway of his flag, and the whole coast of Georgia was held by his squadron. At the siege of Pulaski, one of the batteries on shore was under the command of the officers and crew of the Wabash. He also seized Stone Inlet and River, and thus secured a base of operations against Charleston, and maintained the blockade with a rigor not before exhibited, and did all a man could do with the limited means in his power.

In 1862 he was made one of the nine active rear-admirals. In January of the next year occurred the famous raid of two rebel rams on his blockading squadron off Charleston Harbor. As so many conflicting statements have been given of this affair, we insert the accounts of the two commanders, whose vessels alone were seriously injured. The captain of the Mercedita says, under date of the last day of January :

SIR: I have to report that, at 4.25 this morning, two iron-clad rams, from Charleston, in the obscurity of a thick haze, and the moon having just set, succeeded in passing the bar, near ship channel, unperceived by the squadron, and made an attack upon this ship, being first encountered.

Particular vigilance was exhibited by officers and men in expedition of vessels to run the blockade.

At 3 A. M., we had slipped cable and overhauled a troop steamer, running for the channel by mistake. At 4, I laid down. Lieut. Commander Abbott was on deck giving orders to Acting Master Dwyer about recovering the anchor, when they saw a smoke and the faint appearance of a vessel close at hand. I heard them exclaim, "She has black smoke;" "watch, man the guns," "spring the rattle," "call all hands to quarters." Mr. Dwyer came to the cabin door, telling me a steamboat was close aboard. I was then in the act of getting my pea-jacket, and slipped it on as I followed him out; jumped to poop ladder, saw smoke and a low boat, apparently a tug, although I thought it might be a little propeller for the squadron.

I sang out, "Train your guns right on him, and be ready to fire as soon as I order." I hailed, "Steamer ahoy! Steer clear of us and heave-to. What steamer is that?" Then ordered my men, "Fire on him." Told him, "You will be into us. What steamer is that?" His answer to first or second hail was, "Hallo!" The other replies were indistinct, either by intention or from being spoken inside of his mail armor, until in the act of striking us with his prow, when he said, "This is the Confederate States steam ram." I repeated the order, "Fire! fire!" but no gun could be trained on him, as he approached on the quarter, struck us just abaft our aforemost 32-pounder gun, and fired a heavy rifle through us diagonally, penetrating the starboard side through our Normandy condenser, the steam-drum of port boiler, and exploding against port side of ship, blowing a hole in its exit some four or five feet square.

The vessel was instantly filled and enveloped with steam. Reports were brought to me, "Shot through both boilers," "fires put out by steam and water," "gunner and one man killed, and a number of men fatally scalded, water over fire-room floor, vessel sinking fast." "The ram has cut us through at and below water-line on one side, and the shell has burst at the other almost at water-edge."

After the ram struck, she swung round under our starboard counter, her prow touching, and hailed, "Surrender, or I'll sink you! Do you surrender?" And after receiving reports, I answered, "I can make no resistance; my boiler is destroyed." "Then, do you surrender?" I said, "Yes;" having found my moving power destroyed, and that I could bring nothing to bear but muskets against his shot-proof coating.

He hailed several times to send a boat, and threatened to fire again. After some delay, a boat was lowered, and Lieut. Commander Abbott asked if he should go in her, and asked for orders what to say. I told him to see what they demanded, and to tell him the condition we were in.

He proceeded aboard, and, according to their demand, gave his parole on behalf of himself and all the officers and crew. His report accompanies this. The ram having been detained half an hour or more, ran out for steamer Keystone State, which vessel and three others we had tried to alarm by lights. We saw a shell explode as it hit the ram, without injuring her. Saw the Keystone State was hit several times, and saw the smoke and steam pouring from her. The firing then receded to northward and eastward, and was pretty brisk at the head of the line.

The Keystone State, commanded by Le Roy, was also disabled, and claimed as a prize by the rebels. The details of the fight are thus given by the commander:

Between four and five A. M., 31st January, 1863, a gun was fired near, and supposed to be the Mercedita, and some lights were seen. Soon after discovered a dark object a little ahead of her, and then a column of black smoke was noticed rising from the vessel, but I supposed was either a tug out from Charleston or some stranger passing along. Another column of black smoke was seen more to the north and east of the Mercedita. My suspicions aroused, I ordered the forward rifle trained upon the first steamer, which was standing toward this ship, also other guns to be ready. Gave notice to the engineer of the watch to be ready to move, and, the steamers drawing nearer, ordered the cable slipped, and enough motion to get command of the ship. By this time the stranger was abreast the starboard waist. On hailing, "What steamer is that?" the reply was, "Hallo!" followed by some words that were unintelligible. Satisfied, from the view obtained through my night glasses, that the steamer was a ram, I ordered the starboard bow gun fired at her, which was at once responded to by a shot from the stranger, when I ordered the starboard battery fired as soon as the guns could be brought to bear, putting the helm aport. On heading to the northward and eastward, discovered a ram on either quarter. Soon after the first gun, fire was reported forward below. After extinguishing it, fire was again reported in the same place, when the ship was kept off seaward to enable us to put out the fire and get things in a condition to attack the enemy. Ordered full steam, and about daylight discovered black smoke and stood for it, for the purpose of running her down, exchanging shots rapidly with her, striking her repeatedly, but making no impression, while every shot from her was striking us. About 6.17 A.M., a shell, entering on the port side, forward of the forward guard, destroyed the steam chimneys, filling all the forward part of the ship with steam. The port boiler emptied of its contents, the ship gave a heel to starboard, nearly down to the guard, and the water from the boiler, and two shot-holes under water, led to the impression the ship was filling and sinking, a foot and a half water being reported in the hold. Owing to the steam, men were unable to get supplies of ammunition from forward. Ordered all boats ready for lowering. Signal-books thrown overboard, also some small arms. The ram being so near, and the ship helpless, and the men being slaughtered by almost every discharge of the enemy, I ordered the colors to be hauled down, but finding the enemy were still firing upon us, directed the colors to be rehoisted and resume our fire from the after-battery. Now the enemy, either injured, or to avoid the squadron approaching, sheered off towards the harbor, exchanging shots with the Housatonic, which vessel was in chase. Put fore-and-aft sail on the ship, sent yards aloft and bent sails; there being no wind, drifted along to the north and east, when the Memphis took us in tow. Our surgeon being killed, the surgeon of the Memphis came on board. Having accomplished this much, the rams returned to the harbor. Beauregard issued a proclamation declaring the blockade destroyed, and that foreign governments should so regard it. The pompous manifesto was not regarded by Dupont, and he continued the blockade.

Many blockade runners were captured by Dupont during the year, and he had the entire confidence of the Navy Department and the people.

The successful fight of the Monitor with the Merrimac threatened an entire revolution in maritime conflicts, especially in harbor warfare, and Secretary Welles immediately set about having a fleet of these vessels made, which he believed would put every port on the coast in our possession. In addition to these, a powerful iron-clad, the Ironsides, was built, and, in the spring of 1863, was ready for service. When the fleet was completed, it was determined the first essay of its strength should be against Fort Sumter, in Charleston harbor. Of its success no one seemed to entertain a doubt, for the impenetrability of these vessels to shot was assumed, while it was believed that no mason-work ever built by man could long withstand the tremendous weight of metal they could hurl from their monster guns, the like of which had never before been used on ships of war. This fleet was composed of nine vessels, and placed under the command of Admiral Dupont.

Having rendezvoused in Port Royal, he sailed from there on the 1st of April, 1863, to try the great experiment of the century, and the next day arrived at the embouchure of the Edisto river. The water over Charleston bar not being of sufficient depth in ordinary times to float them, the heavy spring tides of April, which gave a foot more of water, was selected for the passage of the vessels. On Sunday morning at daybreak the fleet moved out to sea, and in a few hours lay off Charleston harbor. The next day Dupont transferred his flag to the Ironsides, and the fleet, taking the flood-tide, passed safely over the bar, and came to anchor inside. The wooden vessels lay outside as a reserve. The rebels having destroyed all the old land-marks by which pilots were guided, the channel had to be buoyed out, which was successfully done by Mr. Boutelle of the Coast Survey. But just as everything was ready, a thick haze settled down over the water, obscuring the range, so that the attack had to be postponed. On the 7th, however, a gentle northerly breeze dissipated the mist, and the bay and forts and distant city lay basking in the clear sunshine. Just two years before, this month, the national flag was hauled down on Fort Sumter, and now it was universally believed that its anniversary day would be celebrated by salutes from national cannon from the same spot and to the same flag.

The officers of the navy, however, were not so sanguine. Dupont, like Farragut, had not unbounded faith in iron clads, least of all in unwieldy monitors. As through his glass he surveyed the work before him, he saw that his little fleet was to be put into a crucible to which no vessels before had ever been subjected. Steeples and roofs, in the far background, and the neighboring shores, were lined with spectators, assembled to witness the Titanic struggle. As Dupont's eye swept around that bristling harbor, it was cannon here, and there, and everywhere. In front, lay Sullivan's Island to the right, and Morris Island on the left, the two points curving in towards each other till they approached within a mile. Midway in the channel between them, built on an artificial island, stood Fort Sumter. Fort Moultrie, on Sullivan's Island, was opposite Sumter, while, above and below, batteries were erected on every available point. On the left, opposite this central fortress, stood battery Bee, on Cummings-Point, while beyond, should the vessels ever get there, battery succeeded battery, clear up to the city, three miles distant. Stretching down towards the fleet were other batteries on Morris Island, and among them Fort Wagner. The sight was enough to daunt the stoutest heart, for uncounted cannon lay shotted and aimed, ready to open on that little fleet. It was Dupont's purpose to pass as quickly as possible up the channel, and get to the west and northwest of Fort Sumter, which was known to be less impregnable than the front face. That there would be great difficulty in reaching this desirable point was well known, for it had been ascertained that torpedoes, and all sorts of obstacles which engineering skill could invent, had been sunk in the channel opposite the fort. To remove these Ericsson had invented a machine which was to be fastened to the bow of the leading vessel, and pushed up amid this net of obstructions, exploding and pulling up whatever might arrest the passage of the ships.

At noon, the signal from the flag-ship to move to the attack was seen, and the little fleet, looking like mere rafts on the water, steamed slowly forward. There was none of the pomp or splendor of grand old frigates, towering proudly over the deep, in these low black monitors, creeping slowly to the conflict.

It was four miles to Fort Sumter, and the batteries of Morris Island commanded the whole distance. The vessels had advanced but a short distance before the Weehawken, leading the way with the strange machine in front, stopped, having got tangled up with the unwieldy, novel thing. It took an hour to free herself, and then the fleet moved on again. The spectators on shore gazed with breathless interest on the spectacle, the music in Fort Sumter ceased, and the rapid roll of the drum was heard beating to quarters, which called every gunner to his place. The fleet kept steadily on till opposite Fort Wagner, where Dupont expected to meet the first blow of the hurricane; but all its guns kept motionless and still in their places, and only curious eyes greeted the advancing vessels. Next they floated by Battery Bee, but silence like death reigned over the low works. What does all this mean? This silence is ominous, and shows a confidence in something yet to come that portends no good. Still the fleet kept on; but just as the Weehawken was rounding-to, to make the entrance of the harbor, she came within the circle of fire from Forts Sumter and Moultrie. Then the crater opened from the top of Sumter, and down came a storm of shot and shell. Moultrie joined in, and thunder answered thunder with awful rapidity. The heavy metal fell like hailstones on the Weehawken; but she kept steadily on towards her assigned position, followed by the whole fleet. But suddenly she stopped in the very vortex of the fire. She had run upon a hawser stretched from Sumter to Moultrie, buoyed up on casks, and strung with nets, cables, and torpedoes. Her propeller, getting entangled in these, became unmanageable, and she drifted helpless through the wild hurricane. The other vessels, as they come up, see the danger, and sheer off to try the channel on the other side of the fort. But here a row of piles is encountered, rising ten feet out of the water—while farther up, the channel is crossed and recrossed with obstructions, backed by three iron-clads, that can hold those vessels under a fire that nothing that ever floated could survive. To add to the perplexity, the Ironsides, in the heavy tide, suddenly refused to obey her rudder, and she drifted towards Fort Moultrie, getting foul of the Catskill and Nantucket in her passage. The plan of the battle was now irrecoverably gone, and Dupont signalled to the fleet to disregard his movements. It was therefore every one for himself; and then was seen what splendid commanders Dupont had to second him in this unprecedented struggle. Five batteries were in full play, and nearly three hundred cannon of the heaviest metal were trained on those monitors, that now had only the simple problem to solve—whether they can knock Fort Sumter to pieces with their enormous guns, before they are carried to the bottom under the tons of metal that fall with a ceaseless crash upon them.

The gallant Rhind, left to act as he pleased, lays the Keokuk boldly alongside of the fort as though it were a ship, and with his little monitor makes a broadside engagement of it. Close behind him comes Rodgers in the Catskill, and, following hard after, the heroic Worden in the Montauk. A little farther off lie the other vessels, all seeking to sound the full terrors of this awful abyss of fire. Within rifle-shot distance of the nearest batteries, they stand and hurl against them their ponderous shells. The gunners, stripped to their waists, and begrimed with powder and smoke, work their monster guns with a coolness and rapidity that tells fearfully on the solid face of Sumter. Shot weighing four hundred and twenty pounds strike like heaven's own thunderbolts the trembling structure, but they are nothing to the answering shots that fall faster than the forge's hammer on their sides. The din of this heavy metal striking and bursting on every side is infernal, and the deafening explosions shake land and sea. It seems one vast volcano, before which everything must be engulfed. Nothing built with mortal hands could long live there, and in thirty minutes the Keokuk came limping out of the fire, fast settling in the waters. One of the port shutters of the flagship was shot away, exposing her gun deck, while a red-hot shot buried itself in her wooden bows. The Nahant was soon disfigured with thirty wounds. The Passaic was in the same plight, with her turret so knocked to pieces that it could not revolve. The Nantucket was reduced to one gun, while the Catskill had been pierced by a rifled shot. Five of the new iron-clads must now be reckoned out of the fight. But what thirty-two guns, (the total armament of this fleet,) against those encircling batteries could do had been done, and now, to put only fifteen or sixteen against them, was downright madness. Besides, night was coming on, and so Dupont wisely signalled the fleet to retire.

During the evening, the commander of the iron-clads came on board the flagship, and Dupont, after a full report of the condition of the vessels, decided that it would be impossible to take Charleston with them alone.

From the following statement, made by him to the War Department, the folly of renewing the attempt with the same vessels is so apparent, that it is a matter of wonder that any one could be found so destitute of common judgment as to uphold it:

"No ship had been exposed to the severest fire of the enemy over forty minutes, and yet, in that brief period, as the Department will perceive, by the detailed reports of the commanding officers, five of the iron-clads were wholly or partially disabled; disabled, too (as the obstructions could not be passed), in that which was most essential to our success—I mean, in their armament, or power of inflicting injury by their guns.

"Commander Rhind, in the Keokuk, had only been able to fire three times during the short period he was exposed to the guns of the enemy, and was obliged to withdraw from action to prevent his vessel from sinking, which event occurred on the following morning.

"The Nahant, Commander Downes, was most seriously damaged, her turret being so jammed as effectually to prevent its turning; many of the bolts of both turret and pilot-house were broken, and the latter became nearly untenable, in consequence of the nuts and ends flying across it.

"Captain P. Drayton, in the Passaic, after the fourth fire from her 11-inch gun, was unable to use it again during the action; and his turret also became jammed, though he was, after some delay, enabled to get it in motion again.

"Commander Ammen, of the Patapsco, lost the use of his rifled gun after the fifth fire, owing to the carrying away of the forward-cap square bolts. On the Nantucket, Commander Fairfax reports that, after the third shot from the 15-inch gun, the port stopper became jammed, several shot striking very near the port, and driving in the plates, preventing the further use of that gun during the action.

"The other iron-clads, though struck many times severely, were still able to use their guns, but I am convinced that, in all probability, in another thirty minutes they would have been likewise disabled.

"Any attempt to pass through the obstructions I have referred to would have entangled the vessels, and held them under the most severe fire of heavy ordnance that has ever been delivered; and while it is barely possible that some vessels might have forced their way through, it would only have been to be again impeded by fresh and more formidable obstructions, and to encounter other powerful batteries, with which the whole harbor of Charleston had been lined.

"I had hoped that the endurance of the iron-clads would have enabled them to have borne any weight of fire to which they might have been exposed; but when I found that so large a portion of them were wholly or one-half disabled, by less than an hour's engagement, before attempting to remove (overcome) the obstructions, or testing the power of the torpedoes, I was convinced that persistence in the attack would only result in the loss of the greater portion of the iron-clad fleet, and in leaving many of them inside the harbor, to fall into the hands of the enemy.

"The slowness of our fire, and our inability to occupy any battery that we might silence, or to prevent its being restored under cover of night, were difficulties of the gravest character, and, until the outer forts should have been taken, the army could not enter the harbor or afford me any assistance."

So unequal was the contest, which lasted less than forty minutes, that the entire fleet of iron-clads fired only one hundred and thirty-nine shots, "though, during that same period, Dupont says the " enemy poured upon us an incessant storm of round-shot and shell, rifled projectiles of all descriptions, and red-hot shot."

The whole affair was so palpable and complete a failure, that the Department dared not directly blame Dupont for not succeeding. Still, reluctant to acknowledge itself any way in fault, it reproached him for not saying beforehand, how impossible success was. The simple truth is, the Secretary of the Navy, as well as the public generally, had come to have such a high opinion of the invulnerability of the iron-clads, that they considered Charleston as virtually ours, the moment the attack commenced. But, instead of complete success, this iron-clad fleet, the first ever set afloat and tested, effected absolutely nothing. It was too mortifying to confess the fact, without putting the blame on some one, and so it was placed on the commander, Dupont. He felt this keenly, and indignantly denounced the injustice of it. A correspondent of the Baltimore American published such a false statement of the whole matter in that paper, that Dupont felt bound, in justice to his officers as well as to himself, to notice it, which he did in a lengthy review. In a clear, concise statement of facts, he fixed the charge of deliberate falsehood against the writer, leaving no doubt as to the motive that instigated the base attack. In conclusion he says, "I now take leave of this, the most odious subject that I ever had occasion to notice. Some other assertions of Mr. Fulton, which might be flatly contradicted, I have not discussed, nor have I thought it worth while to consider his opinions upon purely professional points. To undergo the fire of the enemy and the stabs of an assassin of character, at one and the same time, is too much for my philosophy; and, for further protection against assaults of the latter kind, I look for and expect the countenance of the Department."

Chief-Engineer Stimers joined in the attack on Dupont, and, in the steamer Arago, on which he was a passenger on his way North, indulged in such unwarrantable language towards his commander, that the latter brought charges against him, and he was court-martialled. Though no definite result was reached, the public has long since rendered its verdict in the matter. A lengthy correspondence also followed between Dupont and the Secretary of the Navy, and, although the latter avoided all direct accusation, the tone of his letters wounded the chivalrous old Admiral, who felt that he was being made the scapegoat of other men's sins. He felt especially the censure pronounced against him, some time afterwards, for allowing the guns of the sunken Keokuk to fall into the hands of the rebels, for which he was in no wise to blame; and, said in a letter to the Secretary of the Navy:

"Having indulged the hope that my command, covering a period of twenty-one months afloat, had not been without results, I was not prepared for a continuance of that censure from the Department which has characterized its letters to me since monitors failed to take Charleston.

"I can only add now, that, to an officer of my temperament—whose sole aim has been to do his whole duty, and who has passed through forty-seven years of service without a word of reproof—these censures of the Navy Department would be keenly felt if I did not know they were wholly undeserved."

This was a little evasive; for "he *did* feel them keenly, although they *were* undeserved." The *injustice* stung him, against which there was no redress. Brave and chivalrous himself as a knight of the olden time, this deliberate infliction of wrong by others, in order to shield themselves, wounded most deeply his sensitive nature.

It ended—as all such affairs must end—in the resignation or removal of the commander, and the ultimate condemnation and exposure of those who are really the guilty parties.

In January, he sent Worden down to Great Ogeechee River, in the Montauk, to capture, if possible, Genesis Point, under the guns of which the privateer Nashville lay. During this month, he captured the steamer Princess Royal, while attempting to run the blockade at Charleston. The next month, the celebrated raid of the two iron-clads on the blockading squadron took place, in which the Meredita had her boiler exploded by one of the enemy's guns, and struck her flag; and the Keystone had also her steam-chest injured in the same manner, and also struck her colors, but afterwards escaped. Beauregard declared the blockade broken, and hoped to have it so regarded by foreign powers, but was disappointed.

In June, Dupont was relieved from his command, and Admiral Foote ordered to take his place. The latter, however, was taken sick in New York, just as he was about to leave for his destination, and died.

After the failure to take Charleston with the iron-clads, General Hunter, who was in command of the land forces operating against the city, forwarded the most serious complaints against Dupont, for not coöperating with him, as he desired, in his contemplated movements to take the place. He declares that he has "exercised patience with the Admiral," asks to be liberated from the order to coöperate with the navy, &c., &c., and he would raise colored regiments—take Charleston—in fact, electrify the nation. His after career shows how much he probably would have accomplished.

The sudden death of Admiral Foote compelled the Department to reverse its order of removal, and to direct Dupont to resume his command. During the short interval that elapsed before he was succeeded by Admiral Dahlgren, he sent the Weehawken and Nahant down to Warsaw Sound to look after the rebel ram Atlanta, which was reported to be a most formidable vessel. They succeeded in capturing her on the 17th of June. The next month, Dupont returned to Delaware, and was no more afloat during the war.

Dupont was a superb man physically; of grand and imposing presence, he trod the deck of his battle-ship like one of Nature's noblemen. Even those accustomed to see men of distinguished personal appearance in various parts of the world, were struck with the majesty and grandeur of his mien. A gentleman of the old school, or rather a knight of the olden time, his bearing was that of dignified courtesy to all, and impressed every one that approached him with profound respect. Chivalrous in his own feelings, he was incapable of wounding those of others, while he was keenly sensitive to any censure upon his conduct. Insensible to fear, he never shrunk from encountering any danger, while he was too lofty and noble to rush into it to obtain mere notoriety. Master of his profession, he knew his duty better than the Department that censured him, and experienced his greatest humiliation and suffering in performing it. Proud as he was sensitive, he could not brook unmerited rebuke. Irritated at his manly independence, the Government lost one of its best officers by gratifying its spleen, and under the pretence of maintaining its dignity. Dupont's name, however, will live long after those who persecuted him are consigned to forgetfulness, or to an immortality worse than oblivion.

A. H. Foote

REAR ADM^L A. H. FOOTE.

Engraved expressly for Headley's Naval Work.

CHAPTER VI.

REAR-ADMIRAL ANDREW HULL FOOTE.

HIS NATIVITY, ANCESTRY, AND EARLY EDUCATION.—ENTERS THE NAVY.—FIRST CRUISE.—SECOND CRUISE, UNDER COMMODORE HULL.—THIRD CRUISE TO THE WEST INDIES.—A GREAT CHANGE IN HIS CHARACTER.—DEDICATES HIS LIFE TO GOD.—VOYAGE ROUND THE WORLD.—BECOMES THE CHAMPION OF THE PERSECUTED MISSIONARIES OF THE SANDWICH ISLANDS.—APPOINTED OVER THE NAVAL ASYLUM OF PHILADELPHIA.—GETS THE INMATES TO GIVE UP THEIR GROG.—CRUISE IN THE MEDITERRANEAN.—PREACHES TO THE SAILORS.—LAID UP WITH SORE EYES.—COMMANDS THE SLOOP OF WAR PORTSMOUTH, ON THE EAST INDIA STATION.—BOMBARDS CHINESE FORTS.—COMMANDS THE BROOKLYN NAVY YARD ON THE BREAKING OUT OF THE REBELLION.—SENT WEST TO ORGANIZE A FLOTILLA ON THE MISSISSIPPI.—CAPTURES FORT HENRY.—ATTACK ON FORT DONALDSON.—IS WOUNDED.—SUBSEQUENT OPERATIONS ON THE TENNESSEE AND CUMBERLAND RIVERS.—PHELPS' REPORT.—ADVANCE AGAINST COLUMBUS.—OPERATIONS AROUND ISLAND NO. 10. PASSAGE OF THE BATTERIES BY THE CORONDELET.—MOVES AGAINST MEMPHIS.—IS RELIEVED TO RECRUIT HIS HEALTH.—DOMESTIC AFFLICTIONS.—OUR BUREAU OF EQUIPMENT AND NAVIGATION AT WASHINGTON.—MADE REAR-ADMIRAL.—PLACED OVER THE SOUTH ATLANTIC BLOCKADING SQUADRON.—HIS DEATH AND CHARACTER.

SOME men go through life without ever meeting the circumstances adapted to call forth their greatest powers, while others seem born for those into which they are thrown, and become great men or leaders in the nation. On the other hand, some, apparently, just enter on their true career in life as that life is drawing to a close.

To the latter class Admiral Foote belonged, for his sun was just rising, when it set forever on the earth, and the waves of that mighty struggle, in which he seemed destined to bear so conspicuous a part, rolled over his grave.

Andrew Foote, like so many of our great men, did not spring from obscure parentage. He was born in New Haven, Connecticut, on the 12th of September, 1806, and was the second son of Samuel A. Foote, a graduate of Yale College, and a lawyer by profession; but who, at the time of the birth of this second son, was a merchant engaged in the West India trade. He was distinguished in the political world, having served several times as member of Congress from his district, and once as senator from the State. He was subsequently elected governor.

The grandfather of Andrew was for fifty years pastor of the church of Cheshire, a beautiful village about thirteen miles from New Haven. Here his father was born; and here, having acquired the means of a comfortable subsistence, he returned to live in the old homestead. Andrew was six years old when his father took up his home in this quiet village, and for three years afterwards attended the district school. He was then sent to the academy of the place, an institution of great reputation, and presided over by the learned Rev. Tillotson Bronson, D. D.

He remained in this school for six years, or until he was fifteen years of age. During all this period he was under the strict religious discipline characteristic at that time of Connecticut, and other portions of New England. The rod had not then been banished from the parental roof, and young Andrew often felt its weight, as wielded by his mother; she convinced, him by irrefragable proof, that "he that spareth the rod hateth his son." She was the daughter of General Andrew Hull, a militia general, and gave her father's name to the boy. He was not allowed to play out evenings—forbidden to quarrel, or dicker, as it was called, and allowed very little spending money. Laziness was always punished with an extra amount of work. The Bible, the catechism, and the strict laws of Connecticut, were made equally binding on him when tempted to commit any of the grosser vices, such as violation of the Sabbath, attending the circus, &c. The old New England Sabbath began on Saturday evening at sunset, and ended at the same time on Sunday evening. During these twenty-four hours the ancient Jews were not more strict than were the parents of Andrew. The close restraint was irksome to him, as it always must be to all boys, and an older brother says, "I doubt whether the Admiral ever watched for stars in a storm, or on a lee-shore, with more interest than he was wont, when a boy, to watch for them of a Sunday evening, as a signal that he might begin play."

In the rigid old puritanic way, which has produced so many valiant men, the future Admiral was brought up.

At this early age, he had determined to enter the Navy and pass his life on the sea. Perhaps his father's accounts of his voyages to the West Indies may have had something to do with his desire to become a sailor; but more probably the astonishing victories of our young Navy, when he was fourteen or fifteen years old, were the principal cause. The names of Hull, Bainbridge, Lawrence, Decatur, Perry, Macdonough, and others, made the land rock with loud huzzas, which were quite enough to set every ambitious youth crazy after a sea-faring life.

Be this as it may, Andrew was fixed in his desire to enter the Navy, and, though his parents, especially the mother, opposed it by every argument and inducement in their power, yet, seeing that he was inflexibly set that way, at last wisely yielded. His father, owing to his political influence, was able to procure for him a midshipman's berth, and he was ordered to report on board the schooner Grampus, under the command of Lieutenant, late Admiral Gregory. He had now completed his sixteenth year—a time when life wears only a rose color to the imagination. His father accompanied him on board and presented him to his commander, with a formality common to that time. Said he to the lieutenant: "I have come to put my boy under your care, not only as a commander, but as a friend. He is capable, and I believe he is pure-minded. I hope you will watch over him as carefully and kindly as if he were your brother or son." His parting address to his boy was more lengthy. With true New England faithfulness, he charged him to remember the principles in which he had been brought up, and do nothing that should make his parents, who had watched over and prayed for him, blush; and with grand old puritanic solemnity bade "him remember his duty to his country and to his God." Grave and stern externally, his heart yet overflowed with parental tenderness, and the tears rolled down his cheeks as he bade his boy good-bye, and sent him away to the perils of the deep and into the temptations of a sailor's life. Andrew soon shook off his grief at parting, and entered on his new life, not only with all the ardor of youth, but with visions of glory directly before him, for the Grampus was to sail for the West India station, in the limits of which—the Gulf of Mexico and the Caribbean Sea—a piratical craft was then lurking. But the deadly grapple and glorious victory over these robbers of the sea, which excited his youthful imagination, never took place; and, after a year's cruise, he returned home. He was now transferred to the sloop-of-war Peacock, of glorious memory, which was ordered to the Pacific Ocean. At Callao he was transferred to the frigate United States, the flagship of Commodore Isaac Hull. The education of the commanders who distinguished themselves during the recent war, under those who gave our navy its renown, doubtless had much to do in forming their characters. A son would as soon dishonor his father, as one of these officers the great commander under whom he had served.

He was absent over three years on this cruise, completing his naval education and enlarging his experience, and returned to New York in the spring of 1837. Receiving a short furlough, he now returned home, no longer a boy, but a full-grown, developed young man. For a time the haunts and scenes of his boyhood—the old home—the old schoolhouse, and the old church, and friends, made his time pass pleasantly. But years of active life soon rendered idleness irksome to him, and he was glad when the time came again for him to return to his ship.

He now applied to be attached to the Mediterranean squadron, for he longed to see the Old World. His request was, however, denied, and he was once more ordered to the West Indies. Repairing to Norfolk, he sailed in the latter part of summer, in the sloop-of-war Natches, for his destination. This cruise was not a long one, and in December he returned in the sloop-of-war Hornet.

During this short interval, however, a great change had passed over him. One of the lieutenants was a religious man, and took occasion, before they sailed, to speak with him on the subject of personal Christianity. Young Foote, proud and averse to such conversation—enough of which he thought he had had in his boyhood—closed the interview abruptly by informing him that he intended to do what was right and honorable, and that was enough for him. Of a generous and manly nature, he afterwards felt that he had been uncivil in treating a kind and well-meant act with such coldness, not to say rudeness.

It so happened, that, after they had reached their station, he and this lieutenant were on duty on deck the same night. It was a beautiful evening—the full moon was tranquilly sailing through the cloudless heavens, shedding a flood of golden light on the gently-heaving sea, and revealing a scene of beauty never witnessed except in those tropical regions. It was a night and scene well calculated to hush all the angry feelings, and fill the heart with sad and gentle musings. After a while, he himself introduced the conversation he had so curtly closed before, when his friend talked long and earnestly on the subject so dear to his own heart. His words had a strange power amid the tranquil beauty of that night.

So deep was the impression made on young Foote, that, after the watch was over and he found himself alone, he fell on his knees in prayer, for the first time since he was a sailor. He took up his Bible, and for two weeks he continued to read this, now to him a new book. He had just entered on the great struggle of his life, and truths he had scarcely thought of before, came back upon him with overwhelming power. He knew that prayers at home were ascending for him, and he added his own for light and guidance. The old church and the old pastor were far away, and he must fight this great moral battle alone with his God.

At length, one day, after an hour of solitary reading and thinking, he arose and went on deck. The clouds and darkness seemed to gather thicker and thicker around him, when suddenly there arose in his heart the resolution, "Henceforth, under all circumstances, I will act for God." The struggle was over; the victory won—the most important of his life—and light and peace beamed on his soul. The greatest battles are not fought on the deep, amid the thunder of cannon and the crashing of timbers, nor on the bloody plain, where armies reel and go down in the onset; but on the field of the human heart, unseen by mortal eye, and over which no peans are sung, except the voiceless one: "To him that overcometh, I will give to eat of the tree of life." There, too, are the greatest defeats encountered, from the disastrous effects of which there is no rallying and no recovery.

In this new state of mind his thoughts turned at once to that mother who had so often prayed with him, and wept over him, and he at once wrote to her, commencing his letter with: "Dear Mother,—You may discharge your mind from anxiety about your wayward son; he is safe for eternity as well as for time." The effect of that letter no one can describe—next to the joy that the angels felt, was the joy of that dear mother, and her mute song of praise had in it the harmony of the upper skies.

At the close of this voyage, Foote prepared himself for examination as passed midshipman, and was promoted. During this interval he was married to a young lady of Cheshire, named Caroline Flagg, daughter of Bethuel Flagg.

The next year, Feb. 1829, he sailed in the sloop-of-war St. Louis, for another cruise in the Pacific. During his absence he was commissioned as lieutenant. He returned home in 1831.

Two years after, his desire to visit the Old World

was gratified, and he sailed in the frigate Delaware for the Mediterranean, which, on her way out, carried Edward Livingston, the newly-appointed Minister to France.

During this cruise, which lasted between two and three years, he acted as flag-lieutenant.

He returned in 1836. In 1838, he was transferred to the frigate Columbia, Commodore Read, which, with the sloop-of-war John Adams, sailed on the 6th of May, for the island of Madeira. From this point the voyage was continued by way of Rio Janeiro and Cape of Good Hope to China, thence on to Valparaiso and around Cape Horn, and so home—making the circuit of the world.

He took great interest in the missionary stations at the Sandwich Islands and in the China Sea.

The vessels reached the Sandwich Islands in the heat of the conflict between the missionaries and Captain La Place, who had been sent out by the French Government to compel the Hawaiian Chief to sign a treaty, which permitted Romish priests, contrary to his express command, to reside on the island, and French brandy to be imported. Foote, after investigating the matter, warmly espoused the cause of the missionaries, whom the French commander had included with the chief in his persecutions. He advised them to appeal to Commodore Read, and ask for a court of inquiry to investigate their conduct, which had been grossly misrepresented. The commodore did not feel authorized to take such a step, and the request was denied.

Foote, though he must act alone and take all the responsibility of his conduct, nevertheless determined to make another effort in behalf of the missionaries, for he felt that he owed not only a duty to them as citizens, but as servants of his Master above; and he drew up a paper exonerating the missionaries and expressing the utmost confidence in the good influence of the mission. He also gave a clear and full account of the outrages of La Place, embracing his correspondence with the Hawaiian authorities. To this paper he obtained nearly all the signatures of the officers of both ships. This was published in pamphlet form, and freely circulated. Its clear and truthful narrative of facts helped to open the eyes of the foreign residents, and contributed not a little to the right understanding of the case. Not satisfied with what he had done here, Foote, when he arrived in the United States, gave a public statement of the case, and indirectly caused the Government to take a deeper interest in the welfare of our missionaries in foreign lands.

His arrival at home was marked with circumstances of peculiar sadness. During this long voyage his wife had died, and he found his little girl, whom he had left three years before an infant in her mother's arms, now an orphan.

At the end of a year and a half he married again, his wife being the daughter of Augustus R. Street, of Mott-Haven. He was at this time, and for a year afterwards, on duty at the Naval Asylum of Philadelphia, the inmates of which long had cause to remember his kindness and the interest he took both in their temporal and spiritual welfare. He persuaded them to give up their grog rations, and sign a pledge of total abstinence—and in every way contributed to elevate their moral condition.

From 1843 to 1845 he was attached to the Mediterranean squadron, being executive officer of the Cumberland, the crew of which he persuaded to give up their grog. Like Havelock among his soldiers, he became a voluntary chaplain to them—giving every Sunday a religious address, on the berth-deck, to as many as choose to hear him. Sometimes he would have on these occasions a congregation of two hundred, to whom the sight of a commander turned preacher was a novel one.

After his return from this voyage, he was laid up for awhile with a disease of the eyes, which rendered him unfit for duty.

Although but partially restored, he, at the end of six months, was ordered to the navy yard at Charlestown, Massachusetts, where he remained during the whole of the Mexican war, much to his disappointment. In 1849 he was sent to the West African station, in command of the Perry, to help suppress the slave-trade. His zeal as an officer to perform his duty, was intensified by his strong feelings of abhorrence at the infamous traffic; and his efforts were indefatigable in suppressing it.

He succeeded in banishing liquor from the Perry, in this cruise; and, notwithstanding the unhealthiness of the coast, which was thought to require the use of ardent spirits to some extent, he never lost a man—thus showing their injurious tendency under all circumstances.

For some years after his return, he remained on shore, engaged in no active duty. But in 1856 he again went to sea, as commander of the sloop-of-war Portsmouth, which was ordered to the East India station. During this cruise, he, for the first time, had a taste of actual war, and showed what he was capable of doing by the daring and fierce manner in which he bombarded the barrier forts in the Canton River.

On his return to America, he was placed over the Brooklyn navy yard, where the breaking out of the rebellion found him. His labors were now herculean. To protect it from attack at home and fill all the requisitions of Government, tasked him to the utmost; and it was with a feeling of relief he received orders, in September, 1861, to repair West, and superintend the creation of an inland navy on the Mississippi.

From such motley materials as could be gathered on these waters, he labored night and day to get a respectable force afloat. Having at length got together seven gunboats, four of them iron-clad, he left Cairo, on the 4th of February, 1862, and ascended the Tennessee, to attack Fort Henry, while the rebels thought Columbus, on the Mississippi, to be the point he was aiming at. This delusion had purposely been kept up; and Foote had several partial engagements with the gunboats that were under the protection of its guns. In January he had sent to the Department, saying that he needed a thousand men to man his fleet. They were not furnished, however, and on the 3d of February he forwarded another despatch to the Government, announcing his departure for Fort Henry. In it he said: "It is peculiarly unfortunate that we have not been able to obtain men for the flotilla, as they only are wanting to enable me to have at this moment eleven full-manned instead of seven partially-manned gunboats, ready for efficient operations at any point." But delay was impossible under the circumstances; and with such force as he had he steamed up the river.

The following special order shows how thoroughly he had studied and prepared the attack, which was to be really the first great blow struck at the rebellion:

The captains of the gunboats, before going into action, will always see that the hoods covering the gratings of the hatches at the bows, and sterns, and elsewhere, are taken off; otherwise great injury will result from the concussion of the guns in firing. The anchors, also, must be unstocked, if they interfere with the range of the bow guns.

In attacking the fort, the first order of steaming will be observed, as, by the vessels being parallel, they will be much less exposed to the enemy's range than if not in a parallel line, and by moving ahead or astern, which all the vessels will do by following the motions of the flag-ship, it will be difficult for the enemy to get an accurate range of the gunboats.

Equal distances from one another must be observed by all the vessels in action. The flag-ship will, of course, open the fire first, and then others will follow when good sight of the enemy's guns in the forts can be obtained. There must be no firing until correct sights can be obtained, as this would not only be throwing away ammunition, but it would encourage the enemy to see us firing wildly and harmlessly at the fort. The captains will enforce upon their men the absolute necessity of observing this order; and let it be also distinctly impressed on the mind of every man firing a gun, that, while the first shot may be either of too much elevation or too little, there is no excuse for a second wild fire, as the first will indicate the inaccuracy of the aim of the gun, which must be elevated, or depressed, or trained, as circumstances require. Let it be reiterated that random firing is not a mere waste of ammunition, but, what is far worse, it encourages the enemy when he sees shot and shell falling harmlessly about and beyond him.

The great object is to dismount the guns in the fort by the accuracy of our fire, although a shell in the mean time may occasionally be thrown in among a body of the enemy's troops. Great caution will be observed lest our own troops be mistaken for the enemy.

When the flag-ship ceases firing, it will be a signal for the other vessels also to cease, as the ceasing of firing will indicate the surrender, or the readiness to surrender, the fort. As the vessels will all be so near one another, verbal communication will be held with the commander-in-chief when it is wanted. The commander-in-chief has every confidence in the spirit and valor of officers and men under his command, and his only solicitude arises lest the firing should be too rapid for precision, and that coolness and order, so essential to complete success, should not be observed; and hence he has, in this general order, expressed his views, which must be observed by all under his command. A. H. FOOTE.

That he had a premonition of victory is evident from the following Order, No. 3, to Lieutenant Phelps, who commanded the three gunboats not iron-plated, and which were directed during the action to throw shells from a comparatively safe distance in the rear, into the fort:

Lieutenant Phelps will, as soon as the fort shall have surrendered, and upon signal from the flag-ship, proceed with the Conestoga, Taylor, and

Lexington up the river, to where the railroad bridge crosses, and if the army shall have not already got possession, he will destroy so much of the track as will entirely prevent its use by the rebels. He will then proceed as far up the river as the stage of water will admit, and capture the enemy's gunboats and other vessels, which might prove available to the enemy.

The infantry was landed a few miles below the fort, when Foote made a reconnoissance to ascertain the position of the hostile batteries. He had been told that the bed of the stream, near the fort, was lined with torpedoes; and he ordered it to be thoroughly raked. The swift current at this season of the year had disarranged these engines of destruction—still several were removed, and the channel made clear.

The night before the attack, the fleet anchored abreast of the army under Grant, encamped on the bank. The camp-fires lighted up the gloomy shores, and were reflected on the smoothly-flowing stream—throwing into bolder relief the seven dark hulls, swinging lazily on the bosom of the Tennessee, combining to form a new and thrilling scene to the bold Western men, who, on both land and water, were about to enter on their first conflict. It was the more striking, as the night was dark—heavy, sombre clouds wrapping the heavens,—while the wintry wind surged by in fitful gusts, blending its roar with that of the waters that swept majestically through the gloom. Nature seemed to sympathize with coming events; and before morning a fierce storm burst along the banks of the river, and the rain came down in torrents.

But the tempestuous night at length passed, and the morning broke cold and clear. Foote at once ordered the vessels to be got ready for the attack. Admonishing Grant that he must hurry, or he would not be in time to do his part, which was to cut off the retreat of the enemy, he began about ten o'clock to stem the rapid current. Grant, on the other hand, assuring him that he need not trouble himself about the army being up in time, put his troops in motion. The fort stood on a bend of the river, and commanded it for a long way down. An island lay about a mile below it, behind which Foote kept his boats, so as to avoid the shots of the rifled guns of the fort, which, with their long range, might cripple him before he came to close action. The iron-clads abreast moved slowly up stream, until the fort opened to view directly ahead, when the wooden vessels halted. The commander of the fort, aware of Foote's approach through the force on watch, the moment the latter's appeared, opened on him with his batteries, and shot and shell came hurtling down the river. Foote answered with his heavy bow guns, and the conflict commenced. The rebel gunners, from long practice, had obtained the exact range of every point in view, and hence sent their shot with fearful accuracy against the advancing vessels. Those of the gunboats had to get theirs; but having received orders to fire slowly and deliberately, they were soon able to throw their shells with such precision that the rebel infantry outside of the works retired precipitately. The gunners, however, stood manfully to their work, though the fire to which they were exposed astonished them with its precision and effect.

Foote opened fire at the distance of seventeen hundred yards, using only his bow guns, as he steamed slowly toward the blazing batteries, increasing the rapidity of his fire as he advanced. Leading the way on the flagship Cincinnati, he was followed by the Essex, under Porter; the Carondelet, under Walke, and the St. Louis, Lieutenant Paulding commanding. The fire from the Cincinnati and Essex was most terrific; and to these the enemy gave their chief attention. Shot after shot bounded from their mailed sides, while others crashed amid the timbers; but the boats moved steadily forward, creeping up to the flaming batteries, relentless as fate. Foote saw, by the earth and sand-bags that flew around the hostile guns, and the sudden silence of some of them, that he was slowly grinding them to powder, and steamed still nearer. At length, an unlucky shot entered the porthole of the Essex, and, traversing the boat, carried death and devastation in its track, and plunged at last into the boiler, letting the steam out in a cloud upon the crew. As she drifted helplessly down the current, the rebels sent up a loud cheer, and opened fire with renewed courage. Foote saw that his right hand was gone; but, undismayed, pushed steadily forward, until he lay within six hundred yards of the fort. The firing was now fearful. You could hear the ponderous shot strike, and see the guns lift and tumble from their carriages as the shells exploded under them. Begrimed with powder and smoke, and their faces ablaze with excitement, the gunners worked their pieces with astonishing rapidity. The close proximity of the opposing cannon gave additional terror to the scene, and the heavy explosions, blending into one, made the shores tremble. Tilghman, the rebel commander, fought until nearly every one of his guns were dismounted, when, seeing that longer resistance was useless, he lowered his flag. A boat was sent ashore, and soon the stars and stripes were seen floating in the breeze from the rebel flagstaff, when a loud, long cheer arose from boat after boat, and was borne away toward the Ohio by the swiftly descending current.

The infantry had left some time before, Grant not

having arrived in time to intercept their flight; so that only between sixty and seventy prisoners surrendered, with General Tilghman and his staff.

Foote reported forty-eight killed, wounded, and missing. His ship was struck thirty-one times, the Essex fifteen, the St. Louis seven, and the Carondelet six. The fort was mounted with twenty guns, and had tents and barracks capable of holding fifteen thousand men.

It was a great victory, and Foote's name was repeated with acclamations from one end of the North to the other.

As soon as he had secured the prisoners, he sent off Phelps, as he had previously planned. This gallant officer, taking the Taylor, Lieutenant Gwin commanding, and the Lexington, Lieutenant Shirk, with his own boat, the Conestoga, immediately steamed up the river. But we will let him tell his own story of his expedition.

I arrived after dark at the railroad crossing, twenty-five miles above the fort, having on the way destroyed a small amount of camp equipage abandoned by the rebels. The draw of the bridge was found closed, and the machinery for turning it disabled. About a mile and half above were several rebel transport steamers escaping up stream.

A party was landed, and in one hour I had the satisfaction to see the draw open. The Taylor being the slowest of the gunboats, Lieutenant-Commanding Gwin landed a force to destroy a portion of the railroad track and to secure such military stores as might be found, while I directed Lieutenant-Commanding Shirk to follow me with all speed in chase of the fleeing boats. In five hours the boat succeeded in forcing the rebels to abandon and burn three of their boats loaded with military stores. The first one fired (Samuel Orr) had on board a quantity of submarine batteries, which very soon exploded. The second one was freighted with powder, cannon, shot, grape, balls, &c. Fearing an explosion from the fired boats—there were two together—I had stopped at a distance of one thousand yards; but even there our skylights were broken by the concussion, the light upper deck was raised bodily, doors were forced open, and locks and fastenings everywhere broken.

The whole river, for half a mile round about, was completely "beaten up" by the falling fragments and the shower of shot, grape, balls, &c. The house of a reported Union man was blown to pieces, and it is suspected there was design in landing the boats in front of the doomed home. The Lexington having fallen astern, and being without a pilot on board, I concluded to wait for both of the boats to come up. Joined by them, we proceeded up the river. Lieutenant-Commanding Gwin had destroyed some of the trestle-work at the end of the bridge, burning with them a lot of camp equipage. I. N. Brown, formerly a lieutenant in the navy, now signing himself "Lieut. C. S. N.," had fled with such precipitation as to leave his papers behind. These Lieutenant-Commanding Gwin brought away, and I send them to you, as they give an official history of the rebel floating preparations on the Mississippi, Cumberland, and Tennessee. Lieutenant Brown had charge of the construction of gunboats.

At night, on the 7th, we arrived at a landing in Hardin County, Tennessee, known as Cerro Gordo, where we found the steamer Eastport being converted into a gunboat. Armed boat crews were immediately sent on board, and search made for means of destruction that might have been devised. She had been scuttled and the suction-pipes broken. These leaks were soon stopped. A number of rifle-shots were fired at our vessels, but a couple of shells dispersed the rebels. On examination I found that there were large quantities of timber and lumber prepared for fitting up the Eastport; that the vessel itself—some two hundred and eighty feet long—was in excellent condition, and already half finished; considerable of the plating designed for her was lying on the bank, and everything at hand to complete her. I therefore directed Lieutenant-Commanding Gwin to remain with the Taylor to guard the prize, and to load the lumber, &c., while the Lexington and Conestoga should proceed still higher up.

Soon after daylight, on the 8th, we passed Eastport, Mississippi; and at Chickasaw, further up, near the State line, seized two steamers, the Sallie Wood and Muscle—the former laid up, and the latter freighted with iron destined for Richmond and for rebel use. We then proceeded on up the river, entering the State of Alabama, and ascending to Florence at the foot of the Muscle Shoals. On coming in sight of the town, three steamers were discovered, which were immediately set on fire by the rebels. Some shots were fired from the opposite side of the river below. A force was landed, and considerable quantities of supplies, marked "Fort Henry," were secured from the burning wrecks. Some had been landed and stored. These I seized, putting such as we could bring away on our vessels, and destroying the remainder. No flats or other craft could be found. I found, also, more of the iron and plating intended for the Eastport.

A deputation of citizens of Florence waited upon me, first desiring that they might be able to quiet the fears of their wives and daughters with assurances from me that they would not be molested; and, secondly, praying that I would not destroy their railroad bridge. As for the first, I told them we were neither ruffians nor savages, and that *we were there to protect from violence and to enforce the law ;* and, with reference to the second, that if the bridge were away we could ascend no higher, and that it could possess no military importance, so far as I saw, as it simply connected Florence itself with the railroad on the south bank of the river.

We had seized three of their steamers—one the half-finished gunboat—and had forced the rebels to burn six others loaded with supplies; and their loss, with that of the freight, is a heavy blow to the enemy. Two boats are still known to be on the Tennessee, and are doubtless hidden in some of the creeks, where we shall be able to find them when there is time for the search. We returned, on the night of the 8th, to where the Eastport lay. The crew of the Taylor had already gotten on board of the prize an immense amount of lumber, &c. The crews of the three boats set to work to finish the undertaking, and we have brought away probably two hundred and fifty thousand feet of the best quality of ship and building lumber, all the iron, machinery, spikes, plating, nails, &c., belonging to the rebel gunboats, and I caused the mill to be destroyed where the lumber had been sawed.

Lieutenant-Commanding Gwin had, in our absence, enlisted some twenty-five Tennesseeans, who gave information of the encampment of Colonel Drew's rebel regiment at Savannah, Tennessee. A portion of the six or seven hundred men were known to be "pressed" men, and all were badly armed. After consultation with Lieutenants-Commanding Gwin and Shirk, I determined to make a land attack upon the encampment. Lieutenant-Commanding Shirk, with thirty riflemen, came on board the Conestoga, leaving his vessel to guard the Eastport, and, accompanied by the Taylor, we proceeded up to that place, prepared to land one hundred and thirty riflemen and a twelve-pounder rifle howitzer. Lieutenant-Commanding Gwin took command of this force when landed, but had the mortification to find the camp deserted.

The rebels had fled at 1 o'clock, in the night, leaving considerable quantities of arms, clothing, shoes, camp utensils, provisions, implements, &c., all of which were secured or destroyed, and their winter-quarters of log-huts were burned. I seized, also, a large mail-bag, and send you the letters giving military information. The gunboats were then dropped down to a point where arms, gathered under the rebel "press-law," had been stored, and an armed party, under Second-Master Goudy, of the Taylor, succeeded in seizing about seventy rifles and fowling-pieces. Returning to Cerro Gordo, we took the Eastport, Sallie Wood, and Muscle in tow, and came down the river to the railroad crossing. The Muscle sprang a leak, and, all efforts failing to prevent her sinking, we were forced to abandon her, and with her a considerable quantity of fine lumber. We are having trouble in getting through the draw of the bridge here.

I now come to the, to me, most interesting portion of this report—one which has already become lengthy; but I must trust you will find some excuse for this in the fact that it embraces a history of labors and movements day and night, from the 6th to the 10th of the month, all of which details I deem it proper to give you. *We have met with the most gratifying proofs of loyalty everywhere across Tennessee and in the portions of Mississippi and Alabama we visited. Most affecting instances greeted us almost hourly. Men, women, and children, several times gathered in crowds of hundreds, shouted their welcome, and hailed their national flag with an enthusiasm there was no mistaking; it was genuine and heartfelt.* Those people braved everything to go to the river bank, where a sight of their flag might once more be enjoyed. Tears flowed freely down the cheeks of men as well as women, and there were those who had fought under the stars and stripes at Moultrie, who on this morning testified their joy.

This display of feeling and sense of gladness at our success, and the hopes it created in the hearts of so many people in the heart of the Southern Confederacy, astonished us not a little; and I assure you, sir, I would not have failed to witness it for any consideration. I trust it has given us all a higher sense of the sacred character of our present duties. I was assured, at Savannah, that of the several hundred troops there, more than one-half, had we gone to the attack in time, would have hailed us as deliverers, and gladly enlisted with the national forces.

In Tennessee the people generally braved the secessionists, and spoke their views freely, but in Mississippi and Alabama, what was said was guarded: "*If we dared express ourselves freely, you would hear such a shout greeting your coming as you never heard.*" "We know there are many Unionists among us, but a reign of terror makes us all afraid of our shadows." We were told, too: "Bring us a small organized force, with arms and ammunition for us, and we can maintain our position, and put down rebellion in our midst." There were, it is true, whole communities, who, on our approach, fled to the woods; but these were where there was less of the loyal element, and when the fleeing steamers, in advance, had spread tales of our coming with firebrands, burning, destroying, ravishing, and plundering.

Foote was much encouraged at this report of the state of feeling. On the return of the expedition he steamed down the river to Cairo, and, eight days after the surrender of Fort Henry, was ascending the Cumberland to assist Grant, who was marching across the country to attack Fort Donelson. He was aware of the superior strength of this fort, and his force being now reduced by the loss of the iron-clad Essex, he feared that the attempt to reduce it from the river would prove fruitless. He, however, at the urgent request of Major-General Halleck and Gen. Grant, who regarded the movement as a "military necessity," consented to make it.

The works here were of the most formidable kind, and, it was thought, able to resist any attempt to ascend the river to Nashville. On the river side were two batteries: the lower one mounting eight 32-pounders and a 10-inch columbiad, and the upper, some ten yards above this, two 32-pound carronades and a 32-pound rifled gun. The range of these commanded every foot of the river in sight below the fort.

The day before the attack, Foote sent the Carondelet upon a reconnoissance, and the vessel being fired upon, returned the fire and maintained the unequal contest till she had discharged over a hundred shots, and did not retire until struck by a heavy shot which, entering one of her forward ports, wounded eight men.

Foote knew the desperate undertaking before him, but, on the 14th, moved resolutely up to the batteries with his four iron-clads and two wooden gunboats. He soon found that he was exposed to a different fire than the one he had encountered at Fort Henry. The heavy metal of the batteries fell rapid as hailstones on his vessel, and the water around the boats was beaten into foam by the falling shots and shell. The flagship, as usual, received the chief attention of the enemy. Yet Foote moved steadily forward into the volcano before him, nobly sustained by his other vessels. Noticing that the pilot, under the horrible fire that smote the vessel, was getting nervous, he walked up to him, placed his hand on his shoulder, and spoke some encouraging words, when a heavy shot struck the poor fellow, leaving him a mangled mass beside his broken wheel. Foote, though wounded himself in the foot by a splinter, still limped around, giving his orders with imperturbable coolness, and anxiously watching the effect of the shot on the rebel works. But this unlucky shot had carried away the wheel, with the pilot; and the boat—which had now got within four hundred yards of the fort—became unmanageable; and, swinging to the current, drifted slowly down stream. At the same time, the tiller-ropes of the Louisville were cut, and she, too, floated down stream. The enemy no sooner saw this than he redoubled his fire. Only two boats were now left to maintain the conflict; but they too, being damaged between wind and water, soon followed the flagship, and the fight, that had raged with such ferocity for an hour and a quarter, was over. Fifty-four had been killed or wounded, and the flagship been struck fifty-nine times. Although he could bring but twelve guns to bear on batteries that mounted twenty, Foote thought, but for the untoward accident that destroyed the steering apparatus of the two vessels, he would have succeeded in capturing the works, as the fire of the enemy had materially slackened. Some such accident, however, was to be expected in so unequal a fight.

Leaving two boats here to protect the transports, Foote returned with the ten disabled ones to Cairo, to repair damages and prepare for another attack.

Fort Donelson, however, surrendered a few days after to Grant, and he again advanced up the river to Clarkesville, farther on toward Nashville, which surrendered to him. He found much Union feeling among the inhabitants along the shore, and here issued a proclamation promising security to private property and citizens, and calling on the latter to resume their peaceful avocations. He now, in conjunction with Grant, resolved to move on

Nashville; and the two were about starting, when Grant, "to his astonishment," he says, "received a telegram from General Halleck, not to let the gunboats go higher than Clarkesville." Having received no telegram himself, he could not understand it; and immediately sent a despatch to Halleck's Chief of Staff, saying, "The Cumberland is in a good stage of water, and General Grant and I believe that we can take Nashville. Please, ask General Halleck if we shall do it. We will talk per telegraph, Captain Phelps representing me in the office, as I am still on crutches." But permission was not given him, and he returned to Cairo, and once more turned his attention to Columbus. On the 23d, he made a reconnoissance of the works with four iron-clads, ten mortar-boats, and three transports, containing a thousand men. He found that nothing could be done without an additional force, and returned to Cairo, to wait the completion of other boats.

In the mean time, he had despatched the gunboats Tyler and Lexington up the Tennessee, which attacked the enemy's works at Pittsburg, and captured them with small loss, while there were a hundred and fifty of the enemy killed or wounded. On the 1st of March, Lieutenant Phelps, who had been sent with a flag of truce to Columbus, returned and reported it evacuated, the army having retired to Island No. 10. Foote now transferred his flag to the powerful iron-clad Benton, and advanced against the strong works which had been erected here. Attack after attack followed, and a ceaseless bombardment from the mortar-boats was kept up; but no serious impression could be made on them. General Pope at length arrived below with a large force; but he had no boats with which to transport his troops across to the other side and march against the enemy, and so lay idle on the banks.

For three weeks the fleet lay here, pounding away at the rebel fortifications, and the end seemed as far off as ever, while the public began to weary of hearing of Island No. 10.

The arrival of Pope below made it imperative that a gunboat should be got through to him; but whether one could run the formidable batteries that lined the shore was very problematical. It, however, must be tried, or Pope could never cross and move up to Island No. 10, and compel its evacuation. There was no prospect of capturing the works by our gunboats from above, and so Foote assigned the hazardous duty of running the batteries to the commander of the Carondelet, directing him to avail himself of the first foggy or rainy night to start. If he succeeded, he was to coöperate with Pope, and when the army moved, to attack the fortifications. In closing his directions he used the following solemn language:

On this delicate and somewhat hazardous service to which I assign you I must enjoin upon you the importance of keeping your lights secreted in the hold or put out, keeping your officers and men from speaking at all, when passing the forts, above a whisper, and then only on duty, and of using every other precaution to prevent the rebels suspecting that you are dropping below their batteries.

If you successfully perform this duty assigned you, which you so willingly undertake, it will reflect the highest credit upon you and all belonging to your vessel, and I doubt not but that the Government will fully appreciate and reward you for a service which, I trust, will enable the army to cross the river and make a successful attack in the rear, while we storm the batteries in front of this stronghold of the rebels.

Commending you and all who compose your command to the care and protection of God, who rules the world and directs all things, I am, respectfully, your obedient servant, A. H. FOOTE.

To this was added the following postscript:

P. S.—Should you meet with disaster, you will, as a last resort, destroy the steam machinery, and, if possible to escape, set fire to your gunboat, or sink her, and prevent her from falling into the hands of the rebels. A. H. F.

Everything that ingenuity could devise was done to insure success, for the boat was first to run, head on, to a powerful battery, then take the fire of forty-seven cannon in her daring passage. Chains were coiled around the pilot-house and other vulnerable parts—cord-wood piled against the boilers, and the hose connected with the latter to hurl jets of steam to repel boarders in case of an attack. A boat, loaded with pressed hay, was lashed to the side exposed to the batteries, while, to balance this, and, at the same time, to furnish the steamer with fuel, should she get through safely, a barge loaded with coal was lashed to the other side. Twenty sharpshooters were also added to the crew, who were all thoroughly armed for any emergency.

The night of the 4th of April was dark and tempestuous, and about ten o'clock the Carondelet cut loose from her anchorage, and, rounding slowly to on the stream, turned her head down the Mississippi. The fleet, aware of the expedition, was silent and anxious. Every officer felt the peril into which the intrepid Walke was moving. Darkness soon wrapped his boat from sight; but the blinding flashes of lightning would ever and anon reveal its black form moving forward through the gloom. It was an hour of painful suspense to Foote, for vast results hung on the welfare of that single vessel. As if to impart still greater grandeur to the scene, the thunder rolled heavily overhead, or broke in deafening claps along the shore.

Wrapping itself in the thunder storm, as in a mantle, the Carondelet swept forward into the volcano that awaited her approach. Everything passed quietly for awhile, but suddenly, as she approached the batteries, the soot in the chimneys caught fire, and a blaze, five feet high, leaped from their tops, shedding a broad glare on the surrounding water. "Open the flue caps," passed quietly and quickly to the engineer, and the flames subsided. So suddenly did this strange apparition appear and vanish, that it was either unseen, or, blending in as it did with the lightning, it deceived the guard.

Walke, from his silent deck, gazed intently towards the batteries, expecting every moment to hear the drum beat to quarters, and see the flash of the signal-gun light up the gloom. But, to his great relief, all passed off quietly, and the Carondelet kept on her perilous way. But just as she got abreast of the upper battery, the chimneys caught fire again and blazed like a torch on the breast of the stream. The next moment the report of a musket was heard. In an instant, rockets from island and mainland arose through the storm. The rapid roll of drums was heard in the intervals of the thunder, and then came a single report, followed by a deafening crash that drowned the artillery of heaven. Concealment was now over, and Walke, putting on a full head of steam and hugging the batteries close, to let the shot fly over him, pushed rapidly down the current. A man stood forward with lead and line, coolly calling out from time to time in a low voice the soundings, which a second man on deck repeated, sending the report aft to Walke, who stood beside the pilot, calm and collected, but with every nerve strung to its utmost tension and all his senses keenly alive to every movement and sound. The flashes of the enemy's guns and of the lightning above them, revealed almost momentarily the shores, and thus showed the channel; yet the light coming and going so rapidly, and the utter darkness of the intervals, confused and blinded the pilot, and once the boat was heading straight for the shore. But just then a fierce flash of lightning lit up the scene, and "hard a-port!" fell from the Captain's lips in calm accents, yet so sharp and stern that the pilot threw himself with all his might upon the wheel, and the Carondelet swung back into the channel.

A wilder, sublimer scene cannot be imagined than that boat presented, as, silent as death, she moved steadily on,—one moment painted red on the stream by the flashes of lightning or of artillery, and the next moment lost to sight as completely as though she had gone to the bottom. The rain came down in torrents, the wind swept by in fierce gusts, while the thunder breaking above, and the artillery exploding below, imparted an indescribable terror to this midnight hour.

But at length the last battery was passed, the echo of the last gun died sullenly away up the river, and a heavy load lifted from the heart of Walke. With a cheerful voice he ordered the ports to be thrown open and the guns run out to fire minute guns—the signal agreed on with Foote, should the Carondelet pass the batteries in safety. The latter stood on deck listening to the uproar below, telling him of the fiery ordeal his brave subordinate was enduring, and when it ceased he bent attentively to catch the report of the signal guns. Suddenly it came, but so blent in with the thunder, that he could not certainly tell whether it was not the boom of the latter; others, also, heard it, but the raging storm so drowned it that they too doubted.

At New Madrid, however, there was no doubt, no uncertainty. The soldiers and officers there had also heard the terrific cannonading up the Mississippi, and knew what it meant, and every eye was strained up stream to catch sight of the coming vessel, while lights danced along the shore to guide her course. As the Carondelet, untouched by a single shot, came proudly up to the wharf, the frenzied cheers that arose drowned the voice of the storm, and the soldiers, rushing down, seized the sailors and bore them in their arms up the banks to the nearest hotel, and unbounded joy reigned throughout the army.

Pope immediately despatched a messenger announcing the safe arrival of the Carondelet, and urging Foote in the most earnest manner to send another boat the next night, as its presence was necessary to ensure success. In his ardor, he said, "I am thus urgent, sir, because the lives of thousands of men and the success of our operations, hang upon your decision."

To this, Foote replied in full, stating that it was impossible to send a boat till there came a dark night. He did not like the tone of Pope's letter, and said:

I am sorry to find the expression in your letter, "The success of our operations hangs upon your (my) decision," especially referring to my directing a gunboat to attempt running the blockade in this clear night; for, in my judgment, and that of all the other officers, the boat might as well expect to run it in the daytime. I cannot consider the running of your blockade, where the river is nearly a mile wide, and only exposed to a few light guns, at all comparable to running it here, where a boat has not only to pass seven batteries, but has to be kept "head on" to a battery of eleven heavy guns, at the head of Island No. 10, and to pass within three hundred yards of this strong battery. If it did not sink the gunboat, we would, in the navy, consider the gunners totally unfit for employment in the service; and, therefore, my responsibility for the lives of the officers and men under my charge, induces me to decline a request which would, especially without protection to the boat, were the rebels at all competent to perform their duty, result in the sacrifice of the boat, her officers, and men, which sacrifice I should not be justified in making—certainly not now, when, by your own

12

admission, it will be easy for the new rebel steamers, reported to be on their way up the river, to pass your batteries in the night, and if they meet my squadron, reduced by loss, so as to be unable to cope with them, can continue up the Mississippi or Ohio to St. Louis or to Cincinnati.

In view, however, of rendering you all the aid you request, and no doubt require, while I regret that you had not earlier expressed the apprehension of the necessity of two gunboats, instead of the smaller gunboat, I will, to-morrow, endeavor to prepare another boat; and if the night is such as will render her running the blockade without serious disaster at all probable, I will make the attempt to send you the additional boat requested in your letter of this day's date.

I am, respectfully, your obedient servant, A. H. FOOTE,

Flag-Officer Commanding Naval Forces, Western Waters.

MAJOR GENERAL JOHN POPE,

Commanding Army at New Madrid.

A few days after the 8th, another heavy thunder storm occurring, the Pittsburg, Lieutenant Thompson commanding, started at two o'clock in the morning, and, though exposed to the fire of seventy-three guns, safely passed the batteries.

Previous to these movements, Colonel Bissell, an engineer, had, with incredible labor, cut a canal through sloughs and streams, by which transports were got through, so that now the fate of Island No. 10 was sealed. The gunboats silenced the batteries on the opposite shore, when the troops were carried over and began their march for the rebel works. The commander, Mackall, seeing that all was lost, evacuated the place, and it fell with all its stores and armament into our hands.

While these stirring events were passing on the Mississippi, the terrible battle of Pittsburg Landing was fought, in which two of Foote's fleet did great service. The Tyler and Lexington, under the command of Gwin and Shirk, by the effective manner in which they shelled the rebel left, on the afternoon of the first day, did much towards preventing a total defeat of our arms.

Foote now moved down to Fort Pillow, and while operating here and making arrangements to drive out the enemy, he said, in a letter to the Secretary of the Navy:

"The effects of my wound have quite a dispiriting effect upon me, from the increased inflammation, and swelling of my foot and leg, which have induced a febrile action, depriving me of a good deal of sleep and energy. I cannot give the wound that attention and rest it absolutely requires, until this place is captured."

Another event which soon after occurred, had a still more depressing effect upon him. He had made arrangements that, he thought, with the coöperation of Pope's army, would give him Fort Pillow within six days, when that officer received a despatch from Halleck, to join him at once, with his twenty thousand men, at Pittsburg. In a letter to the Department, the former said: "I am greatly exercised about our position here, on account of the withdrawal of the army of twenty thousand men, so important an element in the capture of the place."

He, however, continued to shell the place, and was busy in devising ways and means preparatory to a successful attack on the fort. But his health continued to grow worse, and, although he managed to limp around on his crutches, it was plain to all, and especially so to his surgeon, that he must be relieved from the cares that pressed upon him, and he finally asked leave of absence. C. H. Davis was placed in command of the fleet till he could recover.

Foote retired to Cleveland, where, with his brothers, he rested for awhile, the subject of anxious solicitude to his countrymen, who felt that he could not yet be spared from the field.

After awhile he proceeded to his home, now saddened by the loss of a bright boy, fourteen years of age, who had been carried to his grave while he was far away, perilling his life for his country. Afflictions rapidly accumulated upon him, seemingly greater than his weakened frame could bear. Before autumn had passed, two young daughters followed their brother to the grave, leaving him a desolate, stricken man. The land was resounding with his praises, yet he heard them not—his heart was in the grave with his children, and the laurels a grateful nation was weaving for him turned to ashes in his sight.

He had, in the mean time, been created a rear-admiral, on the active list, and, in a few weeks after the death of his two daughters, was called to Washington. Though broken in spirits and health, and wholly unfit for duty, he responded to the call, and became engaged in the new "Bureau of Equipment and Navigation." As soon as he saw that he could be spared here, he asked for more active and dangerous service, and was assigned to the command of the North Atlantic squadron. His friends tried to dissuade him from taking it, for they saw that his extreme debility and prostration demanded rest if he wished to save his life. To one and all he replied that his life was not his own, and he was ready to lay it down for his country. He repaired to New York, and made all his preparations to sail, when the disease, against which he had battled so long, overcame him, and he lay down to die. He lingered for ten days in great suffering, and at length expired at the Astor House, June 26, 1863.

Dahlgren, who had been appointed to command the iron-clads under him, and subsequently took his place, came on from Washington to see him just before his death. The following is his account of the last interview with him. He says: "Next morning after my arrival in New York, my first care was to visit my old and dearly beloved friend Foote. Alas! he was delirious—a few words recalled the fast-departing senses—the wandering eye rested on me for a brief moment, and he uttered my name distinctly—even remembered my boys—then he relapsed, and another day ended in this world the life of as *brave* and as *good* a man as ever served any country. No one better knew his virtues than I—no one prized them more dearly. We had been bosom friends for twenty years, and never a cloud between us. What a loss to the country!" A beautiful tribute from a brave and good man to a brave and good man.

The news of his death was received with universal grief, for he had become a favorite with the people, and much was expected of him in the future towards crushing the rebellion, which had received such staggering blows at his hand.

A brave man, an accomplished officer, a noble patriot, and a sincere Christian, he rested from his labors, and passed to that serene abode where the afflictions of this life become blessings to swell his joy and thanksgiving. His fame is secure, and his name will ever stand high in the list of our great naval commanders.

CHAPTER VIII.

COMMODORE CHARLES STUART BOGGS.

EARLY IMPRESSIONS.—HIS NATIVITY AND EARLY EDUCATION.—ANECDOTE.—ENTERS THE NAVAL SERVICE.—HIS FIRST CRUISE.—GREEK PIRATES.—CRUISE TO THE WEST INDIES.—A LIEUTENANT.—SERVICE IN THE PACIFIC OCEAN.—HAS CHARGE OF THE APPRENTICES IN NEW YORK HARBOR.—ORDERED TO THE AFRICAN COAST.—SERVES ON BOARD THE PRINCETON DURING THE MEXICAN WAR.—A DARING ACT.—CRUISE IN THE MEDITERRANEAN.—THE GREEKS ASTONISHED AT A PROPELLER.—SENT TO THE WORLD'S FAIR.—INSPECTOR OF CLOTHING AND PROVISIONS IN NEW YORK HARBOR.—COMMANDS A CALIFORNIA STEAMER.—INSPECTOR OF LIGHTS ON THE COAST OF CALIFORNIA.—HIS POSITION AND FEELINGS ON THE BREAKING OUT OF THE REBELLION.—OFFERS A REWARD TO THE MOST GALLANT SOLDIER OF HIS COUNTRY.—ORDERED HOME.—GIVEN THE COMMAND OF THE VARUNA.—JOINS FARRAGUT'S SQUADRON.—PASSAGE OF THE FORTS BELOW NEW ORLEANS.—HIS GALLANT CONDUCT.—THE BOY OSCAR.—IS PRESENTED WITH A SWORD FOR HIS GALLANTRY.—ON BLOCKADING DUTY OFF WILMINGTON HARBOR.—HIS HEALTH FAILS.—APPOINTED ON ADMIRAL GREGORY'S STAFF AT NEW YORK.—PLANS AND BUILDS TORPEDO-BOATS.—HIS SERVICES SINCE THE WAR.—HIS CHARACTER.

It is curious often to trace the causes which have given bent to a man's whole life, and made or marred his fortunes. Sometimes there seems to be a strong natural tendency to a certain profession or calling; but, on careful examination, it will usually be found that this has arisen from some circumstance—perhaps from a single biographical sketch, which the child has read—making an impression upon him that nothing could efface; often, again, some tradition or character in the family has produced it.

It is more than probable that the subject of this sketch would never have chosen the naval profession had not his mother been sister of the gallant Lawrence, whose last words were: "Don't give up the ship!" It could not be otherwise than that the gallant character of such a man should make an indelible impression on his nephew —especially when the story of his battles and heroic death was told by a mother, who revered the memory of her dead brother. What to the mother was the ideal of a noble man would naturally become so to the son; at all events, he early determined to enter the naval service. It would appear from tradition that other plans had been formed for him, and attempts made to dissuade him from this course, but in vain.

He was born in New Brunswick, N. J., January, 1811, and was sent at an early age to Captain Partridge's celebrated military academy, at Middletown, Connecticut. It is related that one day some of his friends, in attempting to dissuade him from a maritime life, said: "Why, Charles, you can't be a sailor, for you don't know how to climb." He instantly turned, and, for an answer, ascended quickly to the roof of the house, and descended by the lightning-rod. This practical argument was conclusive.

On the 1st of November, 1826, when he was fifteen years old, he was appointed midshipman, and, the next July, joined the sloop-of-war Warren, and sailed for the Mediterranean. The eastern portion of the sea at that time swarmed with Greek pirates, and the vessel in which young Boggs served was very active in protecting our commerce, and suppressing piracy among the Grecian islands. So valuable were the services of Captain Kearney, his commander, that they were spoken of in the British Parliament. At that time, our navy was a sore subject to the English, and it required a strong motive to wring from them a compliment to any of our ships.

This was a good school for the young midshipman. The intricate and narrow channels of those islands furnished hiding-places for the small Grecian crafts, and hence, there were necessarily many boat expeditions sent in search of them, which required the utmost vigilance and calmness to carry out successfully. Young Boggs there learned that quiet, yet quick, prompt resolution, for which he was afterward so distinguished. In these dangerous expeditions, and sudden bold dashes, he saw that perfect self-possession, and the ability to decide on the spur of the moment what course of action to adopt, was as indispensable to a naval officer, as the ability to command a ship.

Winding among the beautiful islands of Greece, and sailing along the classic coast of the Mediterranean, and visiting the cities and mementoes of ancient greatness, Boggs passed three years of his life, and, when he returned, was no longer a boy. He now made two cruises to the West Indies, and, in 1832, passed his examination successfully, preparatory to his promotion. His duties for the next five years did not differ from those common to all officers in times of peace.

In 1836, he joined, as master, the ship of the line North Carolina, which had been ordered to the Pacific coast. When the vessel arrived at Callao, he received an appointment as acting lieutenant, and was ordered as executive officer to the schooner Enterprise, which appointment was confirmed by his promotion in 1833.

For nearly two years, Lieutenant Boggs now saw much active service. The little schooner sailed up and down the coast, from Valparaiso to Lower California, exploring it thoroughly.

In 1839, he returned home in the North Carolina, and served about a year on board of her in New York harbor, as lieutenant, in charge of the apprentices. He here exhibited two very strong traits in his character—mildness and gentleness of manner, and yet strictness in enforcing discipline. The hand was iron in maintaining order; but it was so gloved, that none felt its hardness. Perhaps no man could be more free and easy with his pupils or subordinates, and yet not relax one jot of strict discipline.

He was highly complimented for his conduct and management of these boys.

His next cruise was in the Saratoga, which composed a part of Commodore Perry's squadron, on the coast of Africa, and he took an active part in the bombardment and destruction of the Berreby towns.

When the Mexican war broke out, he was ordered to the steamer Princeton, Captain Eagle, and took part in the grand bombardment of the Castle of St. Juan de Ulloa and of Tampico. The United States brig Truxton, having got aground on the bar of Tuspan River, surrendered to the Mexicans, and the Princeton was ordered down to destroy her. Arriving off the wreck, a boat was manned, and Lieutenant Boggs put in command of it, with orders to destroy the vessel. The boat, impelled by the strong rowers, swept steadily over the water, and had nearly reached the Truxton, when a gale suddenly arose, lashing the sea into fury, and causing it to break with such violence over the stranded vessel that he found it impossible to board her. The current setting strongly in shore, together with the increasing gale, also rendered it impossible to return to the Princeton. The waves were running high; and Boggs, in spite of his efforts, was carried towards the shore. As he approached it, he saw a company of Mexican soldiers drawn up on the beach with a field piece, covering the approach. This was an unexpected dilemma. He could not force the boat out to sea, and he knew, before he could land and charge the soldiers, his little crew would be annihilated. With that quickness of decision which distinguished him, he immediately ordered the only white shirt on board to be torn up, and fastened on a boat-hook, and hoisted as a flag of truce. He then told his men to turn, and pull boldly for shore. Springing on the beach as the bow grazed the sand, he advanced to the Mexican commander with his strange flag of truce, and told him he had been sent to destroy the Truxton—that he was carried against his will to the shore, and had no intention of molesting the town, and that if he was not interfered with, he would do it no injury. If, on the contrary, the former attempted to prevent him from carrying out his instructions, the Princeton would steam in, and open her fire on the place. The Mexican officer, seeing that discretion was the better part of valor, promised not to attempt any interference—on the contrary, he entertained him hospitably till the gale subsided. Boggs then thanked his would-be captor for his civility, and, bidding him adieu, pushed off to the Truxton, and soon she was a mass of flames on the water.

The Princeton was soon after ordered to the Mediterranean, and Boggs visited once more the scenes of his early service. This steamer was a propeller—the first ever seen in the Grecian seas—and when she entered the Piræus, the captain ordered the smoke-pipe lowered. No smoke being visible, as she burned anthracite coal, she moved majestically up the bay, without any apparent means of propulsion, much to the astonishment of the Greeks. Seeing no steam-pipe, and no wheels, she seemed to them a living thing, endued with a vitality of her own.

The Italian revolution of 1848 was now in full progress, and during the cruise Boggs saw much of it.

Two years after, we find him executive officer of the St. Lawrence, which had been designated by the Government to carry the American contributions to the World's Fair in London. On his return, he was appointed First Lieutenant of the New York Navy Yard, and afterwards Inspector of clothing and provisions in the same yard. In this new field of duty, he showed great ability—introducing reforms, and putting a stop to many abuses which had crept into the department.

When the Government made a contract with the California Steam Company to carry the mails, one condition of it was that a United States officer should command their passenger boats, and Boggs was selected to command the Illinois. This was in 1855. The position was a very responsible one, and the duties connected with it most arduous. The gold fever was at its height, and the vessels were crowded with passengers, sometimes a thousand in number; many of whom were rough, lawless adventurers, requiring the greatest tact and nerve to keep proper subordination. But no better man could be found than he for that very duty. He possessed the *suaviter in modo* and *fortiter in re* in a remarkable manner, and he succeeded in maintaining order, and acquiring the esteem and respect of all.

Captain Boggs, with his wife and daughter, were at Panama during the massacre of 1856, and narrowly escaped falling victims to it.

He served as commander of the Illinois for three years, and then was transferred to the coast of California. The light-house system needed extension, and in 1859 and 1860, he was appointed Inspector of Lights. The steamer Shubrick was placed under his command, and he was required to make two annual trips along the coast from Vancouver's Island to Lower California, inspecting old lights, and carrying supplies to them, and surveying sites for new ones.

In performing this duty, he was enabled, at the same time, to complete the exploration of the western coast of the continent, which he had partially carried out so many years before.

In steaming amid the rocks and narrow channels of these comparatively unknown shores, he had several narrow escapes from shipwreck.

He was thus engaged when the rebellion broke out. Commander Boggs now found himself in an unpleasant position, and his feelings respecting it, as well as his views of the rebellion, may be gathered from the following extracts from a letter written at the time to a friend:

> I am heart-sick of the state of our country—we are in a great state of excitement here. * * * The time has arrived for every one to define his position—those who are not for the Government, as it is, should be denounced as traitors, and meet a traitor's doom. I shall stick by the flag that I swore, thirty years ago, to protect. I am disagreeably and peculiarly situated—on special duty—so that I dare not leave and return East, as my

inclinations would prompt; out of funds to carry on this duty—no special orders to govern me in the peculiar state of the country. Should a privateer of Jeff. Davis appear on these waters, my force is not able to meet her, and I have no authority or means to increase my crew, or mount a heavy gun, without which I should be cut to pieces at long shot, by any thing that might come along.

I have obtained a very excellent silver-mounted Mexican saddle, valued at over two hundred and fifty dollars, bridle, spurs, &c., complete. I wish you would present it to the most daring and gallant soldier from our little county of Middlesex, N. J., or from the State, if you learn who distinguishes himself on the side of the Constitution and the Union. * * *

Give my regards to all who know me, and say that I am for the Constitution and Union, and down with traitors! I only wish the Government would order me home. * * *

Thus, from the far-off coast of California, which was trembling in the balance between the North and South, came his voice for the Union. No wonder he chafed in the position in which he found himself—no funds to go on with his peaceful duties—no heart to do it, if he had. Helpless, if attacked, and no authority to place himself in a state of defence, he felt pressed down as by a nightmare.

Fortunately his letter to the Government, begging for active employment afloat, where he could strike, at least, one good blow for the honor of the flag, and the salvation of his country, was favorably received, and he was ordered home. Never was an order more welcome, and it took him but little time to prepare for his departure. On reaching home, he was placed in command of the Varuna, a passenger steamer, which had been bought by the Department, and changed into a gunboat, and ordered to join Farragut's fleet below New Orleans.

When Farragut had determined to run past the forts with his fleet and proceed on up to the city, he gave precise and detailed orders to each of the commanders, and assigned them their respective positions.

Boggs, who knew what a frail thing his gunboat was, sought an interview with him and told him that his vessel would never bear any long pounding from the heavy guns of the fort, which he would be compelled to endure if he was required to move slowly, and asked permission to go ahead of his station, which he knew he could do, as the Varuna was a very fast boat. Farragut good-naturedly complied with his request, provided he would not run down and sink any rebel craft in the channel, as that might obstruct the free passage of the rest of the fleet.

Boggs' plan was now soon formed, and on the morning of the advance he moved up the stream, second from the flag-ship of his division. Ordinary fuel, he knew, would not get up steam fast enough, and he had the pork, which formed a part of his ship's stores, already prepared to throw into the furnace. At the proper time, it was cast on to the hissing coals—the fires blazed up, and with a full head of steam on, he dashed ahead. When abreast of the forts, he fired his starboard battery, loaded with five-second-shell. "Now!" exclaimed Boggs, "fire with grape and canister as fast as possible," and the frail boat shot ahead, wrapped in flame, and was soon above the forts. Looking around him in the early twilight, he saw that he was in a perfect nest of rebel gunboats, ranged on both sides of the river. He instantly gave orders to "work both sides, and load with grape." Cool, and apparently unexcited, the men trained their guns with such precision, that scarcely a shot failed to hit its mark, while the forward and aft pivot-guns also kept up their steady fire. The first rebel vessel that received his fire, seemed crowded with troops. At the first discharge, her boiler exploded, and she drifted ashore. Three other vessels, in quick succession, were now driven ashore in flames, and blew up. At this moment, just as the sun had risen above the horizon, lighting up the strange scene, he saw a vessel, iron-clad about the bows, bearing down full upon him. As the rebel vessel approached, she fired a thirty-two-pound rifled gun, which raked the Varuna terribly, killing and wounding thirteen men. The marines now poured in a galling fire, which swept the gunners clear of the piece, so that it could not be fired again. The next moment she struck his vessel in the port gangway, athwart the mainmast, crushing in her timbers, and causing her to careen over in the water. Backing off, she again came on, hitting nearly in the same place, staving in the side. But Boggs ordered the engineer to go ahead, and the Varuna, pushing up stream, swung the rebel steamer around, leaving her wooden side exposed. Instantly, Boggs poured in abaft her armor eight-inch shells. Five in quick succession entered her side, bursting with such destructive force, that the captain afterwards said they swept his decks of nearly every living object. "This," said Boggs, "settled her, and drove her ashore in flames."

The feeble, but gallant Varuna had hardly recovered from these two staggering blows, when the Stonewall Jackson, an iron-clad, came full upon her, striking her with a tremendous crash, and staving in her sides, so that the water poured in torrents into the vessel. She was also on fire, and there was now no alternative but to run her ashore, and her bow was headed for the banks. The Oneida, Captain Lee, seeing her condition, rushed to her assistance, but Boggs, finding that he could do him no good, waved him on toward the Governor Moore, which, though in flames, kept up a heavy fire, that swept the deck of the Varuna. Fast settling in the water, as she struggled towards the shore, her guns kept booming over the bosom of the Mississippi, until the water was above the trucks—the last shot just skimming the surface. Captain Bailey saw with pride how the wounded thing fought, and says: "I saw Boggs bravely fighting, his guns level with the water, as his vessel gradually sunk underneath, leaving her bow resting on the shore, and above water." The coolness and foresight of Boggs were strikingly shown in running his vessel ashore. When he saw her gun-trucks under water, and knew the last shot had been fired, he hastened forward, and ordered a chain-cable out, and, the moment the bow struck the bank, he had it fastened round a tree, so that the vessel, as she sunk stern first, might not slide off into deep water and carry the crew with her. At the same time, the chief engineer coolly walked up to him, and, touching his hat, reported: "The engine has stopped working, sir." With him came the gunner, who, with the same salute, said: "The magazine is closed, sir, and here are the keys." This shows with what cool deliberation the vessel was fought,—no hurry, no excitement, though the hostile vessels were all around her, shells bursting along her decks, iron-clad bows beating in her sides, and fire raging along her decks.

In fifteen minutes after receiving the last blow, the Varuna went down, with her guns roaring and her flag proudly flying.

During the action, a boy named Oscar Peck, only thirteen years old, whose business was to pass ammunition to the gunners, narrowly escaped death, as one of the enemy's shells burst along the deck. Just then, Boggs came upon him, begrimed with powder, and seeing him running, asked him where he was going in such a hurry. "To get a passing box, sir," he replied; "the other was smashed by a ball." When the Varuna went down Boggs missed the boy, and thought he was among the killed. But a few moments after, he saw the lad gallantly swimming towards the wreck. Clambering on board, the little fellow threw his hand up to his forehead, in the usual salute, for his hat was gone, with the simple exclamation "All right, sir, I report myself on board!" That boy was worthy to be trained under such a man as Boggs. Delighted with his gallantry, he said in his report: "I would particularly recommend to the notice of the Department, Oscar Peck, a second-class boy, and powder-boy of the after rifles, whose coolness and intrepidity attracted the attention of all hands. A just reward for such services would be an appointment at the Naval School."

Boggs was now without a ship, but in losing it had not lost his honor, but, on the contrary, won immortal fame, and showed that he was a worthy nephew of the gallant Lawrence, who lost his life and ship together.

Boggs was now sent by Farragut to General Butler below, to request him to bring his army up, as the fleet had passed the forts. Taking the only iron life-boat of the Varuna which was saved, he passed around the forts by a bayou, and safely delivered his message.

As a reward for his gallantry in this unparalleled naval combat, his native town and state both voted him a sword.

Boggs now came North, and was ordered first to the Juniata, and afterwards transferred to the Sacramento, in which vessel he was senior officer of the blockading squadron off Wilmington. To a man of his enterprise and love of active service, this was a most disagreeable duty, especially as he had an insufficient squadron, or, at least, an inefficient one, in the speed and power of the vessels that composed it. The constant exposure and fatigue attendant on his duties here, at length broke down his health, and he was reluctantly compelled to resign his command, and return home to recruit and receive that medical treatment of which he was in pressing need.

As soon as he was sufficiently recovered, he was appointed one of Admiral Gregory's staff, on duty at New York. Here he was actively engaged in superintending the building and fitting out of a fleet of steam picket-boats of his own planning. One of these, No. 1, was, by him and Engineer Wood, converted into a torpedo-boat. How well it was planned and constructed, may be inferred from the fact that it was the one selected by Lieutenant Cushing to make his memorable attack on the rebel ram Albemarle, in which that dreaded monster was sent to the bottom.

The iron-clad torpedo-boat, Spuyten Duyvil, was also fitted out under Captain Boggs' directions.

After the close of the war, Boggs was put in command of the squadron ordered to the coast of Maine, to watch the Fenian movement. On returning from this duty, he was ordered, with his vessel, the De Soto, to join the West India squadron, and is now on active duty at that station.

Last summer he was made Commodore by seniority. Some of the most striking traits in the character of Commodore Boggs, are clearly exhibited in the manner he fought and handled his vessel in the passage of the Forts below New Orleans. Prompt, fearless, cool, and self-possessed, dangers cannot daunt him, and no obstacles arrest him. But, added to these qualities as a commander, he has those of a man, which make him unusually beloved by those who know him. Gentle, amiable, and indulgent in his family, he is equally so on ship, in every thing that does not interfere with the discipline and good order of the vessel. He overlooks many things that one more of a martinet would notice. Mere technicalities he cares little for, but he exacts the strictest, most thorough, performance of duty. Like many other strong men, he needs a great object to develop his real character. To an ordinary observer, he seems merely good-natured, and inclined to be lazy; but place him amid the smoke of battle, and he is like the roused lion.

Kind and sympathizing in his nature, he is very careful of the health and comfort of his men, and they repay that kindness by affection and supreme devotion.

CHAPTER IX.

REAR-ADMIRAL LOUIS MALESHERBES GOLDSBOROUGH.

HIS NATIVITY.—A MIDSHIPMAN AT SEVEN YEARS OF AGE.—HIS FIRST CRUISE. EARLY SERVICES—A LIEUTENANT AT TWENTY.—PROSECUTES HIS STUDIES AT PARIS.—BATTLE WITH PIRATES IN THE ARCHIPELAGO.—PLACED IN CHARGE OF THE DEPOT OF CHARTS AND INSTRUMENTS AT WASHINGTON.—ESTABLISHES A GERMAN COLONY IN FLORIDA.—TAKES PART IN THE SEMINOLE WAR.—TAKES PART IN THE BOMBARDMENT OF VERA CRUZ.—EXPLORES THE COAST OF CALIFORNIA AND OREGON.—COMMANDS THE BRAZILIAN SQUADRON.—MADE CAPTAIN.—AT COMMENCEMENT OF THE REBELLION, MADE FLAG-OFFICER OF THE NORTH-ATLANTIC BLOCKADING SQUADRON.—COMMANDS THE EXPEDITION SENT TO THE SOUNDS OF NORTH CAROLINA.—STORMS AT CAPE HATTERAS.—ITS DESTRUCTIVE EFFECTS.—SAILS FOR ROANOKE ISLAND.—BOMBARDMENT OF THE WORKS.—HIS SERVICES IN THE CHESAPEAKE BAY AND JAMES RIVER.—RESIGNS HIS COMMAND.—SHORE DUTY.—PRESENT COMMAND.

LOUIS MALESHERBES GOLDSBOROUGH was born in Washington, D. C., on February 18th, 1805. His father and friends, living at the very focus of political influences, were not compelled to work, through some Congressman from a remote district, to secure an appointment for him in the Navy, and he was entered as midshipman, at the extraordinary age of seven years. A mere boy, he could learn but little, and do but little in his profession. It is probable that he was appointed at that time, in order to secure a vacancy that might not again occur for a long time. At all events, he did not enter the service till four years after. When eleven years old, he joined the frigate Independence, under the gallant Bainbridge. From 1817 to 1824, he cruised in the Mediterranean and Pacific, being most of the time in the Franklin, commanded by Stewart. In 1825, he was made lieutenant, being then but twenty years of age. In a time of peace, to reach so early the grade of lieutenant, was almost unprecedented, and shows that his friends had great influence at head-quarters. This was still further evinced by his obtaining leave of absence to visit Europe. He settled himself down in Paris, and prosecuted his studies there for some time, and then joined the North Carolina, in the Mediterranean. He was transferred from this vessel to the schooner Porpoise. The schooner, while cruising in the Grecian Archipelago, fell in with a craft that had been captured by pirates. Lieutenant Goldsborough, then only twenty-two or three years old, was ordered to take the boats of the schooner and recapture it. Thirty-five officers and men, were put under him, and the young officer shoved off to execute the order. It was a hazardous undertaking, for the captured vessel swarmed with pirates. He, however, rowed boldly up to her and opened a close, fierce fire. It was returned, and a severe conflict followed. The vessel was at length taken, but not till every officer and man had killed, upon an average, nearly three pirates apiece. The decks were slippery with blood, and a horrible sight met his gaze as he stepped upon them, for ninety men had fallen in the engagement.

In 1830, he returned to the United States in the Delaware, and was placed in charge of the Depot of Charts and Instruments. This bureau, or whatever it may be termed, was changed on his own suggestion into the National Observatory.

He had some time previously married the daughter of the distinguished orator, William Wirt. The latter had purchased a large tract of land in Florida, on which he wished to found a German colony, and, in 1833, Goldsborough took charge of the emigrants and moved thither. He was there when the Seminole war broke out, and took command of a company of mounted volunteers. He afterwards was placed in command of an armed steamer.

Becoming tired of the kind of life he was compelled to lead in Florida, he resumed his profession, and, in 1841, was promoted to commander.

When the Mexican war broke out, a few years after, he was placed second in command of the Ohio, which formed a part of the fleet that bombarded Vera Cruz.

After the place fell, he took charge of a body of sailors, detached for shore service, at the taking of Tuspan.

At the close of the Mexican war, he was appointed senior naval member of a joint commission, appointed to explore California and Oregon, and report upon various military matters. He showed the same ability here that he had in all the trusts which had heretofore been committed to him, and was, in 1855, made Captain.

At the commencement of the rebellion, he was in command of the Congress, on the Brazilian station. He returned to the United States in August, 1861, and was appointed flag-officer; and, next month, placed in command of the North Atlantic blockading squadron, with the Minnesota as his flagship.

Although we had taken possession of Cape Hatteras, thus cutting off one of the channels of ingress and egress to blockade runners, still, the shallow inlets and sounds on the North Carolina coast furnished other avenues of approach, through which arms, ammunition, clothing, and stores were brought into the Confederacy, and cotton taken out; and hence, it became of vital importance that the waters of Albemarle and Pamlico Sounds should be under our control. A joint expedition of the army and navy was, therefore, organized with great secrecy, to be sent thither; and all through the autumn was being assembled at or near Hampton Roads—the land force to be under Burnside, and the fleet under Goldsborough. Although it was well known that the coast, in the neighborhood of Hatteras, was very stormy and dangerous in winter, by some strange fatality the expedition lingered out the mild autumnal season in Hampton Roads, and was not ready to sail till near the middle of January, 1862. The fleet consisted of twenty-three light-draught vessels, carrying forty-eight guns. The land force numbered sixteen thousand men, and were carried in thirty transports. Five vessels more carried the horses, eight or ten the siege-train, supplies, &c., making in all a fleet of nearly eighty vessels.

This was an imposing force, and, when it was all assembled in Hampton Roads, presented a magnificent appearance, the like of which had never before been seen on our continent.

On Saturday night, the 11th of January, the signal to make sail was hoisted, and by ten o'clock this magnificent fleet was in motion. It was a beautiful moonlight night, and, as the vessels in one vast crowd moved off seaward, it seemed as if nothing along our coast could resist such an armada. As it approached the Atlantic, however, a heavy fog enveloped it, which continued more or less dense all the fore part of the next day, Sunday. But, in the afternoon it cleared up, and just as the sun was sinking in a blaze of glory over the Carolina shore, the fleet swept around Cape Hatteras, and hove-to off the inlet, twelve miles distant, to wait for the morning light, before attempting to cross the bar. Monday morning dawned bright and beautiful, and a gentle south wind breathing of spring stole over the waters. Everything seemed propitious to the expedition. Still, Goldsborough felt some anxiety, as he saw the heavy breakers bursting over the bar—for, although there was but little wind, a heavy swell was rolling in, indicating that a storm was raging not far distant. The lighter vessels, however, one by one passed the bar safely, and anchored inside of the inlet, under the lee of the land. Thus Monday, the 13th, passed, but when night came on several of the heavier vessels were still outside, while a dark cloud in the north, accompanied by a heavy squall, showed that a change of weather must be expected on this tempestuous coast. The next morning—the worst of all winds for that region—a northeasterly gale was upon them, lashing the ocean into fury. Goldsborough saw with the deepest anxiety the increasing storm, for the City of New York lay aground on the bar, loaded with ammunition, tents, blankets, and valuable stores, and wallowing amid the breakers that leaped above her decks, like malignant spirits seeking her destruction. The foremast had been cut away, which, in its fall, carried away the main topmast, while amid the blinding spray a signal of distress was seen flying. In this terrible situation, the long, gloomy day wore away, and night closed in around the ill-fated vessel. With the first gleam of dawn, Goldsborough cast his eye towards the spot where she lay and saw her crew lashed to the masts. All her boats but one had been carried away, and, no help coming from the fleet, two mechanics from Newark, named William and Charles Beach, volunteered to make the desperate attempt, with this one, to pull through the breakers and obtain assistance. They succeeded, with three others, in launching it safely, and though, at times, entirely lost to view amid the combing billows, at length reached the fleet. Life and surf boats were now manned, which, impelled by strong arms, succeeded in reaching the vessel and taking off the crew, when she was left to her fate.

A transport laden with stores went down on the bar; the gunboat Zouave sunk at her anchorage; one transport was blown out to sea, and several got aground.

The Anne E. Thompson, with the New Jersey Ninth Volunteers, lay outside in imminent peril of wreck, and Colonel Allen and Surgeon Weller took a boat and pulled over the bar to ask for help. On their return, the boat swamped, and they both perished. The Pocahontas, with a hundred and twenty-three horses, was wrecked, and all but seventeen drowned. Gale now followed gale in quick succession, and the ships, in their miserable anchorage, lay grinding against each other and tossing heavily on the swell, while the shrieking of the wind through the cordage, and the thunder of billows falling with incessant crashes along the shore, continued to make a scene of terror and gloom sufficient to sadden the stoutest heart. To add to his misery, Goldsborough was taken down with the rheumatism, and groaned aloud over his helplessness in this trying hour. The whole week passed without anything being done. Of course, the destination of the fleet, which had so long and laboriously been kept secret, was now known, and all hopes of surprise were at an end.

When, at last, nearly all the surviving fleet had succeeded in reaching the inlet, Goldsborough found that he still had an almost insurmountable difficulty to overcome, before he could enter the waters of the Pamlico Sound. There was another bar still to be crossed, called the Bulk-Head, or Swash, which, Goldsborough said, under the most favorable circumstances, furnished only seven and a half feet of water, while some of his heaviest vessels drew eight feet. By what strange fatuity vessels were sent where there was not water enough to float them, has never been satisfactorily explained. One by one, however, by taking advantage of high tides, and high winds bringing in a heavy sea, and using every expedient that ingenuity could suggest, Goldsborough finally got his vessels over into deep water.

On Monday the 26th, he sent home a despatch announcing that seventeen vessels were safely within the Sound. But other delays took place, and it was not until three weeks after his arrival at the Cape, that the expedition, which was to be a great surprise, finally got under way.

On the 5th of February, the same day that Foote was moving up the Cumberland River to attack Fort Henry, the fleet of gunboats and transports carrying the army, sixty-five in all, moved off towards Roanoke Island, on which were erected works that commanded the channel leading into Albemarle Sound.

The storms had blown themselves out, and the day was mild and balmy as spring, as the imposing fleet moved majestically forward over the smooth waters.

When within ten miles of the southern point of the

island, it being near sundown, the signal to anchor was hoisted from the flagship, and in a few minutes the fleet lay at rest on the water. It was a beautiful moonlight night, and as the mellow radiance flooded the scene, it did not seem that death and havoc lay slumbering there.

The morning, however, dawned dark and gloomy. Heavy clouds lay along the horizon, as the fleet once more moved slowly onward, and by eleven o'clock a storm broke over the sound, when it again came to a halt. After some time it cleared up, and the signal to advance was given. The weather, however, was too heavy to undertake to pass the batteries that night, and the vessels came to anchor. The next morning the sun rose in a sky mottled with fleecy clouds, indicating a quiet day, and preparations were at once made to attack the enemy's works. As Goldsborough approached them, he came in sight of the rebel gunboats, eight in number, drawn up behind a double row of piles and sunken vessels, placed there to obstruct the channel. Besides these obstructions, and rebel steamers to defend the passage, there were two strong works mounting twenty heavy guns—three of them one hundred pound rifle guns—and four other batteries mounting twenty guns, together with a garrison of from three to five thousand men.

At eleven o'clock the first gun from the flagship broke the ominous silence, and, as the loud report rolled away over the water, Goldsborough ran up Nelson's famous signal: "This day our country expects that every man will do his duty." By noon the combat was raging in all its terror, and the signal for close action was seen flying amid the smoke of the guns that curled lazily up in the atmosphere. Goldsborough directed his fire at first against the rebel gunboats, which gradually fell back to draw his vessels in close range of the works. The fleet steadily advanced until it reached the obstructions, which had been planted just where the rebel forts could pour in their most destructive fire. To these Goldsborough gave his exclusive attention, and the ponderous shell of our vessels dropped thick as hailstones within them. The enemy replied, and soon one eighty-pound rifle shell entered the fore-hold of the Louisiana, setting her on fire. In six minutes however the flames were extinguished, and the vessel was again hurling shot and shell into the rebel works. At half past one the barracks behind the fort at Rock Point were set on fire by our shells. All efforts to extinguish them proved abortive, and the clouds of smoke that arose, making a fearful background to the fire of the batteries, imparted additional terror to the scene. The fire raged for nearly an hour before the buildings were wholly destroyed. In the mean time the bombardment went on, and at a little after 2 o'clock a 32-pounder round-shot struck the steamer Hetzel, Lieut. H. R. Davenport commanding, compelling her to haul off to repair damages. In a little over an hour and a half she was again at her position, pouring in her shot as before.

The bombardment of the forts, which had commenced before noon, was kept up till dark. Goldsborough says:

At 6 p. m. the firing of the enemy being only from Pork Point, and at long intervals, darkness coming on, and, not wishing to waste ammunition, I ordered the signal "cease firing" to be made. In the course of the afternoon, our six launches, under the command of Midshipman Benjamin H. Porter, landed their howitzers and joined the army, for the purpose of commanding the main road and its two forks during the night, and assisting in more active operations the following morning. By midnight some 10,000 of our troops had been safely landed at Ashby's harbor, the Delaware having taken on board from the Cossack some 800, and put them on shore at 10 p. m.

February 8.—As it was arranged by General Burnside that his forces should move, at a very early hour this morning, from where they had been landed, and begin their attack upon the enemy, and, as the direction they were required to take would, in all probability, soon bring them in the line of fire occupied by the navy, it was agreed between us last night that to-day the vessels should not renew operations until I could receive word from him that their missiles would not be destructive to both friends and foes. At daylight none of the enemy's vessels, except the Curlew, could be discovered.

At 9 A. M. a continuous firing in the interior of the island told us that our forces were hotly engaged about midway between Ashby's harbor and Pork Point battery, and, as this intelligence also assured us that our forces were not then in the range of our line of fire, our vessels, without waiting to hear from General Burnside, at once moved up to re-engage the forts. At this work they continued until the firing in the interior evidently slackened. Then, taking it for granted that our troops were carrying everything before them, and thus fast approaching the rear of the batteries, I again ordered the signal "cease firing" to be made. At the time, however, the work on Pork Point was so reduced that it did not use but one gun against us. Shortly afterwards, on being informed by one of General Burnside's aids, of the actual state of things on shore, I was induced to order another demonstration on the part of our vessels, but before firing had generally commenced Commander Rowan came on board the Southfield just from General Burnside, with the suggestion that it would be better to desist, and accordingly they were recalled.

At 1 P. M., judging that the time had arrived for clearing a passage-way through the obstructions alluded to above, by the accomplishment of which both the battery on Redstone Point and the Curlew might be destroyed, and our advance up Albemarle Sound would be secured, the Underwriter, Valley City, Seymour, Lockwood, Ceres, Shawsheen, Putnam, Whitehead, and Brincker, were ordered to perform the service. By 4 P. M., one of them had overcome the difficulty for herself, and reached the other side, and in less than an hour more a sufficient way for all the rest was opened. This important duty could not have been undertaken one moment earlier than it was without exposing our vessels, huddled together, to the converging and crossfire of the four batteries at Pork, Weir's, and Redstone Points, and another one situated between the former two. About the same time that our vessels succeeded in bursting through the barricades the American flag was hoisted over the battery at Pork Point, and in a few minutes afterwards the enemy himself fired the works at Redstone Point, and also the steamer Curlew. Both blew up in the early part of the evening. These events closed the struggle, which had now lasted throughout two days, and were essentially the last scenes enacted in securing to us complete possession of the island of Roanoke.

The casualties were few, considering the length of

the combat, and showed poor firing on the part of the rebels. The Hetzel suffered most, not from the enemy's shot, but from the bursting of her own 80-pounder rifle-gun. This took place at a quarter past five. The concussion was so fearful, that every man at the piece was knocked down and six of them wounded.

The muzzle fell on the deck; a part of the breech leaped into the sea, carrying away the bulwarks in its mad plunge; another portion rose high in the air, and a third went downward, breaking through the deck, magazine, and deck below, and lodged on the kelson. Davenport, the commander, says: "The magazine was set on fire, and only extinguished in time to avoid an explosion by the presence of mind, promptitude, and intrepidity of Lieutenant Charles L. Franklin, Executive Officer." The accident so disabled her, that she had to haul off and anchor out of reach of the enemy's guns. The Commodore Perry was hit seven times, but not materially injured. The Hunchback, Calhoun commanding, was struck eight times, and fired over three hundred shot and shell, yet not a man on board was wounded. All the commanders handled their vessels with great skill. The Stars and Stripes got aground, and remained so for two hours, under the fire of the battery, and all that time returned shot for shot, her officers behaving with great coolness and courage. Goldsborough, who had transferred his flag to the Southfield, remained on deck during the whole of the engagement. The total loss on board the ships was only thirteen, though Midshipman Porter, who commanded a howitzer-battery on shore, lost twenty-three. The works were finally carried by the troops, which had been landed the night before, and advanced in three columns under the command of Reno, Foster, and Park.

The rebel steamers fled up Albemarle Sound, whither, the next day, Monday, Rowan pursued them and sunk or captured all but two.*

Goldsborough now sent off various expeditions into the bays and rivers, to complete his conquest of the coast. A month later, Newbern fell, under a joint expedition of the army and navy; the latter commanded by Rowan. In the mean time, Goldsborough's presence was needed in Hampton Roads, for the Merrimac had made her daring raid in those waters. After the destruction of the Merrimac, he coöperated with McClellan—keeping vessels in both James and York Rivers. Much hard work was done by the various commanders, but the only engagement worthy of particular mention, was that at Drury's Bluff, eight miles below Richmond. Heavy guns were here mounted, which completely commanded the river, so that our vessels could not ascend above it.

In May, Goldsborough sent up the Galena, Aroostook, Naugatuck, Port Royal, and the Monitor, to silence, if possible, the works erected there, called Fort Darling. The Galena in advance, John Rodgers commanding, cleared the shores of the enemy. He says:

We met with no artificial impediments until we arrived at Ward's Bluff, about eight miles from Richmond, where we encountered a heavy battery and two separate barriers, formed of piles and steamboats and sail vessels. The pilots both say that they saw the Jamestown and Yorktown among the number.

The banks of the river we found lined with rifle-pits, from which sharpshooters annoyed the men at the guns. These would hinder all removal of obstructions, unless driven away by a land force.

The Galena ran within almost six hundred yards of the battery, as near the piles as it was deemed proper to go, let go her anchor, and with a spring

* The particulars of this splendid achievement will be found in the sketch of Admiral Rowan.

swung across the stream, not more than twice as wide as the ship is long. Then, at 7.45 A. M., opened fire upon the battery.

The wooden vessels, as directed, anchored about thirteen hundred yards below.

The combat lasted for two hours, the heavy echoes of the guns breaking with startling distinctness over Richmond, filling the inhabitants with terror. But the fight was too unequal, for the shot of the vessels could not be thrown with any accuracy up the hill, a hundred and fifty feet high, while the plunging balls from the fort went through and through the Galena. The vessel being compelled, on account of the narrowness of the river, to remain stationary, the enemy, when he once got the range, made his shots tell so fatally, that in a short time twenty-four of the crew of the Galena were killed or wounded, and she had been struck some eighteen times. The 100-pounder rifle-gun on board the Naugatuck burst early in the action, and she became useless. She had but two wounded, and the Monitor one.

This was the first reverse our iron-clads had met with, and the people of Richmond were highly elated at the result. Rodgers could not run the batteries, on account of the obstructions that were placed across the river, directly under fire of the fort.

Admiral Lee, succeeding Goldsborough (who asked to be relieved on account of disagreement with Wilkes), in the command of the North Atlantic blockading squadron in the forepart of September, the latter was employed afterward on shore duty. At Washington, he rendered the Government good service, and was active in his department until the close of the war. He was then placed in command of the European squadron, which position he at present holds.

CHAPTER X.

COLONEL CHARLES ELLET.

AMERICAN INGENUITY.—ELLET'S NATIVITY.—EARLY EDUCATION.—BECOMES SURVEYOR.—FINISHES HIS EDUCATION IN PARIS.—BECOMES ENGINEER-IN-CHIEF ON THE JAMES RIVER AND KANAWHA CANAL.—PUBLISHES A WORK ON THE LAWS OF TRADE.—PROPOSES TO BUILD A WIRE BRIDGE ACROSS THE MISSISSIPPI.—BUILDS THE FIRST SUSPENSION BRIDGE IN AMERICA.—PLANS OTHERS.—VISITS EUROPE.—PLANS IMPROVEMENTS OF NAVIGATION IN THE OHIO RIVER.—SENT BY THE WAR DEPARTMENT TO SURVEY THE LOWER MISSISSIPPI.—PUBLISHES A WORK ON THE OHIO AND MISSISSIPPI RIVERS.—PLANS THERE THE RAM.—SUBMITS HIS INVENTION TO THE RUSSIAN EMPEROR.—ALSO TO OUR NAVY DEPARTMENT.—PUBLISHES A PAMPHLET ON HIS PROJECTS.—URGES HIS INVENTION ON GOVERNMENT AT THE BREAKING OUT OF THE REBELLION.—ATTACKS M'CLELLAN.—SENT WEST TO BUILD RAMS.—HIS DIFFICULTIES.—HIS FIRST EXPERIMENT AT MEMPHIS.—IS WOUNDED.—HIS SICKNESS AND DEATH.—CHARLES RIVERS ELLET.—HIS BIRTH AND EARLY EDUCATION.—JOINS THE RAM FLEET.—SUCCEEDS HIS FATHER.—HIS BRAVERY.—COMPLIMENTED BY PORTER.—ATTACKS THE CITY OF VICKSBURG.—DESTROYS REBEL TRANSPORTS.—GETS AGROUND, AND LOSES HIS VESSEL.—COMMANDS THE SWITZERLAND. RUNS THE VICKSBURG BATTERIES.—AFTER SERVICES.—HIS SICKNESS AND EARLY DEATH.

AMERICAN ingenuity is proverbial; and, though it is often wasted on worthless objects and impracticable schemes, yet, in great exigencies, it is sure to originate something to meet them. And often what in ordinary times seems useless or impracticable, then becomes of immense value. The inventor may find no encourage-

14

ment from his countrymen, and the Government decline to furnish means to test his proposed experiments, so that he frequently dies without seeing his plans tried—comforted only by the belief that the time will arrive when they will be adopted with gladness.

Of these inventors, Charles Ellet was one who bid fair to die without seeing his favorite scheme carried out. The war however into which we were precipitated, gave to his applications a force that in times of peace they did not possess, and he saw the "Ram" finally adopted as a war vessel by his Government.

Charles Ellet was born at Perry Manor, on the Delaware, about twenty-five miles above Philadelphia. His boyhood was passed on his father's farm, but at sixteen he was sent to Bristol school, where he at once developed his love for mathematics, and indicated clearly his future profession. At eighteen, he became assistant surveyor of Maryland. Here he husbanded his earnings so that he might finish his education in Europe, and at twenty-one he went to Paris, where he remained for two years. Returning to Maryland he was appointed assistant engineer on the James River and Kanawha Canal, which was then being built, and eventually became engineer-in-chief. He proposed to build a wire suspension bridge across the Potomac, but his proposition was declined.

Being now fairly launched in his profession, he married the daughter of Judge Daniel, of Lynchburg, Virginia.

In 1837, he published a book on "The Laws of Trade in Reference to Works of Internal Improvement," which showed great study of the various methods of inland communication. In 1840, he made to the authorities of St. Louis the bold proposition to build a wire bridge across the Mississippi, at that point, but it was rejected. The next year, however, he constructed the wire suspension bridge across the Schuylkill, at Fairmount, the first erected in America. He was now extensively employed and consulted on the great public works going on throughout the country. In 1847, he began the suspension bridge at Wheeling, for the Baltimore and Ohio Railroad, and also threw a temporary bridge over the Niagara River, just below the Falls. In the intervals of his labors he visited Europe several times, to enlarge his experience, and was received there as a distinguished man in his profession. In 1846 and 1847 he was president of the Schuylkill Navigation Company. In 1848 and 1849 he devoted himself a part of the time to making observations and calculations on the Ohio River, for the purpose of devising some method of improving its navigation. Though his plan was not adopted, the results of his labors were published in the Transactions of the Smithsonian Institute.

Soon after, though not belonging to the army, he was selected by the War Department to survey the Lower Mississippi, in consequence of complaints being made to Congress, that the spring floods of the river were injuring the State, and destroying a vast amount of property. He performed the work assigned him with great ability, and published his report, together with the observations he had made on the Ohio, in a book form, entitled, "Ellet on the Ohio and Mississippi Rivers." This is not the place to go into the details of his plan, which was on a gigantic scale, for the improvement of those rivers. By many it was thought chimerical, though he fully believed it would eventually be carried out.

In 1854, Mr. Ellet was in Lausanne, and there being

much discussion at the time respecting the siege of Sebastopol, and the blockade of the harbor by British vessels, his scheming mind was directed to war vessels, and then and there was born in his brain the new and famous ram, which hereafter is to bear such an important part in river and harbor defence. He submitted his plan to the Russian Emperor, declaring that with such vessels the Russians might sink the fleet of the allies. It was well received, though never acted on. The next spring he submitted it to John Y. Mason, then our Minister at Paris. Ellet forwarded it to the Navy Department, but he received no encouragement, and in 1855 published his plan, together with the correspondence with the Government, in a pamphlet form.

The grand idea on which his invention was based, is thus given in the preface of this book: "People are accustomed to regard the art of naval warfare as the art of manœuvering cannon, and throwing shot and shell. I wish them to reflect upon the power of a moving steamboat driven against the enemy, who has no means of resistance but his batteries, and to decide which is the more certain warfare." Again he says: "My plan is simply to convert the steamer into a battering-ram, and enable her to fight, not with her guns, but with her momentum." He proposed to strengthen it, so that it "could run head into the enemy, or burst in his ribs, or drive a hole into his hull below the water line." "This," he said, "would make the combat a short one; for," he added, "a hole only two feet square, four feet under water, will sink an ordinary frigate in sixteen minutes. The pamphlet goes into all the details of his plan, shows how vessels could be converted into rams, and says: "I hold myself ready to carry it out, whenever the day arrives that the United States is about to become engaged in a naval contest."

To Ellet's proposition, Mr. Welch, then acting Secretary of the Navy, said, that "the suggestion to convert steamers into battering-rams, and by the momentum make them a means of sinking an enemy's ships, was proposed as long ago as 1832, and has been renewed many times since by various officers of the Navy." He added that no practical test had been undertaken, but acknowledged that, "with the necessary speed, strength, and weight, a large steamer on the plan proposed would introduce an entire change in naval warfare." Ellet subsequently urged his plan afresh, but Mr. Dobbin, Secretary of the Navy, said that the Department had no power to build vessels for such experiments, except by special vote of Congress. Mr. Ellet did not go on mere theory—he cited numerous cases of accidental collision at sea—some where merely a sailing vessel had sunk large ships, to show what deadly work might be done with a vessel built on purpose to run down an antagonist. He cannot claim originality for his invention, for it had been discussed both here and abroad for years; but it differed from all others in that he did not believe as they did, that great weight was necessary in order to make a ram efficient; he insisted that the momentum required could be obtained by speed, and that river steamers, steam-tugs, and even ferryboats might easily be converted into formidable engines of destruction, and sufficiently strong to sink the heaviest vessels of war that England might send against us.

He was living at Washington at the time of the breaking out of the rebellion, devoting much time to the perfecting of his plans, and urging their adoption. The commencement of war, of course, increased his desire to have them tested, and he vehemently pressed on the Government and Congress the importance of putting them into practical operation. When he learned that the rebels along the coast and on the Mississippi were turning steamers into iron-clad rams, his excitement over the inaction of our Government made his friends almost dread his presence, for his importunity knew no bounds. He printed a memorial to Congress, and laid it on the tables of the members. In it he stated what the rebels were doing, while the Navy Department had not taken the first step to meet this new and threatening evil. In speaking of the Merrimac, then in course of construction, he uses the following remarkable words: "If the Merrimac is permitted to escape from the Elizabeth River, she will be almost certain to commit great depredations on our armed or unarmed vessels in Hampton Roads, and may be even expected to pass out under the guns of Fortress Monroe and prey upon our commerce in Chesapeake Bay. Indeed, if the alterations have been skilfully made, and she succeeds in getting to sea, she will not only be a terrible scourge to our commerce, but also may prove to be a most dangerous visitor to our squadron off the harbors of our southern coast."

Mr. Ellet's active mind, not content with its legitimate work, also undertook to direct the war, and he formed a plan for cutting off the rebel army at Manassas, and submitted it to McClellan for adoption. The latter treating it as he did numerous similar plans which he received, Ellet was very indignant, and wrote two pamphlets against him, in which he spoke in harsh and severe terms of the general-in-chief.

The sinking of the Cumberland and Congress by the

Merrimac, finally woke up the Government to the importance of Mr. Ellet's project and propositions, respecting the building of iron-clad rams. Still, the Navy Department had its hands full, and was spending the appropriation made by Congress for the increase of the Navy, in the building and purchasing of vessels of a different kind. But when Foote reported from Island No. 10 that the rebels had several gunboats on the Mississippi that could be used as rams, the Secretary of War took the responsibility of commissioning Ellet as Colonel of Engineers, and sending him west to buy and convert into rams such vessels as he could find there fit for his purpose. He set out in the latter part of March, and at Pittsburg purchased five heavy tow-boats, and at Cincinnati four side-wheel steamers. The bows of these he strengthened with heavy timbers, and sheathed with iron bars, and built strong bulkheads of oak around the machinery and boilers. The pilot-houses of each were also plated sufficiently thick to protect the pilots from musketry. But though he was able to get his boats in a proper condition, he found it very difficult to obtain crews and officers for them. Neither engineers nor pilots liked to serve on such kind of craft, destined for such new and hazardous work. He finally obtained permission to recruit from the army, and, his brother Alfred being a captain of volunteers, he sent for him. The latter came, bringing his own and another company with him. Ellet's energy and perseverance obtained also pilots and engineers, and he was at last in a condition to test his theory practically.

In the mean time, before he had brought down his rams to join the fleet, commanded by Davis before Fort Pillow, the rebel flotilla attacked our gunboats, and seriously damaged the Cincinnati and Mound City with their rams. What further mischief might be done no one could foretell; and Ellet hastened forward some of his vessels, under the charge of his brother Alfred, and a few days after followed himself with the rest of them. The rebel fleet lay at this time below the fort, and under easy range of its fire, so that Davis could not attack it without at the same time encountering the batteries on shore. Ellet, on his arrival, asked Davis to give him the aid of a couple of gunboats, and he would steam past the fort, and attack the whole rebel flotilla of the enemy. This was a bold proposition, for at this time he had not a single cannon on board of his rams. The fighting force consisted of twenty-three sharpshooters, who were to fire through loopholes.

Soon after, the rebels evacuated Fort Pillow and retired to Memphis, followed by their fleet. Davis now advanced with his gunboats, and when near Memphis was attacked by the latter. Ellet had been detained up the river, but at this time was coming down under a full head of steam, with his ram fleet, each one of which was painted black, to make it look as formidable as possible. The Queen of the West was his flagship, and, standing on her deck as the heavy cannonading from below broke on his ear, he stretched out his arm towards the Monarch, which his brother commanded, and shouted out: "Follow me and attack the enemy." Crowding on all steam that the boilers would bear, he swept like an arrow past the fleet, and, steering for the nearest rebel boat, named the General Lovell, struck her with such awful force, that her sides were crushed in like an egg-shell, and in five minutes she went to the bottom with most of her crew. The Queen of the West staggered back like a drunken man from the shock—her chimneys reeling almost to the water—while the splinters and shivered timbers of her upper works made her deck appear like a wreck. Before she could recover herself and once more get under headway, two rebel rams came full upon her—determined to send her to the bottom after the General Lovell. One struck her near the wheel-house, but inflicted only a glancing blow, and in turn received from her own consort, which ran into her, one which so disabled her that she was compelled to run ashore, when she sunk. The sharpshooters, in the mean time, were busy, while the heavy broadsides of the gunboats shook the shores of the stream. Alfred, in the Monarch, following his brother, struck the Beauregard, but inflicted no serious damage, though the latter soon after blew up, the shot of the gunboats having pierced her boiler.

The combined attack proving too strong for the rebel fleet, it turned and fled. The Monarch and Lancaster gave the Van Dorn a hot chase, but the latter finally got off.

In this sharp encounter, not a man on board the rams was injured but Colonel Ellet. After he struck the General Lovell, he stepped forward to see the amount of injury he had done her, when he was hit in the knee by a bullet, which lodged in the bone. The wound proved to be a dangerous one, for inflammation set in, and the only chance of saving his life was amputation of the limb. This he would not consent to, declaring that he would rather die; at all events, he preferred to take his chances.

His experiment, as far as it went, was successful, but he determined it should have a fuller, more complete trial, and though suffering intensely, prepared to move down with the fleet to Vicksburg. But even his strong will could not resist the inroads the wound had made on his delicate, nervous frame, and he was compelled to abandon his project. Finding himself rapidly sinking, he sent for his family, by whom he was nursed with the greatest care, but he continued to grow worse.

In the mean time, the fleet moved down the river to win new laurels, leaving him behind, to mourn the fate that had laid him aside just as he was on the threshold of his great enterprise.

The command of the ram-fleet now devolved on his brother Alfred, and he told the latter, as he came to bid him farewell before he started, to carry out his plans, saying, as they parted forever: "*Alfred, stand to your post.*" He was now placed on board the Switzerland, and carried to Cairo, but just as the boat reached the wharf he expired, breathing out his gallant spirit in serene composure. Thus, on the 21st of June, 1862, at the age of fifty-two, this ardent, enthusiastic man passed away, leaving to others what he had fondly hoped to do himself.

His broken-hearted wife soon followed him to the grave, leaving a gallant son, only nineteen years of age, to uphold his fame and carry out his project.

CHARLES RIVERS ELLET.

The son followed in the daring footsteps of his father, in command of one of the rams built by the latter, and followed him too, alas! to the grave. Born in Georgetown, District of Columbia, in 1843, he was but eighteen years old when the war broke out. He had formerly accompanied his father to Europe, and remained two years in school at Paris. He was studying medicine when the first battle of Bull Run took place, and volunteered to act as assistant surgeon and nurse to the wounded that came pouring in from that disastrous battle-field.

When his father had just completed at the West the first of his rams, he joined him, and was given a place on board as medical cadet. He was in the battle before Memphis, and witnessed the first triumph of the rams. After it was over, he was sent by his father to demand the surrender of that city.

When the fleet commenced its movement down the river towards Vicksburg, Charles reluctantly left the side of his wounded father, to accompany it. Selected by Davis to carry a despatch to Farragut, anchored below the place, he made his way through swamps and stagnant pools in the darkness, and, after a night of incessant peril and labor, at length in the morning stood on the shore opposite the Hartford. Firing his pistol to attract attention, he was taken on board, where he delivered his message.

While on duty with his uncle Alfred up the Yazoo, he received on the 10th of July the melancholy tidings of the death of both father and mother, and the sickness of his only sister. He, however, felt it his duty to remain with the fleet, and, on the 5th of November, was placed in command of the rams, his uncle Alfred being given the command of the marine brigade.

When Admiral Porter determined to force the Yazoo River at Haines Bluff, he directed young Ellet to destroy a raft of timber that obstructed the stream. Fitting a torpedo-raft of his own invention to the Lioness, the latter, after getting everything ready, reported himself to Porter saying, that he had two tons of powder in the bow of his boat and asked for directions. Porter replied, that he must steam directly up to the raft, which lay right under the enemy's guns, and blow it up. "But," said young Ellet, "don't you expect that the enemy will be firing as I do so, into my two tons of powder?" "Oh yes!" replied the Admiral, "but you must'nt mind bullets and shells, you know." Ellet, a little piqued at the answer, replied that he was not afraid of them—he desired only to know how he wished him to proceed. A more desperate undertaking could not well be imagined, yet Ellet was ready for it and would doubtless have performed it or been blown up, had not a dense fog set in as he was about to start, compelling the expedition to be abandoned. Porter was delighted with the pluck of the youth, for he saw in him a spirit kindred to his own, and wrote to the Department: "I have great confidence in the commander of the rams and those under him, and take this opportunity to state to the Department how highly I appreciate the commander and his associates." This was very extraordinary praise to bestow on a youth only nineteen years old.

The next February, young Ellet was sent down with the ram Queen of the West, to sink, if possible, the "City of Vicksburg," that lay under the guns of the batteries. One of his guns was loaded with turpentine balls, designed to set the rebel vessel on fire. He boldly steamed down into the enemy's fire, and laid his vessel alongside of the City of Vicksburg, and opened on it with his guns, while the batteries on shore played furiously upon him. Although he set the rebel craft on fire, his own vessel also caught fire, and it was with great difficulty that the flames were extinguished.

He did not succeed in destroying the ram, but the manner in which he handled and fought his vessel astonished those who served under him.

Soon after, he was sent down to the mouth of Red River, to destroy rebel transports there, and in three days captured and destroyed three large steamers, valued at nearly half a million of dollars.

On the 15th, he started again for the Red River, accompanied by the De Soto, and, learning that three steamers were lying under the guns of a battery stationed where soon after Fort De Bussy was erected, he determined to capture them. But as he came within range of the guns, their fire was so destructive that he ordered the pilot to back the Queen of the West out of it. But in doing so he ran her aground, where she lay a helpless target. The rebels had the exact range, so that nearly every shot struck the doomed vessel. A frightful scene now followed. Ellet was unable to bring a gun to bear, and he could therefore only stand and see his vessel torn into fragments. On every side shells were bursting—three thirty-two-pound ones exploded one after another on the smoking deck, while one crashed through the machinery below, and another carried away the lever of the engine. The steam-pipe went next, and last, the steam-chest was fractured, letting out a cloud of steam, and prisoners, crew, and engineers, who had crowded into the engine-room for safety, now rushed aft and began to tumble overboard cotton bales, on which they leaped, hoping to float down to the De Soto, a mile below. The negroes with loud cries jumped overboard and were drowned. Some ran for the yawl that was tied to the stern, but a man stood on the bow with a loaded pistol, and threatened to shoot the first man that attempted to enter it. The De Soto steamed up as near as she dared and then sent her yawl to take off those who remained, but the fire of the batteries was so terrific that she had to drop down stream again, before the boat returned. Ellet escaped on a cotton bale, and sorrowfully made his way back to the squadron, blamed by some for his rashness, for the rebels captured the Queen of the West, and soon had her repaired and at work in the Confederate service.

He was soon after put in command of the Switzerland, which, with the Lancaster, commanded by his cousin John A. Ellet, was sent below Vicksburg to coöperate with Farragut. In passing the batteries, the boiler of the Switzerland, just as she got opposite the city, was pierced by two shots. In an instant the vessel was enveloped in a cloud of steam. Ellet's first care was for the crew—when they were safe in the boats he drew his pistol and fired into the cotton bales, for the purpose of setting the vessel on fire, so that she might not, like the Queen of the West, fall into the enemy's hands. He then stepped into the boat and rowed to the Lancaster. The Switzerland however escaped, and, being repaired, acted afterwards as a despatch boat between Generals Grant and Banks.

The exposure and excitement, together with the hot summer, at length proved too much for the constitution of young Ellet, and, obtaining leave of absence to recruit his shattered health, he retired to the residence of his uncle Dr. Ellet, at Bunker Hill, Illinois. He suffered severely from neuralgia in the face, for which he was in the habit of taking some opiate.

On the night of the 16th of October, he complained of feeling very unwell, and said to his aunt as he retired, that he thought he would take something to relieve the pain in his face. In the morning he was found dead in his bed. He had probably taken an overdose of morphine and fallen into a sleep from which he never awoke.

Thus at the early age of twenty, this youth of so much promise closed his labors for his country. Gentle and tender as a woman, he was nevertheless bold and fearless as a lion. His countenance was full of poetic sentiment, to which his large brilliant eyes and long black hair gave additional expression.

Though the career of father and son was so brief, it was glorious, and their names will go down to posterity linked with the navy, and embraced in the same halo of glory that encircles its brave commanders.

CHAPTER XI.

REAR-ADMIRAL THEODORUS BAILEY.

HIS NATIVITY.—EARLY IMPRESSIONS.—APPOINTED MIDSHIPMAN.—SENT TO THE COAST OF AFRICA.—CRUISE IN THE PACIFIC OCEAN.—PLACED ON THE WEST INDIA STATION.—MADE LIEUTENANT.—VOYAGE ROUND THE WORLD.—SECOND VOYAGE ROUND THE WORLD.—STATIONED AT THE BROOKLYN NAVY YARD.—ASSUMES AN INDEPENDENT COMMAND.—SAILS IN THE LEXINGTON FOR THE COAST OF MEXICO.—SHERMAN, HALLECK, AND ORD, THEN LIEUTENANTS, ACCOMPANY HIM.—THEIR APPEARANCE.—AN INCIDENT OFF CAPE HORN IN A GALE.—ARRIVAL IN CALIFORNIA.—MEETS COMMODORE STOCKTON AND FREMONT.—HIS SERVICES ON THE COAST DURING THE MEXICAN WAR.—A PRACTICAL JOKE—CORRESPONDENCE WITH A BRITISH CAPTAIN, ON BLOCKADE RIGHTS.—CRUISE IN THE PACIFIC.—COMPELS ISLAND CHIEFS TO DO JUSTICE.—AT PANAMA AFTER THE MASSACRE OF AMERICANS.—COMMANDS THE COLORADO IN COMMENCEMENT OF THE WAR.—BLOCKADES PENSACOLA.—PLACED SECOND IN COMMAND IN THE EXPEDITION AGAINST NEW ORLEANS.—UNABLE TO GET HIS SHIP OVER THE BAR.—DETERMINES TO LEAD IN SOMETHING.—ANECDOTE OF HIM.—LEADS IN THE CAYUGA.—THE COMBAT.—DEMANDS THE SURRENDER OF NEW ORLEANS.—INTERVIEWS WITH THE MAYOR, LOVELL AND SOULE.—SENT HOME WITH DESPATCHES.—PLACED IN COMMAND OF THE EASTERN GULF BLOCKADING SQUADRON—EXHIBITS GREAT ENERGY AND EFFICIENCY.—COMPLIMENTED BY THE DEPARTMENT.—HIS HOSPITALITY.—ASTONISHES A SECESH VESTRY.—SMITTEN DOWN BY THE YELLOW FEVER.—ATTEMPT TO BRIBE HIM.—RETURNS NORTH.

THEODORUS BAILEY was born in Franklin Co., New York State, in 1805, and received his education in Plattsburgh academy. Although a lad of but eight or nine years of age, when McDonough won his great victory over the British fleet off this place, the excitement caused by the battle and the thousand and one stories connected with it must have made a lasting impression on his mind, and perhaps had more to do with his eventually entering the navy than he himself is aware of. The fame and deeds of such a hero were well calculated to excite the ambition of a boy, living, as it were, in the very focus of the excitement. Be that as it may, four or five years after, in 1818, he entered the naval service as midshipman, and for the next two years and more he was learning his profession off the coast of Africa. He was then transferred to the Franklin, which had been ordered to the Pacific Ocean. He was absent on this cruise a little over one year, when he was transferred to the Shark, and sent to the West India station. Here, at Natchez, and back again, he was on duty nearly two years more.

In 1827, he was promoted to lieutenant and placed on board the Grampus, in which he served for six months. He was then ordered to the Vincennes, about to start on a long cruise in the Pacific Ocean, and thence to China, and so home by the Cape of Good Hope. He was absent two years and two months, and made his first voyage round the world.

He was afterwards transferred to the Constellation, which was ordered on the same cruise. This time he was gone three years and eight months, and made his second voyage round the world. He also served on board receiving ships; and from 1838 to 1841 was stationed at the Brooklyn Navy Yard. He afterwards cruised in the East Indies, and also saw much shore duty.

In 1846, in the 21st year of his lieutenancy, Bailey assumed for the first time an independent command.

We were then at war with Mexico, and he was ordered to the Lexington, which had been fitted up for the reception of troops and military stores, to be conveyed from New York to a certain point on the western coast of Mexico.

On the morning of sailing, writes one who accompanied him, the F company of artillery, a fine body of men, came on board at New York, under the command of Captain Tompkins. The first lieutenant was a tall, spare man, apparently about thirty years of age, with sandy hair and whiskers, and a reddish complexion. Grave in his demeanor, erect and soldierly in his bearing, he was especially noticeable for the faded and threadbare appearance of his uniform. That lieutenant is the present renowned Major-General Tecumseh Sherman. He was characterized at that time by entire devotion to his profession in all its details. His care for both the comfort and discipline of his men was constant and unvaried.

There was another lieutenant, short, rather "pony-built," yet lithe and active as a cat—his intellect bright and keen as his eyes—his movements indicative of nerve and spirit—his name was *Ord*—Edward O. C. Ord, now Brigadier General, United States Army.

A heavy-built, middle-sized man also came on board, with cases containing chronometers, transits, and other instruments. His black velvet trimmings and flat buttons, together with the single bar upon his shoulder-straps, indicated his rank as First Lieutenant of Engineers—Henry Wager Halleck is *his* name. His high forehead was then smooth, his complexion dark and ruddy, his black hair and ample beard were not yet frosted by time and thought. He was never idle at sea or in port, in fair weather or in storm, he was ever at work with book, chart, and pen—for he always read with a pen in his hand. Whether in Brazil, Chili, Mexico, or California, he examined everything with a military eye, taking copious notes and drawings, especially of fortifications and their approaches.

Twenty-six days off Cape Horn, in the winter season, in a succession of gales from the southwest, is not a pleasant experience, even with the best of company.

Here Captain Bailey exhibited conspicuously those high qualities which have ever secured for him in the Navy a reputation for capital seamanship, which implies every phase of judgment, coolness, perseverance, and pluck, with a ready command of resources under all circumstances. Always cheerful and urbane, while full of humor, he never overstepped the line of personal and official dignity, and gentlemanly courtesy.

The decks and lower rigging were encased in ice; the Lexington was deeply laden with heavy guns, shot, shell, &c., for the Army, and though she was what seamen call a comfortable ship, she was often very unsteady.

On one occasion, the whole wardroom mess was precipitated to leeward, by a sudden lurch into Sherman's stateroom—together with the table-crockery, Purser Wilson's iron money-chest and Doctor Abernethy's gold spectacles. All the gentlemen who composed that motley *pile* have since borne the rank of Major General in the Army, or Commander in the Navy. The proprietor of the premises, now Lieutenant-General Sherman, greatly enjoyed, while he participated in the general discomfiture. Storms off Cape Horn, as elsewhere, finally blow themselves out. Clear of " the Horn," the vessel soon reached

Valparaiso, where lay a part of the United States Pacific Squadron. The British and French Admirals were also there, each with a number of ships. Admiral Sir Thomas Seymour called on board the Lexington, and was, of course, received with military honors. He scrutinized closely the "material" of the United States Regular Army, which he saw in the guard of artillerymen in line on the quarter-deck. He certainly found a very good specimen, Lieutenant Sherman commanding that guard.

Here Bailey met Commodore Stockton, who, with his seamen and the mountaineers, under Fremont and his lieutenant, Kit. Carson, had secured possession of what was called Upper California, reinforced as they were, in good season, by General Kearney, who, soon after his arrival on the coast, after his long and perilous march across the continent, was received with his staff on board the Lexington, at San Pedro, and conveyed up the coast. Stoneman, since so distinguished as a cavalry General, was a lieutenant in General Kearney's command.

The Lexington was very actively employed on the western coast during the remainder of the Mexican war.

Positive instructions were given from Washington, that our forces in the Pacific should secure the possession of both Upper and Lower California.

Upon Lieutenant Bailey devolved the duty of conveying troops to the Peninsula of Lower California, and for a long time he remained at La Paz, covering the small force in occupancy of that point, under Lieutenant-Colonel Burton, United States Army, who so gallantly maintained his position when twice attacked by a superior force.

Bailey was fond of a joke, even a practical one, if

good. Many good ones are told of him, of which we give the following, from our pleasant correspondent, as an illustration:

The squadron was in the Bay of Monterey, and about to separate for the performance, by each ship, of its especial work. The general signal had been made from the flagship: "Get under weigh, and proceed as instructed."

The Lexington was by no means *rapid*, but though she never went over nine and a half knots, she could go—five—knots with almost anything, especially with a moderate breeze and smooth water, close hauled.

The wind was from the westward, and it was a dead beat out of the roadstead. The Lexington had an inshore berth, and was the last to get her anchors up; but it was a five-knot breeze, and it soon became evident that she was gaining on the frigates. As she made a stretch from Point Piños, it appeared that she was weathering the Savannah frigate, which was standing in on the other tack. Lieutenant Bailey was delighted at the prospect of astonishing the squadron by the extraordinary sailing qualities of the old Lexington, always noted as being a dull sailer.

It was rather a close thing, but with a fair show he could certainly weather the Savannah. He paced the quarter-deck in high glee, slapping his thigh at each turn with his right hand—as was his custom when pleased—and pleasantly showing his handsome teeth, while his eyes sparkled with fun. Just as he was passing about a cable's length ahead, and to windward of the Savannah, she put her helm down, and came up into the wind's eye, forging ahead. So around she must go, or fall foul.

"'Bout ship!"

"Ready! Ready!"

"Helm a-lee!"

"Raise tacks and sheets!"

Slap comes the frigate right across our bow, and away goes the flying jib-boom.

"Square the main-yard!"

"Box her around, Mr. Macomb!"

"Shift your helm for a stern-board, my man!"

Captain Mervine, on the Savannah's quarter-deck, shouted: "What do you mean, sir, by running into a first-class frigate?" Captain Bailey (*Sotto voce*): "Can't a first-class frigate keep out of the way?" (*Aloud*): "Aye, aye, sir; all aback it is—all clear, sir; no injury done, I hope—quite accidental, of course." (*Sotto voce*): "I accept your explanation." (*Aloud*): "Good-by, sir, I wish you a pleasant passage home."

It frequently happens that Naval officers are required promptly to *decide* very nice points of international law, and it would be fortunate for the country if every officer had as thorough a command of its principles and precedents, as is possessed by Admiral Bailey.

The Lexington was for some time engaged in blockading the Mexican port of San Blas, during which time, two of Her Britannic Majesty's frigates anchored in the roadstead for the purpose of receiving on board a large amount of Mexican dollars to be conveyed to England. It was then, and is perhaps now, the custom for British ships of war to carry bullion or coin for a consideration, which consideration, being a per centage upon the value of the treasure, was divided between certain officers of the ships conveying the same, and the Admiral commanding on the Station from whence the shipment is made.

A correspondence took place, between Captain Bailey and the senior British captain on this occasion, upon the question as to whether a ship engaged in carrying "freight" for a consideration, could be looked upon as a ship of war, and be treated as such by a blockading force, the commander of that force knowing her to be thus engaged. Whether it was not proper to "warn off" such vessels from the blockaded port—endorsing notice upon their "registers;" and, in default of their having registers like other mercantile ships, whether notice might not be endorsed upon the papers under which the ship might be sailing, whether a "sea-letter" pass, or a commission issued to the officer in command.

The correspondence was quite lengthy, and was as humorous as it was able, dignified, and courteous.

The vessels sailed without taking any "freight."

It was in 1848, says our correspondent, that peace with Mexico was concluded, and Henry A. Wise, now Captain, United States Navy, brought the first news direct from the City of Mexico. We landed him at San Blas when he started on his famous ride—during the armistice—and on his return he went up the Coast in the Lexington, at which time we had a peep at the neatly prepared manuscripts of the amusing book in which he so graphically relates his adventures upon that and other occasions.

It was about this time, I think, that the storeship Southampton arrived from Upper California, and John L. Worden, then passed Midshipman, and Acting Master of that ship, called on board the Lexington and exhibited to his friends some nuggets of gold which had been found in cutting a mill-race on Captain Sutter's farm near Sacramento.

Mr. Worden was then rather stout-built, somewhat fleshy, of a light, cheerful disposition, and was considered a very good officer. I should hardly have recognized him in the wiry, muscular, and scarred veteran that he is to-day, carrying upon his face the marks of the first engagement ever fought between iron-clads.

Lieutenant Bailey now received advice of his long-delayed promotion, and returned to his home by the way of the Isthmus of Panama.

During the Mexican war, one of Bailey's duties was the blockading of San Blas—one of the two only ports of entry left open to Mexico. In doing this, he warned all neutrals that the intermediate ports between here and Manzanilla were also blockaded, and the landing of any goods in them would subject such vessels and cargoes to capture and confiscation. This order brought a letter from the British Consul, Wm. Forbes, stationed at Tepic, who protested against the order, as an attempt at paper blockade, without sufficient force—which blockade had been regarded as illegal by American authorities, and also by Lord Stowell. Bailey replied that

"A state of war gives a neutral no rights, which he did not previously possess in time of peace.

"Because, if the belligerent attempts to relieve himself of the pressure of a blockade by opening new ports, he does so in consequence of the pressure of the arms of his enemy, and the neutral, by intervening to relieve that pressure, interferes with the war, to the disadvantage of the other belligerent—which interference the latter cannot tolerate."

He landed four officers and thirty-seven men from the Lexington and a bark, capturing the upper and lower towns of San Blas—spiking guns in the abandoned fort—and brought off two field pieces. He received a few days after a Mexican newspaper, stating that two North American vessels of war had entered the port of San Blas and landed sixteen hundred men, and that a division of five hundred cavalry, stationed in the neighborhood, had, in view of such overwhelming force, retreated to the interior.

From 1853 to '55, Captain Bailey commanded the U. S. ship St. Mary, cruising in the Pacific, and visited most of the prominent seaports, including many of the islands.

At the request of the president of Nicaragua, he visited the capital to confer with him and the U. S. minister, respecting the threatened invasion of the renowned fillibuster, Walker. He was also at Honolulu while important negotiations were being had with Kamehameha III., which however were suddenly terminated by the death of that monarch.

He afterwards visited the Marquesas, Society Islands, Navigator's and Fejee Islands, and at these last two places greatly promoted the interests of American citizens, by seeing that justice was administered—he holding frequent courts, before which many criminals were brought, and after due trial properly and summarily punished.

At Apia, the high chief becoming refractory, and refusing to produce one of his subjects, accused of stealing from an American vessel, every preparation was made for an attack upon the town, and for his arrest, when his unconditional surrender and appearance on board the "St. Mary" prevented a collision.

At the Fejee Islands, Capt. Bailey, finding that Captain Boutwell, of the "John Adams," had, by his injudicious treatment of the natives, created some ill feeling, very maturely considered the matter, and gave such orders to Captain Boutwell as were calculated to promote a more thorough and impartial administration of justice.

Capt. Bailey afterwards visited the principal ports of Chili, Peru, and Ecuador, holding everywhere the most agreeable relations with the chief authorities of each country.

He arrived at Panama after the frightful massacre of April 15, 1856, and here displayed, in a very signal manner, great coolness and good judgment in allaying the excitement existing among his own countrymen.

It would have been an easy matter for him to have bombarded Panama, thereby taking prompt satisfaction for the outrages committed. But forty-eight miles of railroad from thence to Aspinwall, affording the only means of transit between California and the Atlantic states, were entirely unprotected, and would have therefore been exposed to the attacks of an irritated and revengeful populace; he accordingly very wisely refrained, and left to the general government the administration of the proper remedies. He remained, however, for nearly a year at Panama, vigilantly looking after and promoting American interests.

His correspondence with the governor, Don F. de Fabrega, was short and spicy. He first asked an explanation of the outrages committed on American citizens and property. Two or three letters passed, but the governor, with customary Spanish duplicity and pomposity, evading the issue, Bailey closed the correspondence with the following direct and curt letter, which his "Excellency" could ponder on at his leisure:

UNITED STATES SLOOP ST. MARY'S,
PANAMA, *April 25th*, 1856.

His Excellency Don Francisco de Fabrega,
Acting Governor, &c., of Panama.

SIR: I have the honor to acknowledge the receipt of your replies to my communications of the 23d and 24th insts. Apart from the announcement of the restoration to the owners of the cannon and arms illegally taken from the steamer Taboga, I must confess that they afford me little satisfaction. I had expected, when asking for information as to the causes of the frightful occurrences of the 15th inst., that, apart from the immediate origin of the tumult, you would have deemed it due to yourself, as the Chief Magistrate of this community, to state why and wherefore you undertook the fearful responsibility of ordering your police to fire upon my countrymen, women and children, and to state what steps you had taken to punish the guilty, and restore the plunder. Ten days have elapsed since the catastrophe, and I have yet to learn that a single criminal has been arrested, or that any portion of the immense amount of valuables taken from the passengers and railroad company, has been restored. I have yet to learn that your high " conscientious views of duty, and understanding well the great interests which are bound up in this line of universal transit "—extended any further than to order an indiscriminate massacre of the passengers over this transit. I have yet to learn, that when a riot or collision shall here take place between foreigners, on the one side, and natives on the other, that you recognize any higher obligation on your part than to protect and assist the latter, and to disarm, murder, maltreat, and plunder the former.

Is it possible that your Excellency recognizes but one party to a riot? that you shelter yourself under the philosophic assurance, that the fearful catastrophe of the 15th inst. was the result of "*elementas tan heterogeneous como los que forman nuestra poblacion i la emegracion Californiana?*" The deduction, I regret to state, affords me little assurance of the safety of the transit for the future, unless your Excellency shall devise some more speedy and efficacious method for rendering these unfortunate "elements" less "heterogeneous" hereafter. The police who took part in this terrible tragedy now guard the lives and property of the transit passengers. The "*Jendarmena*" who, with the same philosophy as your Excellency, deemed it best, in the late emergency, to destroy the foreign "element," are the reliable means of protection which your Excellency will furnish us to any extent for the future, and it, no doubt, should be a source of gratifiction, that they have, since the 10th inst., permitted the passengers and treasure of the steamers "Uncle Sam" and "Golden Age," to make the transit without murdering the one, or plundering the other. I am, with the force under my command, but from eight to ten days removed from communication with my Government, and am, therefore, bound to submit to their judgment the manner in which the fearful accountability that you have incurred shall be investigated, and to their discretion the indemnity that shall be demanded for the past and security for the future: meanwhile, I shall do all in my power to avert any danger that may occur to the transit passengers, from whatever quarter it may come, and under every emergency. In directing my first communication to your Excellency, I had no desire to listen to apologies for certain parties or certain acts, but an earnest wish to know what you did towards punishing the parties concerned in this frightful atrocity. I wanted not sophistry but action; the names of the criminals arrested—the officers dismissed—and some allusion to plunder restored. That I have not been thus gratified, I have no reason to doubt, arises from the fact that you deem the origin of the affair a sufficient justification for its frightful conclusion.

I shall here take my leave of your Excellency as a *correspondent*, and shall have the honor to submit your two communications to my Government, presuming that they will not be more satisfactory to them than to me.

I am respectfully, sir,

Your obedient servant,

(Signed,) T. BAILEY,

Commander U. S. N.

At the breaking out of the rebellion, he was in the latter part of 1861 ordered to the steamer Colorado, blockading Pensacola, and took part in the subsequent bombardment of the fortifications. After a night reconnoissance he sent a boat expedition to cut out the privateer Judah. The vessel was destroyed, and the battery on shore spiked. The three lieutenants commanding the boats, Russel, Blake, and Sproston, received the highest commendation for their gallantry.

He was subsequently sent to the passes of the Mississippi, second in command under Farragut in the contemplated movement against New Orleans.

Although the general plan of attack had been determined on, Farragut called a council of war just before it occurred, in which Captain Bailey suggested that an attack in the daytime would draw on them the fire of the enemy the moment they came in sight—also, that the advance in double lines would expose the vessels to get fouled. It will be seen that these ideas received the approval of the commander-in-chief.

The way in which Bailey happened to lead his division of eight vessels in the little Cayuga is not generally known. The Colorado was a heavy vessel and one much better calculated to withstand the horrible fire of the batteries than this little gunboat. But it was found impossible to get her over the bar, and so he brought up his men, determined to lead the fleet in the passage of the batteries if he did it in his launch. He was at the time suffering under a painful disease, and the surgeon reported that—

His health would not permit him to take part in the fight. For this act of kindness, he was anything but grateful, and fumed and swore he was not sick, and would go. But the surgeon was firm in the performance of his duty, and asked for a "Medical Survey" upon him, which was ordered in due form.

The "Board" assembled in his cabin, examined his case with great care, retired, talked it over, and made out a written report of his case, closing with the opinion that it would be very dangerous for him to take part in the coming fight, and finally recommended that he should remain quiet, and that severe medical treatment be applied as soon as practicable.

The Board returned to the cabin, (where were assembled Admiral Farragut and other officers, awaiting the result of the examination,) and communicated in due form the result of their consultation.

All remained quiet, waiting to see what effect it had upon "Old Bailey," expecting to see him fume and rage at being prevented from taking part in giving those "d——d rebels a lesson which they would not soon forget." But instead of this, he quietly rose, and in the most dignified manner, said:

"Admiral, I am very much obliged to the gentlemen, and am very grateful to them for their solicitude in regard to my health, for their attention to my case and their kind and considerate recommendation; but, by ——, *I'll lead your fleet up the river, if I burst my boiler.*"

Farragut gave him a division and assigned him the sloop-of-war "Oneida," to carry his flag. The latter had not been long on board when certain matters occurred, which need not now be discussed, but which rendered it undesirable for Bailey to remain on that ship. Lieutenant-commanding Harrison having dined on the "Oneida" on that day, and seeing, in this hitch, a chance for himself, his gunboat having been asigned a place in the rear, he offered Bailey the "Cayuga" and urged him to lead up in her. He promptly accepted the offer, and before sunset was aboard the little vessel, bag and baggage. Now this was an act of the purest patriotism and most unselfish courage; it was giving up, voluntarily, a new, strong, and fast ship (and in this instance speed was of the utmost moment) for a vessel of trifling force and speed, scarcely sufficient to stem the current of the Mississippi; but it was done to prevent agitation, and to produce harmony among the commanders of the fleet, on the eve of a great and uncertain conflict.

The signal for attack was made at 2 A. M., on the morning of the 24th April, 1862. There was too much anxiety on board for sleep; part of the night was spent in steaming up and down the division, in order that Bailey might satisfy himself that nothing was amiss—the river was continually lighted by fire-rafts, as they came down with the current, snapping and cracking with their intense heat—great fires were built at the barrier chains, making the scene and the hour one never to be forgotten. The signal lights had scarcely reached the peak of the Hartford before the "Cayuga" had her anchor atrip, and was heading up stream. The heavier ships were longer in securing their anchors. Much anxiety was felt as to the precise locality of the opening that had been made in the barrier; he, however, steered fairly into it, and just then his vessel was discovered, and the forts opened. The "Cayuga" was now put upon her speed, not much at best, and pointed close under the guns of San Philip, so as to have the shot strike her rigging. Emerging from the dense smoke that filled the river between the forts, Bailey encountered a new, and a most unexpected enemy, nothing less than a flotilla of gunboats, having among them the "Louisiana" and "Manassas," with iron armor. The Cayuga was quite unsupported at this time, and things wore an anxious look. It was now that Captain Bailey exhibited that quiet courage and calm confidence that told so finely on the crew. He could look in no direction without seeing an enemy close aboard. The "Gov. Moore," the best-fought ship of the enemy, was bearing down on his starboard bow, and to her Harrison gave most of his attention. At the same moment a gunboat approached from nearly astern, with the evident intention of ramming. Captain Bailey called to Harrison to "send aft the boarders." The latter replied: "I have no men to spare just now, you must take care of that end of the vessel." With that, Bailey stepped on the arm-chest, and singing out "Surrender, you fool, or I'll blow you out of water!" he opened with his revolver. Almost immediately the reply came back, "Don't shoot! we surrender." "Then stick your d—d nose in the mud until I take possession." The vessel sheered off, ran ashore, and was soon in flames. About the same time a fearful discharge of grape was delivered from the large dahlgren into the "Gov. Moore," raking her from stem to stern, killing many of her men, and causing her to sheer off. Two other vessels of the rebel flotilla were forced to surrender and run on shore before Bailey knew that any other of our ships had succeeded in coming through the fire of the forts—then came the "Varuna" into action, followed in quick succession by the fleet. This was the last effort of the rebels. The victory was complete. "You can fancy the scene, now," says our correspondent, "as the bright day broke over the river, disclosing fourteen vessels of our fleet above the forts, gaily bedecked with the "old flags," while eleven burning hulls were all that remained of the rebel flotilla." As soon as objects on shore were visible Camp Lovell was discovered, having the Chalmette regiment in tents, commanded by Col. Szymanski. Anchoring in front of the camp, and ordering the Colonel on board, Captain Bailey received the surrender of the regiment, He could not but smile at the idea of a regiment on shore captured by a gunboat. He had now no specific orders; but knowing New Orleans to be the objective point, he determined, if possible, to be first before the city. Steaming at full speed, he found himself next day, suddenly, in a tremendous cross fire; this came from the Chalmette batteries, situated on either bank of the river. The Cayuga endured this fire until Farragut could come up and divert it to his own ship. The little gunboat suffered severely here, but her bow was never turned *down stream.*

In speaking of the passage of these latter forts, Farragut says, "Captain Bailey was still far in advance, not having noticed my signal for close order." We rather suspect the gallant captain did not look in the direction where he *could* see it. His eyes were turned up stream towards New Orleans. N. B. Harrison, the lieutenant commanding the Cayuga, than whom a cooler, braver, and more gallant officer never trod the deck of a battle-ship, reported that his vessel was struck *forty-two times*, and that both her masts were so cut up as to be unfit for farther service. Strange as it may appear, only six of his crew were wounded.

The river was now clear to New Orleans; and at one o'clock, on the 25th, the fleet came to anchor in front of the city. The rain was coming down in torrents; but the crowd on shore was dense and turbulent, and blind with futile passion. Directly, a boat was seen to put off from the flagship, and swept towards the shore, impelled by the strong arms of well-dressed sailors. In the stern sat Captain Bailey, with his lieutenant, Perkins, by his side, and Acting-Master Morton, in charge of the boat. He was on his way to demand the surrender of the city. As he approached the levee, the drenched and waiting crowd grew more excited, and deafening cheers were sent up for Jeff. Davis, and groans uttered for Lincoln and the fleet. Now and then a sudden eddy would be seen in some portion of the black, dark mass, as a man was collared or shoved about, who dared to express a Union feeling. Bailey saw at a glance that it was not a pleasant reception that awaited him; but he stepped calmly and firmly ashore, and said he wished to see the mayor of the city. A few came forward, and offered to conduct him. As the little handful moved off, the crowd surged after them, yelling and shouting like demons. A single word, and Bailey and his lieutenant would become the victims of its fury; but they showed no alarm, and reached the City Hall in safety, when the passions of the crowd broke forth. At one time it seemed that they would be set upon by the most infuriated; but some well-dressed citizens, who were aware of the wholesale destruction of the city that would follow such an act, interfered.

Bailey, on being presented to the mayor, and exchanging salutations, said: "I have been sent by Captain Farragut, commanding the United States fleet, to demand the surrender of the city, and the elevation of the flag of the United States over the Custom-House, Mint, Post-Office, and City Hall."

The mayor, Munroe, was in company with Pierre Soulé, and was evidently prompted by him as to questions and replies. Among other things, the mayor wished to know what credentials Bailey had from Flag-Officer Farragut. He replied that he was *second in command*, had led the fleet by the forts, had forced the surrender of three gunboats, and captured the Chalmette regiment;

and as such needed no other credentials—which they appeared to consider sufficient.

Munroe replied that he was not a military man, and had no authority to surrender the place, but that he would send for General Lovell, the military commander, who was out of the city. While the messenger was gone, Bailey engaged in free conversation with those in the mayor's office, interrupted now and then by the yells of the crowd surging to and fro in the pouring rain without. Much property had been destroyed in the city after the news of the passage of the forts was received, and Bailey expressed his regret that it had taken place. The Mayor rudely replied that the property was their own, and its destruction concerned nobody but themselves. Bailey good-humoredly said that such a course looked to him very much like a man biting off his nose to spite his face.

The Mayor did not relish the joke, and grew more disagreeable.

Soon cheers from without heralded the arrival of Lovell, and the next moment he entered the room, and announced his name and rank. He then shook hands with Bailey, who renewed the demand he had a short time before made to the Mayor. To this Lovell replied, that he would not surrender the city; that he intended to fight on land as long as he could; and if they wished to shell the city, filled with women and children, they might do it. Bailey courteously replied, that nothing was farther from Captain Farragut's intentions than shelling the city; that he regretted the destruction of property that had already occurred. To which Lovell answered, with much unnecessary hauteur, that it was done by his own orders. Lovell leaving the affairs of the city in the hands of the civil authorities, Bailey determined to return, and report the situation of matters to Farragut. But as he was about to leave, he turned to General Lovell, and said that he had visited many uncivilized places, such as the South Sea and Fejee Islands—and found even among the savages a decent respect for a herald and flag of truce, which are regarded by all civilized nations as sacred, but that he had been insulted every step of the way from his boat by an unwashed mob. He therefore demanded a safe conduct to his boat. A carriage was then drawn up at a rear door of the City Hall, and he was conducted to it with his aid, Lieutenant Perkins, by two officers, and driven through certain streets entirely depopulated, their inhabitants having thronged to what they supposed would be the scene of his assassination on the route by which he had come.

He arrived without molestation at the landing, where a great crowd was assembled—but the officers, drawing their swords, made way for him, when he shook hands with them and departed.

Bailey was now sent home with despatches to the Government, and on arriving at Fortress Monroe forwarded the following telegraph to the Secretary of War: "I have the honor to announce that, in the providence of God, which smiles upon a just cause, the squadron under Flag Officer Farragut has been vouchsafed a glorious victory and triumph in the capture of New Orleans, Forts Jackson, St. Philip, Lexington, and Pike, the batteries above and below New Orleans, as well as the total destruction of the enemy's gunboats, steam-rams, floating batteries (iron-clad), fire-rafts, obstruction booms, and chains. The enemy with their own hands destroyed from eight to ten millions of cotton and shipping. Our loss is thirty-six killed, and one hundred and twenty-three wounded. The enemy lost from one thousand to fifteen hundred, besides several hundred prisoners. The way is clear, and the rebel defenses destroyed from the Gulf to Baton Rouge, and probably to Memphis. Our flag waves triumphantly over them all. I am bearer of despatches. THEODORUS BAILEY."

The important part that Captain Bailey took in the capture of New Orleans clearly entitled him to receive from the Navy Department some signal recognition of its sense of the value of his services, and, in the fall of 1862, Acting Rear-Admiral Lardner, commanding Eastern Gulf Blockading Squadron, suffering greatly from the weakening effects of an attack of yellow fever, having applied to the Navy Department to be relieved from duty on that station, and ordered North, Commodore Bailey was at once directed to assume the command, and in November, 1862, proceeded to Key West.

The limits of the command comprised a stretch of sea-coast extending nearly a thousand miles, embracing the entire Peninsula of Florida, from Mosquito Inlet on the eastern coast, to St. Andrew's Bay on the western. The headquarters of the squadron were at the important island of Key West—the key of the Gulf of Mexico. Unfortunately, this squadron was the only one, except the West India squadron, that did not contain within its limits some stronghold to be captured. The North Atlantic squadron had its Fort Fisher—the South Atlantic its Sumter—the West Gulf squadron its Fort Morgan—but the East Gulf squadron afforded no sufficient scope for the restless courage that was so distinguishing a trait in the character of its commander-in-chief.

Bailey's orders were to blockade the Florida coast, and

as there was no more active work at hand, he set himself to do this thoroughly. The means at his disposal he found very inadequate to the work, for the squadron had been greatly thinned out by the yellow fever, and a number of the vessels infected with the contagion had been ordered North by Admiral Lardner. The Navy Department found it impossible at that time to supply their places with others, the pressure upon them for vessels being so great for other squadrons, and the material from which to supply this demand, so limited.

In this emergency, finding it useless to apply to the Government for aid, Admiral Bailey set zealously to work to make additions to his force from such materials as he could command. As the Department could not supply him with vessels, he proposed to supply himself. The blockade-running from the Florida coast was, at this time, carried on mostly by swift-sailing schooners that slipped quietly out of the creeks and rivers, under cover of the night, and made for the coast of Cuba. Admiral Bailey determined to make this class of vessels useful, and accordingly, as soon as he caught a particularly fast one, instead of allowing it to be sold at auction, and bought in by the blockade-runners, to be again put upon the contraband line, he took it for the use of the Government at an appraisement, and having sent carbines, cutlasses, a howitzer, and a sufficient number of "blue-jackets" aboard, the American flag was run up at the peak, and the little craft sailed off to astonish her old allies by appearing in her entirely new and unexpected character of a United States vessel. These tenders, for they were all attached to one or another of the larger vessels of the squadron, soon became a distinguishing feature of the Eastern Gulf squadron, and a terror to all the contrabandists along the coast. It was not long before a complete cordon of these vigilant little sentinels was formed, stretching along the entire coast, the cruising-ground of one dove-tailing on to that of the next, and they became the heroes of many bold adventures. Their light draft of water enabled them to run into the creeks and inlets that mark the Florida coast, and they would frequently pounce down upon a nest of blockade-runners,—loading their vessel with cotton up some quiet river, and almost before the latter could recover from their astonishment at the apparition of the unwelcome "Yankees," their vessel would be towed out to sea and under sail for Key West, with a prize crew on board.

Admiral Bailey, by his prompt recognition of every act of gallantry, and of every important service on the part of his officers and men, soon imparted a portion of his own energy to his squadron. There was no more "loafing" on the blockade. It was understood that the vessels were stationed to make captures, and not for fishing purposes, and if a vessel set to guard a particular passage allowed the blockade-runners to slip in and out, the commanding officer was held responsible at headquarters for his negligence; and if, on the other hand, he showed constant vigilance and attention to duty, his good conduct did not fail to receive notice, and to be reported with commendation to the Department at Washington. The vessels of the fleet were likewise, from time to time, personally visited by the commander-in-chief, and his able and vigilant Chief-of-Staff, Commander Temple, and thoroughly inspected. Their efficiency in drill at the great guns and in small arms, and at fire quarters was carefully noted, and every commanding-officer felt that the exact *status* of himself and his ship's company was known and kept in mind at headquarters. In fact, it is not too much to say that the discipline of this squadron was so perfect that the Department highly complimented Bailey, saying: "It was so well governed that it gave them no trouble—it took care of itself." It certainly did its work thoroughly. The coast of Florida was hermetically sealed, and vessels were spared to cruise at large in the Gulf, and intercept the blockade-runners that plied regularly between Mobile and Havana.

Few persons are aware what a very essential part the blockading vessels performed in crippling and dispiriting the enemy. Their work was noiseless, and attracted but little of the public attention; but the pressure brought to bear upon the South was tremendous, and grew every month more intolerable. It was not so much that the rebels were put to the greatest individual discomfort and inconvenience—that indeed was a result, but not the aim or intention of the blockade. The principal pressure was felt where it was intended that it should be—in their military movements—in their armies. They could not purchase military supplies abroad, and they had no adequate means of manufacturing them at home. Their troops were therefore ill-equipped, poorly shod, poorly clothed, and destitute of many of the articles that are necessary to the efficiency of armies in the field.

In 1863, the limits of the East Gulf Squadron were increased by the addition to its jurisdiction of an important part of what had been the cruising-ground of the West India, or Flying Squadron; to wit: the Bahama Banks. The difficulty of communicating by boats with the Admiral, where vessels were lying often at a distance of two miles from the flagship, became so great, that in the spring of this year headquarters were moved ashore, and the flagship was sent to cruise in the Gulf. By this change, the commander-in-chief became rapidly accessible to all those under his command. Whether it was that twenty-odd years on "blue water" had had its effect upon him, or whether Nature in the beginning had implanted in him a kindly heart, certain it was that the Admiral possessed all of those qualities of a large-hearted and open-handed nature that belong traditionally to the sailor. He was the very embodiment of the poetic idea of a son of Neptune, and every human being who crossed the threshold of the great rooms at which headquarters were now located, was sure to find there a hearty, cheerful welcome—except one class, the enemies of his country. When any of the members of his staff heard from their adjoining apartments an unusual noise and declamation, ending with calls for "Orderly," they were pretty certain that one of this class was about being marched out from the indignant presence of Bailey, at the double-quick, and it was usually some time before the waters fairly subsided after one of these storms. The devotion of a sailor to the flag he has served for nearly half a century, has in it an ardor that landsmen fail to appreciate. An amusing instance of the Admiral's dislike of the sympathizers with secession, occurred shortly after the headquarters were moved on shore. It happened that the principal church at Key West was the Episcopal, and that, though the rector was loyal, a majority of the vestry were secessionists, who reëlected themselves to office year after year. This state of things coming to the Admiral's knowledge at the time that the annual election for vestrymen occurred, he resolved to "purge the temple," and, summoning his officers (it being a free church, all who attended there were entitled to vote), he marched up to the annual meeting, on the first Monday after Easter, to the great consternation of the close corporation, who had assembled to vote each other in. As a matter of course, a heavy "Union" vote was cast, and for that year, at least, the church was officered by loyal men, from rector to sexton. The Admiral used laughingly, after this incident, to proclaim himself ex-officio "Bishop of that Diocese."

Though the Admiral and his staff were always on duty, and business was transacted at any hour, from eight in the morning till midnight, there was no lack of mirth at headquarters, and the Admiral's hospitality became so well known through the service, that along the whole coast, from the Potomac to the Rio Grande, there was no naval station visited with more pleasure by officers than that at Key West. As that post lay in the direct track of all vessels bound to the West Gulf Squadron, or from that squadron North, and as the vessels of the West India Squadron were accustomed to put into Key West for provisions and their mails, it often happened that from twelve to fifteen men-of-war were in harbor at the same time. On these occasions, the table of the Admiral's mess was stretched to its largest capacity, and the headquarters became a scene of great animation. In the summer of 1864, however, all this was changed, for the port was again visited by that scourge, the yellow fever. The epidemic commenced in June, and extended from vessel to vessel, and what had shortly before been a scene of bustle, activity, and mirth, became now one of desolation and mourning. A few hours was sufficient to hurry the victims from a state of apparently perfect health to the grave. The vessels were sent North as fast as the infection appeared upon them, and before long the dreaded port of Key West was itself as completely blockaded by the invisible but fearful forces of Yellow Jack, as was any port along the coast by the most vigilant of our cruisers. For weeks there was scarcely any communication with the outer world. No vessel was bold enough to venture in, and there were none to venture out. In the mean time, those on the island sickened, and very many died. The Admiral, after a severe illness, rallied, and, thanks to a fine constitution, recovered. After the abatement of the fever, the Department thought it due to his long service in a sickly climate, to transfer him to a healthier station, and accordingly, in the fall of the same year, he was ordered to the command of the Navy Yard at Portsmouth, New Hampshire.

There is one anecdote told of the Admiral, while engaged in the blockade, which not only illustrates his character, always noble and incorruptible, but explains satisfactorily how so many of our officers, in the South and Southwest, got rich during the war. One day the Admiral received a letter from a merchant in Havana, stating that he desired a personal interview with him, as he had an important communication to make. Not long after, the former, having occasion to send a vessel to Havana, directed the commanding officer to call on the merchant and learn what the important communication was. It turned out to be a proposal to him that he should so arrange his squadron as to allow a vessel to be run into port with contraband goods, the Admiral to receive for so doing forty thousand dollars a trip for six trips, and then have vessel, cargo, and all. The money was to be paid in gold, which then being at $2.50

would have netted the Admiral the nice little sum of about a million of dollars. He could have carried out this nefarious scheme without being detected, with the utmost ease. To most men such a sum of money would seem a large bribe, but to the Admiral a five-dollar bill would have been just as great a temptation. It is needless to say that he took no notice of the proposal, but it would have fared hard with the traitorous merchant, if he had fallen into his clutches. That many officers on land were not superior to much smaller bribes, the military records furnish, alas! too much evidence.

The best proof of the efficiency of the blockade during the period that the Eastern Gulf squadron was under Admiral Bailey's command, is found in the number of prizes captured. With a fleet of some thirty vessels, of which not more than six were steamers in any way fit for cruising, he captured in the course of a little more than a year and a half, more than a hundred and fifty blockade runners of all rates and sizes, from sloops to large and heavily loaded Mississippi steamers. In proportion to the time and the number of vessels employed, this is a larger capture list than is exhibited by any other squadron.

Admiral Bailey remains at present the commandant of the Portsmouth station, although by a law of Congress he is, from his age and length of service, placed on the retired list.

The character of Admiral Bailey is clearly developed in the foregoing sketch. To see him dispensing hospitality at his table, and keeping his guests often in a roar of laughter, one would hardly know him for the same man when leading his line into battle. On the deck of his ship, amid the raining balls of the enemy, he is altogether another being. Stern and inflexible, his orders ring sharply out, and all the lineaments of his kindly countenance reveal the great commander and the fearless man. The confusion and carnage of battle seem to quicken his perceptions, and he is never so much at home as when, amid the thunder of his own broadsides, he presses where the boldest hold their breath. Of great energy, untiring perseverance, quick perceptions—fearless in action, and wise in counsel, he has won a place in the foremost rank of those naval heroes who are at once the pride and glory of the land.

CHAPTER XII.

REAR-ADMIRAL CHARLES HENRY DAVIS.

SCIENTIFIC ATTAINMENTS IN THE NAVAL PROFESSION.—BIRTH AND PARENTAGE OF DAVIS.—HIS EARLY EDUCATION.—ENTERS THE NAVY.—THREE YEARS' CRUISE IN THE PACIFIC OCEAN.—VISITS ITS REMOTE ISLANDS.—ON HIS RETURN RECEIVES HIS WARRANT AND CRUISES IN THE WEST INDIES.—IN THE MEDITERRANEAN.—MADE LIEUTENANT.—ENTERS ON THE STUDY OF THE MODERN LANGUAGES.—FOURTH CRUISE IN THE PACIFIC.—SAILS FOR ST. PETERSBURG.—APPOINTED TO THE COAST SURVEY.—HIS SURVEYS, INVESTIGATIONS, ETC.—HIS REPORTS AND MEMOIRS.—HIS MARRIAGE.—SUPERINTENDS THE PREPARATION OF THE AMERICAN EPHEMERIS AND NAUTICAL ALMANAC.—HIS TRANSLATIONS AND PUBLICATIONS.—ONCE MORE AFLOAT.—RECEIVES THE CAPITULATION OF THE FILIBUSTER WALKER.—SHORE DUTY.—BREAKING OUT OF THE REBELLION.—DAVIS' SERVICES AT WASHINGTON.—PLACED ON A COMMISSION TO INVESTIGATE THE SUBJECT OF ARMORED SHIPS.—DUPONT'S CHIEF OF STAFF IN THE PORT ROYAL EXPEDITION.—HIS GREAT SERVICES.—COMMANDS THE STONE FLEET SUNK IN CHARLESTON HARBOR.—SENT UP THE LITTLE TYBEE.—ENGAGES TATNALL'S FLEET.—RELIEVES FOOTE IN COMMAND OF THE MISSISSIPPI FLOTILLA.—COMBAT OF FORT PILLOW.—DESTROYS THE REBEL FLEET OFF MEMPHIS.—BATTERY OF ST. CHARLES CAPTURED.—DAVIS' DESPATCH.—BEFORE VICKSBURG.—AFTER SERVICES.—RECALLED TO WASHINGTON.—RECEIVES THE THANKS OF CONGRESS, AND MADE REAR-ADMIRAL.—CHIEF OF BUREAU OF NAVIGATION.—SUPERINTENDENT OF NATIONAL OBSERVATORY, ETC.

THE naval profession is not favorable to strict scientific pursuits. Its duties are active and practical, requiring the application rather than the investigation of the principles of science. It is rare that we find the practical accomplished sailor and the abstruse scientific man combined. It is only now and then, in any department of life, that the deep thinker and the effective worker are united in one person. Admiral Davis, however, is one of these men,—combining rare scientific ability with great practical skill and power. But scientific attainments, largeness of view, and thorough knowledge of all the branches and details of the naval profession, being rarer than those qualifications which will make a good commander afloat, they are needed at the centre of influence to guide, direct, and perfect. Hence the man possessing them often performs a greater service to his country than if he won a battle. Yet, that service is wholly unappreciated by the popular mind. So far as mere fame is concerned, his rare endowments are a misfortune to him.

CHARLES HENRY DAVIS was born in Boston, Massachusetts, January 10, 1807. His father was the late Hon. Daniel Davis, for thirty-two years Solicitor-General of that State, and the son of the Hon. Daniel Davis of Barnstable, who was a representative of his town in the Provincial Congress of Massachusetts, during the Revolutionary War, and subsequently Judge of Probate, and Chief Justice of the Court of Common Pleas of his county.

His mother was the daughter of Constant Freeman, Esq., a merchant of Boston; and among her brothers were Colonel Constant Freeman, of the Revolutionary Army, and Rev. James Freeman, of King's Chapel, Boston. Thus on both sides he came of good Revolutionary stock. He received his early education at the Boston Latin School, and entered Harvard College in 1821; but remained there less than two years.

In 1841, he received from the University the degrees

of Bachelor and Master of Arts, and his name may be found in the list of his class of 1825, in the triennial catalogue.

After leaving college, he was appointed an acting midshipman in the United States Navy, by President Monroe, on the 12th August, 1823, being then sixteen years of age, and received in the following October orders to join the frigate "United States," in which vessel he sailed on a cruise of three years and a half in the Pacific Ocean, in the squadron of Commodore Hull. During the cruise, he became one of the officers of the schooner Dolphin, commanded by the late Captain John C. Percival, on the somewhat famous expedition into the remote, and, at that time, little known seas of the Western Pacific, in pursuit of the mutineers of the whaleship Globe. The Marquesas and adjoining group of islands were then almost *terra incognita* to the civilized world, and revealed an entirely new phase of life to the young midshipman.

On his return Acting Midshipman Davis received his warrant, and was ordered to the Erie, Commodore Turner, to do duty in the West Indies. After a year's service in these waters, he again returned and passed his examination for lieutenant; and, on this occasion, received a very handsome letter of approbation from his first commanding officer, Commodore Hull.

In 1829, a few months later, Mr. Davis joined the Ontario, sloop of war, Captain Thomas H. Stevens, as Master, and sailed for the Mediterranean in the squadron of Commodore Biddle. While on board the Ontario, he entered upon the study of the modern languages, especially French and Spanish; and began a life-long friendship with his shipmate, the late Rear-Admiral (then Lieutenant) S. F. Dupont. His commission as lieutenant was received during this his third cruise, and dated March, 1831. His fourth cruise was again in the Pacific, in the Vincennes, the flagship of Commodore Wadsworth. It was on this vessel that Lieutenant Davis began those mathematical studies which have since given him such distinction in the scientific world. On this cruise he was employed as interpreter between Commodore Wadsworth and the authorities of the State of Ecuador, which had sought the aid of the former in settling the embarrassments of a civil war then raging. He returned to the United States in command of the whaleship Vermont, her captain having been killed by a mutineer. In October, 1836, two years and a half after his return from the Pacific, he was ordered to report for duty to the late Commodore Nicholson, and in the following year sailed in the razee frigate Independence, the Commodore's flagship, for St. Petersburg, carrying Mr. Dallas, the American Minister to the Imperial Court of Russia. While the Independence was in the harbor of Cronstadt, she was visited by the Czar, Nicholas I., who sought to improve his own navy by studying the finest specimens of foreign naval architecture. The Independence, after leaving St. Petersburg, proceeded to her own station, the Brazilian, where she cruised for two years.

On his return to the United States from this fifth cruise, Lieutenant Davis, at the age of thirty-three, had completed seventeen years of service in the Navy, and during more than twelve years of that time, had been on active duty at sea. His commanding officer on every cruise had been a hero of the war of 1812. The names of Hull, Turner, Stevens, Biddle, Wadsworth, and Nicholson, are inseparably associated with the exploits of our early naval history; and, as before remarked of other commanders, these associations must have had a strong effect upon the character and patriotism of Davis.

After an interval of repose, Lieutenant Davis, in 1842, was appointed to the United States Coast Survey, then under the superintendence of Mr. Hassler; and he continued on that work under his successor, Mr. Bache, until 1849. The principal investigations which he conducted for seven years in this service, in the command of a Coast Survey vessel, belong more especially to the department of science, and can only be briefly enumerated as follows: 1. Ascertaining the direction, &c., of currents in New York Bay and vicinity, and in the entrances of New York harbor. 2. Hydrographic and physical examination of the Gulf Stream. 3. Surveys and soundings off Martha's Vineyard and Nantucket Islands, resulting in the discovery of shoals and banks in the direct line of navigation between New York and Europe, of which mariners had been hitherto entirely ignorant, numerous losses having thereby occurred; and in the discovery of the rock on Cash's Ledge, which had been long sought for by that eminent British surveyor and hydrographer, Admiral Owen. 4. A memoir communicated to the American Academy in 1848 on the "Geological Action of the Tidal and other Currents of the Ocean"—the result of most careful observations of the formation of shoals, especially on the Nantucket coast; and a second memoir, on the "Law of Deposit of the Flood-tide," published in the Smithsonian *Contributions* in 1851. During his services on the Coast Survey, Lieutenant Davis commenced those investigations into the laws of engineering in tidal harbors, the fruits of which are shown in the numerous reports upon the great harbors of the United States, written by himself and his associates, General Totten, Chief Engineer United States Army, and Professor Bache, Superintendent United States Coast Survey, either as members of an independent commission, or, as in the case of New York harbor, as advisory council to the State commission. The harbors of Portland, Boston, and New York, have been particularly benefited by these investigations and discussions.

In 1842, Lieutenant Davis was married to the youngest daughter of the late Hon. Elijah H. Mills, of Northampton, United States Senator from Massachusetts. He has three sons and three daughters; the second son, bearing his father's name, is a midshipman in the United States Navy, and now serving (May, 1866), on the United States Steamer Colorado.

In July, 1849, Lieutenant Davis was relieved from duty on the Coast Survey, receiving on his departure a strong official expression of appreciation and regret from the Superintendent, Prof. Bache, and was immediately assigned to the duty of superintending the preparation of tho American ephemeris and nautical almanac. Up to this time, the United States naval and merchant marine had been obliged to use the nautical almanac of the English, and this necessity had proved especially annoying in the labors of the United States Coast Survey; so that the establishment of a national ephemeris had long been urged, and by none more earnestly than by Lieutenant Davis. Accordingly, in the last session of the Thirtieth Congress (1849–'50), a law was passed authorizing such an establishment; and in accordance with its provisions Lieutenant Davis was appointed by the Secretary of the Navy, Hon. William B. Preston, to superintend it. In this undertaking were encountered some formidable obstacles to success; but all were at length overcome by energy and perseverance; and the Nautical Almanac, once established, not only fulfilled all the purposes contemplated in its creation, but fostered and stimulated the mathematical and astronomical ability of the country in an eminent degree. The names of Pierce, Chauvenet, Walker, Winlock, Runkle, Bartlett, Wright, and Newcomb, are necessarily associated with the success of an undertaking which their genius and labors so materially assisted to perfect. It is sufficient to say that this work, which, from its nature, must be regarded as a fair exponent of the science of the country, was everywhere abroad received with unqualified approval. Lieutenant Davis, having triumphantly organized the Ephemeris, retained his position as Superintendent for seven years, and during that time, besides the duty of administration, occupied himself in preparing a translation of Gauss' "Theoria Motus," (published in Cambridge, 1857,) as well as treatises on "Mechanical Quadratures," the computation of a planetary orbit, and other mathematical tracts.

In 1854, Davis received his commission as commander, and in 1856, at his own request, prompted by a desire to renew the regular duties of his profession, a love of which he had never relinquished during his scientific pursuits, he was appointed to the command of the sloop-of-war St. Mary, to cruise in the Pacific Ocean.—Professor Winlock, United States Navy, having been named to succeed him as Superintendent of the Nautical Almanac, he sailed for Aspinwall, and joined his ship at Panama in the autumn of 1856. During this cruise,

Commander Davis received the capitulation of General Walker, while besieged by the allied armies of Central America, in the town of Rivas, and reduced to the extremest necessity. He also took possession, in the name of the United States, of Jarvis and New Nantucket Islands, in the remote Pacific, and cruised for some time on the western coast of Mexico, at that time, as usual, distracted by civil wars.

After commanding the St. Mary for two years and a half, Commander Davis returned home from his sixth cruise, and resumed the superintendence of the Nautical Almanac, in which office he remained until the breaking out of the rebellion.

Immediately upon the commencement of hostilities, the Government and the Navy Department perceived the urgent necessity of calling to their aid the counsels of experienced officers, in deciding questions of immediate practical importance, and in forming plans for future conduct.

In May, 1861, Commodore Davis was ordered to Washington on duty connected with the efficiency and discipline of the Naval service, and at about the same time was appointed member of two boards. On one of these he was associated with Commodores Paulding and Smith, with orders to investigate the subject of armored ships and floating batteries. To them were submitted some fifteen or sixteen proposals, of which they accepted but three—one for the building of the Monitor—one for that of the Galena, and the other for the Ironsides. The result showed the wisdom and sagacity of the commissioners.

The other board—of which Captain S. F. Dupont, United States Navy, Major (now Major General), J. G.

Barnard, United States Engineers, and Prof. A. D. Bache, were the other members—was organized for the purpose of considering not only the general blockade of the southern coast, but the seizure of available harbors along it. The result of the labors of this second board, of which Commander Davis was junior member and secretary, was the organization of several combined naval and military expeditions against southern ports. Of one of those, directed against the coast of South Carolina, Captain Dupont was appointed flag-officer, and Commander Davis his chief of staff, and captain of the fleet.

There was no officer in the fleet of more importance to Dupont than Davis, and of this he was fully conscious. In his report from Port Royal, he says "The Department is well aware that all the aids to navigation have been removed, and the bar lies ten miles seaward, with no features on the shore line with sufficient prominence to make any bearing reliable. But owing to the skill of Commander Davis, the fleet captain, and Mr. Boutelle, the able assistant of the Coast Survey, the channel was immediately found, sounded out, and buoyed." And, again, he says: "By three o'clock, I received assurances from Captain Davis that I could send forward the lighter transports, those under eighteen feet, with all the gunboats, which was immediately done." As before, so in the terrific battle that followed, Davis exhibited the same skill and coolness that subsequently distinguished him. He was of more service to Dupont in achieving this great victory than half a dozen gunboats.

The next winter he was placed in charge of the expedition sent to sink the stone fleet in Charleston harbor, and block up the main channel by which blockade runners evaded our squadron. He took sixteen old whale-ships loaded with stone; and, towing them into the channel, scuttled and sunk them. This caused an outcry from the people of Charleston, and provoked a remonstrance from the English Government, which seemed to be shocked at the barbarity of a nation that could thus forever, as it was said, destroy a great seaport.

It was no easy task to get these old, heavily-loaded vessels from Port Royal to Charleston, and sink them in the right spot; but a better man could not have been found to perform the labor than Davis, who, from 1842 to 1849, was chief of a hydrographic party in the coast survey, and who, in 1851, was one of the commanders appointed by the Government, at the request of South Carolina, to superintend the improvement of Charleston harbor, in which work he was engaged for several years. No one knew the channel better; and hence, though his present work stood in singular contrast to the one he was then engaged in, his knowledge was none the less valuable.

A witness of this extraordinary scene says: "It was sufficently novel and striking to satisfy any one. At half-past ten the last plug was drawn, and every ship of the sixteen was either sunk or sinking." None of the vessels wholly disappeared from sight, and those which keeled over farthest, and were most under water, had subsided in a very deliberate manner. An impassable line of wrecks was thus drawn for an eighth of a mile across the channel. All but two or three were soon under water—some on their beam-ends, some down by the head, others by the stern, and the masts, spars, and rigging of the thickly-crowded ships were mingled and tangled in the greatest confusion. They did not long remain so. The boats which had been swarming about the wrecks were ordered to cut away the masts. The snapping of stays and shrouds, as one after another tumbled into the sea, sounded like irregular vollies of musketry. For two hours this work went on, while the heavy boom of cannon from Fort Sumter, as it came down the bay, sounded a requiem to the dying fleet. One ship out of the sixteen had her masts left standing, adding by contrast to the desolation of the scene. As night came on, this was set on fire, and blazed up over the waters of the bay like a funeral pyre. The rebels from Sumter, Moultrie, and Sullivan's Island, could see what was going on, but were powerless to prevent it, and could only vent their indignation in unavailing curses.

A witness of the operation said, "An effort to blockade a tidal harbor like this presented a wholly new problem, which was worked out by Captain Davis, with great ingenuity and scientific skill."

In the following January, Davis was sent by Dupont with some ten vessels, accompanied by three transports, which carried twenty-four hundred men, to flank Fort Pulaski, by the Little Tybee river. On the 26th he passed the fort, the commander of which was so taken by surprise to find vessels on that side of him, that he did not even fire upon them. The telegraph wires were cut leading to the city, and all the surveys and examinations made, necessary to form a conclusion as to the propriety of seizing Wilmington Island.

While he was engaged in this work, Commodore Tatnall, with five rebel steamers, attempted to pass down the river to the fort. Davis at once opened fire upon them, and, after a half hour's engagement, drove two off. The other three succeeded in reaching Pulaski. In two or three hours the latter returned and renewed the attack, and though there was heavy firing, owing to the intervention of the banks of the river which separated the vessels, but little damage was done.

Early in the following month he accompanied Dupont on an expedition against Fort Clinton, and Fernandina, Florida, which were captured with little fighting.

In March, 1862, Captain Davis was detached from the South Atlantic Blockading Squadron, and in April ordered to relieve Flag-Officer Foote, and assume the command of the Mississippi flotilla. He entered upon this duty on the 9th of May. On the following morning, May 10th, he gained the naval victory off Fort Pillow.

Soon after daylight, the mortar-boats were towed down to open on Fort Wright, and had hardly taken their positions, when the rebel ram, Louisiana, appeared round a point below, accompanied by four other gunboats, and made for the Cincinnati, which was in advance. The ram endeavored to run the latter down; but the captain turned the vessel's head, so that his powerful antagonist, instead of striking him, came fairly alongside, when the former opened his batteries; and, drawing his pistol, coolly shot the rebel pilot dead at his wheel. At the same time, however, he himself was struck on the shoulder by a musket-ball, and severely wounded. The opposing crews, now in close proximity, opened a fierce fire of small arms, while shouts and curses helped to swell the din and tumult. The next moment the Cincinnati opened her steam batteries, which sent a cloud of hissing, scalding vapor into the rebel vessel, clearing her decks instantaneously, and causing her to haul off in consternation. Three other boats now joined in the attack, and among them the Mallory; but before she could inflict any damage, the St. Louis, obeying Davis' signal, came down on her under full headway, and, striking her amidships, cut her almost in two, sending her to the bottom with most of her crew. The rest of Davis' fleet now came up, and a close, fierce conflict followed, in which the firing was so rapid, that the loud explosions seemed like one continued report. In a few minutes, there came out of the clouds of rolling and enfolding smoke a report louder than the explosion of cannon. A rebel gunboat had blown up, and in a few moments went to the bottom, leaving only scattered fragments, covered with struggling swimmers, to tell where she had gone down. But a short interval elapsed, when there came out of the bosom of the sulphurous cloud, another report, telling that another rebel vessel had gone to join her consort. Davis, on the flagship Benton, directed every movement—making no mistake from first to last. He handled his fleet amid all this confusion and obscurity, with a coolness and sagacity that elicited the warmest admiration, and showed that Foote had left a worthy successor.

The action lasted for an hour; and, when it was over, the remains of the rebel fleet were seen steaming back to their old position.

After the evacuation of Fort Pillow, Davis passed on down to Memphis. He led the squadron in the Benton, which swept majestically down the river towards Fort Randolph, that lay between it and the city. As the fleet approached it, Davis was seen pacing his quarter-deck with a measured yet impatient step, turning his eye in the direction of the fort. As he drew near, he saw the stars and stripes floating above it—the garrison having fled to Memphis. The city was only twelve miles distant; and yet there were no signs of the enemy, except the smoke and flames along the shore, arising from the burning cotton, which they had set on fire to prevent its falling into our hands. At a little after four o'clock, as he swung around a bend, he saw ahead the rebel steamer-transport Sovereign. The next moment an eighty-four-pound shot passed over her to bring her to. She not obeying the summons, Davis said: "Fire again, Captain Phelps; bring her to." The Benton now fired nine shots in rapid succession, when the Sovereign, unhurt, swept around a bend, and was lost to view. The tug Spitfire started in pursuit; and, after an exciting chase, overhauled and captured her. Davis, in the mean time, kept steadily on with the fleet; and, a little before nine o'clock in the evening, came in full view of Memphis, the lights of which could be seen twinkling along the banks. He then signalled to anchor; and the vessels soon lay gently sleeping on the bosom of the Mississippi. It was a beautiful night; the air was mild and balmy, and the moon sailed quietly above amid her islands of stars. In the mean time the transports landed troops on the Arkansas shore, to serve as pickets during the night, while the men slept beside their guns, ready at a moment's notice to receive the enemy, should he venture on a night attack. The quiet, however, remained unbroken until midnight, when a bright light was seen down the river, near the Tennessee shore, where a rebel tug, which, having got so hard aground, it was found impossible to heave off, had been set on fire by the crew, and now blazed brightly up in the darkness.

At five o'clock in the morning, Davis, from the Benton, which was lying only a mile and a half from Memphis, cast his eye towards the city, glittering in the early rays of an unclouded sun, and saw the bluffs black with citizens, who at that early hour had come forth to witness the battle that they knew was soon to come off.

A little before six, several dark gunboats were seen coming around the bend below. A few minutes later, and Davis issued his orders: "All hands to quarters!" and soon the entire fleet (Davis, in the Benton, leading the van) slowly advanced. Eight rebel rams, commanded by Commodore Montgomery, steamed boldly up to meet him, while the shore was lined with thousands of spectators, gazing with breathless interest on the exciting spectacle. The "Little Rebel," as she came opposite the city, fired the first shot, to which the Benton replied. A moment later, and another of her heavy shot went booming along the Mississippi, and then the conflict opened. In the midst of the heavy firing, down came Colonel Ellet, with the two rams Queen of the West and Monarch; and, passing through the fleet under a full head of steam, drove straight on the rebel boats. The hostile rams now dashed furiously into each other, while the guns of the other vessels poured in their heavy shot and shells. Swift-rolling clouds shut out the morning sun, and out of their involving folds came the crash of colliding vessels, and cries and shouts of men. In an hour and twenty minutes it was all over. The General Beauregard and Little Rebel were blown up, the General Lovell sent to the bottom, while the rest of the fleet was clapping on all steam to escape destruction in flight.

Davis, the victory being won, now pressed after the fleeing enemy, chasing him for ten miles down the river. One vessel after another was captured, until the Van Dorn alone was left of the entire rebel squadron that moved so confidently to battle scarce an hour before. She escaped only by her superior speed.

It was a great victory, and Memphis now lay at the mercy of Davis, and soon the national flag was waving above it.

A few days after, he received the news of the capture of two batteries at the St. Charles, sixty miles up the White River, by a portion of his fleet under Captain Kelty.

The steamer Mound City had her steam-drum exploded in the fight, and blew up, killing and wounding over a hundred and fifty, out of a crew of a hundred and seventy-five. Davis, in reporting the victory to the Department, says:

> The victory at St. Charles, which has probably given us the command of White River, and secured my communication with General Curtis, would be unalloyed with regret, but for the fatal accident to the steam-drum and heater of the Mound City. * * *
>
> After the explosion took place, the wounded men were shot by the enemy while in the water, and the boats of the Conestoga, Lexington, and St. Louis, which went to the assistance of the scalded and drowning men of the Mound City, were fired into, both with great guns and muskets, and were disabled, and one of them forced on shore to prevent sinking. The forts were commanded by Lieutenant Joseph Fry, late of the United States Navy, who is now a prisoner and wounded.
>
> The Department and the country will contrast these barbarities of a savage enemy, with the humane efforts made by our own people to rescue the wounded and disabled, under similar circumstances, in the engagement of the 6th instant.
>
> Several of the poor fellows who expired shortly after the engagement, expressed their willingness to die, when they were told that the victory was ours.

Davis now kept on down to Vicksburg, where he met Farragut, who had, with a portion of his fleet, run the batteries from below. With him he planned an expedition up the Yazoo, to procure correct information concerning the obstructions and the defences of the river. The Carondelet and Tyler, with the ram Queen of the

West, composed the vessels, but they had entered the river only a short distance, when they encountered the rebel ram Arkansas coming down. Their shots had scarcely heralded her approach, when she appeared at the mouth of the stream, steering straight for Vicksburg, although her course lay right through the combined squadron. Guns opened on her from every side, but she passed on unhurt, and anchored safely under the batteries, much to the chagrin of Farragut and Davis. The Benton pursued after; but, as Davis said, "at her usual snail's pace, which renders any thing like pursuit ludicrous." He, however, attacked the batteries, maintaining the bombardment for half an hour. In the course of the morning he renewed the attack with Farragut on board—his object at this time being to reconnoitre the rebel works.

Farragut now determined to run the batteries again, for the double purpose of joining the rest of his squadron below, and destroying the ram Arkansas in his passage. In the mean time, to cover the movement, Davis steamed up, and again engaged the batteries.

The attempt to destroy the ram having failed, Porter, in the Essex, determined to try his hand on her, and the next morning, shortly after daylight, started on his perilous mission, while Davis diverted the rebel fire on himself, by moving boldly against the upper batteries.

This attempt also failed, and, Farragut having gone down the river, followed by General Williams with the army, Davis abandoned his position before Vicksburg as useless and untenable, and moved up to the mouth of the Yazoo River. He here sent out an expedition under Captain Phelps, which succeeded in destroying the fort at Haines' Bluff, and capturing its guns.

With his force now materially reduced by sickness,

he moved up the river to Helena, to close up his lines, now too extended, to open again the sources of communication and supply, and resume his conjunction with the army.

During this time, Davis was occasionally Flag-Officer, Commodore, and Acting Rear-Admiral of the naval forces, on the Mississippi and its tributaries, sending off expeditions here, and coöperating with the army there, until autumn. In July of the same year, Commodore Davis was confirmed by the Senate as Chief of the Bureau of Navigation. After having effected the transfer of the Mississippi flotilla from the army to the navy, under the provisions of an act of Congress, he returned to Washington in November, 1862, and entered upon the duties of his new office, in which he remained until the spring of 1865.

On the 7th Feb., 1863, Commodore Davis received a vote of thanks from Congress, for his services in the war; and, on the same day, was commissioned Rear-Admiral in the U. S. Navy. He also received a vote of thanks for his services from the legislature of his native state.

In May, 1865, Admiral Davis was appointed Super intendent of the National Observatory, a position which he now holds.

He is a member of the Light-House Board, chairman of the Permanent Commission of the Navy Department, and chairman of a Joint Commission of Officers of the Army and Navy on Harbor Obstructions.

He is also one of the United States commissioners of Boston harbor, a fellow of the American Academy of Arts and Sciences, a member of the American Philosophical Society of Philadelphia, and of the National

Academy of Sciences. Although it seems hard to take a commander from active service, in which he is winning distinction, and confine him to shore duty, while his companions in arms are winning fame, yet, men of marked ability must be had at the head of affairs, and personal preferences yield to the public good. As before remarked, there were many afloat to whom our vessels could be trusted without fear, yet, there were few possessing the scientific attainments of Admiral Davis, or those qualities so much needed in the successful administration of affairs at Washington.

CHAPTER XIII.

COMMANDER HOMER C. BLAKE.

A GREAT EXAMPLE WORTH MORE THAN AN ORDINARY VICTORY.—BLAKE'S NATIVITY AND EARLY EDUCATION.—ENTERS THE NAVY.—HIS FIRST CRUISE ROUND THE WORLD.—KEEPS COMMUNICATION OPEN BETWEEN OUR VESSELS IN THE CHINESE SEA.—SERVES ON THE COAST OF AFRICA.—ENTERS THE NAVAL SCHOOL.—PASSED MIDSHIPMAN.—SERVES IN THE WAR WITH MEXICO.—CRUISE TO THE EAST INDIES.—SENT HOME TO RECRUIT HIS HEALTH.—JOINS THE PARAGUAY EXPEDITION.—ANECDOTE.—SECOND CRUISE TO THE AFRICAN COAST.—BREAKING OUT OF THE REBELLION.—BLAKE JOINS THE PORT ROYAL EXPEDITION.—COMMANDS THE R. R. CUYLER.—TRANSFERRED TO THE HATTERAS.—A DESCRIPTION OF HER.—ON BLOCKADE DUTY OFF GALVESTON.—SENT IN PURSUIT OF A STRANGE STEAMER.—HIS FIGHT WITH THE ALABAMA.—CORRESPONDENCE WITH AN ENGLISH CAPTAIN IN KINGSTON.—IS EXCHANGED.—HIS CREW ASK THE GOVERNMENT TO GIVE HIM ANOTHER VESSEL TO CRUISE AFTER THE ALABAMA.—COMMANDS THE EUTAW IN THE JAMES RIVER.—HIS GREAT SERVICES HERE.—NOW OVER THE BUREAU OF NAVIGATION IN PORTSMOUTH, N. H.

It is a curious fact, in our naval history, that a commander never lost a vessel in an engagement not only without being acquitted of all blame, but absolutely winning laurels by his misfortune. The manner in which he fought his ship, the heroism he displayed, and the desperate nature of the contest, made the defeat, by the great example it furnished, worth as much to the country and the navy as a victory would have been.

Thus Lawrence, crying out on the verge of death, "Don't give up the ship," although victory was hopeless, furnished a motto that has been worth more than a dozen victories to the Navy.

Porter, standing on the deck of his shattered vessel, in the harbor of Valparaiso, with his colors struck, was a hero greater than any ordinary victory could have made him, while the example he set of how an American commander should fight his ship, has awakened a spirit of emulation in our commanders that will exert a powerful influence as long as our navy exists. The same is true of the gallant Blake, carrying his frail vessel into a hopeless combat, and then fighting her till she was a wreck and fast sinking.

HOMER C. BLAKE was born in Dutchess County, New York State, on the 1st day of February, 1822. His father's name was Elisha Blake, and his mother's Merilla Crane. When he was but a year old, his father moved into what was then considered the far West, Ohio, and settled in that section called the Western Reserve. Here he grew up from boyhood, attending the schools common to that part of the country, and laboring at intervals, as the youth of that time around him were accustomed to do.

Through the influence of friends, he, at the age of eighteen, March 2d, 1840, received the appointment of midshipman. In the following December, he joined the Constellation frigate, and in her made a cruise round the world. A mere lad, the change from a secluded life in a remote town in the West, to the wide field opened before him in this extended cruise, could not have been greater, and it matured him fast. Active, alert, and always ready for any duty, he showed at the outset that he had chosen the profession for which he was designed.

His first voyage lasted for over three years, and he did not reach home until 1844. In that time he had become a man, having lived twice three years in experience.

When the Constellation reached China, all communication was cut off between the spot where the vessels anchored and Canton. But it was all-important that this should be kept open; and the duty of doing this was committed to young Blake, who, in an open boat, with only twelve men, performed it to the entire satisfaction of his commander. At this time, the price of an Englishman's head was a thousand dollars, and as the Chinamen were not very scrupulous what kind of head they brought to market, and no one could distinguish between that of an Englishman and an American, it required the utmost care and vigilance on the part of the young midshipman to keep his head from going into their basket.

On his return, he was allowed only a short furlough, in which to visit his friends; and in a few weeks was ordered to join the sloop-of-war Preble, about to sail for the coast of Africa. He remained for a year on this inhospitable coast, engaged in the arduous, annoying, and often dangerous duty of suppressing the slave-trade.

On his return from this cruise, he entered the United States Naval School, to add scientific to his practical knowledge, and thus enable him to make the latter broader in its application, and enlarge the field of his future influence.

Here he showed the same devotion to study that he had to practical duties, and the same facility in mastering whatever he undertook. Having completed his education, for which his four years of actual service had been an admirable preparation, he graduated in 1846, as passed midshipman. Six years of practical and scientific training seems a long time before one passes the the threshold of his profession, but none too long to make the accomplished officers we need in the navy.

The war in Mexico now breaking out, young Blake, ambitious of distinction, applied for active service, and was attached to his old vessel, the sloop-of-war Preble, and sent to the coast of California. He would have preferred a different vessel and a destination which placed him more directly in the vicinity of the army, where the hard fighting was expected to take place. As a rule, officers do not like sloops-of-war. In the first place, they are too small to perform any great work, while their armament makes them top-heavy, and anything but pleasant craft to be in in a heavy sea.

His duties were various on the coast of California, but furnished no opportunity for distinguishing himself.

In the mean time the war drew to a close, and in 1848 the Preble was detached from that station, and ordered to the East Indies. But scarcely had the vessel, after her long voyage, reached Canton, when Blake's health became so feeble that he was unfit for duty. There seeming to be no prospect of recovering on board the sloop and in that unfavorable climate, he was permitted to return home.

He was now employed for a short time on shore in the coast survey.

But, in 1850, we find him again afloat in the frigate Raritan, bound once more for the Pacific. He did not, however, complete his cruise in her, but was transferred to the sloop-of-war St. Mary. In this vessel he kept on to the China Seas, and so home by way of the Cape of

Good Hope—thus, in about nine years, making three voyages around the world.

In 1856, he again joined the Raritan frigate, and sailed for the coast of Brazil. This vessel formed a part of the Paraguay expedition. The expedition was devoid of interest; but a little incident occurred, while Blake's vessel lay at Rio Janeiro, which would have been forgotten had it not been related by one of the Russian officers, who visited our country a short time since, and were received with so much display in New York. Several English and French men-of-war were in the port of Rio Janeiro at the same time that the St. Lawrence was there. Soon after, the Russian ship-of-war Diana came into harbor—one of the vessels that bore a prominent part in the repulse of the English and French on the Asiatic coast. One day, some ten or twelve of her crew came ashore on leave, and were walking leisurely along, when they were suddenly set upon by a large party of French and English sailors. Near by, a group of American officers were standing, spectators of the scene. The Russians were getting badly beaten, when one of the officers stepped quickly forward amid the combatants, and, laying his hand on his sword, soon turned the scale, so that the Russian sailors came off victors. It was only a passing incident, forgotten by that officer the next hour, and never perhaps recalled again, till, five or six years after, it was told by a Russian officer on our own soil, to show the friendly relations that existed between the two nations. Forgotten by us, it had been repeated in the Russian navy, and made every sailor who heard it our fast friend. *That officer was Homer C. Blake.*

On his return from this cruise, in 1857, he was employed for a while on shore duty. He was then again sent to the coast of Africa, returning in the latter part of the next year.

For twenty years Blake had now been almost constantly afloat, enriching his experience by almost every species of navigation, till he was fit to command any vessel, yet apparently without any prospect of reaching the grade of captain until he should be almost old enough to be put on the retired list.

But the election of 1860 precipitated the long-threatened collision between the North and South; and when, in 1861, the war actually broke out, Blake applied for active duty. No doubt or vacillation disturbed him in choosing the course he should take. His sword and his life he wished to cast together, if need be, to sustain the old flag he had sailed under in every sea on the globe, and whose folds had been his protection in nearly every harbor of the world.

He was first ordered to the Sabine, which was employed on the coast of South Carolina. This vessel formed a part of the Port Royal expedition; but, being detained in rescuing the crew of the Governor, during a violent storm, she did not arrive in time to take part in the engagement. The Sabine being soon withdrawn from this station, and employed on recruiting duty, Blake, who could not brook such a tame employment amid the vast preparations for deadly combat going on around him on every side, requested to be detached from her and placed at the post of danger.

He was ordered to the command of the R. R. Cuyler, and, though the vessel was not one which he would have selected for active service, it was with feelings of pride that he found himself in separate command.

He was, however, soon transferred from her to the command of the Hatteras. As this vessel went, with all her armament and her brave dead, to the bottom of the sea, a brief description of her may not be out of place, especially as the southern press called her an iron-clad, and the rebel congress passed a vote of thanks to Semmes, for sinking so formidable a ship, and achieving such a transcendent victory.

She was originally built at Wilmington, as a passenger vessel between Galveston and New Orleans, and of the slightest construction, for an iron ship. She was of a thousand tons burden, and drawing but seven feet of water.

The government, which in its sore need purchased everything that could by any transmutation be called a war vessel, bought this also, and, removing the after cabin, put an extra planking on her slight pine deck, to enable it to bear the light guns which were to be placed on board. These consisted of four thirty-two pounders, two thirty-pounder rifles, and one twenty-pounder rifle. The total weight of metal she flung at a single broadside was only one hundred and fourteen pounds, against the Alabama's four hundred and thirty-six, or within a fraction of a quarter as much. The heaviest gun of the Hatteras was a 32-pounder; the heaviest of the Alabama was a 110-pounder rifle gun, and a heavy 68, weighing nine thousand pounds—a gun which could not have been used on the Hatteras without knocking her to pieces.

The Hatteras, however, was strong enough for ordinary blockading duty, to which she was ordered off Galveston, and formed a part of the fleet under command of Commodore Bell.

On Sunday, January 11th, in the afternoon, Blake saw

a signal from the flagship Brooklyn, directing him to sail to the southward and eastward. After steaming in this direction for an hour and a half, the lookout reported a steamer bearing to the southward. Blake immediately ordered all steam on, and took a long and scrutinizing survey of the stranger. As he gradually lessened the distance between them, he saw clearly that she was the far-famed Alabama, and at once ordered his vessel cleared for action —being determined to close with her. She did not try to escape, but kept under easy way to decoy the Hatteras so far from the fleet that no assistance could reach her before the conflict would be over. Blake knew that his frail vessel would not stand her fire more than fifteen or twenty minutes. Almost his only hope therefore in closing with her, was, that he could carry her by boarding before his vessel was hopelessly crippled.— Failing in this, he hoped—though he knew it was only one chance out of a thousand—to be able, by a lucky shot, to detain her until some of the rest of the fleet could come to his assistance. Although the heart of a brave commander exults at the prospect of an even-handed encounter with a foe, it requires the loftiest heroism and the most unselfish patrotism to carry him into an encounter where he knows that defeat awaits him. We cannot conceive of a more trying position, and it awakens the deepest sympathy to see this brave officer steadily and sternly moving up to grapple with his superior enemy. One may look death, but not defeat, calmly in the face. He had said in a private letter to one of his friends, when going down to Galveston: "I have much to live for, but I could not be happy to purchase my life with any neglect of the duty I owe to my country. I shall not seek danger; but if it comes

I shall take it in the line of my duty, and endeavor to do credit to myself, family, and state." That hour had now arrived; and, what adds immeasurably to the interest of this combat, the crew knew perfectly well that it was the Alabama that now lay-to, waiting for them; and knew, moreover, that it was a hopeless contest on which they were about to enter. We all are aware how the hope of success braces men for the combat, and how depressing it is to enter on one when defeat is certain. Blake, fully alive to this, scanned the countenances of his crew with an anxious heart. It was enough for *him* if he could leave a great example to those who should come after, but would the sailors share his feelings? It was with heroic pride, therefore, that he saw every face calm and firmly set for the struggle. He could read there the determination to fight while a plank would float them, and then sink with their brave commander, and their colors flying. No eulogy on the latter could be pronounced so great as this quiet, deep devotion of his crew. He must be a rare officer who can win it.

As the Hatteras pressed forward, night began to gather over the water, and Blake saw that his antagonist had ceased steaming and was lying "broadside on," awaiting his approach. The stranger was now only about four miles off, and loomed clearly up in the darkness. Blake, however, kept silently on, the men at quarters with strings in hand and with orders to fire at the slightest hostile movement on the part of the enemy. When within seventy-five yards, he hailed, "What steamer is that?" Back through the gloom came the hoarse reply: "Her Britannic Majesty's ship Vixen." Blake then said he would send a boat aboard, and, turning, gave the order to have one lowered immediately. But scarcely had the boatman's shrill whistle rung over the water, when the stranger shouted, "We are the Confederate steamer Alabama," followed instantaneously by a full broadside. The darkness had hardly closed over the flash, when the guns of the Hatteras replied, and the terrible conflict commenced. Although almost within pistol-shot, Blake kept straight towards the Alabama, knowing that his only chance was to close with her. If he once could grapple her firmly, he knew his brave crew would sweep her decks like a storm. He at length got within thirty yards, when muskets and pistols were used, and he hoped in a minute more to hear the shout of his boarders. But Semmes knew his advantage too well, and penetrating Blake's design, shot ahead with his swifter craft and poured in his broadsides. Blake continued to hug him close, straining every nerve to lock him in a death grapple, but in vain. With his greater speed Semmes easily avoided it, while his heavy shot was doing fearful execution. A barrel of turpentine lay in the lower part of the hold of the Hatteras, covered with stores; and a shell, entering the vessel, exploded near it, setting it on fire. In an instant the hold was a mass of flame, roaring along the vessel's sides. The alarm was sounded, and the firemen sprang below to extinguish the fire. Blake in a moment saw that this was impossible, and ordered the firemen to return to their guns. With the promptness of men on drill they wheeled into their places, and began to load and fire coolly as ever, though the flames were coming fiercely up the hatchways. The magazine and shell room were above the water-line, and constructed of nothing but thin pine plank, and in a few moments the first lieutenant came on deck and reported that the fire was burning the bulk-heads. Blake, with his heroic nature now thoroughly aroused, replied: "Never mind—she won't blow up for fifteen minutes yet, and we must fight on if we all go to the bottom,"—and they did fight on, firing with a rapidity probably never before equalled in a naval combat. Being close alongside, no training of the guns was necessary, and Blake knew that he must try to make up for disparity in weight of metal, by rapid firing, and so ordered the guns to be fought from a tight heading and not sponged. Before they were so fouled as to be useless, he knew the conflict would be over.

In a few minutes the Hatteras was in flames fore and aft, her walking-beam was shot away, her port wheel smashed to fragments, her decks a mass of splinters, and the brave vessel a hopeless wreck. Blake stood amid the ruins around him calm and collected—determined that the flag, which the flashes of his guns still revealed flying above him, should never be struck—but the next moment, he saw that his vessel was fast settling in the water, and firing his last gun, just as the water was coming on deck, he, out of feelings of humanity for his brave crew, ordered a gun fired to leeward, in token of surrender. The firing at once ceased, and Semmes hailed to know if he wanted help. Blake replied in the affirmative, and at the same time lowered his own boat. Other boats were soon in the water, and the entire crew, with the exception of Blake, were safely placed aboard them. He, with two dead men, remained alone on the wreck until all were out of her, when he also stepped off the submerged deck into a boat and was taken on board the Alabama.

The fight had lasted less than twenty minutes. Scarcely were the prisoners secured, when the Hatteras, with a heavy lurch, went to the bottom, her flag still proudly flying.

Commodore Bell saw the flashes of the guns more than twenty miles distant, and heard the rapid explosions, and immediately sent off three vessels to aid the Hatteras. But utter darkness and silence soon settled over the water, and they cruised at random all night. Next day they found the mastheads of the Hatteras standing upright, and out of water, "tops and gaves awash, and the hurricane-deck adrift." This told the story; but whether her brave commander and crew were below with her, and this was the monument above their watery graves, they could not tell.

In the mean time the Alabama bore away for Kingston, Jamaica, with her prisoners.

Blake, who knew that the short but terrific cannonading of the two vessels must have been heard by our fleet off Galveston, hoped that the Alabama would be overhauled and captured, and every day scanned the waters with an anxious eye. But no help came, and in nine days the crippled pirate reached port. The British steamer Greyhound was in the harbor at the time, and, when she heard that the Alabama had arrived, the band struck up "Dixie's Land." Blake, who was chafing under his captivity, could not brook this fresh insult, and immediately sent the following note to the commander of that vessel.

"*January* 24, 1863.

"*To the Commander of H. B. M. ship Greyhound:*

"Lieutenant-Commander H. C. Blake, of the United States Navy, presents his compliments to the Commander of H. B. M. ship Greyhound, and desires to learn whether or not he may consider the playing of 'Dixie's Land' by the band of the Greyhound, upon the arrival of the Confederate steamer Alabama, on the evening of the 21st instant, as a mark of disrespect to the United States Government, or its officers who were prisoners on board the Alabama, at the period indicated. Lieutenant-Commander H. C. Blake respectfully requests an early response.

"*United States Consulate, Jamaica.*"

To this the former returned the annexed handsome, frank, and satisfactory reply.

"Commander Hickley, R. N., presents his compliments to Lieutenant-Commander Blake, U. S. N., and has to acquaint him that on the evening in question he was on board the A——, dining with Captain Crocroft. Shortly after the time of the officer of the guard reporting the Alabama's arrival, he heard the drums and fifes of H. M. S. Greyhound playing, among other tunes, the tune of 'Dixie's Land.' He immediately repaired on board, causing other national tunes to be played, among which was the United States national air, and severely reprimanded the inconsiderate young officer who had ordered 'Dixie's Land' to be played, calling for his reasons, and writing and forwarding them forthwith, with his report to Commodore Hugh Dunlop, C.B., who severely reprimanded the officer.

"As the officer in question had no idea that any U. S. officer or man was on board the Alabama, it must be evident to Lieutenant-Commander Blake that no insult was intended.

"*H. M. S. Greyhound, Port Royal, Jamaica, January* 24, 1863."

Semmes treated Blake and the prisoners with generosity, but said to another officer that Blake had "more d—d assurance than any man he ever saw," to attack such a vessel as the Alabama with the Hatteras. But weak as the latter was, she, in the short, unequal contest, so severely handled the rebel craft, that she had to remain for a long time in port to be fit for sea again, the repairs costing $86,000 in gold.

Semmes, however, was highly complimented by his Government, and his conduct commended to the notice of Congress. Blake might say, with Paul Jones, who, when he heard that Captain Pearson, of the Serapis, had been made a knight, after the battle with him, remarked: "If I ever catch him at sea again I'll make a lord of him."

Though Blake lost his vessel, he broke up Semmes' plans, which, if carried out, would have caused us more damage than the loss of a dozen such vessels as the

Hatteras. He was short of provisions and coal, and intended to supply himself with these from some of our merchant steamers off Galveston, and then run into the mouth of the Mississippi, and fall in with and capture Banks' expedition.

But, however these plans might have resulted, the noble example set by Blake and his crew was worth more than many such vessels. A great example of self-devotion lives forever, and this brave, hopeless attack of the Alabama will be remembered as long as naval heroism is recorded. Ever present to a commander's mind, he cannot shrink from any contest, however hopeless, when his country's good requires it.

Blake's crew showed their appreciation of his conduct, by sending a petition to the Department, asking that the steamer Eutaw might be given him, and they be allowed to cruise after the Alabama. They say: "We assure you, that if it could be understood that a steamer was actually fitting out, under our able commander, hundreds of seamen now lost to the service would be eager to enlist." * * * And again: "It took the Alabama twenty minutes to sink the Hatteras. But if we once get alongside of her with the Eutaw, and Captain Blake for her commander, we will either sink or capture her in half that time." "*We want satisfaction, and it lies in your power to place us in a position that will give us a chance to take or destroy this notorious pirate.*"

It must be a source of gratification to Blake, to know how the crew that fought this hopeless battle under him, longed once more to stand on the same deck with him, in another encounter with their common adversary. It is higher praise than government officials can bestow. A crew that so loves and trusts their commander, will never see their flag struck, while their guns can carry shot.

The Eutaw was given Blake, but, instead of being sent after the Alabama, was stationed in the James River. Here she was constantly engaged—now in partial engagements with the enemy, and now in transporting troops.

In the latter part of 1863, the rebel press announced that a movement would soon be made on their part which would astonish the world. It actually took place on the 24th of January, 1864.

In order to understand the object and result expected by this movement, it must be remembered, that, with our iron-clads, we could go no further than "Trent Reach," the greatest depth of water beyond being twelve and a half feet, while they drew thirteen and fourteen feet. Finding them useless for a direct attack on Richmond, and the Government requiring them on the coast, a line of strong obstructions was thrown across the river at this point. The iron-clad Onondaga, and a few wooden gunboats, were left to prevent the rebels from removing them (a force fully adequate to the duty, if properly used). The rebels had now their rams, and a number of other vessels. Semmes had returned, and was appointed to the command of their fleet. Longstreet, with twenty-five thousand men, moved to the right of the army of the James; Lee, to the left of the army of the Potomac; and Semmes with his fleet was to force the obstructions, pass down, destroying the pontoons, cutting the connection of the two armies, capture City Point, our base of supplies, and take possession of the James River. On the day fixed, the rebel fleet came down, driving in our pickets, and commenced the removal of our obstructions. The naval commander, instead of taking his vessel to the protection of his defences, retired, and allowed them to be removed, thus leaving a passage for the rebel fleet. Most fortunately for us, two of the rebel rams, waiting for the opening of the channel, got aground, thus frustrating the plan for that night. The enemy, however, prepared for a second attempt at high water the following night. Blake was at this time stationed at Deep Bottom, on the "east side," to protect the right of the "army of the James." On the morning of the 25th, the commander of the naval division having been removed for his conduct on the previous day, Blake took command of it. On going on board the Onondaga, he found her port propeller disabled; yet, with her in this condition, and only a few small gunboats, he was to contend with the rebel fleet. A false step, or a moment's hesitation, would endanger the safety of our armies. Against the advice of almost all the officers, he got the Onondaga, with the assistance of tugs, close to the obstructions, and directly under the fire of the rebel batteries, and in such a position that, if she was sunk either by the rams or torpedo-boats, as he expected, she would take the place of the removed obstructions. This action prevented a second attempt, as he was afterward informed by one of the officers who was attached to the rebel fleet.

A single extract of a letter from Admiral Porter to him, will show how great was the service he performed. The admiral says: "Had your predecessor done as well, we should now be in possession of the entire rebel navy, and on our way to Richmond." On the return of the admiral from the capture of Fort Fisher, Blake was continued in command of the iron-clads and naval picket line, and had the pleasure of taking part in the engagement which caused the fall of Richmond, and saw the old flag assume its proper place on the state house of that city.

He is now at the head of the Bureau of Navigation, at Portsmouth, New Hampshire.

CHAPTER XIV.

COMMODORE JOHN A. WINSLOW.

HIS BIRTH.—ANCESTRY.—ENTERS THE NAVAL SERVICE.—SENT TO THE WEST INDIES.—CRUISES IN THE PACIFIC OCEAN.—SUBSEQUENT SERVICES.—PROMOTION.—SERVES IN THE WAR WITH MEXICO.—FIGHT IN TOBASCO.—GIVEN A CHOICE OF VESSELS FOR HIS GALLANTRY.—SEMMES BECOMES HIS ROOMMATE.—STRANGE CONTRASTS.—IN HAYTI AND YUCATAN.—A CRUISE IN THE PACIFIC.—BREAKING OUT OF THE REBELLION.—WINSLOW SENT WEST TO CO-OPERATE WITH FOOTE.—EQUIPS HIS FLOTILLA.—IS WOUNDED IN TRYING TO GET THE "BENTON" AFLOAT AFTER GROUNDING.—SENT UP THE WHITE RIVER.—DETERS OFFICERS FROM DEMANDING OF THE GOVERNMENT HIS APPOINTMENT TO THE COMMAND OF THE MISSISSIPPI FLOTILLA.—ORDERED EAST TO TAKE COMMAND OF THE KEARSARGE.—HIS CRUISE IN SEARCH OF THE ALABAMA.—BOLD NAVIGATION.—BLOCKADES THE FLORIDA. HIS VESSEL RUN ASHORE BY REBEL PILOTS.—FINDS THE ALABAMA AT CHERBOURG.—IS CHALLENGED BY SEMMES.—BEFORE THE COMBAT.—THE COMBAT.—A BRAVE SEAMAN.—THE VICTORY.—YACHT GREYHOUND.—ENGLISH PERFIDY.—SEMMES' FALSEHOODS REFUTED.—THE ENGLISH PRESS.—THE TWO VESSELS COMPARED.—LETTER OF THE SECRETARY OF THE NAVY.—UNJUST CENSURE.—FEELING OF THE PEOPLE.—WINSLOW'S VINDICATION.—HIS CHARACTER.

OFTEN a man devoted to a single calling or profession passes through life without being known but little outside of the particular sphere in which he moved. The most untiring industry, faithfulness to duty, and signal ability, can, at the utmost, only slowly lift him in mere nominal rank or position. It is only rarely that circumstances so combine as to allow him in one single effort to show to the world what he has been preparing for, or what he is capable of doing. This is more especially true of those whose studies and training look to outward physical results.

Winslow is an illustration of the truth of this statement. Although, for nearly thirty years in the naval service—an accomplished officer—a thorough commander, and a man of great mental ability, yet, but for the fortunate event that brought him in contact with the Alabama, his real worth would not have been known outside of the naval profession.

John A. Winslow is a southerner by birth, having been born in Wilmington, North Carolina, November 19th, 1811. On the mother's side, whose name was Sarah E. Anerim, he came from the celebrated Rhett family of Charleston, but, on the father's, from the best Massachusetts stock, being the seventh generation from John Winslow, brother of Edward Winslow, Governor of Massachusetts Bay, and consecrator of Plymouth Rock. Edward Winslow, the common ancestor of the family which bore such an important part in the early history of the Plymouth colony, was from Droutwitch, England, ten miles from which the family seat is still found. Edward, his son, and afterwards Governor of Massachusetts Bay, joined the pilgrims at Leyden. He had been just married, but his young wife, true to the convictions of duty as himself, left a luxurious home and her native land, to encounter the perils and hardships of a wilderness, whose solitudes were broken only by the cries of wild beasts, and the still more fearful war-whoop of the savage.

Four brothers joined him in Plymouth colony, one of whom was the ancestor of the present renowned commodore. The father of John Winslow was sent from Boston, in 1807, to establish the commercial house of J. Winslow & Co., which was located at Wilmington. This was the way the subject of the present sketch came to be born on southern soil.

When fourteen years of age, he, with his elder brother, was sent North to be educated, and placed under charge of Rev. Mr. Sewall, of Dedham, to prepare for college. The elder brother subsequently entered college; but John's taste inclining to the navy, he, after two years of study, entered the service. He was now only sixteen years old, but was immediately ordered on active duty to the West Indies in the Falmouth. He remained here for nearly three years, being frequently sent on boat expeditions from Cuba against pirates. The excitement and adventure of this kind of life exactly suited him, and showed that he had chosen the right profession. In 1829 he brought Poinsett home from Mexico. The next year he returned, and the year following was ordered, in the same ship, to the Pacific Ocean, where for some two years or more he was engaged in the ordinary duties of a cruise. He returned in 1833, and was examined and promoted to passed midshipman.

For a year and a half he was now employed on naval stations. From 1835 to 1837 he served on the coast of Brazil in the Ontario and Erie. In 1839 he was promoted to lieutenant, and again sent to the coast of Brazil in the brig Enterprise. Returning from this station, he was, in 1842, ordered to the steam-frigate Missouri, Captain Newton commanding, which, after being employed for some time on the coasts of Cuba and Mexico, was sent to convey Mr. Cushing, minister to China, with despatches from President Tyler.

This unfortunate vessel, it is well known, caught fire in the harbor of Gibraltar, and was burned up. Winslow was sent back by Cushing with despatches to the Government, announcing the catastrophe. He was ordered by the Navy Department to return and assist in the removing of the debris, etc. The wreck was finally destroyed by being blown up with gunpowder.

He was afterwards employed on shore stations, till December, 1845, when he was ordered on board the Cumberland, which soon after sailed, as Commodore Connor's flagship, for Mexico. The Mexican War breaking out, he was sent, after the battle of Palo Alto, in a boat expedition up the Rio Grande, to prevent the Mexican army from crossing the river, but which failed to accomplish its object, as the retreating force effected a passage higher up.

Some time after, he was one of a boat expedition sent on shore, fourteen miles from Vera Cruz, to get water for the fleet. The boats were attacked, when the vessels in the distance opened a heavy fire, which drove the assailants back, so that water was obtained.

Soon after, he was drafted with two divisions of the flotilla for Tobasco. Caught in a tremendous gale of wind, the expedition lay for three days at the mouth of the river, unable to enter it. On the 3d, Frontera, three miles up the stream, was captured with two steamers and some other vessels. The next day, Tobasco was reached, and some fourteen vessels captured. Winslow landed with his division, and, advancing to the plaza, was met with a shower of musket-balls. A sharp contest followed, without material advantage to either side.

At night he was ordered to retire, and take down the river one of the captured vessels. The next day, the Mexicans opened from every battery and fort of the city, and a general bombardment followed, which resulted in the fleet dropping back to Frontera.

Winslow's bearing was so fine, and his gallantry so conspicuous on this occasion, that Perry publicly complimented him, and as a token of his high appreciation of his conduct, gave him the choice of vessels. He selected the Morris, and sailed to join the fleet at Vera Cruz.

He was next drafted with a division, to sail for Tampico and capture it. The city, seeing the boats advancing, capitulated. Here he remained for six weeks, guarding the arsenal, until the arrival of troops from New Orleans. He then returned to the fleet at Vera Cruz, and there found *Raphael Semmes*—whose vessel, the Somers, had been capsized in a squall, and all but thirty of the crew lost—*occupying his room.* The two afterwards shared it together, until other arrangements could be made. Under what widely different circumstances the same men are sometimes brought together! To-day, a young officer, having lost his vessel and crew, without any assigned place, occupies the room of his brother officer and friend, until his return. Fighting under the same flag, they have a common feeling and sympathy. Winslow especially feels for the unfortunate lieutenant, whose vessel, with all her armament, is sleeping at the bottom of the Gulf.

Twenty years pass by, and those two officers meet off the coast of France as deadly enemies, sailing under different flags. A fierce conflict follows, and when it is over Semmes is again swimming for his life, not towards the flag of his country, to find shelter in his friend's room, but away from it, and from that former friend, to seek protection under a foreign flag. The two meetings stand in strange and striking contrast to each other.

In February, 1847, Winslow was drafted into the Mississippi, Commodore Perry commanding, and not long after returned home. All hands being detached from the vessel, as she was ordered to be altered for a flagship, he was sent to Boston on ordnance duty. In March, the following year, he sailed as first lieutenant in the Saratoga for Mexico. The vessel stopping at Hayti, where the revolution was then in progress, he landed at night in a boat to bring off the refugees, which he succeeded in doing, marching unmolested through the town, though dark visages crowded around his little band. These being sent to Jamaica, he sailed for Yucatan, where he was actively engaged in supplying the inhabitants with arms, &c., to enable them to repel an invasion of the Mosquito Indians. Having completed this task, he went to Tampico, Vera Cruz, and other ports, to gather up and send home what belonged to the United States, and which had been left there at the close of the war.

Returning in the summer of 1849, he had a rest of two years, and was then ordered to the frigate St. Lawrence, and sailed on a cruise in the Pacific. Visiting the various ports of South America, the islands of the Pacific, San Francisco, &c., he was absent three years and five months, engaged in active duty all the while. Returning in the spring of 1855, he was ordered on recruiting duty to Boston. In the following September, he was promoted to commander. From that time till the breaking out of the rebellion, he performed various duties along the coast, acting, in the mean time, as light-house inspector. With that patriotism and devotion to duty which have always distinguished him, the moment he heard that the flag he loved so well had been fired upon, he hastened to Washington, and applied for active service. He was ordered to join Foote at St. Louis, where the latter was fitting out a flotilla. To extemporize, equip, and man a fleet on the Mississippi, in the short time required, was no ordinary task, yet the whole work was put on him, and a half dozen other officers. Not only were the vessels to be constructed out of such material as they could at once lay hands on, but gun-carriages had to be made, guns cast, and cordage and anchors procured, and then western boatmen taken and drilled into "men-of-war's men." Foote had great confidence in him, and when the fleet was ready, he directed him to make an experimental trip with it. He did so, and reported the result to the former, who expressed great gratification with it. He then took the first division of the flotilla down the river, and joined Grant at Cairo, Foote remaining in charge of the second division. Having performed this duty, he was ordered back to St. Louis to relieve Foote, and bring down the second division also. While in charge of this, and in command of the flagship Benton, which had got hard aground, he met with an accident, which came near depriving the country of his valuable services. While superintending the work of getting the unwieldy monster off shore, the chain attached to it parted with the tremendous strain put upon it, and the broken link, flying with the force of a cannon ball, struck his left arm, tearing out the tendons, and making a frightful wound. Crippled and bleeding, he was carried to his couch, where he lay helpless for some time. As soon as he was able, he went home to recover; but, just as Foote was leaving for Fort Pillow, he joined him again. After the action at this place, he was ordered up to hurry down the rams, and did not rejoin the fleet till after the action at Memphis. He was then ordered to relieve the officer in command of the division at St. Charles, White River, where the Mound City had been blown up, in the capture of the place. The object of this expedition, aided by one regiment under Colonel Fitch, was to succor General Curtis. But the enemy was in too great force, and attacked the fleet with rifles every day, keeping the shores aflame with their fire. In the mean time, the river began to fall rapidly, and, in order to detain the fleet until it would be left aground, the enemy sunk vessels in the channel. For awhile, it seemed probable that Winslow would be caught as Porter was up the Red River, but by great effort he succeeded in destroying the sunken hulks, and reached the Mississippi in safety. He now took the Cincinnati, and joined the fleet en route for Vicksburg. Effecting a junction with the lower fleet, in the action that followed he covered the mortar boats. Remaining here two weeks, he was sent back to Memphis to coöperate with Sherman and take charge of the river above. While he was engaged in sending out various expeditions against the guerillas, and moving backward and forward to keep the river free of obstructions from the pestilent gangs, Davis was relieved from command of the fleet. Winslow now applied to the Department to be transferred to sea-service, as one more congenial to his tastes. The pilots and volunteer officers, hearing of this, waited upon him, and informed him that they were about sending a delegation to Washington, to request the President to give him command of the fleet, and to say that, if he refused, they should in a body resign. They also informed him, to his surprise, that a similar application had been made after the battle of Fort Pillow, and now, if their request was not granted, they should leave the service. Though gratified at this voluntary, strong testimonial of the attachment of the officers to him, he was grieved at the action they contemplated. In the first place, he wished no promotion obtained in this way. In the second place, a true patriot himself, he desired that the country should have the services of these gallant men, no matter what became of him. He told them so, and that they must on no account let any personal matter come between them and their country—*that* had the first and last claim on them. Inspiring them with his own unselfish and patriotic spirit, he succeeded in dissuading them from their purpose.

Fortunately for his own fame, and the honor of his country, and especially of the navy, his request to be transferred to sea service was granted, and he was shortly afterwards ordered to take command of the Kearsarge. He joined the vessel in the early part of the year 1863, and was ordered to the coast of Europe to watch rebel cruisers. It was with a sense of relief and freedom he found himself once more on the broad bosom of the ocean, which had been his home for so many years. A man, who, all his life, had been accustomed to the deck and armament of a man-of-war, felt ill at ease in the cramped-up, nondescript craft that composed the western flotilla. Besides, this dodging about up crooked narrow streams, fighting guerillas on shore, and raking for torpedoes on the bottom of rivers, is to the thorough-trained sailor and commander very much what bushwhacking and guerilla fighting is to a brave and able commander on shore.

In command of a fine vessel, with a noble crew under him, and out on the open sea, Winslow lacked nothing to complete his happiness but to meet a rebel cruiser, his equal in size and armament, in a fair sea-fight.

The rebel vessel Florida, having been heard of off the coast of South America, he was sent in search of her.

Subsequently, he cruised in the channels off the coast of England and France. Here he was constantly kept in hot water by the French and English Governments, which complained of his violations of the neutrality laws. The French, petulant and complaining, ordered the French pilots not to serve him, and he had to become his own pilot, which, fortunately, he was perfectly able to be, showing these gentlemen that he knew the waters that washed their coast quite as well as they did. Finding the Florida in Brest, and about to sail, he blockaded the port, and, though it was midwinter, the stormiest season of the year, he boldly carried his ship into intricate bays, along leeshores, through races where the eddying currents swept at the rate of seven knots an hour, and where ships had never been before, with a skill and daring that made the French pilots stare with surprise. They could not comprehend what to them seemed the recklessness of the American commander, who, without a pilot, would undauntedly steam through channels along which the sea ran like a torrent, the breakers foaming and thundering on each side of him, and where a vessel had never before been known to go. In any commander but one who knew the ground thoroughly, it would have been madness; for he was more than once caught in these dangerous channels in gales that strewed the shores of England with wrecks.

In the presence of such a bold and vigilant enemy the Florida dared not leave port. The duty that Winslow performed was, in this cold and stormy season, a most trying one. Yet the crew, inspired with his own energy and enthusiasm, cheerfully seconded all his efforts.

At length, however, he got short of provisions, and was reluctantly compelled to set sail for Cadiz, to obtain supplies. Taking advantage of his forced absence, the Florida slipped out of port and put to sea. Winslow, however, was soon back, and steamed in search of the fugitive. Overhauling one vessel after another only to find them French vessels, he was compelled at last to acknowledge that the enemy which he had watched so long and faithfully was beyond his reach.

Having been foiled in his efforts to capture the Florida, he proceeded to Calais, where he had learned that the rebel steamer Rappahannock was. He lay off this port for two long months, watching and waiting in vain for the rebel to put to sea.

At length, one day on running into Ostend—a short trip, which would not interfere with his keeping the Rappahannock from putting to sea—a pilot in the employ of the rebels ran the vessel plump ashore, breaking through the piers. Winslow saw at once that it was done on purpose, and, divining the object, was roused by it into tenfold energy and determination. He sternly ordered every pilot from the ship, resolved to be his own pilot, and, summoning all hands, went to work, and by great efforts hove off his ship before morning.

The commander of the Rappahannock, who was waiting for this calamity to befall Winslow, the moment he heard of it accepted the French terms that had been dictated to him, and prepared to put to sea. Winslow, however, who was kept informed of his movements, heard of it, and immediately hoisted anchor, and, without waiting for some of his officers and crew who were on shore to come on board, steamed out of the harbor. When the morning sun broke over the sea, the rebel commander, to his astonishment, saw his enemy once more off the port of Calais. He now gave it up, and taking everything out of the ship finally dismantled her.

Seeing this enemy disposed of, Winslow went to Flushing to repair in dock. He had scarcely completed his repairs when he received a telegram stating that the Alabama had arrived in Cherbourg. This was exciting news—all hands were called, and the bow of the Kearsarge was quickly cleaving the waves towards Cherbourg. Two days after, he lay off the port.

Semmes, the commander of the Alabama, when he was informed of the arrival of the Kearsarge, sent Winslow the following challenge;

CONFEDERATE STEAMER ALABAMA,
CHERBOURG, *June 14th*, 1864.

SIR,—I hear that you were informed by the United States Consul that the Kearsarge was to come to this port solely for the prisoners landed by me, and that she was to depart in twenty-four hours. I desire you to say to the United States Consul that my intention is to fight the Kearsarge as soon as I can make the necessary arrangements. I hope these will not detain me more than till to-morrow evening, or next morning, at the farthest. I beg she will not depart before I am ready to go out.

I have the honor to be, very respectfully, your obedient servant,

R. SEMMES, Captain.

Semmes may have *heard* that the mission of the Kearsarge was the peaceful, timid one he represents, but we do not believe he, for one moment, credited the rumor. He knew perfectly well that his old friend had been chasing him half round the globe to get a fight out of him, and had heard too that he had said that, if they ever met, one ship or the other would go to the bottom, and the introduction of this pretended "hearsay" was meant as a taunt. Irritated at being so long chased and held up to the world as a pirate, and now confronted by his old messmate and present foe, he thought he would irritate in turn, by hinting that the Kearsarge would hasten to get out of harm's way. He knew better—he knew that he had got to remain a prisoner in that port, or sneak away clandestinely, which would be a confession of weakness and fear, or fight. Winslow quietly waited for five days, perfectly willing to give the Alabama ample time to complete all her arrangements.

The Sabbath morning of the 19th of June was a lovely one. No strong wind lashed the sea into waves, but a gentle breeze came drifting in from the ocean, bringing a slight haze, through which the summer sun shone with a softened radiance upon the deep. Semmes had made no concealment of his intended fight, nor of the time it would come off, and the news that it was expected to take place on this Sunday morning had spread over the surrounding country, so that an excursion train was sent down from Paris, loaded with passengers to witness it. A photographer perched himself with all his apparatus in a church tower that overlooked the neighboring sea, in order to obtain a sketch of the approaching combat. The port swarmed with boatmen offering their boats to those who wished to go out and witness it, and the quiet town of Cherbourg looked as if some great fête was about to come off. There were two, however, who did not feel so—Captains Semmes and Winslow. Each knew the other well—his bravery and resolution—and that the approaching struggle would be a desperate and decisive one. Semmes was determined to fight his ship to the last, and was well aware that the proud American flag swaying far out to sea would never go down before his guns, except it went to the bottom. The night before, he had told M. Bonfils, the agent of the Confederate government in port, that he was a Roman Catholic, and, as he would not be able to attend divine service the next day, requested him to attend mass and have it offered up for him. He did so, but the prayers, it seems, were unanswered.

Winslow was equally serious, for, notwithstanding his confidence in his ship, the crew, and himself, he knew how often the fate of a battle turns on a chance shot. His life, his reputation, and the honor of his flag, he was well aware, were in jeopardy, and were all to be cast at once on the doubtful issue of an even-handed fight. Of only one thing he was certain, that, ere that Sabbath sun touched the western waves, his fame would be secure, his flag victorious, and the scourge of the ocean no more, or he and his good ship would be lying together on the bottom of the deep. But quietly making all his preparations, he seriously committed himself and the flag of his country to Him who lifts up or casts down, according to His sovereign pleasure. The Alabama bore the motto, "Aide toi et Dieu t'aidera," "Help yourself and God will help you."

Semmes, in his plundering career, had accumulated *sixty* chronometers, which he took the precaution to send ashore, that they might be saved in case of disaster to his ship.

Spectators, in the mean time, crowded every spot that commanded a view of the neighboring sea, and the most intense excitement prevailed among the vast throng. A little after nine, as the church bell's were ringing, calling people to the house of prayer, the Alabama cast loose, and began to steam out of the harbor. As the graceful vessel slowly drifted past the mole, black with the eager crowd, a mighty shout rent the air, and "God speed you!" rolled over the quiet waters of the bay. For a response, came back the stern roll of drums beating to quarters. About ten o'clock, Winslow, through his glass, saw the head of the steamer coming round the end of the mole, some three miles distant, and immediately beat to quarters. The French steamer Couronne accompanied the Alabama, till she reached the limits of French waters, and then steamed back without waiting to witness the combat. The English yacht Deerhound also followed after—the owner of which, having received a telegraph at Caen, informing him of the expected fight, had hastened down with his wife and family to witness it. Determined to be a close spectator, at the risk of receiving a random shot, he kept on after the Couronne had turned back. By a singular coincidence this yacht was built by the famous, or rather infamous, house of Laird & Co., that had also built the Alabama, with which the rebels had driven our commerce from the ocean. She was now to witness what the handiwork of these rebel sympathizers would do.

Winslow, as soon as he descried his antagonist approaching, turned his vessel and steamed slowly seaward, for the double purpose of avoiding the question of jurisdiction, and to have the battle take place so far from shore that his adversary, if crippled, could not take refuge in port, before he had time to finish him. The Alabama followed after, and for awhile it looked from

SINKING OF THE PIRATE ALABAMA BY THE KEARSAGE.

shore like a chase, rather than a fight. But when Winslow had got about seven miles out, he turned short about, and, putting on steam, steered straight for his enemy, intending to run him down. Semmes, discovering his design, slowed his engines and sheered off, thus presenting his starboard battery to the Kearsarge. The latter was now about a mile off and was moving steadily ahead, when there suddenly came sharp puffs of smoke from the side of the Alabama, followed by the deep thunder of her guns rolling over the tranquil sea. The shot and shell flew over the Kearsarge, cutting up her rigging, but effecting no serious damage. Like the gallant Hull, in the first sea-fight of the war of 1812, Winslow made no reply, but sternly ordered the engineer to put on more steam, and the noble steamer the next moment was dashing the foam from her bows, as she pressed forward for a death grapple. In two minutes came another broadside, and then another, yet not a gun replied. Silently and sternly Winslow kept on his way, but, as he approached, bows on, he saw that he was in danger of being raked, and therefore, when about a half a mile distant, he sheered, so as to bring his own broadside to bear, and fired his first gun. The crashing shot and bursting shell, that made the rebel ship tremble, showed Semmes that his adversary intended to throw away no shot in this deadly encounter. Wheeling, Winslow again pressed on under a full head of steam, in order to get in close range, but soon sheered and poured in another broadside. In about ten minutes, the spanker gaff of the Alabama and the ensign came down on a run. These were immediately replaced, and the fight went on. The two vessels were now steaming at the rate of seven or eight miles an hour—and every few minutes sheering, so as to bring their broadsides to bear, they were forced to fight in circles, swinging steadily around an ever changing centre. The firing, when within a quarter of a mile of each other, was rapid and terrible. Two guns of the Kearsarge, carrying eleven-inch shells, did fearful damage, making great gaps in the hull of the enemy. The former, in the mean time, received but little injury from the wild firing of her antagonist. But, about twenty minutes after the conflict began, a sixty-pound Blakely shell passed through her bulwarks, and, bursting with a terrific explosion on the quarter-deck, wounded three of the crew of the pivot-gun. One of them was named William Gowin, who, though pale and suffering acutely, was carried to the surgeon with a smile on his face: "It is all right," said the brave fellow, "we are whipping the Alabama. I willingly lose my leg or life, if necessary;" and, as the heavy broadsides shook the deck, he would comfort his two wounded comrades by telling them that "victory was certain." And as ever and anon the cheers of the crew were borne to his ears, when they saw the shell and shot planted in a vital part of the Alabama, he would wave his hand over his head, and give a faint cheer in reply. A true hero to the last, when the battle was over, and he found himself dying, he exclaimed, "I am willing to die, for we have won a glorious victory!" With a crew composed of such men, a commander can never suffer defeat.

The difference between the firing of the two vessels was very marked. The Alabama fired rapidly—almost two guns to the Kearsarge's one—but very wild. Now a shot would enter the starboard gangway, a shell here, and another there, cut away planking, or crash through the engine house, while the rigging seemed alive with the hissing, exploding missiles, yet none of them doing but little damage. Winslow, on the contrary, fought his ship as coolly as though engaged in mere practice. To the different officers he said, "Don't let the men fire too rapidly. Point the heavy guns below rather than above the water-line, and sweep the decks with the lighter ones." It is astonishing to see how the character and bearing of a commander affect the conduct of the crew. Receiving their inspiration from him, the gunners pointed their pieces with the coolness and precision they would have done if firing at a target, the only evidence of excitement being the cheers that rose over the thunder of the guns, as they saw a huge gap open in the side of the Alabama, where an eleven-inch shell entered at her water-line. Besides her regular armament, the Kearsarge had a twelve-pound howitzer, which was wholly useless in the fight, unless the vessels came to such close quarters that grape could be used. This piece was put in charge of two old quartermasters, "the two Dromios" of the ship, as they were laughingly called, with orders not to fire until directed to do so. The jolly old salts, however, had no intention of remaining idle, while their messmates were having, as they said, "all the fun." So when the combat thickened, and the enemy's shells and shot came bursting and tumbling about their ears, they forgot their orders, and loaded and fired their howitzer, as though the battle rested solely on their exertions. They knew perfectly well that it was a mere waste of ammunition, yet they greeted each discharge with a loud cheer, and between the shots would curse and swear at each other, for not making better hits, in the most approved man-of-war style.

This droll exhibition drew peals of laughter from the crew, that sounded strangely amid the din and uproar of the awful cannonade that shook the deep. The officers saw at a glance in what excellent condition for cool, effective fighting, this jolly humor kept the men, and, amused themselves at the ludicrous picture which these old privileged favorites of the ship presented, did not interfere, and let them fire on until their entire box of ammunition was exhausted.

On the Alabama, a very different scene presented itself. Stripped to their shirts and drawers, the heated gunners worked their pieces with desperate energy; for the ripping planks and shuddering hull, and splintered masts, and bloody decks, told them that this mode of fighting could not last long. One shot alone disabled a gun, and killed and wounded eighteen men. Another exploded in the coal bunks, completely blocking up the engine-room, while on every side the ship seemed to be incessantly struck with Titanic sledge-hammers. Thus round and round in their fiery, cloudy circles, the well-matched steamers swept—the Kearsarge edging nearer and nearer as she moved on her pathway of flame, Winslow straining every nerve to get to closer quarters, where he could sweep the decks of his adversary with grape. At the seventh rotation, as the American commander was just getting warmed to his work, or rather when, as he said, he "*supposed the action for hot work had just commenced*," he saw the Alabama set her fore trysail and two jibs, and turn her head towards the shore. He knew at once that it was all up with her, for she limped heavily on her way, and, steaming after her, poured in shot and shell with such destructive power, that in a few moments the rebel flag came down, and a white flag was run up. He at once ordered the firing to cease. But, in less than two minutes, the enemy opened again with two guns, when the Kearsarge suddenly belched forth flames, and, steaming grandly ahead, was laid across her adversary's bows, for raking, just as the white flag was a second time run up.

In a few moments, boats were seen lowering into the water, and an officer in one of them rowed quickly alongside, saying that the ship had surrendered and was sinking, and that with Winslow's permission he would return and bring off the prisoners.

But scarcely twenty minutes passed, when the Alabama threw her bows high out of the water, like some huge drowning animal making a last struggle for life—the mainmast, which had been half cut in two by a shot, breaking off in the effort—and then with one heavy lurch went to the bottom, with all her armament and a part of her crew, leaving only the swirling waters to tell where she had gone down. Amid the eddying waves that clashed above her descending form, a crowd of human heads were seen struggling for life. Winslow immediately ordered the only two boats he had left, to be lowered, and hasten to the rescue of the drowning men. Observing the yacht Deerhound steaming towards the scene of disaster, he called out, "For God's sake, do what you can to save them!" She immediately began to pick up the swimmers, and soon the boats of the Kearsarge were on the spot engaged in the same humane work. Semmes, nearly exhausted, was picked up by the Deerhound. The moment he was on board, he begged not to be delivered up to Winslow, and was placed in the bottom of the boat and covered with hammock cloths. As soon as she had got her load, the Deerhound steamed rapidly away for the English coast. Mr. Lancaster knew that in doing this he was carrying off our prisoners, and had Winslow anticipated such faithlessness, or want of honor, he would have brought the Englishman to with a shot.

Captain Semmes, in his report, written while smarting under his defeat, said, "The enemy fired on me five times after my colors had been struck. It is charitable to suppose that a ship-of-war of a Christian nation could not have done this intentionally." Why, then, does he mention it at all, or in a way that clearly shows that he wants the reader believe it was done on purpose? A man of any sagacity would have left this out, for he would have known that so preposterous a supposition would not be believed by any one, and would damage nobody but himself.

The disparity of loss in this engagement was very remarkable—the Kearsarge, though receiving twice as many shots as she gave, had only three killed and wounded in all, while, according to Semmes' own report, his loss was thirty, or ten times as great as that of his adversary. If the same proportion had been preserved, under an equal number of shots, the loss would have been as one to about twenty.

This naval engagement, which lasted only a little over an hour, and resulted in such a triumphant victory, created a most profound sensation in Europe, and the English papers discussed it in a manner and spirit that at this time only provokes a smile of derision. One said that the Alabama, having just returned from a long voyage, was not in a condition to fight—forgetting that this reflected quite as severely on Semmes as his defeat, for he was not compelled to fight till he was prepared. He could have staid in Cherbourg a month, if he liked, or until he was in a condition to go to sea. An officer who knowingly and unnecessarily takes his ship into action, when she is not in a seaworthy condition, is not fit to command one.

Another, apparently seeing the dilemma in which this placed the rebel commander, said that it was probable that Semmes knew that his ship was not only in a dilapidated condition, but that she was too far gone ever to be rendered fit for service again, and, in the true spirit of chivalry, resolved to give her a glorious death, and so go out and sink her alongside with her colors flying. This is a worse explanation than the other, for it makes Semmes a barbarian. Rather than his ship should rot in the port of Cherbourg, he would destroy all that gallant crew which had followed him so long. Besides, the ship did not go down with her colors flying, but with the white flag of surrender alone fluttering in the breeze. But the great explanation of the defeat was the disparity between the two vessels. It was affirmed, without the least knowledge of the facts, that the Kearsarge was the heavier vessel, with heavier armament, and a larger crew. This was the stereotyped excuse offered by Englishmen for those astounding victories in almost every single-handed sea-fight that occurred between the national vessels in the war of 1812.

Although this attempt to pluck away Winslow's well-earned laurels, was owing in some measure to the sympathy generally felt in England towards the South, it is, doubtless, mainly to be attributed to the fact that the Alabama was an English ship, armed with English guns, and fought by an English crew, so that they felt it was a combat between an English and American ship-of-war. It was this that made them feel so sore. If the Alabama had been victorious, it would have been claimed really as an English victory. But, unfortunately, the English vessel having gone to the bottom, there was nothing left them but the old absurd cry of an unequal fight.

Again, Semmes and his English friends endeavored to lessen the victory, by saying that the Kearsarge was iron-plated, the former asserting that he did not know, till the action was over, that she was iron-clad. Now, this iron-plating was simply some spare chain-cable, hung over the vessel amidships, and boxed over with planking. Its main object was to protect the engines, as the Kearsarge was lightly loaded with coal, while the Alabama was so deeply loaded, that her engines were protected without it. This, doubtless, is the reason Semmes did not resort to the same expedient, for it had become a custom among all vessels to do so, ever since Farragut had set the example at New Orleans.

Semmes exhibits his own character in a painful light in his report, which abounds in transparent falsehood, either direct or implied. He was perfectly aware of the existence of these chains, for he said, some days previous to the fight, "that they were only attached together with rope-yarn, and would drop into the water with the first shot." If these chains were really of such vast service, and he neglected to put them on his own ship, it would have been much better for his reputation had he said nothing about it.

The following figures show how much reliance can be placed on Captain Semmes' statements. He says, "The enemy was heavier than myself, both in ship, battery and crew:"

	ALABAMA	KEARSARGE.
Length over all,	220 feet.	214½ feet.
Length in water-line,	210 "	198½ "
Beam,	32 "	33 "
Depth,	17 "	16 "
Horse-power—two engines,	300 each.	400
Tonnage,	1150	1031

Thus, it will be seen that the Alabama was the longest vessel, deepest vessel, possessing greater engine power, and the heaviest vessel. Besides, she had one more gun than the Kearsarge, although the latter, by her large guns, threw the heaviest broadside. But, during the engagement, the Kearsarge fought only five guns, while the Alabama fought seven. The latter also fired nearly double the number of shots that the former did. Hence, so far as the amount of metal thrown, the Alabama had clearly the best of it. It is true the Kearsarge had one great advantage, which we cheerfully concede: she carried American guns, chiefly Dahlgrens, while the Alabama's armament was wholly English. Thus much as to Semmes' statement that the Kearsarge was heavier both in ship and battery.

We will now examine the captain's statement that his antagonist outnumbered him in the crew. It is a matter of small moment, however, in an engagement like this, which was fought by shot and shell alone; for in such an encounter, any more men than are necessary to work the guns and handle the ship, are in the way. It is only in boarding, or close quarters, where the numerical superiority of the crew gives any advantage.

But be that as it may, the Kearsarge's vast superiority in crew consisted of just sixteen men. Winslow reports his crew, including officers and sick, *one hundred and sixty-three.* Many of the English papers made the crew of the Alabama to consist of only about one hundred persons. Mr. Mason, Confederate representative in London, declared, over his own signature, that it numbered just one hundred and twenty. But three days after, the Liverpool *Mercury* published a complete list of the crew of the Alabama, giving the names of all, except those picked up by the Deerhound, and this list sums up one hundred and three. Now, the latter picked up forty-four, thus making in all one hundred and forty-seven against one hundred and sixty-three. The simple truth is, that there never was, and probably never will be, a naval duel between two vessels more equally matched than these. The secret of success lay here, as it did in the single-handed fights between British and American frigates in the war of 1812, not in superior bravery, or seamanship, or vessels, but in superior gunnery. Dahlgren's guns here vindicated themselves.

The Constitution was ready to go again into action in a few hours after the Guerriere went to the bottom—so, subsequently, every spar was standing in her, while the Java lay a helpless wreck on the ocean. So now, the Kearsarge had hardly begun to fight, when the Alabama went down with all her dead on board.

A great deal of noise was made over Semmes' chivalrous character, because he threw his sword into the sea, rather than surrender it to his enemy—on which the London *News* sarcastically remarks, "he had better *thrown over his trumpet* with the sword."

The conduct of Mr. Lancaster, owner of the yacht, met with universal condemnation on both sides of the water. Urged by Winslow to help those who he knew had surrendered themselves prisoners of war, he no sooner got Captain Semmes and some forty more aboard his vessel, than he steamed away, at the rate of thirteen knots an hour, for Southampton. He dared not return to Cherbourg, for he knew he was acting the part of a thief, and so made haste to get into an English port. So hard was he scourged for his dishonorable conduct, that he found it necessary to publish a defence, which only made the matter worse. He says, "Captain Winslow's request to help save the crew was not accompanied with any stipulation, to the effect that I should deliver up the rescued men to him as prisoners. If it had been, I should have declined the task, because I should have deemed it dishonorable—that is, inconsistent with my notions of honor—to lend my yacht and crew, for the purpose of rescuing those brave men from drowning, only to hand them over to their enemies for imprisonment, ill treatment, and perhaps execution."

What a confession is this for a member of the Royal Yacht Squadron to make? Because Winslow made no stipulation that he should deliver up to him men who had surrendered and were prisoners of war, and hence just as much his, by the laws of nations and the laws of honor, as though they were on board his vessel, he therefore felt justified in running away with them! That is, if Winslow saw a large amount of his own property floating about, and in danger of being lost, and should ask Mr. Lancaster to help him save it, the latter, after picking up a good boat-load, would run away with it, because the request to save it was not accompanied with a stipulation that he should return it to the lawful owner!

One hardly knows which to admire most in this barefaced statement—its morals or its logic. Again he says: "I should have deemed it inconsistent with my notions of honor to lend my yacht and crew for the purpose of rescuing those brave men from drowning, &c." His sense of honor would have forced him to look stolidly on and see those men drown, rather than save them, if they were to be held as prisoners. This certainly is a most extraordinary exhibition of honor, and exists nowhere, we apprehend, except in the British Isles. One would think that a proper feeling of honor, not to say of humanity, would prompt a man to consult the men struggling for life, to know whether they preferred to go to the bottom, or be saved as prisoners. They had already taken their choice, and surrendered rather than sink with the ship, and now asked to be saved. But this Englishman, with his notions of honor, thinks that they did not know what was best for themselves, and rather than save them on the very terms they had accepted, he would have allowed them to drown.

One can imagine this pompous Englishman moving off with his yacht, while the half-drowning crew is despairingly calling on him to save them, with the reply: "Captain Winslow has ordered me to give you up as prisoners, and it is inconsistent with my sense of honor to save you on those terms—and you had better go to the bottom."

If Captain Winslow had dreamed how little sense of honor the man possessed, he would have wakened him up to the sense of it with shot and shell, in a manner that would have taught him better logic and better manners.

We venture to say that it will be the last time a vessel of the Royal Yacht Squadron will be a close spectator of a naval engagement in which one of the combatants is an American ship of war.

Captain Winslow received the following highly complimentary letter from the Secretary of the Navy, who did not attempt to conceal his great delight at the summary destruction of this vessel, which almost alone had driven our commerce from the seas.

"NAVY DEPARTMENT, *July* 6, 1863.

"SIR;—Your brief despatches of the 19th and 20th ultimo, informing the Department that the piratical craft Alabama, or "290," had been sunk, on the 19th of June, near meridian, by the Kearsarge, under your command, was this day received. I congratulate you on your good fortune in meeting this vessel, which had so long avoided the fastest ships, and some of the most vigilant and intelligent officers of the service, and, for the ability displayed in this combat, you have the thanks of the Department.

"You will express to the officers and crew of the Kearsarge, the satisfaction of the Government at the victory over a vessel, superior in tonnage, superior in number of guns, and superior in the number of her crew. The battle was so brief, the victory so decisive, and the comparative results so striking, that the country will be reminded of the brilliant actions of our infant Navy, which have been repeated and illustrated in this engagement.

"The Alabama represented the best maritime efforts of the most skilful English workshops. Her battery was composed of the well-tried thirty-two pounders, of fifty-seven hundred weight, of the famous 68-pounder of the British Navy, and of the only successful rifled 100-pounder yet produced in England. The crew were generally recruited in Great Britain, and many of them received superior training on board her majesty's gunnery ship, the Excellent.

"The Kearsarge is one of the first gunboats built at our Navy Yards, at the commencement of the rebellion, and lacks the improvements of vessels now under construction. The principal guns composing her battery had never been previously tried in an exclusively naval engagement, yet, in one hour you succeeded in sinking your antagonist, thus fully ending her predatory career, and killed many of her crew, without injury to the Kearsarge, or the loss of a single life on your vessel. Our countrymen have reason to be satisfied, that in this as in every naval action of this unhappy war, neither the ships, the guns, nor the crews, have been deteriorated, but that they maintain the abilities and continue the renown which ever adorned our naval annals.

"The President has signified his intention to recommend that you receive a vote of thanks, in order that you may be advanced to the grade of Commodore. Lieutenant Commander James S. Thornton, the executive officer of the Kearsarge, will be recommended to the Senate for advancement ten numbers in his grade, and you will report to the Department the names of any others of the officers and crew, whose good conduct on this occasion entitle them to especial mention.

Very respectfully,

GIDEON WELLES,

Secretary of the Navy.

"CAPTAIN JOHN A. WINSLOW,

Comd'g. U. S. Steamer Kearsarge, Cherbourg, France."

But if the Government was delighted and Europe excited over the result of this naval conflict, the people of this country were filled with unbounded enthusiasm. This vessel had seemed as ubiquitous as the Flying Dutchman—so erratic were her movements, and rapid her transitions, that the most experienced officers that were sent in pursuit of her invariably returned baffled. The swiftest steamers scoured the ocean in search of her, but always failed to find her. Yet she did not hide away in obscure places, but boldly stood along the track of our commerce, and made the ocean lurid with the flames of our merchantmen, which she burned because there was no port that dared to receive the prizes. One day she would be on the Atlantic seaboard—the next, lost in the intricate mazes of the West India Islands, and, when the search for her was about to be abandoned, news would come that she was flaunting her flag in the Indian Ocean, sending terror amid our vessels in that remote part of the world. The people were irritated, indignant, and mortified, that this bold rover should so put to defiance our fleetest steamers and best commanders. But now her career was ended—not by the storms of heaven, or hidden sea-rocks, nor yet by being ignominiously shut up in a neutral harbor—but in fair, open combat had been sent to the bottom by a vessel inferior in size—in a fight, too, not forced on her by circumstances, but one of her own choosing. Her commander had sent an open challenge, thus inviting spectators to come and witness our defeat. The national feeling was satisfied, and the name of Winslow was mentioned with pride by every tongue.

Yet, right on the top of this, the Secretary of the Navy wrote to Winslow: "I notice by the last mail from England that it is reported that you have parolled the foreign pirates, captured on board the Alabama. I trust you have not committed this error of judgment." And again: "In parolling the prisoners, however, you committed a grave error." How did the Secretary of the Navy know this, for he had never yet received Winslow's report of his proceedings? What right had he to censure a gallant officer on mere rumor? It never occurred to him that this brave commander, whose whole life had been spent in the naval service, knew vastly better what was proper and right under the circumstances than he could who had been but three years or so in the Navy Department. It always has been a source of annoyance to our naval commanders that they are under the orders of an officer wholly ignorant of the naval profession. A lawyer, or editor, or politician, is placed at the head of the navy, and, seemingly thinking that all necessary qualifications come with the office, conveys or gives orders or proposes measures that a naval officer would never think of doing. That the War and Navy Departments of this great country should, every four years, be put under a new man, to whom the duties of both are wholly unknown, is an error that has cost us and will cost us in the future millions of treasure and oceans of blood.

Winslow, in reply to this censure, said that his decks were crowded with the bedding of the wounded and prisoners under guard; moreover, the ship was damaged both in rigging and hull. A shot had entered the stern-post, raising the transom frame and binding the rudder so hard as to require four men at the helm. It was therefore important that an examination should be made of the damages sustained. This, of course, could not be done without clearing the ship. This was the more important, as he continued, "I received information from our consul, in London, that the Florida was in the channel on the French coast, and at the same time information came that the Yeddo was out, and the Rappahannock was expected to follow." He had heard that the sea around him was alive with rebel cruisers, with no vessel but the Kearsarge to take care of them. "It therefore became," he says, "in my mind, of the utmost importance that the Kearsarge should at once be put in a state to meet these vessels and protect our commerce. This could not be done with prisoners on board equalling half of our crew, and the room occupied by the wounded, to the exclusion of our own men; to have kept them would have required a quarter watch as guards, and the ship would have been wholly ineffective as a man-of-war to meet this emergency which threatened. Under these circumstances, and without an American vessel in port, by which arrangements could be made for transhipping the prisoners outside, I felt it my duty to parole them." Of course it was his duty to do so—not to act as jailor to thirty or forty men, but strip his vessel for another fight, and keep rebel cruisers from these waters.

Commodore Winslow has all the qualities that go to make up a great naval commander—a naturally strong intellect, cultivated by careful training and long practical experience. Quiet in his manner, he is yet capable of intense excitement, but which shows itself only in increased energy and determination. Apparently destitute of fear, he is, notwithstanding, never rash. When once fairly roused, no obstacles can stop him, no dangers daunt him. Of great powers of endurance, and a courage that never flags, there seems no limit to his exertions. Rock-fast in his resolution he moves to his purpose with a firmness before which everything must give way. His remark that he was just getting ready for "warm work" when the Alabama surrendered, reminds one of Paul Jones, who, when asked if he had surrendered, replied that he had just begun to fight, and throws a flood of light on the character of the man. Without being vain, he has a supreme confidence in himself—a self-reliance growing out of the consciousness of power. Scorning cant, trickery, and humbug, in others, he never blows his own trumpet, and, instead of overestimating, underrates his own actions. He sees only the simple performance of duty where others are dazzled with the heroism of his conduct, and hence did not fully appreciate the enthusiasm of the people at his victory over the Alabama. His fame is secure, and his name, which in one hour he made known the world over, will go down to posterity on the same historic roll with Hull and Bainbridge, and Perry and McDonough, and other naval heroes of the nation.

CHAPTER XV.

VICE-ADMIRAL DAVID D. PORTER.

HIS BIRTH AND EARLY EDUCATION.—ACCOMPANIES HIS FATHER TO THE WEST INDIES IN SEARCH OF PIRATES.—ENTERS THE MEXICAN NAVY AS MIDSHIPMAN.—HIS FIRST FIGHT ON THE CUBAN COAST.—IS TAKEN PRISONER AND PLACED IN CONFINEMENT.—PAROLLED AND RETURNS TO MEXICO.—RETURNS HOME.—ENTERS THE NAVAL SCHOOL.—MIDSHIPMAN IN THE U. S. NAVY.—HIS SUBSEQUENT SERVICES AND CRUISES.—SENT BY BUCHANAN TO HAYTI TO INVESTIGATE THE CONDITION OF THE DOMINICAN REPUBLIC.—MADE FIRST LIEUTENANT ON THE SPITFIRE IN THE MEXICAN WAR.—AT VERA CRUZ.—HIS GALLANT ATTACK OF TOBASCO.—AT TUSPAN.—COMMANDS THE PACIFIC MAIL STEAMSHIP PANAMA, AND SAILS THROUGH THE STRAITS OF MAGELLAN.—COMMANDS THE GEORGE LAW STEAMER GEORGIA, FOR THREE YEARS.—COMMANDS THE STEAMER GOLDEN AGE.—REMARKABLE VOYAGE TO AUSTRALIA.—SENT BY THE SECRETARY OF WAR TO IMPORT CAMELS.—BREAKING OUT OF THE REBELLION.—SENT TO RELIEVE FORT PICKENS.—A CURIOUS PIECE OF HISTORY.—BLOCKADES THE MISSISSIPPI.—LONG CHASE AFTER THE PRIVATEER SUMTER.—COMMANDS THE MORTAR FLEET UNDER FARRAGUT IN THE ATTACK ON NEW ORLEANS.—THE BOMBARDMENT.—GOES TO PENSACOLA AND MOBILE.—AIDS FARRAGUT IN PASSING THE BATTERIES OF VICKSBURG AND PORT HUDSON.—PUT IN COMMAND OF THE MISSISSIPPI FLEET.—CO-OPERATES WITH FARRAGUT, SHERMAN, AND GRANT.—ARKANSAS PORT.—WHITE RIVER.—BATTLE OF GRAND GULF.—AIDS GRANT IN THE SIEGE OF VICKSBURG.—EXPEDITION TO THE SUNFLOWER COUNTRY.—FALL OF VICKSBURG.—RECEIVES THE THANKS OF CONGRESS.—MADE ADMIRAL.—SUBSEQUENT OPERATIONS ON THE MISSISSIPPI RIVER.—THE RED RIVER EXPEDITION.—A NEW CHAPTER IN ITS HISTORY.—PASSAGE OF THE FALLS NEAR ALEXANDRIA BY THE FLEET.—BAILEY, ENGINEER OF THE DAMS, REWARDED BY PORTER.—RENDERS SHERMAN VALUABLE AID IN HIS MARCH TO CHATTANOOGA.—VARIOUS OPERATIONS IN HIS EXTENSIVE DISTRICT OF COMMAND.—RETURNS NORTH TO VISIT HIS FAMILY.—PLACED OVER

David D. Porter

VICE ADL DAVID D. PORTER

THE NORTH ATLANTIC BLOCKADING SQUADRON.—THE FIRST EXPEDITION AGAINST FORT FISHER.—THE BOMBARDMENT.—SECOND EXPEDITION.—THE ATTACK.—THE VICTORY.—AIDS GRANT IN HIS LAST MOVEMENT AGAINST LEE.—HIS CHARACTER.—PRESENT COMMAND.

THE saying has almost passed into a proverb that great men seldom beget great sons. The renowned Commodore Porter of the war of 1812, however, is a notable exception, for he gave to his country two sons as famous as himself, David D. and William D., and distinguished too for the very traits of character that made him so remarkable. The former, in addition to the great qualities of his father, had the advantage also of being trained in his profession directly under his eye, where he could feel the force of his example.

He was born June 8th, 1813, in the town of Chester, Delaware County, Pennsylvania. He received the first rudiments of education at that place, and entered Columbia College in the city of Washington, at the early age of eleven years. His college course, however, was a short one, for, in 1824, he accompanied his father, Commodore Porter, to the West Indies, where the latter was sent by the Government to break up the gang of pirates that infested those seas, and there imbibed his first taste for sea life. In 1826, Commodore Porter, at the solicitation of the Mexican Government, took command of the Mexican Navy, and appointed his son David a midshipman in the service. The latter spent one year in the city of Mexico, learning the Spanish language, and at the end of that time reported himself for active service afloat. His father was about to sail with the Mexican fleet for the coast of Cuba, but it being unable to go to sea, for want of supplies, he fitted out several small prizes, in one of which, the Esmeralda, with his cousin, D. H. Porter, as captain, young Porter sailed to destroy the Spanish commerce around the island of Cuba. After a cruise of sixty days, in which he had many narrow escapes, the schooner, laden with a cargo of sugar and coffee taken from thirty captured vessels, sailed for Key West. But the crew, consisting of twenty-nine men, mutinied while the vessel was on her way, and attempted to take possession of her. The captain, however, D. H. Porter, a powerful and determined man, cut some of them down, and shot several others, and finally succeeded in getting the remainder in irons, and, with Midshipman Porter and a faithful Swede, brought the vessel into Key West.

In 1827, Commodore Porter returned with the Mexican fleet to Vera Cruz, and fitted out afresh for a new expedition, having in the first one almost destroyed the coast commerce of Cuba.

Midshipman David D. Porter was detailed to the brig Guerrero, with his former captain, D. H. Porter. The Guerrero, built in New York, by Henry Eckford, was a fine vessel and mounted twenty guns. She sailed in June, 1827, for the coast of Cuba, and on sighting the island, the fourteenth day out, discovered a large convoy in shore, in charge of two brigs-of-war. The Guerrero was immediately cleared for action, and chase given to the enemy. The Spaniards and their convoy ran into the port of "Little Mariel," fifteen miles west of Havana. This snug harbor was defended by shoals and a two-gun fort; but, although the two brigs ran in and got springs on their cables, the Guerrero boldly followed them, and, anchoring outside, opened with her guns, to which the brigs and the fort both replied.

The action lasted one hour and a half, in which the brigs were completely dismantled and cut to pieces by the Guerrero's shot. The fort still kept up a galling fire, and the latter had to haul out of range—the captain intending to go in at night with boats, and finish the combat.

In the mean time, the heavy cannonading had been heard in Havana, and a large sixty-four-gun frigate, the Lealtad, slipped her cables and put to sea.

The Guerrero was standing in shore to take possession of her prizes, when the frigate hove in sight, coming on with a fresh breeze, while the former lay becalmed. The names of the two brigs were the Marte and the Amelia, and they were so knocked to pieces that they were never used again in the Spanish Navy. They mounted, together with the fort, six more guns than the Guerrero.

The frigate finally came up with the Guerrero, and one of the most desperate and unequal battles on record took place between the two vessels, which ended in the capture of the brig, but not till she had bravely held her own against her huge antagonist for two hours and a half. The brig did not surrender until all her masts were shot away, and she was in a sinking condition. Eighty-six men were killed and wounded, out of one hundred and eighty in this desperate conflict. The captain was killed, and all the officers wounded, and there was not a shot left in the locker to fire.

Young Porter was badly hurt in the first fight, but performed the duty of captain's aid in the second battle, where he was also wounded. A mere lad, he had, like Farragut, under his father, received a bloody baptism into the naval service, and in his first combat learned how a ship should be fought.

The vessel, after her capture, was towed into Havana,

where the officers and crew were imprisoned in a filthy hulk, at the base of the Moro Castle, and kept in close confinement many months, suffering a great deal both in mind and body. They had the consolation, however, of knowing that the Spanish frigate had lost more men than they, and was finally dismasted at sea, owing to the injuries to her spars, received during the fight.

Midshipman Porter, owing to his ill-health, was finally allowed to go to Vera Cruz on parole, where, finding no chance of getting exchanged, he returned to the United States.

After going to school for a year, he obtained, in 1829, an appointment as Midshipman in the United States Navy, and sailed with Captain Alexander Wadsworth, in the Constellation, for the Mediterranean.

In 1832, he joined the frigate United States, flagship of Commodore Patterson, and spent three years in her, when he returned to the United States to stand his examination. From the time of passing his examination, until his promotion to lieutenant, he was employed on the Coast Survey. In 1840, he sailed in the frigate Congress to the Mediterranean and coast of Brazil. On his return from this cruise, he was employed at the Naval Observatory, under Lieutenant Maury. In 1846, he was sent by Mr. Buchanan, then Secretary of State, to the island of Hayti, the Dominican Republic, to ascertain the exact condition of affairs in that country. He was three months on the island, and during that time travelled nineteen hundred miles on horseback, taking the census of every town, and returning with much information useful to the Government.

While Lieutenant Porter was absent on this duty,

the war between the United States and Mexico broke out, and he applied for immediate service afloat.

He was ordered to proceed to New Orleans and raise men for Commodore Conner's fleet. This duty he performed, and carried the men to Vera Cruz, where he was made First Lieutenant of the steamer Spitfire, Captain Tatnall. Lieutenant Porter had great difficulty in getting Commodore Conner to order him into service, the latter not liking his full whiskers, which the lieutenant declined to part with, never having shaved more than once or twice in his life.

Lieutenant Porter was with Tatnall, as First Lieutenant of the Spitfire, when the latter attacked the Castle of San Juan de Ulloa, and the town batteries.

A few days after, the Spitfire attacked the batteries again, and did material service to the army, by withdrawing the Mexican fire from our batteries on shore.

No vessel performed more active service than the Spitfire while Lieutenant Porter was in her. When Commodore Perry moved on Tobasco, the Mexicans barricaded the river, and so it was determined to land the troops, or sailors, eighteen hundred in all, and attack the city by land. But the Spitfire, disregarding the obstructions, made a dash through them, and pushed on up the river, in advance of the landing party, amid the hearty cheers of all.

Eight miles up, the vessel encountered a heavy fort, commanding the river. It mounted eight large guns, while the Spitfire had only one heavy gun (8-inch), and two thirty-two-pounders.

The first shot from the fort cut the Spitfire's wheel in two, but the little steamer sped on, firing rapidly, and gained the rear of the battery, where, letting go her anchor, she soon cleared the works.

Lieutenant Porter, under the fire of the steamer's guns, boarded the fort with sixty-five men, and carried it with a shout.

The landing party arrived four hours afterwards, and found the town and batteries of Tobasco in possession of the Spitfire, and the Scorpion, a steamer commanded by Captain Bigelow, which vessel came up behind the former.

Lieutenant Sidney Smith Lee, who commanded the Spitfire, being ordered to the steamer Mississippi, Lieutenant Porter was given the command of her, which he retained while the American forces held Tobasco, and until ill-health obliged him to go home after the fall of Vera Cruz.

He was engaged in every operation that took place during the Mexican war, and was first lieutenant of the steamer Spitfire, the leading vessel when our little fleet of steamers fought their way up Tuspan River and captured that place.

On his return to the United States, he was again ordered to the Coast Survey, but, having been offered the command of the Pacific Mail Company's steamer Panama, he took charge of her and sailed for the Pacific, through the Straits of Magellan. He left the steamer at Panama, after a most successful voyage, and returned to the United States, when he was placed in command of George Law's steamer, the Georgia, which vessel he successfully commanded for three years, without an accident of any kind. Having got into a difficulty with the Spanish authorities at Havana, in which he made them respect the American flag, he left the service of the company by which he was employed, and took command of the steamer Golden Age, belonging to the Australian Steamship Company.

Proceeding to England, he made a successful voyage thence to Australia in fifty-six days, thirty days quicker than it had ever been made before.

He ran the Golden Age six months on the Australian coast, and then crossed the Pacific with a load of English passengers, and arrived safely at Panama.

Having taken the Chagres fever, he was obliged to return home, and it was many months before he regained his health. The Secretary of War, Jefferson Davis, then selected him to go abroad to import camels. He performed this duty successfully, bringing over two loads, eighty-four in all, and then (1859) was ordered to the Portsmouth (N. H.) Navy Yard.

Just before the breaking out of the war of the rebellion, Lieutenant Porter was directed to bring the old frigate Constitution to Annapolis. This being done, he was about to proceed to California, to take charge of the Coast Survey vessels there, when the Southern States seceded. Sumter was now threatened by the rebels, who had seized upon many of our best forts. Fort Pickens was also in great danger, although gallantly defended by Lieutenant Slemmer of the artillery.

And here occurs one of the most curious pieces of history that has ever seen the light. It really reflects on no department of the Government, but it illustrates the total confusion into which everything was thrown at the commencement of the rebellion:

It may be recollected that Mr. Fox, Assistant Secretary of the Navy, identified himself with an expedition that was fitted out by the Government and some merchants in New York, to throw supplies into Sumter.

The expedition was badly planned and worse executed, and it was necessary to lay the blame on some one. Mr. Seward came in for the greatest share, when in fact he had nothing whatever to do with it.

While at dinner, on the very day Porter was to have started for California, he received a letter from Captain (now General) Meigs, asking him to call on Mr. Seward, who wished to see him. He did so without delay, and, after some preliminary conversation, Mr. Seward asked him if he thought it possible to get a ship into the harbor of Pensacola and reinforce Fort Pickens, and thus prevent the rebels from making use of the most important harbor on the Atlantic. He replied that there was no difficulty about the matter, provided he could have his own way. He then unfolded his plan, when Mr. Seward took him to see Mr. Lincoln, with whom he discussed the whole matter thoroughly. His plan was, for the President to give him authority to proceed to New York and take command of the Powhatan, then lying partly dismantled at the Navy Yard; also to invest him with power to give such orders in the Navy Yard as he deemed proper—in fact, placing for the time being the officer in command there under his directions. This was perhaps a high-handed measure—going over the head of the Secretary of the Navy, and fitting out a ship without his authority or cognizance. Still, it was the only way to accomplish the object. Secretary Welles was new in the office, and had no knowledge of the men about him. Half of them were traitors; and had a single individual in the Department known that such an expedition was fitting out, it would have been flashed along the wires in a very short time, and Bragg, the rebel commander at Pensacola, would at once have overpowered Lieutenant

Slemmer with his handful of men, and taken possession of the fort.

The President, after carefully weighing all the circumstances of the case, and listening to all the arguments offered him, finally took the responsibility, and wrote an order directing him to proceed to New York without delay, and take command of the "Powhatan," or any other vessel that he deemed necessary for his purpose. The Commandant of the Navy Yard and the naval officers were directed to give him all the aid and facilities he desired, to enable him to get the vessel to sea with the least possible delay. In conclusion, the President said, "You will not show these orders to any naval commanding officer superior in rank to yourself, unless there is danger of your being interfered with. When inside of the harbor, you will call upon the senior naval officer at Pensacola for such reinforcements as you may deem sufficient to hold the place."

Other orders were also issued, one to the commander of the Powhatan, Captain Mercer, ordering him to give up his vessel, and one to the commandant of the yard at New York, ordering him to give him secret despatch, &c., &c. Armed with these extraordinary orders, he hastened at once to New York.

In the mean time, Captain Meigs, who was the originator of the scheme to relieve Fort Pickens, also proceeded to New York and chartered one of the Atlantic steamers, which he prepared for sea without delay, to carry two thousand regulars. Under the guns of the Powhatan these were to be thrown into Fort Pickens, to reinforce Lieutenant Slemmer.

When Porter reached New York, he found the Powhatan had just been put out of commission, her crew sent to the receiving-ship, and all her officers detached. Her sails were unbent, her machinery all apart, her powder and gun-gear on shore, and her coal-bunkers empty. A survey had been held on her, her boilers and hull had been condemned, and she was to go in dock for repairs, when Porter presented his orders to Commodore Foote, who then commanded the Yard. The latter was quite taken aback at the unusual, extraordinary proceeding, and Porter had very great difficulty in getting him to pay that attention to them which they demanded. Foote considered it impossible to send the vessel to sea, she was so unseaworthy, and her boilers were actually dangerous, while her rigging was all rotten, and her boats would not float. However, there was no other vessel, and Porter, with that determination which characterizes him, shoved the President's orders at Foote so hard, and insisted so pertinaciously on a compliance with them, that the latter finally had to give in, and went to work with a will to get the ship ready for sea. She was, without question, in a horrible condition, but there was no remedy, and she had to go. For six days and nights, Porter sat in Commodore Foote's office, directing the different operations, and urging on the work. Foote, in the mean time, telegraphed for the officers the former wanted to go with him. Captain Mercer, who was let into the secret, took charge of the vessel for the time being, and made it appear that he was going out in her, and it was rumored that she was getting ready to carry a Minister to Mexico. In fact, Porter's boxes and trunks, labelled as the property of the Minister to Mexico, were sent on board in open day, no one suspecting even that he was going out in the ship, or had any connection with her.

On the sixth day after commencing to fit her out (working night and day, including Sunday,) the vessel was ready to sail. But just as Porter was about going on board, an order came from the Navy Department to "*fit the Powhatan for sea with all despatch, and report her when ready to proceed.*" Here was a dilemma. The Secretary evidently knew nothing of what was going on, and to give up the ship would be to imperil the whole expedition, for Captain Meigs depended on the guns of the Powhatan to cover his landing. Besides, the vessel had a large part of the artillery and ammunition belonging to the troops, on board.

On receiving the Secretary's order, Commodore Foote sent for Captain Mercer, and showed it to him, but he agreed with Porter that the order of the President was paramount to all others, and it was decided that the ship should proceed on her destined mission. Porter at the time supposed that the order of the Secretary was given as a matter of form, and that he had been made acquainted with the whole affair.

In half an hour after this, he stepped on board the ship, as if to bid the captain good-by, and in the confusion was unnoticed. He remained in the cabin until the Powhatan reached Staten Island, where the captain (Mercer) left her to go on shore. But just as they were hoisting the boat on board, and about to proceed, a swift steamer came puffing alongside with an officer on board, who delivered Porter the following despatch:

"*Give up the Powhatan to Captain Mercer.* (*Signed*,) SEWARD."

But Porter still held grimly to the President's order; no other order, he said, could take precedence of that. It was no time to stand on trifles, the country was in danger, and, if he gave up the ship, the expedition would have to be abandoned, and Captain Meigs, who had sailed just ahead, would go on a bootless mission. It took but a moment for Porter to decide, and he telegraphed back: "My orders were from the President, and I must look to him to support me," explaining at the same time how matters stood.

It will be seen from Mr. Seward's telegraphic despatch, that he threw no obstacle in the way of the Powhatan's going to the relief of Fort Sumter, which he at the time was accused of doing. The Powhatan could not have been got ready for the expedition to relieve Sumter, had she commenced preparations at the time Mr. Welles' order came to fit her out. That order (as things were going on) would have found her all in pieces, and in dock. In five days after Porter sailed in her, Fort Sumter fell.

The Powhatan, under any circumstances, would have been of no use in such an expedition, for she could not cross the bar at Charleston, while her boats were worthless, as they would not float; and when Porter lowered them into the sea off Pensacola, the seams were so open that they all filled with water.

The ship could only have laid off the harbor, and her officers and men would have witnessed the bombardment as others did, without being able to do any good.

It will be seen, therefore, that it was a very unjust thing to lay the blame of the failure on Mr. Seward, who, in saving Fort Pickens, performed a more important service than the relieving of Sumter would have been.

Porter had heavy weather all the voyage out, and

the ship was almost knocked to pieces, yet in eight days he appeared off the harbor of Pensacola, disguised as an English steamer, and so altered that, with English colors up, the officers of the fleet lying off the place did not know the vessel. The troops in the Atlantic Company's steamer arrived just before him, and had got close to the beach, ready to be landed. Porter was standing in *over the bar*, with the batteries all manned, and would have been inside or sunk in twenty minutes more, when General Meigs intercepted him in a tug, and wished him to cover the landing. He still clung to the President's order, to go inside and take the place, but Meigs showed him another order from the President, directing him to comply with any requisition made upon him by the army landing party, and he was reluctantly obliged to give up his plan of going inside. He proceeded at once to cover the landing, and in half an hour Fort Pickens was safe in our possession. With a strong force of regulars thrown in, there was no longer any chance of General Bragg's attacking it. Thus the most important fort in the South was kept in our possession.

Had the rebels succeeded in getting into it, (which they would have done that night, but for this opportune arrival,) Pensacola would have proved a greater thorn in our side than either Charleston or Wilmington.

In justice to Mr. Seward, he deserves all the credit of the achievement, notwithstanding the abuse heaped upon him.

As soon as Porter got all the troops on shore, he urged the senior naval officer, Captain Adams, to blockade the port, and permit no vessels to go in with supplies. He would not do so himself, but told Porter that he might. The latter fitted out at once a small pilot-boat, and, lying in close with the Powhatan, closed the port effectually.

He could have gone into Pensacola at any time, ten days after his arrival, and anxiously desired to do so, but the army officers in Fort Pickens *protested* against it, urging as a reason, that the fort was not in a condition to resist the fire of Bragg's batteries, which Porter knew he could silence. He had made a reconnoissance inside the harbor, on a bright moonlight night, and with a night-glass saw that there were very few guns. It was a great disappointment to him not to be able to take the place, when he knew how easily it could have been done, but he could not attempt it with the army and navy commanders (both his seniors) opposed to it. He has, no doubt, since regretted a hundred times that he paid any attention to such timid counsels, and did not take the responsibility.

On the arrival of Commodore McKean, the Powhatan was ordered to blockade the mouth of the Mississippi, at the Northwest Pass, which she did successfully for ten months, no vessel getting in or out.

Finally, the Sumter ran by the United States steamer Brooklyn, at Pass a l'Outre, and escaped to sea. A short time afterwards, the Powhatan's boats captured a prize to the Sumter, endeavoring to get into Barrataria Bay. From the prisoners, Lieutenant Porter learned that the Sumter was on the south side of Cuba, committing depredations on our commerce.

By permission of Commodore McKean, he went in pursuit of her, and finally arrived at the mouth of the Surinam, the day after the Sumter sailed from there. He then concluded to steer for Maranham, but met with the same disappointment at the latter place. Thence he tracked the privateer all the way back to the West Indies, where she escaped among some of the French islands.

The Powhatan, having steamed over ten thousand miles with her condemned machinery, was now obliged to return to the United States, where she was laid up at about the time of the Dupont expedition to Port Royal, and Lieutenant Porter was detached. He immediately sought other active service, and, the capture of New Orleans being proposed by him, he was put in communication with General McClellan and General Barnard of the engineers, to talk the matter over. They were unanimous in their opinion that the city could be taken, and preparations were accordingly made to attempt the capture of the forts at or near the mouth of the Mississippi River. Admiral Farragut was ordered to command the naval forces, and Lieutenant Porter, having recommended a large force of mortar vessels, was directed to equip them without delay. In thirty-six days thereafter, twenty-one mortar schooners and seven gunboat steamers sailed from New York for Key West, to join the New Orleans expedition.

Only the mortars were cast. The iron carriages had all to be made, twenty thousand shells to be cast, and the vessels to be fitted. The fleet arrived at Ship Island, and found the squadron still there, and not over the bar of the Mississippi, as Porter feared it would be, and so was in time.

After entering the river, the gunboats of Commander Porter's flotilla were constantly employed in helping the large vessels over the bar. He devoted himself personally to the matter, and when the pilots failed, time after time, he succeeded in getting the Mississippi and Pensacola over, and up to Pilot Town. His fleet being all ready to move, he sailed up to within three miles of the forts, and tied up to the bank.

As stated in a previous chapter, under the order of Porter, Messrs. Harris and Oltmanns were detailed by Mr. Gerdes, assistant on the coast survey, to make a minute survey of the river, from "Wiley's Gap," as it was called, up to the forts. Lieutenant-commanding Guest, in the Owasco, was detailed to protect them in their work. These brave engineers surveyed and triangulated over seven miles of the river, taking in both Forts Jackson and St. Philip. A part of the time they were under fire of shot and shell from the batteries, as well as exposed to riflemen concealed in bushes on shore, yet they finished their work successfully, and established with great precision the positions which the mortar-boats were to occupy.

Before these took their assigned places, Porter directed the masts to be dressed off with branches, which would intermingle them so with the trees or vines, behind which they were to be placed, as to render them invisible to the enemy. This showed admirable foresight, and afterwards so distracted the fire of the enemy that it was far less destructive than any one expected it would be.

The wood behind which Porter concealed his mortar-boats, was three hundred yards across, and so dense that the rebel shot could with difficulty pierce it, while Porter's shells rose over it to drop with mathematical accuracy into the hostile works. The fleet was divided into three divisions, under the command of Lieutenants Watson Smith, K. R. Breese, and W. W. Queen, and when the signal to "commence action" was made, they opened in order, each one firing every ten minutes. The forts immediately replied with all the guns they could bring to bear, and the rebel shot crashing through the forest, and the shells of the mortars rising in graceful curves above it, presented a magnificent spectacle.

About noon, Porter, seeing that the enemy was getting the range of Queen's division, and the shot falling too near, went on board to move it, and found that a hundred-and-twenty-pound shot had passed through Queen's vessel, damaging the magazine.

At five o'clock the fort was discovered to be in flames, and the fire of the enemy ceased.

Night coming on and the wind rising, Porter ceased firing, having sent over fourteen hundred shells into and around the rebel works. On the south shore, the mortars could be pointed only by sights fixed to the mastheads, "and many curious experiments," remarks Porter, "were resorted to, to obtain correct firing."

The next morning, the 19th, he opened fire again and kept it up steadily all day. During the day the schooner Maria G. Carleton was sank by a rifle shell passing through her deck, magazine, and bottom, while Porter was alongside.

Each day now was a repetition of that which preceded it. Porter, seeing that the fuses of the shells were bad, ceased timing them, and ordered full-length fuses, so that they would burst after they had entered the ground. Although there were great disadvantages in this arrangement, it prevented shells from bursting in the air.

The ground being wet and soft, they descended eighteen and twenty feet into the soil, and, exploding some time after they were landed, lifted the earth up in huge masses. The effect was like that of an earthquake. For three days and nights the commanders and crews got but little rest, and few meals, and hence would often be found by Porter in his rounds fast asleep, even while a mortar beside them was thundering away, and shaking everything around like an earthquake. Seeing that this strain could not be borne long he ordered each division into three watches of four hours each. By this arrangement the firing was more accurate, and fifteen hundred shells were thrown every twenty-four hours. Under this tremendous explosion, windows were broken in Balize, thirty miles distant.

On the night of the 20th, Porter covered the expedition sent to break the chain across the channel, with a tremendous fire from his mortar fleet. On the 23d, he urged Farragut to commence the attack with his ship that night, as ammunition was getting low, and the crews were well nigh worn out, while the enemy was daily adding to his naval force and power of defence.

As the fleet of Farragut, towards morning, steamed past the batteries, Porter's flotilla of steamers, the Westfield, Owasco, Clifton, and Merwin, moved up and maintained a galling fire with shrapnell on the forts, until the last vessel had got beyond range of the rebel guns.

Porter had hardly ordered the firing to cease, when it was reported to him that the celebrated ram Manassas was coming down to attack him. She was steaming slowly along shore, as if preparing for a dash, and fire was opened on her. But Porter soon saw that she was a dying monster, and ordered the commanders to spare their shot. The smoke now began to pour from her, showing that she was on fire, while her hull, badly cut up with shot, slowly settled in the water. Porter tried to save her as a curiosity, and got a hawser around her, but just before she reached the bank she exploded, and, "like some huge animal, gave a plunge and disappeared under the water." Next came a steamer on fire, followed by two others, burning as they slowly drifted by, while "fires seemed to be raging all along up river," showing what wild work Farragut's fleet was making with the rebel vessels. Porter now sent a flag of truce to the forts, demanding their surrender. The answer was, "the demand is inadmissible."

Giving the men a day to rest, and, having heard in the mean time from Farragut, Porter again opened on the forts. He then sent another demand for their surrender, with the terms he would grant. This time the answer indicated a great change in the temper of the commander, for he replied that, after receiving instructions from the authorities of New Orleans, he probably would comply with his summons. On the 28th, a flag of truce came on board, the bearer of which announced that the terms offered by Porter would be accepted.

While he was engaged in the capitulations, an officer approached him, and reported that the iron floating battery Louisiana, of four thousand tons burthen, and mounting sixteen heavy guns, had been set on fire. Porter turned to the rebel commander, and quietly remarked that the act was in no way creditable to him. The latter replied that he was not "responsible for the acts of naval officers." Porter then went on with the negotiations, when an officer again approached him, saying that the ropes which fastened the vessel to the bank had been burned off, and that all in flames she was drifting slowly down on them. Porter turned to the commander and asked if the guns were loaded, and if there was much powder on board. The latter replied, "I presume so, but I know nothing about the naval matters here." At that moment the heated guns began to go off, throwing shot and shell, as though engaging a battery. The heavy thunder of the explosions, foretelling what would happen when the magazine was reached, aroused a little of the sleeping tiger in Porter, and, turning to the rebel military officers, he coolly said: "If you don't mind the explosion which is soon to come, we can stand it," and went on with the conference, amidst the stern music, as calmly as though nothing else was going on. In speaking of it afterwards, he said: "A good Providence, which directs the most unimportant events, sent the battery off towards Fort St. Philip, and, as it got abreast of that formidable fort, it blew up with a force which scattered the fragments in all directions, killing one of their own men in the fort, and when the smoke cleared off it was nowhere to be seen, having sunk immediately in the deep water of the Mississippi. The explosion was terrific, and was seen and heard for many miles up and down the river. Had it occurred near the vessels, it would have destroyed every one of them." Porter denounced this dastardly act in scathing language.

Like all brave, magnanimous men, willing to accord the high qualities they possess to others, even though fighting in a bad cause, he said, the "*military* commanders behaved honorably to the end. * * * The most scrupulous regard was paid to their promises. They defended their works like men. Had they been fighting for the flag under which they were born, instead of against it, it would have been honor enough for any man to have said, he had fought by their side."

After the capitulation of the forts, and the surrender of the few remaining steamers, Porter visited the former to see what had been the effect of his bombardment. He found that one thousand three hundred and thirteen bombs had struck in the centre and solid parts of the works, two thousand three hundred and thirty in the moat, near the foundations, shaking the whole structure to its base, nearly one thousand exploded in and over the works, and one thousand three hundred and fifty-seven struck about the levees, and in the marsh close around, and in the paths and near the water's edge, where the steamers attempted to come. Porter says:

It was useless for them to hold out; a day's bombardment would have finished them; they had no means of repairing damages; the levee had been cut by the thirteen-inch bombs, in over a hundred places; and the water had entered the casemates, making it very uncomfortable, if not impossible, to live there any longer. It was the only place the men had to fly to out of reach of the bombs. The drawbridge over the moat had been broken all to pieces, and all the causeways leading from the fort were cut and blown up with bomb-shells, so that it must have been impossible to walk there, or carry on any operations with any degree of safety. The magazine seems to have been much endangered, explosions having taken place at the door itself, all the cotton bags and protections having been blown away from before the magazine door. Eleven guns were dismounted during the bombardment, some of which were remounted again and used upon us. The walls were cracked and broken in many places, and we could scarcely step without treading into a hole made by a bomb-shell; the accuracy of the fire, is, perhaps, the best ever seen in mortar practice; it seems to have entirely demoralized the men, and astonished the officers. A water battery, containing six very heavy guns, and which annoyed us at times very much, was filled with the marks of the bombs, no less than one hundred and seventy having fallen into it, smashing in the magazine, and driving the people out of it. On the night of the passage of the ships, this battery was completely silenced, so many bombs fell into it, and burst over it.

Many remarkable escapes and incidents were related to us as having happened during the bombardment. Colonel Higgins stated an instance, where a man was buried deep in the earth, by a bomb striking him between the shoulders, and directly afterwards another bomb exploded in the same place, and threw the corpse high in the air. All the boats and scows around the ditches and near the landing, were sunk by bombs; and when we took possession the only way they had to get in and out of the fort to the landing, was by one small boat to ferry them across.

Porter did full justice in his report to his brave commanders Renshaw, Guest, Wainwright, Hanell, Baldwin, and Woodworth, of the steamers, and Smith, Breese, and Queen, of the flotilla.

Unstinted praise of others connected with him, whether military officers or subordinates, who perform their duty nobly, is a peculiarity of Porter. His impulses are so generous and noble that he always seems afraid that he shall take too much credit to himself, and not do full justice to others.

The flotilla now took on board General Butler's troops, and conveyed them to New Orleans, where the mortar vessels were also orderd to assemble.

Commander Porter was anxious to push on to Vicksburg with his force, which he thought would have resulted in the capture of that place, but he was sent to Ship Island, to await the attack on the Mobile forts. In the mean time, he sent the mortar schooners to cruise off the coast, and captured several prizes loaded with cotton.

As Admiral Farragut was detained in New Orleans, Commander Porter determined to attempt the capture of the forts at Mobile, alone, and for this purpose got under way from Ship Island, with the mortar vessels and gunboats, and steered for Mobile Bay. The wind however dying away, and the weather looking bad, the schooners put back into port, but the gunboats went in and tried their range on the works, hitting them almost every time, while only a few shots were fired in return.

Not designing to do anything more than exhibit a little practice, the gunboats retired at sunset. Some went back to Ship Island, and the Harriet Lane drifted along up to Pensacola.

Next day, two deserters came off in a boat, and informed the blockading officer that there was only a small fire-company in the fort, who had all intended to surrender. The day after, it was strongly reinforced.

In the mean time, the telegraph conveyed the news to Pensacola that a strong force of gunboats was coming to that place, upon which the rebels set fire to everything, and evacuated it. Commander Porter arrived off there while this was going on, and ran in and assisted to transport the troops across from Santa Rosa Island to the mainland.

The mortar fleet all rendezvoused at Pensacola, but their anchors were hardly down when Porter received orders from Admiral Farragut to join him at Vicksburg. He immediately proceeded thither and bombarded that place on the passage of the fleet, as he did at Forts Jackson and St. Philip. One of his steamers, the Jackson, being disabled by a rifle shell, the Clifton went to her assistance, when a shot pierced her boiler—the escaping steam scalding six men and wounding many others.

The mortar fleet laid two weeks before Vicksburg, at a distance of eighteen hundred or twenty-two hundred yards from the batteries, and always succeeded in silencing them when they opened fire.

Porter had three of his vessels disabled, and twenty-nine men killed and wounded on his steam flotilla, during the passage of the fleet, accompanying each vessel as far as the water batteries, where they were exposed to a heavy fire.

In July, 1862, Commander Porter was ordered by

the Secretary of the Navy, to proceed with twelve mortar boats to Fortress Monroe, and there await orders. He arrived there in ten days, and there being nothing for the vessels to do, he obtained leave of absence, and was finally detached from the command of the mortar flotilla, a little fleet of which he was very proud, and which had rendered most excellent service. Wilkes took the command, and eventually broke it up, an act, in Porter's judgment, very injurious to the navy.

In September, 1862, he was ordered to command the Mississippi squadron, as Acting Rear-Admiral, and entered upon his duties the next month.

Admiral Porter found the fleet quite inadequate for the defence of such long rivers. There were only thirteen good vessels in all, and these required heavy repairs. He immediately improvised a navy-yard at Mound City, and in a short time his fleet numbered one hundred vessels. These were common river boats, armed with heavy guns, and covered with light iron to resist field pieces and rifle balls.

Admiral Porter, immediately on his arrival in the west, notified General Grant that it was proposed at head-quarters to send General McClernand to attempt the capture of Vicksburg, which would have been an invasion of his (Grant's) command. In consequence of this information, the General hastened to Cairo and arranged a plan of attack on Vicksburg, which was at once carried out. He marched from Holly Springs, while Sherman embarked thirty thousand men in transports, and, under cover of the gunboats, proceeded to surprise Vicksburg.

The gunboats under Admiral Porter joined Sherman

at Memphis, from whence they proceeded together direct to Vicksburg, while General Grant was marching on with 50,000 men from Holly Springs.

The rebels had filled the Yazoo River with torpedoes, and the gunboats were sent in at once to clear them out, which they did, under a murderous fire of musketry from hidden sharpshooters.

On the 12th of December, 1862, while this work was going on, the Cairo, one of the finest vessels, was blown up by a torpedo, and sunk out of sight in three minutes.

The officers and men deserved great credit for their successful efforts in clearing out torpedoes, and, on the 18th of December, two landings had been secured for General Sherman's troops, both well protected by the gunboats.

In the mean time, the rebels had burned the army stores at Holly Springs, so that General Grant was obliged to fall back again to protect his base and obtain further supplies.

The force that had left Vicksburg, under Joe Johnston, to meet him, now fell back again on Sherman, who, instead of finding about ten thousand men, found forty thousand in possession of the place.

The army, after landing and meeting with great success, had to retire with loss. The rains, setting in very heavily at the same time, obliged them either to reëmbark or swim for it.

Admiral Porter made an attack on the Yazoo batteries; but, owing to a heavy fog that set in, accompanied by heavy rains, it was not successful.

General Sherman now proposed to the Admiral to withdraw from before Vicksburg and attack Arkansas Post—

a strong work up the Arkansas River. In the mean time, General McClernand came down and assumed command; but the army virtually remained under the control of Sherman, and Admiral Porter refused to coöperate unless it was so.

The fleet and transports arrived in the Arkansas River about the 2d of January, 1863, and, after the army had gained its desired position, the gunboats went in and attacked the fort at close quarters—seventy-five yards. After a sharp and sanguinary fight of three hours, all the enemy's guns being dismounted, and our army surrounding it ready for an assault, the rebels surrendered. The fort surrendered to the navy, and the troops on the outside to the army. Porter had twenty-six killed and wounded in the engagement. He showed here, not the long practice of mortar vessels, but the close combat of vessels when lying broadside to broadside.

After the capture of the fort, destruction of all war material, and embarkation of the prisoners—seven thousand in all—the army and navy returned to Vicksburg.

Previous to this, Admiral Porter sent his vessels up White River and captured all the enemy's remaining batteries, which left the Arkansas and White Rivers open to the gunboats whenever they chose to go there. For his success on this occasion, he received the thanks of Congress.

On the return of the fleet and army to Vicksburg, regular operations were commenced against it—the Yazoo being held by the navy. Fifteen heavy mortar floats were towed down from Cairo, gunboats were fitted out and added to the fleet as fast as possible, and, finally, the whole river was so well protected, from Cairo to Vicksburg, that transports came and went with perfect security.

General Grant now came in person to take command of the army, and there was from the first the most perfect accord between him and Admiral Porter, the latter being at all times ready to carry out his slightest wish. Never did a military commander have the aid of a more persevering, energetic, unconquerable, tireless, and able naval commander than Grant, in the long and arduous work that followed.

Great patience and endurance were shown on both sides; but nowhere can history exhibit a more indomitable spirit than that manifested by our navy.

Admiral Porter led his fleet into almost inaccessible places. The heart of the Yazoo or Sunflower country was reached in a great overflow of the Mississippi, by pulling up and cutting down the forest trees, and the gunboats traversed a distance of one hundred miles over ground where the keel of a canoe even had never before been seen.

The Yazoo pass was opened by cutting the levee, and a fleet passed through in that direction, to meet the one working its way through Steele's Bayou.

This last expedition was a most arduous one and full of peril. Leaving the Yazoo below Haines' Bluff, it entered Steele's Bayou, designing to keep north into the Rolling Fork, then eastward through it into the Sunflower River, and pass in a southerly direction into the Yazoo, again striking it above Haines' Bluff instead of below, where it started from. Such inland navigation was never before attempted by war vessels. The expedition consisted of four gunboats, four mortars, and four tugs. For thirty miles the little fleet passed up Steele's Bayou, then a mere ditch, to Black Bayou, in which, for four miles, the trees had to be torn out or pushed over by the iron-clads, or the branches cut away, when Porter at last reached Deer Creek. It took twenty-four hours to make these four miles. Some idea of the difficulties of the route may be obtained when it is remembered that, with the utmost exertion of the crews, the vessels for twenty-four consecutive hours averaged a speed of only about *fifty rods* an hour. Up this stream to Rolling Fork it was thirty-two miles. To the same point by land, was twelve miles, over which Sherman marched, in order to coöperate with him. The channel was narrow and filled with small willows, which so retarded the progress of the boats that with his utmost exertions Porter could average only about a half a mile an hour. At length he got within seven miles of the Rolling Fork, from whence there would be water enough to the Yazoo.

The inhabitants were filled with amazement to see a war fleet sailing through the heart of a country where a vessel of any kind had never before been seen, while the negroes flocked in crowds to the shore to gaze on the unwonted spectacle. But as soon as the Confederate official in that section was informed of the expedition, he gave the alarm and ordered the torch to be applied to all the cotton along the shore, and Porter was lighted on his strange course by a continuous conflagration.

Negroes were also set to work cutting down trees to arrest his progress, until troops and guns could be brought up. Porter, made aware of the movement, pushed on the tug Thistle, with a howitzer on board, which reached the first tree before it was cut down. The tug then kept on to keep the way open, but the enemy at length succeeded in getting one large tree across the creek, and thus for a time stopped all further progress. Being now safe from our guns, the negroes, under the orders of their masters, continued to chop down trees until it was thought that Porter could make no farther advance. He, however, by working night and day—chopping and sawing them in two, or hauling them one side, at length cleared the channel and pushed on until he got within three miles of the Rolling Fork. Here he saw smoke rising over the tree tops in the direction of the Yazoo, and learned that the enemy was landing troops to dispute his passage. He immediately sent Lieutenant Murphy, with two boat howitzers and three hundred men to hold Rolling Fork until he could reach it with his boats.

After working all night, (says Porter,) and clearing out the obstructions, which were terrible, we succeeded in getting within eight hundred yards of the end of this troublesome creek; had only two or three large trees to remove, and one apparently short and easy lane of willows to work through. The men being much worn out, we rested at sunset.

In the morning we commenced with renewed vigor to work ahead through the willows, but our progress was very slow; the lithe trees defied our utmost efforts to get by them, and we had to go to work and pull them up separately, or cut them off under water, which was a most tedious job. In the mean time, the enemy had collected and landed about eight hundred men, and seven pieces of artillery, (from 20 to 30-pounders,) which were firing on our field pieces, from time to time, the latter not having range enough to reach them.

I was also informed that the enemy were cutting down trees in our rear, to prevent communication by water, and also prevent our escape; this looked unpleasant. I knew that five thousand men had embarked at Haines' Bluff for this place, immediately they heard that we were attempting to go through that way, and, as our troops had not come up, I considered it unwise to risk the least thing; at all events, never to let my communication be closed behind me. I was somewhat strengthened in my determination to advance no further, until reinforced by land forces, when the enemy, at sunset, opened on us a cross-fire with six or seven rifled guns, planted somewhere off in the woods, where we could see nothing but the smoke. It did not take us long to dislodge them, though a large part of the crew being on shore at the time, we could not fire over them, or until they got on board.

I saw at once the difficulties we had to encounter, with a constant fire on our working parties, and no prospect at present of the troops getting along. I had received a letter from General Sherman, informing me of the difficulties in getting forward his men, he doing his utmost, I know, to expedite matters.

The news of the felling trees in our rear was brought in frequently by negroes, who were pressed into the service for cutting them, and I hesitated no longer about what to do. We dropped down again, unshipped our rudders, and let the vessels rebound from tree to tree.

As we left, the enemy took possession of the Indian mound, and in the morning opened fire on the Carondelet, Lieutenant Murphy, and Cincinnati, Lieutenant Bache; these two ships soon silenced the batteries, and we were no longer annoyed.

The sharpshooters hung about us, firing from behind trees and rifle pits; but with due precaution we had very few hurt—only five wounded by rifle balls, and they were hurt by being imprudent.

On the 21st, we fell in with Colonel Smith, commanding Eighth Missouri, and other parts of regiments; we were quite pleased to see him, as I never knew before how much the comfort and safety of iron-clads, situated as we were, depended on the soldiers. I had already sent out behind a force of three hundred men, to stop the felling of trees in our rear, which Colonel Smith now took charge of. The enemy had already felled over forty heavy trees, which Lieutenant-Commander Owen, in the Louisville, working night and day, cleared away almost fast enough to permit us to meet with no delay.

Colonel Smith's force was not enough to justify my making another effort to get through; he had no artillery, and would frequently have to leave the vessels in following the roads.

On the 22d, we came to a bend in the river, where the enemy supposed they had blockaded us completely, having cut a number of trees altogether, and so intertwined, that it seemed impossible to move them. The Louisville was at work at them, pulling them up, when we discovered about three thousand rebels attempting to pass the edge of the woods to our rear, while the negroes reported artillery coming up on our quarter.

We were all ready for them, and, when the artillery opened on us, we opened such a fire on them, that they scarcely waited to hitch up their horses. At the same time, the rebel soldiers fell in with Colonel Smith's troops, and after a sharp skirmish fled before the fire of our soldiers. After this we were troubled no more.

Although he now met Sherman's advancing forces, he

saw it would be folly to attempt to retrace his steps, and the expedition, after having sailed for upwards of a hundred and forty miles, right through the plantations of rebels, at length found itself once more at the starting point; and the last attempt to get around Vicksburg from the north had been made and abandoned. Porter made several efforts to send vessels past the batteries at Vicksburg, to cut off the enemy's supplies from Red River, but, owing to mismanagement, they fell into the hands of the enemy. The Queen of the West and the Indianola were both lost to the squadron, but this did not deter the Admiral from pursuing his intentions.

The orders issued on these occasions show how well he calculated, and what would have been the consequences had they been carried out. The particulars of the loss of the Queen of the West, under Ellet, are given in the sketch of him. The Indianola was sent down past the batteries at Vicksburg, to coöperate with Ellet, but met him returning in the Era, and the commander, Lieutenant Brown, thus learned, for the first time, that he had lost his vessel. The Indianola then proceeded down the Mississippi to the mouth of Red River, and blockaded it for several days, when Brown, having learned that the Queen of the West had been repaired, and was on her way, with several other rebel boats, to attack him, he started to join Porter's fleet above Vicksburg. He was, however, overtaken on the night of the 28th February, and two vessels struck the Indianola at the same time, bows on. A fierce engagement followed, but crash succeeded crash as the rebel vessels kept driving on her, and in a short time Brown found that she was sinking, when he ran her ashore and surrendered her. The rebels immediately began to repair her, as they did the Queen of the West. The two boats would make a formidable addition to their navy, and interfere seriously with some of Porter's plans. A ludicrous incident, however, broke up this part of their programme, and almost repaid Porter for the mortification he felt over the loss of the vessel. To break up the monotony of the siege, and furnish some amusement to the men, as well as play a good joke on the enemy, he rigged up a sort of scow as a monitor, and set her afloat down the river. The strange craft so alarmed the rebels that they blew up the Indianola, and fled. We will, however, let the Admiral tell his own story. He says—

"Ericsson saved the country with an iron Monitor—why could I not save it with a wooden one? An old coal barge, picked up in the river, was the foundation to build on. It was built of old boards in twelve hours, with pork barrels on top of each other for smoke-stacks, and two old canoes for quarter-boats. The furnaces were built of mud, and only intended to make black smoke and not steam.

"Without knowing that Brown was in peril, I let loose our Monitor. When it was descried by the dim light of the morn, never did the batteries of Vicksburg open with such a din. The earth fairly trembled, and the shot flew thick around the devoted Monitor. But she ran safely past all the batteries, though under fire for an hour, and drifted down to the lower mouth of the canal. She was a much better looking vessel than the Indianola.

"When it was broad daylight they opened upon her again with all the guns they could bring to bear, without a shot hitting her to do any harm, because they did not make her settle in the water, though going in at one side and out at the other. She was already full of water. The soldiers of our army shouted and laughed like mad."

The news of the safe passage of the batteries by this "Turreted Monster," was sent down to Warrenton, under the batteries of which the Queen of the West and Indianola were lying, causing the greatest consternation. The Queen of the West instantly got up steam, and hurried off as fast as her wheels could carry her. The Indianola, left alone, was, by direction of the authorities, at once blown up, to prevent her falling a victim to the slowly and majestically approaching Monitor. When the rebels found out the hoax that had been played on them, their rage and mortification knew no bounds. The Richmond Examiner, after reporting the fact, said—"Laugh and hold your sides, lest ye die of surfeit of derision, O Yankeedom! Blown up, because forsooth a flatboat or mud-scow, with a small house taken from the back garden of a plantation put on top of it, is floated down the river." The Dispatch said, grimly, "Truly, an excellent joke; so excellent that every one connected with the affair should be branded with a T. M. 'Turreted Monster.'" The whole affair reminds one of the famous "Battle of Kegs" in our war of Independence, and should be immortalized in as stirring a ballad.

Everything had been tried that the ingenuity of man could suggest, and there seemed no prospect of the capture of Vicksburg, until General Grant, in opposition to the views of the most of his officers, determined to turn it by landing his troops below.

To Admiral Porter was entrusted the task of getting the gunboats and transports past the batteries, which he succeeded in accomplishing (only losing one transport) under a tremendous fire of an hour and a half's duration. His escape seemed almost miraculous, for the enemy had collected a large pile of combustibles on the bank, which they set on fire, just as the vessels came to a point, on which the fire of the batteries was concentrated. The conflagration lit up the whole bosom of the stream, throwing into distinct outline every dark hull. The Forest Queen was riddled with shot, and had to be towed down stream. The Henry Clay was set on fire, and blazed like a beacon through the gloom, while the crew, leaping into the boats, made their escape on the western bank. Of the three transports, the Silver Wave, alone, escaped unhurt. Porter, however, succeeded in getting others through, by lashing barges to their sides, and Grant, who had marched below inland, had now gunboats and transports to take him over the river. But, thirty miles below Vicksburg, he found another obstruction in his path, the batteries of Grand Gulf, of which it was necessary to get possession, before the army could proceed.

At General Grant's request, Admiral Porter attacked these batteries with six heavy gunboats, and, after a fight of five hours and a half, completely silenced them, took all the transports by in safety, and next morning with his gunboats and transports, conveyed the army to Bayou Pierre, where commenced that march which, after a series of beautiful moves, ended in the destruction of the city of Jackson, the dispersion of Joe Johnston's forces, and the investment of Vicksburg in the rear.

The fight at Grand Gulf was one of the hardest, if not the hardest stand-up fight during the war. The enemy's guns were very heavy, and placed in most commanding positions for a mile along the river, and although some of the gunboats were literally cut to pieces, there was not one that did not get at close quarters. The current was very powerful, and would whirl them around like tops, distracting the aim, and exposing every side to the rebel batteries; but they maintained a distance of from forty to three hundred yards, and never retired until the enemy was silenced.

The severity of the battle is shown by the heavy loss sustained in three ships—seventy-nine killed and wounded. Twenty-six were killed and wounded on the flagship Benton, though iron-clad.

After the army was landed at Bayou Pierre, Admiral Porter got under way again with his fleet, to end the matter of the Grand Gulf, but the rebels decamped on seeing him coming, and their guns and munitions of war fell into the hands of the navy. Thirteen guns were the fruits of this victory.

The same day of the capture of Grand Gulf, the Admiral pushed on down the river, with six gunboats, to communicate with Admiral Farragut, at the mouth of Red River, where, learning that General Banks was marching on the town of Alexandria, he pushed up the river to await him.

Fort de Russey and Alexandria fell into the hands of the navy, and, General Banks arriving a day or two after, the city was delivered over to him.

After this successful raid, in which much valuable property belonging to the rebel government was destroyed, Admiral Porter returned to Vicksburg, to coöperate with General Grant.

He destroyed the works and town of Warrenton, a place that had given our vessels considerable trouble, and deserved no mercy.

While the Admiral was below at Grand Gulf, he had all the upper fleets to regulate, one on the Tennessee, one on the Cumberland, one on the Yazoo, coöperating with General Sherman, while one long line stretched from Vicksburg to Cairo, the various reports of which would of themselves make a lengthy article. All his plans were carried out, and there was not an instance of any mishap to any of his vessels, or to the transports. Guerilla warfare was kept down on all the rivers, and the gunboats were dreaded by the rebels far and near.

When General Grant put himself in the rear of Vicksburg on the 18th of May, 1863, Admiral Porter immediately placed himself in communication, and supplied him with all the necessary stores wanted in his army.

On the evening of the 21st of May, the Admiral received a communication from General Grant, informing him that he intended attacking the rebel works on the following morning, and asked his coöperation.

At seven o'clock next day, the gunboats moved against the batteries, Admiral Porter leading in a small tug. The firing was kept up until one o'clock, at which time all the batteries along the river were silenced; but General McArthur was not permitted to take advantage of the naval success, and, General Grant's plans having been thwarted in other respects, the combined attack was a failure.

The naval operations in the siege that followed, were chiefly confined to occasional attacks on the batteries, which could be of little avail without a coöperating force from the army.

One of the noblest spectacles of the war was the attack of the Cincinnati on the rebel batteries, when there was scarcely a hope that she could stand for five minutes the fire of the hundred guns which were concentrated on her. This was done at the request of General Sherman, who wished to get possession of that flank of the rebel works. He thought the heavy guns had been moved into Vicksburg, but was mistaken. Porter feared that he was, but with that readiness to make any sacrifice for the army, especially for such leaders as Sherman and Grant, which characterized him, he packed the steamer with logs and hay, and sent her down. Bache, her commander, carried her gallantly into the terrible fire, but in a few minutes she was completely riddled with shot, and began to sink. The flagstaff being shot away, Bache had the colors nailed to a stump of the foremast, and himself steered his vessel up stream towards the right-hand shore, but before she could be made fast, she went down, carrying fifteen of the crew with her. These, with the killed and wounded, made his loss over forty men.

Sherman from a hill top saw the terrific engagement, and its sad termination, and, in a letter to Porter, said the conduct of the Cincinnati "elicited universal praise, and I deplored the sad result as much as any one could."

Porter, at the request of Grant, now landed twenty 9-inch, 8-inch, and hundred-pounder rifles, in an incredibly short space of time, and transported them to the rear of Vicksburg. Most of them were worked by sailors and their officers, and did excellent service.

That was a glorious Fourth of July, 1863, when the rebel flag was at last hauled down at Vicksburg, at 10 A. M., and the stars and stripes floated in its place.

Admiral Porter, in his flagship, and the fleet following, passed down until he came abreast of the town, the guns firing, and the flags waving from every masthead. As he rounded to at the levee, General Grant and all his general officers came on board, and the warmest felicitations took place. It was a beautiful sight to see so many gallant men of the army and navy assembled together.

The country was electrified, when the telegraphic despatch of Admiral Porter announced that Vicksburg was in possession of the Union forces. Grant was rewarded, as he deserved to be, with a high position, and with votes of thanks, and Acting Rear-Admiral Porter again received the thanks of Congress, and was created a full Rear-Admiral, the commission dated July 4th, which intelligence was conveyed to him in an autograph letter from the President.

The Secretary of the Navy, in his public despatch to him, complimented him highly, and in conclusion said: "To yourself, your officers, and the brave and gallant sailors who have been so fertile in resources, so persistent and enduring through many months of trial and hardship, and so daring under all circumstances, I tender, in the name of the President, the thanks and congratulations of the whole country, on the fall of Vicksburg."

After this great event, there was much to do to keep the banks of the Mississippi River free from guerrillas. Fourteen different districts were constituted with a regular naval officer in command of each. The White, Arkansas, and Red Rivers, were traversed by the gunboats as far as water would permit them to go, and the most dogged perseverance was shown by them to kill all rebels, or make them quit the country.

In no part of the country did harder stand-up fighting take place than in the Mississippi fleet. The rebels would bring numerous batteries on the rivers to blockade them and stop commerce, but Admiral Porter always had gunboats ready to drive them off or capture them.

In but one instance did a "tin-clad" succumb to the rebels. On several occasions they went down fighting, with colors flying, but they kept the river clear.

When the rebels marched suddenly into Helena with eighteen thousand men, under Price, and surprised the weak garrison there, and were putting them to the sword, Admiral Porter, who had heard of the move, and prepared for it, sent his gunboats up at the right moment, and defeated the rebels with great slaughter. This occurred on the 4th of July, at the hour when our flag was just going up on the flagstaff at Vicksburg.

General Prentiss wrote Admiral Porter a strong letter commendatory of the officer, Lieutenant Prichett, who had carried out the Admiral's orders. Porter also sent an expedition to Yazoo city, and, though the Baron De Kalb was sunk by a torpedo, the frightened enemy set fire to five of their largest boats and left one to be captured.

Active operations were carried on in the heart of the enemy's country in the seizure of Confederate cotton and steamers, by which the sailors were stimulated to renewed zeal, and secured a snug little sum of prize money. It is impossible in a single article to go over the whole field occupied by the forces under Porter.

The fleets in the upper Ohio and Tennessee, were kept very actively employed, and, owing to the perseverance of Lieut.-Commander Fitch and his attention to orders, the rebel guerrilla Morgan, and all his gang, were captured. Strange to relate, all the artillery and wagons fell into the hands of the navy, one of the gunboats surprising them and causing the men to stampede.

After the fall of Vicksburg, Admiral Porter went to work raising from the bottom of the river the different vessels that had been sunk, among them the "Cincinnati." He refitted her, and she subsequently formed a part of Commodore Thatcher's fleet in the attack on the enemy's works at Mobile city.

The year 1864 opened with apparent quiet all along

the Mississippi river, from Cairo to New Orleans. Occasionally there would be an attack of guerrillas or field pieces on a harmless merchant steamer, but the gunboats kept everything quiet. The rebels could not stand the shrapnell which was poured into them whenever they came in sight, for Porter's fleet was ubiquitous and his blows fell on every side.

Sometime in the month of February, General Banks wrote to Admiral Porter and informed him that he was going up Red River as far as Shreveport, and asked the coöperation of the gunboats. This matter had been discussed by Porter and General W. T. Sherman, and it was proposed that, after the general made his first raid near Atlanta, he would suddenly return, and with the admiral make a dash up to Shreveport, destroy the rams and forts, bring off the cotton, and be back in Memphis on the 10th of April.

General Sherman, who was an old campaigner on Red River, and knew all about the rise and fall of water there, suggested that as the only feasible plan—consequently, the plans of the admiral were made to conform with this arrangement. General Sherman had agreed to meet the admiral at Vicksburg, on the 29th of February, and so confident was the latter of the general's punctuality, although he had hundreds of miles to travel with his army, that he made his arrangements to meet him at that time.

Sherman arrived exactly on the day he said he would, and was quite surprised to learn that Banks was about to go to Shreveport. As McClernand was to be second in command, and he would not serve under him, he (Sherman) determined to go to New Orleans. On his return, General Sherman told Porter that he would have to give up the expedition, but that he would send General Andrew J. Smith, along with ten thousand men, to represent him, and that Gen. Banks had promised to be in Alexandria on the seventeenth day of May, and to push right on to Shreveport without delay. It was necessary to be governed by the height of water in Red River.

Porter landed General A. J. Smith, in the Atchafalaya, while gunboats pushed up Red River, to clear out the obstructions. The army and navy arrived about the same time, at Fort de Russey, which had been rebuilt since Porter's destruction of it the preceding year, and heavily armed. The army assaulted and carried it as the shells of the leading gunboat drove the enemy from the water batteries which they had turned upon our troops. This was on the fifteenth of May. Porter then at once pushed on up to Alexandria, with the naval part of the expedition, and captured it on the 16th, one day before he promised to meet General Banks there. General A. J. Smith came up shortly after, and held the town while Porter prepared to get the vessels over the "falls." The water was very low though rising slowly, but he saw that it was too late in the season for the gunboats to go any further. He supposed that Banks would give up the expedition when he got to Alexandria, and allow Sherman to have his troops again, with which to carry out General Grant's plans. These plans were, for General Sherman to push on to Atlanta, while Banks made an attack on Mobile, open the Columbia railroad, and join the former in his march through the South. This plan was defeated by Banks pushing on to Shreveport, after cotton, and allowing the rebels to hold Mobile.

Had the latter place been captured, Sherman's march

—supplied, as he would have been, with provisions from Mobile—would have been an easy task. Banks, however, cared for no plans but his own. Instead of being, as he had promised, in Alexandria on the 17th of May, he did not leave New Orleans until the 22d. His army, under General Franklin, reached the place on the 20th; but. although well organized and ready to proceed, they could do nothing until the arrival of the general commanding. On the 20th the water was rapidly falling, and Porter told General Stone (Banks' Chief-of-Staff) that it would be impossible to reach Shreveport, if he depended on the gunboats. Stone asserted (for Banks) that the gunboats were *a necessity*, and that without them the expedition could not succeed; and that all the failure to wipe out the rebel army in Louisiana would be due to the navy. Porter, who never allowed an army man to call on him in vain, determined at once to get the gunboats over the "falls," if he broke all their backs. So he went to work, trying to pull the Eastport, the largest boat, over, and after great labor succeeded. In the mean time, on the 20th of May, General Banks arrived in a steamer loaded with champagne and ice, cotton speculators and brandy, and professing to be in a great hurry to get away on his march.

Porter had all his vessels over, ready for a start; but instead of moving right on, Banks started an election! He forced all the male inhabitants to go to the polls, threatening those who were supposed to be disloyal with his displeasure if they refused to vote, and promising the loyal to stay in the country and protect them, if they did vote. This affair occupied several days, and was the finishing blow to the expedition.

When at length the army started, Porter pushed the

gunboats up to Grand Ecore, and captured that place before the arrival of the troops.

Five or six more days were wasted in electioneering at Grand Ecore, the water in the river still falling.

Porter now did all he could to persuade General Banks to give up the hope of getting the gunboats up, and to push on to Shreveport by himself; but the latter dared not move without them.

Selecting vessels of the lightest draft, and the proper kind of transports, drawing little water, Porter now pushed on to a point where Banks proposed to meet him with his army, having it perfectly understood that no other transports would follow. But he had not gone twenty miles, when six large transports joined the expedition, for the purpose of taking *on board cotton.* This delayed the vessels; but Porter could not get rid of them without sending a couple of gunboats back to protect them, and not a single gun could be spared, so he dragged them through.

No one can imagine the difficulties of that river for two hundred miles, as without pilots Porter had to thread his way through snags and shoals. It was a wonder he ever reached the appointed place, where he expected to find a victorious army.

He was much annoyed with rebel sharpshooters on his way up; but, by maintaining a fire of shells into the brush, he kept them at a respectful distance.

When he arrived at the landing where Banks expected to meet the fleet, he found a large steamer thrown across the river, from bank to bank, to stop his progress, while the silence of the grave reigned around.

Porter had with him, in command of the troops, General Smith, who landed with him and proposed landing his men. The former said, "No, General, there is something wrong; an army like that of Banks should have been here, and he has met with a check."

So they rode out to the front to reconnoitre, and at a short distance perceived a number of rebel horsemen watching their movements. Porter made up his mind that our army was nowhere near, and so they returned on board the vessels. He there met a messenger who had left General Banks the day before, and who informed him that the whole army was retreating. Here was an awkward dilemma for Porter—fifty vessels in a narrow river, and a victorious rebel army, with some fifty pieces of artillery, between him and safety. But there was no time to be lost, and, although the night was coming on, he ordered a return, issuing the most stringent instructions about the movements of the vessels. He also distributed the different gunboats among the transports, to protect the latter.

One has observed how a rain shower comes on—first a drop or two, then a slight pattering rain, then a heavy shower, and, finally, a torrent. So now commenced the bullets from the rebel sharpshooters—first a few, then in companies of twenty, then by hundreds, then by thousands.

The soldiers and sailors, screening themselves as best they could, drove off these fellows with their bullets, while the gunboats kept shelling them all day and night. It was a most tedious and harassing retreat.

Porter had succeeded in getting about half-way down the river, when a heavy fire of artillery and musketry was opened on the middle of the line by the rebels. Fortunately this happened to be where Porter had two good gunboats, the Lexington, under Lieut. George M. Bache; and a small iron-clad, under Lieut. Commander Thomas O. Selfridge. Some of the army boats had field-pieces on their upper decks, and all these vessels opened heavily on the rebels.

Porter was just getting his gunboats below in position to attack a battery that the enemy had thrown up to stop him, when he heard heavy firing behind him. He at once left his work to return and see what was going on, and arrived just in time to see the army retreating in all directions, and completely routed.

The rebels had made their attack at the most difficult part of the river, where four or five of our vessels were fast in the mud, and others alongside of them trying to pull them off. The advance consisted of three thousand men, with a reserve of seven thousand a mile back, ready to come to their assistance. They were commanded by General Green, their best general, and one who had given our people a great deal of trouble.

He soon found that his men could not stand our fire; but he determined not to retreat, and forced his troops up to the edge of the bank, where our gunboats fairly mowed them down. He finally got his head shot off, and, nearly all his officers having been killed around him, the rest retreated in disorder, cut up as they fled. Their artillery and all the killed and wounded were left on the field of battle. The seven thousand in reserve never advanced at all, and soon followed the retreating mob, losing a number of men by our far-reaching shells.

This was the victorious army that had defeated Banks the day before, and, flushed with victory, pounced on Porter. They calculated that the high banks and low water, and the grounding of his vessels, would give them an easy victory. They were then to fall on Banks' army again, and capture the provisions and medical stores, and thus compel its surrender. The death of General Green defeated this plan.

The management of the rebel army now fell into the hands of drunken Dick Taylor, who was entirely incompetent to conduct it. He did really nothing, except hang on Banks' rear and pick up a few barrels of whiskey, and a few stragglers.

When Porter arrived at Grand Ecore, three days after the above fight, he found the army perfectly demoralized, and Banks ready to run any where. He advised him to hold on, and not retreat, and to occupy the country until the spring rains, when they could go up again. He told him that he could supply him with his light vessels; but Banks chose to retreat, and, finally, reached Alexandria in safety!

Porter knew he could not get out of the river *then* without help. But, in a conversation with Colonel Bailey, a plain, common-sense man, the latter assured him he would have no difficulty about getting the vessels over the "falls."

The Admiral now had to fight his way back, overcoming difficulties that would have disheartened any other man. He finally reached Alexandria, with all his gunboats, except the Eastport, and his own "tin-clad" steamer, the Cricket, which was so cut up that there was scarcely any of her left. Half her crew were killed and wounded, and some of the other vessels had fared almost as badly.

Porter's efforts to save the Eastport show, not only the indomitable character of the man, but that chivalric feeling which belongs to the whole race. After she had been lightened and got afloat she again grounded. Although she was taken several miles down the river, grounding in all eight times, he would not abandon her. Had he acted on his own judgment he doubtless would have blown her up before he did; but, seeing the determination of her commander, Lieutenant E. T. Phelps, and his crew to save her, and admiring the ceaseless herculean efforts they put forth, he stuck to them like a brother. He said: "I determined that I would never leave this vessel to her fate, as long as her commander felt a hope of getting her down." The army was sixty miles ahead of him, and a snaggy, shallow river, with its banks filled with sharpshooters, lay between. The Eastport was finally brought down sixty miles from the place where she first sunk, and he had strong hopes of getting her through, when she ran fast aground, with a bed of logs under her, and had to be blown up. Phelps himself applied the match.

Porter now fought his way back to Alexandria, at one point under a heavy fire.

Finding (he says) the guns not firing rapidly, I stepped on the gun-deck, to see what was the matter. As I stepped down, the after gun was struck with a shell and disabled, and every man killed or wounded. At the same moment, the crew from the forward gun were swept away by a shell exploding, and the men were wounded in the fire-room, leaving only one man to fire up.

I made up a gun's crew from the contrabands, who fought the gun to the last moment. Finding that the engine did not move, I went into the engine-room and found the chief engineer killed, whose place was soon supplied by an assistant. I then went to the pilot-house, and found that a shot had gone through it, and wounded one of the pilots. I took charge of the vessel, and, as the battery was a very heavy one, I determined to pass it, which was done under the heaviest fire I ever witnessed.

The moment he arrived at Alexandria, and found that he could not get over the falls, he called to see what General Banks was going to do. He found him determined to leave as soon as he could gather all the cotton in and about Alexandria, and talked to Porter about blowing up his gunboats, which the latter laughed at.

Seeing how things were going, he sent a bearer of despatches to Washington, which were telegraphed from Cairo. On Porter's representations, General Canby was sent out to relieve Banks, and with orders to stay with the army in Alexandria, until the gunboats were relieved.

The same orders came to Banks, much to his surprise, as he knew nothing about Porter's action. In the mean time, the latter called on Banks and laid Colonel Bailey's proposition, for getting the boats over the falls, before him. He looked at it kindly enough, but took no steps towards doing anything, until General Franklin urged it. Then, after three days' vacillation, he gave the proper orders, placing at Colonel Bailey's disposal three thousand men, and two or three hundred wagons. All the neighboring steam-mills were torn down for material, two or three regiments of marine men were set to work felling trees, which soon were coming down with great rapidity, teams were moving in all directions bringing in brick and stone, quarries opened, flatboats built, and the forest became a human hive, while the shouts of men resounded on every side.

In the mean time, General Hunter came up to see how matters stood, and he and Banks called to see Porter. General Hunter said to Porter: "Admiral, which of your vessels above the falls can you best afford to blow up?" He answered, "Not one of them, sir; not even the smallest. If I can't get over the 'falls,' and

PORTER'S GUN BOATS PASSING THE FALLS OF RED RIVER.

the army leave me, I can take care of myself, and will get out at the first rise."

Still, it would have subjected him to great inconvenience for a couple of months, but he knew that before that time had elapsed, General Sherman would come up there, if he was in danger.

We cannot do better than give the account of the building of the dams and passage of the falls, in Porter's own graphic and eloquent language.

These falls are about a mile in length, filled with rugged rocks, over which, at the present stage of water, it seemed to be impossible to make a channel.

The work was commenced by running out from the left bank of the river, a tree-dam, made of the bodies of very large trees, brush, brick, and stone, cross-tied with other heavy timber, and strengthened in every way which ingenuity could devise. This was run out about three hundred feet into the river; four large coal barges were then filled with brick, and sunk at the end of it. From the right bank of the river, cribs filled with stone were built out to meet the barges. All of which was successfully accomplished, notwithstanding there was a current running of nine miles an hour which threatened to sweep everything before it.

It will take too much time to enter into the details of this truly wonderful work. Suffice it to say, that the dam had nearly reached completion in eight days' working time, and the water had risen sufficiently on the upper falls to allow the Fort Hindman, Osage, and Neosho, to get down and be ready to pass the dam. In another day it would have been high enough to enable all the other vessels to pass the upper falls. Unfortunately, on the morning of the 9th instant, the pressure of water became so great, that it swept away two of the stone barges, which swung in below the dam on one side. Seeing this unfortunate accident, I jumped on a horse, and rode up to where the upper vessels were anchored, and ordered the Lexington to pass the upper falls, if possible, and immediately attempt to go through the dam. I thought I might be able to save the four vessels below, not knowing whether the persons employed on the work would ever have the heart to renew their enterprise.

The Lexington succeeded in getting over the upper falls just in time, the water rapidly falling as she was passing over. She then steered directly for the opening in the dam, through which the water was rushing so furiously that it seemed as if nothing but destruction awaited her. Thousands of beating hearts looked on, anxious for the result. The silence was so great, as the Lexington approached the dam, that a pin might almost be heard to fall. She entered the gap with a full head of steam on, pitched down the roaring torrent, made two or three spasmodic rolls, hung for a moment on the rocks below, was then swept into deep water by the current, and rounded-to safely into the bank. Thirty thousand voices rose in one deafening cheer, and universal joy seemed to pervade the face of every man present.

The Neosho followed next; all her hatches battened down, and every precaution taken against accident. She did not fare as well as the Lexington, her pilot having become frightened as he approached the abyss, and stopped her engine, when I particularly ordered a full head of steam to be carried; the result was, that for a moment her hull disappeared from sight under the water. Every one thought she was lost. She rose, however, swept along over the rocks with the current, and fortunately escaped with only one hole in her bottom, which was stopped in the course of an hour.

The Hindman and Osage both came through beautifully without touching a thing, and I thought if I was only fortunate enough to get my large vessels as well over the falls, my fleet once more would do good service on the Mississippi.

The accident to the dam, instead of disheartening Colonel Bailey, only induced him to renew his exertions, after he had seen the success of getting four vessels through.

The noble-hearted soldiers, seeing the labor of the last eight days swept away in a moment, cheerfully went to work to repair damages, being confident now that all the gunboats would be finally brought over. These men had been working for eight days and nights, up to their necks in the water in the boiling sun, cutting trees and wheeling bricks, and nothing but good humor prevailed among them. On the whole, it was very fortunate the dam was carried away, as the two barges that were swept away from the centre swung around against some rocks on the left, and made a fine cushion for the vessels, and prevented them, as it afterwards appeared, from running on certain destruction.

The force of the water and the current being too great to construct a continuous dam of six hundred feet across the river in so short a time, Colonel Bailey determined to leave a gap of fifty-five feet in the dam, and build a series of wing-dams on the upper falls. This was accomplished in three days' time, and on the 11th instant the Mound City, Carondelet, and Pittsburg, came over the upper falls, a good deal of labor having been expended in hauling them through, the channel being very crooked, scarcely wide enough for them. Next day, the Ozark, Louisville, Chillicothe, and two tugs, also succeeded in crossing the upper falls. Immediately afterwards, the Mound City, Carondelet, and Pittsburg, started in succession to pass the dam, all their hatches battened down, and every precaution taken to prevent accident. The passage of these vessels was a most beautiful sight, only to be realized when seen. They passed over without an accident, except the unshipping of one or two rudders. This was witnessed by all the troops, and the vessels were heartily cheered when they passed over. Next morning at 10 o'clock, the Louisville, Chillicothe, Ozark, and two tugs, passed over without any accident, except the loss of a man, who was swept off the decks of one of the tugs. By 3 o'clock that afternoon, the vessels were all coaled, ammunition replaced, and all steamed down the river, with the convoy of transports in company. A good deal of difficulty was anticipated in getting over the bars in lower Red River; depth of water reported only five feet; gunboats were drawing six. Providentially, we had a rise from the back-water of the Mississippi, that river being very high at that time; the back-water extending to Alexandria, one hundred and fifty miles distant, enabling us to pass all the bars and obstructions with safety.

Words are inadequate to express the admiration I feel for the abilities of Lieutenant-Colonel Bailey. This is, without doubt, the best engineering feat ever performed. Under the best circumstances, a private company would not have completed this work under one year, and to an ordinary mind the whole thing would have appeared an utter impossibility. Leaving out his abilities as an engineer, the credit he has conferred upon the country, he has saved to the Union a valuable fleet, worth nearly two million dollars. More, he has deprived the enemy of a triumph, which would have emboldened them to carry on this war a year or two longer; for the intended departure of the army was a fixed fact, and there was nothing left for me to do, in case that event occurred, but to destroy every part of the vessels, so that the rebels could make nothing of them. The highest honors the government can bestow on Colonel Bailey, can never repay him for the services he has rendered the country.

The Signal and Covington were unfortunately lost below Alexandria, although they were fought to the last. The commander of the latter was compelled to blow her up, but the former was surrendered, as her decks were so covered with the wounded, that Lieutenant Morgan refrained, from feelings of humanity, from blowing her up.

Porter not only complimented Bailey in his report, but got him promoted to Brigadier General. Not satisfied with this, he presented him with a splendid sword, costing seven hundred dollars. He also, with the officers of the fleet, presented him with a silver vase, emblematic of the event, that cost sixteen hundred dollars, and has never lost his interest in him from that time to this.

It was the opinion of the army and of the country, that the fleet would have been destroyed in case the army left; but this was a mistake. The fleet had nearly four months' provisions, and could have maintained itself easily until the next rise of water, which took place two months afterwards. Porter did not attempt to discourage this belief; for he was determined not to stay there. His fleet was needed on the Mississippi—in fact, the Government could not do without it.

There was a stretch of river above the falls, of forty miles extent, where the vessels could have gone up and down without hindrance. The guns of the fleet were too heavy and too numerous to permit the rebels to erect any batteries, and they had no heavy guns of any kind with which to do the fleet much harm. Some inconvenience might have been felt from sharpshooters, but the rebels had too wholesome a dread of gunboats and shrapnell, to venture within reach of the navy batteries, and Porter would have stood at bay there till the last ounce of provision was gone.

The friends of General Banks attempted to break his fall, by laying a part of the blame of the failure of the expedition on the navy; but it would not do, and praise instead of censure is meted out to Porter for the management of his part of the unfortunate undertaking.

The latter part of Admiral Porter's command on the Mississippi, was spent in chasing the rebels from river to river, giving them no rest by night or day. He also opened communication with the army, and supplied it with provisions.

While General Grant was preparing to attack the rebels at Chattanooga, Admiral Porter accidentally heard that General Sherman had left Memphis with thirty thousand men, to join him by the Corinth road.

It was usual with General Sherman to keep the Admiral notified of his movements, in case he should want assistance; but the former supposed that he would have no difficulty in crossing the Tennessee, as it was the stage of low water, and he did not think, moreover, that the light-draught gunboats could get up to Florence, a place somewhat above where he intended to cross. But Admiral Porter thought otherwise. The moment he heard of Sherman's move from Memphis, he selected the lightest-draught gunboats, and took off some of their guns, so that they would draw the least possible water. He then planked over some empty coal barges to serve as bridges, and sent along a light-draught ferry-boat. Light-draught transports were also added with stores for the army, and the fleet was despatched up the Tennessee, under the command of Captain Phelps, an able officer.

When the advance guard of General Sherman arrived at Corinth, he rode over to the Tennessee and found the river rising. A heavy rain-storm set in, and in a few hours it was booming. All efforts to construct a bridge failed, while the wagons that attempted to ford the stream were damaged and had to give it up. Finally, the current became so strong that Sherman felt that he would have to wait patiently for the waters to subside. He rode back to camp quite disheartened, and throwing himself on his camp bed, felt, he said, "as if he had a thirty-pound shot in his stomach." He was thinking of the mutability of human affairs, when an orderly rode up at full speed and informed him that the admiral was in sight, coming up with the gunboats. The orderly had mistaken the divisional flag of the district commander for that of the admiral. It was like an electric shock to Sherman, and jumping up he rode over immediately to the river, when Captain Phelps, in the name of the admiral, placed the vessels at his disposal.

With the flatboats, ferryboats, gunboats, and transports, only a few days were occupied in crossing the river, and, with a fresh supply of stores and forage, General Sherman marched with elated spirits forward. As it is well known he did not arrive at Chattanooga a moment too soon. But for Porter's forecast and thoughtfulness, what a different result might have been reached.

After the great victory of Missionary Ridge, the state of Tennessee became comparatively quiet. Still the upper part of the Tennessee River was much infested with rebels, and Admiral Porter armed and equipped four steamers that had been built by the army above Muscle Shoals, and formed a little squadron there under a lieutenant of the regular navy, which did good service during the campaign, and rendered material aid to our forces. He also sent fifteen vessels of different kinds to Admiral Farragut, some of which performed an important part in the attack on Mobile.

Admiral Porter found it necessary to rule on the Mississippi with an iron hand. He constantly came in contact with dishonest speculators, cotton stealers, and swindlers of all kinds, to whom he showed no mercy.

These persons hired hostile presses to abuse him, which had about as much effect on him as pouring oil on fire to put it out.

He performed his duty faithfully and fearlessly, to the satisfaction of the government.

After an active and harassing service of two years on the Mississippi, Admiral Porter was invited by the Secretary of the Navy to pay a visit to Washington, and see his family, with whom he had only been a few days during the war, and then under circumstances where he could not enjoy their society. He now spent three months at the North, quietly enjoying the rest he so much needed, and, when his health was somewhat improved, started, *via* Washington, to return to his duties in the West. But while at the capital, he was tendered the command of the North Atlantic squadron, which he disliked to accept, as it interfered with another officer, but the matter was not left to him.

The capture of Fort Fisher, long a cherished object with the Secretary of the Navy, was now taken up again, and Porter and Mr. Fox, assistant secretary, were sent to City Point in September, 1864, to confer with Grant about it. The latter agreed to furnish eight or nine thousand men to be placed under Weitzel.

A large fleet was at once ordered to assemble in Hampton Roads. A powerful force was soon gathered and organized into five divisions, under five commodores, each of whom had charge of the fitting out of his own squadron, and in a few days Porter was ready to move. But long delay followed, as General Grant just then could not spare the troops. This delay, however, did the navy no harm. It gave the commanders an opportunity to discipline and exercise their crews, and to become familiar with the plans of the Commander-in-chief, which were given in full to every officer in command.

The smaller vessels were in the mean time placed on blockade duty, off the Cape Fear inlets, and the system adopted by Porter almost broke up the blockade running.

The steamers were placed in three half-circles, one outside of the other. The first circle was near the bars, the second about twelve miles outside of that, and the third one hundred miles outside of all. All the vessels in the circles were within signal distance, so that a steamer could not pass between them without being seen.

If a blockade runner got out of Wilmington at or before daylight, she would be seen by the middle circle. If she left Wilmington after sunset, she would be picked up by the outer circle at daylight the next morning, &c. This plan succeeded admirably, and, in less than thirty-five days, over seven millions of the enemy's property were either captured or destroyed.

Other portions of the squadron were actively engaged during the time the larger vessels were lying in Hampton Roads.

He sent Lieutenant Cushing to Plymouth, N. C., to attempt to blow up the rebel ram Albemarle, and, at the same time, gave instructions to Commander Macomb, the senior officer in the Sounds, to assist him with boats, and to take advantage of the opportunity if he succeeded. Cushing did succeed; and Macomb, like a brave officer, availing himself of the consequent confusion, attacked the forts at Plymouth with his small force, capturing them and everything in the town. The fruits of this victory were: twenty-two heavy cannon, thirty-seven prisoners, and over four hundred stand of arms. There were more guns in the forts than were carried by the fragile vessels that made the attack.

In the middle of December, the fleet, which had been lying all winter in Hampton Roads, sailed.

No American commander, and scarcely any European one, ever led so imposing a fleet as Porter now had under him. Over seventy vessels of various kinds composed it; and, when it was all assembled near Fort Fisher, it presented a grand and imposing spectacle. And never did a fleet have a nobler captain at its head.

Before the attack commenced, a powder-boat, with sufficient powder aboard, it was thought, to blow up the magazine of the fort, was towed up to the neighborhood of the works by Commander A. C. Rhind and Lieutenant S. W. Preston, and fired. These gallant men never expected to return alive, yet they unflinchingly performed the perilous task assigned them, and received the warmest commendation of Porter.

No adequate description of the bombardment that followed can be given.

The attack was made with thirty-seven vessels, with nineteen more in reserve; and when they took up their respective positions, and opened fire, the spectacle was one of the grandest ever witnessed on earth. The shells, crossing and recrossing each other in every direction, made the heavens one great fretwork of fire, while the explosion of so many cannon made land and sea tremble. The hostile batteries at first responded, but as soon as Porter got all his guns to bear, he poured such a horrible, ceaseless storm of shells into the works, that the gunners took refuge in their casements, and the fort stood and received the remorseless pounding in silence.

The bombardment was kept up for five hours, and

during that time six one-hundred-pound Parrott guns burst on board the vessels, killing and wounding several men.

The troops not all having arrived, Porter, at night, withdrew his fleet. The next morning, Christmas, he again signalled to form line of battle, and the awful fire of the day before was repeated. Under cover of it, part of the troops were landed, and some daring soldiers actually walked inside the works. But Weitzel, after a reconnoissance, pronounced them too strong to be carried by assault, and Butler, who had taken command, resolved to abandon the attempt, and reëmbark the troops. When this decision was reported to the Admiral, he was at the table, after a hard day's work, eating a Christmas turkey. "Well," said he, "that don't spoil my appetite," and, turning to an officer near him, quietly asked, "What part of the turkey will you have?" and said no more about it. The fact was, he thought the sooner General Butler went back the better. He continued filling up with ammunition, confident that Grant would not let the affair end so. In reporting it to the Department, he said that he did not wish to put his opinion against so able an engineer as Weitzel. "But," he dryly added, "*I can't help thinking it was worth while making the attempt after coming so far.*" In an after report he said, "there never was a fort that invited soldiers to walk in and take possession more plainly than Fort Fisher."

It is useless, in the light of subsequent events, to go over Butler's report, and show how false Porter found his statements to be. A charlatan, and ignorant of military matters, the former never should have been allowed any command in the expedition. With such men as Grant and Sherman, Porter could always act with perfect accord, but, with military leaders like Banks and Butler, it was impossible—for gallantry and ability cannot harmonize with cowardice or imbecility.

Porter now went on to prepare for another attack, which the government determined should be made. In the mean time a succession of gales swept over him, which the enemy thought would drive him off, but they little knew the man. He held on, though at times it seemed impossible to do so.

On the 13th of January, another military force having arrived under General Terry, preparations were at once made to take the fort, and, under cover of the fire of the iron-clads, the troops were landed. The next day Porter again formed his line of battle, and, with all the ships carrying eleven-inch guns, opened on the fort. He rained a horrible tempest on it till sunset, when, as he said, "the fort was reduced to a pulp, and every gun silenced." That evening Terry came on board his ship, to arrange for the assault next day.

It was determined that Porter should furnish sixteen hundred seamen and four hundred marines, to constitute a storming party against the sea side, while Terry assaulted the land side.

The next day, at eleven o'clock, Porter was again in line of battle, and, with his anchors down, once more rained his shells into the fort. A fire that nothing human could stand was kept up till three o'clock, when the long-expected signal from shore came, that the troops were ready to assault.

The vessels then changed their fire to the upper batteries; all the steam-whistles were blown, and the troops and sailors dashed ahead, nobly vying with each other to reach the top of the parapet; we had evidently (we thought) injured all the large guns, so that they could not be fired to annoy any one. The sailors took to the assault by the flank along the beach, while the troops rushed in at the left, through the palisades that had been knocked away by the fire of our guns.

All the arrangements on the part of the sailors had been well carried out; they had succeeded in getting up to within a short distance of the fort, and lay securely in their ditches. We had but very few killed and wounded to this point. The marines were to have held the rifle-pits and cover the boarding party, which they failed to do. On rushing through the palisades, which extended from the fort to the sea, the head of the column received a murderous fire of grape and canister, which did not, however, check the officers and sailors who were leading. The parapets now swarmed with rebels, who poured in a destructive fire of musketry. At this moment, had the marines performed their duty, every one of the rebels would have been killed.

I witnessed the whole affair, saw how recklessly the rebels exposed themselves, and what an advantage they gave our sharpshooters, whose guns were scarcely fired, or fired with no precision. Notwithstanding the hot fire, officers and sailors in the lead rushed on, and some even reached the parapet, a large number having reached the ditch.

The advance was swept from the parapet like chaff; and notwithstanding all the efforts made by commanders of companies to stop them, the men in the rear, seeing the slaughter in front, and that they were not covered by the marines, commenced to retreat, and as there is no stopping a sailor if he fails on such an occasion on the first rush, I saw the whole thing had to be given up.

The troops, however, kept on; and, fighting from traverse to traverse in the darkness, at length cleared the works. Terry's signal torch blazed from the ramparts, announcing the victory, which Porter, with rockets in turn, announced to the fleet, when there arose such thundering cheers as never before shook the waters of that bay.

The fleet in this bombardment had thrown fifty thousand shells; its great loss was in this assault. Among the killed, were the gallant lieutenants, S. W. Preston and B. H. Porter.

General Butler was in Washington, before the Committee on the Conduct of the War, giving the reasons why it was unwise and hopeless to attempt to carry Fort Fisher by assault, when the astounding news came that

BOMBARDMENT AND ASSAULT OF FORT FISHER.

it had fallen. His able exposition was cut short, and the country lost the benefit of the whole argument he had planned. The shout of victory that went up closed the controversy that had been carried on between him and Porter, and raised the latter still higher in the popular estimation. A greater triumph, after all his harassing difficulties, could not have been awarded him.

The navy captured in the various works here one hundred and sixty-eight cannon.

After the capture of Fort Fisher and the adjacent works, Admiral Porter, by direction of the Navy Department, sent off all the vessels he could spare to points where they were most wanted, and, leaving proper officers in command, proceeded with an increased force to join General Grant, at City Point. There was little that the navy could do there, except to keep the rebel rams in check, for a heavy barricade in the river barred all progress toward Richmond.

Porter remained at City Point until Lee surrendered and Richmond fell, giving what aid he could. When the war was ended, he applied to be detached from the North Atlantic Squadron, having seen the first and last gun of the war fired. During the whole war he was constantly in service; and, although at times his mind and body required rest, he never applied for leave of absence. He received the thanks of Congress for the Fort Fisher affair, and those of many of the State legislatures; this being the fourth vote of thanks received from Congress during the war, including the general one for the capture of New Orleans.

Admiral Porter possesses in an eminent degree all those distinguished qualities found in a great and successful commander. Of consummate nautical skill, he adds to it an originality of conception and a boldness of execution that always ensure success. Joined to all these is an inflexibility of purpose that nothing can move. Having once made up his mind to a course, he will admit of no impossibilities, but drives toward his object with a fierceness and power that bear down all opposition. Buonaparte said that *moral* force is half, even when every thing seems tò depend on hard blows. All this is true; yet it is a force which few can calculate. The power to do this, Porter possesses in an eminent degree. A bold and confident bearing, where others would fail—the assurance of victory which he exhibits to his own men, and at the same time to the enemy, impart courage and strength to the former, and corresponding doubt and vacillation to the latter. He is aware of this, and acts on the knowledge. Hence, his plans and attempts sometimes seem rash to those who do not comprehend this quality, and they attribute to luck what is due to genius. He is the *beau idéal* of a commander to sailors, who never seem to doubt that he will accomplish every thing which he undertakes.

He takes care of his subordinates, and delights in their promotion as much as in his own. Just and generous to the brave, he is severe and unsparing to the timid and reluctant. Frank and outspoken, one always knows where to find him. A strong writer, his reports and journal would make an interesting book by themselves. The government appreciated his great services and abilities by making him Vice-Admiral, so that he now stands next to Farragut in rank, and in time will, doubtless, occupy his place.

At present, he is President of the Naval School a Annapolis.

CHAPTER XVI.

COMMANDER WILLIAM B. CUSHING.

HIS NATIVITY.—ENTERS THE NAVAL ACADEMY.—HIS RESIGNATION.—ENTERS THE NAVAL SERVICE.—EXPEDITION AGAINST FRANKLIN, IN VIRGINIA.—A SECOND EXPEDITION.—LOSES HIS VESSEL.—ATTEMPT TO CAPTURE WILMINGTON PILOTS.—TAKES A FORT BY ASSAULT.—COMMANDS A GUNBOAT IN THE NANSEMOND.—A SEVERE BATTLE.—CHARGES REBEL CAVALRY.—ANECDOTES OF HIM.—DESTROYS A BLOCKADE-RUNNER.—PLANS THE DESTRUCTION OF THE ALBEMARLE BY A TORPEDO.—HIS BOLDNESS AND SUCCESS.—MIRACULOUS ESCAPE.—COMPLIMENTARY LETTER OF THE SECRETARY OF THE NAVY.—SENT TO DESTROY THE RALEIGH.—TAKES PART IN THE BOMBARDMENT OF FORT FISHER.—HIS PRESENT POSITION.

It is seldom that a man is given the command of a ship who had seen so little sea-service as Cushing did before one was entrusted to him.

William B. Cushing was born in Wisconsin, in the year 1842, and entered the Naval Academy in 1857, where he remained four years. He received his appointment from New York State, though he claims Pennsylvania as his residence. In March, 1861, he resigned, under circumstances that did not promise much for his naval fame.

But the breaking out of the war opened to him a field of distinction, and he applied for service, promising the Secretary of the Navy that he would prove worthy the confidence reposed in him. From that time, the Secretary took a personal interest in him, seeming to regard him as his protégé. Attached to the North Atlantic Blockading Squadron, he soon exhibited that daring spirit and love of perilous adventure which marked his career throughout the war.

In October of this year, Acting Rear-Admiral Lee put him in command of the gunboat Ellis, in the expedition against Franklin, Virginia, and for his bravery and skill he was recommended by him to the Department. The next month he entered the New River Inlet, for the purpose of capturing vessels, with the town of Jacksonville, and destroying salt-works, &c. He was completely successful, capturing the place and three vessels; but on his return he got aground, just after he had driven the enemy from two pieces of artillery with which they had opened on him at close range. After trying in vain to get the steamer afloat, and knowing that the enemy would soon be on him, in overwhelming force, he took every thing out of her but her pivot-gun and coal and ammunition, and, sending it aboard one of his prize schooners, told the crew to follow. He then called for six volunteers to remain with him and fight that single gun to the last. They at once stepped forward, though they knew that certain death awaited them. He then ordered the schooner to drop down the river, and, if she saw he was overpowered, to proceed on her way back.

Early next morning, the enemy opened on him from four different points, exposing him to a terrible cross-fire which cut him up fearfully. It was an heroic spectacle to see that little band of half a dozen stand in that fiery tempest, and work that single gun which had to be turned in every direction. Cushing soon saw it was a hopeless fight, and he must decide on one of two alternatives—surrender, or pull in an open boat for a mile and a half under the hostile fire. Scorning to do the first, he resolved on the second—and training his gun on the enemy to go off when the flames reached it, and firing the steamer in five places, he left her with her battle-flag still flying, and started down the river. The brave fellows bent to their oars with a will, and he succeeded in reaching the schooner in safety, and made sail for the sea. It was low water on the bar, over which the surf was rolling with a deafening sound, and the schooner struck bottom several times; but the wind forced her over, and in four hours she reached Beaufort in safety.

He was again commended to the Department for "his courage, coolness, and gallantry."

Early next January, Acting Rear-Admiral Lee allowed him to undertake an enterprise that he himself had planned—which was the capture of Wilmington pilots. He failed in the attempt, owing, as he said, to his schooner getting becalmed three times in shore, at the points where he desired to act. He, however, determined not to return without accomplishing something, and, learning that there was a pilot station thirty miles below Fort Caswell, made sail for it, reaching it on the 5th. At eight o'clock that night, he took three cutters and twenty-five men, and crossing the bar kept on quietly up the river in hopes of capturing pilots, and also some schooners which he heard were there. But he had proceeded but a half mile, when he was observed from shore, and a volley of musketry poured into his boats. He immediately ordered the prows turned to the beach, and landing his men formed them about two hundred yards from the point from which the fire came, and shouted: "Forward, double-quick, charge!" He did not know on what he was charging in the darkness, but he pressed forward with his brave two dozen, till he cleared a piece of wood in front, when he suddenly came upon a fort, with camp fires blazing brightly through the gloom. Nothing daunted at this unexpected sight, he still shouted, "Forward, charge!" The enemy thinking that at least a regiment was upon them, turned and fled—escaping over one side of the fort, as Cushing entered the other. He never fired a shot. He found he had captured an earthwork, surrounded by a ditch ten feet broad, and five feet deep—with a blockhouse in the centre, pierced for musketry. It was held by a company of infantry, who fled in such haste, that they left all their stores, clothing, ammunition, and part of their arms. Destroying what he could not bring off, he then proceeded up the river, where he had another skirmish, when, getting out of ammunition, he returned.

In the spring, General Peck, stationed at Norfolk, heard of the advance against him of Longstreet with a heavy force, and telegraphed to Lee to send him some gunboats. These were immediately forwarded, under the command of Lieutenants Lamson and Cushing. Here, on the 14th of April, the latter had a severe engagement with a rebel battery, which he at last silenced, though with the loss of ten of his crew. He received eight raking shots in this fierce contest, but fortunately his engine was not injured, and he reported: "I can assure you, that the Barney and her crew are still in good fighting trim, and will beat the enemy, or sink at our post." He and Lamson did Peck good service and prevented the enemy from crossing the river.

Hearing on the 21st that a boat from the Stepping Stones had been decoyed on shore by a white handkerchief and then fired into, he determined to avenge the treacherous act. Organizing a boat expedition, composed of seven boats, and manned with ninety sailors, he in the afternoon put off, and, under cover of the fire of the vessels, landed with one 12-pound howitzer. Leaving a part of his force to guard the boats, he boldly marched inland, and, setting on fire three houses with their adjoining barns, moved towards Chuckatuck Village, three miles distant, where four hundred cavalry were posted. Driving in their pickets, he secured a mule cart, and, "toggling the trail-rope of the howitzer to the rear," started the animals on a trot and shouted "Forward, double-quick!" Driving everything before him, he at half past four entered the town. Suddenly he saw a body of cavalry coming down the street at a sabre charge, and shouting like madmen. Quickly unlimbering his howitzer, he poured in a round of grape, while at the same time his little band gave a volley of musketry. This frightened the mules, which rushed, cart and all, directly into the rebel ranks, taking all the ammunition with them. Giving them the charge already in the howitzer, Cushing again cried, "Forward!" and with a cheer the sailors drove down the street, clearing it with a bound, and recovering the cart and ammunition. Remaining master of the town the rest of the day, he towards evening returned leisurely to his boats, having lost but one man.

For his services here, in the Nansemond, he received a congratulatory letter from the Secretary of the Navy, in which the latter said: "Your conduct adds lustre to the character you had already established for valor in the face of the enemy." Lamson also gave him high commendation.

Many anecdotes are told of him while in service here, illustrative of his daring, energetic spirit. Uneasy at General Peck's quietness, he urged him to make some decided move. The latter replied that he could not, for lack of information. Cushing replied that he would furnish him with some; and organizing a party he surprised and captured a small force of the enemy, and forwarded the prisoners to Peck with his compliments, saying, that he sent him some information.

At another time, he, with Lamson and the quartermaster, were out reconnoitering, when they came upon three cavalry men, whom they captured. Mounting the horses, they kept on and soon came in sight of the main force. The commander of it, thinking them to be the advance of a large body of cavalry, ordered the bugle to sound the recall. Lamson and Cushing at once halted, but the horse of the quartermaster, hearing the bugle-call, immediately started off towards the rebel line. Being no horseman, the sailor could not manage him, and, finding that he was taking him straight to the enemy in spite of all his efforts, drew a pistol from the holster, and, placing the muzzle to the animal's head, shot him dead. He then took off the bridle and saddle, and shouldering them moved back to Lamson and Cushing. The latter laughingly asked him what was the matter. The quartermaster replied, with a sailor's usual emphatic language, that he never again would have anything to do with a craft that he could neither steer, turn about, nor stop.

The cavalry men Cushing sent to Peck, saying, that he forwarded more information. He was afterwards placed in command of the United States steamer Shokokon. In August, a few miles from Fort Fisher, he saw the Anglo-rebel steamer Hebe ashore, and the Niphon near by, making preparations to board her. But it was blowing a gale from the northeast, so that the Niphon's boats were swamped, and their crew drowned or taken prisoners. He at once sent a boat in, and rescued two of the men. He then lay off, and, under a tremendous fire from the rebel artillery, continued to throw shells into the steamer, until he set her on fire, and left her a wreck. He also destroyed another blockade runner about the same time, and exhibited a vigilance and energy that brought the highest commendations from his superiors.

But the achievement that has won for him the greatest renown, both for the skill with which it was planned, the consummate daring and coolness with which it was carried out, and the great results accomplished by it—entitling him to a place among those so much above him in rank—was the destruction of the rebel ram Albemarle.

This powerful iron-clad had, in the spring, come out of the Roanoke River, and boldly attacked our naval force near Plymouth, sinking the Southfield, disabling the Miami, and killing the gallant commander Flusser. One hundred-pound rifle shot had no effect on her mailed sides, and she threatened to get control of the waters of the Albemarle Sound. At all events, her presence there required a large naval force on our part. Melancthon Smith had an engagement with her in May, and an attempt was made to destroy her with torpedoes, but she bade defiance to all our efforts, and was a constant menace to our fleet in the Sound. It was, therefore, of the utmost importance she should in some way be disposed of. Nothing, however, was effected, and in the summer Lieutenant Cushing was sent to New York to Admiral Gregory, to have a torpedo boat constructed, with which he proposed to put an end to this apparently invulnerable monster. He found one contrived by Boggs, who was under Gregory in the port of New York, which, with such alterations as he suggested, he thought would answer the purpose. Having completed it to his satisfaction, he took it to Albemarle Sound, and, on the 27th of October, prepared for his desperate undertaking. The ram, at this time, was lying at Plymouth, and, after dark, he with thirteen officers and men, part of them volunteers, started in a steam-launch for that place. The distance from the mouth of the river to where the ram lay, was about eight miles. The stream was only about a rifle-shot across, and lined with pickets, which rendered his chance of reaching the ram undiscovered very improbable. He took with him a cutter, so that in case he was not observed he could land at the wharf, board the ram, and, cutting loose her fastenings, bring her safe out of the river.

The night was dark and rainy, just fitted for his purpose, and he put off with strong hopes of success. He proceeded cautiously on his way, passed the pickets without giving any alarm, and arrived within a mile of the place without being discovered, when he came upon the wreck of the Southfield, sunk the spring previous by the Albemarle. This was surrounded by schooners, and he knew it was very doubtful if he would be able to pass them unseen. If he did not, he ordered the cutter to cast off and board the wreck, which he understood was mounted with a gun that commanded the bend of the river. But, by an extraordinary piece of good fortune, he passed unnoticed, though he steamed so near he could have thrown a biscuit aboard. All seemed locked in sleep, for a dead silence reigned.

Fate thus far had smiled on his desperate undertaking, and, keeping cautiously on, he soon saw, by the light of a large fire on shore, the dark form of the ram tied up to the wharf, and surrounded by a pen of logs thirty feet broad, placed there on purpose to keep any daring craft from running into her while at her moorings. He now steered straight for her, but, as his boat came within the circle of light from the fire on shore, it was seen, and immediately the guard hailed, "What boat is that?" Cushing returning an evasive answer, they sprung their rattles, and, rushing to the rope of the alarm-bell, startled every sleeper with its clang. It was now about three o'clock, and dark as Erebus. Cushing immediately ordered the cutter to cast loose and drop below. In the mean time the guard poured a volley of musketry into the shadowy object that was moving so swiftly and in such mysterious silence towards them. The next moment the dark waters gleamed in the sudden blaze of a cannon, and a shower of grape whistled over the heads of the gallant little crew. Every minute now was fraught with destiny. The crew of the ram were already at their quarters, and Cushing knew that he had not a minute to waste. The air was alive with shot, and shouts, and cries of alarm; but, as he approached the black mass, towering high above him in the gloom, he saw by the course he was going that he would not strike her fair, and perhaps not reach her, over the intervening logs—so he gave the quiet order to steam past. As he stood in his little launch, amid that wild uproar, his men saw by the flash of the enemy's guns that his face, though set like iron, was calm and tranquil. Paymaster Swan fell by his side, three bullets pierced his clothes, but not a movement of haste or alarm was seen in him. The scene, the hour, the issues at stake, and the deadly peril awaiting them, made that boat, with its gallant commander and crew, an object at once fearful and sublime.

Steaming swiftly past the huge structure, after giving the crew one charge of canister, Cushing, though he knew it gave the enemy time to prepare to receive him, shot up the river till he could make a complete circuit, then wheeling, came down with all steam full on the ram. As the launch struck the logs it forced them half way back to the ram by the severity of the blow, and running up on them, rested there. In an instant, the torpedo boom was lowered, and Cushing, by a vigorous pull, succeeded "in diving it under the overhang," and at the same time exploded it. At the same moment a heavy gun, which had been depressed so as to bear on him, was fired, and the huge shot crashed through his boat, while the water flung up by the torpedo came rushing like a cataract into it, filling and completely disabling it.

The rebels, now only fifteen feet off, poured a terrible fire into the little crew, and a hoarse voice shouted out, "Do you surrender?" "No!" thundered back Cushing, and the firing went on, dropping the men on every side, yet, strange to say, missing Cushing. Again came the call to surrender, and again Cushing with a shout of defiance refused. Finding the launch useless, and seeing that to remain in it longer was madness, he told the men to save themselves the best way they could. Then, coolly taking off his coat and shoes, he sprang overboard into the water, and swam with others for the middle of the river, while the shot fell like hailstones around him. He now struck boldly down stream, and was soon out of the reach of the fire. When about half a mile below the town, he came upon Acting-Master's-Mate Woodman, also swimming, but much exhausted. Cushing cheered him up, and with his fast-failing strength strove to get him ashore. But the poor fellow at length gave entirely out, and, bidding his commander "good-by," sank to the bottom. Cushing at length reached the shore, but so completely exhausted that he was unable to drag himself out of the water, and rested with his head on the beach till daylight. He then crept into a swamp near the fort, and lay down, wet and weary, to recover his wasted strength. A path ran a few feet from where he lay, but the autumnal foliage hid him from view. While reclining there, he heard voices approaching, and soon two officers from the Albemarle passed him, and he judged, by their conversation, that he had destroyed the vessel. This somewhat revived him, and he soon arose and started on, still keeping the swamp, and travelled for several hours, till well below the town, when he came out. Meeting a negro, he questioned him, and, finding he could trust him, sent him back to Plymouth to find out the truth about the ram.

One would think that he might have waited a few hours for the news, and made use of the negro to aid him to escape, or furnish him with food to strengthen him. He was beset with foes,—a rebel prison, and perhaps death, awaited him; but these he could not think of until he had heard whether his desperate enterprise had succeeded. Nothing shows the indomitable character of the man more than this. Death alone can conquer such an iron will. Right there on the edge of the swamp he lay, until that negro returned and told him the ram was at the bottom of the river. He then got his direction, and, taking to another swamp to avoid capture, kept on down the river until he came to a creek, where he found a skiff belonging to a picket of the enemy. Loosing this, he shoved off, and, keeping the stream, finally came out into the bay.

Footsore and weary he had toiled on, and now, as night approached, pulled slowly towards the ships. It was a long row, and he did not reach the Valley City till eleven o'clock at night. His appearance on board, all alone, created the greatest astonishment. He was the bearer of his own despatches, and reported the Albemarle destroyed.

Only one man escaped besides himself, and he in another direction. The rest were all killed, drowned, or taken prisoners. When it is considered that Cushing at this time was only twenty-one years of age, one is astonished at the coolness, nerve, and desperate daring of the man. The act would have been the sublimest heroism in a veteran; but in this youth it was almost miraculous.

The Secretary of the Navy wrote him the following complimentary letter:

NAVY DEPARTMENT,
November 9, 1864.

SIR: Your report of October 30th has been received, announcing the destruction of the rebel iron-clad steamer Albemarle, on the night of the 27th ultimo, at Plymouth, North Carolina.

When, last summer, the Department selected you for this important and perilous undertaking, and sent you to Rear-Admiral Gregory, at New York, to make the necessary preparations, it left the details to yourself to perfect. To you and your brave comrades, therefore, belongs the exclusive credit which attaches to this daring achievement. The destruction of so formidable a vessel, which had resisted the combined attack of a number of our steamers, is an important event touching our future naval and military operations. The judgment, as well as the daring courage displayed, would do honor to any officer, and redounds to the credit of one of twenty-one years of age.

On four previous occasions, the Department has had the gratification of expressing its approbation of your conduct, in the face of the enemy, and in each instance there was manifested by you the same heroic daring and innate love of perilous adventure; a mind determined to succeed, and not to be deterred by any apprehensions of defeat.

The Department has presented your name to the President for a vote of thanks, that you may be promoted one grade, and your comrades, also, shall receive recognition.

It gives me pleasure to recall the assurance you gave me at the commencement of your active, professional career, that you would prove yourself worthy of the confidence reposed in you and of the service to which you were appointed. I trust you may be preserved through further trials; and it is for yourself to determine, whether, after entering upon so auspicious a career, you shall, by careful study and self-discipline, be prepared for a wider sphere of usefulness, on the call of your country.

Very respectfully, &c.,

GIDEON WELLES,
Secretary of the Navy.

Lieutenant W. B. CUSHING, U. S. N.,
Washington.

The phrase, "The Department has presented your name for a vote of thanks, that you may be promoted one grade," seems cold, in view of the service he had performed. Still, he was very young to hold the rank he did, but such a man is older than mere years can make him. He who could accomplish *what* he did, and in the *manner* he did, might be entrusted with a frigate in a broadside engagement with any vessel of equal size that ever floated. He had actually achieved more than many a squadron in a year's service. His name was now heard in every man's mouth, coupled with the warmest eulogies on his gallantry and heroism. Cushing's success in destroying this formidable ram, naturally caused him to be selected to perform a similar undertaking the following summer. Another rebel iron-clad, the Raleigh, was known to have been built, and, though there were rumors that she had been wrecked, it was not certain that they were true, and Cushing proposed to settle the matter by actual experiment. One thing was certain, if she were not destroyed, he would ascertain the fact, and in all human probability end her existence before he finished his investigations. We will allow him to give in his own words the results of this expedition. He says in his despatch to the Secretary of the Navy:

SIR: In consequence of permission received from you to attempt the destruction of the iron-clad ram Raleigh, I proceeded to the blockade at that point, with the intention of doing so, judging it prudent to make a thorough reconnoissance first, to determine her position.

I left this ship on the night of the 23d, in the first cutter, with two officers (Acting Ensign J. D. Jones, and Acting Master's Mate William Howorth,) and fifteen men, and started in for the west bar. I succeeded in passing the forts, and also the town and batteries of Smithville, and pulled swiftly up the river. As we neared the Zeke Island batteries, we narrowly escaped being run down by a steamer, and soon after came near detection from the guard boat; evading them all, we continued our course. As we came abreast of the Old Brunswick batteries, some fifteen miles from the starting point, the moon came out brightly and discovered us to the sentinels on the banks, who hailed at once, and soon commenced firing muskets, and raising an alarm by noises and signal lights. We pulled at once for the other shore, obliquing so as to give them to understand that we were going down; but, as soon as I found that we were out of the moon's rays, we continued our course straight up, thereby baffling the enemy and gaining safety. When within seven miles from Wilmington, a good place was selected on the shore; the boat hauled up, and into a marsh, and the men stowed along the bank. It was now nearly day, and I had determined to watch the river, and, if possible, to capture some one from whom information could be gained. Steamers soon began to ply up and down, the flagship of Commodore Lynch, the Gadkin, passing within two hundred yards. She is a wooden propeller steamer of about three hundred tons, no masts, one smoke-stack, clear deck, English build, with awning spread fore and aft, and mounting only two guns; did not seem to have many men.

Nine steamers passed in all, three of them being fine, large blockade runners. Just after dark, as we were preparing to move, two boats rounded the point, and the men, thinking it an attack, behaved in the coolest manner. Both boats were captured, but proved to contain a fishing party returning to Wilmington. From them I obtained all the information that I desired, and made them act as my guides in my further explorations of the river.

Three miles below the city I found a row of obstructions, consisting of iron-pointed spiles, driven in at an angle, and only to be passed by going into the channel left open, about two hundred yards from a heavy battery that is on the left bank.

A short distance nearer the city is a ten-gun navy battery, and another line of obstructions, consisting of diamond-shaped crates, filled and supported in position by two rows of spiles; the channel, in this instance, being within fifty yards of the guns. A third row of obstructions and another battery, complete the upper defences of the city. The river is also obstructed by spiles at Old Brunswick, and there is a very heavy earthwork there. Discovering a creek in the cypress swamp, we pulled, or rather poled up it for some time, and at length came to a road, which, upon being explored, proved to connect with the main road from Fort Fisher and the Sounds to Wilmington. Dividing my party, I left half to hold the cross-road and creek, while I marched the remainder, some two miles, to the main road and stowed away. About 11.30 A. M., a mounted soldier appeared with a mail-bag, and seemed much astonished when he was invited to dismount; but, as I assured him that I would be responsible for any delay that might take place, he kindly consented to shorten his journey. About two hundred letters were captured, and I gained such information as I desired of the fortifications and enemy's force. An expedition was contemplated against Fisher by our army about this time, and the information was of much value. There are thirteen hundred men in the fort; and the unprotected rear that our troops were to storm, is commanded by four light batteries. I enclose rebel requisitions, and report of provisions on hand.

I now waited for the courier from the other direction, in order that we might get the papers that were issued at 1 P. M. in Wilmington; but, just as he hove in sight, a blue jacket exposed himself, and the fellow took to instant flight. My pursuit on the captured horse was rendered useless, from the lack of speed, and the fellow escaped after a race of some two miles.

In the mean time, we captured more prisoners, and discovered that a store was located about two miles distant, and, being sadly in need of some grub, Mr. Howorth, dressed in the courier's coat and hat, and mounted upon his horse, proceeded to market. He returned with milk, chickens, and eggs, having passed every one, in and out of service, without suspicion, though conversing with many. At 6 P. M., after destroying a portion of the telegraph wire, we rejoined the party at the creek, and proceeded down, reaching the river at dark. In trying to land our prisoners upon an island, a steamer passed so close that we had to jump overboard, and hold our heads below the boat to prevent being seen. As we had more prisoners than we could look out for, I determined to put a portion of them in small boats, and set them adrift without oars or sails, so that they could not get ashore in time to injure us. This was done, and we proceeded down the river, keeping a bright lookout for vessels, in order to burn them, if possible. None were found, but I found a pilot to take me to where the ram Raleigh was said to be wrecked. She is indeed destroyed, and nothing now remains of her above water. The iron-clad North Carolina, Captain Muse commanding, is in commission, and at anchor off the city. She is but little relied upon, and would not stand long against a monitor. Both torpedo boats were destroyed in the great cotton fire some time since. One was very near completion. As I neared the forts at the east bar, a boat was detected, making its way rapidly to the shore, and captured after a short chase. It contained six persons, four of whom were soldiers. Taking them all into one boat, I cut theirs adrift, but soon found that twenty-six persons were more than a load. By questions, I discovered that at least one guard boat was afloat, containing seventy-five musketeers, and situated in the narrow passage between Federal Point and Zeke Island. As I had to pass them, I determined to engage the enemy at once, and capture the boat if possible.

The moon was now bright, and as we came nearer the entrance, I saw what we supposed to be one large boat just off the battery; but as we prepared to sail into her, and while about twenty yards distant, three more boats suddenly shot out from that side, and five more from the other, completely blocking up the sole avenue of escape. I immediately put the helm down, but found a large sail-boat filled with soldiers to windward, and keeping us right in the glimmer of the moon's rays. In this trying position, both officers and men acted with true coolness and bravery.

Not the stroke of an oar was out of time; there was no thought of surrender, but we determined to outwit the enemy, or fight it out. Suddenly turning the boat's head, we dashed off as if for the west bar, and, by throwing the dark side of the boat towards them, were soon lost to view. The bait was eagerly seized, and their whole line dashed off at once to intercept us. Then again turning, by the extraordinary pulling of my sailors I gained the passage of the island, and, before the enemy could prevent, put the boat into the breakers on Caroline Shoals. The rebels dared not follow, and we were lost to view, before the guns of the forts, trained on the channel, could be brought to bear upon our unexpected position. Deeply loaded as we were, the boat carried us through in fine style, and we reached the Cherokee just as day was breaking, and after an absence from the squadron of two days and three nights.

I am now posted in regard to the city, land, and water defences, and everything that it will interest the Department to know.

In the operations against Fort Fisher the next winter, he commanded the Monticello. In the first attack, he was sent to buoy out the channel, and afterwards took part in the bombardment. In the second attack, after guarding and assisting the troops in landing, he joined in the shelling of the fort until the final assault, when, at the head of forty men, he landed, and, with Lieutenant Porter commanding another force, led the storming party. When Lieutenant Porter fell, Cushing became the senior officer, and at once rallied as many men as could be gathered in the confusion, and placed them in the trenches, thus relieving regiments that were needed in the front.

He was afterwards sent by Admiral Porter to receive the capitulation of Fort Caswell, but found it deserted. Hoisting the national flag upon it, he proceeded to Little River, North Carolina, and surprised and captured some rebel soldiers.

But all naval operations north, of any importance, ending with the fall of Fort Fisher, Cushing's active career was ended. The collapse of the rebellion soon after left him, like so many other naval officers, in the rank and position they were to occupy in time of peace.

Promoted to commander, he was attached to the Pacific Squadron, and is now on duty in the Pacific Ocean. Still a young man, he has a bright future before him, and if he lives will doubtless reach the highest rank in the navy. Bold, daring, and self-collected under the most trying circumstances—equal to any emergency—never unbalanced by an unexpected contingency, he possesses those great qualities always found in a successful commander. No man in our navy, at his age, has ever won so brilliant a reputation, and it will be his own fault if it is not increased until he has no superior.

CHAPTER XVII.

REAR-ADMIRAL STEPHEN C. ROWAN.

HIS NATIVITY.—APPOINTED MIDSHIPMAN.—CRUISE ROUND THE WORLD.—ON DUTY IN NEW YORK.—PASSED MIDSHIPMAN.—SERVES IN THE WEST INDIES.—HIS SERVICES IN THE FLORIDA WAR.—JOINS THE SOUTH SEA EXPLORING EXPEDITION.—PROMOTED TO LIEUTENANT.—ON THE COAST SURVEY.—CRUISES ON COAST OF BRAZIL AND IN THE MEDITERRANEAN.—SERVES UNDER DUPONT ON THE COAST OF CALIFORNIA.—MEXICO.—AT MONTEREY.—AT MAZATLAN.—LAND MARCH AND FIGHT WITH MEXICANS.—IS WOUNDED.—OTHER SERVICES DURING THE WAR.—INSPECTOR OF ORDNANCE IN NEW YORK NAVY YARD.—COMMANDS RECEIVING SHIP NORTH CAROLINA.—AT BREAKING OUT OF THE REBELLION PUT IN COMMAND OF THE PAWNEE.—COVERS WASHINGTON, ETC.—SENT TO RELIEVE SUMTER.—IN THE POTOMAC.—FIRES THE FIRST NAVAL GUN IN THE WAR.—MATTHIAS POINT.—GALLANT CONDUCT.—FORT HATTERAS.—COMMANDS A DIVISION IN BURNSIDE'S EXPEDITION.—DESTROYS THE REBEL FLEET.—A DARING ACT.—AFTER SERVICES.—COMMANDS THE FLEET.—COÖPERATES WITH BURNSIDE IN THE ATTACK ON NEWBERN.—ORDERED TO FIT OUT THE ROANOKE.—COMMANDS THE IRONSIDES UNDER DAHLGREN AT CHARLESTON.—HIS SERVICES.—A GALLANT FIGHT.—PROMOTED TO COMMODORE.—THE IRONSIDES DAMAGED BY A TORPEDO.—ROWAN RETURNS WITH HER TO PHILADELPHIA FOR REPAIRS.—PROMOTED TO REAR ADMIRAL.—NOW COMMANDS THE NORFOLK NAVY YARD.

ADMIRAL ROWAN, though he now claims Pennsylvania as his place of residence, is a native of Ireland, and was appointed midshipman in the Navy from Ohio, in February, 1826. Though an Irishman by birth, he came to this country when a mere child. His first cruise was in the Vincennes, Captain Finch commanding, who afterwards changed his name and became Commodore Bolton. In the Pacific Ocean and East Indies, he was learning his profession for four years. From Callao, this vessel sailed by way of the South Sea Islands, and, keeping on to the Cape of Good Hope, thence to St. Helena, completed a voyage round the world—the first ever made by a national vessel. In 1830 he returned home, and for the two following years was attached to a cutter in the waters of New York. In 1832 he was promoted to passed midshipman, and ordered to the West Indies, where he served as acting master or acting lieutenant, for four years. At the breaking out of the Florida war he was attached to the Vandalia, and, when the news of the massacre of Dade's command was received, the ship hurried to Tampa Bay to aid the small garrison stationed there, in case of an attack by the Indians. Here he was busily employed in boat expeditions along the coast, to prevent the Indians from passing from the Withlacooche to the everglades. In one of these expeditions, he united his little command with Colonel, late Major General Persifer Smith, and marched into the interior in search of Indians. In 1836 he joined by invitation the South Sea exploring expedition, and remained attached to it until, after various delays and vexatious changes, it was the next year finally reorganized, when he was ordered to other duty.

The spring of this year he was promoted to lieutenant, and in the following spring ordered to the coast survey, in the duties of which he was engaged, when he was transferred to the line-of-battle ship Delaware, Captain McCauley, bearing the flag of Commodore Morris, which cruised on the coast of Brazil and in the Mediterranean for nearly six years. It will be seen, from the foregoing succinct account, that young Rowan had long cruises, and saw but little shore duty. For the first twenty years of his naval life, he was afloat most of the time.

From 1844 to 1845, he served on board the Ontario, and, the three subsequent years, in the Cyane, under the then Captain Dupont, on the Coast of California and Mexico, or to the close of the Mexican war. He helped to hoist the American flag at Monterey, and with the crew of his ship, built a blockhouse and stockade for its defence. He afterwards blockaded Mazatlin—commanded the naval brigade under Stockton and Kearney, on the march from San Diego to Los Angelos, and, at the latter place, defeated the enemy.

In a fight at the Mesa with the Mexicans, he was wounded, but kept the field, and not long after commanded a boat expedition in a night attack on the advanced post of the enemy, near Mazatlin. He also bombarded a small town on the Mexican coast, and destroyed two gunboats.

When Dupont marched to the relief of Lieutenant Heywood, then closely besieged by a superior force, Rowan joined him with a body of sailors from the Cyane, and helped to swell the shout that went up in reply to the cheers of the beleaguered little band.

After the close of the Mexican war, he was ordered to the Navy Yard of New York, as Inspector of Ordnance, and organized that department. In 1852 he was detached from this service, and placed in command of the Relief. He cruised in this vessel for three years, when he was promoted to the rank of commander by the Retiring Board, and put in charge of the receiving-ship North

Carolina, which position he retained for three years, or till the close of 1857. The two subsequent years, he was on ordnance duty at the Navy Yard, New York. The year previous to the breaking out of the war, he was awaiting orders. When it actually occurred, he applied for service afloat, and, in January, 1861, was put in command of the Pawnee, whose commander, being a southern man, had resigned. The next month he was ordered to Washington, and his vessel became the strongest naval protection to the Capital that we had in the Potomac, and the chief reliance in keeping this channel of communication open. By order of General Scott, he covered the landing of our troops at Alexandria, at the time that Ellsworth fell.

Soon after, Rowan was ordered off Charleston, to coöperate with the army in landing stores for the garrison at Fort Sumter. He found in the offing the Baltic, under charter to the army, and the Harriet Lane.

On the very morning of his arrival, the rebels opened fire on Sumter. The heavy boom of the cannon, as it rolled down the bay, and the flashes that rent the darkness towards the rebel city, told him too well that the brave Anderson and his gallant little band had entered on their hopeless struggle. As the deepening roar made the waters tremble, he ordered the vessel to be run in, and anchored in the mouth of the nearest channel. As daylight broadened over the bay, and the tossing clouds of smoke were revealed, rent ever and anon by the terrific explosions, he could hardly restrain himself from steaming boldly in and lying broadside to the enemy's batteries. He knew the smallness of the garrison in Fort Sumter, and though he saw, by the puffs of smoke from its side, that the few men that composed it were bravely battling for the old flag, he knew also that they could not long withstand the concentrated fire of the batteries, with which they were assailed. He paced his deck with a stern and passionate step; one moment resolved to brave the worst, and sail in, and lie alongside of the fort; but the next moment he checked himself, with the reflection that his orders did not permit such action on his part. Hoping, however, that he might find some loophole in them that would justify him in such a case, he read them over again. His heart sunk within him as he saw that his orders were peremptory—no permission to act on his own judgment being given him.

He was to await the arrival of the frigate, with means for carrying out the object of the expedition. He felt that he had no right to hazard the only naval ship present in the opening fight, and thus derange the whole plan for reinforcing the fort. But it was a trying position for a gallant and intrepid commander like Rowan to be placed in. To stand within sight of the beleaguered garrison, whose desperate situation called to him so pleadingly for help, and listen to the frightful cannonading that he knew was steadily pounding the fort to pieces, and find his hands tied by orders that he dared not break, was far harder to bear than the concentrated fire of a dozen batteries.

While this fearful bombardment was going on, the preparations were completing rapidly as possible to reinforce the garrison, and by next morning everything was ready, and the vessels waited only for the night to cover the movement. That was a long morning to Rowan, and he paced his deck impatiently. A little while after, as he stood watching the clouds of smoke that wrapped

Sumter, ever and anon parted before the explosions of its own cannon, and was rejoicing to see how gallantly Anderson was defending his post, there suddenly leaped up through the murky atmosphere a vast volume of flame, and the "fort is on fire" burst from his lips. It was true—help had come too late—and by two o'clock the old flag came down, and the rebel flag went up amid the cheers of Charleston.

Rowan's mission was now ended, and with a sad heart he turned the prow of his vessel north. On his arrival at Washington, he was directed to take on board a number of officers, and to receive further orders from Flag Officer Paulding.

That same evening, the Pawnee steamed down the river, and the next evening, at eight o'clock, was alongside the navy yard wharf at Norfolk. The following morning, she left with the Cumberland in tow, and the work of destruction in the navy yard was begun.

Paulding left the vessel at Old Point, and Rowan returned with her to Washington. While lying at anchor off Alexandria, he was informed that the rebels were erecting batteries at Acquia Creek, to obstruct the free passage of the Potomac. He immediately volunteered to go down and attack them. The Government gave permission, and, at nine o'clock the next morning, he lay off the battery and opened his broadsides. The enemy replied, and all day long the thunder of the guns echoed up and down the Potomac, filling all hearts with anxiety. The sky in this direction had been full of omens for a long time; but this was the first open, hostile act. Just before sundown, Rowan hauled off, having been struck nine times. He thus had the honor of firing the first gun of the navy at the rebels. He afterwards continued to blockade the river, and make reconnoissances along its banks.

In the fight at Matthias Point, in which Ward was killed, Rowan sent a party on shore, under Lieutenant Chaplin, to assist in the attack. When the latter was compelled to retreat, he first collected all his men, "steady and cool," said Rowan, "among a perfect hail of musketry from hundreds of men." The last man left the shore with him, and not being able to swim to the boat with his musket, Lieutenant Chaplin took him on his shoulders, musket and all, and safely reached the boat without a scratch, save a musket-hole through the top of his cap.

John Williams, captain of the maintop, while waiting for the retreating crew, told the sailors that every one must die on his thwarts, sooner than leave a man behind. The bullets dropped like hailstones in the boat, and one soon pierced his thigh. Another cut his flagstaff in two, letting the ensign fall. Though suffering severely from his wound, he instantly seized it and waved it over his head in defiance, to show that his colors were not struck.

But when the expedition under Stringham against Cape Hatteras was organized, Rowan was ordered to join it, and took part in the action that gave us possession of the rebel works, and the control of the Inlet. The Pawnee after the victory was ordered to remain on the spot, and Rowan fitted out an expedition which destroyed the fortifications, &c., at Acracoke Inlet.

The Pawnee was afterwards ordered to Washington, and Rowan detached from her, and placed in command of the Brooklyn, at Philadelphia. He, however, had been in command of the latter but a short time, when he was ordered to Hampton Roads, to help Goldsborough organize a flotilla to operate in the sounds of North Carolina. He shared in all the perils and anxiety of what seemed at first this ill-fated expedition.

After the engagement that gave us Roanoke Island, and sent the rebel fleet in flight up the sound, Rowan was selected to pursue the enemy, and complete the victory. The rebel vessels, seven in number, had taken refuge behind some works near Elizabeth City, about thirty-seven miles north. Rowan, who had command of a division, with the Delaware for his flagship, took such vessels as were fit for immediate service and could be spared, and started on Sabbath morning to find the enemy. Seeing the smoke of two rebel steamers ahead, he gave chase, when they disappeared up the Pasquatank River. He followed after, but, night coming on, he anchored about fifteen miles below the city in the river. The inhabitants, never dreaming that our vessels could pass the obstructions at Roanoke, were terrified at the news that they were approaching the place.

The rebel gunboats were now fairly entrapped, and Rowan could take his own time in preparing for the attack. It was a beautiful night in which he lay at anchor; not a cloud obscured the sky, and the bright moon sailed serenely through the heavens, flooding with her mellow light the placid waters of the river and the little fleet of fourteen vessels riding quietly on its bosom. Rowan now called all the commanders on board his vessel, and told them that the enemy was either drawn up behind a battery on Cobb's Point, ten miles further up the river, or had escaped through the Dismal Swamp Canal, which joins Elizabeth City to Norfolk. He also informed them that they were short of ammunition, having only twenty-four rounds, which was not sufficient for a long combat, and therefore what was done must be done quickly. He consequently gave positive orders, that, in the attack which he proposed to make in the morning, not a shot should be fired until he gave the signal; and, moreover, that each vessel as she approached the enemy should, instead of engaging him at even short range, run him down, and make a hand to hand fight of it. "With this understanding," says Rowan, "these noble spirits returned to their ships to await the events of the morrow." The night passed off quietly, and the next morning at daylight, the signal to weigh anchor was hoisted, and soon the "Yo! heave ho!" of the sailors rang over the water. Rowan in the Delaware, with the Underwriter, Perry, and Morse, moved off in advance, followed by the remaining vessels, which had orders, the moment the battery was passed, to leave the line and attack it in the rear. Proceeding cautiously up the river, he at eight o'clock came in sight of the rebel steamers, commanded by Lynch—noted in times past as the leader of the Dead Sea expedition—drawn up behind the battery, which mounted four heavy 32-pounders. On the opposite shore, in close range, was moored the schooner Warrior, armed with two more 32-pounders. Rowan was compelled to carry his vessels between these, before he could reach the rebel gunboats beyond. As the fleet moved forward, the hostile batteries and the heavy guns from the steamers opened fire, and the balls came skipping along the water, or dropped amid the vessels. Not a shot replied, and the little fleet kept on in dead silence. The enemy seemed astonished at this, but, as Rowan steadily drew nearer, opened with smaller guns till the air around the vessels was full of shot and shell, screaming and bursting on every side. All eyes were turned on the flagship to catch her signal to commence action, but she still moved silently on through the fire, until she got within half a mile of the battery. Rowan then ran up the signal, "*Dash at the enemy.*" In an instant all steam was crowded on, and it became a swift race between the vessels to see which should close first with the enemy. The foam parted and rolled away from the bows, as, put to their utmost speed, they drove into the fiery opening between the fort and schooner, while every gun that could bear poured in a storm of shot and shell. The sudden, swift dash forward, and the almost simultaneous opening of the heavy guns, confounded the enemy, who had expected a long bombardment. Rowan, leading in the Delaware, delivered his broadsides right and left, and, passing swiftly abreast of the fort, saw the garrison fleeing from it in affright, while on the other side the Warrior was on fire, and the crew rushing for the shore. The vessels in the mean time kept moving on in flame, driving straight for the rebel fleet. The Perry, commanded by the gallant Flusser, made for the rebel flagship Seabird, and striking her full amidships, crushed her like an eggshell —finishing her with one terrible blow. The Ceres took the Ellis, the crew boarding her with a fierce shout and sweeping her decks like a storm, while Rowan captured the Fanny. A shell entered the Valley City, and, passing through the magazine, exploded on the berth-deck, setting it on fire. Chaplin, the commander, jumped down into the magazine himself, and, while giving directions to the men who were dashing water on the fire, passed up loose cylinders of powder. The fire-works on board ignited, and rockets whizzed and shot off, blue-lights blazed up amid the ammunition, while the vessel reeled to the heavy broadsides that never slackened. The shell-room caught fire, and for a few moments it seemed as if the vessel must be blown out of the water. But Chaplin kept the men steady, working himself like a common sailor to extinguish the fire. John Davis, the gunner's mate, seeing the flames leaping up on every side, jumped on an open barrel of powder, and sat down on the head to cover it with his person. Chaplin, seeing him quietly seated there, ordered him in a peremptory tone to get down and help put out the fire. The brave fellow replied: "Don't you see, sir, I can't, for if I do, the sparks will fall on the powder. If I get *down*, Captain, we shall all go UP." Though the danger was imminent, and the scene terrific, Chaplin could not refrain from smiling at the imperturbable coolness of the man. A more daring act cannot be conceived, and he was promoted for it, as he ought to have been. The fight was so quickly over, that Rowan did not fire even his twenty-four rounds.

It will be noticed that he has the honor of setting the example in this war, of not waiting to engage batteries, but of running past them, and thus rendering their fire harmless.

When the master's-mate planted the stars and stripes on the fort, one long, loud cheer went up from the whole flotilla.

The rebel steamers were all captured and sunk but one, which escaped up the river past the city. Leaving most of his vessels to try and save the burning steamers, Rowan now pushed on up to Elizabeth City. As he came alongside of the wharf, he saw a battery wheeling off at a gallop down the street. The crew jumped ashore, and, dashing along the street, captured its commanding officer, who had staid behind to compel the inhabitants to set fire to their dwellings. The flames were soon extinguished, when Rowan ordered all on board, lest he should be accused of Vandalism. Some of the inhabitants, and among them women and children, rushed to the wharf, and implored him to save their houses and property from destruction; but he would not allow a man to move.

The three following days were spent in destroying the fort and machinery of those vessels which could not be raised.

Rowan followed up this victory by sending off expeditions in various directions, to complete the conquest of the coast. When Goldsborough returned to Hampton Roads, Rowan took command of the fleet, and coöperated with Burnside.

In February, he made a reconnoissance up the Chowan River, having Hawkins' Zouaves on board. At four in the afternoon of the 10th, he came in sight of the wharves and landing of the town of Winston. He ranged up past the wharf, and was just letting go his anchor, when suddenly two batteries opened on him, accompanied by a perfect hailstorm of musketry. Volley followed volley, in rapid succession, the bullets striking the vessel like pattering rain. Being too close under the high land to return the fire, he steamed ahead, and, running up a short distance, succeeded, after much trouble, in turning round in this narrow river, when he came down and opened on the enemy with shells. The next morning he entered the town and destroyed the military stores, etc. The following month he coöperated with Burnside in the attack on Newbern. After landing the troops, he proceeded up the Neuse, toward Newbern, shelling the woods in advance of the army. The river was lined with batteries, and in one place so filled with obstructions and torpedoes, that it was thought by the enemy no vessel could pass. Fort Dixie, which was first encountered, after sustaining a bombardment all one day, was abandoned, when a boat was sent ashore to raise the stars and stripes. Rowan then steamed slowly ahead till he came under the fire of Fort Ellis. This he returned with such fierceness, that it soon blew up with a terrific explosion. He then passed on to Fort Thompson—the last fort before reaching the obstructions. He soon silenced this also, and then making signal, "follow my motions," passed slowly through the first line of obstructions. It was a bold movement, for he did not know but that at any moment a torpedo would lift his vessel out of the water. There was a line of thirty of them, each containing two hundred pounds of powder, at this point.

As he cleared them, he saw our troops mount the ramparts of Fort Thompson, cheering and waving their colors. Fort Lane was abandoned, and Rowan now steamed rapidly up towards Newbern. A second barrier, composed of sunken vessels, was also passed, although some of his vessels were injured by striking the submerged timbers. He passed six forts before he reached the city, all mounting rifle guns, ranging from 32 to 80 pounders.

Rowan also furnished Burnside with a naval battery, manned by sailors, which did good service in the battle—a quarter of the whole number being killed and wounded.

He sent home nine ships, freighted with stores, captured by him at Newbern. The subsequent fall of Beaufort gave us entire command of the waters of the North Carolina coast, and Rowan, having finished the work assigned him, was in July detached from the command of the flotilla, and ordered at first to the Susquehannah, and afterwards to New York to fit out the iron-clad Roanoke. In the mean time Congress passed a vote of thanks for his signal services. When Dahlgren took command of the South Atlantic blockading squadron, Captain Rowan was placed in command of the New Ironsides.

In the subsequent attacks on Forts Wagner and Gregg, the Ironsides bore a conspicuous part, as the numerous dents in her mailed sides evinced.

In the action of the 16th of August, she was struck thirty-nine times. The next month, however, Rowan showed what he could do with his ship unsustained by the other vessels. The Weehawken having got aground in the pass between Sumter and Cummings Point, where she was exposed to a horrible fire, Dahlgren ordered Captain Rowan to go to her help. He immediately steamed up, and, placing his vessel right between the Weehawken and the enemy's fire, cast anchor. As the bows of the noble vessel slowly swung round towards Moultrie, a concentrated and terrific fire was opened on her. The water seemed alive with bursting shells, while the heavy bolts fell with ceaseless clatter and awful power on her mailed sides. As soon as Rowan got his port broadside to bear, he directed the gunners to fire slowly at first, till they got the exact range. When this was done, he bade them pour in their shells rapidly as possible. Such a horrible tempest was now rained on the fort, that its fire soon began to slacken. But, in the mean time, other batteries of 10-inch guns between this fort and Beauregard were pounding him fearfully. Opening suddenly on these, he soon dismounted one of their heaviest guns. He thus stood grandly at bay, his guns thundering on the right, and on the left, until all the forts ceased firing, except an occasional gun. He then directed a slow fire to be kept up on Moultrie with shells. As soon as the enemy saw this, they jumped up from behind their sand bags, and opened a rapid fire, but, Rowan immediately pouring in his shells as before, they soon retired to their shelter again. The huge missiles were sent with the unerring certainty of rifle balls, and burst around the hostile guns with such destructive force, that not a man dared to show his head. For nearly three hours he lay here and protected the Weehawken, that otherwise would have been knocked to pieces; and did not leave till he had expended all his ammunition.

His vessel was under fire fourteen times in Charleston harbor, and, in the actions of Sept. 7th and 8th, fired over three hundred rounds, and was hit ninety-four times.

While on service here, Captain Rowan was promoted to Commodore, his commission dating back to the vote of thanks by Congress.

During the first part of the year 1864, Admiral Dahlgren was absent on leave of absence, and Commodore Rowan was left in command of the South Atlantic blockading squadron.

The Ironsides, though apparently impervious to shot, came very near being destroyed by a torpedo, which exploded against her sides, inflicting considerable damage. Active operations having ceased in Charleston harbor, she was ordered to Philadelphia for repairs.

Commodore Rowan was subsequently placed in command of the Nadowasca, and promoted to Rear-Admiral. His sea service covers nearly twenty-five years.

He is now in command of the Navy Yard at Norfolk.

CHAPTER XVIII.

COMMODORE S. P. LEE.

HIS BIRTH.—COMMANDS THE ONEIDA IN THE PASSAGE OF THE FORTS BELOW NEW ORLEANS.—DEMANDS THE SURRENDER OF VICKSBURG.—PLACED OVER THE NORTH ATLANTIC BLOCKADING SQUADRON.—HIS SERVICES HERE.—FIGHT BETWEEN THE RAM ALBEMARLE AND OUR VESSELS IN THE ALBEMARLE SOUND.—PLACED OVER THE MISSISSIPPI FLEET.—COÖPERATES WITH THE ARMY IN THE CAMPAIGN AGAINST HOOD.—COMPLIMENTARY LETTER FROM GENERAL THOMSON.

COMMODORE LEE was for so long a time Acting Rear-Admiral of the North Atlantic Blockading Squadron and Mississippi Flotilla, that his reports fill a large space in the naval documents. But during his command over this extensive district, he was engaged in no general important movements, while the principal events that occurred in its limits are given in the sketches of those subordinate officers who were principally engaged in them.

SAMUEL PHILLIPS LEE is a Virginian by birth, and was appointed midshipman from that State in November, 1825, and hence had been thirty-five years in the national service when the war broke out. Though a Southerner by birth, he did not, like so many other officers, join the Confederacy; but remained true to the old flag.

When Farragut organized his expedition against New Orleans, Lee was given the command of the United States steamship Oneida, and was assigned to Bailey's division, that led the fleet. After the latter found that he could not get the Colorado over the bar, he selected the Oneida as his flagship in the approaching struggle; but, finding that this arrangement was displeasing to Lee, who felt that whatever honor his vessel might win, he would get no share of it, he transferred his flag to the Cayuga. Lee carried his vessel gallantly into action, standing on the forecastle and directing all the movements of the ship from that exposed position, until the obstructions in the river were passed. He says:

The Oneida was steered in for the Fort St. Philip side, passed up quickly in the strong eddy, and close under the guns of that fort, (so that the sparks from its immense battery seemed to reach us,) fired rapidly bolts from two rifled guns, (we had no shell for them,) grape and canister from the forward 32's, and shrapnell from the two 11-inch pivot guns, whilst passing this long line of works. (It was, perhaps, the burning of the sulphur in our 11-inch shrapnell, which occasioned the officers in Fort St. Philip to inquire, after the surrender, if our shells were not filled with Greek fire.)

The terrific fire from the heavy batteries of Fort St. Philip passed over us, their guns seeming to be too much elevated for our close position.

* * * * * * * * *

When just above the forts, we encountered the gunboats and transports of the enemy. The former, it seems from the subsequent reports of our prisoners, were tied to trees along the steep bank above Fort St. Philip; thence passing over to the Fort Jackson side, these gunboats came down to meet us. It was very thick from darkness and smoke. We had now got on the Fort Jackson side. A flash revealed the ram Manassas, gliding down our port-side below our guns, and passing too close and swiftly, aided by steam and the current, to enable us to bring our heavy guns to bear on her. Next came a gunboat quite near, and passing from the Fort Jackson to the Fort St. Philip side, across our bow. Ran into it with a full head of steam, and cut it down with a loud crash on its starboard quarter. Clear of our guns in a moment, it drifted down stream in the darkness. We now slowed down, and afterwards used the steam as necessary to get or keep position in fighting the gunboats, firing right and left into them as we could ascertain (from other indications than black smoke, on account of the Varuna), that we were not firing into one of our steamers; forebore to fire into those steamers that appeared to be river transports, and ceased firing into others when they made no return.

In this manner we fired into and passed several rebel boats on the right bank, leaving it for those who came after to pick up the prizes. A black gunboat, with two masts—a converted sea-steamer—ran ahead after a brief contest. At or near daybreak, we found the Cayuga on our port-side. After consultation with Captain Bailey, we concluded to wait for the fleet to come up and form in order. Captain Bailey afterwards hailed that the Varuna might be ahead. Looked for her, but could not make her out, and received reports from the first lieutenant and the officer on the forecastle, that she was not in sight. When we had steamed a mile or more ahead of the Cayuga, saw her general signal No. 80, but, as there was nothing in sight of us needing assistance, supposed the signal to refer to some vessel astern of the Cayuga. Moving ahead, reconnoitring, came up with what, in the gray of the morning, appeared to be a fort, but what, on nearer approach, proved to be a rebel camp on the right bank, with a large rebel flag flying over it. Fired into it, but no reply was made, no one was seen moving, and the camp seemed deserted. Passed on, leaving the trophy flag flying, and soon received a report that the Varuna was ahead, and that the enemy was trying to board her. Went ahead with all speed to her assistance. Approaching rapidly, saw the Varuna ashore on the left bank of the river, where she had been driven by two rebel gunboats. At 5.30 A. M. fired on one of them—the black gunboat, our previous acquaintance—with the forecastle rifle gun. He had hoisted his jib (his wheel-ropes being gone) and was trying to escape up river; but both rebel gunboats, finding they could not get away, ran on shore—the black one, which proved to be the Governor Moore, Commander Kennon, on the left bank, above the Varuna, and the ———, (name yet unknown,) on the right bank, opposite the Varuna, with her head up stream. After we had driven them ashore, their crews deserted, but not before setting fire to their vessels.

With our boats, captured Commander Kennon, (formerly of our navy,) one first lieutenant of artillery, one chief engineer, and fourteen of the crew of the Governor Moore; also, a rebel signal-book and some official papers, showing that the rebel gunboats were ordered to ram our vessels, and to distinguish themselves by showing lights, which they must soon have found prudent to haul down. Seeing that the Varuna was sinking, sent our boats and went to her assistance. Brought on board Oneida the first lieutenant, two acting masters, two mates, and forty petty officers and seamen of the Varuna, and sent ten others, seven of whom were wounded, to the Pensacola.

The Varuna had been rammed and badly stove by both of these rebel gunboats, which had kept with or after her up river, and she was filling, with her magazine flooded, when the Oneida drove off her assailants, prevented her officers and crew from being captured, and was received by them with loud and hearty cheers.

The Cayuga (Captain Bailey's flag) also cheered the Oneida heartily for opportunely coming to his support that morning.

Lee passed up the river with Bailey, and shared in the action of the 25th, against Fort Chalmette. After the capitulation of New Orleans, Farragut sent him forward to demand the surrender of Vicksburg. The authorities refusing to obey his summons, Lee threatened to bombard the town, but forebore.

In the subsequent passage of the batteries by Farragut, January 28th, he carried his ship steadily through the fire, receiving but four shots.

Lee having been promoted, was soon after transferred to the command of the North Atlantic Blockading Squadron, taking the place of Goldsborough, who was relieved at his own request, and became Acting-Rear-Admiral. Here he continued "discharging his duties," said the Secretary of the Navy, "in a position of great responsibility, and in some respects of great embarrassment." * * * "The rivers of Virginia, and the sounds of North Carolina have been penetrated, watched and guarded, as well as the entire coast, so that all intercourse with the rebels has been cut off, with the single exception of the port of Wilmington." Various expeditions were fitted out; rivers were explored; guerillas dispersed, and blockade runners captured in the limits of his jurisdiction; but no naval movements of a decisive character made. While here, he received a letter from Alexander Stephens, who wished to be allowed to proceed to Washington as commissioner from Jefferson

Davis. After communicating with Washington, Admiral Lee informed him, that his request was inadmissible.

When Butler commenced his movement on Bermuda Hundreds, Lee coöperated with him, and afterwards with Grant. While his subordinates were active in maintaining the blockade along the coast, and our supremacy in the sounds of North Carolina, he personally superintended affairs in the James River and adjoining waters. His correspondence with Grant, Butler, and the authorities at Washington, covers the whole field of operations, though the duties of the navy were quite subordinate to those of the army. Keeping communications open; clearing rivers of batteries; transporting troops, and covering their landing, and holding the enemy's vessels in check, are quite as important as naval battles; yet, a detailed narrative of all the proceedings possesses but little interest to the general reader.

Lee was anxious to have the rebel fleet come down the James and attack him; but no such opportunity was given him to distinguish himself, and he was reluctantly compelled to submit to a comparatively inactive life personally—his time being chiefly occupied in giving orders to subordinates in the various portions of his wide command, and in receiving their reports.

As a fair illustration of the character of his duties in the James River, we give one of his despatches:

FLAGSHIP N. A. B. SQUADRON,
HAMPTON ROADS, JULY 9, 1864.

SIR: I transmit, enclosed, three (3) reports from Captain Smith, of 4th, 5th, and 6th instants, as follows: (1) enclosing report from Lieutenant-Commander Quackenbush of the capture, by a boat's crew from the Pequot, of three confederate prisoners. A large body of cavalry approaching after the capture, the Pequot and Commodore Morris opened fire and drove them off. The prisoners had little information. (2) 5th instant, enclosing copies of two telegrams, (A and B,) dated 4th and 5th instants, from General Weitzel to General Foster, warning him of a probable attack by a rebel force of about five thousand, which the second despatch states is probably meant as a feint to cover a heavy attack on Meade's left; also a despatch (C) from General Butler, of 5th instant, requesting the assistance of the naval vessels in destroying the enemy's forage and grain in their vicinity. (3) of 6th instant, reports the destruction of a considerable amount of hay and grain on Aiken's farm, and an attempt to capture the rebel guard stationed to protect the reapers; they escaped, however, their arms, ammunition, and clothing only being taken.

Acting-Master Lee, commanding the Commodore Morris, reports to Captain Smith, that, while destroying a field of wheat near Turkey Bend, an escaped Union prisoner, John H. Bond, who had been sent from Richmond to aid in cutting the grain, claimed his protection, and stated that there were seven (7) other prisoners sent with him for the same purpose. Richard D. Lee, Justice of the Peace for Warwick County, Virginia, was taken prisoner at the same time, and turned over to General Butler. Captain Smith also reports that he is informed that the man Aiken, upon whose premises the grain was destroyed, had assisted a party of five (5) to escape to the rebel lines. This man gave a strict pledge of neutrality, when our forces first went up the river. This report also encloses the statement of three (3) deserters from the rebel iron-clad Virginia, who came off on the 5th; they furnish no new information.

There has been no change in the naval situation, and all was quiet at the last date.

I have the honor to be, sir, very respectfully,

S. P. LEE,

Acting Rear-Admiral, Commanding N. A. B. Squadron.

Hon. Gideon Welles,

Secretary of the Navy.

Such events as these would be varied by an attack on a rebel battery planted on the banks of the river. The rebel ram Albemarle, in the Roanoke River, caused him much anxiety, and the engagements with her, and attempts to dest. oy her, were the chief naval events in the waters of North Carolina. This powerful vessel had attacked our force there, and sunk the Southfield; hence, Admiral Lee was very anxious to dispose of her in some way. On the 5th of May, she again came out of Roanoke River, when Melancthon Smith, senior officer in the sound, boldly advanced to meet her with his little squadron, but failed to capture her.

When the Department determined on the capture of Wilmington, Admiral Porter was put in Lee's place and the latter given the former's command on the Mississippi. The severe fighting had all been done here, but still it required a good deal of hard work to keep what we had got. The Tennessee River especially caused Lee much trouble.

In the fall of 1864, the steamer Undine was captured here, while three "tin-clads" had to be burned to prevent them from falling into the hands of the enemy.

Lee's important command extended from the Ohio to the mouth of the Mississippi, embracing not only the tributaries of the latter, but the Tennessee and Cumberland Rivers. This was divided into several districts, with a separate commander over each. The eleventh district embraced the Tennessee River, and here the most valuable services were rendered by the Acting Rear Admiral, in coöperating with the army under Thomas, in the campaign against Hood. The former acknowledged those services, in a complimentary letter to Lee, in which he says: "Your official coöperation on the Tennessee, has contributed largely to the demoralization of Hood's army," and further says: "In conclusion, it gives me great pleasure to tender to you, your officers and men, my hearty thanks for your cordial coöperation during the operations of the past thirty-five days."

At the close of the war, Lee received the surrender of the last of the rebel fleet on the western waters.

CHAPTER XIX.

COMMODORE THORNTON A. JENKINS.

HIS NATIVITY.—ENTERS THE SERVICE.—FIRST CRUISE.—ON THE COAST SURVEY.—LIGHT-HOUSE DUTY.—SERVES IN THE MEXICAN WAR.—COMMANDS HYDROGRAPHIC PARTY IN COAST SURVEY.—BRINGS HOME PRISONERS FROM MEXICO.—EMPLOYED IN SECRET SERVICE IN VIRGINIA.—HIS SERVICES IN THE JAMES RIVER.—IN THE WEST GULF BLOCKADING SQUADRON.—MADE FLEET CAPTAIN TO FARRAGUT.—HIS SERVICES.—IS WOUNDED.—IN THE ACTION BELOW MOBILE.—FARRAGUT'S OPINION OF HIM.—CHIEF OF BUREAU OF NAVIGATION.

COMMODORE JENKINS was born in Orange County, Virginia, December 11th, 1811. He entered the navy as midshipman, November 1st, 1828, and was ordered to the Natchez, in which he served for two years—a part of the time cruising in an open boat along the coast of Cuba, in search of pirates. In 1833 he received his warrant as passed midshipman, standing No. 1, and was ordered to the coast survey, in which he afterwards became assistant. In 1842 he was detached from it, and made a cruise in the Congress as lieutenant. In 1845 he was on special duty connected with the examination of light-houses in Europe, and the next year made inspector of light-houses on our coast. He served gallantly in the Mexican war, participating in the capture of Tuspan and Tobasco. In 1850 he was placed in command of the hydrographic party on the coast survey—commanding the schooner John Y. Mason. In 1858 he commanded the Preble in the Paraguay expedition. In 1860, when Miramon bombarded the Fort of San Juan d'Ulloa, the Saratoga and Preble captured one hundred and twelve men, whom Jenkins took to New Orleans, and delivered up as pirates.

The next year he was ordered to report to the Secretary of the Treasury as Secretary of the Lighthouse Board, and from April to November was employed on special duty and secret service in Virginia, in connection with the rebellion. But the great exposure and labor connected with it, broke down his health, and he was, for a long time, laid up with the typhoid fever. On his recovery, he applied for active service, and was given the command of the Wachusett. When the rebels attacked McClellan at Harrison's Landing, he drove them off, and afterwards did good service in the James River. Being promoted to captain, he was, in September, ordered to the Oneida, and joined the West Gulf Blockading Squadron. The next February he was detached from this vessel and ordered to report on board the Hartford at New Orleans as captain of the fleet, and Chief of Staff to Farragut.

He led the fleet in the passage of the batteries of Port Hudson in March. A few days after, he engaged the batteries of Grand Gulf, as well as those of Warrenton. In May, in the Monongahela—the temporary flag-ship—he attacked the batteries of Port Hudson, and remained before the place until called to Donaldsonville.

The next month he was ordered to Port Hudson, to assume command. In July, the Monongahela, with the tug Ida in company, silenced a battery of fifteen field pieces about twelve miles below Donaldsonville, which opened on the vessel at only two hundred yards distant. In the engagement, Commander Read was killed, and Jenkins, who was on board on his way up to take command of the Richmond, was wounded "by the same shot, breaking a cutlass which struck him on the thigh." He commanded the naval force at Port Hudson, when the place surrendered. From January, 1864, to 1865, he was in command of a division blockading Mobile, and took an active part in the engagement with the forts in the following August. He commanded the Richmond in that most fearful conflict of modern times, and no higher praise can be awarded him than that bestowed by Admiral Farragut, who said:

"Before closing this report, there is one other officer of my squadron of whom I feel bound to speak, Captain T. A. Jenkins of the Richmond, who was formerly my chief of staff, not because of his having held that position, but because he never forgets to do his duty to the government, and takes now the same interest in the fleet as when he stood in that relation to me. He is also the commanding officer of the second division of my squadron, and, as such, has shown ability, and the most untiring zeal. He carries out the spirit of one of Lord Collingwood's best sayings: "Not to be afraid of doing too much; those who are, seldom do as much as they ought." When in Pensacola, he spent days on the bar placing buoys in the best position, was always looking after the interests of the service, and keeping the vessels from being detained one moment longer in port than was necessary. The gallant Craven told me, only the night before the action in which he lost his life: 'I regret, Admiral, that I have detained you; but had it not been for Captain Jenkins, God knows when I should have been here. When your order came, I had not received an ounce of coal.'

"I feel I should not be doing my duty did I not call the attention of the Department to an officer who has performed all his various duties with so much zeal and fidelity."

In January, 1865, he was ordered north, and in August, the same year, he was appointed Chief of Bureau of Navigation in the Navy Department, having been promoted the month previous to Commodore.

CHAPTER XX.

REAR-ADMIRAL HENRY KNOX THATCHER.

RANK A TEST OF MERIT AS WELL AS VICTORIES.—THATCHER'S BIRTH AND EARLY EDUCATION.—ENTERS THE NAVY.—FIRST CRUISES.—CRUISE TO SUPPRESS THE SLAVE-TRADE.—PROMOTION.—BREAKING OUT OF THE REBELLION.—COMMANDS IN THE GULF BLOCKADING SQUADRON.—HIS GALLANTRY IN THE BOMBARDMENT OF FORT FISHER.—PORTER'S EULOGY OF HIM.—COMMANDS THE SQUADRON IN MOBILE BAY.—SINKING OF VESSELS BY TORPEDOES. — CAPTURE OF MOBILE. — HIS AFTER SERVICES ON THE MISSISSIPPI AND AT GALVESTON.—DESTRUCTION OF THE REBEL VESSEL WEBB. —COMMANDS THE GULF SQUADRON.

MANY of our accomplished commanders had no opportunity during the war of performing any isolated brilliant action, they either being kept on stations at points where it was necessary to have a portion of our navy, or on blockading duty, where no opportunity occurred of meeting the enemy. Others were very little known outside of the navy until their names suddenly appeared near the close of the war, they then for the first time having an opportunity to show their capacity for commanding a fleet, and conducting active operations. Their services, however, were none the less valuable because not connected with any brilliant action. These may be known from the high rank which was given them. Among the latter is Rear-Admiral Thatcher. Born in Maine, he received his education in the schools of Boston, and in 1823 entered the naval service as midshipman.

He made two cruises in the Pacific Ocean, the West Indies, and the Gulf of Mexico. He afterwards made three cruises in the Mediterranean, and one on the coast of Africa to suppress the slave-trade. He also, as lieutenant and captain, saw much duty on shore in our navy yards and recruiting stations.

After the breaking out of the rebellion he was engaged in active service, being promoted to commodore, in July, 1862.

In 1863, he commanded the Colorado, and under Commodore Bell, commanding for the time the Western Gulf Blockading Squadron, he endeavored to destroy a blockade-runner, which had got aground directly under the guns of Fort Morgan, Mobile bay. It was on the 12th of October, a dark and rainy morning, when he saw her aground, and instantly despatched his executive officer, Lieutenant Miller, in his tender—a boat of scarcely a hundred tons burden—to reconnoitre. The Kanawha, under Lieutenant Commander Mayo, observed the blockade-runner at the same time, and instantly steamed in and boldly attacked her. The fort opened a tremendous fire upon the Kanawha, and soon sent an eight-inch shell through her. She still, however, maintained her fire, while the little tender, disdaining to be outdone in boldness, though the shot and shells of the fort rained around her, kept up a vigorous fire with her howitzers, and retired only with the Kanawha. Though the attempt to destroy the blockade-runner failed, it was gallantly executed. The first important action in which Thatcher was engaged was the bombardment of Fort Fisher, under

Porter. In this attack he carried his ship gallantly into action, and on the first day fired fifteen hundred and sixty-nine projectiles, his ship being hulled several times. The cool and deliberate manner in which he handled his ship and fought her to the close, received the warm commendations of his commander. In the second attack, the Colorado, in the second line, was directed to advance next to the leading ship, Minnesota, under Commodore Lanman. The latter, however, while moving up, got her propeller foul with a hawser, and Thatcher took the lead and led the line, and for an hour lay abreast of the formidable batteries, raining shot and shell in an incessant shower on the fortifications. Now, a hundred and fifty pound shot went crashing through his berth-deck, soon another tore through his gun-deck, making an ugly opening. A third pierced the port side of his ship, above the water line; two more struck the sheet chain, cutting it through, while shells were incessantly exploding above and around him. But though under such an awful fire, and receiving such a terrible pounding, Thatcher fought on as coolly as though only testing the range of his guns. In the midst of the fire, he ordered Lieutenant M. L. Johnson to carry a hawser to the Ironsides, to warp round his vessel so as to bring all his guns from the port battery to bear. This gallant officer, with a crew of volunteers, rowed away, and for half an hour was the target of the guns of the enemy, who had observed his movements. It was a bold and hazardous act, and highly complimented by Thatcher.

Ensign Perry, after assisting in landing the troops, and though worn out with fatigue and drenched to the skin, took up his position, and in the language of Thatcher, "fought his guns splendidly through the action." Strange to say, that, although the vessel was hulled six times, and received several other shots, only three were killed or wounded. Of the force spared from his ship to compose the assaulting party, twenty-three were reported killed, wounded and missing. In his report of the action, Porter says: "First and foremost on the list of commodores is Commodore H. K. Thatcher. Full of honest zeal and patriotism, his vessel was always ready for action, and when he did go into it his ship was handled with admirable skill; no vessel in the squadron was so much cut up as the Colorado; for some reason the rebels selected her for a target. I believe Commodore Thatcher would have fought his ship until she went to the bottom, and went into the fight with a full determination to conquer or die. There is no reward too great for this gallant officer; he has shown the kind of ability naval leaders should possess, a love of fighting and an invincible courage." Fort Fisher having fallen, Thatcher was detached from Porter's fleet and placed in command of the squadron in Mobile bay, to coöperate with Canby and Granger, commanding the land forces, in the reduction of this last port that still acknowledged the authority of the Confederate Government. After landing the troops under General Canby at Danby's Mills, and shelling the woods along the shore in the vicinity, to clear them of the enemy, he advanced upon the rebel forts commanding the inner bay of Mobile. Before sending his Monitors over the shallow bar into the river, he had it thoroughly dragged for torpedoes, for it was well known that the enemy had lined the bottom with these hideous engines of destruction. Having dragged till no more could be found, the Milwaukie, Lieutenant commander E. H. Gibbs, was sent up the Blakely river, to shell a rebel transport supposed to be conveying supplies to the lower fort. Having caused the steamer to retreat up the river, he was slowly dropping down, stern first, to avoid accident—for in turning he would sweep over more ground. He had reached, as it was supposed, a place of safety, as the iron-clad Winnebago had turned there not ten minutes before, and the boats had dragged for torpedoes, when a sudden shock was felt, and the next moment the water came pouring through the bottom of the vessel. At first there was some confusion on board, for the hatches were down. But Gibbs promptly restored order, the hatches were pried open, when the men rushed on deck; and though but three minutes elapsed from the time the torpedo exploded, before the vessel went down, the entire crew was saved.

The very next day the iron-clad Osage, Lieutenant Wm. M. Gamble commanding, was also sunk inside of Blakely bar. The vessel was anchored alongside three other iron-clads in a heavy gale. Gamble, seeing that the Winnebago was dragging her anchor, drifting slowly against him, weighed anchor and moved off to a safe distance, and stopped in two fathoms water. He then ordered three bells, the signal to back, and the crew to stand ready to drop anchor, when suddenly a torpedo exploded under the bow, and in an instant the vessel began to settle in the water. Gamble immediately sent a portion of the crew to search for the killed and wounded, and ordered all the rest on the hurricane deck, except two to each boat to haul them alongside.

Two were killed and eight wounded. The latter were quickly lifted into the boats, but were scarcely safe aboard, before the vessel went down. As the spot had been thoroughly dragged, it was supposed that the torpedo was a floating one. Three days after this sad accident, the United States steamer Rodolph was also sunk. This vessel was on its way to help raise the Milwaukee, sunk a few days before, when a torpedo exploded under the bow, staving a hole ten feet in diameter, and killing and wounding twelve men. Sinking in only twelve feet of water, the most valuable part of her armament, &c., was saved.

Scarcely ten days elapsed, before the gunboat Scioto, tug Ida, and a launch of the Cincinnati, shared the same fate, losing nearly twenty men. The Althea had also been previously sunk. It will be seen by these casualties occurring so rapidly, and that, too, after the water had been thoroughly dragged, and quantities of torpedoes taken up, what a difficult and dangerous service Thatcher was called upon to perform. Nothing could be more unpleasant to a naval commander. Officers and men had rather face any battery, however powerful, or meet any vessel, however superior in strength, than to be thus constantly dreading an unseen foe. To be in momentary expectation of feeling the vessel lifting beneath you, or with one great shudder sink to the bottom, is more trying to the nerves than the most desperate engagement. The very mystery that envelops these hidden messengers of death, renders them more terrible.

Thatcher, however, worked his way steadily forward against all opposition—thanks to the indefatigable exertion of Commander Pierce Crosby, who dragged Blakely River till he took out one hundred and fifty torpedoes—and at last got his iron-clads abreast of Spanish Fort, from whence he shelled Forts Huger and Tracy with such precision, from a rifled gun under Commander Low, that both were evacuated. Taking possession of these, he conveyed eight thousand men under Granger, to the west side of Mobile Bay to attack the city. The rebels retreated, and the two commanders sent in a formal demand for the surrender of the place. It was granted, and the stars and stripes were hoisted over the city.

The capture of Fort Alexis and the Spanish Fort, completed the conquest, and the rebel iron-clad Nashville and gunboat Morgan retreated up the Tombigbee River. The two powerful rams Huntsville and Tuscaloosa had been previously sunk in Spanish River.

Thatcher immediately went to work blowing up and removing the obstructions in the main channel.

On the 4th of May, the rebel naval commander, Farrand, surrendered all the vessels that remained, four in number, to Thatcher, who had followed him up the Tombigbee River, and was ready to open on him with his heavy guns.

Admiral Thatcher now proceeded to New Orleans. Here, on the 24th of April, he was aroused by the startling intelligence, that the rebel ram Webb, that had run the blockade of the Red River, was passing the city under a full head of steam, with the United States flag at half-mast. At first she was supposed to be an army transport; but as soon as her true character was discovered, he sent several vessels in hot pursuit.

The Webb kept dashing on at a high rate of speed—with a torpedo suspended at her bow—making for the open gulf. But suddenly she came upon the Richmond, on her way up, when she turned for the shore and, running her bows into the left bank of the river, was set on fire by her commander. The crew of forty-five escaped to the shore with the exception of three, two of whom were captured, while the third perished with the vessel. Her cargo consisting of cotton, rosin and turpentine, she was soon a mass of flames shooting through thick clouds of black smoke, and in a few minutes blew up with a terrific explosion. Detachments from the navy and land force pursued the fugitives through the swamps into which they plunged for shelter, capturing two of the crew, and taking the commander and five other officers prisoners.

Thatcher, in the mean time, had despatched several vessels, to convey a force of thirteen thousand men under General Steele, to Selma and Montgomery. A month later he received a despatch from the fleet captain, E. Simpson, at Mobile, announcing that on the afternoon of the 25th of May, an awful explosion of ordnance stores took place at Marshall's warehouse, setting the city on fire, and causing a great destruction of life. The conflagration, fanned by a fierce south wind, spread with great rapidity, carrying terror and desolation in its path.

Amid the exploding shells on every side and the blinding smoke and flames shooting heavenward, quarter-master John Cowper, belonging to the Brooklyn, seeing a wounded man lying where certain death awaited him, dashed fearlessly in, at the imminent risk of his life, and lifting him in his arms, bore him to a place of safety.

The surrender of the defences of Sabine Pass followed, and the last stones of the Confederacy crumbled to the ground.

Admiral Thatcher now proceeded to Galveston, where Kirby Smith surrendered to our land forces, and the national flag was soon flying over all the forts of the harbor. Thatcher, not having a sufficient force to garrison them, laid his light-draught gunboats abreast of them, until troops could arrive. This being done, he directed Captain Sands to buoy out the harbor.

Since the war, he has been most of the time commanding the Gulf squadron.

CHAPTER XXI.

COMMODORE WILLIAM D. PORTER.

HIS NATIVITY.—BREAKING OUT OF THE REBELLION.—HIS LETTER TO THE GOVERNMENT.—SENT TO THE WESTERN DEPARTMENT.—TURNS A FERRY-BOAT INTO A GUNBOAT.—NAMES HER THE ESSEX.—ON WATCH ABOVE COLUMBUS.—CHALLENGES THE ENEMY.—ATTACK ON FORT HENRY.—IS WOUNDED.—OVERHAULS THE ESSEX.—DESIGNS TWO OTHER GUNBOATS.—JOINS DAVIS BEFORE VICKSBURG.—THE RAM ARKANSAS.—PORTER'S BOLD ATTACK ON HER.—DESPERATE UNDERTAKING.—AIDS GENERAL WILLIAMS AT BATON ROUGE.—DESTROYS THE RAM ARKANSAS.—AT BAYOU SARA.—ASKS FOR AID TO PREVENT THE ERECTION OF WORKS AT PORT HUDSON.—BURNS BAYOU SARA.—BOMBARDS NATCHEZ.—RUNS THE BATTERIES AT PORT HUDSON.—MADE COMMODORE.—HIS SICKNESS.—OBTAINS LEAVE OF ABSENCE.—HIS DEATH.

As the father illustrated the navy in our second war with England, so the two sons have shed glory on it during the unholy rebellion of 1861. The story of the illustrious sire's heroic fight in the port of Valparaiso, doubtless had much to do in fixing the profession of the sons, and also in forming their characters, distinguished for desperate daring and unconquerable resolution.

William D. is a native of New Orleans, where he was born in 1809. He was educated, however, in a Free State—Pennsylvania—and was appointed to the navy from Massachusetts, in 1823.

When the rebellion broke out he was cruising in the sloop-of-war St. Mary; and, being a Southern man by birth, his loyalty was suspected. Being informed of this, he wrote a characteristic letter to the Government, defending himself from the aspersion. This letter caused a good deal of comment at the time. Recalled from the Pacific, he was afterward sent to the Western Department to serve under Foote, who was preparing a fleet with which to open the Mississippi. The vessel selected for his command was a St. Louis ferry-boat, which he was expected to convert into a formidable iron-clad gunboat. Named after the ship his gallant father fought so desperately in the harbor of Valparaiso in 1813, it was destined, notwithstanding its ignominious birth, to win a reputation as great. The manner in which she was transformed into the powerful gunboat she became, cannot be better described than in Porter's own amusing language.

He says: "The commander-in-chief (Flag-Officer A. H. Foote) gave me only eighteen days to get her together. So in that time I had her off the docks, and in three days was steaming down the Mississippi River. Of course there was much to be done in that time, and no place to do it. I therefore set up on my own hook; seized three large scows, and converted them into a locomotive navy-yard. One of these I made a blacksmith's shop and iron-working establishment in general; another, my boat-shed, and carpenter's establishment; and another, my coal depot. When I move up stream, I tow them all with me; if down stream, they follow. I sometimes go into action fighting at one end, while carpenters, calkers, blacksmiths, and painters are working at the other. You see therefore that the Essex *has been built about in spots.*

I have my crew divided off into gangs—wood-choppers, coal-men, carpenters, calkers, etc.; and we are a perfect workshop in ourselves."

We venture to say a vessel was never put in a fighting condition in such a way before; and it needed no prophet's ken to foretell that a vessel commanded by such a man would become illustrious, either by her victories, or, like her great namesake, in her death. He made her sides two feet thick with timber, packed in also india-rubber, and over all laid a thick plating of iron, so that, although she was an uncouth-looking and somewhat unwieldy thing, she possessed formidable powers of resistance. She was of five hundred tons burthen, and had for her armament three nine-inch Dahlgren shell guns, one ten-inch Dahlgren, two fifty-pound rifled guns, one long thirty-two pounder, and one twenty-four-pound howitzer. Thus, though she had but few guns, she threw heavy metal.

Foote assembled his fleet in the Ohio River, near Paducah, preparatory, it was thought, to an attack on Columbus, the highest point in the Mississippi fortified by the rebels.

In January, 1862, Foote, on watch above Columbus, was informed by General McClernand that several rebel vessels were coming up the river, towing a battery. He immediately signalled Lieutenant Paulding, of the St. Louis, to get under way and prepare for action. But just as he was starting, a thick fog settled down on the steamer, compelling him to steam slowly. A little after ten, however, it lifted, and through the thin haze he saw a large steamer at the head of Lucas Bend, which immediately blew the whistle, a signal to two other steamers, which in a few minutes hove in sight, and joined her. Porter kept steadily on, when a large shell came ricochetting towards him, and burst some fifteen rods from him, with a loud explosion. Paying no attention to it, Porter swept boldly down until he got within fair range, when he opened his bow guns. The three rebel vessels now brought all their broadsides to bear, and the cannonading became furious. In less than half an hour, the enemy, finding the contest becoming too warm, hauled off. Porter and the St. Louis pressed after, working their guns with great precision. The rebel steamers occasionally rounded-to, to bring their broadsides to bear, but they could not stop the impetuous Porter, and he finally drove them crippled under the protection of their batteries.

While on duty at this point, he endeavored in vain to get a fight out of the enemy. He steamed down to their batteries, and fired a shot in challenge; and, having again and again chased the steamer Grampus back to her shelter, at length sent the commander a challenge to come out and meet him in a fair fight. The latter accepted it, and it was thought for a while that there would be an action between the two vessels; but the rebel commander refused to keep his promise.

When Foote was ready for his great move up the Tennessee, Porter was ordered to join him; and the Essex constituted a part of the fleet that advanced against Fort Henry. The day previous to the attack, he was sent up the river in advance, with two other gun-boats, to make a reconnoissance and ascertain the exact position of the rebel batteries. Running up to within a mile and a half of them, he opened fire, which was immediately returned. The enemy, bringing a twenty-four-pound rifled gun to bear on the Essex, succeeded, in the third fire, in sending its huge missile right through Porter's cabin. He then dropped down to join the fleet, and prepare for the grand attack the next day.

As Foote moved up against the fort the next morning, the Essex hugged him close, and, when fire was opened, at a thousand yards distant, she lay alongside. In the tremendous fire that followed she became a special target for the enemy's guns. The heavy shot and shell pounded her mailed sides with fearful violence, causing her to quiver from stem to stern; yet Porter, side by side with the flagship, kept creeping nearer to the batteries, boldly pushing into the very vortex of the fire. Amid the horrid uproar caused by the explosion of the heavy guns, the crashing of shot and bursting of shells above, around, and against the ship, his bearing was grand and heroic. The firing of his gunners was steady, cool, and accurate, and in half an hour he had dismounted five of the enemy's guns. The Essex was now within a few hundred yards of the fort, and was sending her enormous shot with appalling effect into the garrison, when a thirty-two-pound shot struck just above the porthole, through which Porter was watching the effect of his fire, and, breaking through the bow, flew along the ship—crashed through the bulk-heads that protected the machinery, and landed with a heavy thud in the middle boiler. Young Brittain, an aid of Porter, was standing with his hand on the shoulder of his commander, when the shot entered the ship. The huge missile struck his head, carrying away half of it, scattering the brains over the paymaster standing alongside of him. But its last mad plunge into the boiler was the climax of terror. The steam instantly rushed forth with a sound more terrific than the crash of cannon, and filled all the vessel. The sailors, who had stood unmoved at their guns through the fearful fire of the last half hour, were appalled at this new foe. Shrieking with pain, many plunged through the port-holes into the river below for safety, others fell writhing along the deck. Porter himself lay senseless and scalded on deck. The two brave pilots, standing firmly at the wheel, keeping the vessel's bows dead on the rebel batteries, were so absorbed in their duties, that they forgot to close the trap-door that led from their house below. The unimprisoned steam rushed up this aperture, and, quick as thought, wrapped them in its fatal embrace. They made desperate but vain efforts to get out. Locked firmly in, with no way of escape but the trap-door, through which the scalding vapor was rushing, they thrust their arms through the narrow look-outs, and, forgetful of the raining shot, strove frantically to push their heads through, in order to get fresh air. But, held as firmly as though in an iron chamber, their struggles were vain, and soon ceased altogether, and the brave fellows lay scalded to death alongside of the wheel. Twenty-nine officers and men were disabled by this single shot. The noble vessel at once began to pay off before the current, and drifted helplessly out of the fight. Animated at the sight, the rebels sent up a loud cheer, and sprang to their guns with renewed vigor. Foote's right-hand man was gone; yet, as we have seen, he did not abandon the contest.

The boilers of the Essex were not below the water line, or this disaster would not have happened. Porter had foreseen just such a catastrophe; but, whatever else he could do with his ferry-boat, he could not get his boilers beyond the reach of danger, though he protected them in every way in his power.

The manner in which the boat was handled may be gathered from the fact that, in the short time she was in action, Porter had fired seventy-five rounds. The next day the Essex dropped down the river, carrying her sad load with her.

Porter's wounds were thought at first to be mortal, or at least so severe as permanently to disable him. It was feared that he would become totally blind. Weeks of suffering followed; but, owing to good care and a fine constitution, he at length began to recover. The news of further naval triumphs was borne to his ears, and, though he rejoiced at every victory won by our brave tars, the feeling that he could not share in their dangers and successes made his long confinement tenfold more wearisome.

It was now determined to overhaul the Essex thoroughly and make her much stronger than ever, and she was ordered to St. Louis and put on the stocks. Porter, though partially blind, resolved to go with her to superintend, as far as possible, the work. Here, besides attending to his own vessel, he designed and built two gunboats, the Fort Henry and Choctaw, for the Government. His original designs were not fully carried out, much to his regret, for he confidently believed that had they been, they would have proved the most powerful boats on the Western waters.

The Essex was lengthened forty feet; the pilot-house placed low, and admirably protected, and her casemates made higher, while her boilers were placed below the water-line. By the last of June she was again ready for service, and so was her gallant commander. Her forward casemate of wood was two feet and a half thick, plated with india-rubber one inch thick, and iron an inch and three-quarters thick. Her side casemates had about half the thickness of wood, the same plating of rubber, and iron three-quarters of an inch thick. She had false sides to protect her against rams, and forty-two water-tight compartments, so as to render her secure against sinking, even though she should be half knocked to pieces.

Foote, having been disabled in the attack on Fort Doneldson, was at length compelled to withdraw from active service, and Davis was placed in chief command. With the aid of the army the Mississippi was cleared by him down to Vicksburg.

On the 9th of July, Porter started down the river, and, on the 13th, joined the fleet before this place. Farragut was below with Porter's brother, who commanded the mortar fleet.

It was well known by our naval officers there that a powerful ram, called the Arkansas, had been built by the rebels, and was towed down the river after the fall of Memphis, and now lay concealed upon one of the tributaries of the Mississippi. It was also believed that she was a more formidable vessel than any we had on the Mississippi, and hence a good deal of anxiety was felt concerning her whereabouts. On the evening of the 14th, soon after his arrival, Porter took one of his officers and went ashore opposite Vicksburg to make a reconnoissance. In prosecuting it, he took two rebel prisoners, or deserters, who told him the Arkansas was up the Yazoo. These prisoners were sent to Davis, on board the flag-ship, and he, the next day, at daylight, sent the Tyler and Carondelet and ram Lancaster up the Yazoo, to ascertain where she lay, and what was her condition. These vessels had not proceeded far when they descried the rebel monster slowly steaming down the stream. Fearing they would be sunk, they wheeled and retreated, firing their stern guns as they fell back. The Arkansas immediately opened on them with her heavy guns, and soon the Carondelet was so disabled that she had to seek safety in shallow water, where she grounded. The fleet below heard the firing, and soon discovered that it was steadily coming nearer. Immediately everything was astir, and the vessels got in line of battle across the river, to prevent her passage down to Vicksburg. Soon only a narrow strip of land separated the heavy explosions from the Mississippi, and in a few minutes the three vessels hove in sight around this point under a full head of steam. All eyes were now turned in that direction, when, lo! the head of the monster shoved around the point, and, a moment later, her huge form lay clearly exposed as all alone she headed boldly towards the whole fleet, that seemed to cover the bosom of the stream. Conscious of her strength and invulnerability, she proudly flung down the gauntlet to the whole. There was something grand in this solitary vessel thus sending her challenge to our combined fleet, for Farragut, with several vessels, had run the batteries, and was now with Davis. As she approached, every gun that could bear was levelled at her. Keeping on her stately way, she approached the Richmond, which gave her a broadside; but the heavy shot rattled like peas against her mailed sides. Other vessels followed suit, and at length she approached Farragut's ship, the Hartford, when another broadside was poured in. She, however, did not deign a reply. The Essex, which was to know more of her in the future, also gave her a broadside. The ram Lancaster was disabled; but nothing availed to stop the Arkansas, and she kept on her way, pursued by the Benton, till she was safe under the protection of the Vicksburg batteries. It was a strange spectacle which those gallant commanders witnessed on that pleasant July morning. The whole fleet had been bearded by a single boat, and it was evident there was mischief in her which must in some way be warded off. Besides, her haughty bearing had roused the indignation of the officers and men, and the insult must be wiped out. A general council of war was called of all the commanders, to take into consideration what should be done. This formidable vessel might make her way to New Orleans and destroy our entire fleet there, and take possession of the city. She seemed more impregnable than the Merrimac, the terror of whose name still filled the land. She was about one hundred and eighty feet long, with sixty feet breadth of beam, and pointed with an enormous beak of iron fastened forward, weighing 18,000 pounds, and so firmly fixed that scarcely any shock would dislocate it. Her armament consisted of six eight-inch and four fifty-pound rifled guns. She lay now in the water with slanting sides, inclining at an angle of about forty-five degrees, though not coming to a point, like the Merrimac, but ending in a flat top. These sides were eighteen inches thick, of solid timber, covered with rail-road iron, which rendered her so impervious that our shot rattled like hail on her as she passed. She had two propellers that worked independently of each other, so that if one gave out or was disabled, the other would still move the vessel. Her engines were below the water-line, and well protected against shot and shell. It was very plain that such a formidable enemy must in some way be got rid of, or all our lighter armed boats and vessels would be in constant jeopardy.

After mature deliberation, it was resolved to make a combined attack on the batteries, and during the engagement destroy the Arkansas, which lay under their protection. This was done that very evening, and a tremendous bombardment opened on Vicksburg, during which Farragut again passed below to the remainder of his fleet, though without inflicting any damage on the Arkansas. It was becoming more palpable every day that the two fleets alone could never take Vicksburg. They needed the coöperation of a powerful land force. But it was felt on all hands that our naval reputation in the West demanded that no rebel fleet or vessels of war should exercise any control there or menace the existence of our own. Yet this ram had dared to pass leisurely through our whole fleet, compelling the lighter vessels to take refuge in flight. She was now evidently employing her time in strengthening herself still more, and was taking on munitions of war preparatory to some decided move; but, if allowed to get under way, there was no certainty of being able to stop her.

While matters were in this unsettled and perilous shape, Porter offered to go down alone, and, under the concentrated, overwhelming fire of the batteries on shore, engage single-handed this monster, that unprotected had defied the whole fleet. Officers, that no danger could daunt, looked amazed at this desperate proposition; but Porter was so confident that he could hold his own against the batteries on shore, and the ram to boot, that it was finally resolved to grant his strange request. When it is remembered that the Arkansas mounted fourteen and the Essex but seven guns, and that the crew of the former trebled that of the latter, making the encounter between the vessels alone a desperate undertaking, and that over a hundred guns on shore, trained on the Essex, increased this disparity a hundredfold, one can imagine what sort of undertaking Porter proposed to himself, and what a bold and daring commander he was. Everthing being ready, he, at four o'clock on the morning of the 22d, weighed anchor, and slowly steamed down the river. Moving steadily through the fleet, greeted with many a warm wish for success, the Essex passed down alone, her flag flying proudly in the morning breeze. As she rounded the point that hid her from the enemy's batteries, the astonished foe beheld a single gunboat in broad daylight, deliberately entering the volcano ready to receive her. The next minute her upper batteries opened, and the echoes of the heavy guns rolling up and down the river, announced to the fleets above and below that Porter had entered on his daring undertaking. Shot and shell fell fast as rain-drops on the mailed sides of the Essex, creating a din like the pounding of workmen on a boiler. Not a shot replied. Silent and stern, her flag gayly kissing the summer air, that dark form headed straight for the terrible water batteries, under the guns of which the Arkansas lay moored. It seemed impossible that under such a fire as was poured into her, she would ever be able even to reach the object she was aiming at, much less withstand the broadsides that awaited her. But she never swerved nor faltered, but kept silently, steadily, on her terrible way, till she got within close pistol-shot, when she opened her forward battery of nine-inch guns, and the ponderous shells were hurled with awful power into the motionless ram. Porter, however, had no intention of settling the conflict with his guns—he was determined, while under full headway, to strike her with his armed bow, and sink her at her moorings. The commander of the Arkansas, divining his object, suddenly let go his bow-line, when the ram, caught by the current, swung out into the stream, so that the Essex missed her blow, and, grazing along the sides of her antagonist, was carried by her great headway plump into the bank, where she remained fast aground. Her engines stopped, and for a few minutes she became the target of the most terrific fire that ever was concentrated on a single vessel. Soon, however, the two vessels floated so close together that a tow-line could have been thrown aboard of either, when most of the shore batteries dared not fire lest they should hit the Arkansas. In this close proximity Porter opened his nine-inch battery. The heavy shot, backed by the most powerful charges the guns could bear, and fired with the muzzles almost touching the sides of the ram, tore up her iron plating as if it had been nothing but so much pine lumber. A yell of terror arose from the terror-stricken crew as these ponderous missiles of death crashed and burst among them. Wrapped in her own smoke, the Essex maintained this terrific conflict for some time, when, drifting down by the force of the current, she again became the target for the batteries on shore. Porter expected the fleets to divert their fire by making a combined attack on them; but, seeing no evidence that this had taken place, and fearing that he would soon become disabled in this unequal contest, he dropped down the river, running the gauntlet of the hostile fire.

The result showed that Porter had not overrated the impregnability of his vessel, for, notwithstanding the overwhelming fire to which she had been exposed, only two shots pierced her. One shell exploded in her sides, tearing away her timbers and disabling several of her crew. The other, a sixty-eight pound shot, struck her aft quarter, and, crashing through her mailed side, passed through the captain's cabin, scattering destruction in its path, and finally stopped in the other side against the iron plating. The smoke-stack was riddled with shot, while indentations in the iron casing in every direction, showed how terrible had been the iron hail.

Porter had failed in his great object, yet he had tested the power of his vessel; and, notwithstanding the formidable character of the ram, determined, if he ever got a chance for a single-handed combat with her, he would fight her till one or the other went to the bottom of the river.

The small land force under General Williams, which was to coöperate in the capture of Vicksburg, having become a prey to the malaria that prevails in this region in the hot summer months, it was resolved to remove it. Thus the siege of Vicksburg was abandoned for the time, and Farragut with his fleet dropped down to New Orleans. But the Essex belonged to Davis' fleet above the city, and Porter wrote to his commander for orders what to do. In reply, he received permission to cruise between Vicksburg and Baton Rouge. He was not destined to remain idle long, for, General Williams having repaired to Baton Rouge, Breckenridge determined to attack him there, assisted by the ram Arkansas and other gunboats; and, on the fifth of the next month, made his appearance before the place, driving our troops before him. Porter, who had been informed of this, stationed the Essex and two other gunboats so as to arrest the progress of the enemy. The Arkansas, while at Vicksburg, had her deck plated with iron, and still further protected with cotton bales, which the experience she had gained in that fierce encounter with the Essex, had taught her was necessary. Having communicated with Breckenridge, she left her moorings and started for Baton Rouge, to assist in the attack. But one of the engines gave way before she reached the place, and she was obliged to stop for repairs, so that she could not take part in the engagement. Porter expected her down, and had kept a sharp lookout, well knowing that if the ponderous structure once fairly struck him, he would be inevitably sunk. At length, when the rebels were repulsed—the gallant Williams falling in the very hour of victory—he determined to hunt her up. Proceeding up stream, he, at ten o'clock, came in sight of her, and at once opened fire. The Arkansas at the time was moored to the shore, and at once cleared for action. After a short conflict, Porter all the while steaming nearer, the engineer of the Arkansas reported that her engines were repaired, so that they would last half a day. This was most welcome news to her commander, and he immediately ordered the lines cut away; and moved straight down towards the Essex, determined, with one resistless blow of his iron beak, to send her to the bottom. Porter saw her coming, and, bidding his gunners take good aim, sent the heavy shot and shell from his nine-inch bow guns, which, mailed as she was, went through and through her. One of these struck either her engines or steering apparatus, so that she became partially unmanageable; and Reed, her commander, ordered her to be run ashore. This was done, when with her stern guns she continued the combat. This was just what Porter wanted. No longer compelled to manœuvre his vessel so as to prevent being run down by his more powerful adversary, he steamed up so close that his heavy shot could pierce the mailed sides of his antagonist, and raked her with a terrible fire. At length, finding a spot where he could send in, as he says, an incendiary shell, he set her on fire, when the crew, fearful of an explosion, escaped in wild alarm to the shore. The flames made rapid headway, the smoke puffing out of her ports in vast volumes. It was soon evident that this terror of the Western waters, and hope and pride of the rebels, on which such labor and experience had been lavished, was beyond human help. As the fire gained headway, and burst forth in vast sheets of flame on every side, shooting up in the air, and wreathing in their fiery embrace the blackened form, the ropes that held her to the shore burned off, she swung heavily into the stream, and began to drift slowly downward—a deserted, helpless thing. The raging fire lit up her interior like a furnace, exposing to view the ragged holes made by Porter's shot. Casting a baleful light on the water, she kept on her flaming pathway, till within four miles of Baton Rouge, when the fire reached the magazine, containing *eighteen* thousand pounds of powder! A sudden lift of the mighty monster, with a great convulsive throe—a swift rush into the air of a vast mass of smoke and flame, mingled with burning timber and fragments of iron, followed by an explosion that shook the shores, and was heard miles away—and down went the long-dreaded ram Arkansas to the bottom of the Mississippi. In reporting to the Department, Farragut said: " It is one of the happiest moments of my life that I am enabled to inform the

Department of the destruction of the ram Arkansas, not because that I held the iron-clad in such terror, but because the community did."

The Essex having made the necessary repairs, steamed up the Mississippi on the 9th of August, to procure coal at Bayou Sara, some thirty miles distant. Anchoring before the town, Porter was waited on by the mayor of the place, with whom he made arrangements by which private property was to be respected if the inhabitants remained peaceable, delivering up the coal lying on the wharf and releasing the Federal prisoners confined on shore. He remained here till the 14th, when, being joined by the Sumter, he left her in charge of a guard, and returned to Baton Rouge. Hearing that it was the intention to evacuate the place, he remonstrated against it, and moreover wrote to New Orleans, begging that gunboats might be sent him, so that he could prevent fortifications being erected at Port Hudson, which he represented as a most important point. He sent a dispatch also to Washington, begging only for a small force with which he would prevent the place being fortified. He said that it was the principal point for the transmission of supplies to the Confederate armies from Texas, and the rich valley of the Red River. His representations however were unheeded, and the rebels, as he foretold, soon made it one of the strongest places on the river. The stupidity of the Government in not heeding his advice cost us afterwards thousands of brave men, whose death lies at the door of those in power at Washington.

Lying off Baton Rouge till the 23d, Porter again went up to Bayou Sara after the coal he had left there. The Sumter, which was appointed to stand sentinel over it, got aground, and the commander, fearing an attack, had abandoned her, when she was set on fire by the inhabitants.

On his arrival, he found the greatest part of it had been burned. Sending a boat's crew on shore to see if any more could be found, it was fired upon by concealed guerrillas. The crew immediately fell back to the shore, when Porter opened on the place with shot and shell, which soon scattered the enemy. He then ordered the houses on the levee to be burned, near which the coal lay, in order to keep back any lurking guerrillas; then, taking in what fuel he wanted, steamed down to Port Hudson to see what progress the enemy was making in erecting batteries there. As he predicted, they were fast going up. He cannonaded them for awhile, when unfortunately his ten-inch pivot-gun burst. He, however, continued to lay near the place for two days, shelling the woods and the earthworks going up. Returning to Bayou Sara to get some coal he had left behind, and being again attacked by guerrillas, he burned the town to the ground, and, leaving it a desolation, proceeded up to Red River for the purpose of ascending it. The low state of water, however, prevented his crossing the bar at the mouth of the stream. But hearing that two transports loaded with cattle, cotton, and other commodities, and convoyed by a gunboat, had left the day before for Natchez, he immediately started in pursuit, but on reaching Natchez on the 1st of September he found the vessels gone. The next day he sent ashore a portion of his crew to procure ice for his sick and wounded men. No hostilities were anticipated, as heretofore the inhabitants had been peaceable and orderly. But just before the unsuspecting crew reached the shore, a sudden volley from two hundred citizens, armed with muskets, was poured into them. One seaman was instantly killed, and five others, with the officer in charge, were wounded. As these pale and bleeding men were brought over the vessel's side, Porter's brow grew dark as wrath, and the stern, sharp order to clear for action and to beat to quarters, showed that there was to be no demand for explanations, but swift, terrible vengeance. The next moment the heavy guns of the Essex broke the stillness, and shells went bursting along the streets of the city. For nearly an hour and a half an incessant fire was kept up, carrying havoc and destruction. The enemy, concealed in houses near the shore, swept, in the mean time the deck of the Essex with a steady fire of musketry. During the bombardment, the Essex exploded another nine-inch gun. Probably it would have been better had Porter first given the women and children time to leave the place; but the treachery of the act and the bleeding forms of his men borne back to the ship, left no room in his heart for any other feeling but vengeance. If he was to blame, much more was the mayor, who refused to hoist a flag of truce, which would have stopped the fire.

Having taught the people of Natchez a severe lesson, Porter steamed up to Vicksburg, to see what could be done there. Finding the fortifications immensely strengthened, and that Davis' fleet had left the place, he deemed it imprudent to join it by running the batteries, for, should he suceed in getting through, it might be in a disabled state; and, being already reduced by sickness to one officer and thirty men, and, some of these, negroes who had been trained to work the guns, he determined to go to New Orleans, which he was permitted to do in case of necessity, and recruit his exhausted stores, and repair his vessel. And so, after bombarding the batteries below Vicksburg for a couple of hours, he turned the bow of the Essex down stream; and, on the 6th of September, anchored once more in the port of Natchez. He immediately despatched a letter ashore to the mayor, demanding the surrender of the city. An arrangement was soon effected, by which the city stipulated hereafter to respect the flag of the United States. Porter then kept on towards New Orleans, and the next day approached Port Hudson, where new, heavy batteries were erected. No sooner did he come within range of their heavy guns, than a tremendous fire was opened on him. The Essex returned it, keeping steadily on till she came to the central battery, located in the extreme end of the river, which at that point was not over five hundred yards across. Porter had to come within thirty yards of this, when he received a terrible pounding. Iron and timber gave way before the heavy shot; and for awhile it seemed as if the Essex, strong as she was, would be knocked to pieces. Porter, however, held slowly on his way, returning the fire with such precision, that he made a wreck of one of the batteries. For an hour and a half he maintained the unequal fight, when, finding his ammunition getting low, he dropped down beyond range, and kept on to New Orleans. Here he found awaiting him his promotion to the rank of Commodore, although the navy advisory board, for some extraordinary reason, had omitted his name among those proposed for promotion. The President, however, could understand his merits and appreciate his conduct without any advisory naval board.

This promotion did not come a moment too soon, for

disease was rapidly undermining his naturally strong constitution, and in a short time he was compelled to ask to be relieved, that he might go East to get medical advice. He, however, continued to grow worse, and soon after died in St. Luke's Hospital, New York, into which he was received for the purpose of giving him the care he needed. Thus, at the age of fifty-three, in the prime of his life, passed away this able commander. A brave man, a thorough officer, a fearless fighter, had he lived he would have placed his name foremost among those naval heroes that adorn our history.

CHAPTER XXIII.

REAR-ADMIRAL JOHN A. DAHLGREN.

HIS BIRTH AND ANCESTRY.—ENTERS THE NAVY.—FIRST CRUISE.—ON THE COAST SURVEY, UNDER HASSLER.—DISTINGUISHED AS A MATHEMATICIAN.—HASSLER'S ESTIMATION OF HIS ABILITY.—MADE SAILING-MASTER IN THE SOUTHERN EXPLORING EXPEDITION.—DECLINES THE APPOINTMENT.—LOSES THE USE OF HIS EYES.—GOES TO PARIS.—PAIXHAN GUN.—GOES ON A FARM.—CRUISE IN THE MEDITERRANEAN.—ASSIGNED TO ORDNANCE DUTY.—PLACED OVER THE ROCKET DEPARTMENT.—HIS LABORS.—TESTS THE RANGE OF THE 32-POUNDERS OF THE NAVY.—ORIGINATES THE BOAT HOWITZER.—RESOLVES TO REVOLUTIONIZE NAVAL ARMAMENT.—HISTORY OF HIS DIFFICULTIES AND FINAL SUCCESS.—SHELL GUNS.—PUBLISHES HIS WORK ON BOAT ARMAMENT.—OTHER WORKS.—"SHELLS AND SHELL GUNS."—SAILS IN THE PLYMOUTH TO TEST HIS OWN GUNS.—SETTLES DIFFICULTIES IN MEXICO.—DESIGNS A FOUNDERY.—RIFLED GUNS.—PLACED OVER THE NAVY YARD AT WASHINGTON.—PREPARES FOR AN ATTACK.—ACCOUNT OF HIS SERVICES HERE.—INTERVIEW WITH PRESIDENT LINCOLN.—CHIEF OF THE BUREAU OF ORDNANCE.—HIS SON ULRIC.—PLACED OVER THE SOUTH ATLANTIC BLOCKADING SQUADRON.—HIS SERVICES BEFORE CHARLESTON, AND HIS DIFFICULTIES WITH GILLMORE.—CLOSE OF THE WAR.—IMPRESSIVE FUNERAL CEREMONIES OF HIS SON.—HIS CHARACTER.

It is not often that, after a series of great naval victories by others, a man who took little part in them can point back to years of peace, and say, "Then I was laying the foundation of them all;" but this Dahlgren can with perfect truth assert. In almost every action that has been fought, he can see the triumph of his inventive genius, and, in the trial of all kinds of ordnance in actual combat, the complete success of his own. A ship's armament cannot be given, without mentioning the name of Dahlgren, and it occurs in the report of almost every combat that has occürred, till he seems to be omnipresent in the navy.

It is a little singular, that our navy should be so much indebted to Sweden for the great changes that have come over it. Ericcson, a Swede, gave us the monitors, and the son of a Swede has entirely revolutionized the armament of our vessels of war, för the father of Dahlgren was a native of Sweden, and educated at Upsala. A ripe scholar, he emigrated while still a young man to this country, and engaged in mercantile pursuits in Philadelphia. He married into one of the old wealthy families of that city—distinguished in our War for Independence for their patriotism. Rowan, Dahlgren's grandfather, fought bravely at Princeton and Germantown. John, the eldest son, was born in November, 1809, in Philadelphia, on the spot where now stands the City Exchange.

The father died in 1824, leaving only enough property to support the widow, and John early sought to obtain a midshipman's berth in the navy. His application was at first refused, and he came very near giving up all hopes of securing the appointment. But fortunately for the country, he at last succeeded, and received his warrant, Feb. 1st, 1826. His first cruise was in the Macedonian, the British ship captured by us in the war of 1812. Her commander was Commodore Biddle, who in the same war captured the sloop-of-war Penguin. Dahlgren served six years, and then passed his examination, and received the warrant of passed Midshipman. He was remarkable for his proficiency in mathematics, and hence was detached from the regular service, and put on the coast survey, under Mr. Hassler, who at the time had no equal as a mathematician in the country. He was selected to serve in the triangulation of the survey, and assist in the astronomical observations, as well as the measurement of the base on Long Island—the first base line ever measured scientifically in this country—that of Mason and Dixon being merely a chain and compass measurement.

So high was Hassler's opinion of his mathematical skill, that he chose him to make the counter calculations of the base, to compare with and verify his own. He was engaged in these labors from 1834 to 1836, when he was selected to assist in making observations of the solar eclipses of that year. In the autumn, he was offered the appointment of sailing-master in the Macedonian, which had been selected as the flag-ship in the Southern Exploring Expedition. He declined it because he did not think it would ever sail until reorganized. His views proved to be correct, for it was deferred, remodelled, and eventually sailed under Wilkes.

He was now detailed from the second triangulation, to assist in the first trials of the great theodolite of Houghton which had just been completed for Hassler. On this occasion heliotropes were first used in this country in the survey, instead of tin cones, and their glittering points could be seen by the naked eye from stations at the astonishing distance of thirty or forty miles.

In the winter of 1837, he was engaged in bringing up the work of the summer. This being done, Hassler made him second assistant in the survey, and gave him charge of a party of triangulation. No higher compliment could be paid his mathematical ability than this, for no other naval officer has ever held this position.

In the spring he was promoted to lieutenant, and received sailing orders. But his naturally strong eyes began now to show the evils of overwork, and he had to give up everything in order to save them. It was hard—just as he was about to receive the reward of his incredible labor, to see it slip from his hands, and be compelled to sit down in idleness. The weary summer passed away, but his disease seemed beyond the reach of medical skill. As a last resort he went to Paris to consult Sichel, the celebrated oculist. Here, to his great joy, his eyes began to improve. About this time Paixhan was trying to draw the attention of the French Government to his system of firing shells, and Dahlgren, finding that he could work again, translated his pamphlet, and had it printed at his own expense, to distribute in our navy. He also sent a copy to the board of commissioners; but the red-tape system still had sway, and we did nothing but follow French and English precedent.

In 1839, Dahlgren married, and retired for a time into the country to establish his health. For two years this man of untiring industry and keenly active mind never read a word, but labored diligently on a farm to regain his health. This course saved his eyes, and he was at length able to return to the service, when he was detailed to the receiving-ship at Philadelphia.

In 1843, Dahlgren, leaving his family of three children, one of whom was Ulric, went to sea in the frigate Cumberland under Commodore, now Admiral, Joseph Smith, and cruised in the Mediterranean. Foote was first lieutenant, and a friendship on this cruise sprung up between the two officers, which lasted for twenty years, unmarred by a single misunderstanding.

Returning at the commencement of the war with Mexico, he was assigned to ordnance duty, though he applied for active service.

In 1847 he was placed over the Rocket Department just then being introduced. Everything was in confusion, yet he was able by his great energy to manufacture and send off, in a short time, a lot of rockets to the Mexican coast.

Seeing the want of system in the ordnance work, Dahlgren proposed to collect the scattered parts into a department. The bureau approved of his views and directed him to take charge of the matter. He could not wait to put up large buildings, and so he had the ship timber cleared out of one end of a timber shed, and there set up the first ordnance workshop of the country. For seven years he occupied these limited quarters, and there devised the present armament of the navy. From such small beginnings arose the present great establishment. There too commenced the most important revolution in the arming of ships that ever occurred. Dahlgren could with difficulty obtain a room to write in; but, as he said, "the field was ample and almost untouched, and my will was good."

A board of officers in 1845 had recommended the introduction of guns of a uniform size in the navy—32-pounders, in imitation of the English system—and Dahlgren was now to fix sights on these and ascertain their range. But there being no level ground near, sufficiently extensive for his purpose, he proposed to substitute for it the smooth surface of the river. But such an experiment for accurate results had never been tried, and he had to devise some means to determine with precision the jet of water thrown up by the shot when it struck the surface. The ingenious method by which he overcame all difficulties is too scientific for popular apprehension—it is sufficient to say that his success was perfect—for nothing seemed too difficult for his inventive mind. With no aid but a mechanic, he worked out his problem, a full account of which may be found in his report to the Bureau. He soon discovered that this unit system of 32-pounders robbed us of some of our best guns, and was a foolish imitation of a false system, and hence began to plan his great revolution in naval armament.

But another subject of almost equal importance began at the same time to occupy his teeming brain. The navy had no boat guns—some old carronade or army piece serving as such in case of necessity—and he determined to create a "naval light artillery." Carrying out his project, he submitted to the Bureau a system of howitzer boat armament, and asked leave to prosecute the work. He knew the difficulties that he would have to encounter in introducing changes in the navy; but he resolved to make the attempt. He had, up to this time, never seen a gun cast, or finished, or drafted, or had computed one himself. Although he had only the most primitive means at hand, yet the first gun was made—and there being no boring lathe in the yard, he had it finished on an ordinary lathe. It required a peculiar carriage, and this he also devised.

Having at length completed his experimental piece, he invited Warrington, the chief of the Bureau, to come down and see it. The old hero had been delighted at his success in sighting the 32-pounders, and his ingenious method of getting their ranges, and was, therefore, in a mood to look favorably on any scheme which Dahlgren might propose.

The practice of the piece equalled his most sanguine expectations, and it was afterwards constantly exhibited to officers and tried in every possible way. Vindicating its claims under every ordeal, it had to be pronounced a complete success, and from that time dates the boat howitzer system. Though he met with after opposition, he triumphed over it all, and in 1850, the Navy Department recognized the system and ordered a full compliance with it, and it remains at this day unaltered from its first design.

A full and interesting account of the whole matter, together with a description of the piece, its mode of firing, plates, &c., will be found in a book published by him, entitled "Boat Armament of the United States Navy." It is full of interest, even to the non-professional reader.

Dahlgren had now made one great stride forward; he had, besides, got the entering wedge into the old, clumsy, stereotyped system, and he meant to drive it home. Stepping out in the bold originality of true genius, he planned no less than the overthrow of the whole system of naval armament. Penetrating with his acute mind the weakness of that of England and France, which we had tamely copied, he determined to show to the world one of his own, and invoke the test of actual experiment to prove its value.

No one but a person similarly situated, can appreciate how herculean was the task which Dahlgren had assigned himself; for he needed the lever of Archimedes to lift the world of prejudice opposed to him. Like

Galileo, who, after long watching the heavens through his diminutive telescope, at last exclaimed "*il muove*," "it moves;" so Dahlgren, after his long reflection and observation said, it moves—the world moves, and by its motion overthrows systems hoary with age, and strengthened by the verdict of generations.

Archimedes said he would lift the world, if he had anything to stand on—so with Dahlgren; he wanted something to stand on in his gigantic effort, and that was *influence*. This he knew he could not secure from the Navy; for those who represented it had recently decided on the 32-pounder system. He must, therefore, fall back on actual facts to get it, and he set to work to amass such a body of these, as even prejudice could not override. This he did, unobserved by any one, as he watched each day's practice. An accident, in the mean time, unexpectedly came to his aid. He had stated to the chief that the *powerful* guns of the 32-pounder system lacked accuracy, and the *accurate* ones lacked power.

On the 13th of November, 1849, a new heavy 32-pounder burst, on being fired, killing the gunner, while a fragment of it weighing two thousand pounds tore up the earth within a foot of Dahlgren. Dahlgren had previously asked leave to submit a draft of a gun of his own, and this accident gave force to his request, and he drafted the 9-inch shell gun. This was in 1850—the same year in which he published his first work on ordnance, being the report on "practice with 32-pounders," —and before it closed he had the satisfaction of seeing his first 9-inch gun laid on the wharf of the Navy Yard. During the session of Congress, being applied to by the chairman of the naval committee for some information respecting war steamers, he sketched a large propeller, to be armed with the heavy cannon on hand, "going," he said, "as far as he considered safe in intrenching on old ideas."

His 9-inch gun proving to be a success in every way, he asked for the casting of an 11-inch gun. The chief, Warrington, granted his request, saying that he "*never gave his confidence by halves.*" This liberality of view does him great credit, for he had to stand almost alone by Dahlgren, who was looked upon by many as a dangerous innovator—his pieces being uncouth in form compared to ordinary cannon, while to talk of an entire battery of shell-guns, was downright heresy. He, however, finished his 11-inch gun, and his firm friend Warrington lived just long enough to know of its completion, when he suddenly died. His death was a great misfortune to Dahlgren, and delayed the fulfilment of his plans for several years.

This year, being one of a board of commissioners appointed by the Secretary of War to investigate and report on coast defences, he, in his paper, introduced his plan of a screw frigate with 9-inch guns on the gun deck and a pivot 10 or 11-inch on the spar deck—all shell guns—but to be capable of firing shot if necessary. This was printed by order of Congress.

Thus he was gradually preparing the way for more decided action. In 1852, at the request of the chairman of the Naval Committee, Mr. Stanton, he gave his views in full to Congress. The latter made an able speech, in which he fortified his views with lengthy quotations from Dahlgren's paper, and moved an appropriation to carry out his plan. But meeting the opposition of the Navy Department and some of the bureaus, his resolution failed, and Dahlgren had still to wait and hope on. This year he published his work on boat armament.

In 1853, while maturing his plans and collecting facts, he published his third work on ordnance, "Percussion Primers and Locks."

The necessity of steam instead of sailing frigates becoming more palpable every day, an appropriation for building them was obtained. They were to be 3000 tons burthen, the largest ever built; but it was found that the regulation cannon, thirty-two pounders, would not answer for them, and here, as if to meet this very exigency, came in Dahlgren's armament. Although a facetious old gentleman called the queer-looking cannon tadpoles, Dahlgren told him he would find they would be full grown frogs in time. He proposed to place nine-inch guns on the main deck, and to put eleven-inch ones above them. This last proposition was pushing matters too far, and the bold innovation had to bide its time. He was told, however, that if he would draft a ten-inch gun it should be carried as a chase gun, one at each end. Dahlgren remonstrated against interfering with his plan in this way, but it was of no use. The result was, that the Merrimac had his main-deck battery, and the Niagara his spar-deck battery, and thus made his plan, as Dahlgren said, "like a circus rider that rides around the ring with a foot on each horse."

The next year he was hard at work getting the guns for the six new frigates that were to be built, besides attending to other ordnance duty. In the midst of his labors he was stricken to the earth by the death of his wife, leaving him with five orphan children.

In the fall, he was promoted to Commander. In the beginning of '56, Commodore Morris, chief of the bureau of ordnance, died, and the President wished to give Dahlgren the post; but, as the law required that officer to be at least a captain, he proposed to defer the appointment till it could be changed. Dahlgren, however, objected to this, and it was not done.

This year he published his second edition of Boat Armament, making his fourth work on ordnance; and before it closed he gave to the world his chief work, "Shells and Shell Guns." This is a very full and exhaustive work, and though containing many new ideas which at the time seemed chimerical, time and experience have proved their soundness and value.

Dahlgren, seeing how impossible it was to get his system fairly tried at sea by others, in 1857 applied for a command afloat, that he might test it himself. After much opposition he obtained command of the Plymouth, a sloop-of-war, with full permission to alter and arrange her at his pleasure. Although his eleven-inch guns were too large for a frigate of 3,000 tons, he boldly mounted one on his sloop-of-war, and put to sea. Making a gunnery-ship of her as he sailed, he cruised along the European coast, touching at various ports and visiting the principal founderies, and navy yards, and ships-of-war of the old world.

On his return he reported that the monster gun was perfectly manageable at sea. Thus by actual experiment he had overthrown the last objection, and so finally disappeared the last vestige of opposition to his system, and it soon after was adopted in the arming of our national vessels. Long years of thought, labor, experiment, and of "hope deferred that maketh the heart sick" had been passed, but victory came at last—not partial and qualified, but complete and triumphant.

In 1858, when the news came of the liberties that British cruisers were taking with our merchantmen, Dahlgren was sent in the Plymouth to look after the matter. Fortunately, no collision occurred—the trouble was amicably settled—and he sailed for Port-au-Prince to settle a difficulty about the Guano Island of Nevassa. From thence he went to Vera Cruz to convey our Minister to Mexico, and while there took upon himself the responsibility of settling difficulties at Tampico, growing out of outrages committed on American citizens, and for his services received the thanks of the merchants, whose property he had saved.

Returning to Washington, he had the satisfaction, during the year, of seeing his 11-inch guns ordered to most of the new screw sloops-of-war of the Brooklyn class that were then building.

The next year, 1859, he proposed the building of a large and suitable foundery—the interior of which he designed himself,—and the work was begun.

During the year, the Armstrong gun of England was much talked about, and rifled cannon, for a while, threatened to throw Dahlgren's improvements into the background. He at once took up the subject and proposed two rifled cannon—one iron and the other bronze—the latter of which, designed for boat armament, was adopted, and still holds its place.

In 1860, still devoting himself to the question of rifled cannon, he, after careful study, adhered in the main to his old system. The subject, however, of monster rifled guns still occupied him, when his investigations were cut short by the breaking out of the rebellion. One of his last acts was to urge on the Department the necessity of providing some iron-clads for the navy, and referred to a proposition which he had made eight years before. By accident this memorial found its way to Congress, instead of his report on rifled cannon which had been called for, and awakened a great deal of attention; but nothing was or could be effected towards their construction till imminent danger demanded that something should be done, and that speedily. It seems strange that the views of a man who, for so many years, had shown that he knew more than the Department and all the naval Bureaus put together, should have been thus ignored; but it is only one of the countless blunders of the same kind which have been committed.

At the beginning of the war, the navy yards of the country were generally under the command of officers whose homes were near them—hence most of the stations South were controlled by those who sympathized with the secessionists. This was also the case at Washington, which Dahlgren observed with considerable anxiety. Rumors were abroad that the navy yard was to be seized, and ill-looking fellows whom nobody knew, began to cluster about the corners and places of resort in the city. Dahlgren saw that it behooved him to look to his charge, and so selecting the most defensible building, he secretly removed into it all the breech-loading rifles and light artillery, and barricaded all the doors except two, which he commanded by his howitzers. No one was allowed to enter it but a small body of seamen employed in the ordnance, and who he knew would obey his orders whatever they might be. The powder he had carried into the cock-loft of the large ordnance shop, which was in range of his guns in the shell-house, and could be fired in a moment, if necessary. He then sent all his spare money to Philadelphia for the use of his family, and calmly awaited the forthcoming events.

Mobs, incendiary fires, and rumors of sacking Washington, kept the inhabitants in a state of feverish excitement during the winter. April came with its stirring events, and at last the storm broke, and the sound of cannon around Fort Sumter fell on the country like a thunder-clap at noon-day. The Government awoke from its dream of security;—volunteers were called for—and the land shook to the tread of armed hosts. In the mean time, our troops were driven back from Baltimore, the capital became isolated, and a cloud, black as night, hung over the country. At last the arsenal of Harper's Ferry was seized, and now the Navy Yard at Washington might be next attacked.

One afternoon Dahlgren was sitting in his office, occupied in making dispositions of arms and ammunition, when a confidential messenger from the Navy Department entered with a message that it distrusted the state of affairs in the yard, and wished him to take immediate command. He sent back word that the Department might fully rely on him, and at once sallied out to take such measures as might be necessary. While thus employed, a messenger approached and said that the commandant wished to see him. On going to his office, this officer said he was about to resign, and wished to turn over the command to him. Very few words passed, and Dahlgren resumed his preparations for defence, for the yard was so exposed on almost every side to attack, that four or five hundred resolute men might have easily seized it. There were only about ninety seamen and marines altogether, to defend it, with such little aid as might be obtained from two war steamers in the river, whose crews did not probably exceed one hundred and fifty men. With the fall of the Navy Yard, an easy road was open to the city, and yet it furnished no support to the former. The capital was never in so much danger afterwards, as at this critical period, when Dahlgren took command. He, however, determined with his handful of seamen to defend it to the last, and if it fell, to fall himself amid its ruins. He placed howitzers at commanding points, while he brought up the mail steamers to assist him in keeping open the Potomac, now the only channel of communication between the capital and the North. He hurried forward matters with such energy, that by midnight of the day he took command, he had manned and equipped one of these steamers, and placing her in charge of an old boatswain, whose locks had grown white in the service of his country, sent her down the Potomac to capture suspicious looking crafts, and to furnish pilots to any vessels loaded with Northern troops who might be coming up to the relief of the capital.

The rest of the week was one of constant toil and excitement to Dahlgren, for everything was quivering in the balance; but at last the troops arrived, and shortly after the road was open through Baltimore.

During this brief period, Dahlgren was constantly on the move, eating and sleeping anywhere, except in his quarters, and though his work was unheralded by the smoke of battle and unaccompanied by the shouts of victory, it was nevertheless the most important one he ever performed.

In the movement on Alexandria on the 24th of May, he coöperated with some steamers, and personally superintended the operations. When at daybreak the Zouaves jumped ashore, and the possession of the place was assured, Dahlgren lay down on a sofa in his steamer to snatch a few moments' repose, but had hardly closed his eyes when the quartermaster awoke him with the startling news that Ellsworth was killed. Springing ashore, he met a detail of Zouaves bearing the body to the wharf. Directing them to his own steamer, he returned to the Navy Yard.

In the afternoon, the President drove down to the Yard, and after speaking with a great deal of feeling for Ellsworth, and showing how shocked he was at his sudden and violent death, he asked Dahlgren if it would be proper to have the funeral services at the White House. The latter replied it would be proper to consult his own feelings entirely. He did so, and had the services in the Presidential mansion.

In the occupation of Alexandria, a troop of Virginia cavalry were taken prisoners, and lodged in the Navy Yard. These Dahlgren treated with the utmost kindness, until their release at his own earnest request in June.

On that memorable Sunday of the battle of Bull Run, the Navy Yard being almost deserted—as the Seventy-first Regiment quartered there had gone to the front—the President drove down towards evening for a ride, and in a conversation with Dahlgren, said the battle had begun; that he had telegrams from the field, and all was going on well. But before he had been gone half an hour, Dahlgren also had a telegram from General Mansfield, asking him to send a vessel with despatch to Alexandria, to cover the approaches. The former knew at once that all was not going on well; for this despatch showed plainly that the army was falling back. Hurrying down the Perry, the only vessel on hand, he had not long to wait before the full extent of the calamity became known.

"Black Monday," with Washington crowded with refugees, followed. Dahlgren was now called on to help man the lines in front, and he sent down three 8-inch ship-cannon and five howitzers, under a body of trained seamen and some marines, which formed a naval battery that proved to be of great service. His son Ulric, only nineteen years of age, here began that brilliant career which had so tragic an end, being volunteer aid to Captain Foxhall Parker, who commanded the battery.

In August, Congress, by a special act, enabled him, though only a commander, to hold command of the Navy Yard. During the year and some months that he held this appointment, he was not called upon to take any very active part in naval operations, except as connected with the quiet duties of the yard. His position, however, threw him into constant contact with the principal actors in the great drama going on, and his reminiscences of events and conversations would make an interesting book in itself.

The transforming of merchant vessels into war ships to help keep open the Potomac, occupied much of his attention, and made a busy scene of the Navy Yard.

Foote, out west, was hard at work, but in great want of seamen, and Dahlgren sent to him during the winter the naval force which had been on the lines and in Fort Ellsworth. The former had previously written to his old friend: "I expect of course to be shot by a Kentucky rifleman; but I mean to die game, as there must be a providence in all these things."

The autumn and winter passed with its usual excitements, and with the return of spring came the great raid of the Merrimac into the waters around Fortress Monroe. On the Sunday that the tidings were received of the terrible destruction she was making with our vessels of war, Dahlgren was sitting in the ordnance office, attending to public business that could not be postponed, when the President was announced. He stepped out to the carriage, when Mr. Lincoln said, "Get your hat and ride up with me." As he took his seat by the President's side the latter said, "I have frightful news to tell you," and then in a calm though earnest manner related to him what the Merrimac had done and threatened to do. In half an hour they were at the White House, where assembled in cabinet meeting were several of the secretaries and General McClellan. After some desultory conversation, the telegrams that had been received were carefully read over and discussed. The President then turned to McClellan, Meigs and Dahlgren, and said: "Now you are a committee to advise measures; just step into the next room and talk it over." But the conclusions they came to were of no consequence, as the arrival of the Monitor settled the matter.

When in the following May the President rode through Fredericksburg and reviewed McDowell's army, Dahlgren accompanied him, and remarked as it filed away that it would soon be at Hanover Junction, to give McClellan a helping hand. So thought the President. But next morning just at daylight, as they reached the Navy Yard, on their return, and the President crossed the plank from the boat, a telegram was handed him. Glancing at it, he said "Good-morning" to Dahlgren, and stepping into the carriage, drove off with the Secretary of War. That telegram announced the onslaught of Jackson at Harper's Ferry. Soon after, Dahlgren received a telegram from Washington, asking him if he could send some howitzers to Harper's Ferry to help defend it. He replied, "Yes, and heavy cannon, too," and that evening, both, with a choice body of seamen, were being whirled fast as steam could carry them on the railroad to the threatened point. The only officer he could spare was a young Master, who, with his son Ulric, soon had them planted, and the 9-inch shells sending consternation among the rebel troops, to whom such enormous missiles of death were the more terrific as they were new. On Thursday, late at night, Ulric came to the War Department with the news of the repulse of Jackson, and returned a captain.

On the 18th of July, 1862, Dahlgren was commissioned Chief of Bureau of Ordnance. A year before it had been offered him, but he declined it, preferring the Navy Yard, if he could not be given more active service. It seems hard at first glance, that an officer who had done so much to make the navy efficient, and shown such great capacity, should be kept on shore, while others scarcely known before were winning a world-wide reputation. But it should be remembered in the first place, that somebody of ability must hold this post, and to whom did it more properly belong than to him? In the second place, there would be manifest injustice in taking a gallant officer from the field where he was winning renown, and shutting him up in a bureau, in which he would be wholly lost sight of. Such an officer would say, and rightly too, that Dahlgren, having secured a reputation second to no naval officer in the world in the ordnance department, should be satisfied with it, and leave to others, less fortunate, the field where rank and renown were to be won by

Engraved expressly for Headley's Naval Work.

gallant deeds. Though the country has a right to the services of her best men in the way she chooses, yet to have good officers, justice must be done to all

Dahlgren's new position necessarily brought him into connection with all the navy yards, founderies of cannon, &c., of the country, and his field became as wide as the theatre of military operations.

Meanwhile, in August, he was made Captain. Soon after, the news of Pope's battles in front of Washington began to throw the city into the wildest alarm. On the 19th of August, the President sent for Dahlgren on official business, and after it was finished, began to talk over the situation of affairs, closing with the remark "Now I am to have a sweat of it for five or six days." Dahlgren, in the mean time, felt very anxious about his son Ulric, who was fighting on the lines in front, and of whom he could hear but little. But one day the latter burst unexpectedly into his office beaming with health and spirits. Soon after, passing out of the department, they suddenly came upon President Lincoln, who took Ulric warmly by the hand, while a pleasant smile lighted his countenance—now worn and anxious—and drawing him inside the door, said, "Come now, tell me what you have seen." The young soldier rapidly and clearly narrated the events of the past few days, while the President, leaning forward, lost not a word. When he was through, the latter shook him by the hand, and asked him to come and see him again. Not long after, this gallant youth galloped into Fredericksburg with fifty or sixty cavalrymen, and returned with half his number, prisoners.

Among the incorporators of the National Academy of Science, authorized by Congress this session, Dahlgren was named as one, but he declined the honor, because his public duties required all his time.

In the spring he visited the naval ports in the West, to see to the arming of the ironclads, and while at Cairo, heard of the failure of Dupont before Charleston.

When the Government finally relieved Dupont from the command of the South Atlantic Squadron, and put Foote in his place, the latter came to his old friend Dahlgren and urged him to go with him. Though Dahlgren wanted sea service, he preferred an independent command, but he finally consented to command the iron-clads of the fleet. The sudden illness and death of Foote broke up this plan, and Dahlgren was ordered to take his place.

This was the 22d of Jan., 1863, and two days after he started for New York to set sail for Charleston. The next week, having purchased a small screw steamer from a packet line, he hurried away with but one staff officer, and not a single domestic, or scarcely the equipment and outfit of a midshipman.

Reaching Port Royal and assuming command of the fleet, he was told by General Gillmore that he wanted him to coöperate immediately in a movement designed to effect a lodgment on Morris Island. Dahlgren had not yet seen the vessels that would be required in the attack—three monitors, he knew, were in the hands of mechanics undergoing repairs—he had not yet formed a staff, he knew nothing of the locality by actual inspection, and was without instructions, yet he was determined that no delay should be charged on him, and he told Gillmore to name the day. The latter said Wednesday, and Dahlgren at once put forth every energy to be ready for battle. The next day Gillmore asked to have the attack deferred for one day. Wednesday night Dahlgren was off Charleston Bar, and the following morning received word from Gillmore that he had postponed the attack for another day, as he was not ready. At length, on Friday morning, the movement began; our troops were landed, and the enemy breaking fled up to Fort Wagner. Dahlgren, seeing this, steamed after, rolling his ponderous shells along the beach behind the fugitives, and in a short time laid his own monitor abreast of Fort Wagner, followed by the others in line of battle, and opened a terrific fire, which he kept up till noon. Had Gillmore followed up his first success, he doubtless could have entered the fort in triumph. All the southern defences had fallen, and a vigorous assault on the astonished enemy gave every promise of success. At all events, it should have been made then or not at all.

Dahlgren renewed the attack after giving his men a little refreshment, and kept it up till six o'clock, when he withdrew, for he saw that Gillmore intended to make no further effort that day. The severity of the rebel fire may be judged from the fact, that Dahlgren's vessel was struck sixty-seven times. Although disappointed in Gillmore's neglect to seize the auspicious moment and dash over the rebel works, he was delighted with the powers of endurance shown by the monitors. Gillmore, in his official report, said that the work of occupying the island could have been done without the navy—then why blame Dupont as he did for not coöperating with him? Either this was not true, or he was guilty of unnecessary delay in putting off the attack till the arrival of Dahlgren, and then making him wait day after day. But he knew that but for the presence of the monitors, the rebel iron-clads would have come down from Charleston and scattered his forces to the winds. However, the next morning Gillmore thought he would try and see what he could do independent of the navy, and ordered an assault without even notifying Dahlgren, and was sadly defeated.

At length, on the 18th of July, came that last fatal assault. Gillmore had signalled in the morning that he would be ready at noon, and at half past eleven Dahlgren got under way in the Montauk, followed by the Patapsco, Katskill, Weehawken, and the Ironsides. At half past twelve he opened with the first gun, and in a few minutes the action became general, and it flamed and thundered from land and water all that hot summer afternoon, while the army inland stood and listened to the uproar. At first the tide was low, so that Dahlgren could not get nearer than twelve hundred yards; but at four o'clock it had flowed so as to give deeper water, and, ordering his anchor up, he steamed to within three hundred yards, closing steadily and sternly with the fort. So rapid and well directed was the fire, that the rebel guns were silenced, and Dahlgren, mounting to the top of the turret to survey the hostile batteries, could not see a head exposed. Night came on, and through the darkness our brave columns surged up to the blazing works, only to melt away and disappear in the gloom.

The next morning Dahlgren sent ashore a flag of truce with a surgeon, to ask for our wounded, and if the request was refused to offer medical aid. Both proposals were rejected. Two days after, he heard that his son Ulric had been dangerously wounded at Gettysburg.

Gillmore now began his regular but slow approaches towards Wagner, which gave the enemy time to strengthen Sumter.

Gillmore, at times, seemed quite independent of the navy, yet on the 11th of August he signalled Dahlgren that Wagner had opened on him with grape and canister, and evidently intended an assault; and asked him to be ready with his gunboats. In a half hour came another telegram, "Open as soon as possible, the enemy's fire is heavy." Dahlgren did so, sweeping with his terrible fire the whole ground between our lines and the fort.

At half past three in the morning he went up the harbor in his barge, to examine matters personally, as it was his custom to do, and on returning came very near being sunk by the heavy guns of Wagner.

Dahlgren, generous and noble, like most of our naval officers, who are ever willing to give the coöperating land forces all the honor they deserve, endeavored to remove the ill feeling which had been produced at Washington against Gillmore, for his ill-judged, badly managed assault on Wagner; and requested his flag lieutenant Preston, who was obliged to return North for his health, to see the President, and by explanations remove the bad impressions which he had received. He did so, and the result was, Mr. Lincoln ordered five thousand men to reinforce Gillmore, although Halleck was opposed to it.

In striking contrast with this noble conduct, Gillmore soon began to shift the responsibility of the delays in taking Charleston on Dahlgren and the navy.

In the bombardment of the 18th of August, the latter, after silencing Fort Wagner, shifted his flag from the Weehawken to the Passaic, and with the Patapsco steamed up to Sumter and opened fire. Although the latter, with Gregg and Moultrie, concentrated a terrible fire on these two vessels, he had by noon silenced it. As he withdrew, he learned with grief that Captain Rodgers, his fleet captain, had been killed.

The shore batteries having at length made sad breaches

in Sumter, Dahlgren, on the 22d and 23d, again moved against it, but it was found to be impregnable as ever, in fact the lower casemates, mounted with heavy guns, were in excellent condition.

On the night of the 26th Dahlgren determined to feel the defences at the entrance of the harbor, on his own responsibility, but a heavy squall of wind and rain, succeeded by a heavy fog and blinding storm, kept him groping helplessly about all night, and nothing was accomplished.

An after effort was equally unsuccessful, but in the engagement that followed, he had another fleet captain shot.

The siege of Wagner and bombardment of Sumter went on, and Gillmore, impatient of success and annoyed that he could make no more headway, began to insist that no guns were mounted on Sumter, and therefore the fleet could go past it. This was mere conjecture on his part, for he had never been anything like as near to it as Dahlgren. He also insinuated that a programme had been agreed on between him and the naval commander, and that he had performed his part, and now it remained for the latter to do his, when in fact there had been no such programme at all. Dahlgren's orders were explicit—to coöperate with and assist Gillmore, which he did.

The whole question is, however, too absurd to be treated seriously. For six weeks the fleet and army had tried in vain to take Wagner alone, and yet the former unaided, according to Gillmore, was quite able to go inside, carry all the batteries that lined the shore clear up to the city—each more powerful than Wagner and commanding each other—or else pass them. But if he could have done the latter, the ironclads would have been cut off from coal and ammunition, and all succor from the troops. It was a new military maxim he was introducing, "divide and conquer."

At length on the 6th of September, the rebels evacuated Fort Wagner, and Morris Island fell into our possession. All hoped that Sumter would now be abandoned, but the bombardment of it by Gillmore's heavy guns, two and two and a half miles distant, instead of making clean breaches through the walls, as it would have done at short ranges, and with a concentrated fire, had only pounded it into sand, that falling to the base simply converted a stone fort into a sand work like Wagner. When Dahlgren ascertained this fact, he determined to try and carry it by storm. By accident he learned that Gillmore intended to assault it also, on the same night. It was then determined that the attack should be a combined one.

On the night agreed upon, Dahlgren advanced his column in boats, and waited to hear from Gillmore, to whom he had sent his fleet captain, Preston, to see that everything was well understood. The latter returning and reporting all was right, Dahlgren gave the order to advance. Preston asked to lead his division, to which the former reluctantly consented, as it left him without a staff officer, except one who was very young. Before starting, however, he said, "Are you sure *that all is right, and no mistake with the General?*" He replied, "Yes." Then said Dahlgren, "Go." He never saw him again. In the mean time he steamed up nearer, and then got into his boat and pulled for the fort. It was half an hour or more after midnight, and, just as the oarsmen were dipping their blades, a heavy volley of musketry broke from Sumter; then a rocket shot into the air, followed by a red light that blazed up in the darkness. The next moment the batteries on Sullivan and James Islands opened. Dahlgren kept on, but all was still in Sumter; the conflict was over. The rowers paused, while the shells from the neighboring batteries and rebel ironclads blazed and screamed, and burst over and around his boat, lighting up the waters of the harbor like day.

The assault had failed, and Dahlgren now attempted to regain his steamer, but it had moved off, and he spent the whole night in searching for it.

Gillmore's column never came up at all, owing, as he said afterwards, to the state of the tide, it being too low for his boats. A sad comment this on his own sagacity. Had he never thought of the tide, when a few hours before he told the gallant Preston, that his column would be up in time?

Dahlgren had before become sadly weakened in his naval force, by damage to his vessels, &c., so that he had but four monitors left, with the Ironsides, fit for duty, and now, by those lost in the assault, he was weakened in men. Of this small fleet, one, the Montauk, was sadly in need of repairs, and another had her smoke-pipe nearly carried away.

The failure of this assault awakened a great deal of senseless clamor against Dahlgren, brought about in a great measure by the statements of newspaper correspondents, who hovered around Gillmore's headquarters to manufacture public opinion. The former was blamed for attempting the only thing that remained to be done; for, to endeavor with his few vessels to force the entrance of the harbor, would have been simply suicide.

On the 5th of October, a torpedo exploded under the Ironsides, which came very near being a very serious accident.

The public being greatly dissatisfied that Charleston was not taken, and the Navy Department coming in for its share of abuse—the more severe, because of its treatment of Dupont—it ordered a council of war to be called in the fleet, to decide upon the propriety of an attempt to force an entrance into the harbor. In this Dahlgren took no part, except to submit all the papers, &c., necessary to come to a just conclusion. Its decision was "that there would be extreme risk without adequate results, by entering the harbor of Charleston with seven monitors, the object being to penetrate to Charleston."

After this decision by the gallant commanders of those vessels, who had been so long on the spot, it is a waste of words to discuss the propriety of Gillmore's assertion, that they could and ought to do it. An admiral who should take the opinion of a military officer, whose operations are all on land, against the decision of a board of naval commanders, would deserve to be dismissed the service. If any other proof were wanted of the wisdom of Dahlgren's course, we might cite a letter of General Sherman to him, when operating from Savannah, in which he declares, "it would be unwise to subject his ships to the heavy artillery of the enemy, and his sunken torpedoes." The truth is, the passage of the forts below New Orleans and off Mobile, had greatly misled the public, in its judgment of the whole matter. In both the other cases, when the point of danger was passed, there was a clear river or open water beyond, where the vessels were safe from attack; but in Charleston harbor, they could only silence batteries—not get away from them—a useless business, unless there was a land force to occupy them. Sherman, who knew

Charleston harbor well, corroborates this view. He says, that if Dahlgren "had gone into the inner harbor, and up Cooper River, the enemy could easily have held all his works on James and Sullivan's Islands without trouble, &c." We think that General Sherman and the decision of the council of war, *versus* the opinion of General Gillmore, will be all that any man of common sense will need to come to a just decision on Dahlgren's course. The assertion of Gillmore was an after-thought to shield himself from the blame that always attaches to a commander who fails to meet the public expectation.

In November, while in obedience to Gillmore's request to keep the rebels from an attack by boats on the face of Cummings Point, the Lehigh got aground in the darkness, when all the batteries on Sullivan's Island opened on her. Dahlgren at once signalled the other ironclads to engage the batteries, while he went up in the Passaic to investigate matters. Finding the Nahant nearer the grounded vessel than he could get in his own, he took his barge and rowed to her. Dr. Longshaw and two seamen then took a line in an open boat, and passed through the fire to the Lehigh. Three hawsers, which were carried aboard her, were cut in succession; one by shot and the other two by the sharp edges of the deck. The shells fell in a perfect shower around the two vessels, but a hawser was at length secured, and the Nahant steamed ahead, but the Lehigh would not stir. Dahlgren then ordered the Montauk to make fast to the Nahant, and both pull together. They started, and he watched the struggle with intense interest, for if this effort did not succeed, the poor monitor would have to lie there for twelve hours, the target of the enemy, before another could be made. But the hawser held fast, and under the tremendous strain the Lehigh moved off amid the cheers of the crews, and once more floated in deep water.

The latter part of this month Dahlgren was cheered as well as saddened, by a visit from his gallant son Ulric, who had recovered from his long illness, resulting from his wound at Gettysburg, but at the sacrifice of his leg. In the mean time he kept pounding away at Sumter, though effecting nothing. On the 6th of December, a gale arose, and he saw with grief the Weehawken go down, almost alongside, with between twenty and thirty of her crew. Winter was now on them with its gales, and the monitors were almost constantly under water, the sea breaking clean over their decks, leaving only the tops of the turrets dry. The men, when wishing a little fresh air, clustered around the stacks to keep warm, making the duty of keeping watch and ward here a most cheerless and trying one. At night this was 'still worse, for torpedo boats had to be guarded against, and blockade runners prevented from entering. Drenched, and chilled, and wearied, they thus passed the long weeks, while men before their cheerful fires at home criticized the naval commander, and wondered that more was not done.

In February, another vessel, the Housatonic, was sunk by a torpedo.

Dahlgren had other duties besides those in Charleston harbor. Three hundred miles of coast, including seventeen ports, were under his charge, and had to be kept blockaded by a fleet seldom numbering less than seventy vessels. The varied and multiplied duties required of him, to direct and manage all this, were of the most exhausting kind. During this trying period he lost four chiefs of staffs, thus necessarily increasing his burdens.

In the latter part of February, he visited Washington at the request of the Secretary of the Navy. He reached the capital the 2d of March, the very night that his son Ulric was killed below Richmond. When the sad news was received, President Lincoln sent for him, and expressed the deepest sympathy with his great loss. Dahlgren saying that he wished to go to Fort Monroe to learn more of his boy and recover his body, "Go," replied the President, "ask no one, I will stand by you." He went, but failed in his mission, and in the middle of April prepared to return to the squadron. Before leaving, he complained to the President of the abuse heaped upon him, to which Mr. Lincoln replied, "Well, you never heard me complain, did you?" The latter spoke with tears in his eyes of the fate of Ulric. As he pressed his hand for the last time, he little dreamed that the fatal bullet would soon bring him to a similar end. Dahlgren never saw him again, but he will remember those last kind words forever.

Arriving at Port Royal on the 2d of May, he found Gillmore had left with the tenth corps to join Butler. A week later he was in Charleston harbor, when he again convened a council of war to determine what course to pursue, in which it was decided that no serious attack on Sumter should be made. Dahlgren therefore went down the coast to look after the blockade. During the summer he forwarded to the committee on the conduct of the war his answer to their queries respecting operations around Charleston. We refer the reader who wishes to see a complete vindication of Dahlgren, to this document. Foster having succeeded Gillmore, the latter planned an expedition to Stone River, in which Dahlgren assisted with his monitors. Although it failed of success, the latter performed his part thoroughly, and to the satisfaction of the commander.

In August he had the gratification of receiving the fifty prisoners that had been kept under fire in Charleston, who cheered him as they came alongside. In the mean time he received a photographic copy of the paper said to be found on his son when killed, in which the burning of Richmond was ordered. He never believed for a moment the foul calumny on his noble-spirited boy; but it was a satisfaction to find that the paper itself, without further evidence, proved it to be a forgery, for the signature was written *Dalhgren*, instead of Dahlgren—a mistake impossible for Ulric to have made. Dahlgren made it the occasion of writing a reply to the slander of the rebels, which he published in the *Herald* of Aug. 8th. But while the summer passed thus without interest around Charleston, Dahlgren's squadron was busy along the Southern coast. Toward the latter part of November, it being known that Sherman had cut loose from Atlanta, Foster determined to make a diversion in his favor. To assist him Dahlgren organized a fleet brigade. Although it numbered but five hundred men, it was complete; for Dahlgren drilled it himself. On the 29th of November the expedition started, Dahlgren taking a squadron of light draft steamers, and his fleet brigade. It moved up Broad River, and then struck inland for the Savannah and Charleston Railroad. The enemy were met and a severe conflict followed, in which Dahlgren's fleet brigade, with their destructive howitzers, did good service, and won the highest commendation.

On the 12th of December a messenger reached Dahlgren from Sherman, who was near Savannah. Two days after, Sherman himself met him in the Warsaw Sound, having come down to communicate with him the moment Fort McAllister fell. They returned together to Ossabaw Sound, and talked over the situation thoroughly. Sherman then went back to the lines; but soon after, again came down to see Dahlgren, when they arranged for a united attack on the works around Savannah.

They went together to Port Royal to complete the arrangements, and the next day returned in the Harvest Moon; but finding a gale outside, Dahlgren put into Tybee, and tried the inside passage. Getting aground, he took Sherman in his barge and pulled for Ossabaw Sound. Just before reaching it, a little tug was seen puffing away under a full head of steam. As she came alongside the captain held up a slip of paper on which was written: "Savannah has surrendered." Two days later, Dahlgren had the pleasure of lunching with Sherman in the captured city. But, soon after, hearing that the iron-clads of Charleston were coming out in a last death-struggle with his vessels, he hastened back; but found it was only a sensation rumor.

In the beginning of the new year he went to Savannah, to superintend the embarkation of the right wing of the army under Howard, destined for Beaufort. It took place on the narrow winding creek of St. Augustine; the banks of which, crowded with 20,000 or 30,000 men, presented a stirring spectacle. Dahlgren, struck with the dead silence that reigned through the waiting ranks, said to Sherman: "They seem to have no tongues." "Ah," replied the latter, with a grim smile, "*they can make noise enough when they choose.*"

Dahlgren now bent all his efforts to assist Sherman in carrying out his plans, and, before the army was ready to move, he went to Charleston, to commence clearing out the obstructions in the harbor.

The day before the hazardous work was to begin, Dahlgren had been constantly on the move, attending to every thing; and, wearied with his labors, about bed-time dropped to sleep on the sofa. He had been asleep only a short time, when he was suddenly aroused by the commander of the Patapsco, who stood before him, and startled him with the brief announcement that his vessel had just gone to the bottom, sunk by a torpedo. In one minute from the time it exploded, the vessel was under the waves. One man below was saved; he saw much in the fleeting moments allowed him to dart along the lower deck. He happened to have his eyes directed to the ward-room, where many officers were gathered around the table—one being seated upon it. In a twinkling the deck was blown open, and the table and all around it dashed violently upward against the deck above, that formed the ceiling of the apartment. The lights went out, and he heard the men struggling desperately, but in vain, to get up the hatch. He made for it himself, and, finding it free, dashed up it. The sea was pouring over it, and some one, pressing close behind him, was borne back by the torrents of water that rushed down, and never rose again. He himself struggled on deck, reaching it just as it sunk beneath the surface; and, floating off, was picked up by the boats.

Such was the brief, sad story told to Dahlgren, who, aroused from his sleep by the startling intelligence, jumped into his barge and pulled to the spot. It was midnight; not a sound broke the Sabbath stillness of the scene; all was silent as death. The story was told—the brave crew were sleeping their last sleep beneath the waves.

Soon after, he received a letter from Sheramn, announcing the commencement of his grand march, and the direction he was taking. Dahlgren at once placed suitable forces in the Edisto and Stono, to coöperate with him, and was everywhere superintending the movements required to meet the exigencies arising in various quarters.

The Daiching in the mean time grounded in the Combahee, right under the guns of a rebel battery. Chaplin, the commander, fought her bravely to the last, and, when he found her a wreck, set her on fire, and escaped with his crew. On the 1st of February, Dahlgren jots down: "Nothing from Sherman; he is marching on, I know." At the same time he received a letter from his son Charles, who landed with a detachment from his vessel to assist in the assault on Fort Fisher. The latter wrote: "I fired my rifle thirty-four times from a rest, and you know I never miss." This brave son participated in the siege of Vicksburg.

Dahlgren's vessels were scattered all along the coast at this time, requiring him to move almost continually from one point to another—one day being in the North Edisto, another in the Stono, and a third in Bull's Bay; one day superintending the fire of those vessels engaged with the enemy, and another seeing to the landing of troops.

Gillmore now came down to supersede Foster, and Dahlgren, much to his regret, found himself once more in communication with an officer in whose integrity and truthfulness he had no confidence. However, it was the public interest first, and private griefs afterwards; and he immediately consulted with him on the movements required to assist Sherman, and a demonstration at Bull's Bay was determined on. While engaged in covering the landing of the troops, he received a despatch from Sherman, in cypher, dated at Midway, on the railroad. On the 17th, he sent some vessels into the Stono to aid Schimmelfennig, and, at the same time, ordered the naval battery on Morris Island to open fire, and all night the booming of his heavy guns broke over the water

The end was now approaching; Charleston was evacuated, and Dahlgren steamed up the harbor with all his captains aboard, and landed in the city. The streets were silent, the houses shut; but a fire, kindled by the rebels, was still raging. This he soon extinguished, and saved the city from further ruin. Next day he learned that Lieutenant Bradford, who had been mortally wounded in the unsuccessful night assault on Sumter and died in a Charleston hospital, had been dug up, after being buried by a friend in the Magnolia Cemetery, and thrust ignominiously into the Potter's-field. He had him disinterred at once, and buried with the honors due an American soldier.

Not knowing but that Sherman would wish to open communication with the seaboard farther up the coast, he at once sent some vessels and marines to seize Georgetown and hold it.

In the mean time he examined the defences of Charleston, and found ocular proof of what he knew before—that an attempt to force his way up to it with his vessels would have been simply foolhardiness and ended in defeat and disgrace. He then went to Georgetown, and established everything on a firm footing there.

On the 1st of March, as he was steaming out of the harbor, on his return to Charleston, and pacing the cabin while breakfast was preparing, he was startled by a loud noise and shock, that made everything rattle, and blew in the partition. He hurried out, and, observing the men rushing for the boats, was about to ascend himself to the upper deck, when he saw a great gap beside him, and felt the vessel sinking. A torpedo had exploded under the boat, and she was fast settling in the water. A tug near by, witnessing the disaster, steamed alongside, and took off the crew. In a few minutes the Harvest Moon set forever.

Hoisting his flag on another vessel, he proceeded to Charleston to witness the dispersion of his command—for his long and weary work in Charleston Harbor was drawing to a close.

A correspondence now followed between him and General Gillmore respecting the official report of the latter, in which he reflected unjustly on Dahlgren and the navy in the operations before Charleston, and also on the statement of his correspondents to the same effect. We cannot give it here, and will only say that it was characterized on the one hand by that straightforward, frank manner, so universal with naval officers, and on the other with a disingenuousness always attached to one who, having done wrong, will neither retract nor fairly meet it.

The balance of the time previous to Lee's and Johnston's surrender, Dahlgren was employed in removing obstructions in Charleston Harbor and in buoying out the channel and in sending forces up the various rivers to protect the inhabitants and preserve order.

On the 17th of June, having sent home most of his vessels, he set sail for Washington, and on the 12th of next month struck his flag as admiral of the South Atlantic Blockading Squadron. The Navy Department, in relieving him, complimented him for "the ability and energy" he had shown in his arduous command for two years, and expressed its high "appreciation of his services and those associated with him in the efficient blockade of the coast and harbors at a central and important position of the Union, and in the work of repossessing the forts and restoring the authority and supremacy of the Government in the Southern States." Sherman also said, before the Committee on the Conduct of the War: "On the morning of the 3d of May, we ran into Charleston Harbor, where I had the pleasure of meeting Admiral Dahlgren, who had, in all my previous operations, from Savannah northward, aided me with a constancy and manliness that commanded my entire respect and deep affection." In what striking contrast does this grand and noble testimony stand with the unjust statements and Jesuitical language of Gillmore, whom he had aided in the same manly, unselfish spirit, from beginning to end.

As soon as Dahlgren was free from official duty, he devoted himself to caring for the remains of his gallant son, which had been identified and brought on. Owing to the heat of the weather the funeral ceremonies were deferred till October.

From the council chamber where he lay, covered with the flag to uphold the honor of which he had given his young life, it was but a short distance to the church. "Every spot was alive with the memories of former days," for it had been pressed over and over again by his young feet. His lifeless body was borne close by the door where he had passed most of his brief life. From the windows, now crowded with sympathizing spectators, had been witnessed day by day his boyish outgoings and incomings. The church which was to witness the parting services had held him each Sabbath as it came. The President and

Cabinet, and high officers were present. From Washington he was carried to Philadelphia, and laid in the Hall of Independence. There the pastor who had baptized him delivered a discourse, when with notes of solemn music, and surrounded by glittering bayonets, he was carried to the grave, and gently, tenderly laid close beside his mother. Peace to his ashes! Unselfish, noble, good, and gallant, he was beloved by all, and almost adored by his father.

In February, Dahlgren was made a member of a joint board to consider the defences of our harbors. Gillmore was a member of the same board, but Dahlgren refusing to serve with him, he was detached; once with him was enough for Dahlgren. In May, he was named as President of the Board of Visitors to the Naval School at Annapolis. He is now in command of the South Pacific squadron.

Dahlgren, by his inventive genius in the construction of ordnance, and his bold and original plan of arming vessels of war, has done more for the Navy of our country, than probably any single man in it. At the same time he has given it *éclât* abroad, for every European writer on ordnance and ship armament, has to recognize his genius and improvements.

It is curious to see the strange contradiction which is sometimes presented in the same man, between his mental and moral character. Dahlgren, whose whole life seems to have been spent in inventing and forging the most terrible instruments of death, increasing the destructive power of cannon fourfold, is yet possessed of the gentlest, tenderest feelings of our nature. To go over his works, and see how coolly and scientifically he guages destructive force, one might imagine him to be a man of blood, one who loved carnage; whereas a kinder, gentler, nobler heart never beat in a human bosom. His inventions and improvements are the result of careful study of his profession, of scientific skill combined with original genius. In any other profession in which his great mathematical ability and originality could have had free scope, he would have made similar discoveries, and worked out and introduced equally astonishing improvements.

One of the most remarkable characteristics of his mind is its completeness. It does not advance one step, and then wait to see that tested before proceeding to another. His plans, when completed in his own brain, are also complete for actual adoption in all their details. The inventions of most men reveal, on actual trial, some defect not provided for—show some point overlooked. But everything proceeding from Dahlgren's mind comes, like Minerva from the head of Jupiter, completely panoplied. Indeed, so perfect has every improvement he has made been, that he himself can hardly see where an alteration could be made. Nothing could show more forcibly with what mathematical accuracy and certainty his mind works, and how perfect is the intellectual machinery which has produced such wonderful results.

CHAPTER XXIV.

REAR-ADMIRAL HIRAM PAULDING.

A NAVY-YARD IN TIME OF WAR.—PAULDING'S BIRTH AND PARENTAGE.—ENTERS THE NAVY.—SWORD VOTED HIM BY CONGRESS FOR HIS GALLANTRY IN THE BATTLE OF LAKE CHAMPLAIN.—CRUISE AFTER MUTINEERS IN THE ISLANDS OF THE PACIFIC.—PUBLISHES A JOURNAL OF IT.—PROMOTION.—BREAKS UP WALKER'S FILIBUSTERING EXPEDITION TO NICARAGUA.—HIS ACTION NOT WHOLLY APPROVED BY GOVERNMENT.—THE PRESIDENT OF NICARAGUA PRESENTS HIM WITH A SWORD.—NOT ALLOWED TO ACCEPT A TRACT OF LAND.—AT THE BREAKING OUT OF THE REBELLION SENT TO DESTROY THE NAVY-YARD AT NORFOLK.—DESCRIPTION OF THE SCENE.—APPOINTED COMMANDANT OF THE NAVY-YARD AT NEW YORK.—CONTRACTS FOR THE FIRST ARMORED VESSELS.

THE commander of the chief navy-yard of a country, in time of war, holds a post of great responsibility, and is compelled to do much hard work. Hence one of the ablest officers of the navy is usually selected to fill it. His work, however, is of a kind that neither interests nor attracts the public. He is aware of this, and therefore much prefers to be afloat and in active service. The daily routine of a navy-yard, and the superintending the repairs or building of ships, furnish tame employment compared with the bold cruise in search of an enemy, or the stern conflict, in which fame and glory may be won. But he has no choice in the matter; he must stay where the Government places him, and perform those duties which bring no renown, but yet are as essential in time of war to the welfare of the nation as those which command the public eye.

Admiral Paulding, though ranking as one of our ablest officers, was doomed during the war to this monotonous life, as Commander of the Brooklyn Navy-Yard.

He was born in Westchester County, about the year 1800, and entered the navy in September, 1811. His father was John Paulding, one of the captors of Major Andre. A young midshipman, in the second war with England, he early saw some hard fighting with McDonough, in the battle on Lake Champlain, and so distinguished himself by his bravery, that Congress voted him a sword.

After the war he made several cruises, possessing no especial interest, until 1825. In 1824, the crew of the whale ship Globe, of Nantucket, mutinied while in the Pacific Ocean, and, murdering the officers, took the ship to Mulgrave Island, where they proposed to burn her and form a settlement. Here they landed a great part of the stores and rigging; but, before she was entirely dismantled, some of the crew—who took no part in the mutiny—cut the cable one night, just at dark, while the rest were on shore, and, under a fine breeze, stood out to sea. The mutineers, seeing her moving off, pursued in boats; but soon gave up the chase. All the nautical instruments had been taken out of her, so that those on board had nothing but the stars and prevailing winds to guide them in navigating the broad Pacific. They, however, at length reached Valparaiso in safety, and reported to the United States Consul there what had been done. There being no Government ship on hand that could be spared to go after the mutineers, the matter was reported to

Government, which directed Commodore Hull, then in the Pacific, to send the schooner Dolphin in search of them, and bring them home as prisoners. Lieutenant Percival was put in command of her, and Paulding made his chief officer. It was a long cruise, for the islands of the Pacific were not so well known at that time as now. The Marquesas and neighboring islands were then almost *terra incognita*, and, as the vessel passed from one to another, a new world seemed opening to Paulding. One day embraced by the dusky wife of a chieftain, in return for some beads that he had given her; another, carried by an island king on his back to his boat, his cruise was made up of novel and ever-varying incidents.

At length one mutineer was discovered on the shore of an island, who warned Paulding off. The latter asked him his name. He replied, "William Lay." Paulding then told him to come to the boat; but he refused, saying that the natives would not let him. "Run, then;" said the former. The poor fellow still declined, saying that the natives would kill him with stones the moment he moved. Paulding then disembarked, and, with loaded pistols, marched up to the place where Lay was standing, and, seizing him with the left hand, with the other presented a cocked pistol to his breast, and sternly demanded, "Who are you?" He replied, "I am your man," and burst into tears. The natives, thinking violence was intended, rose angrily, when Paulding levelled his pistol at them, and marched his prisoner off to the boat.

A few miles to windward of this island he found another mutineer, by the name of Huzzy, who was stark naked, like the natives. The latter somehow had got wind of Paulding's search, and hence knew what he was after, and planned that very night to board the vessel and murder the crew. Huzzy, however, dissuaded them from it. Paulding boldly landed, and, marching up to the chief, levelled a pistol at his breast and demanded that Huzzy should be delivered up. He yielded, and Paulding took his prisoner on board, when the latter informed him that all the other mutineers were dead. Paulding afterwards published a book, entitled "Journal of a Cruise among the Islands of the Pacific," in which he gave a minute account of this cruise, describing the various islands that he visited, and the customs of the inhabitants, &c., which were then new to the public.

In 1844, he was promoted to Captain. Many years after, in 1857, Paulding figured in the famous filibustering expedition of Walker. The main body, commanded by Walker in person, landed at Punta Arenas, in the harbor of Greytown. Commodore Paulding, commanding the Home Squadron, arrived in the Wabash the next month, when Walker, with one hundred and thirty-two men, surrendered to him.

Paulding acted in the matter without specific instructions, and his conduct was not fully approved by the government, especially in arresting Walker on foreign soil.

Subsequently, the President of Nicaragua presented him with a sword, and offered him a large tract of land as a reward for his services, but the government would not allow him to accept the latter gift.

At the breaking out of the rebellion, Commodore Paulding was ordered to supersede Captain McCauley, in the command of the Navy Yard at Norfolk, then threatened by the rebels, but, as it turned out, not to save it but to superintend its destruction. This Navy Yard was one of the most extensive in the United States, being three quarters of a mile long, a quarter of a mile wide, and covered with machine shops and buildings of various kinds. In the harbor were the new steam frigate Merrimac, the line-of-battle-ship Pennsylvania, the Germantown, the Dolphin, and other vessels. Nine millions of property were supposed to be in the yard, and among it three thousand cannon. All this the rebels expected to have, and troops were assembled to seize it. On the night of the 16th of April a large number of boats loaded with stones, were towed into the channel and sunk, so that the large vessels could not be towed out, and two days after, the rebel general Taliaferro arrived to take charge of the troops, when the federal naval officers resigned their commissions, and passed over to the confederate government. This state of things being reported at Washington, it was determined to destroy the yard and all its material, to prevent it from falling into the hands of the rebels. The Pawnee, Captain Rowan commanding, had just arrived from its fruitless endeavor to reinforce Sumter, and six hundred men were immediately put on board the vessel with Paulding as flag officer, and she ordered down to the yard. She started on the night of the 21st, with a bright moon to guide her on her course, and steamed down the Potomac. The next evening at eight o'clock she reached the wharf, and was received with thundering cheers by the loyal gallant crews, while the traitors were seized with alarm, lest the Pawnee should open her broadsides on everything within reach. Whether the government could have saved the yard, had it possessed more confidence and boldness, it is impossible to say, but the attempt was not made.

Paulding ordered the troops, as soon as the Pawnee was made fast to the dock, to land and seize all the gates of the yard. He thought the Cumberland might be saved, and determined to try and tow her out. Everything that could be carried and was valuable, was taken out of the Pennsylvania and the other vessels, and then the work of destruction began. Some three thousand men sprang to their task with a will, and shot and shells and stacks of arms were thrown overboard, while the heavy guns could only be spiked. All night long the work of destruction went on, and it was nearly morning when the Pawnee, taking the Cumberland in tow, and with all the men on board except those left behind to fire the trains, cast loose and moved off a short distance. Everything being ready, Paulding ordered a rocket to be sent up, the signal agreed on for the torch to be applied. It rose gracefully into the air with its silent message, and as it "burst in shivers of many-colored lights," the men who watched its ascent, fired the trains. In an instant the flames leaped up in every direction, revealing the whole yard as by magic, and turning night into day. Startled by the mighty conflagration from their sleep, the citizens of Norfolk and Portsmouth rushed into the open air, and saw the whole heavens illumined as though the fires of the last day had been kindled. The flames leaped from the pitchy, smoking decks to the shrouds, and curled like fiery serpents round the tall masts, while on every side piles of material and dwellings became a mass of fire. Says a spectator of the terrific scene, "It was not thirty minutes from the time the trains were fired, till the conflagration roared like a hurricane, and the flames from land and water swayed and mingled together, and darted high, and fell, and leaped up again, and by their very motion showed their sympathy with the crackling, crashing roar of destruction beneath. But in all this magnificent scene, the old ship Pennsylvania was the centre-piece. She was a very giant in death, as she had been in life. She was a sea of flame, and 'when the iron entered her soul' and her bowels were consuming, then did she spout forth from every port-hole of every deck, torrents and cataracts of fire, that to the mind of Milton, would have represented her a frigate of hell, pouring out unremitting broadsides of infernal fire. Several of her guns were left loaded but not shotted, and as the fire reached them they sent out on the startled morning air, minute guns of fearful peal, that added greatly to the alarm that the light of the conflagration had spread through the surrounding country. The Pennsylvania burned like a volcano for five hours and a half, before her mainmast fell. I stood watching the proud but perishing leviathan, as this emblem of her majesty was about to come down. At precisely half past nine, the tall tree that stood in her centre tottered and fell, and crushed deep into her burning sides, while a storm of sparks flooded the sky."

Paulding, with the Cumberland in tow, succeeded in getting out of Elizabeth river. His work was then done, and he left the Pawnee at City Point.

Not long after this he was placed over the Navy Yard at Brooklyn, where he remained. He was one of the three appointed by the Secretary of the navy to investigate the subject of armored vessels, and to contract for the three first that were built:—viz. the Ericsson, Galena, and Ironsides. He is now on the retired list.

CHAPTER XV.

REAR-ADMIRAL JAMES S. PALMER.

HIS NATIVITY.—ENTERS THE NAVY.—LENGTH OF SEA-SERVICE.—AT THE BEGINNING OF THE WAR SENT IN THE IROQUOIS IN SEARCH OF THE PRIVATEER SUMTER.—BLOCKADES HER IN THE HARBOR OF ST. PIERRE.—HER ESCAPE.—CONDEMNATION OF PALMER.—HIS VINDICATION.—JOINS FARRAGUT ABOVE NEW ORLEANS.—DEMANDS THE SURRENDER OF BATON ROUGE.—OF NATCHES.—LEADS THE LINE IN PASSING VICKSBURG.—COMMANDS THE FLAG-SHIP IN THE PASSAGE OF PORT HUDSON.—COMMANDS THE WEST GULF BLOCKADING SQUADRON.—WITH ADMIRAL THATCHER IN THE CAPTURE OF MOBILE.—HIGHLY COMPLIMENTARY LETTER OF THE LATTER.

ADMIRAL PALMER is a native of New Jersey, from which State he entered the Navy, the 1st of January, 1825. Between this date and the breaking out of the war, he saw nearly twelve years of sea service—was engaged on shore duty about five, and was unemployed between eighteen and nineteen years. Altogether, he had been about thirty-six years in the service.

Soon after the commencement of hostilities, the Confederate Government sent the privateer Sumter to sea, to prey on our commerce, when Palmer, in the Iroquois, was despatched in search of her. His cruise was a fruitless one; and constantly led astray by false reports, he had almost begun to despair of stopping her depredations; when, in the fall of 1861, while coaling in St. Thomas, he heard that she had just put into Port

Royal, Martinique. This time the information came so direct, that he gave it full credence, and immediately ceased coaling—got his engines together, and started off for Martinique—arriving in St. Pierre in thirty-six hours. As he turned into the harbor, he saw a suspicious looking steamer moored to the wharf, which, on nearer approach, proved to be the notorious Sumter, boldly flying the secession flag. His arrival threw the town and shipping into the greatest excitement; for it was not certain that Palmer would not attack this bold rover even in a neutral port. This, however, he could not well have done, had he been so inclined, without firing into the houses of the inhabitants. But fearing that she might slip out under cover of darkness, Palmer cruised around the harbor all night, never going more than half gunshot from her.

In the morning, a French man-of-war came round from Port Royal, the seat of government, some twelve miles distant. The Sumter had been there for two days, and although the government had refused to give her any coal, allowed her to come around to St. Pierre, where she easily obtained it from some English merchants. Palmer said "she had evidently been received with courtesy at the seat of government, and this farce of the non-recognition of the Confederate flag is played out in both France and England." He at once addressed a note to the governor, in which he said: "As your Excellency cannot be aware of the character of this vessel, I denounce her to you as one who has been, for some time, engaged in pirating upon the commerce of the United States, robbing, burning, and otherwise destroying all American vessels that come within her reach. May I not hope, therefore, that your Excellency, upon this representation, will not allow her to enjoy the privileges I complain of, but direct her to leave the protection of the French flag, and the immunities of the French port."

To this the governor replied that he could not depart from strict neutrality. The captain of the French war steamer also addressed Palmer a note, in which he said that he had been requested by the governor to ask him not to compromise the neutrality of the French waters by establishing a blockade within their jurisdiction, but come to anchor, when every hospitality and facility would be afforded him, or else take up his position a marine league from shore. He decided to anchor, when the French commander visited him, and after the usual exhibitions of national courtesy, politely called his attention to the law of nations that one belligerent could not depart till twenty-four hours after the other had sailed.

Suspecting that the Sumter, aware of this fact, was about to slip away, as her steam was up, he immediately weighed anchor and put to sea until he had reached the marine league, when he hove to. He passed the night in much anxiety, fearing that in the darkness and under cover of the high land, the Sumter would escape. He knew the people of the town generally sympathized with the rebel craft, and hence he need expect no aid or information from them. Besides, where he lay was almost an open roadstead fifteen miles wide, while the surrounding land was very high, with bold shores. He needed at least two more steamers to keep watch and ward over the rebel cruiser. Although the nights were moonlight, he knew she could steal out under shadow of the land in spite of him. It was a very disagreeable position to be placed in; for, while painfully conscious it would be almost impossible to prevent her escape; he was also aware that it would be equally impossible to convince his countrymen that he was not to blame if she did. He thus lay off for nine days, waiting for her to put to sea, while she all the time lay moored to the wharf surrounded by sympathizing crowds, who wished her to escape.

At length, on the 23d of November, when the moonlight nights had ended, the Sumter prepared to leave. Signals which Palmer had arranged beforehand were at once made from shore that she was under way, and steering to the northward. He immediately steamed in that direction, but found no Sumter. Probably, made aware of the course Palmer was pursuing, she doubled like a hare in the chase, and shot out to sea in the opposite direction. The next morning Palmer cruised in every direction, but the privateer was nowhere to be seen, while it was impossible to guess whither she had gone.

The public were irritated at her escape, and great injustice was done Palmer for a time. The people were impatient and unreasonable, and the Government, if not equally so, was more or less influenced by the state of feeling, and nothing short of impossibilities would satisfy either. Palmer was at once relieved from command of the Iroquois; but subsequent investigation showed the injustice of the act, and that he had done all that a wise and efficient officer could do.

The next year he was given his vessel again, and just after the passage of the batteries below New Orleans, joined Farragut, and was sent by him up the river to demand the surrender of Baton Rouge. He did so, but the mayor returning a pompous, ridiculous answer, Palmer said: "I was determined to submit to no such nonsense, and accordingly weighed anchor and steamed up almost abreast of the arsenal, landed a force, took possession of the arsenal, barracks and other public property of the United States, and hoisted over it our flag." From this point he proceeded to Natchez and demanded its surrender, offering the same terms which had been granted to Baton Rouge. But the authorities refused to receive the communication at the landing, which conduct, Palmer said, "being rather more dignified than wise, I instantly seized the ferryboat, then on this side, occupied in filling herself with coal, which I intended to secure also, and placing on board of her a force from this squadron of seamen and marines, and a couple of howitzers, under the command of Lieutenant Harmany of this ship, sent her across to the landing, with orders that if there were not some of the authorities to receive my communication, he was to land his force, march up to the town, which was about half a mile distant, with colors flying, and there cause the mayor to receive and read my letter. But when the party had reached the landing, they found two members of the common council, sent with an apology from the mayor, to receive my communication. They begged that the force should not be landed, as they intended to make no resistance, and seemed disposed to acquiesce in anything I demanded."

This settled the matter. The next month, June, hearing that earthworks were being thrown up at Grand Gulf, he sent down the Wissahickon and Itasca, under command of De Camp, who had commanded the Iroquois in the passage of the forts below New Orleans, to ascertain the fact. The latter found there a battery of rifled guns, and five hundred artillerists to defend it. A sharp conflict ensued, in which one vessel was hulled twenty-five times, and the other seventeen. Palmer then dropped down abreast of the town with his squadron, which composed the advance division of Farragut's fleet, and shelled the enemy out of it.

In the passage of the batteries of Vicksburg this month, Palmer, in the Iroquois, led the line. In speaking of it, he says, in the most business-like manner: "We so fought our way up, running close into the town, having a raking fire from the fort above, and a plunging fire from the batteries on the hill, together with broadsides from the cannon planted in the streets; and, what is most strange, through all this heavy concentrated fire, with the exception of cutting away both our mainstays, and some other immaterial damage to the rigging, we escaped without injury. One shell burst on board of us, scattering its fragments around, and yet no casualty occurred.

"We remained off the upper battery until joined by the flag-ship, when, following your motions, we anchored out of range. My men and officers behaved with the same coolness which, I learn, so distinguished them in the attack on the forts below New Orleans."

In speaking of the action, Farragut said: "No one behaved better than commander J. S. Palmer of the Iroquois."

When, in the following month, Farragut determined to drop down below Vicksburg, and endeavor in his passage to destroy the ram Arkansas, which, coming out of the Yazoo, had boldly passed through the combined fleets, and anchored under the batteries of the city,

Palmer was again selected to lead the line in the Iroquois. When under the concentrated fire of the enemy, his worn-out engines suddenly stopped, and for nearly half an hour he lay helpless under it, and had it been better directed, would probably have sent him to the bottom. But being wild, and hence comparatively harmless, it "very soon gave him no concern." The moment he could get his engines in working order again, he stood up for the batteries, thinking the flag-ship was above; but learning that she had passed below in the darkness, he also dropped down and anchored beside her. The high estimation in which Farragut held Palmer may be inferred from the fact that the next spring, in March, when he resolved to run the terrible batteries of Port Hudson, Palmer commanded his ship, and stood on the poop-deck by his side in the awful conflict that followed. Farragut, in reporting it, said: "This ship moved up the river in good style, Captain Palmer governing with excellent judgment her fire according to circumstances, stopping when the smoke became too dense to see, and re-opening whenever a fresh battery fired upon us; but we always silenced their batteries when we fired."

In 1864, Palmer was commodore, commanding at New Orleans. The next year he commanded the Western Gulf Blockading squadron. While here, he captured and destroyed several blockade runners. Later in the season, he coöperated with Admiral Thatcher in the movements that resulted in the fall of Mobile. With the overthrow of this last stronghold of the rebellion, he returned north. To show the high estimation in which he was held by Admiral Thatcher, and the important aid he rendered him, we quote the following highly complimentary letter of the latter to the Secretary of the Navy:

UNITED STATES FLAG-SHIP STOCKDALE,
WEST GULF SQUADRON, MOBILE, ALA., *May* 3, 1865.

SIR: The Department was informed by Commodore Palmer, under date of February 10, 1865, that he would avail himself of the permission granted by it, to return north after the fall of Mobile; and as he is now about to leave this squadron, I beg leave to say that he has rendered me most efficient and untiring service throughout the attack upon the defences of the city, which has resulted so favorably to our arms; and I am indebted to him for the admirable manner in which the vessels to be employed for this service were prepared under his supervision, previous to my arrival on the station, and I part with him with reluctance and regret.

It was the belief of the enemy that it would be impossible for our monitors and gunboats to cross the Blakely River bar, owing to the shallowness of the water; but should we succeed in doing so, their hope rested in our entire destruction by the innumerable torpedoes with which they had filled the river, combined with their marsh batteries; and they well knew that our success in overcoming these obstacles would be fatal to them; but by great exertions night and day, under fire, we succeeded.

Commodore Palmer commanded the first division, consisting of the monitors and Octorara, and successfully ascended the Blakely with them, coming down the Tensas, directly in front of the city; the remainder of the gunboats, led by the flag-ship, convoying General Granger's command, for the purpose of making a joint attack in flank and front. These movements having been anticipated by the enemy, led to the evacuation; and although Commodore Palmer did not have the satisfaction of bombarding the city, he had placed himself in position to do so effectually, had not the rebels deprived him of the opportunity by flight.

Very respectfully, your obedient servant,

H. K. THATCHER,
Acting Rear-Admiral, Com'dg West Gulf Squadron.

Hon. GIDEON WELLES,
Secretary of the Navy, Washington, D. C.

Notwithstanding the rank to which Admiral Palmer has attained, he may, in one respect, regard himself an unlucky man. Had fortune favored him in the commencement of the war, when he so faithfully blockaded the Sumter, and enabled him to catch her as she steamed out of the harbor, he would have been promoted at once, and placed at the head of some of those expeditions in which the leaders of them won such renown. From the bravery, resolution and ability of the man, we may be assured that he would have won a reputation second to none.

In 1866 he commanded the West India Squadron.

CHAPTER XXVI.

CAPTAIN JOHN LORIMER WORDEN.

HIS NATIVITY.—EARLY SERVICES.—SERVES IN THE WAR WITH MEXICO.—FIRST LIEUTENANT IN THE BROOKLYN NAVY YARD.—BEFORE HOSTILITIES COMMENCED IN 1861, WAS SENT TO PENSACOLA WITH SECRET DESPATCHES.—HIS SUCCESS AND AFTER IMPRISONMENT.—EXCHANGED.—LOSES HIS HEALTH.—PUT IN COMMAND OF THE NEW MONITOR.—FIGHT WITH THE MERRIMAC IN HAMPTON ROADS.—IS WOUNDED.—COMMANDS THE MONTAUK.—ATTACKS FORT M'ALLISTER.—DESTROYS THE PRIVATEER NASHVILLE.—TAKES PART IN THE ATTACK OF THE IRON-CLADS ON FORT SUMTER.—HIS PRESENT COMMAND.

THE hero of the first Monitor, and the first prisoner of war, was born at Mount Pleasant, Dutchess County, March 12, 1818. He entered the navy in 1834, and was promoted to lieutenant in 1840. After nine years of service, he was ordered to the National Observatory at Washington, where he remained till the Mexican war, when he was transferred to the store-ship Southampton, of the Pacific squadron. At the close of the war, he was made first lieutenant of the Brooklyn Navy Yard.

In April, 1861, when war was found to be inevitable, he was sent by the Government as bearer of despatches to Captain Adams of the frigate Sabine, commanding the fleet at Pensacola. These despatches he committed to memory and then destroyed them. This fleet had been sent to Fort Pickens with two companies of artillery, to reinforce it whenever orders were sent to do so. These despatches contained such orders, and were destroyed lest the rebels should get possession of them, and prevent them reaching their destination. Lieutenant Worden arrived at Pensacola by way of Richmond and Montgomery on the 11th of the month. He here had an interview with General Bragg, and obtained from him a permit to visit Captain Adams, stating in reply to an interrogation as to his object, that he had a verbal communication from the Secretary of War to him. Going on board he delivered his message, and received a written reply in return, acknowledging the reception of the despatches, and stating that they should be carried out.

Fort Pickens was reinforced by Captain Vogdes that night. In the meantime, Worden was on the cars, whirling north. But when within five miles of Montgomery, five officers of the rebel army came in and arrested him, and took him to the Adjutant General. Montgomery was at that time the rebel capital, and a cabinet meeting was immediately called to consult on his case. He was finally remanded to the custody of the Deputy Marshal, in whose rooms he remained a prisoner for two days, and was then placed in the county jail. Worden boldly demanded the reason for his arrest and confinement, but could get no answer. He heard, however, it was because he had violated his word of honor, as well as Captain Adams, who, Bragg declared, had made an agreement with him, that no attempt either to reinforce or take the fort without previous notice, should be made by either party. It afterwards turned out, that Bragg had actually resolved to seize the fort the very night it was reinforced.

Worden remained in prison for seven months, or until the 13th of November. He was well treated and allowed to purchase such provisions as he chose. A great many Southern officers who were formerly acquainted with him in the service visited him, and used every effort, but in vain, to obtain his release on parole. Until mail connection with the North was cut off he was allowed to write to his friends and receive letters from them, but all except those from his family were opened and read before he was allowed to see them. After the fight at Santa Rosa Island, Major Vogdes and twenty-two of Wilson's men were placed in prison with him.

His confinement during the hot summer months broke down his health, and on the 13th of November, Quartermaster Calhoun informed him that he was released on parole, and ordered to report himself to the Adjutant General at Richmond. Having given his word not to divulge anything which he might learn on his journey to the disadvantage of the Confederacy, he next morning set out for Richmond, where he arrived on Sunday evening the seventeenth. After an interview with the Adjutant General and Acting Secretary of War, Benjamin, he was sent to Norfolk and exchanged.

His health was so much impaired, that he was compelled to remain in New York till the next February, to recruit.

The following month, March, he was placed in command of Ericsson's Monitor, and ordered to proceed to Hampton Roads. He arrived there on the evening of the eighth, and immediately went out to the protection of the Minnesota, lying hard aground just below Newport News.

Worden found a terrible state of things on his arrival. The iron-clad Merrimac had come out that very day, and sent two of our vessels to the bottom. The most intense excitement prevailed, and all wondered what the morning would bring forth. Lieutenant Morris, in temporary command of the Cumberland, had fought his ship bravely, but his terrific broadsides had no effect on the monster, and she kept on her way shaking the heavy shot like peas from her mailed sides, and struck the frigate with a force that careened her far over, and stove a hole in her side as big as a hogshead. Delivering a broadside as she backed off, she came on again, striking her amidships. She then lay off and deliberately hurled the shells from her 100-pound Armstrong guns into the sinking ship. These monstrous missiles of death tore through the wooden sides of the Cumberland with a destructive power that was awful to witness. Guns went spinning over the deck—great masses of splintered timbers flew about like straws in a gale, while dismembered, mangled bodies lay strewed over the gory deck. But Morris, aided by Lieutenants Davenport, Selfridge, and other subordinate officers, disdained to surrender, and poured in the heavy broadsides with a rapidity and power that would have sent any wooden vessel that ever floated to the bottom. But they made no impression apparently on this mailed monster. To the report that the ship was sinking, these noble officers replied only with fiercer broadsides. They determined that the flag above them should never be struck, and like Paul Jones, when told that his vessel was on fire and sinking, replied: "If we can do no better, we will sink alongside," they too resolved to fight on, while a gun could be fired, and then go down with their colors proudly flying. At length the waters rushed through the port-holes, as the noble frigate slowly settled over them. Still not a man faltered, and the pivot-guns on deck gave a last shot as with a sudden lurch the vessel went to the bottom, carrying her dead and wounded with her.

Some attempted to escape by swimming, and many were picked up by a propeller, but nearly a hundred of the gallant crew went to the bottom with her, and among them the Chaplain.

The work of destruction had been completed in forty-five minutes, and then the Merrimac turned to the Congress, which, seeing the fate of the Cumberland, hoisted sail and endeavored to escape, but got hopelessly aground. The Merrimac now steamed to within about a hundred yards, and then lay to and deliberately raked the frigate from stem to stern with her enormous shells. The carnage was awful. The rebel steamers Jamestown and Yorktown also came up and poured in their fire, and soon the decks of the Congress presented a ghastly spectacle. Added to all, she was set on fire in three places, and the flames, fanned by a brisk wind, soon roared along her decks. Out of feelings of humanity to the wounded, who would be roasted alive in the burning ship, the colors were hauled down. But while a boat was coming to take off the prisoners, some sharpshooters on shore kept up their fire, which so incensed the commander of the Merrimac, that he ordered another broadside to be poured into the surrendered vessel, which caused great slaughter.

Leaving the Congress to consume away until her

magazine was reached, the Merrimac now turned to the Minnesota and Lawrence, both of which had unaccountably got aground. That all these vessels should get aground, and thus become helpless targets for the enemy, is certainly very strange.

As the Merrimac approached the Minnesota, she received one of the broadsides of the latter, and fired in turn, but she could not get within a mile, and fearing to get aground in the dark she retired to her anchorage, behind Craney Island, to wait till morning before completing her work of destruction.

This was the state of things at the time of Worden's arrival. The Monitor was a small vessel, mounting only two guns in her revolving turret, and wholly untried in combat. Those who hailed her arrival as a saviour, were confounded at her insignificant appearance. It required a great deal of faith to believe she could cope with a vessel that had just destroyed two frigates.

It was a sad Saturday night—Fortress Monroe was thronged with fugitives—the heavens were aflame with the burning Congress, which at last exploded with the sound of thunder—the Merrimac was apparently uninjured, and, "What will the Sabbath morning bring?" was the mournful question that trembled on every lip.

Worden lay all night alongside of the Minnesota, in case a nocturnal attack should be attempted.

The morning broke bright and beautiful—not a cloud obscured the sky, and every glass was turned in the direction from which the Merrimac was expected to come. Soon she was seen approaching, accompanied by her consorts of the day before. The Minnesota at once beat to quarters. Worden ordered the iron hatches to be closed, the dead light covers put on, and the little

Monitor put in perfect fighting trim, while he and some of his officers stood on the top of the turret and watched the movements of the approaching vessels. These were followed by steamers filled with gentlemen and ladies from Norfolk, who were coming out to see the crowning victory. As the Merrimac approached the Minnesota, Worden steamed out and ran boldly down to meet her. The enemy seemed non-plussed at the bold approach of what seemed scarcely big enough to be a New York ferryboat. It looked more like a raft with a round tub upon it nine feet high, and twenty feet in diameter. The commander of the Minnesota watched her progress with the deepest anxiety, for on the success of this new, untried experiment rested the salvation of his ship. To his astonishment, he saw Worden lay her right alongside of the Merrimac, where she looked like a fly beside an ox. But small as she was, her guns threw shot weighing a hundred and seventy pounds, and the first that struck the Merrimac woke her commander up to a sense of the danger that menaced him, and he opened a whole broadside on the tiny structure; heavy enough, one would think, to blow her out of the water. But the turret was the only thing to fire at, and most of the shot flew harmlessly over her, while those that did strike the turret, glanced off. It was a marvellous spectacle—that little thing holding at bay and worrying such a monster.

The Merrimac, finding that she could do nothing with her pertinacious little adversary, turned her attention once more to the Minnesota, and steaming towards her, received a broadside from the latter, which, as Van Brunt, her commander, said, "would have blown out of the water any timber-built ship in the world."

The heavy shot, however, rattled harmlessly against the sides of the Merrimac, when she, in turn, sent a rifled shell into the Minnesota, which tore through the chief engineer's state-room, the engineers' mess-room, amidships, and bursting in the boatswain's room, knocked four rooms into one in its headlong passage, and set the vessel on fire. A second exploded the boiler of the tug Dragon alongside, causing for a while, great alarm. But all this time, Worden in his "cheese-tub," as the rebels called her, was crowding all steam to overtake his powerful adversary, and by the time the latter had fired his third shell was again between the two vessels, covering with amazing audacity the Minnesota. Exasperated at her inability either to shake off her puny antagonist or cripple her, the Merrimac now determined to run into and over her, and sink her by mere weight—and turning, ran full speed upon her. She struck the little Monitor with tremendous force, and her bow passed over the deck. But at that close range Worden planted one of his heavy shot square on the iron roof, with such resistless force that it went clean through. The monster backed off with a shudder, and then, enraged at the invulnerability of her antagonist, concentrated her entire fire on the turret. Worden was stationed at the pilot-house, while Green managed the guns, and Stimers turned the turret. The two vessels at times almost touched, and the explosion of their monster guns at this short range was most terrific. Titanic hammers seemed incessantly falling on their iron armor—so fierce and fast flew the shot. One shot struck the turret with such force that it knocked down Lieutenant Stimers and two men. Another struck the pilot-house, breaking in two an iron log a foot thick. It hit just outside of where

Worden had his eye, knocking him senseless, while the small particles of iron driven off by the concussion, flew into his eyes, completely blinding him for the time being. But it was soon evident that the Merrimac was getting the worst of it. Worden had found his way into her vitals, and would soon send her to the bottom, and so she wheeled out of the conflict and under the convoy of two tugs, limped away to her moorings. The Monitor followed her a short distance, but Worden having received orders to act strictly on the defensive, and not leave the fleet, he soon ceased to follow his thoroughly humbled antagonist.

Lieutenant Wise, who had watched the conflict from the shore, now jumped into a boat and rowed off to the Monitor. As he descended through the "man hole" to the cabin below, everything was as calm and quiet as though nothing extraordinary had happened. One officer stood by the mirror, leisurely combing his hair, another was washing some blood from his hands, while the gallant commander lay on a settee with his eyes bandaged, but giving no sign of the excrutiating pain that racked him. The first words he uttered on recovering from the stunning effect of the shot was:

"Have I saved the Minnesota?"

"Yes," was the reply, "and whipped the Merrimac."

"Then," said he, "I don't care what becomes of me."

He had saved *more* than the Minnesota—how *much* that more was, one shudders to contemplate. It is a wonder—when we remember how the iron-clads afterwards suffered before Charleston—that the turret did not get jammed so that it would not revolve; or one, at least, of the two cannon, did not have its muzzle broken off under the close and awful cannonade to which she was exposed.

Some will call it a wonderful piece of luck, while the devout man will see in it a remarkable interference of Providence in our behalf. Never was a government so warned as ours had been of this very catastrophe, and never did one show such apathy under it.

Lieutenant Worden was now laid up for some time; but as soon as he was able, he again asked for active service, and being promoted to commander, was placed in command of the Montauk, attached to the South Atlantic Blockading Squadron. In January, 1863, Dupont sent him down to operate up the great Ogeechee River; to capture, if he could, the fort at Genesis Point, and destroy the Nashville that lay under its protection. With four other vessels, he for nearly four hours bombarded the fort, and withdrew only after his ammunition was expended—very little damage, however, was done on either side. A few days after he renewed the attack with like results—though his vessel was hit forty-six times.

The last of this month, having ascertained that the Nashville had got aground just above Fort McAllister, he steamed up, and though under a tremendous cannonade from the latter, set her on fire with his shells, completely destroying her.

In the attack of the iron-clads on Sumter the following April, he carried his ship into action with his usual gallantry, and retired only on the signal of Dupont. He was hit fourteen times, and though no one had had greater experience than he in the power of iron-clads, he said that if the attack had been continued, it would have ended in disaster.

Worden was afterwards detached from this ship—his health having failed him, and he was engaged in no other important action during the war.

He is now on duty on the coast of South America.

CHAPTER XXVII.

REAR-ADMIRAL HENRY H. BELL.

HIS NATIVITY.—AVENGES AN INSULT OFFERED TO THE NATIONAL FLAG IN CHINA.—AT THE SECESSION OF THE SOUTH DISOWNS HIS NATIVE STATE.—SERVICES IN NEW YORK.—APPOINTED FARRAGUT'S FLEET CAPTAIN.—A BOLD RECONNOISSANCE.—CUTS THE BARRIER ACROSS THE MISSISSIPPI.—LEADS ONE DIVISION OF THE FLEET IN THE PASSAGE OF THE FORTS.—HOISTS THE NATIONAL COLORS OVER THE CUSTOM HOUSE IN NEW ORLEANS.—COOLNESS IN PASSING THE VICKSBURG BATTERIES.—SUCCEEDS FARRAGUT IN COMMAND OF THE WEST GULF BLOCKADING SQUADRON.—ORDERED NORTH.—SERVICE IN NEW YORK.—HIS HEALTH BREAKS DOWN.—HIS PRESENT POSITION.

ADMIRAL BELL is a native of North Carolina, from which State he entered the navy the 4th of August, 1823. His early cruises differed little from those of other young officers. He was distinguished for devotion to his profession, and steadily rose in it till, at the breaking out of the war, he ranked as captain.

In 1855, he commanded the frigate San Jacinto, then attached to the East India Squadron, under Commodore Armstrong. While on this station, one of the ship's boats returning one day from the shore—whither it had been sent—was fired upon by the Barrier forts in Canton River. The Commodore was inclined to negotiate on the matter, but Captain Bell and Captain (since Admiral) Foote, were aroused at this insult to the American flag and urged the former so vehemently to avenge it on the spot, that he finally consented to let these gallant officers do it in their own way. They at once manned their boats and pulled for the forts. The latter opened fire as they approached; but the rowers bent steadily to their oars until they were beached near the hostile works. Bell and Foote then formed their men, and leading them in person, rushed to the assault with such fury, that the Chinese, terror-stricken, left their guns and fled in every direction. Captain Bell then laid the trains and fired them with his own hand, blowing the forts into fragments. He thus taught the Chinese that it was a dangerous thing to touch the American flag where his ship floated.

Although Captain Bell was a Southerner by birth, and married a Southern woman, and one connected with the leading families and secessionists of Virginia, he never wavered a moment in his duty. Indeed, it can scarcely be said it got so far as a question of mere duty with him. Intensely loyal, his whole soul was aroused at the rebellious attitude of the South. The first gun fired at the old flag at Sumter, stirred his blood as did the hostile shot aimed at it in Canton River. When his native State seceded and joined the Southern Confederacy, he wrote to Washington requesting to have his name registered as coming from the loyal State of New York, as he was unwilling to appear in any way as belonging to a secession State.

In 1861, Captain Bell was employed in the responsible duty of fitting out and arming the nondescript vessels that the agent of the Navy Department was buying to be used in blockade duty.

When Farragut took command of the West Gulf

Blockading Squadron, Captain Bell was appointed his fleet captain, and took part in all the operations that led to the fall of New Orleans.

The month previous to the passage of the forts, he ran up to inspect the cable that stretched across the river, and the batteries. This bold movement drew a furious fire from the forts, but Bell coolly finished his reconnoissance. Some time after, Farragut wanted to get a peep at them himself, and so Bell took him up. He steamed up in broad midday, and could see through his glass the forts thronged with officers watching his movements. But to obtain a fairer view, Bell and Farragut mounted the rigging, and getting astride the cross-trees, began to take observations. In a few moments a puff of white smoke was seen to issue from Fort Jackson, and before it had melted into the air a 100-pound rifle shell came screeching towards them, striking the water about one hundred yards ahead of the vessel. After a short interval there came another puff of smoke, and another monster shot shrieked overhead, passing only fifty feet above Farragut and Bell. This was getting rather too close, for Bell had the Admiral with him, and "Back her" came from aloft. The vessel drifted down two or three ship's lengths, when a third shell struck and burst on the very spot they had just left. In a few minutes, Bell steamed ahead again into the fire, when a 100-pound shell came like a sudden gust of wind between the smoke-stack and mainmast—its windage actually rocking one of the boats hanging to the vessel's side.

When everything was ready for the squadron to advance, it was necessary, as a preparatory step, to cut the cable, which was strung across the river on hulks below the forts. This daring and difficult enterprise was entrusted to Captain Bell. It was a dark night, when, taking the Pinola and Itasca gunboats, he steamed up to the barrier. Petards had been brought from the north, which were to be thrown aboard one of the hulks, and discharged by electric wires from one of the gunboats—this part of the plan failed, owing to the heavy gale that was blowing.

As Bell steamed past the line of mortar schooners Porter opened fire; and, canopied by blazing shells, arching the sky overhead, the boats ran boldly up to the cable, and commenced the work of destruction. Sledges and chisels were soon busy sundering the chain; the anchors of the hulks were slipped, and the work went steadily on. But, in the meantime, they had been discovered; a rocket from one of the forts shot into the air, and then both opened a tremendous fire. The gallant men, however, paid no heed to it till their task was accomplished.

It is said that Farragut threw his arms around Bell in delight, when he once more stepped safely on board his vessel.

In the final passage, Bell led the second division in the Sciota. His vessel set fire to two steamers in her passage, and captured a third. She was the fourth in the attack and capture of the forts at the city of New Orleans on the 25th, and the third in passing up in front of the city.

The victory having been won, he, on the 26th, hauled down his pennant, and repaired on board the Hartford to resume his duties as fleet captain. He gave Captain Donaldson of the ship, and his officers and crew great praise for their conduct while passing the forts.

It is well known what an excitement followed the pulling down of the American flag from the custom-house, after it had been raised there by order of Farragut. The New Orleans papers praised the daring act, and Mumford, who had committed it, was regarded as a hero. As the surging multitude gazed on the rebel flag flying in its place, they declared that the man who attempted to haul it down should die. Knowing that some action would be taken in the matter, the crowd assembled in large numbers in the immediate neighborhood of the custom-house; and angry, savage faces scowled out from the turbulent mass, and oaths, and threats of vengeance filled all the air. In the midst of this excitement, Bell landed on the levee with two officers and a handful of marines, and took his course for the custom-house. The mob opened as he advanced, but closed up behind him, cursing him and his little band, and swearing that the moment a head appeared above the roof of the custom-house, a bullet would pierce it. But Bell, unmoved and erect, and like Abdiel amid the rebel angels, passed

> "Long way through hostile scorn, which he sustained,
> Superior, nor of violence feared aught."

Reaching the custom-house, he demanded the keys. They were given him; but every one refused to show him the way to the roof. He then stationed his little band in front of the building, and taking one of his officers and his coxswain, groped his way along the passage, and finally mounted to the roof. In the meanwhile, the excited multitude below watched the roof of the building, to see if he dared to show his head above it. As it appeared above the opening a deep murmur of vengeance rolled through the streets. Slowly, and with a dignified carriage, as became his solemn task, Bell rose to view, and his tall, commanding form stood in full relief against the sky. With no theatrical display—not even deigning a glance to the excited multitude below, thirsting for his blood—without haste, but calmly and slowly, he, with his own hands, lowered the rebel flag in sight of all, and hoisted the stars and stripes in its place. All expected to see a bullet pierce him, but the calm, dignified, fearless bearing of the man; the sublimity of the scene as he stood there pencilled against the sky, overawed the angry passions of the mob, and breathless silence fell upon it. Here there was no excitement of the combat; no clangor of trumpets, or shouts of men to brace up the nerves and stimulate to daring deeds; nothing but love for the dear old flag, and of the honor of his country. Nothing could exceed the moral grandeur of the act—it would make a subject for a great picture. The national ships at the levee, with their guns bearing on the city; the heaving, turbulent mass blocking all the streets; the little band of marines, with firm-set front, standing across the door-way; the tall, erect form of Bell pictured against the sky from the top of the custom-house, as he slowly sends the national colors up the flagstaff, form a group of objects from which some artist will yet give us a great historical painting.

When Bell descended again to the street, he quietly locked the door behind him, and putting the key in his pocket, placed himself at the head of his marines and marched back to his ship.

When, in the June following, Farragut ran the batteries of Vicksburg, Bell stood on the poop by his side, to direct the movements of the fleet, but the darkness and smoke soon shut the vessels from his sight, and he could tell where they were only by the thunder of their broadsides, or their blaze as it illumined the gloom, and so gave his attention to looking up the batteries of the enemy, and pointing them out to the officers in charge of the guns, and directing where to fire.

After the fall of Vicksburg and Port Hudson, Farragut, accepting a respite tendered him by the Government, turned over to Admiral Porter the entire control of the western waters above New Orleans, and Bell, who had been made Commodore, was placed in command of the squadron during his absence.

His duties were now of the most arduous kind, though connected with no important movement in which he was personally engaged. His blockading fleet stretched with intervals from Mobile to Galveston. After dark, he always kept his ships on the move, so that blockade runners never knew where to find them. While off Galveston, he had the misfortune to lose the Hatteras—Blake commanding—which was sunk by the Alabama. He heard the cannonading, and saw the flashes of the combat, and hurried off in the Brooklyn in the direction from whence they came; but could find no traces of either vessel until next morning, when he saw the masts of the Hatteras standing out of the water, telling him of her fate.

He detailed a portion of his force to coöperate with Banks in his movements against Brownsville, Brazos, Aranzas, and Cabello Passes. Commander J. H. Strong had charge of it, and received the thanks of Banks, and the commendations of the Government for the skill, ability, and energy with which he performed his part in the expeditions. In storm and calm, under vexations, delays, and countless embarrassments, he executed every task imposed on him.

On Farragut's return to take command of the squadron, previous to the attack on the defences of Mobile, Bell was ordered north to the Brooklyn Navy Yard. Here his incessant labors, joined to the exposures on the Mississippi and off the coast, completely broke him down, and, for a while, his friends feared he had made his last cruise. But his health rallied in the bracing air of the Highlands at Newburg, and he gradually recovered his strength.

With the old battered Hartford for his flagship, he now commands the Asiatic Squadron in the China seas, as Rear-Admiral.

Admiral Bell is a man of dignified deportment, frank, genial, unassuming manners, and a kind, noble heart. A better officer, a more gallant man, or one more beloved by all who serve under him, never trod the deck of a battle ship.

Between him and Farragut there exists the warmest affection and esteem.

CHAPTER XXVIII.

COMMODORE MELANCTHON SMITH.

HIS BIRTH AND ANCESTRY.—ENTERS THE NAVY.—HIS EARLY SERVICES.—COMMANDS IN FLORIDA.—SENT TO THE GULF BLOCKADING SQUADRON IN 1861.—DRIVES THE ENEMY FROM SHIP ISLAND.—COMMANDS THE STEAMER MISSISSIPPI IN THE PASSAGE OF THE FORTS BELOW NEW ORLEANS.—CAPTURES THE RAM MANASSAS.—LOSES HIS VESSEL IN PASSING PORT HUDSON.—HIS GALLANT CONDUCT.—TAKES PART IN THE SIEGE OF THE PLACE.—ON COURT-MARTIAL DUTY.—ORDERED NORTH.—ON PICKET DUTY IN THE JAMES RIVER.—COMMANDS IN THE NORTH CAROLINA SOUNDS.—BATTLE WITH THE RAM ALBEMARLE.—CAPTURES THE BOMBSHELL.—DIVISIONAL COMMANDER ON JAMES RIVER.—TAKES PART IN THE TWO ATTACKS ON FORT FISHER.—SUBSEQUENT SERVICES.—PRESENT POSITION.

MELANCTHON SMITH was born in New York city, May 24th, 1810. His father, Fauquier Smith, was from Long Island, and his mother, Cornelia Jones, daughter of Dr. Gardiner Jones, from New York city. His father served as colonel in the war of 1812, and commanded a fort at the battle of Plattsburg. Sidney Smith, Captain in the United States Navy, and his uncle, was in the naval battle that took place on Lake Champlain, at the same time, under McDonough. His grandfather, Hon. Melancthon Smith, was one of the most prominent political debaters of the day, and in 1777, was the first Sheriff of Dutchess County. In 1788, he represented this county in the convention which met at Poughkeepsie, to take into consideration the Constitution of the United States, which had been prepared the year before in Philadelphia. He was one of the most prominent debaters in that convention, and chief antagonist of Alexander Hamilton.

The subject of the present sketch, having received an academic education, entered the navy March 1st, 1826.

His first service was on board the frigate Brandywine, from which he was transferred to the sloop-of-war Vincennes. In 1830, he was sent to the naval school of New York; but the next year ordered to the frigate Potomac, in which he served but little over a month, when he was ordered to the Navy Yard of Brooklyn. In 1832 he received his warrant as passed midshipman, and joined the sloop-of-war St. Louis; but in the following winter was detached from her and sent to the Navy Yard at Pensacola. The following year, however, he was ordered to the schooner Porpoise, and then to the sloop Vandalia, in which he served till 1837. The next year he was, for a short time, on duty in the Navy Yard at New York, from which he was transferred, in 1836, to the sloop-of-war Natchez, in which he served as sailing master. The same year he received his warrant as master in the navy, and the following year was promoted to lieutenant, in which capacity he served in the sloop Vandalia, till 1838. In 1839, he was attached to the steamer Poinsett, and a part of the time commanded a fort, and a twenty-oared barge on the Miami River, Florida.

The next year he was stationed in the Navy Yard at New York; but from 1841 to 1843, served on board the Fairfield and Preble, when he was ordered to the store-ship Erie. He remained here a year, and during the following year was, part of the time, on the Vandalia and Colonel Harney, and a part of the time executive officer of the Pensacola Navy Yard. From 1848 to 1855 he served, first on the frigate Constitution, and then on the Potomac, as executive officer. Being promoted to commander in 1855, he was detached from the latter vessel, and two years after ordered on special duty as light-house inspector; which position he held until just before the breaking out of the rebellion. In May, 1861, he was ordered to the Gulf Blockading Squadron, and in the following September moved against Ship Island with the steamer Massachusetts, when the rebels fired the barracks, destroyed the light-house lantern, and escaped to the mainland. He had an engagement also with some Confederate steamers, but his first serious action was in the passage of the forts below New Orleans. He commanded the steamer Mississippi in this terrific encounter, and received ten shots, eight going clean through the vessel, wounding six of her crew. Seeing the ram Manassas, he signalled for permission to attack her. Farragut granting it, he boldly made for her. The ram advancing to the contest, struck the steamer, inflicting a severe damage below the water line. The monster in return received a terrific broadside from the heavy guns of the Mississippi, which carried away her smoke-stack, and crashed through her mailed sides with such awful power, that the crew ran her ashore and fled in affright. Smith immediately boarded her, but finding his machinery so disabled that he could not take her in tow, and a steamer on fire drifting down on him, he recalled his boats after setting her on fire. He then riddled her with shot, when she swung loose from the bank, and drifting below the forts, blew up with a tremendous explosion. He afterwards passed up the river, and engaged, with other vessels, the batteries above.

His next important engagement, was in the terrible passage of Port Hudson, in which he lost his ship. A full account of this, together with a description of his gallant bearing on the occasion, are given in the sketch of Farragut. Nothing could test his great qualities as a commander, more than the trying position in which he found himself here, when his vessel grounded in twenty-three feet of water, right under the concentrated fire of the hostile batteries. When, after the most desperate efforts, it became evident that she could not be made to float again, and the rebel shells were bursting in and around her, the cool manner in which, with lighted cigar, he removed his crew to the boats, and then set fire to her, showed that no danger or adversity could shake his steady nerves. He felt keenly, however, the loss of his noble vessel. A man loves the good steed which has once carried him right gallantly and safely through a deadly struggle; but a sailor has a still warmer affection for his ship, whose heavy broadsides have spoken at his command, and which has borne his flag triumphantly through a great combat. No wonder then his heart was filled with sadness, when he saw his noble vessel perish before his eyes. The manner of her death, too, appealed strongly to his sympathies. When relieved from the weight of her crew, she again floated, and swinging slowly down stream, brought her other broadside to bear. Her guns, heated by the raging flames, soon began to go off, as if still remembering her old commander, and thundered away in stern response to the rebel batteries. A pyramid of flame, she towered grandly through the gloom, and drifting with the current, moved majestically past him. He watched her blazing form lighting up the bosom of the stream, the banks, and the murky heavens, till Prophet's Island shut her from view. A few minutes more he could trace her course by the illumination made by her burning hull, and then came a deafening explosion that shook the shores, followed by utter darkness, that told him that his noble ship was sleeping beneath the waters of the mighty river whose name she bore.

He was afterwards given the command of the Monongahela, and joined in the attack on Port Hudson, from the 1st to the 20th of June. In January, he was on a court of inquiry, to investigate the "Galveston matter," relating to the failure to capture the Harriet Lane. He was afterwards transferred east, to the North Atlantic Blockading Squadron. Here, in the Onondaga, he was on picket duty for some time, and coöperated with General Butler in the movement of troops at Dutch Gap and Deep Bottom. But the ram Albemarle in the Sounds of North Carolina seriously threatening the existence of our squadron there, Lee sent him down to look after her. The ram, having previously sunk the Southfield, now came out again to renew her attack, when Smith, with his little squadron, boldly advanced to meet her.

The following is his account of the engagement:

"The ram Albemarle, steamer Cotton-Plant, with troops, and the armed steamer Bombshell, laden with provisions and coal, came out of Roanoke River to-day at two o'clock, P. M., and, after being tolled ten miles down the sound by the picket force left to guard the entrance of the river, the Mattabesett, Wyalusing, Sassacus, and Whitehead, got under way and stood up to engage them; the smaller boats falling into position in accordance with the enclosed programme.

The engagement commenced at 4.40, by the ram firing the first gun, which destroyed the Mattabesett's launch and wounded several men. The second shot cut away some of the standing and running rigging. At 4.45, the Bombshell surrendered to the Mattabesett, and was ordered to fall in our wake; at 4.50, fired a broadside into the ram at a distance of one hundred and fifty yards; at 5.50, the Sassacus delivered her fire in passing and then rammed his stern, pouring in a broadside at the same time. The Sassacus was seen soon afterwards enveloped with steam, when she hauled off, evidently disabled. The colors of the ram at this moment came down, and it was some time before it was ascertained whether he had surrendered, or they had been shot away. During the contact, it was, of course, impossible for the other vessels to fire; but when the Sassacus became disengaged, and resumed her firing, the engagement became general; the smaller vessels firing so rapidly, that it was dangerous for the larger ones to approach; and they appeared also to be ignorant of all signals, as they answered without obeying them. The engagement continued until about 7.30, when, it becoming dark, the Commodore Hull and Ceres were then sent ahead to keep the ram in sight, and to remain on picket duty off the mouth of the Roanoke River, if he succeeded in entering it; the Mattabesett, Wyalusing, Miami, and Whitehead, coming to anchor in the sound, two miles and a half below. Eight torpedoes had been furnished by the army, and an attempt was made last night to place them in the mouth of the river; the entrance being watched, it was found impracticable. Another effort was made to-day at two o'clock, P. M., when the ram was discovered two miles above, on his way out. During the engagement, a seine was laid out across the ram's bow, in obedience to orders, to try and foul his propeller, but he passed over it without injury. A torpedo was rigged out from the bow of the Miami, and she was ordered to go ahead and attempt to explode it, but, from some cause yet unexplained, it was not done. She ran up, however, sheered off, and delivered her broadside, and continued to fire at him rapidly. The injuries sustained by the ram are thought to be considerable, but his motive-power is evidently uninjured. His boats were knocked off from the decks, and his stack riddled, and it is also believed that one of his guns was disabled. The ram is certainly very formidable. He is fast for that class of vessel, making from six to seven knots, turns quickly, and is armed with heavy guns, as is proved by the 100-pounder Brooks projectile that entered and lodged in the Mattabesett, and 100-pounder Whitworth shot received by the Wyalusing, while the shot fired at him were seen to strike fire upon the casemates and hull, flying upwards and falling into the water without having had any perceptible effect upon the vessel. I had tried the effect of ramming (as suggested by the Department) in the case of the Sassacus, and was deterred from repeating the experiment by the injury she had sustained, and a signal from the Wyalusing that she was sinking, which, if the latter had been correct, (and I was not informed to the contrary until after the vessels came to anchor,) would have left too small a force of efficient vessels to keep the control of the sound, which I now hold, and shall be able to maintain against any rebel force that they will be able to organize at this point, when present damages are repaired. I am convinced that side-wheel steamers cannot be laid alongside of the Albemarle, without totally disabling their wheels, which is the reason for not adopting the suggestion contained in your order to me of the 23d instant. It is reported that the rebel barges with troops were at the mouth of the Croatan River, ready to come out, and *a steamer was seen* in that direction; but in regard to the first I have no positive information."

Lieutenant Commander Roe, of the Sassacus, also struck the ram, and gives the following account of the collision:

"As the Mattabesett had passed around the stern of the ram, and was heading down the sound again, the ram had turned partially round with a port-helm, and now lay broadside to me. As the Sassacus had been drawn off some little distance by her operations and capture of the Bombshell, she had a good distance to get headway; and, seeing the favorable moment before me, I ordered full steam and open throttle, and laid the ship fair for the broadside of the ram to run her down. The Sassacus struck her fairly just abaft her starboard beam in the position of the rear of the house or casemate, with a speed of nine to ten knots, making twenty-two revolutions with thirty pounds of steam. As I struck, she sent a 100-pounder rifle shot through and through, from starboard bow to port-side, on the berth-deck.

"The collision was pretty heavy, and the ram

careened a good deal—so much so that the water washed over her deck forward and aft the casemate. At one time I thought she was going down; I kept the engine going, pushing, as I hoped, deeper and deeper into her, and also hoping it might be possible for some one of the boats to get up on the opposite side of me, and perhaps enable us to sink her, or at least to get well on to her on all sides; I retained this position full ten minutes, throwing grenades down her deck-hatch, and trying in vain to get powder into her smoke-stack, and receiving volleys of musketry, when the stern of the ram began to go round, and her broadside-port bearing on our starboard bow, when the ram fired and sent a 100-pounder Brooks rifle shot through the starboard side on the berth-deck, passing through the empty bunkers into the starboard boiler, clean through it fore and aft, and finally lodging in the wardroom. In a moment the steam filled every portion of the ship, from the hurricane-deck to the fire-rooms, killing some, stifling some, and rendering all movement for a time impossible. When the steam cleared away so I could look around me, I saw my antagonist was away from me, and steaming off. In the meantime the engine was going, as no one could do anything below, some sixteen men being scalded. I then put the helm hard a-port, headed up the sound, and around to the land, in order to clear the field for the other boats. Soon as the steam cleared up, and the effect of the explosion was over, the officers and men immediately went to the guns, and kept them going upon the enemy until we drifted out of range. I tried to ricochet several 9-inch shot, so that she might be struck on her bottom by the upward bound of the shot, but I had the mortification to see every shot strike the water inside of her, and rise on the opposite side of her. While alongside of her, and almost simultaneous with the fatal shot of the enemy, Acting-Ensign Mayer sent a 100-pounder solid shot at her port, which broke into fragments, one of which rebounded and fell on our deck, as did also some fragments of grenades. While thus together, I fired three separate shots into one of her ports; we clearly observed the muzzles of two of her guns broken very badly. After the separation of the two vessels, the Sassacus was finally headed down the sound, and continued to move very slowly, working on a vacuum, and finally stopped, when I dropped anchor. In the meantime the Mattabesett and Wyalusing gallantly went in, and the fight was nobly maintained by those vessels."

The other vessels joined in the engagement, but their shot seemed to have but little effect on the ram.

Smith lost eight in killed and wounded, while Roe, on the Sassacus, had some twenty scalded by the escaping steam.

Smith, in a subsequent report, states that Lieutenant Roe was mistaken as to the speed he was going when he struck the ram; also, that he overrated the injury he had done her, especially her guns.

In July, 1864, he returned to the James River, and was made divisional officer, with the Onondaga as his flagship. In October, he was transferred to the frigate Wabash, in which vessel he participated in both of the attacks on Fort Fisher. In the last one he had eleven killed and wounded, besides those lost in the storming party furnished by his vessel. In 1865, he was detached from the Wabash, and during a part of the year was engaged on court-martial duty. In July, of this year, he was appointed Executive Officer of the Navy Department at Washington, and the same month promoted to Commodore. In September, 1866, he was appointed Chief of the Bureau of Equipment and Recruiting in the Navy Department, which position, we believe, he at present holds.

CHAPTER XXIX.

COMMODORE JOHN RODGERS.

HIS NATIVITY.—ENTERS THE NAVY.—AT THE COMMENCEMENT OF THE WAR SENT WEST TO SUPERINTEND THE BUILDING OF IRON-CLADS.—PLACED IN COMMAND OF THE GALENA.—FIGHT AT DRURY'S BLUFF.—COMMANDS THE WEEHAWKEN.—ATTACK ON FORT SUMTER.—CAPTURES THE ATLANTA.—COMPLIMENTARY LETTER FROM THE SECRETARY OF THE NAVY.

COMMODORE RODGERS is a native of Maryland, but was appointed to the navy from the District of Columbia, of which he is a resident. He entered the service as midshipman in March, 1825.

At the breaking out of the war he was sent West to assist in the building of an iron-clad fleet, in which he exhibited the enterprise and skill which distinguish him.

Having done such good service here, he was given the command of the Galena, one of the three first armored vessels built on the Atlantic coast, and sent to Hampton Roads. As in one of these, the Monitor, Worden had tested their power of resistance in combat with another mailed vessel, so he now was to prove their strength in conflict with shore batteries, and in May, 1863, steamed up the James River to engage Fort Darling. If this could be silenced the obstructions above could be removed, and our war vessels pass up to within a short distance of

Richmond. He had with him the Aroostook, the Monitor, Port Royal, and Naugatuck. The wooden vessels anchored thirteen hundred yards below, while the Galena ran up to within about six hundred yards, and let go her anchor, and with a spring swung across the stream, which here was not more than twice as wide as the ship was long. The Monitor also anchored near her, and the commander, Lieutenant Jeffers, gallantly engaged the batteries, but found it impossible to elevate his guns sufficiently to make them effective until he dropped farther down stream. The Galena, being unable to change her position in the narrow river, became a stationary target for the Rebel guns mounted on Drury's Bluff, and hence took a terrible pounding. The heavy shot coming from so great a height fell with tremendous power, while the sharp-shooters picked off every man that showed his head. Yet Rogers lay here motionless for nearly four hours, exposed to this plunging fire. In that time he lost twenty-four men killed and wounded, while thirteen shot and shell pierced the iron armor of his vessel, shattering her bulwarks and starting the seams in her side and deck.

Rodgers held on in his desperate position until he had but six Parrott charges left, and not a single filled nine-inch shell.

He was afterward placed in command of the Weehawken, and ordered to bring her from New York around to Fortress Monroe. Although the pilots attempted to dissuade him from starting, predicting bad weather, he determined to go, wishing to test the sea-going qualities of the vessel. When two days out he encountered a terrific gale, and Rodgers, cutting the line that united his vessel to the tug Boardman, determined to ride out the storm alone. Captain Case, who was convoying him in the Iroquois, then offered to tow him; but Rodgers declined the proffered aid. Case, however, would not leave him, and stood nobly by him through all the fearful night that followed. Lashed by the tempest the waves rose thirty feet high, and poured in such wild torrents over the shuddering vessel that no one could go on deck to heave either log or lead. In a private letter to his father-in-law describing the gale he said: "I stood on the turret and watched her movements with great interest. * * * No boat from the Iroquois could have lived, for she was rolling her guns under; our fate, therefore, depended on the safety of our own vessel. The waves swept over the deck with great violence, an iron plate two inches thick and eleven feet long, weighing three thousand pounds, was broken loose from its lashings and carried forty feet against the iron stanchions, and another plate, as much as two men could slide along the deck, was lifted and thrown upon some kedges. We could neither throw the log nor sound, as no one could live on the deck to do either."

It was a fearful night, and a commander never witnessed a more appalling sight than that which met the eyes of Rodgers as he stood on the top of the turret, and watched the great angry black waves fall one after another with the sound of thunder over the shivering deck, burying it from sight and surging up around him until the spray swept like a driving rain over his high perch.

He was delighted with the behavior of his vessel, and brought her safely into port, though leaking badly.

In the following April the Weehawken formed part of the iron-clad fleet in the attack on Fort Sumter. The raft with the torpedo which was to blow up the obstructions was attached to her, and impeded very much her movements. It proved useless, yet, crippled as he was with this bungling apparatus, Rodgers boldly laid his vessel alongside of the rebel batteries, and was struck fifty-three times, withdrawing from the horrible fire only as he saw the signal to do so.

In the following June, Rodgers distinguished himself by capturing the rebel ram Atlanta. This vessel, sometimes called the Fingal, ran the blockade of Savannah a few days after the forts of Port Royal were taken, and was now ready to attempt a passage by Wilmington River into Warsaw Sound, and attack our blockading vessels there as well as those farther south. To prevent this dangerous movement Rodgers in the Weehawken and Downes in the Nahant were despatched to look after her.

A little after daylight on the 7th of June Rodgers saw this formidable iron-clad coming down at the mouth of Wilmington River, accompanied by two other steamers. He immediately beat to quarters and cleared for action. In a few minutes the bow of his vessel was pointing toward the Atlanta, followed by the Nahant. When about a mile and a half distant the Atlanta fired a rifle-shot which passed across the stern of the Weehawken. The hostile vessel at this time was lying across the stream waiting the approach of Rodgers, who kept silently and steadily on, determined to waste no time or ammunition in firing at long range. At a quarter past five, being then within three hundred yards, he commenced firing—planting his huge shot with an accuracy probably never before equalled in a naval combat. The first, a 15-inch cored shot, broke with a crash through the iron plating and wooden backing, strewing the deck with splinters, knocking down forty men by the concussion, and wounding several others with the broken iron and shivered timbers it hurled on every side. Making a hole nearly four feet in circumference, it was as if the head of a barrel had been driven through the side of the vessel, and caused consternation among the crew.

The second, an 11-inch solid shot, broke some of the iron plates. The third, a 15-inch cored shot, struck like a falling rock the pilot-house, knocking it into fragments, and killing two pilots and stunning the men at the wheel. The fourth struck a port stopper in the centre, breaking it in two and driving the fragments through into the vessel. Appalled at the destructive power of these enormous shot, before which his iron-clad became no more than a wooden vessel, the rebel commander hauled down his flag. It was all over in fifteen minutes. So quickly did Rodgers do his work that Downes in the Nahant, though steaming gallantly forward to join the combat, was too late to share it.

The Atlanta had a crew of over a hundred and fifty men, of which sixteen were wounded.

It was a great victory, and, had the battle been a long and doubtful one, would have made the land echo with applause. But Rodgers did his work so quickly, the public could not feel that it had required much effort. Not so, however, with the Department. This iron-clad had caused it much anxiety; and when it heard that she was not only overpowered, but in good condition for efficient service in our own navy, it was highly gratified and sent the following complimentary letter to Rodgers. After speaking of the engagement of the Monitor with the Merrimac, the Secretary of the Navy says:

"Your connection with the Mississippi flotilla, and your participation in the projection and construction of the first iron-clads on the western waters—your heroic conduct in the attack on Drury's Bluff—the high moral courage that led you to put to sea in the Weehawken upon the approach of a violent storm, in order to test the sea-going qualities of these new craft, at the time when a safe anchorage was close under your lee—the brave and daring manner in which you, with your associates, pressed the iron-clads under the concentrated fire of the batteries in Charleston harbor, and there tested and proved the endurance and resisting power of these vessels, and your crowning, successful achievement in the capture of the Fingal, *alias* Atlanta, are all proofs of a skill, and courage, and devotion to the country and the cause of the Union, regardless of self, that cannot be permitted to pass unrewarded. To your heroic daring and persistent moral courage, beyond that of any other individual, is the country indebted for the development, under trying and varied circumstances on the ocean, under enormous batteries on land, and in successful rencontre with a formidable floating antagonist, of the capabilities and qualities of attack and resistance of the monitor class of vessels and their heavy armament. For these heroic and serviceable acts I have presented your name to the President, requesting him to recommend that Congress give you a vote of thanks, in order that you may be advanced to the grade of commodore in the American navy."

Soon after this great victory, Rodgers was detached from the Weehawken. Next winter she went down in a gale in Charleston harbor.

* The lapse of twenty pages after 547 is accounted for by the omission to number the illustrations in their order. See list of illustrations.

CHAPTER XXX.

REAR-ADMIRAL THOMAS T. CRAVEN.

THERE are some rear-admirals whose biographies are not given in the foregoing sketches, not, as remarked in the preface, because they are inferior in any of the great qualities that distinguish our naval commanders, but because their services happened to be of a kind during the war which possess but little interest to the public. Others have attained their rank by seniority. Among the latter is Admiral Craven. He distinguished himself, however, as commander of the Brooklyn, in the passage of the forts below New Orleans, of which he gives the following account:

"In consequence of the darkness of the night and the blinding smoke, I lost sight of your ship, and when following in the line of what I supposed to be your fire, I suddenly found the Brooklyn running over one of the hulks and rafts which sustained the chain barricade of the river. For a few moments I was entangled and fell athwart the stream, our bow grazing the shore on the left bank of the river. While in this situation I received a pretty severe fire from Fort St. Philip. Immediately after extricating my ship from the rafts, her head was turned up stream, and a few minutes thereafter she was feebly butted by the celebrated ram Manassas. She came butting into our starboard gangway, first firing from her trap-door, when within about ten feet of the ship, directly towards our smoke-stack, her shot entering about five feet above the water-line and lodging in the sand-bags which protected our steam-drum. I had discovered this queer-looking gentleman, while forcing my way over the barricade, lying close into the bank, and when he made his appearance the second time I was so close to him that he had not an opportunity to get up his full speed, and his efforts to damage me were completely frustrated, our chain armor proving a perfect protection to our sides. He soon slid off and disappeared in the darkness. A few moments thereafter, being all the time under a raking fire from Fort Jackson, I was attacked by a large rebel steamer. Our port broadside, at the short distance of only fifty or sixty yards, completely finished him, setting him on fire almost instantaneously.

" Still groping my way in the dark, or *under* the *black cloud* of smoke from the fire raft, I suddenly found myself abreast of St. Philip, and so close that the leadsman in the starboard chains gave the soundings "thirteen feet, sir." As we could bring all our guns to bear, for a few brief moments we poured in grape and canister, and I had the satisfaction of completely silencing that work before I left it—my men in the tops witnessing, in the flashes of their bursting shrapnells, the enemy running like sheep for more comfortable quarters.

"After passing the forts we engaged several of the enemy's gunboats; and being at short range—generally from sixty to a hundred yards—the effects of our broadsides must have been terrific. This ship was under fire about one hour and a half. We lost eight men killed, and had twenty-six wounded, and our damages from the enemy's shot and shell are severe."

He afterwards commanded the Niagara, which captured the rebel privateer Georgia after she had been turned into a British merchantman. Born in the District of Columbia, he entered the navy in 1822, and hence has been in the service over forty years. He is distinguished as a gallant, able commander.

REAR-ADMIRAL CHARLES H. BELL

commanded most of the time during the war the Pacific squadron, and although his position was an important one to the country it afforded no opportunity for him to distinguish himself. A native of New York State, he entered the navy in the opening of the war of 1812, and hence at the beginning of the rebellion had been nearly fifty years in the service. Although on the retired list, he near the close of the war was put in command of the Navy Yard at New York.

REAR-ADMIRAL GEORGE F. PEARSON,

who succeeded him in the command of the Pacific squadron, was most of the time stationed at the Portsmouth navy yard, and hence took little part in active operations afloat. He succeeded in 1864 in capturing a gang of desperadoes under the leadership of an officer of the rebel navy, who had embarked in disguise on board of the steamship San Salvador at Panama for the purpose of seizing her, and then capture treasure-ships, and prey on our commerce in the Pacific Ocean. For this he received the thanks of the secretary of the navy. The officer who had direct charge of the business was Commander H. K.

Davenport. A native of New Hampshire, he entered the navy in 1814, and hence has been over half a century in the service.

REAR-ADMIRAL SYLVANUS GODON

has won his way up by meritorious service, having distinguished himself in the first great naval combat of the war—the capture of Port Royal by Dupont, and in the last action, the bombardment of Fort Fisher, in which as Commodore he commanded a division under Porter. A thorough officer and a gallant man, it is not his fault that he never won renown as the leader of a great expedition. Born in Pennsylvania, he entered the service in 1819. At the close of the war he was given the command of the Brazilian squadron.

REAR-ADMIRAL LARDNER

for a while commanded the gulf blockading squadron, but fell sick under his exposure and hard labor, and was succeeded by Admiral Bailey. He afterwards commanded in the James River, and subsequently was placed over the West India squadron, and continued to command it till near the close of the war, when it was broken up by the Department. A native of Pennsylvania, he entered the service in 1819, and now, under the law which limits the term of service afloat to 47 years, is on the retired list.

REAR-ADMIRAL GREGORY,

who died during the last year at the advanced age of seventy-six, was a native of New Haven, and entered the service in 1800. He distinguished himself in the war of 1812, and was taken prisoner and impressed into the English service, but soon effected his escape. His name was prominent before the public in the celebrated Amistad case, in which he rescued a cargo of Africans from a slaver, and brought them to this country, where they were subsequently released, and returned to their homes by the Government. On the breaking out of the rebellion, although he had reached his threescore and ten, he hastened to Washington to offer his services to the Government. He was given charge of the construction of all the gunboats built in New York and Brooklyn, and took great interest in the building of the first monitor at Greenpoint. He was subsequently charged with the supervision of the East in connection with Commodore Hull. He was an able officer and universally beloved.

REAR-ADMIRAL WILLIAM RADFORD

was another Southerner by birth, who maintained his loyalty when so many went over to the Confederacy. Born in Virginia, he entered the navy in 1825, and hence had been in the service about thirty years when the war broke out. With the new Ironsides as his flag-ship, he commanded the ironclad division in the attack on Fort Fisher. He now commands the navy yard at Washington.

There are several others on the retired list, all gallant officers, the notice of whom, however, does not come within the scope of this work, which has to do only with those who took an active part in the recent war. Their record belongs to a naval history in which their names will hold a conspicuous place.

COMMODORE HENRY WALKE.

What has been said of the admirals would apply also to our commodores, excepting that most of the latter won their rank for gallant services under other commanders, in the biographies of whom a detailed account of those services is given.

A separate sketch of these, therefore, to be lengthy, would require a recapitulation of what has been said previously, and could not have been omitted in an account of the events narrated. Among these, Commodore Walke stands conspicuous.

His first command was the Tyler, a wooden gunboat constantly on duty between Cairo and Columbus, protecting our pickets and advanced posts. This boat, with the Lexington, conveyed the transports which carried the troops under Grant and McClernand to Belmont, and, after the battle, covered their embarkation. He also boldly advanced against the batteries, and for some time took their concentrated fire. His boat and the Lexington doubtless saved the crowded transports, in the retreat, from destruction.

He was soon afterwards transferred to the ironclad Carondelet, and took a prominent part in the attack on Fort Henry—his vessel firing over a hundred shots. His bold diversion in favor of Grant, and single-handed fight with Fort Donaldson, are mentioned in the sketch of Admiral Foote. In the subsequent fight his vessel suffered severely—having her wheel-house shot away, her rudder broken, and over thirty of her crew killed and wounded. This however was the first gunboat to take possession of the enemies' works; and it being Sunday when the surrender was made, Captain Walke had divine service on board for the purpose of publicly thanking God for the great victory. Foote wrote a warm letter to the Department, eulogizing Walke highly and urging his promotion. But the passage of the batteries of Island No. 10 at midnight, in the midst of a terrible thunder-storm, a full description of which is given in the sketch of Admiral Foote, was the great act that distinguished him during this war. In this he stands out in all the sublime, grand proportions of a true hero, and will ever be held up as a model to be studied by our young naval officers. So also much might be said of

COMMODORE JAMES ALDEN,

who, in the Brooklyn, was appointed to lead the fleet in the passage of Fort Morgan, and joined in the bombardment of Fort Fisher; but these services are mentioned in other places.

Commodores James McKinstry, Oliver S. Glisson, Augustus H. Kilty, John B. Marchand, Wm. Rodgers Taylor, Benjamin F. Sands, Daniel B. Ridgely, and others, stand high in the roll of honor, and have received the warm commendation of their superiors.

CAPTAIN PERCIVAL DRAYTON.

Most of the present captains in the navy have won their rank by gallant services in the various engagements which have been described in the sketches of those commanders who fought them. Captain Drayton, had he lived, would, doubtless, have received by this time a high rank. A South Carolinian by birth, he, nevertheless, stood nobly by the old flag, and in his first action—that of Port Royal—hurled his shot against the fort commanded by his own brother. He served with distinction under Dupont, who sent him to Fernandina and the adjacent waters to complete the conquest of the Southern coast. In such high estimation was he held, that Farargut selected him to command his flag-ship—the Hartford—when he forced the entrance to the harbor of Mobile.

There are always some officers who, from oversight or neglect, fail to get the promotion they deserve. How many in our navy stand in this category we are unable to say, but one or two, we are certain, ought to feel themselves hardly used, and among them Captain JAMES H. STRONG. Few were more constantly on duty or oftener under fire than he, and, as commander of the naval force that co-operated with General Banks, in his movement against Texas, he won the commendation of that general as well as of the commodore of the fleet. But the act which, in any navy in the world, would have secured his promotion, was his daring attack, single-handed, of the ram Tennessee, after he had passed Fort Morgan. Before Farragut had signalled the fleet to ram her, he wheeled out of line and ran with a full head of steam on straight into the ironclad monster, crushing in his own bows fearfully. Battered and broken, he wheeled again and drove his shattered bow a second time into her, while the shot tore through his decks. It was a gallant deed, and should have secured his promotion to commodore in the final action on the merit roll.

The same might be said of WM. LE ROY, who was the last to strike the ram, and received her surrender.

Statement of vessels captured and destroyed for violation of the blockade, or in battle, from May, 1861, to May, 1865, from the Official Report of the Secretary of the Navy.

Class.	Name.	Cargo.	When captured.	Where captured.	By what vessel.
			1861		
Schooner	A. J. Russell	Cotton	May 3	Hampton roads	Cumberland
Ship	Argo	Tobacco	May 14	"	"
Schooner	Arcola	Corn, &c.	May 22	"	Minnesota
Schooner	Almira Ann	Timber	May 17	"	"
Schooner	Aid		June 5	Mobile bay	Niagara
Ship	Amelia	Assorted	June 18	Charleston	Wabash and Union
Brig	Amy Warwick	Coffee	June 10	Hampton roads	Minnesota
Sloop	Alena		June 15	Potomac river	Mount Vernon
Schooner	Achilles	In ballast	June 17	Chandeleur island	Massachusetts
Schooner	Ann Ryan	Timber	July 4	Galveston	South Carolina
Brig	Alvarado		Aug. 6	St. Mary's river	Jamestown
Schooner	Abbie Bradford		Aug. 13	Mississippi river	Powhatan
Schooner	Albion	Coffee, &c.	Aug. 16	Charleston	Roanoke & Seminole
Schooner	Aigburth	Molasses	Aug. 31	Lat. 30°, long. 80°	Jamestown
Schooner	Aristides	None	Sept. 27	Key West	
Schooner	Alert	Salt, fruit, &c.	Oct. 6	Charleston	Roanoke and Flag
Brig	Ariel		"	"	Vandalia
Brig	Ariel	Salt	Oct. 20	Wilmington, N. C.	Gemsbok
Schooner	Argonaut		Sept. 13		Susquehanna
Schooner	Adeline	Coffee, sugar, &c	Nov. 17	Off Cape Carnaveral	Connecticut
Schooner	Albion	Assorted	Nov. 25	Coast of S. Carolina.	Penguin & Alabama
Ship	Admiral	Coal, salt, &c.	Dec. 12	Tybee	Alabama
Steamer	Anna	Rosin, turpentine, &c.	Nov. 22	Mississippi sound	New London & R. R. Cuyler
Schooner	A. J. View	Turpentine and tar	"	"	New London & R. R. Cuyler
Sloop	Advocate	None	Dec. 1	"	New London, &c
			1862		
Schooner	Anna Smith	Turpentine and rosin	Jan. 10	Cedar Keys	Hatteras
Schooner	Arrow	Salt, &c.	Feb. 25	St. John's, Florida	Bienville & Mohican
Sloop	Atlanta			West coast of Florida	Ethan Allen
Yacht	America	None	March	East coast of Florida	Ottawa, &c.
Steamer	Albemarle		Mar. 14	Newbern, N. C.	Rowan's expedition
Schooner	A. H. Partridge	Rosin & shingles	"	"	"
Schooner	Alphonsina				
Schooner	Anna Belle	Coffee, spirits, &c	March	Cape Blass	Pursuit
Schooner	Alert	Assorted	Feb. 26	St. John's, Florida	Bienville
Schooner	Active	Salt and coffee	April 26	Stono, S. Carolina	Flambeau
Steamer	Alfred Robb		April 19	Florence, Alabama.	Tyler
Ship	Alliance	Assorted	April 26	Captured at Fort Macon	Daylight and Chippewa
Schooner	Albert	Soap, salt, &c.	May 1	Charleston	Huron
Sloop	Annie	Cotton	April 29	Gulf of Mexico	Kanawha
Steamer	Alice	Bacon	May 14	Roanoke river	Perry, Lockwood & Ceres
Schooner	Actor	Machinery	Mar. 6	Pamlico river, N. C.	Ceres
Schooner	Andromeda	Cotton, &c.	May 26	Mural, Cuba	Pursuit
Schooner	Agnes H. Ward	"	June 1	Coast of S. Carolina	Northern Light
Schooner	Amer'n Coaster	None	June 7	Pamunkey river	Currituck
Schooner	Agnes	Cotton, &c.	July 16		Huntsville
Schooner	Aquilla	Turpentine	Aug. 4	Charleston	Huron
Steamer	Adela		July 7	Bahamas	Quaker City and Huntsville
Steamer	Ann	Arms and ammunition	June 19	Mobile	Susquehanna & Kanawha
Schooner	Albemarle		Mar. 25	Pungo river, N. C.	Delaware
Sloop	America	None	April 10	Newtogan c'k, N. C.	Com. Perry, &c
Schooner	Anna Sophia	Assorted	Aug. 27	Gulf of Mexico	R. R. Cuyler
Schooner	Arctic			Potomac river	Freeborn
Schooner	Agnes		Sept. 25	St. Andrew's sound, Ga.	Florida
Sloop	Ann Squires	Assorted	Oct. 1	Wicomico bay	William Bacon.
Tug	Anglo American		Aug. 23	Mississippi river	Essex
Ram	Arkansas			"	"
Schooner	Adventure	Rope, &c.	Oct. 1	Pensacola	Kensington, &c.
Steamer	A. B.		Aug. 15	Corpus Christi	Arthur

Class.	Name.	Cargo.	When captured.	Where captured.	By what vessel.
			1862.		
Schooner...	Annie Dees.....	Turpentine, &c.	Nov. 7	Charleston..........	Seneca
Schooner...	Adelaide	....	Oct. 21	Sounds of N. Car. ..	Ellis
Steamer....	Anglia	Drugs, &c......	Oct. 24	Bull's bay..........	Flag & Restless
Schooner...	Ariel...........	Assorted........	Nov. 15	Lat. 24°, long. 83° ..	Huntsville
Schooner...	Agnes..........	None	Nov. 24	Indian river........	Sagamore
Schooner...	Alicia...........	Cotton..........	Dec. 10	.... "	"
Schooner...	Ariel...........	Salt.............	Nov. 18	Shallotte inlet, N. C.	Monticello
Schooner...	Ann Maria.....	"	... " ...	.... "	"
Sloop.......	Ann............	Salt, &c........	Dec. 30	Jupiter inlet........	Gem of the Sea
			1863.		
Sloop.......	Avenger	Coffee, salt, &c.	Jan. 5	.... "	Sagamore
Steamer....	Antona.........	Munitions of war	Jan. 6	Cape St. Blas.......	Pocahontas
Steamer....	A. W. Baker ...	....	Feb. 3	Mississippi river....	Queen of the West
Schooner ...	A.W.Thompson	Sutler's stores..	Feb. 28	Piney Point........	Wyandank
Boat	Alligator.......	....	Feb. 8	Caloosahatchie river	Julia
Schooner ...	Avon...........	Salt............	Feb. 14	Abaco..............	Tioga
Schooner...	Annie..........	.. "	Feb. 25	Wilmington........	State of Georgia
Brig........	Atlantic........	....	Mar. 15	Havana............	Sonoma
Steamer....	Aries...........	Dry Goods, &c.	Mar. 28	Bull's Bay, S. Car..	Stettin
Schooner...	Antelope.......	....	Mar. 31	Charleston	Memphis
Schooner...	Agnes	Cotton..........	"	Tortugas...........	Two Sisters
Sloop.......	Aurelia........	.. "	Mar. 23	Mosquito inlet......	Arizona
Schooner...	Anna...........	Coffee, salt, &c..	Feb. 26	Suwanee river......	Fort Henry
Schooner...	Ascension	....	April 14	Havana............	Huntsville
Schooner...	Annie B........	Cotton.........	April 17	Lat. 27°, long. 83° ..	Wanderer
Schooner...	Alabama.......	Brandy, &c.....	April 18	Lat. 29°, long. —°...	Susquehanna
Schooner...	A. Carson......	Assorted	April 24	Chesapeake bay	W. World and S. Rotan
Schooner...	Alma...........	.. "	May 8	....	Perry
Schooner...	Amelia.........	Cotton..........	"	Charleston.........	Flag, Canandaigua, Wamsutta
Sloop.......	Angelina	.. "	May 16	At sea..............	Courier
Schooner...	A. J. Hodge....	Assorted........	May 13	Lat. 28°, long. 86°..	Huntsville
Ram	Arkansas.......	....	May 20	Yazoo city..........	Yazoo Pass expedition
Steamer....	Argo...........	....	"	.... "	"
Iron-clad, rebel.....	Atlanta.........	....	June 17	Savannah..........	Weehawken and Nahant
Schooner...	Anna Maria....	Cotton..........	June 28	Steinhathee river...	Fort Henry
Schooner...	Arctic..........	None...........	May 28	Great Yiocomico....	Satellite
Schooner...	Ann	Cotton..........	July 6	Charlotte Harbor, Florida...........	Restless
Schooner...	Artist..........	Drugs, &c......	Aug. 15	Lat. 28°, long. 95° ..	Bermuda
Brig........	Atlantic........	....	Aug. 10	Rio Grande.........	Princess Royal
Steamer....	Alice Vivian....	Cotton	Aug. 16	Gulf of Mexico	De Soto
Schooner...	Ann............	Assorted........	Aug. 8	Gilbert's bar	Sagamore
Steamer....	Alonzo Childs ..	....	....	....	Mississippi squadron
Steamer....	Arabian	....	Sept. 15	New inlet, N. Car..	Shenandoah
Brig	Atlantic........	....	Aug. 14	Off the Rio Grande.	
Steamer....	Alabama	Assorted	Sept. 12	Chandeleur island ..	Eugenie
Steamer....	Argus..........	....	Oct. 7	Red river...........	Black Hawk
Boat	Alice...........	....	July 13	....	Fort Henry
Schooner...	Arctic..........	....	Nov. 15	At sea..............	Ladona
Schooner...	Anita	Cotton..........	Oct. 27	At sea..............	Granite City
English sch.	Amelia Ann.....	Assorted........	Nov. —	Brazos Santiago....	"
Schooner...	Albert, or Wenona	.. "	Nov. 30	Off Mobile..........	Kanawha
British sch..	Antoinette	....	Dec. 8	Cumberland beach..	Braziliera
Steamer....	Antonica.......	....	Dec. 20	Off Wilmington	Gov. Buckingham
			1864.		
Sloop.......	Annie Thomps'n	Assorted........	Jan. 16	St. Cath.'s sound...	Fernandina
Schooner...	Arietta, or Martha...........	Coffee..........	Mar. 3	Off Tybee island....	
Steamer....	Alliance........	Assorted........	April 12	Off Savannah	S. Car., T. A. Ward
Mexican sch	Alma	.. "	April 19	Coast of Texas......	Virginia
Schooner...	Amanda........	.. "	May 14	Off Espiritu Santo Pass..............	Kanawha
Schooner...	Agnes	....	May 3	Off Velasco, Texas..	Chocura
Schooner...	Ann C. Davenport..........	Lumber	May 12	Alligator river......	Ceres and Rockland
Steamer....	Arrow..........	Cotton & tobacco	July 28	Gatesville, N. C....	Naval and army capture

Class.	Name.	Cargo.	When Captured.	Where captured.	By what vessel.
			1864.		
Steamer....	A. D. Vance....	Cotton..........	Sept. 10	At sea..............	Santiago de Cuba
Steamer....	Annie..........	Cotton, &c......	Oct. 31	Off New inlet.......	Kansas, &c.
Schooner...	Annie Virden...	Cotton..........	Oct. 5	Off Valasco.........	Mobile
Steamer....	Annie..........	....	Oct. 7	Near Cape Fear.....	Aster
Schooner...	Ann Louisa....	....	Sept. 6	Lat. 26° 30' N.; long. 89° 30' W.........	Proteus
Rebel ram..	Albemarle......	....	....	Roanoke river......	Torpedo boat (Lieut. Cushing)
Rebel steam	Alabama.......	Armed vessel...	June 19	Off Cherbourg, Fr..	Kearsarge
Schooner...	Albert Edward.	Cotton..........	Oct. 31	Lat. 27° N.; long. 94° W...............	Katahdin
Steamer....	Armstrong......	Cotton, &c......	Dec. 4	Lat. 32° N.; long. 77° W...............	R. R. Cuyler and others
Schooner...	Alabama........	Assorted........	Dec. 7	Off St. Louis Pass...	Princess Royal and Chocura
			1865.		
Schooner...	Augusta........	Assorted........	Jan. 17	Suwanee river, Fla.	Honeysuckle
Steamer....	Amazon........	Cotton	Mar. 2	Savannah river.....	Pontiac
Schooner...	Annie Sophia...	.. „	Feb. 7	Galveston Bay	Bienville and Princess Royal
Rebel sch...	Anna Dale	Ammunition,&c.	Feb. 18	Pass Cavallo........	Panola
Sloop.......	Annie..........	Cotton..........	April 11	Crystal river, Fla..	Sea Bird
			1861.		
Schooner...	Belle Conway..	Tobacco	May 15	Hampton roads.....	Minnesota
Schooner...	Brilliante......	Flour...........	June 23	Mississippi sound...	Massachusetts
Schooner...	Basilde.........	Salt and oats....	„	.... „	„
Schooner...	Brunette.......	Iron and vitriol.	July 16	Coast of Maryland..	Potomac flotilla
Schooner...	Baltimore......	Salt and sugar..	Sept. 29	Hatteras inlet......	Susquehanna
Schooner...	Beverly.........	....	Oct. 3	....	Gemsbok
Schooner...	Bachelor	....	....	Potomac river......	Potomac flotilla
Schooner...	Buena Vista....	Assorted	July 17	.... „	Resolute
Schooner...	Beauregard.....	None...........	Nov. 13	Bahama channel....	W. G. Anderson
Brig........	B. F. Martin ...	....	July 28	Hatteras...........	Union
Sloop.......	Blooming Youth	....	Dec. 18	Alexandria, Va.....	Perry
			1862.		
Schooner...	Black Warrior..	....	Feb. —	Elizabeth City.....	Rowan's expedition
Schooner...	British Queen...	Salt and coffee..	Mar. 1	Wilmington.........	Mount Vernon
Steamer....	Bermuda.......	Powder, &c.....	April 27	Hole-in-Wall.......	Mercedita
Schooner...	Belle...........	Salt, &c........	April 26	Charleston.........	Uncas
Schooner...	British Empire..	Provisions, &c..	....	Maratanzas inlet....	Isaac Smith
Schooner...	Baigorry	Cotton..........	June 9	Lat. 23°, long. 83° ..	Bainbridge.
Sloop.......	Beauregard.....	Lumber........	....	Coast of Texas......	Rachel Seaman
Sloop.......	Blossom........	Wheat	Aug. 12	Potomac river......	Reliance
Schooner...	Breaker........	None...........	„	Coast of Texas......	Arthur
Sloop.......	Bellefont.......	....	Feb. —	.... „	„
Sloop.......	Belle Italia.....	None...........	July 10	.... „	„
Schooner...	Brilliant........	Salt............	Nov. 3	New Topsail inlet..	Daylight
Schooner...	By George......	Coffee, salt, &c.	Dec. 1	Indian river........	Sagamore
			1863.		
Steamer....	Bloomer........	....	Jan. 1	Pensacola..........	Naval and army capture
Schooner...	Brave	....	Jan. 15	....	Octorara
Steamer....	Burton.........	....	Jan. 19	New Orleans, La....	Admiral Farragut's fleet
Steamer....	Berwick Bay...	Sugar,cotton,&c	Feb. 3	Mississippi river ...	Queen of the West
Schooner...	Belle...........	Coffee, salt, &c.	Feb. 23	Sapelo sound.......	Potomska
Schooner...	Brothers........	Assorted........	Mar. 22	Abaco.............	Tioga
Schooner...	Bangor.........	....	Mar. 25	....	Fort Henry
Sloop.......	Bright..........	Cotton..........	April 24	Gulf of Mexico	De Soto
Sloop	Blazer.........	.. „	May 27	Lat. 26°, long. 96°..	Brooklyn
Steamer....	Britannia.......	„	June 25	Lat. 25°, long. 74°...	Santiago de Cuba
Ship.......	Banshee........	....	July 29	New Inlet.........	Niphon
Schooner...	Bettie Cratzer..	None...........	June 23	Coast of N. Car....	Flambeau
Sloop.......	Blue Belle......	Sugar, &c......	July 2	Sabine Pass........	Cayuga
Boat.......	Buckshot.......	....	Aug. 7	....	San Jacinto
Steamer....	Banshee	Assorted.......	Nov. 21	„	Grand Gulf and Fulton
Schooner....	Bigelow.........	None...........	Dec. 16	Bear Inlet.........	Not known
			1864.		
Steamer....	Bendigo........	....	Jan. 3	Off Wilmington....	Blockading squadron
Sloop.......	Buffalo.........	Cotton..........	Feb. 1	St. Andrew's sound Ga....	Braziliera

Class.	Name.	Cargo.	When captured.	Where captured.	By what vessel.
			1864.		
Steamer....	Bombshell......	....	May 5	Off Plymouth, N. C.	Mattabesett and others
Steamer....	Boston..........	Assorted........	July 8	Off Wilmington....	Fort Jackson
Steamer....	Bat.............	Machinery......	Oct. 10	,, ...	Montgomery, &c.
Schooner...	Badger..........	Cotton....	Nov. 6	St. George's Sound, Fla.......	Adela
Steamer....	Beatrice........	....	Nov. 27	Off Charleston, S. C.	Picket boats
Schooner...	Belle...........	Cotton........	Dec. 27	Galveston, Texas...	Virginia
			1865.		
Steamer....	Blenheim.......	Assorted........	Jan. 24	Cape Fear river....	N. Atlantic squadron
Schooner....	Ben Willis.	Cotton..........	Feb. 2	Lat. 28° N., long, 92° W....	Panola
Gunboat. ..	Beaufort........	Ammunition,&c	Mar. —	Richmond, Va.....	Part of N. Atlantic squadron
Rebel st'r..	Baltic..........	,, ...	May 10	Tombigbee river....	Part of West Gulf squadron
Rebel st'r..	Black Diamond	,, ...	,,	,, ...	,,
			1861.		
Schooner...	Cecilia..........	....	Sept. 24	....	Dart
Schooner...	Cambria.........	Coal............	April 23	Hampton roads....	Cumberland
Schooner...	Carrie..........	,, ...	May 2	,, ...	,,
Schooner...	Crenshaw..... ..	Tobacco...... ...	May 17	,, ...	Minnesota
Schooner...	Catherine..... ..	....	May 27	,, ...	,,
Schooner....	Caroline........	General....	July 5	Galveston....	South Carolina
Schooner...	C. P. Knapp....	....	Aug. 8	....	Santee
Sloop.......	Charles Henry.	Fish....	April 7	Chandeleur island..	Massachusetts
Schooner...	Col. Long......	Assorted........	Sept. 4	At sea..............	Jamestown
Schooner....	Cheshire........	Blankets, &c...	Dec. 6	Savannah..........	Flag, Seneca, Pocahontas, Augusta, and Savannah
Schooner....	Charity....	Assorted........	Dec. 15	Hatteras inlet......	Stars and Stripes
Schooner....	Capt. Spedden..	Lumber..	Dec. 31	Biloxi.............	Harry Lewis, Water-Witch and New London
			1862.		
Steamer....	Calhoun...... ...	Powder, rifles, &c..........	Jan. 23	Southwest Pass.....	Colorado, Rachel Seaman, and tender of Samuel Rotan
Steamer....	Curlew.........	....	Feb. —	Roanoke island.....	Rowan's expedition
Sloop.......	Caroline.... ...	....	Mar. —	West coast of Fla...	Ethan Allen
Schooner....	Cora.......... ...	Cotton..........	,,	Lat. 26°, long. 84°..	Panola
Schooner....	Clifton.........	....	Mar. 14	Newbern...........	Rowan's expedition
Sloop.......	Coquette.......	Assorted......	April 3	Charleston bar.....	Susquehanna
Pilot boat..	Cygnet.........	....	April 2	Apalachicola........	Mercedita and Sagamore
Schooner....	Columbia........	Cotton.........	April 5	Coast of Texas.....	Montgomery
Schooner....	Charlotte......	,, ...	April 10	Mobile.............	Kanawha
Schooner....	Cuba............	Powder, &c....	,,	,,	,,
Steamer....	Circassian..	Assorted...... ...	May 4	Coast of Cuba......	Somerset
Steamer....	Constitution....	....	May 22	Lockwood's Folly inlet...............	Mount Vernon, Victoria, and State of Georgia
Steamer....	Cambria........	Rifles, drugs, &c	May 26	Charleston........	Huron
		Cotton, 45 bales	....	At Sea.............	Arletta and Dan
Schooner...	Cora....	Salt............	May 31	Charleston....	Keystone State
Gunboat....	Corypheus......	....	May 13	Bayou Bonfouca....	Calhoun
Steamer....	Clara Dolson...	....	....	....	Mound City
Schooner...	Catalina........	Cotton..........	June 20	Charleston.........	Alabama and Flambeau
Schooner....	Curlew.........	Dry goods, &c..	June 16	Cedar Keys....	Somerset
Schooner....	Chance.........	Salt............	June 28	Warsaw Sound.....	Braziliera
		Cotton, 30 bales	Mar. 14	Sounds of N. Car....	Naval expedition
Schooner...	Caroline Virginia	None..........	,,	Newbern...........	Rowan's expedition
Schooner...	Comet.........	None...........	April 10	Newtogan c'k N. C..	Commodore Perry and others
		Cotton, 52 bales	July 9	Coast of Texas.....	Arthur
Propeller...	Columbia.......	Cannon, rifles, &c..........	Aug. 3	Lat. 28°, long. 76°...	Santiago de Cuba
Schooner. ..	Corelia.........	Assorted........	Aug. 23	Lat. 23°, long. 84°..	James S. Chambers
Schooner....	Chapel Point...	....	Sept. 20	Potomac river......	Jacob Bell
Schooner....	Conchita....	....	Oct. —	Coast of Texas.....	Crocker's expedition

Class.	Name.	Cargo.	When captured.	Where captured.	By what vessel.
			1862.		
Steamer	Carolina	Munitions of war	Oct. 28	Lat. 29°, long. 87°	Montgomery
Sloop	Capitola	None	Nov. 8	Glymont, Md	Resolute
Sloop	Caperton		„		„
Schooner	Corse	Drugs, &c	Nov. 11	Sabine Pass	Velocity, Dan Kensington, and Rachel Seaman
Schooner	Courier	Salt, coffee, &c.	Dec. 22	Lat. 24°, long. 83°	Huntsville
Brig	Comet	Assorted	Dec. 26	Abaco	Santiago de Cuba
Schooner	Carmita	„	Dec. 27	Marquesas keys	Magnolia
			1863.		
Ship	C. A. Farwell		Jan. 19	New Orleans, La	Admiral Farragut's fleet
		Coal, 16,000 tons	„	„	„
Steamer	Ceres		„	„	„
Schooner	Chatham		Feb. 27	Alexandria, Va	Adolf Hugel
Steamer	Curlew		Feb. 28		New Era
Schooner	Charm	Cotton	Feb. 23	Indian river	Gem of the Sea
Schooner	C. W. Worrell		Feb. 24		Wyandank
Schooner	Clara	General	Mar. 25	Mobile	Kanawha
		Cotton, 179 bales	Mar. 30	Deer creek	Mississippi squadron
Schooner	Clyde	Cotton, &c	April 14	Campeachy bank	Sonoma
Sloop	Crotilda	Cotton	April 16	Lat. 28°, long. 80°	McClellan
Steamer	Cherokee	do	May 7	Charleston bar	Canandaigua and Flag
		Cotton, 12 bales, 2 bags, and 1 crate	April 20	Apalachicola	Port Royal
Steamer	Cuba		May 17	Lat. 28°, long 87°	De Soto
Brigantine	Comet	Assorted	May 15	Fort Morgan	Kanawha
Boat	Crazy Jane	Cotton, &c	May 8	Tampa bay, Florida.	Tahoma
Sloop	C. Ronterean	„	May 16	Charleston	S. Atlantic block-ad'g squadron.
Schooner	Clarita	Assorted	April 26	Lat. 26°, long. 83°	De Soto
Steamer	Calypso	„	June 11	Wilmington	Florida
		Cotton, 57 bales	June 1	Crystal river	Fort Henry and Beauregard
		Cotton, 39 bales.	June 3	„	Fort Henry and Beauregard
		Cotton, 52½ bales	June 21	At sea	Octorara and Tioga
		Cotton, 22 bales.	June 19		Fort Henry
		Cotton, 138 bales	July 26		Hendrick Hudson
		Cotton, 116 bales	July 11		De Soto
		Cotton, 5 bales	Aug. 7		San Jacinto
		Cotton, 15 bales.	July 29		Port Royal
		Cotton, 5 bales			
		Cotton, 17 bales.			
		Cotton, 54 bales.			
		Cotton, 50 lbs			
		Cotton, 13 bales	April 20		Port Royal
		Cotton, 12 bales.	July —	Near Apalachicola	„
		Cotton, 14 bags.	July —	„	„
		Cotton, 64 bales, &c	July —	St. Joseph's bay	J. L. Davis
		Cotton, 150 bales	Dec. —	Mississippi squadron	Osage
		Cotton, 18 bales.	Dec. —	„	„
Steamer	Charleston		July 11	Wilmington	Seminole
Schooner	Cassandra	Whiskey, &c	„	Rappahannock river	Yankee.
Sloop	Clara Ann	„	Aug. 1	Cone river	„
Sloop	Clotilda	Cotton	July 26	Mosquito inlet	Sagamore, &c
		Cotton, 22 bales.	July 17	Wacassassa river	Fort Henry
		Cotton, 138½ bales	do. 19-26	Cape San Blas	Hendrick Hudson.
Steamer	Cronstadt	Cotton, &c	Aug. 16	Lat. 27°, long. 76°	Rhode Island
Schooner	Carmita	Cotton	Aug. 14	Lat. 26°, long. 95	Bermuda
Sloop	Clara Louisa	Whiskey, &c	Aug. 8	Indian River inlet	Sagamore
		Cotton, several lots			Mississippi squadron
Schooner	Charmer		July 26	Mosquito inlet	Sagamore, &c.
Steamer	Cornubia		Nov. 8	Off New Inlet	Jas. Adger and Niphon
Steamer	Chatham	Cotton	Dec 16	Dobey sound	Huron
Eng. stem'r.	Ceres		Dec. 6	Cape Fear river	Conn. and others

Class.	Name.	Cargo.	When captured.	Where captured.	By what vessel.
			1863.		
Schooner....	Caroline........	Cotton..........	Dec. 28	Oclockney river, Fla.	Stars and Stripes
Schooner....	Concordia.......	....	Oct. 5	Calcasieu Pass......	Granite City
			1864.		
Sloop........	Caroline........	Salt, &c........	Jan. 18	Jupiter inlet........	Roebuck
		Cotton, 50 bales.	Jan. 6	At sea..............	Vanderbilt
		Cotton, 67 bales.	Feb. 26	Suwanee river, Fla..	Clyde
		Cotton, 2,129 bales.........	....	....	Mississippi squadron
		Molasses,28 brl's	....	....	"
		Cotton, 450 bales	Feb. —	Port Pemberton.....	Expedition up Yazoo
Steamer....	Cumberland....	Assorted........	Feb. 5	At sea..............	De Soto
Schooner....	Camilla.........	Cotton..........	Feb. 29	San Luis Pass......	Virginia
Sloop.......	Cassie Holt.....	....	"	.... "	"
Steamer....	Caledonia	....	May 30	At sea..............	Massachusetts and Keystone State
Sloop....	Caroline........	....	June 10	Jupiter inlet........	Union
Sloop.......	Cyclops	Cotton..........	June 12	Off Charleston......	Flag
Schooner....	Coquette........	....	Oct. 26	Potomac river......	Adolph Hugel
Steamer....	Condor	....	Oct. 1	....	
Steamer....	Constance	....	Oct. 5	Off Charleston......	
		Cotton, 78 bales and 2 half bls.	May 31	At sea..............	Vicksburg
		Cotton,109 bales.	April 23	Suwanee river......	Sagamore
		Cotton, 88 bales.	June 4	Off Cape Lookout..	Keystone State
		Cotton, 34 bags.	June 14	Wacassassa river....	J. S. Chambers and Clyde
		Cotton, 27 bales.	June 20	.... "	"
		Cotton, 40 bales.	June 26	At sea..............	Quaker City
		Cotton, 4 bales and 152 bags.	July 7	.. "	Fort Jackson
		Cotton, 94 bales.	"	Suwanee river	Sagamore and Clyde
		Cotton, 90 bales.	July 11	At Sea.............	Connecticut
		Cotton, 2 bales..	July 13	.. "	Massachusetts
		Cotton, 161 bales and 3 half bls.	July 26	.. "	Keystone State
		Cotton, 90 bales.	July 28	Gatesville, N. C....	Whitehead
		Cotton, 82 bales.	July —	At sea..............	Aries
		Cotton,235 bales.	Aug. 7	.. "	Keystone State
		Cotton, 12 bags.	Aug. 8	.. "	"
		Cotton, 43 bales and 3,500 lbs. loose..........	Aug. 7	.. "	Santiago de Cuba
		Cotton, 30 bales.	Aug. 10	.. "	Monticello
		Cotton, 30 bales.	"	.. "	Gettysburg
		Cotton,12,000lbs. good, 1,200 lbs. pickings	"	.. "	Monticello and Mt. Vernon
		Cotton, 22 bales and 2 bags....	"	Lat. 33° 9′ N.; long. 76° 36′ W.	Mount Vernon
		Cotton, 23 bales.	Aug. 13	Off Beaufort........	"
		Cotton, 42 bales and 11 bags...	Aug. 24	Suwance river......	Clyde
		Cotton, 80 bales.	Aug. 25	At sea..............	Keystone State, Gettysburg
		Cotton, 52 bales.	Aug. —	.... "	R. R. Cuyler
		Cotton, 83 bales.	Sept. 9	Off Galveston.......	Sciota
		Cotton, 81 bales.	Sept. 11	Off Velasco.........	Augusta Dinsmore
		Cotton, 38 bales.	Sept. 13	Gulf of Mexico.....	Aroostook
		Cotton, 4 bales..	Sept. 30	Albemarle sound...	Wyalusing
		Cotton, 4,000 or 5,000 pounds.	Sept. 16	Yellow Bluff, Fla...	Hendrick Hudson
		Cotton, 5 bales..	Mar. 13	Up St. John's River	Pawnee and others
		Cotton, 93 bales.	Mar. 14	"	"
Schooner....	Cora Smyser....	Assorted.......	Oct 28	Off Velasco, Texas..	Sciota and Chocura
Schooner....	Carrie Mair	....	Nov. 30	Pass Caballo, Texas.	Itasca
		Cotton, 133 bales	Dec. 5	Lat. 32° N., long. 77° W.	Gettysburg and others
		Cotton 27 bales.	"	At sea..............	Mackinaw
Schooner....	Cora............	Cotton..........	Dec. 19	Off Galveston island	Princess Royal

Class.	Name.	Cargo.	When captured.	Where captured.	By what vessel.
			1865.		
		Cotton, 14 bales.	Jan. 5	Lat. 33° N., long. 75° W.	Horace Beals
Steamer....	Charlotte.......	Arms, blankets, &c.	Jan. 19	Cape Fear river.....	Malvern and others
Schooner....	Coquette........	Cotton..........	Jan. 26	Combahee river, S. Carolina	Dai-Ching and Clover
Steamer.....	Celt............	Cotton..........	....	Stranded on Sullivan's island	
Schooner....	Comus..........	Cotton..........	Mar. 31	Lat. 23° N., long. 83° W.	Iuka
Sloop.......	Cath. Coombs...	Whiskey, &c....	Feb. 27	Yorktown, Va......	Crusader
Steamer.....	Cora............	Lumber.........	Mar. 24	Near Brazos de St. Iago.	Quaker City
		Cotton, 5 bales..	April 27	Mississippi river....	Huntress
		Cotton, 50 bales.	April 20	Off Galveston, Texas	Gertrude
Schooner....	Chaos..........	Cotton..........	April 21	"	Cornubia
		Cotton, 140 bales	April 19	"	Cornubia and Gertrude
Steamer....	Cotton Plant....	....	....	Roanoke river......	Boat expedition
		Cotton, 99 bales.	....	"	"
Rebel iron-clad	Columbia.......	....	....	Charleston, S. C....	
			1861.		
Schooner....	Dorothy Haines	Hay.............	May 11	Hampton roads.....	Cumberland
Schooner....	Delaware Farmer	Tobacco.........	May 14	"	"
Schooner....	Dart............	None............	July 4	Galveston..........	South Carolina
H. brig.....	Delta...........	Salt............	Oct. 27	"	Santee
Schooner....	Delight.........	....	Dec. 9	Mississippi sound...	New London
			1862.		
Sloop.......	Dudley or Pinkney	....	Jan. 10	Cedar keys.........	Hatteras
Steamer....	Darlington.....	Wagons, mules.	Mar. 3	Fernandina.........	Naval expedition
Schooner....	Dixie...........	Cotton..........	April 15	Georgetown	Keystone State
Schooner....	Deer Island.....	....	May 13	Mississippi sound...	Bohio
Schooner....	Director........	....	May 4	York river..........	Corwin and Currituck
Schooner....	Director........	None...........	July —	....	
Schooner....	Defiance........	Oil, soap, &c....	Sept. 7	Sapello sound......	Braziliera
Schooner....	David Crockett.	Turpentine, &c..	Oct. 13	Charleston..........	America and Flag
Schooner....	Dart..	Salt, rope, &c...	Oct. 6	Coast of Texas......	Kensington, &c
Steamer....	Dan............	....	Oct. —	"	"
Schooner....	Diana..........	Assorted........	Nov. 26	Pass Cavalo........	Kittatinny
	Dove..........	....	....	....	Magnolia
			1863.		
Steamer....	Diana..........	....	Jan. 19	New Orleans........	Admiral Farragut
Propeller...	Douro..........	Cotton	Mar. 9	Lat. 33°, long. 77°...	Quaker City
Steamer....	Dolphin........	....	Mar. 25	Lat. 19°, long. 65° ..	Wachusett
	D. Sargent.....	Cotton..........	Mar. 12	Galveston..........	Kittatinny
Schooner....	Dart...........	Assorted........	May 1	Mobile............	Kanawha
Steamer....	Dew Drop......	....	May —	....	Yazoo expedition
Schooner....	Don Jose.......	....	July 2	At sea..............	Juniata
Schooner....	Director.......	....	Sept. 30	Point Rossa........	Gem of the Sea
Steamer....	Duoro.........	Assorted.........	Oct. 11	New inlet..........	Nansemond
Steamer....	Diamond.......	....do..........	Sept. 23	St. Simon's sound...	Stettin
Brig........	Dashing Wave.	Medicines......	Nov. 5	Off Rio Grande.....	Owasco, Virginia.
			1864.		
Steamer....	Dare...........	In ballast......	Jan. 9	....	Aries
Schooner....	Defy...........	....	Feb. 3	Off Doboy light, Ga.	Midnight
Steamer....	Dee...........	Assorted........	Feb. 6	Near Masonboro'...	Cambridge
Steamer....	Don...........	"	Mar. 4	Off Beaufort, N. C...	Pequot
Steamer....	Donegal, or Austin.	Munitions of war.	June 6	Off Mobile bay......	Metacomet
			1865.		
Schooner....	Delia..........	Lead and sabres.	Feb. 17	Near Bayport, Fla..	Mahaska
Schooner....	Delphina.......	Cotton..........	Jan. 22	Calcasieu river.	Chocura
Steamer....	Deer...........	Copper, arms, &c.	Feb. 18	Charleston, S. C.....	Monadnock and others
Steamer....	Dolly..........	....	....	Roanoke river, N. C.	Naval expedition
Steamer....	Denbigh.......	....	May 25	....	

Class.	Name.	Cargo.	When captured.	Where captured.	By what vessel.
			1861.		
Schooner....	Elite...........	Coal....	May 4	Hampton roads.....	Cumberland
Schooner....	Emily Ann.....	Tobacco........	May 14	"	"
Schooner....	Elizabeth Ann..	....	....	Coast of Virginia....	Albatross
Schooner....	Enchantress....	Assorted........	July 22	....	"
Schooner....	Extra..........	Wheat..........	Aug. 29	Rappahannock river	Daylight
Schooner....	Eagle....	....	Aug. 12	....	Resolute
Schooner....	Edwin.........	Molasses........	....	Beaufort, N. C......	Cambridge
Schooner....	Ezilda.........	Arms and coffee.	Sept. 30	Barrataria bay......	South Carolina
Schooner....	Ewd. Barnard..	Turpentine.....	Oct. 16	Pass à l'Outre......	"
Bark.......	Empress	Coffee..........	Nov. 26	Northeast Pass, Miss	Vincennes and Miss.
Schooner....	E. J. Waterman	"	Nov. 30	Tybee light.........	Savannah
Sloop.......	Express........	None...........	Dec. 9	Mississippi sound...	New London
Sloop.......	Ellen Jane.....	Marketing.......	Dec. 18	Alexandria, Va.....	Perry
Sloop.......	Eugenia Smith.	....	Dec. 7	Off Rio Grande.....	Santiago de Cuba
			1862.		
Schooner....	Emma..........	Assorted........	Jan. 17	Coast of Florida....	Connecticut
Schooner...	Eugenia Smith.	Coffee, &c.......	Feb. 7	Lat. 28°, long. 91°...	Bohio
Steamer....	Ellis..........	....	Feb. —	Roanoke island.....	Rowan's expedition
Sloop.......	Edisto.........	Rice............	Feb. 14	Bull's Bay..........	Restless
Schooner...	Elizabeth.......	.... ,, ...	,,	.... ,, ...	,,
Schooner...	Eva Bell.......	....	Mar. 14	Newbern..........	Rowan's expedition
Schooner...	Eothen.........	....	,,	.... ,, ...	,,
Schooner...	Eugenie........	Cotton..........	Mar. 16	Off the Mississippi..	Owasco
Ship........	Emily St. Pierre	Gunny Cloth...	Mar. 18	Charleston..........	Blockadi'g squadron
Propeller...	Eureka.........	Cotton, &c......	April —	Potomac river......	Potomac flotilla
Steamer....	Ella Warley....	Arms, &c.......	April 25	Lat. 28°, long. 97°...	Santiago de Cuba
Schooner...	Eugenia.......	....	May 20	North Carolina.....	Hunchback and Whitehead
Schooner...	Ella D..........	Salt	May 22	.... ,, ...	Whitehead
Steamer....	Elizabeth.......	....	May 29	Charleston..........	Keystone State and Jas. Adger
Schooner...	Emily..........	Salt............	June 26	Wilmington.........	Mt. Vernon, Penobscot, Mystic, and Victoria
Steamer....	Emily..........	Assorted........	July 7	Bull's bay..........	Restless and Flag
Schooner...	Emma..........	Salt, &c........	July 23	Lat. 27°, long. 75°...	Adirondack
Schooner...	Elizabeth.......	Cotton.........	July 5	....	Hatteras
Schooner...	Eliza..........	Salt............	Aug. 21	Charleston..........	Bienville
Schooner...	Elmira C'rnelius	Assorted........	Oct. 11	Bull's bay..........	Flag and Restless.
Sloop.......	Eliza..........	....	....	....	Crocker's expedition
Armed sch..	Elmer.........	....	Aug. 12	Coast of Texas......	Arthur
Schooner...	Elias Reed......	Cot'n, rosin, &c.	Nov. 5	Lat. 26°, long. 77°...	Octorara
Schooner...	Emma.........	Cotton, &c.....	Sept. 26	Velasco, Texas.....	Kittatinny
Schooner...	Emma Tuttle...	Assorted........	Nov. 3	New inlet..........	Mt. Vernon and Cambridge
Sloop.......	Ellen.........	....	Nov. 24	Indian river........	Sagamore
Schooner...	Exchange.......	....	Dec. 28	Rappahannock river	Anacostia
			1863.		
Schooner...	Emma Tuttle...	Saltpetre........	Jan. 27	....	Hope
Schooner...	Emily Murray..	Merchandise....	Feb. 9	....	Cœur de Lion
Sloop.......	Elizabeth.......	Salt............	June 28	Jupiter inlet........	Sagamore
Steamer....	Evansville......	....	Feb. 12	Carson's landing....	Conestoga & Duchess.
Sloop.......	Enterprise......	Cotton..........	Mar. 8	....	Sagamore
Sloop.......	Express........	Salt, &c.........	May 4	Coast of S. Carolina	Chocura and Maratanza.
Schooner...	Emma Amelia..	Wines, &c......	May 2	St. Andrew's bay, Fla..............	Roebuck
Sloop.......	Elias Beckwith..	Assorted........	April 23	Mobile.............	Pembina
Steamer....	Eugenie........	.... ,, ...	May 6	.... ,, ...	R. R. Cuyler
Sloop.......	Emeline........	Cotton	May 16	At sea.............	Courier
Schooner...	Emily..........	General.........	May 21	Urbana, Va.........	Currituck, &c.
Schooner...	Echo..........	Cotton.........	May 31	Lat. 25°, long. 83°..	Sunflower
Steamer....	Eagle..........	....	May 18	Lat. 25°, long. 77°..	Octorara
Steamer....	Emma Bett.....	....	May —	....	Yazoo expedition
Sloop.......	Evening Star...	Cotton..........	May 29	Warsaw sound, Ga..	Cimarron
Schooner...	Elizabeth.......	....	June 14	Lat. 23°, long. 83°..	Juniata
Schooner...	Emma.........	Assorted........	June 19	Mosquito inlet......	Para
Sloop.......	Emma.........	Tar, &c.........	July 3	Cedar keys	Fort Henry
Steamer....	Eureka.........	....	July 2	Commerce..........	Covington
Steamer....	Emma.........	Cotton	July 24	Lat. 33°, long. 76°..	Arago, army transport

Class.	Name.	Cargo.	When Captured.	Where captured.	By what vessel.
			1863.		
Steamer....	Elmira..........	Sugar, rum.....	July —	Red river...........	Red River expeditn'
Schooner...	Excelsior.......	Cotton	July 13	Galveston...........	Katahdin
Steamer....	Elizabeth.......	....	Oct. —	Lockwood's Folly inlet................	
Steamer....	Ella and Anna.	....	Nov. 9	....	Niphon
Steamer....	Ella............	....	Nov. 10	Off Fort Fisher.....	Howquah
Steamer....	Eureka.........	Cotton..........	Nov. 22	At Sea..............	Aroostook
Schooner...	Ella............	....	Nov. 26	Masonboro' inlet, N. Carolina..........	James Adger
British sch..	Edward.........	Lead and salt...	Dec. 24	Near Suwanee river.	Fox, tender to San Jacinto
British sch..	Exchange.......	Assorted........	,,	Coast of Texas......	Antona
			1864.		
Schooner...	Ellen...........	.... ,, ...	Jan. 16	Off Mobile..........	Gertrude
British sch..	Eliza...........	Cotton..........	Jan. 19	Jupiter inlet, Fla...	Roebuck
Steamer....	Emily..........	Salt............	Feb. 10	Masonboro' inlet....	Florida
Schooner...	Experiment.....	Cotton	May 3	Coast of Texas.....	Virginia
Steamer....	Emma.........	....	June 9	Near Charlotte har.	Rosalie, tender to Gem of the Sea
Steamer....	Elsie...........	Cotton..........	Sept. 4	At sea..............	Keystone State, Quaker City
Schooner...	Emily..........	.... ,, ...	Oct. 19	Off San Luis Pass...	Mobile
Steamer....	Emma Henry...	.... ,, ...	Dec. 8	Lat. 33°N., long. 77° W...............	Cherokee
Steamer....	Ella............	Munitions......	Dec. 3	Off Wilmington, N. Carolina..........	Emma
			1865.		
Schooner...	Elvira..........	Cotton & tob'cco	Feb. 25	Bull War sound....	Chenango
Brig........	Eco............	Coffee, rice, &c..	Feb. 19	Off Galveston, Tex.	Gertrude
Steamer....	Emma No. 2....	....	Mar. 20	Rodney, Miss.......	
Steamer....	Egypt Mills.....	....	....	Roanoke river, N. C.	Naval expedition
			1861.		
Schooner...	F. W. Johnson..	Iron............	June 1	Chesapeake bay.....	Union
Brig........	Forest King....	Coffee..........	June 13	Key West..........	Mississippi
Schooner...	Fanny..........	Bricks..........	June 23	Mississippi sound...	Massachusetts
Schooner...	Falcon..........	General........	July 5	Galveston...........	South Carolina
Schooner...	Favorite........	....	July 16	Eastern Shore, Md..	Potomac flotilla.
Ship........	Finland.........	....	Aug. 26	Apalachicola bay....	R. R. Cuyler
Schooner...	Falcon.........	....	....	....	
Schooner...	Fanny Lee.....	Rice, &c........	Nov. 6	St. Simon's island...	St. Lawrence
Schooner...	Fairwind........	....	Aug. 29	....	Quaker City
Schooner...	Fashion.........	Green turtle....	Nov. 29	....	Ethan Allen
Sloop.......	Florida.........	....	Dec. 11	Tumbalin lighthouse...........	South Carolina
			1862.		
Steamer....	Forrest.........	....	Feb. —	Roanoke island.....	Rowan's expedition
Steamer....	Fanny	....	,,	.... ,, ...	,,
Schooner...	Florida.........	Coffee, &c......	Mar. 10	Lat. 27° N., long. 84° W...............	J. L. Davis
Schooner...	Fairplay........	Fish, &c	Mar. 12	Georgetown, S. C...	Gem of the Sea
Schooner...	Floyd	....	April 2	Apalachicola	Mercedita and Sagamore
Schooner ...	F. J. Capron...	....	April 29	....	Potomac flotilla
Schooner...	Falcon..........	None...........	April —	Potomac river......	,,
Steamer....	Florida.........	Cotton..........	April 6	St. Andrew's.......	Pursuit
Schooner...	Farren..........	....	....	....	Ethan Allen
Schooner...	Flash..........	Salt, &c........	May 2	Charleston	Restless
Steamer....	Fashion	Cotton, &c......	May 6	....	Hatteras
Bark	Fannie Laurie..	Salt............	Sept. 4	South Edisto	Shepherd Knapp
Schooner...	Fanny..........	.. ,, ...	Aug. 22	St. Simon's.........	Keystone State
Schooner...	Frances.........	Powder, salt, &c	Oct. 23	Coast of Florida....	Sagamore
Sloop.......	Flying Cloud...	....	Dec. 29	....	Magnolia.
Sloop.......	Flying Fish.....	....	Dec. 30	....	"
			1863.		
Schooner...	Five Brothers...	Cotton..........	Mar. 16	Lat. 27° N., long. 77° W...............	Octorara
Schooner...	Florida.........	....	Jan. 11	....	
Schooner...	Florence Nightingale........	Cotton..........	Jan. 13	Lat. 25° N., long. 77° W...............	Tioga and Octorara
Sloop.......	Fashion.........	.. ,, ...	May 23	Apalachicola	Port Royal
Sloop.......	Flying Cloud...	None	June 2	Potomac river......	Primrose

Class.	Name.	Cargo.	When captured.	Where captured.	By what vessel.
			1863.		
Schooner...	Frolic..........	Cotton, &c......	June 25	Crystal river, Fla...	Sagamore and Two Sisters
Boat.......	Florida.........	.. „	June 3	St. Mark's light....	Stars and Stripes
Schooner...	Fashion	Salt, &c.........	June 13	Lat. 23° N., long. 83° W...............	Juniata
Schooner...	Flying Scud....	Cotton..........	Aug. 12	Near Matamoras....	Princess Royal
Steamer....	Fulton	....	Oct. 7	Red river...........	Black Hawk
Steamer....	Fanny..........	Assorted........	Sept. 12	Near Pascagoula....	Genesee
Schooner...	Florrie.........	Drugs, &c......	Oct. 2	Near Matagorda....	Bermuda
Schooner...	Friendship......	Munitions of war	Oct. 10?	Off Rio Brazos......	Tennessee
Schooner...	Friendship......	.. „	Oct. —	At sea	„
Schooner...	F. U. Johnson..	....	Dec. 1	Off Alexandria, Va.	A. Hugel
			1864.		
English sch.	Fly............	....	Jan. 11	Jupiter inlet, Fla...	Honeysuckle
Steamer....	Fanny & Jenny.	....	Feb. 10	Off New inlet.......	Florida
Sloop	Florida........	Assorted........	Mar. 20	At sea..............	Honeysuckle
English sch.	Fanny..........	.. „	April 19	Off Velasco.........	Owasco
Schooner...	Fred. the Second	Cotton..........	May 8	Off Brazos river.....	Chocura
Sloop.......	Fortunate......	.. „	May 30	Near Indian river..	Bermuda
Rebel steam.	Fort Gaines....	Armed vessel...	Aug. 5	Mobile Bay	W. Gulf blockading squadron
Rebel arm'd steamer ..	Florida.........	.. „	Oct. —	Bahia, Brazil.......	Wachusett
Steamer....	Flora...........	Assorted........	Oct. 22	Off Charleston, S. C.	Picket launches
Schooner...	Flash...........	Cotton	Nov. 27	Lat. 23° N., long. 97° W	Princess Royal
			1865.		
Schooner...	Fannie McRae..	Assorted........	Jan. 23	Off St. Mark's, Fla..	Fox
Sloop.......	Florida.........	Cotton..........	April 11	Crystal river, Fla..	Sea Bird
Rebel Iron-clad.	Fredericksburg .	....	April —	Richmond, Va.....	
Steamer....	Fisher..........	....	....	Roanoke river, N.C.	Naval expedition
			1861.		
Schooner...	George M. Smith	Gun carriag's, &c	April 24	Hampton roads.....	Cumberland
Bark.......	General Green..	Sugar, &c......	June 4	Cape Henry........	Quaker City
Ship........	General Parkhill	Assorted........	May 12	Charleston.........	Niagara
Schooner...	General Knox..	Oak timber.....	June 25	....	Dawn
Schooner...	George G. Baker	Assorted........	July 6	Galveston..........	South Carolina
Schooner...	Georgiana......	....	June 25	....	Dawn
Schooner...	George B. Sloat.	....	June 5	St. Mark's, Fla.....	Mohawk
Steamer....	Gipsey.........	....	June 24	Potomac river......	
Schooner...	Good Egg	....	Aug. 29	Rappahannock river	Daylight
Schooner...	Gypsey.........	Cotton..........	Dec. 28	Pascagoula.........	New London
Schooner...	Garonne	Tobacco........	Dec. 30	Galveston..........	Santee
			1862.		
Schooner...	Grace E. Baker.	Cotton..........	Mar. 29	Coast of Cuba	R. R. Cuyler
Schooner...	G. H. Smoot....	....	Mar. 17	Potecay creek, N. C.	Hunchback, &c.
Schooner...	Guide..........	Cotton, &c......	April 19	Charleston	Huron
Ship	Gondar.........	.. „	April 26	Capture of Fort Macon	Gemsbok
Bark.......	Glenn..........	....	„	.... „	„
Schooner...	Gen. C. C. Pinkney	Cotton, &c	May 6	At sea..............	Ottawa
Steamer....	Gov. A. Moulton	Provisions, &c..	May 12	Berwick's bay......	Hatteras
Steamer....	General Lovell.	....	June 6	Memphis...........	Western flotilla
Steamer....	Gen. Beauregard	....	„	.... „	„
Steamer....	General Price..	....	„	.... „	„
Steamer....	General Bragg..	....	„	.... „	„
Sloop.......	G. L. Brockenborough......	Cotton	Oct. 15	Apalachicola river..	Fort Henry
Sloop.......	Grapeshot......	None...........	Nov. 6	Chesapeake bay.....	Teazer
Sloop.......	G. W. Green....	Shoes, &c	Nov. 16	....	T. A. Ward
Steamer....	Gov. Morton....	....	....	St. John's river.....	Joint expedition
			1863.		
Sloop	Goodluck.......	Assorted........	Jan. 6	Cape Florida	Ariel
Schooner...	Galena.........	....	....	....	
Schooner...	George W. Grice	Assorted	Jan. 11	....	
Bark.......	George Alban...	....	Jan. —	New Orleans	Admiral Farragut's fleet
Steamer....	Gov. Mouton...	....	Jan. —	.... „	"
Schooner...	Georgia........	Assorted	Jan. 11	....	

Class.	Name.	Cargo.	When captured.	Where captured.	By what vessel.
			1863.		
Schooner...	General Taylor.	Suspicious......	Feb. 20	Chesapeake bay....	Crusader and Mahaska
Schooner....	Glide..........	Cotton....	Feb. 23	Tybee creek........	Marblehead and Passaic
Steamer....	Granite City...	Assorted.... ...	Mar. 22	At sea............	Tioga
Steamer....	Georgiana......	....	Mar. 19	Charleston........	Wissahickon
Steamer....	Gertrude.......	Assorted...... ..	April 16	Eleuthera..........	Vanderbilt
Schooner....	Gipsey.........		Mar. 20	St. Joseph's bay....	Ethan Allen
Schooner....	Golden Liner...	Flour, Sugar, &c	April 27	Morrell's inlet, S. C.	Monticello
Schooner....	General Prim...	Cotton..........	April 24	Gulf of Mexico.....	De Soto
Steamer....	Golden Age.....	....	May 24	....	Yazoo Pass expedition
Schooner....	Glen...........	Cotton.........	June —	Lat. 35°N., long. 73° W...............	Cambria
Schooner....	George.........	None......	July 29	Caloosahatchee river	Gem of the Sea
Schooner....	General Worth	General........	Aug. —	Lat. 24°N., long. 82° W...............	Sunflower
Schooner....	Gold Leaf.......	None....	Aug. 23	....	Jacob Bell
Steamer....	General Beauregard..........	....	Dec. 12	Off Wilmington....	
Steamer....	Grey Jacket....	Cotton..........	Dec. 31	Off Mobile..........	Kennebec
			1864.		
Sloop........	G. Garibaldi....	,, ...	Feb. 4	Jupiter inlet........	Beauregard
Steamer....	Gen. Sumter...	....	Mar. 12	Lake George.......	Daffodil and others
Schooner...	Good Hope.....	Salt & dry goods	April 18	At sea.............	Fox, tender to San Jacinto
Steamer....	Greyhound.....	Assorted........	May 10	At sea..............	Connecticut
Sloop........	Gen. Finnegan.	,, ...	May 28	Chashcowitzka river	Ariel, tender to San Jacinto
Steamer....	Georgiana McCaw..........	....	June 2	Off Wilm., N. Car.	Maratanza
Steamer....	Georgia......	....	Aug. 15	Coast of Portugal..	Niagara
Brig........	Geziena Hilligonda.........	Assorted..... ...	Dec. 4	Off Brazos, St. Iago, Texas............	Pembina
			1865.		
Schooner....	Gen. Burkhart.	Cotton....	Mar. 17	Lat. 26°N., long. 96° W...............	Quaker City
Bark........	Geo. Douthwaite	Sugar &c........	May 8	Coast of Florida....	Isonomia
			1861.		
Schooner....	H. M. Johnson.	Assorted........	May 31	Near Cape Lookout.	Perry
Schooner....	Haxall..........	....	....	Hampton roads.....	Minnesota
Bark........	Hiawatha.......	....	May 20	,, ...	,,
Schooner....	H. E. Spearing.	Coffee...........	May 29	Mouth Miss. river..	Brooklyn
Brig........	Hallie Jackson.	Molasses.......	June 10	Savannah...........	Union
Schooner....	Herbert........	....	....	....	
Brig........	Herald.........	Naval stores....	July 16	Coast N. Car.......	St. Lawrence
Sloop........	H. Day.........	....	....	Potomac river......	Thomas Freeborn
Brigantine..	Hannah Balch..	....	....	Charleston........	Wabash
Schooner....	H. Middleton...	Turpentine, &c.	Aug. 21	,, ...	Vandalia
Schooner....	H. C. Brooks...	Cotton, &c......	Sept. 9	Hatteras inlet......	Naval expedition
Schooner....	Henry Nutt....	Mahogany......	,,	,, ...	"
Schooner...	Harriet P. Ryan	Rum, salt, &c..	,,	,, ...	Pawnee
Schooner....	Harmony.......	Fish....	April 24	Hatteras...........	Gemsbok
Schooner....	Harford........	Wheat, &c.....	Sept. 18	Pope's creek, Md...	Resolute
Steamer....	Henry Lewis...	Sugar, molasses, &c..........	Nov. 22	Mississippi sound...	New London and R. R. Cuyler
Schooner....	Havelock.......	Cigars and coffee	Dec. 15	Cape Fear..........	Jamestown
Boat........	Henrietta.......	....	Nov. 13	Chincoteague.......	Louisiana
			1862.		
Schooner....	Harriet & Sarah	....	May 14	Newbern, N. Car.	Rowan's expedition
Schooner....	Henry Travers.	Coffee, &c......	Mar. 8	Lat. 28°N., long. 91° W..............	Bohio
Steamer....	Havana........	....	June 5	Dead Man's bay....	Isilda
Armed sloop	Hannah........	....	Aug. 12	Corpus Christi......	Arthur
Schooner....	Hermosa.......	Drugs, &c......	Oct. 30	Sabine river........	Connecticut
			1863.		
Schooner....	Hampton.......	Assorted........	Jan. 13	Dividing creek, Va.	Currituck
Schooner....	Harriet.........	....	Jan. 22	Chuckatuck creek..	Commodore Morris
Schooner....	Hettiwan.......	Cotton....	Jan. 21	Charleston.........	Ottowa
Steamer....	Home..........	....	....	....	
Sloop.......	Hortense.......	Assorted........	Feb. 18	Lat. 29°N., long. 84° W..............	Somerset, &c.

Class.	Name.	Cargo.	When captured.	Where captured.	By what vessel.
			1863.		
Sloop	Helen	Corn	Mar. 24		Naval expedition
Rebel armed steamer	Hart		April —	Berwick's bay	Estrella
Schooner	Handy	Salt, &c	April 22	Lat. 26°N., long. 76° W	Octorara
Schooner	Harvest	Cotton	April 30	Lat. 28°N., long. 75° W	Juniata
Schooner	Hunter	"	May 17	Mobile	Kanawha, &c.
Schooner	Helena		June 30	"	Ossipee
Sloop	Henry Wolcott		June 22		Satellite
Schooner	Hattie	Cotton, &c	June 21	Coast of N. Car	Florida
Schooner	Harriet		June 18	Lat. 28°N., long. 82° W	Tahoma
Bark	H. McGuin		July 18	Bay St. Louis	Vincennes & Clifton
Steamer	Havelock (?)		June 10	Charleston	S. Atlantic blockad'g squadron
Steamer	Herald	Assorted	Sept. —	At sea	Tioga
Steamer	Hebe		Aug. 18	Off New inlet, N. C.	Niphon and others
Schooner	Herald	Assorted	Oct. 23	Off Fryingpan shoals	Calypso
Sloop	Hancock	"	Dec. 24	Tampa bay	Sunflower
			1864.		
Sloop	Hope	Cotton	Feb. 4	Jupiter inlet	Beauregard
Sloop	Hannah	"	Mar. 11	Off Mosquito inlet	"
Schooner	Henry Colthurst	Powder	Feb. 20	San Luis Pass	Virginia.
Steamer	Hattie	Assorted	Mar. 14	Near St. John's Fla.	Daffodil and others
Steamer	Hard Times	Lumber	Mar. —	St. Mary's river	Para
Sloop	Hope	Cotton & tobacco	July 10	Sapelo sound	Ladona
Steamer	Hope	Machinery	Oct. 22	Off Wilmington	Eolus
Rebel st'r	Hampton			Richmond, Va	
Gunboat unfinished	Halifax			Roanoke river, N. C.	Naval expedition
			1861.		
Schooner	Industry	Hay, &c	May 15	Hampton roads	Minnesota
Schooner	Iris	Naval stores	May 27	"	"
Schooner	Island Belle	Sugar & molass.	Dec. 31	Bull's Island light	Augusta
			1862.		
Schooner	Isabel or W. R. King	Sugar, &c	Feb. 1	Atchafalaya bay	Montgomery
Brig	Intended	Salt, &c	May 1	New inlet, N. Car	Jamestown
Schooner	Ida	Assorted	July 12	Lat. 26°N., long. 76° W	Mercedita
			1863.		
Schooner	Ida		Mar. 4	Charlotte harb'r Fla.	J. S. Chambers
Schooner	Inez	Salt, &c	April 18	Indian River inlet	Gem of the Sea
Schooner	Isabel		May 18	Mobile	R. R. Cuyler
Brig	Isabella Thompson	Cotton, &c	June 19	Lat. 41° N., long. 67° W	United States
Sloop	Isabella	None	May 22	Wacassassa bay	Fort Henry
			1864.		
English sch.	Indian		April 10	At sea	Vicksburg
Steamer	Isabel	Munitions of war.	May 28	Off Galveston	Admiral
Steamer	Ivanhoe		July 4	Off Mobile	Fleet off Mobile
Steamer	Ida	Cotton	July 8	Sapelo sound	Sonoma
			1861.		
Schooner	J. H. Etheridge	Tobacco	May 15	Hampton roads	Minnesota
Schooner	John Hamilton	None	July 5	"	Daylight, &c.
Schooner	Jane Wright		Aug. 2	Potomac river	Thomas Freeborn
Schooner	Julia	Drugs, &c		Beaufort, N. Car	Cambridge
Schooner	Joseph H. Toone	Arms, &c	Oct. 1	Barrataria bay	South Carolina
Schooner	Judith		Sept. 13	Pensacola navy yard	Boat expedition from Colorado
Bark	Jorgen Lorentzen	None	Dec. 26	Lat. 6° N., Long 37° W	Morning Light
Schooner	Jane Campbell	Assorted	Dec. 14	Beaufort, N. Car	State of Georgia
			1862.		
Schooner	J. W. Wilder	Coffee, lead, &c.	Jan. 20	Mobile bar	R. R. Cuyler
Schooner	Julia	Cotton	Jan. 24	New Orleans	Mercedita, &c.
Schooner	Joanna Ward	"	Feb. 24	Lat. 30° N. long. 80° W	Harriet Lane
Schooner	J. J. McNeil	Coffee, &c	Jan. 25	Corpus Christi	Arthur
Schooner	Julia Worden	Rice, corn, &c	Mar. 27	Cape Roman passage	Restless

Class.	Name.	Cargo.	When captured.	Where captured.	By what vessel.
			1862.		
Schooner...	Jesse J. Cox....	Cotton, &c.	Mar. 25	Mobile..............	Cayuga.
Schooner...	Julia...........	"	May 11	....	Kittatinny
Schooner...	Jane...........	Pig lead, &c....	May 3	Lat. 26° N., long. 83° W...........	R. R. Cuyler.
Steamer....	Jeff. Thompson.	....	June 6	Memphis...........	Western flotilla
Sloop..... ..	Jeff. Davis......	....	Mar. 14	Newbern...........	Vessels in sounds of North Carolina
Schooner...	John...........	Corn............	April 8	Pasquotank river, N. Carolina......	Commodore Perry, &c.
Schooner...	J. J. Crittenden	None	April 10	Newtogan creek, N. Carolina	"
Schooner...	James Norcon..	Corn...........	Mar. 28	Little River, N. C...	Shawsheen, &c.
Brig........	Josephine.......	Cotton..........	July 28	Ship Island, Miss...	Hatteras
Schooner...	John Gilpin....	"	....	Mississippi sound...	Katahdin
Sloop.......	John Thompson	Turpentine.... .	Sept. 2	....	Restless
Schooner...	J. C. Rozer.....	Salt............	Dec. 3	Wilmington........	Cambridge
			1863.		
Sloop.......	Julia...........	Salt............	Jan. 8	Jupiter inlet........	Sagamore
Sloop.......	John C. Calhoun	Contraband.....	Jan. 22	Chuckatuck creek ..	Commodore Morris
Schooner...	J. C. McCabe...	....	Jan. 18	James river........	Zouave
Schooner...	John Williams..	Iron, &c........	Mar. 19	Lat. 26° N., long. 76° W...........	Octorara
Steamer....	J. D Clark.....	....	April 8	Red river...........	Hartford
Schooner...	Joe Flanner....	Assorted........	April 24	Mobile.............	Pembina
Schooner...	Juniper.........	"	May 4	"	Kanawha
Sloop.......	Jane Adelie	Cotton..........	April 24	Gulf of Mexico.....	De Soto
Sloop.......	Justina.........	"	April 23	Lat. 28° N., long. 78° W...........	Tioga
Steamer....	John Walsh....	....	May 24	....	Yazoo Pass expedition
Sloop..	John Wesley...	Cotton....	June 16	Lat. 28° N., long. 83° W...........	Circassian
Schooner...	Julia..........	....	....	Lat. 25° N., long. 76° W...........	Tioga
Steamer....	James Battle...	Cotton..........	July 17	....	De Soto, &c.
Schooner...	J. T. Davis.....	"	Aug. 10	Rio Grande.........	Cayuga
Steamer....	Juno...........	Assorted........	Sept. 22	Off Wilmington, N. Car..............	Connecticut
Schooner...	Jenny..........	154 bales of cotton...........	Oct. 6	Off Rio Grande.....	Virginia
Schooner...	Jupiter.........	Assorted..	Sept. 13	At sea..............	Cimarron & Nantucket
Schooner...	Jane...........	....	Oct. —	Off Rio Brazos......	Tennessee
Schooner...	Jenny..........	Cotton..........	Oct. 6	Coast of Texas......	Virginia
			1864.		
Steamer....	John Scott......	Assorted........	Jan. 7	Off Mobile..........	Kennebec and others
Schooner...	John Douglass..	Cotton..........	Feb. 29	Off Velasco, Texas..	Penobscot
Sloop..... ..	Josephine......	"	Mar. 24	Saversota sound....	Sunflower
Mexican sch	Juanita.........	....	April 11	Off San Luis Pass...	Virginia
Schooner...	Julia A. Hodges	Stores..........	April 6	Matagorda bay.....	Estrella
Schooner...	Judson.........	Cotton..........	April 30	Off Mobile bar......	Conemaugh
Steamer....	Jupiter....	....	June 27	At sea..............	Proteus
Sloop.......	Julia..........	Salt............	"	Off Sapelo sound....	Nipsic
Schooner...	James Williams	Assorted........	July 12	Off Galveston.......	Penobscot
Schooner...	John...........	Cotton..........	Sept. 11	Off Velasco.........	Augusta Dinsmore
Sloop.......	James Sandy...	....	Oct. 28	Off Alexandria, Va.	Adolph Hugel
Schooner...	John A. Hazard	Medicines, &c..	Nov. 5	Lat. 26° N., long. 96° W...........	Fort Morgan
Schooner...	Julia...........	Assorted........	Dec. 5	Near Velasco, Texas	Chocura
Steamer....	Julia...........	Cotton..........	Dec. 23	Alligator creek, S. C.	Acacia
			1865.		
Schooner...	Josephine......	Cotton....	Jan. 14	Off Brazos, St. Iago, Texas...........	Seminole
Schooner...	John Hale......	Lead, &c.... ...	Feb. 3	Coast of Florida	Matthew Vassar
			1862.		
Schooner...	Kate...........	Salt............	April 2	Wilmington........	Mount Vernon
Schooner...	Kate...........	Salt, &c........	Dec. 27	St. Mark's river....	Roebuck
			1863.		
Schooner...	Kate...........	Assorted........	Feb. 25	....	Potomac flotilla
Sloop.......	Kate.......	Cotton..........	May 28	Point Isabel light...	Brooklyn
Sloop.......	Kate....	Assorted........	June 23	Indian river........	Pursuit
Steamer....	Kate......... ..	None...........	Aug. 1	New Inlet, N. C....	James Adger, &c.

Class.	Name.	Cargo.	When captured.	Where captured.	By what vessel.
			1863.		
Steamer....	Kate Dale......	....	July 14	....	R. R. Cuyler
Steamer....	Kaskaskia......	....	....	....	Mississippi squadron.
Sloop.......	Kate Dale......	....	Oct. 16	Tampa bay.........	Tahoma and Adela
			1861.		
Schooner...	Laurie..........	Wood...........	May 4	Hampton roads.....	Cumberland
Schooner...	Lynchburg.....	Coffee...........	May 30	Chesapeake bay....	Quaker City
Schooner...	Louisa..........	Lumber.........	July 4	Galveston..........	South Carolina
Sloop.......	Leon............	....	July 25	Potomac river......	Thomas Freeborn
Schooner...	Louisa..........	....	Aug. 11	Cape Fear river....	Penguin
Schooner...	Louisa Agnes...	Fish............	Sept. 9	Beaufort, N. Car....	Cambridge
Schooner...	Lida............	Coffee, cigars, &c.	Dec. 1	Off St. Simonds.....	Seminole
			1862.		
Schooner...	Lizzie Weston..	Cotton	Jan. 19	....	Itasca
Propeller...	Labuan	.. "	Feb. 1	Boca Chica.........	Portsmouth
Schooner...	Lynnhaven.....	....	Feb. 0	Elizabeth City, N. C.	Delaware
Schooner...	Lion	Coffee, powder, &c	Feb. 5	Lat. 26° N., long. 93° W...............	Kingfisher
Schooner...	Lizzie Taylor...	....	Mar. 4	Newbern...........	Rowan's expedition
Schooner...	Lydia and Mary.	Rice and corn..	Mar. 9	Cape Roman passage	Restless
Schooner...	Lookout.........	Corn...........	April —	Potomac river......	Potomac flotilla
Sloop.......	Lafayette.......	Cotton	April 4	....	Pursuit.
Schooner ...	Liverpool.......	....	April 10	Georgetown	Keystone State
Steamer....	Lewis Whitemore.........	....	May 6	....	Colorado
Schooner...	Lucy C. Holmes.	Cotton	May 27	At sea..............	Santiago de Cuba
Schooner...	Lion	Shingles........	Mar. 28	Pantago creek, N. C.	Delaware
Schooner...	La Criolla......	Assorted........	May 29	Charleston..........	Bienville
Steamer....	Little Rebel	....	June 6	Memphis	Western flotilla
Schooner...	Louise	Cotton..........	June 19	....	Albatros
Schooner ...	Lucy...........	Cotton, &c......	June 20	Lat. 29° N., long. 83° W...............	Beauregard
Brig........	Lilla	Drugs, &c......	July 3	Hole in the Wall....	Quaker City
Sloop.......	L. Rebecca.....	Sugar, &c.......	June 21	....	Bohio
Sloop.......	Lizzie	Assorted........	Aug. 2	Coast of North Carolina...............	Penobscot
Steamer....	Lodona.........	Salt, &c........	Aug. 4	Ossabaw sound.....	Unadilla
Schooner...	Lonely Bell.....	Corn............	Mar. 21	Powell's Point......	General Putnam
Schooner...	Louisa	Assorted........	Aug. 23	Charleston	Bienville and Pembina
Bark........	La Manche.....	Tobacco.........	"	Lat. 38° N., long. 69° W...............	Ino
Schooner...	Lavinia	Turpentine.....	Aug. 27	Lat. 27° N., long. 76° W...............	Santiago de Cuba
Schooner...	Lilly............	Powder, &c.....	Aug. 31	At sea..............	W. G. Anderson
Schooner...	Levi Rowe......	Salt	Nov. 30	New inlet..........	Mount Vernon
			1863.		
Steamer....	Landis	....	Jan. 19	New Orleans, La....	Admiral Farragut's fleet.
Steamer....	Little Magruder.	....	Jan. 8	White House.......	Mahaska, &c.
Schooner...	Lightning	Assorted........	Mar. 15	....	Bienville
Sloop.......	Laura Dudley..	.. "	April 27	Lat. 27° N., long. 86° W...............	McClellan
Schooner...	Ladies' Delight.	.. "	May 14	Urbana, Va.........	Currituck, &c
Schooner...	Linnet	.. "	May 21	Lat. 26° N., long. 84° W...............	Union
Steamer....	Lady Walton...	....	June —	White river........	Naval boat exp'n
Steamer....	Lizzie..........	Assorted........	July 15	Lat. 27° N., long. 75° W...............	Santiago de Cuba
Schooner...	Lady Maria.....	Cotton..........	July 6	Bay Port, Fla......	De Soto and others
Steamer....	Louisville......	....	....	Red River..........	Red river expedit'n
Sloop.......	Last Trial......	Salt............	Oct. —	....	Beauregard
Steamer....	Lizzie Davis....	Lead, &c........	Sept. 16	Lat. 25° 58' N., long. 85° 11' W.........	San Jacinto
Steamer....	Leviathan......	....	Sept. 22	Off Southwest Pass..	De Soto
			1864.		
Steamer....	Laura..........	Merchandise....	Jan. 18	Ockockney river....	Stars and Stripes
Boat........	Lydia..........	Cotton and turpentine.......	Feb. 4	Jupiter inlet	Beauregard

Class.	Name.	Cargo.	When Captured.	Where captured.	By what vessel.
			1864.		
Schooner...	Louisa	Munitions of war........	Feb. 11	Off Brazos River Pass	Queen
Schooner...	Linda..........	Assorted.......	Mar. 11	Off Mosquito inlet..	Beauregard and Norfolk packet
Schooner...	Lilly...........	.. "	Feb. 28	Off Velasco, Texas..	Penobscot
Schooner...	Lauretta	Salt...........	Mar. 1	Off Indian River....	Roebuck
English sch.	Lilly...........	....	April 17	Off Velasco.........	Owasco
.. "	Laura..........	....	April 21	.... "	"
Sloop.......	Last Resort.....	Cotton....	June 30	Jupiter inlet........	Roebuck
Steamer....	Little Ada.....	Assorted........	July 9	At sea.............	Gettysburg
Steamer....	Lilian.........	Cotton.........	Aug. 24	"	Keystone State and others
Steamer....	Lynx..........	....	Sept. 25	Off New inlet, N. C.	Niphon and others
Steamer....	Lucy..........	Cotton, &c.....	Nov. 2	Lat. 32° 40′ N., long. 77° 48′ W........	Santiago de Cuba
Schooner ...	Louisa.........	Assorted........	Oct. 15	Off San Luis Pass...	Mobile
Schooner....	Louisa.........	"	Oct. 12	Near Aransas Pass.	Chocura
Steamer....	Lady Sterling...	Cotton.........	Oct. 31	Off Wilmington....	Calypso, Eolus, Fort Jackson
Schooner....	Louisa.........	Assorted........	Oct. 12	Off Aransas Pass, Texas...........	Chocura
Schooner....	Lucy..........	Assorted........	Oct. 21	Off Bayport, Fla....	Sea Bird
Sloop.......	Little Elmere...	"	Nov. 9	Mobjack bay, Va...	Stepping Stones
Schooner....	Lone..........	Medicines, &c..	Nov. 6	Lat. 28° N., long. 95° W...............	Fort Morgan
Schooner ...	Louisa.........	....	Nov. 24	Bar of St. Bernard..	Chocura
Schooner....	Lowood........	Cotton.........	Dec. 4	Near Velasco, Texas	"
Schooner....	Lady Hurley...	Assorted.	Dec. 6	Off Velasco, Texas..	"
			1865.		
Schooner...	Lilly...........	Bagging & Salt	Jan. 6	Off Galveston, Texas	Metacomet
Schooner...	Louisa.........	Crockery, &c...	Feb. 18	Arkansas Pass, Texas	Penobscot
Schooner...	Lecompte.......	....	May 25	Galveston, Texas...	Cornubia
Steamer....	Lady Davis.....	....	....	Charleston, S. C....	
			1861.		
Schooner...	Mary & Virginia	Coal...........	May 4	Hampton Roads....	Cumberland
Schooner...	Mary Willis....	Tobacco........	May 14	"	Minnesota
Schooner...	Mary..........	"	May 15	"	"
Schooner...	Mary Clinton...	Rice, &c.......	May 30	Mouth of Mississippi	Powhatan
Schooner...	McCanfield.....	Lumber........	July 4	Galveston..........	South Carolina
Schooner...	Mary..........	None..........	July 13	North Carolina....	Roanoke
Schooner...	Monticello	....	July 26	Rappahannock river	Daylight
Longboat...	Morning Star...	....	....	Potomac river......	Freeborn
Schooner...	Mary Alice.....	....	Aug. 3	....	Wabash
Bark	Macao.........	Coffee.........	Sept. 5	Mouth of Mississippi	Brooklyn & St.Louis
Schooner...	Mary Wood....	Salt, &c.......	Sept. 9	Hatteras inlet......	Pawnee
Schooner...	Mary E. Pindar	....	Sept. 22	....	Gemsbok
Schooner...	Mabel.........	Contraband.....	Nov. 15	Lat. 31°N., long. 80° W...............	Dale
			1862.		
Schooner...	Major Barbour..	Powder, &c.....	Jan. 28	Racoon Point, La...	De Soto
Schooner...	Mars..........	Salt...........	Feb. 5	Fernandina........	Keystone State
Sloop.......	Mary Lewis....	....	Jan. 25	Mantle river, Fla...	Kingfisher & others
Sloop.......	Margaret, *alias* Wm. Henry..	Cotton.........	Feb. 6	Isle au Briton......	Sciota
Steamer....	Magnolia.......	.... "	Feb. 19	Pass a l'Outre......	Brooklyn and others
Pilot boat..	Mary Olivia....	....	April 2	Apalachicola........	Mercedita, &c.
Schooner...	Monterey.......	None...........	April --	Potomac river......	Potomac river
Schooner...	Mersey.........	Salt, coffee......	April 26	Lat. 31° N., long. 79° W...............	Santiago de Cuba
Schooner...	Maria..........	Salt, cigars, &c..	April 30	Charleston..........	"
Schooner...	Magnet.........	Cotton..........	....	Fernandina.........	Dupont's expedition
Schooner...	Mary Teresa....	Drugs, &c......	May 10	Charleston..........	Unadilla.
Schooner...	Magnolia.......	Cotton.........	May 1	Berwick bay........	Hatteras
Sloop.......	Monitor........	....	June —	Piankatank river...	Anacostia
Schooner...	Mary Stewart...	Salt, &c........	June 3	Santee river........	Gem of the Sea
Schooner...	Morning Star...	Salt, acids, &c...	June 27	Frying Pan shoals..	Bienville
Steamer....	Modern Greece..	Munitions of war	"	Near Fort Fisher...	Cambridge, Stars & Stripes
Steamer....	Memphis.......	Cotton, resin...	July 31	At sea.............	Magnolia
Schooner...	Mail...........	....	Aug. 1	....	Freeborn
Schooner...	Mary Elizabeth.	Salt, fruit, &c..	Aug. 24	Wilmington........	Stars & Stripes, &c.
Schooner...	Monte Christo..	Cotton.........	July 10	Coast of Texas......	Arthur

Class.	Name.	Cargo.	When captured.	Where captured.	By what vessel
			1862.		
Schooner...	Mary Ann......	....	....	....	Kensington, &c.
Sloop.......	Mustang........	....	Feb. —	Coast of Texas......	Arthur
Schooner...	Maria...........	Assorted........	Nov. 12	Sabine Pass.........	Kensington, &c.
		Molasses, 10,170 gallons........	Dec. 3	Baton Rouge.......	Essex
Schooner...	Mary Grey.....	....	Dec. 19	....	T. A. Ward
Schooner...	Mont Blanc.....	Salt............	Dec. 25	Bahamas............	Octorara
			1863.		
Ship........	Metropolis......	....	Jan. 19	New Orleans, La....	Admiral Farragut's fleet
Ship........	Milan...........	....	„	.... "	„
Sloop.......	Music...........	....	Jan. 22	Chuckatuck creek...	Commodore Morris.
Sloop.......	Mercury........	Turpentine.....	Jan. 4	Charleston..........	Quaker City
Schooner....	Matilda	....	....	Matagorda bay......	Henry Janes, &c.
Schooner....	Margaret.......	Cotton..........	Feb. 1	Lat. 27° N., long. 83° W...............	Tahoma, &c.
Steamer....	Moro...........	Pork, salt, &c...	Feb. 3	Mississippi river....	Queen of the West
Schooner...	Mail............	....	Feb. 23	....	Potomac flotilla
Brig........	Minna..........	Salt, drugs, &c..	Feb. 18	Shallot inlet........	Victoria
Brig........	Magicienne.....	....	Jan. 28	Lat. 22° N., long. 28° W...............	Onward
Schooner...	Mary Jane.....	Salt, soap, &c...	Mar. 24	Wilmington..........	State of Georgia, &c.
Schooner...	Minnie.........	Cotton..........	April 6	Lat. 26° N., long. 82° W...............	Huntsville.
Schooner...	Mattie..........	Coffee, salt, &c..	April 13	Lat. 23° N., long. 83° W...............	Annie
Schooner...	Maggie Fulton .	General.........	April 8	Indian river inlet...	Gem of the Sea
Brig........	Minnie.........	Salt............	April 20	Bull's bay..........	Ladona
Schooner...	Major E. Willis	....	April 19	Charleston..........	Powhatan
Schooner....	Martha Ann....	Assorted........	April 24	Chesapeake bay.....	Western World, &c.
		Merchandise, lot of............	May 13-14	Urbana, Va.........	Currituck, &c.
Schooner....	Maria Bishop...	Cotton..........	May 17	At sea..............	Courier
Schooner....	Mignionette....	Sutler's stores..	May 19	Piney Point........	Sophronia
		Money, $10,455.	June 1	Lawson's bay, Va...	Primrose, &c.
Schooner....	Mississippian...	Cotton..........	May 19	Gulf of Mexico.....	De Soto
Steamer....	Mobile..........	....	....	Yazoo City.........	Yazoo Pass exped'n
Steamer....	Magnolia........	....	....	....	„
Schooner....	Mary Jane......	....	June 18	Clearwater harbor..	Tahoma
Schooner ...	Miriam.........	Cotton..........	„	Brazos Santiago.....	Itasca
Steamer....	Merrimack......	Turpentine, &c.	July 24	New inlet, N. C....	Iroquois
Steamer....	Massachusetts..	....	July 2	Baltimore, Md.......	Yankee
Sloop.......	Music...........	Assorted........	Sept. 17	Potomac river......	Adolph Hugel
Steamer....	Montgomery....	.... „	Sept. 13	Lat. 28° 32′ N., long. 89° 12′ W.........	De Soto
Schooner....	Mack Canfield..	Cotton..........	Aug. 25	Rio Grande.........	W. G. Anderson
Schooner....	May............	Cargo of........	....	....	Cœur de Lion, &c.
British stmr	Mail............	Cotton & specie.	Oct. 15	At sea..............	Honduras & others
British stmr	Martha Jane....	.... „	Oct. 20	Near Cedar Keys....	Anne, tender to Fort Henry
Steamer....	Margaret and Jessie........	....	Nov. 5	Off Wilmington....	Keystone State and others
Schooner....	Matamoras.....	Assorted........	Nov. 4	Off Rio Grande.....	Owasco and Virginia
Schooner....	Marshal J.Smith	Cotton..........	Dec. 9	Off Mobile..........	Kennebec
Schooner....	Maria Alberta..	....	Nov. 27	Bayport, Florida....	Two Sisters, tender to San Jacinto
Sloop.......	Magnolia.......	Spirits and medicines.........	Dec. 16	Lat. 26° 15′ N., long. 82° W...........	Ariel, tender to San Jacinto
Schooner...	Mary Ann......	Cotton..........	Nov. 26	Lat. 26° 22′ N., long. 97° W...........	Antona
Steamer....	Minna..........	Assorted........	Dec. 9	Lat. 23° 48′ N., long. 78° 3′ W.........	Circassian
Schooner...	Mary Campbell.	....	Nov. 14	Near Pensacola.....	Bermuda
			1864.		
Steamer....	Mayflower......	Cotton..........	Jan. 13	Sarasope Pass, Fla..	Union
Schooner...	Minnie.........	Assorted........	Jan. 15	Mosquito inlet......	Beauregard
Sloop.......	Maria Louise...	Cotton..........	Jan. 10	Jupiter inlet........	Roebuck
Sloop.......	Mary...........	.... „	Jan. 19	.... „	„
Schooner...	Mary Ann......	.... „	Mar. 6	Off Wilmington....	Grand Gulf
British sch..	M. P. Burton...	Iron and shot...	Mar. 11	Lat. 28° 50′ N., long. 95° 5′ W.........	Aroostook
Schooner...	Marion.........	Assorted........	Mar. 12	Gulf of Mexico.....	

Class.	Name.	Cargo.	When captured.	Where captured.	By what vessel.
			1864.		
Schooner...	Mary Sorley....	Cotton.........	April 4	Off Galveston.......	Scioto
Schooner...	Maudoline......	.... „	April 13	Atchafalaya bay....	Nyanza
British sch..	Maria Alfred...	Assorted........	„	Lat. 28° 50′ N., long. 95° 5′ W..........	Rachel Seaman
Eng.steamer	Minnie..........	Cotton, gold, tobacco, &c.....	May 9	Lat. 34° N., long. 75° 28′ W............	Connecticut
English sch.	Miriam.........	....	April 29	Lat. 25° 25′ N., long. 84° 30′ W.........	Honeysuckle
Schooner...	M. O'Neill......	....	May 5	Off Washington, N. Carolina.	Valley City
Steamer....	Matagorda......	....	July 8	Off coast of Texas..	Kanawha and others
Steamer....	Matagorda......	Cotton..........	Sept. 10	Lat. 22° 50′ N., long. 85° 47′ W.	Magnolia
Schooner....	Mary Bowers...	....	Oct. 29	Off Charleston, S. C.	S. Atlantic Block. Squadron
Schooner....	Medera.........	Cotton....	Dec. 8	Pascagoular bar.....	J. P. Jackson and Stockdale
Schooner....	Mary...........	Cotton, &c......	Dec. 3	Lat. 32° N., long. 78° W.	Mackinaw
Sloop.......	Mary Ann......	Cotton..........	Dec. 8	Off Pass Cabello, Tex	Itasca
Schooner....	Morris..........	„	Dec. 19	Gulf of Mexico.....	Pocahontas
			1865.		
Schooner....	Mary Ellen.....	In ballast.......	Jan. 3	Off Velasco, Texas..	Kanawha
Schooner...	Matilda.........	Cotton, &c......	Feb. 11	Off Pass Cabello, Tex	Penobscot
Schooner...	Mary Agnes....	Cordage, wines, &c...........	Feb. 18	Aransas Pass, Texas	„
Schooner....	Matilde.........	Rope, liquors, &c.	Feb. 11	Near Pass Cabello, Texas.	„
Schooner....	Malta...........	Cotton.........	Mar. 3	Bayou Vermillion, Louisiana.	Glide
Schooner...	Mary...........	Shoes, rum, &c.	Mar. 16	Indian river, Fla...	Pursuit
Steamer....	Morgan.........	....	....	....	
Steamer....	Mab............	....	....	Charleston, S. C.....	
Iron-clad (rebel)	Missouri........	....	June 3	Red river...........	
Steamer....	Mary T. Cotton.	....	„	.... „	
			1861.		
Ship........	North Carolina.	In ballast......	May 14	Hampton roads.....	Minnesota
Brig........	Nahum Stetson.	Specie, $2,000...	June 19	Mouth of Mississippi river.	Brooklyn, &c.
			1862.		
Schooner....	Napoleon.......	Cotton, &c......	Mar. 14	Newbern	Rowan's expedition
Schooner....	New Island.....	....	April 2	Apalachicola........	Mercedita, &c.
Schooner....	Newcastle.......	Turpentine, &c.	May 11	Lat. 23° N., long, 83° W.	Bainbridge
Sloop.......	New Eagle.....	Cotton.........	May 15	Coast of Cuba......	Sea Foam
Steamer....	Nassau.........	Rifles, &c.......	May 28	Wilmington........	State of Georgia, &c.
Brig........	Napier..........	Salt.............	July 29	„	Mount Vernon, &c.
Schooner....	Nathan'l Taylor	....	April 8	Pasquotank river, N. Carolina.	Commodore Perry, &c.
Schooner....	Nellie..........	Drugs, &c.......	Sept. 23	Ossabaw Sound, Ga.	Alabama
Schooner...	Nonsuch........	Coffee, &c......	Dec. 1	Bahama Banks......	Tioga
Steamer....	Neustra Sonora de Regla.	....	„	Port Royal.........	General Sherman, &c.
Steamer....	Naniope........	Sugar, &c.......	„	....	Diana
			1863.		
Steamer....	Nashville.......	....	Feb. 28	Fort McAllister.....	Montauk
Steamer....	Nicolai 1st......	Am'nition, &c..	Mar. 21	Cape Fear river....	Victoria, &c.
Sloop.......	Neptune........	Cotton..........	April 19	Charleston..........	S. Atlantic Block. Squadron
Schooner....	Nellie..........	„	Mar. 29	Port Royal.........	South Carolina
Schooner....	New Year......	Cotton, &c.....	April 26	Tortugas...........	Sagamore
Schooner....	Nymph.........	General.........	April 22	Coast of Texas.....	Rachel Seaman
Steamer....	Natchez.......	....	May —	....	Yazoo Pass exped'n.
Schooner....	Nanjemoy.......	None...........	July 15	Cone river..........	Yankee
Steamer....	Nita............	Pork, beef, &c..	Aug. 17	Gulf of Mexico.....	De Soto
Steamer....	Neptune........	....	June 14	Lat. 25° N., long. 85° W.	Lackawanna
			1864.		
Steamer....	Nutfield........	M'nitions of war	Feb. 4	New river inlet.....	Sassacus
Steamer....	Nan-Nan.......	Cotton..........	Feb. 24	Suwannee rive	Nita
Sloop.......	Nina...........	Assorted........	Feb. 27	Indian river........	Roebuck

Class.	Name.	Cargo.	When captured.	Where captured.	By what vessel.
			1864.		
Sloop.......	Neptune........	Cotton..........	May 6	Tampa bay.........	Sunflower
Steamer....	Night Hawk....	....	Sept. 29	....	Niphon
Schooner....	Neptune........	In ballast.......	Nov. 19	Off Brazos de Santiago, Texas.	Princess Royal
			1865.		
Steamer....	Nansemond.....	....	April —	Richmond, Va......	
Iron-clad (rebel)....	Nashville.......	....	May 10	....	
			1861.		
Bark	Octavia.........	....	May 16	Hampton roads.....	Star
Schooner....	Olive Branch...	Turpentine.....	June 23	Mississippi sound...	Massachusetts
Schooner...	Ocean Wave....	Coffee..........	Sept. 9	Hatteras inlet......	Pawnee
Pungy......	Ocean Wave....	....	July 18	Potomac river......	Resolute
Schooner....	Olive...........	Lumber.........	Nov. 22	Mississippi sound...	New London, &c.
Sloop.......	Osceola.........	None...........	Dec. 9	.... ,, ...	,,
			1862.		
Schooner....	Olive Branch...	Turpentine.....	Jan. 21	Coast of Florida....	Kingfisher, &c.
Schooner....	Ocilla...........	....	Jan. 10	Cedar Keys.........	Hatteras
Sloop.......	O. K...........	....	Feb. —	.... ,, ...	Santiago de Cuba
Steamer....	Old North State.	....	Mar. 14	Newbern...........	Rowan's expedition
Sloop.......	Octavia.........	None...........	April 2	Appalachicola......	Mercedita
Schooner....	Orion...........	Assorted........	July 24	Lat. 22° N., long. 87° W.	Quaker City
Steamer....	Ouachita........	Arms, &c.......	Oct. 14	Coast of Carolina...	Memphis
Schooner....	Orion...........	....	Dec. —	....	Calhoun
			1863.		
Barkantine.	Ocean Eagle....	....	Jan. 19	New Orleans........	Admiral Farragut's fleet
Schooner...	Odd Fellow.....	Turpentine, &c.	April 15	Little River inlet, N. Carolina.	Monticello
Schooner...	Oliver S. Breeze	....	May 16	Anclote Key........	Two Sisters
Steamer....	Oconee	Cotton..........	Aug. —	Near Savannah.....	
British sch..	Ocean Bird.....	Salt.............	Oct. 23	Off St. Augustine inlet.	Norfolk packet
			1864.		
Sloop.......	Oscar...........	Cotton..........	May 1	Lat. 26° 5′ N., long. 83° 20′ W.	Fox, tender to S. Jacinto
Eng. schn'r.	O. K............	Assorted........	April 27	Coast of Florida....	Union
Schooner...	Oramoneta......	M'nitions of war	April 18	Off St. Augustine, Florida.	Beauregard
Schooner...	Oregon.........	....	Aug. 24	Biloxi bay..........	Narcissus
			1861.		
Bark.......	Pioneer.........	Salt.............	May 25	Hampton roads.....	Minnesota.
Ship........	Perthshire......	Cotton..........	June 9	Gulf of Mexico.....	Massachusetts.
Bark.......	Pilgrim.........	Liquor.........	June 7	Pass à l'Outre......	Brooklyn.
Schooner...	Petrel..........	None...........	July 28	Charleston.........	St. Lawrence.
Schooner...	Prince Leopold.	....	Aug. 22	New York..........	Collector of the port
Schooner...	Prince Alfred...	Rum, sugar, &c.	Sept. 28	Hatteras inlet......	Susquehanna
Schooner...	Prince of Wales.	Salt and oranges	Dec. 24	Georgetown........	Gem of the Sea
			1862.		
Schooner...	P. A. Sanders...	....	Mar. 14	Newbern...........	Rowan's expedition
Schooner...	Palma..........	....	,,	.... ,, ...	,,
Sloop.......	Pioneer.........	....	Feb. 20	Rio Grande.........	Portsmouth
Schooner...	President.......	Cotton.........	Mar. 16	Mississippi river....	Owasco
Steamer....	P. C. Wallis....	Rosin, pitch, &c	April 4	Pass Christiana.....	Hatteras, &c.
Sloop.......	Poody..........	Assorted........	May 17	Vermillion bay.....	Hatteras
Steamer....	Patras..........	Pow'r. arms, &c	May 26	Charleston.........	Bienville
Schooner...	Providence.....	Salt, cigars, &c.	May 29	.... ,, ...	,,
Schooner...	Princeton.......	Drugs, &c......	June —	Tortugas banks.....	Susquehanna
Schooner...	Planter.........	....	May 7	Pamunkey river ...	Currituck
Steamer....	Post Boy.......	....	Mar. 14	....	Vessels in sounds of N. Carolina
Schooner...	Pathfinder......	....	Nov. 2	....	Penobscot
Sloop.......	Pointer	Assorted........	Oct. 31	....	Reliance
Boat	Prize...........	....	Dec. 20	....	Octorara
			1863.		
Sloop.......	Potter..........	Oysters, &c.....	June 3	Potomac river......	Currituck
Schooner...	Pride...........	Salt, drugs, &c.	June 21	Frying Pan shoals..	Chocura
Steamer....	Pearl...........	....	June 20	....	Tioga
Steamer....	Princess Royal.	Assorted........	June 29	Charleston.........	Unadilla, &c.
Steamer....	Peterhoff.......	.... ,, ...	Feb. 25	St. Thomas........	Vanderbilt
Sloop,......	Petee...........	Salt............	Mar. 10	....	Gem of the Sea

Class.	Name.	Cargo.	When captured.	Where captured.	By what vessel.
			1863.		
Schooner...	Pacifique......	....	Mar. 27	St. Mark's.........	Stars and Stripes
Schooner...	Pushmataha....	Cotton	June 13	Tortugas..........	Sunflower
Steamer....	Planter........	Cotton, &c	June 15	Lat. 27° N., long. 86° W...............	Lackawanna
Steamer....	Powerful	....	Dec. 20	Suwannee river....	Fox, tender to S. Jacinto
Steamer....	Phantom.......	....	Sept. 23	Near Rich inlet, N. Carolina..........	Connecticut
			1864.		
Steamer....	Presto.........	....	Feb. 2	Sullivan's island....	Lehigh and others
Steamer....	Pet............	....	Feb. 16	Off Lockwood's Folly inlet..........	Montgomery
Sloop.......	Persis..........	Cotton	Mar. 12	Off Wassaw sound, Ga..............	Massachusetts and others
Steamer....	Pevensey.......	....	June 9	....	Newbern
Schooner...	Pocahontas.....	Cotton & tobacco	July 8	....	Azalia and Sweet Brier
Schooner...	Prince Albert...	....	Oct. 29	Off Charleston, S. C.	S. Atlantic Blockading squadron
Schooner...	Pancha Larispa.	Gunny bags, &c	Oct. 27	Off Velasco, Texas..	Sciota
Small boat..	Peep O'Day....	Cotton..........	....	Near Indian river, Fla..............	Pursuit
Steamer....	Petrel..........	Munitions......	Dec. 15	New inlet, N. C.....	
Sloop.......	Pickwick.......	Contraband of w.	Dec. 6	Coast of Florida....	Sunflower
			1865.		
Schooner...	Pet............	Cotton.........	Feb. 7	Galveston bay......	Boat expedition
Sloop.......	Phantom.......	Iron, liquors, &c	Mar. 3	Suwannee river.....	Honeysuckle
Steamer....	Philadelphia....	....	Jan. —	Sounds of N. Car...	
Rebel steam.	Patrick Henry .	....	April —	Richmond, Va......	
			1863.		
Ram	Qu'n of the West	....	April —	Red river, Ark.....	Estrella, &c.
			1861.		
Schooner...	Ring Dove.....	Iron, &c........	July 16	Eastern Shore, Md.	Potomac flotilla
Sloop.......	Richard Lacey..	Wood..........	....	Potomac river......	Thomas Freeborn
Schooner...	Remittance.....	Tobacco, &c....	Aug. 28	.... ,, ...	Yankee
Schooner...	Revere.........	Salt, fish, &c....	Sept. 10	Beaufort, N. C.....	Cambridge
Schooner...	Reindeer	Salt............	....	....	Dart
Armed rebel schooner..	Royal Yacht....	Fire-arms......	Nov. 7	Galveston..........	Expedition from Santee
			1862.		
Sloop.......	Rattler.........	....	Jan. 10	Cedar Keys........	Hatteras
Schooner...	Rose	Cotton..........	April 2	Appalachicola	Mercedita, &c.
Schooner...	Reindeer	None	April 20	Potomac river......	Potomac flotilla
Schooner ...	R. C. Files.....	Cotton..........	,,	Mobile.............	Kanawha
Schooner...	Rebecca........	Salt............	May 29	Charleston.........	Bienville
Schooner...	Rowena........	Lead, &c.......	June 6	Stono inlet.........	Pawnee and others
Schooner...	Rich'd O. Bryan	Drugs, &c......	June 1	Coast of Texas......	Rhode Island
Schooner...	Resolution......	Wood..........	April 4	Pass Christian......	Hatteras
Schooner...	Reindeer.......	Cotton.........	July 9	Coast of Texas......	Arthur
Steamer....	Reliance........	.. ,, ...	July 21	....	Huntsville
Schooner...	Rambler	.. ,, ...	Sept. 9	Lat. 28° N., long. 94° W...............	Connecticut
Schooner...	Rising Sun.....	....	Sept. 5	....	Wyandank
Schooner...	Revere.........	Salt, &c........	Oct. 11	Cape Fear river....	Monticello, &c.
Brig........	Robert Bruce ..	Shoes, &c......	Oct. 22	Shallot inlet, N. C..	Penobscot
Schooner...	Reindeer.......	Cotton	Sept. 17	....	W. G. Anderson
Schooner...	Racer..........	Salt............	Oct. 30	New inlet, N. C.....	Daylight
			1863.		
Schooner...	Rising Dawn...	Salt............	Jan. 10	....	Octorara
Sloop.......	Richards	Salt, coffee, &c.	Feb. 1	Bocos Grande	Two Sisters
Schooner...	Rowena........	....	....	....	New Era
Steamer....	Rose Hamilton.	....	Feb. 12	Carson's landing....	Conestoga, &c.
Sloop.......	Relampago......	Coffee, &c......	Mar. 4	Charlotte harbor, Fla	J. S. Chambers
Sloop.......	Rosalie........	Assorted........	Mar. 16	Lat. 26° N., long. 76° W...............	Octorara
Sloop.......	Ranger.........	Powder, &c.....	Mar. 25	Crystal river........	Fort Henry, &c.
Schooner...	Rising Dawn...	Salt, &c........	,,	New inlet..........	Mount Vernon, &c.
Schooner...	Royal Yacht....	Cotton..........	April 15	Galveston..........	W. G. Anderson
Schooner...	Ripple.........	.. ,, ...	May 18	Mobile.............	Kanawha
Schooner...	Rapid..........	.. ,, ...	April 24	Gulf of Mexico.....	De Soto
Steamer....	R. J. Lockland.	....	May 24	....	Yazoo Pass exped'n.
Ram	Republic.......		....	Yazoo City.........	,,

Class.	Name.	Cargo.	When captured.	Where captured.	By what vessel.
			1863.		
Sloop.......	Richard Vaux..	Old iron, &c....	June 20	Potomac river......	Primrose
Schooner...	Rebekah	....	June 18	Lat. 27° N., long. 83° W	J. S. Chambers
Sloop.......	Relempago.....	Assorted...	July 14	Lat. 25° N., long. 82° W...............	Jasmine
Schooner...	Revenge	Sugar, &c......	July 21	Calcasieu	Owasco
Schooner...	Renshaw.......	....	July —	Washington, N. C..	Louisiana
Sloop	Richard........	Cotton....	Aug. 31	Charlotte harbor...	Gem of the Sea
Schooner...	Robert Knowles	....	Sept. 15	....	Cœur de Leon
Steamer....	R. E. Lee, formerly Giraffe.	Munitions of w'r	Nov. 9	Off Wilmington....	James Adger
British sch..	Ring Dove.....	Salt, &c........	Dec. 17	Off Indian river, Fla	Roebuck
Mexican sch	Raton del Nilo.	Coffee, sugar, &c	Dec. 3	East of Padre island, Texas.	New London
			1864.		
Steamer....	Rosita..........	Assorted........	Jan. 28	Gulf	Western Metropolis
Schooner...	Roebuck........	.. ,, ...	Jan. 7	Lat. 26° 23′ N.; long. 83° 59′ W.	San Jacinto
Steamer....	Ranger.........	....	Jan. 11	Near Lockwood's Folly inlet.	Minnesota and others
Sloop.......	Racer..........	Cotton..........	Jan. 31	Off Cape Canaveral.	Beauregard
Schooner...	Rebel	Assorted	Feb. 29	Indian river........	Roebuck
Sloop.......	Rosina	....	April 13	San Luis Pass......	Virginia
Sloop.......	Resolute........	None...........	May 12	Cape Canaveral....	Beauregard
Steamer....	Rose...........	Assorted	June 2	Off Georgetown	Wamsutta
British sch..	R. S. Hood.....	....	June 9	Lat. 28° 2′ N.; long. 77° W.	Proteus
British st'r.	Rouen..........	....	July 2	Lat. 32° 50′ N.; long. 75° 40′ W.	Keystone state
Sloop.......	Racer	....	Aug. 2	Off Bull's Bay......	Hope
Sloop	Reliance........	Assorted........	Nov. 9	Mobjack bay, Va...	Stepping Stones
			1865.		
Steamer....	Ruby...........	Lead, &c.......	Feb. 27	At sea..............	Proteus
Schooner...	Rob Roy	....	Mar. 2	Steinhatchie river, Fla.	Fox
Iron-clad, rebel.	Richmond......	....	April —	Richmond, Va......	
Iron-clad, rebel.	Roanoke........	....	April —	.... ,, ...	
Brig........	R. H. Vermilyea	Coffee, shoes, &c	Mar. 12	Lat. 27° N., long. 96° W.	Quaker City
			1861.		
Schooner...	Soledad Cos.....	Coffee	Sept. 11	Galveston..........	South Carolina
Schooner...	Sarah and Mary	Coal	May 1	Hampton roads.....	Cumberland
Bark.......	Star...........	Tobacco	May 17	.... ,, ...	Minnesota
Schooner...	Savannah......	None...........	June 3	Charleston.........	Perry
Bark.......	Sallie Magee....	Coffee, &c......	June 26	Hampton roads.....	Quaker City
Schooner...	Sally Mears....	....	July 1	.... ,, ...	Minnesota
Schooner...	Sam Houston...	In ballast.......	July 7	Galveston..........	South Carolina
Schooner...	Shark	Assorted........	July 4	.... ,, ...	,,
Bark.......	Solferino	....	June 26	Rattlesnake shoals..	Vandalia, &c.
Schooner...	Sarah Starr.....	Turpentine.....	Aug. 3	Wilmington........	Wabash
Schooner...	Susan Jane.....	Assorted........	Sept. 10	Hatteras inlet......	Pawnee
Schooner...	San Juan.......	Salt, sugar, &c..	Sept. 28	.... ,, ...	Susquehanna
Schooner...	Specie..........	Rice............	Oct. 12	Lat. 31° N., long. 80° W.	Dale
Steamer....	Salvor..........	Arms, &c.......	Oct. 13	Tortugas...........	Keystone State
Schooner....	Somerset.......	....	June 8	Maryland	Resolute
Schooner...	S. T. Garrison..	....	....	....	Louisiana
Schooner...	Sarah & Carol'e	Turpentine.....	Dec. 11	St. John's river.....	Bienville
			1862.		
Schooner...	Stephen Hart...	Arms, &c.......	Jan. 29	Lat. 24° N., long. 82° W.	Supply
Schooner...	Stag...........	....	Jan. 10	Cedar keys.........	Hatteras
Schooner...	Star...........	....	Feb. 8	Bayou Lafourche...	De Soto
Steamer....	Sea Bird.......	....	Feb. —	Roanoke island.....	Rowan's expedition
Schooner....	Spitfire.........	....	Mar. —	West coast of Fla...	Ethan Allen
Schooner....	Sarah A. Falconer.	....	Mar. 14	Newbern...........	Rowan's expedition
Schooner....	Sarah Ann.....	Corn...........	April —	Potomac river......	Potomac flotilla
Schooner....	Sidney C. Jones	None...........	,,	.... ,, ...	,,
Schooner....	Sea Foam	Assorted........	,,	.... ,, ...	,,

Class.	Name.	Cargo.	When Captured.	Where captured.	By what vessel.
			1862.		
Schooner	Southern Independence.	Cotton, &c	April 10	Off Mobile	Kanawha
Schooner	Sarah		May 1	Bull's bay	Onward
Steamer	Stettin	Saltpetre, drugs, &c.	May 24	Charleston	Bienville
Steamer	Swan	Cotton & rosin.	,,	Lat. 23° N., long. 82° W.	Bainbridge, &c.
Sloop	Sarah	Cotton	May 15	Coast of Cuba	Sea Foam
Steamer	Sovereign		June 5	Memphis	Western flotilla
Steamer	Sumter		June 6	,,	,,
Schooner	Sereta		June 14	Shallow inlet, N. C.	Penobscot
Steamer	Sarah	Cotton	June 20	Charleston	Keystone State, &c.
Steamer	Sarah	Sugar, &c	June 3	Berwick bay	Hatteras
Steamer	Susan Ann Howard.		Mar. 14	Newbern	Vessels in sounds of N. Carolina
Steamer	Scuppernong	Lumber	June 9	Indian Town, N. C.	General Putnam
Steamer	Sabine		April 19		
Steamer	S. C. Jones		Aug. 11		
Steamer	Southerner		Sept. 22	Cone river	Wyandank
Steamer	Sunbeam	Arms, &c	Sept. 28	New inlet, N. C.	State of Georgia, &c.
Sloop	Swan		Feb. —	Coast of Texas	Arthur
Steamer	Scotia	Assorted	Oct. 24	Bull's bay	Restless
Bark	Sophia		Nov. 4	Masonborough inlet	Daylight, &c.
Sloop	S. W. Green		Nov. 16		T. A. Ward
Steamer	Southern Merchant.	Sugar, &c	Dec. —		Diana
			1863.		
Steamer	St. Charles		Jan. 19	New Orleans, La	Admiral Farragut's fleet
Steamer	Sallie Robinson.		,,	,,	,,
Schooner	Silas Henry		Jan. 8		Tahoma
Bark	Stonewall	None	Feb. 20	Point Rosa, Florida.	Julia, &c.
Schooner	Springbok	Assorted.	Feb. 3	Lat. 25° N., long. 73° W.	Sonoma
Schooner	Sue	Salt, &c	Mar. 30	Little River inlet	Monticello
Schooner	Surprise	Cotton	Mar. 13	Lat. 26° N., long. 83° W.	Huntsville
Steamer	St. John's	Assorted	April 18	Cape Romain inlet	Stettin
Schooner	St. George		April 22	Fort Fisher, N. C.	Mount Vernon, &c.
Schooner	Samuel First	None	May 6	Potomac river	Dragon
Schooner	Sarah Lavinia	,,	May 8	Curritoman river	Primrose
Schooner	Sea Bird		May 13	Lat. 29° N., long. 87° W.	De Soto
Schooner	Sea Lion	Cotton	May 9	Mobile	Aroostook, &c.
Sloop	Secesh	Cotton, &c	May 15	Charleston	Canandaigua
Steamer	Scotland		May 24		Yazoo Pass exped'n
Steamer	Star of the West				,,
Schooner	Star	None	May 30	Brazos Santiago	Brooklyn
Schooner	Sea Drift	Drugs, &c	June 22	Matagorda island	Itasca.
Schooner	Statesman		June 6	Tampa, Florida	Tahoma
Schooner	Sarah		May 28	Great Wicomico	Satellite
Sloop	Southern Star	Turpentine	Aug. 6	St. Martin's reef	Fort Henry
Schooner	Southern Rights	Assorted	Aug. 8	Gilbert's bar	Sagamore
Schooner	Shot	,,	,,	,,	,,
Steamer	Sir William Peel	Cotton	Aug. —	Off Rio Grande	Seminole
Steamer	St. Mary's			Yazoo City	Mississippi squadr'n
Steamer	Spaulding	Assorted	Oct. 8	Lat. 31° N., long. 80° W.	Union
Steamer	Scottish Chief		Oct. 16	Tampa bay	Tahoma and Adela
British bark	Saxon		Oct 30	Coast of Africa	Vanderbilt
British sch.	Sallie	Salt	Dec. 20	Off Wilmington	Connecticut
Bark	Science	Assorted	Nov. 5	Off Rio Grande	Owasco & Virginia
			1864.		
British sch.	Silvanus		Jan. 2	Doboy sound, Ga	Huron
Eng. sch'ner	Susan	Salt	Jan. 11	Off Jupiter inlet	Roebuck
Schooner	Swift	Salt fish	Feb. 9	Wassaw sound	Patapsco
Steamer	St. Mary's	Cotton	,,	St. John's river	Norwich and others
Steamer	Spunky		,,	Fort Caswell, N. C.	
Schooner	Stingray	Cotton	Feb. 29	Off Velasco, Texas	Penobscot
Steamer	Scotia	180 bales cotton.	Mar. 1	Lat. 32° 34′ W., long. 77° 18′ W.	Connecticut
Schooner	Sophia	Assorted	Mar. 3	Altamaha sound, Ga.	Dan Smith & others

Class.	Name.	Cargo.	When captured.	Where captured.	By what vessel.
			1864.		
Schooner...	Sylphide	Assorted........	Mar. 9	Off Coast of Texas.	Virginia
Sloop........	Swallow........	Cotton, &c.......	Mar. 20	Off Elbow Light....	Tioga
Schooner....	Spunky.........	Cotton..........	April 7	Off Cape Canaveral.	Beauregard
Steamer....	Siren...........	Liquors, &c.....	June 5	South of Cape Lookout.	Keystone State
Sloop........	Sarah Mary....	Cotton..........	June 26	Mosquito inlet......	Norfolk packet
Steamer....	Selma..........	....	Aug. 5	Mobile bay.........	W. Gulf blockading squadron
Schooner....	Sea Witch......	Coffee, &c......	Dec. 31	Lat. 27° N., long. 93° W.	Metacomet
Schooner...	Sybil...........	Cotton..........	Nov. 21	....	Iosco
Steamer....	Susanna........	.... „	Nov. 27	Off Campeachy b'ks	Metacomet
Schooner...	Sorts...........	.... „	Dec. 10	Anclote keys.......	O. H. Lee
			1865.		
Steamer....	Stag............	Arms, shoes, &c.	Jan. 19	Cape Fear river....	Malvern & others
Steamer....	Syren...........	Assorted........	Feb. 18	Charleston, S. C....	Gladiolus & others
Schooner...	Salvador........	.... „	Feb. 25	At sea.............	Marigold
Schooner...	Sort............	.... „	Feb. 28	Cedar keys, Fla.....	Honeysuckle
Brig........	Sar. M. Newhall	....	....	S. A. squadron.....	
Rebel stm'r	Shrapnell.......	....	April —	Richmond, Va......	
Rebel stm'r	Spray..........	....	....	....	
			1861.		
Schooner....	Theresa C......	Cotton..........	May 4	Hampton roads.....	Cumberland
Schooner....	Tropic Wind....	....	May 20	.... „	Minnesota
Schooner....	Tros Freres.....	Iron............	June 23	Mississippi sound...	Massachusetts
Schooner...	Tom Hicks.....	Lumber.........	July 9	Galveston....	South Carolina
Schooner...	T. J. Chambers.	.... „	....	.... „	„
Schooner...	Teaser..........	....	July 5	Potomac river......	Dana
Sloop........	T. J. Evans.....	Pistols, &c.....	Sept. 1	Chesapeake bay.....	„
Ship........	Thomas Watson	Salt............	Oct. 15	Charleston.........	Roanoke, &c.
Sloop.......	T. W. Riley....	....	Nov. 6	Rappahannock river	Cambridge
			1862.		
Span. bark..	Teresita........	Assorted........	Jan. 30	Yucatan bank......	Kingfisher
Schooner....	Theo. Stoney...	Rice............	Feb. 14	Bull's bay.........	Restless
Steamer....	Tubal Cain.....	Contraband.....	July 24	Lat. 31° N., long. 78° W.	Octorara
Schooner....	Telegraph.......	....	....	....	
Tug.........	Teaser..........	....	July 4	James river........	Maratanza
Schooner....	Troy...........	Cotton..........	Aug. 13	Sabine Pass........	Kensington
Sloop.......	Thomas Reilly..	....	Oct. —	Quantico Creek.....	Freeborn
Schooner....	Two Sisters.....	Gunny bags, &c.	Sept. 21	Rio Grande.........	Albatross
Schooner....	Theresa........	Salt, &c........	Sept. 4	Lat. 28° N., long. 93° W.	W. G. Anderson
Schooner...	Trier...........	General	Oct. 28	....	Sagamore
	Tobacco, 4 boxes	....	....	Mobjack bay........	Crusader
			1863.		
Steamer....	Tennessee......	....	Jan. 19	New Orleans, La...	Admiral Farragut's fleet
Schooner....	Time...........	Salt............	Jan. 23	New inlet..........	Cambridge
Schooner....	Theresa........	....	Mar. 16	Lat. 27° N., long. 83° W.	H. Hudson
Schooner...	Tampico........	Cotton..........	Mar. 3	Sabine Pass........	Cayuga, &c.
Schooner...	Three Brothers.	None...........	Aug. 17	Great Wicomico....	Satellite
	Turpentine, 11 barrels.	....	July 24	Cape Canaveral....	Sagamore
Steamer....	Tom Sugg......	....	July —	Tensas river........	Mississippi squadr'n
Steamer....	Three Brothers.	....	Oct. 21	Potomac river......	Currituck & Fuchsia
Span. bark..	Teresita........	Cotton..........	Nov. —	Near Rio Grande...	Granite City
			1864.		
British sloop	Two Brothers...	Salt, &c........	Feb. 25	Off Indian river....	Roebuck
Schooner...	Three Brothers.	....	April 11	Homasassa river....	Nita
Steamer....	Tristr'm Shandy	Cotton, tobacco, &c.	May 15	Lat. 34° 6′ N., long. 77° 27′ W.	Kansas
Steamer....	Thistle.........	....	June 4	Lat. 32° 38′ N., long. 75° 55′ W.	Fort Jackson
Eng. sch'ner	Terrapin........	Cotton and turpentine.	July 10	Off Indian riv. inlet.	Roebuck
Rebel ram..	Tennessee......	....	Aug. 5	Mobile bay.........	W. Gulf blockading squadron
			1865.		
Schooner....	Triumph........	Assorted........	Jan. —	Perquimon's river, N. Carolina.	Wyalusing

Class.	Name.	Cargo.	When captured.	Where captured.	By what vessel.
			1865.		
Sloop.......	Telemico.......	Cotton..........	Mar. 16	Lat. 25° N.; long. 96° W.	Quaker City
Rebel ram..	Texas..........	....	Mar. —	Richmond, Va......	Part of N. A. B. squadron
	Torpedo........	....	Mar. —	Richmond, Va......	
Steamer.....	Transport	....	....	Charleston, S. C.....	
			1861.		
Schooner...	Union..........	Provisions......	June 5	....	Harriet Lane
			1862.		
Schooner...	Uncle Mose.....	Cotton..........	July 7	Coast of Yucatan...	Tahoma
Steamer.....	Union..........	"	Aug. 25	Lat. 23° N.; long. 85° W.	J. S. Chambers
			1863.		
Steamer.....	Union..........	Assorted........	May 19	Lat. 27° N.; long, 85° W.	Huntsville
			1861.		
Schooner....	Venus..........	Lumber	July 4	Galveston..........	South Carolina
Schooner....	Velasco	Sugar..........	July 18	Coast of N. Carolina	Albatross
Schooner....	Venus..........	Lead, Copper, &c	Dec. 26	Lat. 28° N.; long. 93° W.	Rhode Island
Schooner....	Victoria........	Cotton..........	Dec. 3	Point Isabel........	Santiago de Cuba
			1862.		
Schooner...	Victoria........	.... "	April 10	Mobile.............	Kanawha
Schooner...	Venus..........	.... "	May 15	Lake Ponchartrain.	Calhoun
Schooner....	Volante........	Salt, fish, &c...	July 2	Georgetown, S. C...	Gem of the Sea, &c.
Schooner...	Victoria........	Cotton..........	July 12	Lat. 26° N.; long. 76° W.	Mercedita
Sloop.......	Venture........	Flour, rice, &c..	June 19	Mobile bay.........	Morning Light
Schooner...	Velocity........	Rope, &c.......	Sept. 30	....	Crocker's expediti n
			1863.		
Steamer....	Virginia........	Assorted........	Jan. 18	Mugue's island.....	Wachusett
Schooner...	Vesta...........	Sutler's stores..	Feb. 28	Piney Point........	Wyandank
Steamer....	Victoria........	....	May 28	Havana............	Juniata
Sloop.......	Victoria........	Assorted........	May 30	Point Isabel........	Brooklyn
Steamer....	Victory.........	Cotton, &c......	June 21	Lat. 25° N.; long. 75° W.	Santiago de Cuba
Steamer....	Venus..........	Lead, bacon, coffee, &c.....	Oct. 21	New inlet, N. C.....	Nansemond
Brig	Volante	Assorted........	Nov. 5	Off Rio Grande.....	Owasco & Virginia
British sca.	Volante........	Salt, &c.........	"	Off Cape Canaveral.	Beauregard
			1864.		
Steamer....	Vesta	....	Jan. 12	Between Tubb's river and Little inlet, N. Carolina.	
Steamer....	Vixen..........	....	Dec. 1	Lat. 32° N.; long. 78° W.	Rhode Island
			1865.		
Rebel iron-clad	Virginia........	....	Mar. —	Richmond, Va......	
			1861.		
Schooner....	William & John	Tobacco........	May 15	Hampton roads.....	Minnesota
Schooner...	William Henry.	"	"	.... "	"
Bark.......	Winifred	Coffee..........	May 25	Cape Henry........	Quaker City
Yacht......	Wanderer.......	....	May 14	Key West..........	Crusader
Schooner...	William H. Northrop.	Coffee, drugs, &c	Dec. 25	Cape Fear..........	Fernandina
			1862.		
Schooner....	Wyfe or Nye....	....	Jan. 10	Cedar keys.........	Hatteras
Sloop.......	William H. Middleton.	....	"	.... "	"
Schooner....	Wave	Assorted........	Feb. 1	Boca Chico.........	Portsmouth
Schooner....	Wandoo........	Rice............	Feb. 14	Bull's bay..........	Restless
Schooner....	William Mallory	Assorted........	May 5	St. Andrew's bay...	Water Witch
Schooner....	Wave	Cotton	April 19	Georgetown	G. W. Blunt
Schooner...	W. C. Bee......	.... "	April 23	....	Santiago de Cuba
Schooner...	Winter Shrub...	Salt, herrings, &c	May 21	Keel's creek, N. C ..	Hunchback, &c.
Steamer....	Whiteman......	....	May 6	Lake Pontchartrain.	Calhoun.
Schooner....	Will o' the Wisp	Powder, caps, &c.	June 3	Rio Grande.........	Montgomery
Sloop.......	Water Witch...	....	May 5	....	Currituck, &c
Sloop.......	Wave..........	Salt, &c	June 27	Mississippi sound...	Bohio.
Steamer....	Wilson.........	....	July 9	Hamilton, N. C.....	Com'dore Perry, &c.
Schooner....	William........	Cotton..........	July 1	Sabine lake, La.....	De Soto

Class.	Name.	Cargo.	When captured.	Where captured.	By what vessel.
			1862.		
Schooner....	West Florida...	....	....	....	Kensington, &c.
Schooner....	Water Witch...	Assorted........	Sept. 27	Corpus Christi......	Arthur
Schooner....	Wave..........	Cotton, &c.....	Nov. 4	....	E. B. Hale
Schooner....	Water Witch...	Salt, &c........	Aug. 24	Arizona Pass.......	Corypheus
Sloop.......	Wm. E. Chester	Cotton..........	Nov. 20	....	Montgomery
			1863.		
Schooner...	Wm.H.Harrison	....	Jan. 24	....	
Steamer....	Wm. A. Knapp.	....	....	....	New Era
	White Cloud...	....	....	....	
Steamer....	Wave Queen....	Assorted	Feb. 25	North Santee.......	Conemaugh
Schooner...	Wanderer......	Salt and fish....	May 2	....	Sacramento
Schooner....	W. Y. Leitch...	Salt	April 20	Lat. 26° N.; long. 76° W.	Octorara
Schooner...	Wonder	....	May 13	Port Royal, S. C....	Wabash, &c.
Steamer....	Wm. Bagley....	Cotton..........	July 18	....	De Soto, &c.
Schooner...	Wave..........	.... ,, ...	Aug. 22	Lat. 26° N.; long. 96° W.	Cayuga
British sch.	William........	....	Oct. 28	....	Mercedita
Steamer....	Warrior........	Coffee, cigars, & dry goods.	Aug. 16	Lat. 26° N.; long. 86° W.	Gertrude
			1864.		
British sch.	William........	Salt, &c........	Jan. 13	Off Suwannee river.	Two Sisters, tender to San Jacinto
Schooner...	Wm. A. Kain...	Cotton & tobacco	Jan. 22	St. Andrew's bay...	Restless
Steamer....	Wild Dayrell...	Assorted........	Feb. 1	Stump inlet, N. C...	Norwich, &c.
Schooner....	Wm. Douglass..	....	Feb. 15	San Luis Pass......	Virginia
Schooner....	Wild Pigeon....	....	Mar. 21	Florida coast.......	Hendrick Hudson
Steamer....	Wando	Cotton	Oct. 21	Lat. 33° 5′ N. ; long. 76° 40′ W.	Fort Jackson
Schooner....	Watchful.......	Lumber, oil, &c.	Sept. 27	Lat. 28° 46′ N.; long. 90° 53′ W.	Arkansas
			1865.		
Steamer....	Will o' the Wisp	....	Feb. 9	Off Galveston, Texas	
Steamer....	Winona........	....	Jan. 21	Mississippi Squadr'n	
			1861.		
Tug........	Young America.	None..	April 24	Hampton Roads....	Cumberland
Rebel priv'r schooner.	York...........	....	Aug. —	Cape Hatteras......	Union
			1864.		
British slo'p	Young Racer...	....	Jan. 14	Near Jupiter's inlet.	Roebuck
Steamer....	Young Republic	Cotton & tobacco	May 6	Lat. 32° 10′ N.; long. 78° 49′ W.	Grand Gulf
Sloop.......	Yankee Doodle.	Cotton..........	June 10	Entrance to Pearl river, Miss.	Elk
			1861.		
Schooner...	Zeland	Ballast-laden...	Nov. 21	Off Tampico bay....	Connecticut
Schooner...	Zavala	....	Oct. 1	Vermillion bay.....	Huntsville
Schooner...	Zulima	....	....	....	New London
Steamer....	Zouave........	....	....	....	Mississippi squadr'n
			1864.		
Sloop.......	Zion...........	....	Nov. 2	....	Adolph Hugel

MISCELLANEOUS CAPTURES.

Description.	Cargo.	When captured.	Where captured.	By what vessel.
		1861.		
Schooner		Dec. 11	Off St. John's river, Fla.	Bienville
Schooner		May 28	Potomac river	Resolute
Schooner		Oct. 5	Chincoteague inlet	Louisiana
Schooner		Oct. 11	Quantico creek	Union
Sloop		Aug. 16	Potomac river	Yankee
Schooner		Nov. 15	St. Lone bar	Sam Houston
Schooner			Pass Cavallo	Arthur
Schooner	Coffee, &c.	Dec. 15	St. Andrew's	Bienville
		1862.		
Bark	Cotton	Jan. 24		Mercedita, &c.
Schooner	"	Jan. 23	Mobile bar	Huntsville
Sail-boat		Jan. 10		Hatteras
Launch		"		"
Ferry scow		"		"
1 iron windlass		Mar. 14	Roanoke, N. C	Naval expedition
5 barrels of lard, &c.				
Schooner		Feb. 10	Elizabeth City	Commodore Perry
Schooner		Jan. 22		Ariel.
New gunboat		Feb. —		Rowan's expedition
Schooner		Feb. 12	Edenton, N. C.	Louisiana, &c.
Schooner		"		"
Schooner		"	"	"
Schooner				Lieut. Jeffer's expedition
Schooner				"
2 fishing schooners			Isle au Pied	New London
9 fishing sloops			"	"
Schooner		Mar. 3	Fernandina	
Schooner			Sullivan's island	S. Atlantic Blockading Squadron
Sloop	Shad, &c.	April —	Rappahannock river	Jacob Bell, &c.
Schooner	"	"	"	"
Schooner	"	"	"	"
Schooner				Hatteras
Schooner		April 12	Coast of South Carolina	Huron
Schooner		April 26	Bull's bay	"
Schooner		May 8	Light-house inlet	Alabama
Schooner	Cotton			Santiago de Cuba
Schooner	Powder	April 24	Cedar keys	Tahoma
Steamer		June 6	Memphis	
Steamer		"	"	
Steamer		"	"	
Steamer		"	"	
Schooner	Cotton	Mar. —	Near Sabine river	Santiago Cuba
Bark	800 slaves	June 17	Table land of Mariel	Amanda
Schooner, (supposed to be Monticello.)		June —	Fort Morgan	Kanawha
Long gig		May —	West Point, Virginia	Corwin, &c.
Launch	Army stores	May 4	Coppohosal	"
Schooner		July —	Coast of Texas	Rhode Island
1,200 bars railroad iron.			St. Simon's sound, Ga.	Naval expedition
Steamer			Newbern, N. C.	"
Steamer		Mar. 21		Delaware
Sloop	Salt, &c.	Aug. 11	Potomac river	
Schooner		Aug. 12	Sturgeon creek	
Sloop		"	"	
Sloop	Cotton	July 10		Arthur
A wharf boat		July 29	Eunice	Pittsburg
Schooner	Arms	Sept. 26	New inlet, N. C	State of Georgia
An old launch		Oct. 1	Quantico creek	Eureka.
Three boats		Oct. 3-5		T. A. Ward
One seven-oared boat		Oct. 9		"
Metalic life-boat	Merchandise	Oct. 17		Jacob Bell
Two canoes		Oct. 24	Potomac river	Matthew Vassar

Description.	Cargo.	When captured.	Where captured.	By what vessel.
		1862.		
Three boats		Nov. 1		Freeborn
One seine boat		Nov. 16		T. A. Ward
Schooner		Nov. 17	Masonborough inlet	Cambridge
Brig		"		Daylight
Schooner	Rosin, &c	Nov. 19	Shallow inlet	Chocura
Bark		Nov. 4	Masonborough inlet	
Pilot schooner		Oct. 21	Nassau river	E. B. Hale
Schooner		Nov. 25	North river	General Putnam, &c.
Schooner		"	"	"
Vessel on stocks		"	"	"
Schooner		Nov. 23	East river	"
Schooner		"	"	"
Schooner		"	"	"
Scows and boats		"	"	"
Two sloops		"		Crusader
Schooner		Nov. 3	New inlet	Mt. Vernon, &c.
Flat-bottomed boat	Contraband	Nov. 30	Floro creek	Dan Smith
Launch	Howitzer, &c	Nov. 26	Bell river	Calhoun
Two sloops		Dec. 5		Sagamore
Sloop		Dec. 19	York river	Mahaska, &c.
Nine boats		"	"	"
Fifteen boats		"	"	"
Five boats		Dec. 20	"	"
Sloop		"	"	"
Eight boats		"	"	"
Scow		"	"	"
Lighter	Sugar, &c	Dec. —		Diana
Boat	Cotton	Dec. 20	Indian river, Fla	Octorara
		1863.		
Sloop		Jan. 8	White House	Mahaska
Sloop		"	"	"
Bark		"	"	"
Bark		"	"	"
Scow		"	"	"
Sloop	Merchandise	Jan. 18	Newport News, Va	Minnesota, &c.
Rebel vessel, (bldg.)		Jan. 19	Capture of New Orleans	Admiral Farragut's fleet
Rebel vessel, (bldg.)		"	"	"
Rebel vessel, (bldg.)		"	"	"
Rebel vessel, (bldg.)		"	"	"
Rebel vessel, (bldg.)		"	"	"
Canoe	Assorted	Jan. 13	Dividing creek, Va	Currituck
Sloop	Contraband	Jan. 20	Chuckatuck creek	Commodore Morris
Four clinker-built boats.		Jan. 23	"	"
Two small boats		"	"	"
Two canoes	Assorted	Jan. 20	Indian creek	Currituck
Nine canoes	"	Jan. 25	Tabb's creek	"
Three boats		Jan. 24-25.	Potomac river	George Mangham
Schooner		Jan. 21	Topsail inlet	Daylight
Vessel	Whiskey, coffee, &c.	Feb. 12		George Mangham
Sloop	Assorted	Jan. 20		Commodore Morris
Two boats	Merchandise	Feb. 9		Dan Smith
Schooner		Feb. 2	Topsail inlet	Mt. Vernon
Canoe	Assorted	Mar. 13		Cœur de Leon
Schooner	Cotton	Mar. 2	Mosquito inlet	Sagamore
Schooner	"	Mar. 24		Boat expedition
Schooner	Salt	April 19	Charleston	
Brig	"	"	"	
Sloop		April 10	Sabine Pass	New London
Wharf boat		April 8	Warrenton	Hartford
Sloop	Cotton	April 24	Wassaw sound, Ga	Cimmaron
Schooner	Salt, &c	May 2	Rich inlet	Perry.
Schooner		May 14	Urbana, Va	Currituck, &c.
Steamer		May 20	Charleston	
Six vessels, &c		May 1-8		Western World, &c.
Steamer "35th Parallel"				Yazoo Pass expedition
Schooner		May 10	Morrell's inlet	Conemaugh, &c.
Two transports		May —		Yazoo Pass expedition
Monster ram		May 20	Yazoo City	Naval expedition

Description.	Cargo.	When Captured.	Where captured.	By what vessel.
		1863.		
Horses and Wagons.				Mississippi squadron
Fishing scow		May 30		Brooklyn
Schooner		"		"
Flat-boat	Sugar, &c	June 24	Mantau river, Fla	Tahoma
Sloop boat	Corn	June 9	Withlacoochee river, Fla	Fort Henry
Scow boat	57 bales cotton	June 1		"
Skiff and flat	Corn	June 10	Withlacoochee river, Fla	"
Barge	Cotton	June 2	Crystal river, Fla	"
Flat	Corn	May 14	Wacassassa bay	"
Sloop boat		May 30	"	"
Schooner		July —	White House	Shokokon
Sloop		July 3	Cumberland	Commodore Morris
Sloop	Cotton	July 6	Charlotte harbor, Fla	Restless
Canoe		July 13	Rappahannock river	Yankee, &c.
Flat-boat		"	"	"
Lot of Merchandise.		"	"	"
Dry-goods and shoes		July 17	Charles county, Md	Cœur de Leon
Four canoes	Whiskey, &c	July 20-21.	Dividing creek, Va	Currituck
4 schooners		July 8-9	Coast of Texas	Sciota
11 bbs. of turpentine		July 24		De Soto
Schooner		July 8	Coast of Texas	Sciota
Schooner		July 9	"	"
Schooner		"	"	"
Schooner and launch		June 22	Neuse river	Boat expedition
Row-boat		July 14		Annie
3 rolls bagging				
Scow	Sugar, &c	June 24		Tahoma
Scow	Cotton	July 19		Fort Henry
Sloop		July 8		Restless
Schooner		Sept. 28	Old Haven creek	Currituck
Steamer		June 30		
Schooner	Powder	Oct. —	Coast of Louisiana	Cayuga
Schooner	"	"	"	"
Schooner		Oct. 7	Off Sabine Pass	"
Sloop		"	"	"
Steamer		Dec. 31	Matagorda bay	Granite City, &c.
Sloop boat	Salt, &c	Dec. 14	Indian river, Fla	Roebuck
		1864.		
Schooner	Turpentine	Jan. 1	Morrell's inlet, S. C	Nipsic
Twelve oyster boats.		Feb. 1	York river	Morse
Boat		Feb. 13	"	"
Sloop		"	"	"
Skiff		"	"	"
Schooner		"	"	"
Schooner	Cotton	Mar. 11	Lat. 24° N.; long. 83° W.	San Jacinto
Schooner		Feb. 8	Caney creek, Texas	Queen
Two canoes		Feb. 23	Running from Va. to Md.	Dragon
Schooner	Cotton	Mar. 28	Matagorda bay	Estrella
Twenty-two boats		April 18	Up the Rappahannock	Potomac flotilla
Twenty-six small boats.		May 15	Turkey creek	Commodore Perry
Large barge		"	"	"
Seven boats (bldg.).		"	"	"
Three boats	Cotton and turpentine	July 4	Lat. 27° 41′ N.; long. 78° 54′ W.	Magnolia
Steamer		Aug. 9	Off Charleston	Katskill
Sail-boat	Merchandise	Sept. 2	Potomac river	Primrose
Twenty-two boats		Oct. 4	"	Potomac flotilla
Nine boats		"	Piankatank river	"
Rosin	25 barrels	Mar. 11	Up St. John's river	Pawnee's launch
Turpentine	13 barrels	Mar. 11	"	"
Sugar	5 barrels	Mar. 16	"	Pawnee and others
Railroad iron	500 or 600 bars	Mar. 21	"	"
Sugar	2 barrels	"	"	"
Bacon	1,000 pounds	April 18	Up Rappahannock	Potomac flotilla
Horses	2	"	"	"
Wheat	60 bushels	"	"	"
Tobacco	80 boxes	July 28	Gatesville, N. C	Whitehead
Schooner		June 30	Mobile	Glasgow
Four scows		Aug. 5	Mobile bay	W. G. B. squadron
Rifles—9	160 rounds	Aug. 24	Masonboro' inlet	Niphon

Description.	Cargo.	When captured.	Where captured.	By what vessel.
		1864.		
Rifles, &c.		Nov. 21	Bruinsburg, Miss.	Avenger
Schooner	Assorted cargo.	Oct. 24	Tampa bay, Fla.	Nita
Sloop boat	Salt, shoes, &c.	"	Off Little Malco, Fla	Rosalie
Sloop	Cotton and turpentine.	Nov. 5	Off Charleston, S. C.	Patapsco
Schooner		Nov. 29	Decross's Point, Texas.	Itasca
Steamer		Dec. 3	Off Cape Fear river	Emma and others
Steamer		Dec. 27	Western bar	Monticello
		1865.		
Boat	Cotton & sugar.	Jan. 27	Manitee river	Ino and Ariel
Steamer		Feb. 4	Beach inlet, S. C.	Wamsutta, &c.
Cargo of sloop, name unknown.		Feb. 27	Wando river, S. C.	Jonquil and others
Rebel torpedo boat.			Columbus	
3 rebel torpedo boats			Charleston, S. C.	
One lighter			"	
Iron, cables, anch'rs, &c.			Wilmington, N. C.	
Flat-boat	Dry-goods	April 6	Windmill Point, Va	Mercury
Machinery, &c.		April —	Richmond, Va.	N. A. B. squadron

The number of the prizes adjudicated to this date (Jan. 27, 1867), is seven hundred and thirty. The total amount of money involved—including that for distribution to the captors, and that which is passed to the credit of the United States—is about $25,000,000.

Payment has already been made to nearly ten thousand different claimants, in sums varying from twenty-five cents to thirty-eight thousand dollars. There still remain to be adjudicated about six hundred prizes, the most of which will probably be condemned and the proceeds paid to the captors.

PAY TABLE OF THE UNITED STATES NAVY.

Grades.	Pay per annum.
VICE-ADMIRAL.	
When at sea	$7,000
When on shore duty	6,000
On leave or waiting orders	5,000
REAR-ADMIRALS, (ACTIVE LIST.)	
When at sea	5,000
When on shore duty	4,000
On leave or waiting orders	3,000
On RETIRED LIST	2,000
COMMODORES, (ACTIVE LIST.)	
When at sea	4,000
When on shore duty	3,200
On leave or waiting orders	2,400
On RETIRED LIST	1,800
CAPTAINS, (ACTIVE LIST.)	
When at sea	3,500
When on shore duty	2,800
On leave or waiting orders	2,100
On RETIRED LIST	1,600
COMMANDERS, (ACTIVE LIST.)	
When at sea	2,800
When on shore duty	2,240
On leave or waiting orders	1,680
On RETIRED LIST	1,400
LIEUTENANT COMMANDERS, (ACTIVE LIST.)	
When at sea	2,343
When on shore duty	1,875
On leave or waiting orders	1,500
On RETIRED LIST	1,300
LIEUTENANTS, (ACTIVE LIST.)	
When at sea	1,875
When on shore duty	1,500
On leave or waiting orders	1,200
On RETIRED LIST	1,000
MASTERS, (ACTIVE LIST.)	
When at sea	1,500
When on shore duty	1,200
On leave or waiting orders	960
On RETIRED LIST	800
ENSIGNS, (ACTIVE LIST.)	
When at sea	1,200
When on shore duty	960
On leave or waiting orders	768
On RETIRED LIST	500
MIDSHIPMEN	500
FLEET SURGEONS	3,300

Grades.	Pay per annum.
SURGEONS—	
On duty at sea—	
For first five years after date of commission as surgeon	$2,200
For second five years after date of commission as surgeon	2,400
For third five years after date of commission as surgeon	2,600
For fourth five years after date of commission as surgeon	2,800
For twenty years and upwards after date of commission	3,000
On other duty—	
For first five years after date of commission as surgeon	2,000
For second five years after date of commission as surgeon	2,200
For third five years after date of commission as surgeon	2,400
For fourth five years after date of commission as surgeon	2,600
For twenty years and upwards after date of commission	2,800
On leave or waiting orders—	
For first five years after date of commission as surgeon	1,600
For second five years after date of commission as surgeon	1,800
For third five years after date of commission as surgeon	1,900
For fourth five years after date of commission as surgeon	2,100
For twenty years and upwards after date of commission	2,300
RETIRED SURGEONS—	
Surgeons ranking with captains	1,300
Surgeons ranking with commanders	1,100
Surgeons ranking with lieutenants	1,000
RETIRED PASSED AND ASSISTANT SURGEONS—	
Passed	850
Assistant	650
PASSED ASSISTANT SURGEONS—	
On duty at sea	1,500
On other duty	1,400
On leave or waiting orders	1,100
ASSISTANT SURGEONS—	
On duty at sea	1,250
On other duty	1,050
On leave or waiting orders	800
FLEET PAYMASTERS	3,300
PAYMASTERS—	
On duty at sea—	
For first five years after date of commission	2,000
For second five years after date of commission	2,400
For third five years after date of commission	2,600
For fourth five years after date of commission	2,900
For twenty years and upwards after date of commission	3,100
On other duty—	
For first five years after date of commission	1,800
For second five years after date of commission	2,100
For third five years after date of commission	2,400
For fourth five years after date of commission	2,600
For twenty years and upwards after date of commission	2,800
On leave or waiting orders—	
For first five years after date of commission	1,400
For second five years after date of commission	1,600
For third five years after date of commission	1,800
For fourth five years after date of commission	2,000
For twenty years and upwards after date of commission	2,250
PAYMASTERS RETIRED—[Under acts of Aug. 3 and Dec. 21, 1861.]	
Paymasters ranking with captains	1,300
Ranking with commanders	1,100
Ranking with lieutenants	1,000
ASSISTANT PAYMASTERS—	
On duty at sea—	
First five years after date of commission	1,300
After five years from date of commission	1,500
On other duty—	
First five years after date of commission	1,000
After five years from date of commission	1,200

Grades.	Pay per annum.
ASSISTANT PAYMASTERS—Continued.	
On leave or waiting orders—	
First five years after date of commission	$800
After five years from date of commission	1,000
CHAPLAINS—To be paid as lieutenants.	
PROFESSORS OF MATHEMATICS—	
On duty	1,800
On leave or waiting orders	960
BOATSWAINS, GUNNERS, CARPENTERS, AND SAILMAKERS—	
On duty at sea—	
For first three years' sea-service from date of appointment	1,000
For second three years' sea-service from date of appointment	1,150
For third three years' sea-service from date of appointment	1,250
For fourth three years' sea-service from date of appointment	1,350
For twelve years' sea-service and upwards	1,450
On other duty—	
For first three year's sea-service after date of appointment	800
For second three years' sea-service after date of appointment	900
For third three years' sea-service after date of appointment	1,000
For fourth three years' sea-service after date of appointment	1,100
For twelve years' sea-service and upwards	1,200
On leave or waiting orders—	
For first three years' sea-service after date of appointment	600
For second three years' sea-service after date of appointment	700
For third three years' sea-service after date of appointment	800
For fourth three years' sea-service after date of appointment	900
For twelve years' sea-service and upwards	1,000
FLEET ENGINEERS	3,300
ENGINEERS—	
CHIEF ENGINEERS, (on duty)—	
For first five years after date of commission	2,200
For second five years after date of commission	2,500
For third five years after date of commission	2,800
After fifteen years from date of commission	3,000
On leave or waiting orders—	
For first five years after date of commission	1,500
For second five years after date of commission	1,600
For third five years after date of commission	1,700
After fifteen years from date of commission	1,800
FIRST ASSISTANT ENGINEERS—	
On duty	1,500
On leave or waiting orders	1,100
SECOND ASSISTANT ENGINEERS—	
On duty	1,200
On leave or waiting orders	900
THIRD ASSISTANT ENGINEERS—	
On duty	1,000
On leave or waiting orders	800
NAVY AGENTS, commissions not to exceed	3,000
NAVY AGENT at San Francisco	4,000
TEMPORARY NAVY AGENTS	
NAVAL STOREKEEPERS	
Officers of the navy on foreign stations	1,500
NAVAL CONSTRUCTORS	2,600
NAVAL CONSTRUCTORS, when not on duty	1,800
SECRETARIES to commanders of squadrons	1,500
CLERKS to commanders of squadrons and commanders of vessels	500
CLERKS TO COMMANDANTS AT NAVY-YARDS—	
First clerk, Portsmouth, N. H	1,200
Clerk of yard	900
First clerk, Boston	1,200
Second clerk, Boston	960
Clerk of yard	1,200
First clerk, New York	1,200
Second clerk, New York	960

Grades.	Pay per annum.
CLERKS TO COMMANDANTS AT NAVY-YARDS—Continued.	
Clerk of yard	$1,200
Clerk, Philadelphia	1,200
Clerk of yard	1,200
First clerk, Washington	1,200
Second clerk, Washington	960
Clerk of yard	1,200
Clerk, Norfolk	1,200
Clerk of yard	1,200
First clerk, Pensacola	1,200
Clerk of yard	1,200
Clerk, Mare Island	1,500
Clerk of navy-yard	1,500
CLERKS—	
To paymasters at Boston, New York, Washington, and Philadelphia stations	1,200
At other stations	1,000
To inspectors in charge of provisions and clothing at Boston, New York, and Philadelphia	1,200
At other inspections	1,000
To receiving ships at Boston and New York	1,200
In other receiving ships, and in vessels of the first rate, and at the Naval Academy	1,000
To fleet paymasters and to paymasters of vessels of the second rate	800
To paymasters of vessels of the third rate, when allowed	700

PAY TABLE, COMMENCINNG JULY 1, 1864.

	PAY PER MONTH.			
	1st rate.	2d rate.	3d rate.	4th rate.
Chief Boatswain's Mates	$30	$30	..	..
Boatswain's Mates in Charge	30	30	$30	$30
Boatswain's Mates	27	27	27	27
Chief Gunner's Mates	30	30	..	..
Gunner's Mates in Charge	30	30	30	30
Gunner's Mates	27	27	27	27
Chief Quartermasters	30	30	28	28
Quartermasters	25	25	25	25
Coxswains to Commanders-in-Chief	30	30	30	30
Coxswains	25	25	25	25
Captains of Forecastle	25	25	25	25
Captains of Tops	25	25	25	25
Quarter Gunners	25	25	25	25
Carpenter's Mates	30	30	30	30
Carpenters, including Caulkers	20	20	20	20
Sailmaker's Mates	25	25	25	25
Painters, 1st Class	25	25	..	..
Painters, 2d Class	22	22	22	22
Coopers	22	22	22	22
Armorers	35	30	..	..
Armorer's Mates	22	22	22	22
Captains of Hold	25	25	25	25
Captains of Afterguard	25	25	25	25
Ship's Cooks	30	30	26	26
Bakers	25	25	22	22
Yeomen	45	40	35	30
Master-at-Arms	40	35	30	25
Surgeon's Stewards, in charge	40	40	40	40

PAY TABLE, COMMENCING JULY 1, 1864—Continued.

	PAY PER MONTH.			
	1st rate.	2d rate.	3d rate.	4th rate.
Surgeon's Stewards	$40	$33	$25	$25
Paymaster's Stewards	33	33	33	33
School Masters	35	30	25	20
Ship's Writers	30	25	20	18
Ship's Corporals	22	22	22	22
Masters of the Bands	35	30	..	..
Musicians, 1st Class	20	20	..	..
Musicians, 2d Class	16	16	..	..
Stewards to Commanders in Chief	40	40	40	40
Cooks to Commanders-in-Chief	35	35	35	35
Cabin Stewards	35	35	35	35
Cabin Cooks	30	30	30	30
Wardroom Stewards	30	30	30	30
Wardroom Cooks	25	25	25	25
Steerage Stewards	20	20	20	20
Steerage Cooks	18	18	18	18
Warrant Officers' Stewards	18	18	18	18
Warrant Officers' Cook	14	14	14	14
Seamen	20	20	20	20
Ordinary Seamen	16	16	16	16
Landsmen	14	14	14	14
Nurses	14	14	14	14
Boys, 1st Class	10	10	10	10
Boys, 2d Class	9	9	9	9
Boys, 3d Class	8	8	8	8
Firemen, 1st Class	30	30	30	30
Firemen, 2d Class	25	25	25	25
Coal-Heavers	20	20	20	20

NOTES.—All officers, while at sea or attached to a sea-going vessel, shall be allowed one ration.

No rations shall be allowed to any officers of the navy on the retired list.

The pay of all naval officers appointed by virtue of an act entitled "An act to provide for the temporary increase of the navy," approved July 24, 1861, shall be the same as that of officers of a like grade in the regular navy.—(See act July 16, 1862.)

TESTIMONIALS

FOR

Headley's Grant and Sherman.

From the Pittsburgh Daily Gazette.

The great success which has attended the author's former works is an assurance of the popularity of the present. Advance sheets which have been sent us show that there has been no falling off in Headley's graphic style.

From the New York Observer.

Our readers need no commendations of the writings of this popular author. There is no more graphic pen wielded at the present day than that of Mr. Headley, who has the happy faculty of spreading the scenes he describes visibly before the eye. He is altogether at home in military matters and in describing battle scenes. The present work is peculiarly in his line, and all who have read "Washington and his Generals," &c., will anticipate a literary treat in reading a work by the same author on Grant and Sherman and their Generals.

From the Newburgh (N. Y.) Daily Journal.

The name of the author is a sufficient guarantee that it will be all that it is represented to be. From the host of publications that are now flooding the country relative to the war, we can confidently single out this work and recommend it to our readers.

From the Chicago Daily Republican.

We have before us a portion of the new book, "Grant and Sherman," from the vigorous and graphic pen of Hon. J. T. Headley; the author's name alone gives it a position as a reliable and standard work.

From the North-Western Christian Advocate and Journal, Chicago, Ill.

Headley's "Grant and Sherman" we are satisfied will have a "fine run." Mr. Headley's pen is graphic, and he has a wonderful faculty in deluding a reader into the belief that he is an actual spectator of the scenes described. The deeds of Grant and Sherman deserve a record as imperishable as themselves, and Headley is especially the author to teach these epic-materials to the people.

From the New York Daily Tribune.

The campaigns of Grant and Sherman have found a popular historian in the Hon. J. T. Headley. The pen of the author of "Washington and his Generals" will find ample scope for vivid descriptions of the battles and stirring incidents of these memorable campaigns.

"Mr. Headley's qualities as a biographer and historian are well known to the reading public."—*Cleveland Herald.*

"The brilliant descriptive powers of the author, and his thorough appreciation of men, will make this one of the most readable records of the war. His personal acquaintance with many of its prominent characters will add to its value and interest."—*New York Journal of Commerce.*

"The campaigns of Grant and Sherman, by J. T. Headley, is intended to be the most complete work on the subject. The brilliant and picturesque style of Mr. Headley will very happily set forth all that was remarkable in their romantic campaigns."—*Hartford Daily Press.*

"The advance sheets give evidence of the writer's skill in word-painting.—*Springfield Republican.*

"The author has a congenial subject, affording ample scope for his descriptive powers, and will produce an attractive book."—*N. Y. Independent.*

"It promises to be one of the most popular books which the war has inspired, and the only one that can lay claim to completeness as a panorama of the war."—*Cleveland Leader.*

"This book is destined to arouse a greater interest than any other work from the pen of this distinguished author."—*N. Y. Evangelist.*

"Grant and Sherman and their Generals, in Headley's thrilling style, will be read by many with an unusual degree of interest."—*Hartford Daily Times.*

www.ingramcontent.com/pod-product-compliance
Lightning Source LLC
LaVergne TN
LVHW021103110826
845150LV00001B/158

* 9 7 8 1 4 2 5 5 6 5 1 6 9 *